Changing Organizations

Foundations of Social Inquiry

SCOTT MCNALL AND CHARLES TILLY, SERIES EDITORS

Changing Organizations: Business Networks in the New Political Economy, David Knoke

War, Peace, and the Social Order, Brian E. Fogarty

Faces of Feminism: An Activist's Reflections on the Women's Movement, Sheila Tobias

Criminological Controversies: A Methodological Primer, John Hagan, A. R. Gillis, and David Brownfield

Immigration in America's Future: Social Science Findings and the Policy Debate, David M. Heer

What Does Your Wife Do? Gender and the Transformation of Family Life, Leonard Beeghley

Forthcoming
Race, Gender, and Discrimination at Work, Samuel Cohn
Social Change: The Long-Term View from Sociology and Anthropology, Thomas D. Hall, Darrell La Lone, and Stephen K. Sanderson

Changing Organizations

Business Networks
in the
New Political Economy

David Knoke
University of Minnesota

Westview
PRESS

A Member of the Perseus Books Group

Copyright © 2001 by Westview Press, A Member of the Perseus Books Group

Published in 2001 in the United States of America by Westview Press, 5500 Central Avenue, Boulder, Colorado 80301-2877, and in the United Kingdom by Westview Press, 12 Hid's Copse Road, Cumnor Hill, Oxford OX2 9JJ

Find us on the World Wide Web at www.westviewpress.com

Library of Congress Cataloging-in-Publication Data
Knoke, David
   Changing organizations : business networks in the new political economy / by David Knoke.
     p.   cm. — (Foundations of social inquiry)
   Includes bibliographical references and index.
   ISBN 0-8133-3453-5 (pbk.)
   1. Business networks—United States.   2. Strategic alliances (Business)—United States.
3. United States—Foreign economic relations.   I. Title.   II. Series.

HD69.S8 K58   2000
658'.044—dc21   00-63302

The paper used in this publication meets the requirements of the American National Standard for Permanence of Paper for Printed Library Materials Z39.48-1984.

10   9   8   7   6   5   4   3

This one is for Maggie

Contents

Figures and Tables

Figures

Tables

Acronyms

ADR	alternative dispute resolution
CAS	complex adaptive systems
CAD/CAM	computer-assisted design and manufacturing
ESOP	employee stock ownership plans
FEC	Federal Election Commission
FILM	firm internal labor market
GIS	global information sector
HRM	human resources management
IPO	initial public offering
JIT	just-in-time
LBO	leveraged buyout
LTIP	long-term incentive plan
MDF	multidivisional form
MNC	multinational corporation
MSF	multisubsidiary form
NBF	new biotechnology firm
NLRB	National Labor Relations Board
PAC	political action committee
PIG	public interest group
QC	quality circle
SFN	small-firm network
SIC	Standard Industrial Classification
SMO	social movement organization
SPC	statistical process control
TQM	total quality management

Preface

Mr. Gittes, you may think you know what you're dealing with, but believe me, you don't.

—Robert Towne, *Chinatown* (1974)

The origins of this book lie in the three decades I spent teaching, reading about, and conducting research on organizations ranging from small neighborhood associations, to national lobbying coalitions, to strategic alliances among international information sector corporations. Two overarching themes integrate the seemingly divergent facets of this volume. First, understanding changing organizational behavior requires observers to view the U.S. political economy as a system within which money and power intimately interconnect across all levels of analysis. Organizations are not just the unitary, utility-maximizing production functions depicted by neoclassical economic models. They also consist of numerous social actors pursuing divergent interests and goals that conflict and realign over time. The collective actions emerging from such malleable systems are best analyzed as joint outcomes of market processes and political power interacting within and between organizations.

Second, network relations are indispensable for explaining the continual transformations of organizational structures and processes. Network analysis encompasses wide-ranging phenomena, from employee careers and work team relations to collective action in organizational populations. This multilevel scope, combined with an emphasis on recurring interactions among social actors, gives network analysts vigorous conceptual and empirical tools for investigating dynamic organizational change. The information exchanges and resource transactions at the heart of network analysis reveal how economic and political influences shape organizational behaviors, from international corporations forming joint ventures, to business and labor coalitions lobbying the government, to employees cooperating within high-performance work teams. The dual themes of political economy and network analysis, interweaving the diverse trends and developments in organizations throughout the twentieth century, help us to anticipate plausible directions for organizational change in this century.

However, the general orientations offered by the political economy and network perspectives lay an insufficient foundation on which to build a comprehensive account of changing organizations. Additional primary approaches are indispensable to constructing more thorough analytic interpretations. Many key concepts, ideas, principles, theories, and methods useful in explaining organizational actions come from a loose collection of disciplines best described as "organization studies." Their practitioners span traditional fields, including sociology, business management, economics, law, political science, public administration, social psychology, history, and journalism. Rather than treating these disciplines as competing and irreconcilable perspectives, I tried to determine where those diverse schemas might contribute toward more inclusive explanations of events. Some applications of these alternative perspectives yielded contradictory implications, whereas others simply offered few insights into specific components of organizational change. Still, these incomplete accounts should spur organization studies theorists and researchers to stronger efforts at integrating their distinct approaches into more comprehensive explanations.

For an overview of the book's specific substantive conclusions, readers should consult the concluding section of each chapter. Here I briefly describe the common elements in their format. Each chapter focuses on specific topics in organizational change, primarily at the macro level of whole organizations, organizational fields, or populations, rather than at the level of individual persons or organizational roles. An introductory anecdote illustrates these topics, followed by explicit definitions of key concepts and principles relevant to analyzing the issues under consideration. Where available, time-series charts graphically display trends in particular organizational behaviors. I gather eclectic evidence about these issues from journalistic accounts, censuses, governmental reports, in-depth case studies, sample surveys, and quantitative data analyses. The bulk of this evidence concentrates on the large U.S. corporations that dominated the American political economy during the twentieth century. My relative neglect of smaller, entrepreneurial, nonprofit, voluntary, governmental, and international organizations reflects not only the more meager research attention paid to these other organizational forms but also the limited space available to treat them in greater depth.

I review relevant research literatures, concentrating on recent publications, from the many disciplines that make up organization studies. I try to contrast alternative theoretical explanations and interpretations of organizational change. I hope that I fairly represent various analysts' views, despite my particular biases toward network and power explanations. Most chapters include one or more detailed data analyses that illustrate how applications of research methods lead to substantive conclusions. Because my disposition toward organizational networks motivated several such analyses, the Appendix offers an introduction to basic network analysis concepts and methods. I try to assess the range of empirical findings about the substantive topics and their implications for alternative theoretical explanations of organizational change. I offer suggestions about how conflicting results might be reconciled and where future research efforts could contribute to explicating the causes and consequences of organizational change.

I spend much of my professional life trying to squeeze a few grains of insight into organizational behavior from the stubborn stones of reality. If the conjectures in this book inspire others to take up the study of changing organizations, then I will consider my time well spent.

Acknowledgments

I greatly appreciate the research grants provided by the National Science Foundation to myself and several co-investigators to conduct the National Associations Survey, two National Policy Domain Studies, and two National Organizations Studies. Grants-in-aid from the University of Minnesota's College of Liberal Arts and Graduate School supported research on the global information sector, and a single-quarter leave and a sabbatical gave me time to begin and to finish writing this book.

During the many years this project gestated, I benefited greatly from the steadfast counsel of talented editorial staff at Westview Press: Jill Rothenberg, Margaret Loftus, Lisa Wigutoff, Adina Popescu, Andrew Day, David McBride, Michelle Trader, and Sharon DeJohn. Sage advice from series editors Scott McNall and Charles Tilly and from manuscript reviewers Dan Chambliss and John Lie significantly enhanced the final product.

I owe an immense intellectual debt to the authors of the countless articles, chapters, reports, and books cited in this volume, which taught me almost everything I know about organization studies. I especially thank my collegial friends who read individual chapters and gave much encouragement and many useful suggestions, which I tried to incorporate, not always successfully: Howard Aldrich, Paul Burstein, Joseph Galaskiewicz, Anne Genereux, Arne Kalleberg, Naomi Kaufman, Patrick Kenis, David Krackhardt, Nicole Raeburn, Verta Taylor, Emanuela Todeva, Andrew Van de Ven, and Song Yang.

Most important, I am grateful to Margaret Frances Knoke for her exceptional editorial work on the manuscript, which vastly improved its quality; for sharing her passionate and brilliant insights about organizational life; and, best of all, for being a wonderful daughter to Joann and me.

Edina, Minnesota
June 19, 2000

1

Generating Change

> Nothing of him that doth fade
> But doth suffer a sea-change
> Into something rich and strange.
> —William Shakespeare, The Tempest (1611)

As they entered the twenty-first century, American business corporations and their employees were increasingly buffeted, battered, and bewildered by dramatic changes. The U.S. economy enjoyed its longest period of uninterrupted expansion, with bullish stock markets making many investors overnight millionaires. Following decades of stagnating family incomes and widening inequality, real earnings finally began growing again. The accelerating march of technological innovations and the rapid succession of new production and distribution processes forced organizations to reinvent themselves continually. The chaotic turmoil in formerly stable product markets and industries left many companies vulnerable to relentless pressures from domestic and foreign competitors, stakeholders, and governments. Interorganizational alliances increasingly bound once and future rivals together in uneasy collaborations. The fates of local communities were susceptible to decisions about investments and relocations made by distant geopolitical actors. The loss of social capital through dwindling organizational reputations combined with wrenching internal reorganizations to flatten corporate hierarchies and erode personal statuses and privileges.

Periodic waves of corporate downsizings, restructurings, mergers, and divestitures tore up the employment contract binding employers and employees. Many workers, especially in white-collar occupations, experienced the swift disappearance of lifetime job security. Increased project length and temporary employment eroded traditional attachments at the same time that new high-performance work designs placed heavier demands for highly skilled, self-directed workers. Blue-collar union ranks shrank to a tiny fraction of the labor force, while social movements by various identity groups demanded enhanced legal protections in the workplace. To many observers, U.S. public policymaking seemed held captive by the business, labor, and other interest groups making bloated campaign contributions to gain special access and influence over public officials. The primary aim of this book is to examine these trends and developments in the U.S. political economy to understand and explain changing organizations at the end of the twentieth century. An ultimate, although perhaps unattainable, goal is to understand better some possible paths of future change as the new century begins.

What Happened to Big Blue?

The spectacular upheavals at International Business Machines (IBM) in the last decades of the twentieth century represented a microcosm of the many organizational transformations explored in great detail throughout this book. Big Blue dominated the mainframe computer market from the 1950s until the 1980s, but it failed to anticipate the enormous expanding personal computer market of the 1980s. Its several midrange systems were unable to "talk" to one another, sharing information and application programs. Small start-up companies gained toeholds in various niche markets and began to develop diverse products, including networking capabilities, more responsive to customer demands, which eventually ate IBM's lunch. As a result of Big Blue's lapses, the corporation and its employees struggled through wrenching changes to adapt to the 1990s environment of relentless technology innovation and ferocious international competition. Some key events in this cautionary tale:

- In the "best-known episode in Microsoft's history" (Stross 1996:8), Bill Gates signed a 1980 contract promising to provide IBM with operating system software (MS-DOS) for its new PC Jr. Lacking such a system, Gates bought one from a smaller company and licensed it to IBM under terms that allowed Microsoft to sell DOS to other companies and consumers. The PC Jr. flopped, forcing IBM out of the market. By the mid-1990s, Microsoft had gained control of more than 85 percent of all PC software installations (Zachary 1994).
- Two subsequent IBM and Microsoft joint ventures—to create a successor operating system (OS/2) and to build a sound-equipped CD-ROM machine—ultimately shattered under incompatibilities between the two firms' corporate cultures, costly production overruns, and numerous delays in delivery dates.
- IBM then launched two joint ventures with Apple Computer in 1991 to compete against the suddenly dominant "Wintel" colossus

(the MS Windows–Intel Corp. alliance). The agreements called for IBM to reimburse Apple for converting its Macintosh PC software to enable it to run on IBM's renamed Warp OS/2, using IBM's new PowerPC microprocessor chip developed with Motorola. But Apple's own troubles—rapidly deteriorating revenues and shrinking market share, forcing it to lay off 20 percent of its workforce (Carlton 1996)—sank both ventures, leaving IBM to foot most of the $40–60 million bill.

- Gushing red ink, IBM slashed its workforce from a peak of 406,000 employees in 1986 to 219,000 workers by 1994. Yet it managed to boost the revenues generated from each remaining employee by 58 percent (Ziegler 1997). IBM achieved this huge productivity gain by a draconian internal restructuring that ended its cherished and highly visible "no-layoffs" policy. Managers pressured younger employees to quit, while sweetening the incentives for voluntary early retirees. Big Blue reorganized its slimmed-down workforce into 13 autonomous business lines, concentrating on personal computers and services to its core market, large corporation customers such as LTV Steel and Budget Rent a Car Corp. (Boyett et al. 1993:187–193).
- After an intense three-year effort, IBM's Rochester, Minnesota, production plant won the coveted 1990 Malcolm Baldrige National Quality Award from the U.S. Commerce Department for creating a customer-driven approach to its new Application System/400 and hard disk storage devices (Boyett et al. 1993). But many IBM employees and customers continued to complain about prevalent divisional infighting, plodding response times, insensitivity to customer specifications, and loss of extensive free consulting.

IBM shareholders, who formerly counted on continually rising stock prices and dividends, saw the value plummet from a peak $175 per share in 1987 to $40 in 1993. The corporation lost $12 billion in 1992 and 1993. Between 1986 and 1994, IBM fell from first place to 354th place in *Fortune* magazine's annual poll of America's Most Admired Companies (Fombrun 1996:8). On April Fool's Day 1993, Chairman and Chief Executive Officer John Akers resigned and was replaced by Big Blue's first outsider CEO, John Gerstner Jr. from RJR Nabisco. Executive headhunters had unsuccessfully dangled the top IBM job before several corporate legends, including General Electric's Jack Welch and Motorola's George Fisher. "Nobody—but nobody—wanted to save this company" (Morris 1997:70). Citing "bureaucracy run amok" and considering his primary mission to boost revenues quickly, Gerstner announced a massive 38,500-person layoff. He assembled a new inner circle of five senior vice presidents, all IBM lifers and all white males (Hays 1995). The highest-ranking woman executive, software head Ellen Hancock, unexpectedly resigned after 29 years with the firm.

By 1997 Big Blue appeared to have stopped hemorrhaging red ink. Profits returned but only to a mere 3.2 percent of the total revenue of $76 billion in 1996. Although still the sixth largest U.S. company by sales income, and with twice the software revenue of Microsoft, IBM was growing much slower than many of its domestic and international rivals. It no longer held a commanding position in any key market segment, and a return to dominance seemed elusive. After sinking nearly $2 billion over 10 years to develop Warp OS/2 for desktop PCs, IBM had built a base of just 6 million customers compared to Microsoft Windows' 60 million copies. Big Blue also lagged in client-server software that coordinated corporate PC local networks, and Oracle and Sybase were stealing IBM's mainframe and minicomputer customers. With cash reserves below $11 billion, the company faced a dilemma: whether to continue alone, to ally with competitors, or to acquire a major software company in hopes of challenging the Wintel juggernaut. "They're still trying to figure out where they're a player and where they're not," said one corporate customer. "They're not the IBM of the past—but I don't think they're the IBM of the future" (Ziegler 1997).

The sad story of Big Blue was just one gloomy dispatch from the trenches of corporate warfare. Journalists, business leaders, politicians, and academic observers all sought to describe and explain the vast sea changes that eroded the insular society of our parents. In its place arose a rich and strange new world whose contours grew darkly visible only toward the end of the twentieth century. I contend that one useful approach to solving the puzzle of where the United States, and the rest of the globe, may be heading lies in viewing our political economy as a complex social system involving intricately intertwined networks of organizational and personal relationships. Multilayered webs of diverse ties connect citizens, communities, corporations, and countries into one dynamic, planet-girdling social structure. The structural perspective I apply asserts that social behavior largely consists of repeated actions that give rise to relatively stable, dependable patterns over time. But these structural patterns are liable to change in collisions between individual and collective human wills responding to altered environmental conditions.

The central task for social structure analysts must be the accumulation of careful observations of numerous organizational activities with the aim of (1) providing accurate, nuanced descriptions of the crucial factual details; (2) distilling from these bewildering surface events and personalities the deeper underlying analytical patterns; and (3) developing and testing theories about the large- and small-scale economic, political, and social forces causing both persistence and change in organizations' structured relationships. The remaining sections of this chapter prepare the stage for the many-storied narrative to unfold in this book.

Organizational Structures and Environments

Formal organizations are "goal-directed, boundary-maintaining, activity systems" (Aldrich 1979:4). Boundaries separate the persons and property over which an enterprise exercises some control from the people and goods over which it exerts no legal authority. As the archetypal sociologist of economic activity, Max Weber emphasized understanding social actions by uncovering the subjective meaning of social relationships. Membership rights, such as working conditions and employment benefits, make up the essential criterion for discerning where an organization's boundary ended and its external environment began:

> A [social] relationship will be called "closed" against outsiders so far as, according to its subjective meaning and the binding rules of its order, participation of certain persons is excluded, limited or subjected to conditions.... A party to a closed relationship will be called a "member." ... A social relationship which is either closed or limits the admission of outsiders by rules, will be called a "corporate group" (*Verband*) so far as its order is enforced by the action of specific individuals whose regular function this is, of a chief or "head" (*Leiter*) and usually also an administrative staff. These functionaries will normally also have representative authority. (Weber 1947:139–146)

Applied to a modern profit-making corporation, Weber's definitions identify its production workers, middle managers, professional employees, top executives, board of directors, and shareholders (owners) as members. The excluded social actors—who thus make up part of the environments lying outside the organizational boundary—include the company's suppliers, industrial customers, individual consumers, governmental agencies, cultural and legal institutions, and local and international communities.

The crucial point is that any organization's relationships can be conceptually divided into internal and external dimensions. Unlike Weber, who concentrated his efforts on explaining participant interactions inside organizational boundaries, most contemporary theorists embrace an implicit "open system" perspective, in which "the systems are embedded in—dependent on continuing exchanges with and constituted by—the environments in which they operate" (Scott 1998:28). Hence, any thorough investigation of organizational change requires us to pay serious attention to external sources. Specific corporations are exposed to unique micro-

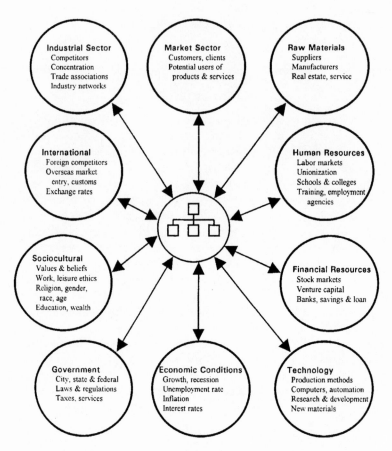

FIGURE 1.1   Organization's Environment
SOURCE: Modified from Daft (1995:80)

environments that vary, for example, in their relative levels of resources, uncertainty, and turbulence (see Aldrich [1979:63–73] for a discussion of six analytical environmental dimensions). The schematic diagram in Figure 1.1, displaying 10 conceptually distinct environmental sectors, barely hints at the enormous diversity and complexity of conditions and relationships within which a particular organization might be embedded. Later chapters overflow with illustrations of specific organizational environments. Given the potentially great consequences of national and international economic and political conditions for organizations, throughout this book I use the term *political economy* to indicate a complex intertwining of these macrolevel environmental dimensions. This label draws analytical attention to the dual impacts of power and money in shaping organizational structures and actions.

An organization's internal structural anatomy may be just as complex as its external environments. Henry Mintzberg's (1979) classic icon classified these relationships into five fundamental functions, as shown in Figure 1.2. The central stem is a vertical line of authority whose three types of participants directly engage in making and implementing decisions about the corporation's core products and services. The top executives in the strategic apex serve the firm's mission and forge networks of power relations to the important external actors affecting the organization's fate, such as suppliers, customers, and governmental regulatory agencies. The middle-line managers try to coordinate the activities within and across various internal work units. The lowest-level managers directly supervise the operating core of employees who actually produce and distribute the company's physical goods and services. The two side circles represent auxiliary components not directly involved in production activities. The engineers and personnel administrators staffing the technostructure seek to control uncertainty by standardizing hiring, training, and performance standards. Support specialists provide various services—ranging from building security to advertising—that might well be (and often are) purchased through external market relationships. As later chapters reveal, a major component of organizational change is periodic internal restructuring that drops or adds, shrinks or expands internal functions as companies search for optimal structural designs to enhance productivity and profitability.

Forces Driving Changes

Every theorist proffers a favorite list of the fundamental forces driving changes over the past quarter century (roughly from the economic disruptions caused by the 1973 Arab oil boycott to the present). Lester Thurow characterized the Earth's new economic surface by a metaphor of five tectonic plates: the end of communism; a technological shift to an era dominated by man-made brainpower industries; a demographic split between impoverished nations and the affluent elderly of rich countries; a globalizing economy; and an era without a dominant economic, political, or military power (Thurow 1996:8–10). George Ritzer (1989) argued that a "permanently new economy" emerged in the United States, generated by changes in technology and knowledge, demographic shifts, external changes in the world economy, and internal changes in U.S. labor and industrial relations. The Hay Management Consultants' diagnosis identified "six major changes common to almost every organization" (Flannery, Hofrichter and Platten 1996:8–9):

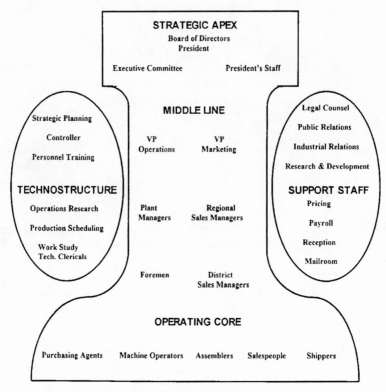

FIGURE 1.2   Five Basic Parts of an Organization
SOURCE: Modified from Mintzberg (1989:20 & 33)

- rapidly expanding technologies
- growing global competition
- increased demand for individual and organizational competencies and capabilities
- higher customer expectations
- ever-decreasing [product-development] cycle times
- changing personnel requirements

Expecting any two analysts to assemble a consensual catalog of the important dimensions of organizational change, much less agree about their underlying causes, is clearly mission impossible.

Every conceptual scheme draws our attention to a handful of key processes at the cost of simplifying complex realities. Still, by the first definition of *analysis*—breaking a whole into its component parts—reduction is unavoidable in any investigation. Not to be left behind, I present my own broad outline, involving nine interlocking forces that drive contemporary organizational changes. These topics appear under two broad headings: macro-environmental trends occurring outside corporations and micro-organizational trends taking place within their boundaries. Note the overlap between several of my conceptual categories with those identified by the analysts cited above. Of necessity, I paint these nine pictures using thick paints and some very broad brushstrokes, leaving to later chapters the task of filling in their many fine details.

Macro-Environmental Trends

My purpose in this section is to summarize five key environmental trends over the past quarter century that transformed many organizations, regardless of their specific manifestations. I discuss these major macro-environmental changes under five topical headings: the globalizing economy; accelerating technological innovation; slowing productivity growth; demography may be destiny; and market capitalism trumps political democracy.

The Globalizing Economy.   A single global, capitalist economy increasingly connects the planet's 6 billion inhabitants, who live in more than 200 sovereign nations. The globalization dynamic snares everything in its web. Americans have long been familiar with the penetration of foreign automotive and electronic brands (Toyota, Volkswagen, Sony, Samsung). But even purportedly pure "domestic" service enterprises such as neighborhood restaurants and beauty salons face competition from foreign firms marketing cheeseburgers and hair care products. Today all basic factors of production—technology, labor, physical and financial resources—and their output of goods and services move across political borders with unprecedented ease. Modern communication and transportation systems enable entrepreneurs to reap enormous profits by finding new opportunities to substitute cheaper labor and materials for higher-priced components. Over the long run, these dynamic gales of creative destruction processes may eventually compress wage differentials and narrow the gap in living standards between the high-income and the Third World of developing societies (Thurow 1996:166–180). But, as in dancing and stand-up comedy, timing is everything in the modern world system. By the end of the twentieth century, the handful of high-income economies still produced and consumed the lion's share of wealth in the globalizing economy.

Two simple graphs capture this situation. Figure 1.3 divides the 1998 world's gross national product (GNP) pie among the six largest national economies, 20 other high-income nations (about half of which were members of the European Union), China (including Taiwan and Hong Kong), and the rest of the world.[1] Although the United States at 27.4 percent oper-

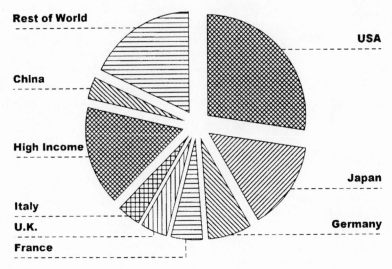

FIGURE 1.3   Shares of World GNP, 1998
SOURCE: World Bank (1999)

ated the largest economic engine, the biggest change over the preceding quarter-century was Japan's expanding share, from barely 7 percent to 14 percent of world GNP despite a decade-long stagnant economy. Huge inequalities prevailed. Although only one-sixth of the planet's people lived in its 26 wealthiest nations, because their citizens enjoy average per capita incomes of more than $25,000, they garnered almost four-fifths of the world's $28.9 trillion GNP (in 1998 U.S. dollars).

Figure 1.4 splendidly illustrates how the social network perspective captures complex relationships in succinct visual images. The input data to construct this image take the form of a matrix with the aggregate dollar amount of $3.1 trillion in goods and services exchanged in 1997 between eight economic units: the United States, Japan, and six geopolitical blocks defined by the United Nations (1997). A computer program reduces these 56 pair-values to a two-dimensional map of the world's economic space.[2] Just as a geographic map shows inter-city flying distances, pairs of trading regions appear close to one another whenever they have high volumes of exchange. For example, the United States' exports to the rest of the Americas (including Canada) account for 4.8 percent of world trade transactions, and imports from that region into the United States account for another 5.5 percent. In contrast, pairs with low trade flows are located great distances apart (e.g., Eastern Europe and the Oceania region, mainly Australia and New Zealand, which exchanged just 0.01 percent of total world

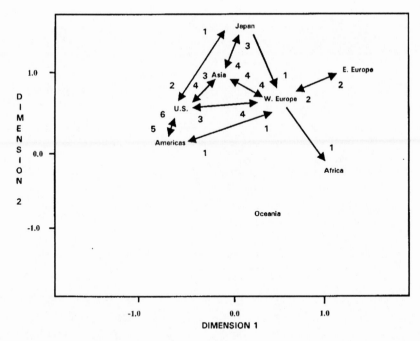

FIGURE 1.4   Structure of World Trade Flows, 1997
SOURCE: United Nations (1997)

trade). Superimposed on the spatial image are directed lines, where the dec-
imals next to each arrowhead report the trade percentages coming from the
block or country where the arrow originates. (To avoid clutter, I show only
the 18 highest-volume exchanges, involving at least 1 percent of world
trade.) For example, the numbers on the U.S.–Japan arrow indicate that the
United States imports 2 percent of world trade from Japan and exports 1
percent in return (and Japan's export-import flow with the United States is
just the reverse).

No single nation or block dominates the 1997 world trade network.
However, the United States is involved in three distinct triads: (1) with Western Europe and the Asian block, (2) with Japan and Asia, and (3) with Western Europe and the Americas block. Japan is directly connected to three
partners, but is located away from the core group involving Asia, Western
Europe and the United States. Japan's export-driven economic policies resulted in several asymmetric relationships, reflecting its exports of almost 50
percent more than it imported from other countries in 1997. The United
States, having become the world's largest debtor nation during the preceding
quarter century, reveals the opposite trade pattern. Western Europe has the

most numerous high-volume exchanges (with six partners), followed by the United States (four partners). Three blocks consisting of mostly developing nations (Eastern Europe, Africa, and Oceania) are only weakly connected to the four core players, whereas the Americas, primarily because of Canada, are somewhat better integrated into the world trade network.

The globalizing economic structure displayed in Figure 1.4 is a vast simplification. Nations and regions don't directly exchange goods and services with one another. Rather, world trade consists of billions of annual transactions between organizations, both as intermediate business customers and as ultimate consumers of goods and services. Because the diagram uses only aggregated dollars, it conceals the diversity of goods and services sent and received. Further, substantial trading occurs among nations *within* each regional block; for example, more than $1.4 trillion in goods and services moved among the Western European countries in 1997. Finally, cross-border exchanges ignore such international dynamics as factories shutting down in high-wage nations and re-opening in low-wage countries, as well as multinational corporations engaged in joint production ventures with overseas partners.

Despite these oversimplifications, the snapshot developed in Figure 1.4 depicts a clear core-periphery structure. If similar networks could be projected as a motion picture spanning 50 years, the central image would probably reveal a growing connection of Asia to the U.S.-West European axis. For decades, alarmists made comfortable livings by warning that Japan Inc. would inevitably surpass the United States as the world's leading economic super power (e.g., Vogel 1978; Kennedy 1987:458–471). Alas, the bursting speculative "bubble" sent Japanese stock prices and Tokyo real estate values plummeting in the early 1990s. A decade of nongrowth exposed Japan as just another high-income player struggling to find a competitive edge. Meanwhile, the four Little Tigers (South Korea, Singapore, Taiwan, and Hong Kong before its reversion to China) roared onto the world economic stage, closely followed by Thailand, Malaysia, and Indonesia. Their bellows became muted groans when their 1997–1998 currency debacles and sharp recessions disclosed their rickety crony-capitalist underpinnings. After China abandoned its centralized economic planning system in 1978 for a free enterprise economy, its accelerating development lured numerous Western corporations lusting after untapped markets despite Beijing's authoritarian politics and abysmal human rights record (Johnson 1997). At century's end China was poised to surge past a stagnating Japan as the United States' second-largest international trading partner (behind Canada). However, although China's 1.2 billion population was five times larger than the United States' 0.25 billion inhabitants, its tiny per capita income ($750, compared to Americans' $29,340 in 1998) implied that full maturation of China's potentially gargantuan consumer markets would lie far in the future.

Accelerating Technological Innovation. The twentieth century's successive explosions in technology radically changed work, family, leisure, government, warfare, and all other facets of social life. Early applications of scientific principles to machine manufacturing processes boosted the productivity of steel mills, automobile factories, chemical works, and airplane plants. An information technology (IT) revolution exploded in the 1970s, opening a "technological divide" (Castells 1996:46) that split the last quarter century from its forerunners. It was built on computers, but also embraced telecommunications, biotechnology, and materials sciences. Key innovations include the microprocessor (1971), the microcomputer (1975), and gene cloning (1973). The Internet, launched in 1969 as a Department of Defense project to link research computers, morphed into a worldwide, decentralized network of personal computers whose ultimate intellectual and commercial consequences were yet unfathomable in 2000. The speed of IT computations grew exponentially while costs per byte of information plummeted precipitously (Scott Morton 1991:9). Moore's Law, fabricated by Intel co-founder Gordon Moore, asserted that the number of transistors engineers could squeeze onto a silicon chip (and hence the speed of microprocessor operations) doubled every 18 months. The rapid succession of PC generations pushed typical desktop machine prices well below $1,000 by 1997, threatening to squeeze the profits of chip manufacturers, ironically including Intel itself (Clark 1997; Takahashi 1997).

By the early 1990s, a global information sector had emerged to break down traditional boundaries among seven industries: film studios, television networks, newspaper and book publishers, telecommunication, computer, cable, and consumer electronics companies. This $350 billion industry replaced jet engines as America's chief export (Auletta 1997:x). Software, hardware, wetware, content, and marketing and delivery systems—all churned together as deep-pocket corporations and upstart companies floundered toward new combinations that might bring vast riches to a few and oblivion to the many. These high-tech companies and industries furnish many of the exciting illustrations of organizational change scattered throughout this book.

Although the technologies undergirding the information superhighway might begin as pure science, their applications are fundamentally social construction processes. Interorganizational networks clutch at the reins needed to ride risky technological tigers without being eaten alive. As an example, consider why commercialization of the multimedia digital video disc (DVD), to supplant computer CD-ROMs and home VCR taping systems, was delayed for several years in the early 1990s (De Laat 1999). Two rival consumer electronics producer alliances fought to establish their prototype designs as the industry's standard. The design pushed by a Japanese research and development group (comprising Toshiba, Hitachi, Pioneer, JVC, and Matsushita) was endorsed by such movie and music firms as Time Warner, MGM, and MCA. A second alliance, between Sony and the Dutch high-tech company Philips, pushed for an alternative design. Most neutral image, sound, and information companies rated the two systems as equally satisfactory on purely technical criteria. But, remembering the 1980s debacle over competing VHS and Betamax videotape systems, they wanted to avoid a "broken" DVD standard entering the consumer market. Using its central position in a cluster of info-tech alliances, IBM brokered a secret agreement in 1995 on patents and licensing fees. This compromise allegedly merged bits and pieces of both camps' technologies into a hybrid standard for DVD consumer products. Thus, organizational network dynamics ultimately shaped the implementation of a technological innovation.

IT innovations continually forced fundamental changes in the ways companies and their employees worked. Although I explore these impacts at the micro level in greater detail in the next section, two macro trends are worth noting here. First, the global information and communication revolutions drastically shortened manufacturing firms' development and production cycles while enabling them to operate profitably in customized, rather than mass product, markets. Instead of competing on high volumes and low prices, firms strove to satisfy business customers and consumers who demanded highly specialized goods and services. Careful and constant attention to quality performance became essential for organizations to survive and thrive. Second, because IT communication networks enabled managers to coordinate efforts across many physical locations, employees increasingly found themselves competing for jobs in worldwide labor pools at *all* occupational levels. American high school graduates vied directly with Koreans, Chinese, and Malays with superior basic schooling. Even highly skilled technical and professional workers were not immune from the World Wide Web's reach. Overnight, a New York bank could electronically subcontract data entry tasks to clerks in Jakarta and coding assignments to computer programmers in New Delhi, at a fraction of prevailing U.S. wages.

Slowing Productivity Growth.   Economists puzzled over the ominous slowdown in U.S. productivity growth in the final decades of the twentieth century. Productivity measures the relationship between the inputs (amounts of material, machinery, and human capital skills) used to produce outputs (goods built and services rendered). Over the long run, virtually the only way to raise a nation's standard of living is by increasing its per capita productivity (Krugman 1994; Thurow 1996). The most commonly used measure, *labor productivity,* is the value of output that an average worker can produce in one hour. Figure 1.5 plots the annual percentage changes in

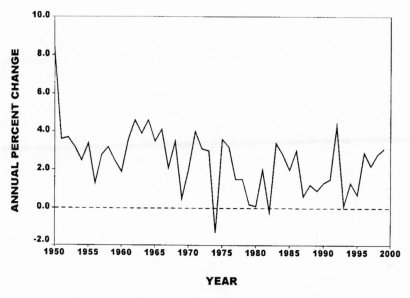

FIGURE 1.5   Falling Productivity Growth Rates
SOURCE: *Economic Report* (1995, 1999)

the output per hour for all persons in the business sector from 1950 to 1999. Fluctuations in both directions are evident around economic recessions and booms, but the long-term trend across the five decades was clearly downward: 3.5 percent in the 1950s, 3.2 percent in the 1960s, 2.1 percent in the 1970s, 1.6 percent in the 1980s, and 2.0 percent in the 1990s. These differences may seem small but, like a compounding savings account, their consequences are enormous. A 3.5 percent growth doubles living standards within just 21 years, but a 1.6 percent rate takes 44 years to double, almost two human generations or roughly the U.S. pace during the first half of the twentieth century. Small wonder that many Americans looked back with nostalgia at the two post-World War II decades as a prosperous golden age! Every advanced industrial economy experienced a similar productivity slowdown after 1973, suggesting that its causes were not unique to the United States. But even after the fall-off, the German and Japanese rates still remained higher than the growth in American productivity.[3] Although U.S. workers maintained a higher average *level* of productivity, their lower productivity *growth* meant that standards of living in many high-income nations were catching up with the United States.

Analysts propose numerous explanations for persistently poor labor productivity performance (Baumol, Blackman and Wolff 1989; Krugman 1994). Whatever the 1973 Arab oil boycott's initial impact on triggering worldwide energy price rises, the productivity decline persisted much too long for that one event to be the sole culprit. Some conservative economists blamed the U.S. government for excessively taxing and regulating business, but the 1980s supply-side and monetarist economic policies of Presidents Reagan and Bush did not reverse the stagnant productivity trend. A small productivity up-tick in the late 1990s coincided with the longest economic expansion in U.S. history, but the average annual gains remained substantially below the 1950–1969 rates. Other analysts rebuked workers for bringing too few skills to the workplace, perhaps the result of poor public schooling and too much time in front of the boob tube. Included among the other usual suspects were a decline in entrepreneurial vigor; inadequate research and development spending; too little savings and insufficient capital investments; and the drag of such social problems as unwed single mothers, an allegedly wasteful welfare system, and an insidious criminal underclass. Another perpetrator that some economists blamed was inaccurate official government statistical data, especially about service sector productivity (Bollier 1998:12). These varied alleged causes defied measurement and imputation of their precise contributions to the puzzle. Anyway, the political system generally just ignored stagnating productivity as a policy issue requiring drastic solutions (Krugman 1990:17).

One controversial interpretation connected the high-tech changes noted in the preceding subsection to shifts in the U.S. economy's industrial structure. Only about 20 percent of the U.S. labor force remained in manufacturing industries, where technological innovations could more easily produce dramatic productivity gains, often equaling the national rates of the 1950–1970 period. A large and expanding majority of the labor force worked in services such as banking, retailing, personal and business services, education, and health care, where boosting worker output was often much more difficult to achieve (see summary in Wolff 1985:50). Despite businesses spending $500 billion on information technology in 1996 alone, payoffs in lowered labor costs and better quality service remained hard to detect (Gibbs 1997). Employees often continued to perform numerous routine tasks in old-fashioned ways (think of college professors still using the lecture method going back to Plato's Academy in ancient Athens).

IT problems went far beyond office workers who futzed away their work hours at computer Solitaire and Minesweeper. Although a majority of office personnel used local area networked PCs, many organizations still hadn't learned how best to apply them to increase efficiency in workers' daily activities. When offices installed or upgraded their LANs, mid-career managers typically scrambled frantically to acquire new skills already familiar to their entry level employees. Resistance to bone-headed supervisory demands was reflected in the bitter humor of *Dilbert* cartoons plastering the cubicle world. IT could also breed its own pathologies. Hospitals, for example, built higher administrative staff-to-patient ratios than 30 years earlier because they devoted so much effort to processing forms and filing reports with insurance companies and government health bureaucracies (Strassman 1997).

Redesigning social relationships in the workplace might hold the ultimate keys for fully realizing the new technologies' productivity possibilities. Electronic networks could empower corporate employees to connect in better ways with suppliers and customers. Restructuring internal authority lines might encourage abolishing "business as usual" via paper memos and personal contacts. Making user-centered offices and factories the workplaces of the future promised to reverse the U.S. productivity slowdown, but no one should expect dramatic overnight transformations. Even the new millennium may not provide enough time.

Demography May Be Destiny. During the last half of the twentieth century, the gender, race, and ethnic composition of the U.S. labor force changed dramatically. White males made up the large majority in 1950. Relatively few women with children under 18 years of age worked outside their homes. Many white, middle class families actually resembled those depicted on such popular TV sit-coms as *Father Knows Best* and *Leave It to Beaver*: one employed (male) spouse, a second full-time (female) homemaker, and their two-and-one-half offspring. Starting in the 1960s, the most significant generational change was the mass entry of women into the paid labor force. By 1990, three-quarters of women with school-aged kids worked for pay, as did half the women with children under two years old. Two main factors propelled this transformation: (1) skyrocketing divorce rates and increasing out-of-wedlock childbirths fostered female-headed, single-parent households, many living below the official poverty line; and (2) married couples discovered that the lifestyles to which they wished to become accustomed were increasingly difficult to purchase with a single earner's paycheck (more follows about stagnant wages).

With their women employees facing conflicting work and family demands, employers responded slowly to these new workplace demographic realities. Although a few progressive corporations of the 1990s such as IBM and AT&T initiated generous family services—maternity leave, child- and elder-care, and "flextime" work scheduling—most companies gave only stingy and begrudging recognition to real burdens and barriers (Lamphere, Zavella and Gonzales 1993; Ingram and Simons 1995). United States government policies explicitly sought to maintain a facade of "gender neutrality" regarding working conditions, which probably worsened the economic vulnerabilities of women workers (Bailyn 1992). By socially constructing women's work-family concerns as equivalent to those faced by men, businesses could persist in acting neither responsibly nor responsively by accommodating their female employees' welfare needs. Only if social norms supporting family-friendly employment practices became more widely diffused would corporations come under greater institutional pressures to adopt them.

A second dramatic demographic change was the U.S. labor force's increasing racial and ethnic diversification. Through immigration (both legal and illegal) and natural increase, the diverse Hispanic American segment was expected to surpass African Americans as the nation's second largest population group by the 2010 Census. The heterogeneous Asian-ancestry segment—Chinese, Vietnamese, Japanese, Filipino, and others—grew more rapidly than both native white and black racial groups. The new ethnic employees often brought into their workplaces vastly divergent cultural understandings regarding appropriate work behaviors, as well as significant problems of language and technical skill deficits. Multicultural diversification wasn't unique to the United States. Several high-income nations were economic magnets for poor people from Eastern Europe, Africa, Asia, and Latin America willing to toil in low-paid menial jobs shunned by native-born citizens. Thus, France and Germany contended with torrents of Islamic immigrants from Algeria and Turkey, respectively, not to mention Polish, Romanian, and Ukrainian "guest workers." Even insular Japan attracted Korean, Filipino, and increasing numbers of Chinese sojourners.

All high-income nations faced impending demographic challenges in their steadily aging populations. In the early decades of the twenty-first century, the proportion of populations past age 60 might reach 20 percent in the United States and 30 percent in Japan and Germany. A rising tide of retiring U.S. "baby boomers" will put increasing fiscal burdens on a relatively smaller labor force to subsidize heavier social security and Medicare transfer payments. By avoiding such necessary but painful remedies as sharply raising the retirement age and means-testing eligibility, pusillanimous politicians have only worsened the looming fiscal crunch. Many corporations also abetted a similarly precarious predicament, promising generous retiree benefits but greatly underfunding their pension obligations. When elderly workers eventually discover their inability to make ends meet with paltry government and company pension checks, more of them may stay in the labor force past the traditional retirement age. However, if senior employees remain in their jobs, the upcoming generations could experience slower progress up the corporate ladder. Not all implications of an aging workforce are ominous: Companies often believe older employees are more loyal, reliable, and competent than younger replacements. Enough intergenerational tinder is lying around to ignite a social conflagration that could make the 1960s look like a weenie roast.

Market Capitalism Trumps Political Democracy.   When the citizens of Berlin tore down their infamous Wall in October 1989, they lowered the Iron Curtain on a 40-year Cold War that had drained vast wealth and political energies from both sides of the ideological conflict. The Soviet Empire's death was quickly followed by Russia's descent into a thuggish kleptocracy from which economic and political recovery could take decades. Exhausted from "imperial overstretch" (Kennedy 1987), American political leaders doubted that the public would stand to see its soldiers die on television while trying to police countless tribal conflicts from Somalia to Rwanda and Haiti to Bosnia. In the absence of meaningful threats from powerful foes spurred by an aggressive ideology, the United States shrank its armed forces and cut its defense budget. Bases closed across the South and West, airplane competitors Boeing and McDonnell-Douglas merged, and military research and development budgets were re-engineerd for civilian applications. With North Koreans starving, Cubans on the ropes, and both Chinese and Vietnamese commissars courting U.S. and Japanese corporate investors, capitalism had apparently trumped communism for good. Burying the Red Menace even deeper, developing nations from Mexico to India sold such state-owned enterprises as banks, airlines, steel mills, and telephone companies to the private sector (Solomon 1994). New regional trading blocks struggled to take shape in North America (NAFTA) and Western Europe (EU). Lacking a dominant political authority to settle international disputes, the world fumbled to construct a new trading system without significant tariffs and quotas.

In every high-income nation, organized labor movements played major roles in creating and expanding the twentieth-century social welfare state (Rueschemeyer, Stephens and Stephens 1992). In the political struggles between employers and workers to control labor market conditions, elected officials and bureaucrats were both the targets of influence and key players in shaping collectively binding legislative, regulatory, and judicial decisions. In the United States, the AFL-CIO had allied at mid-century with northern Democrats to formulate such New Deal and Great Society policies as social security, union recognition, collective bargaining, minimum wage, unemployment compensation, and occupational safety and health. However, business groups allied with the Republicans exercised substantial veto power over much social welfare spending. The domination of corporate over labor interests could be traced to America's political "exceptionalism": the absence of a strong socialist labor party along European lines, low election turnouts by working and lower class voters, fragmented federal political authority, and weak central government bureaucracies.

During the last third of the twentieth century, control of the U.S. federal government remained largely divided between Republican presidents and Democratic congresses, a sure recipe for political gridlock. The main political thrust was away from government regulation toward market direction of private-sector employment conditions. Reeling under the impacts of the globalizing economy while morphing from a manufacturing into a service-sector labor force, U.S. union membership declined from a peak of 35 percent of the nonagricultural labor force in 1954 to less than 20 percent by the mid–1980s. Employers fought to prevent further union intrusions on management control of workplace activities; for example, in 1987 blocking risk assessment legislation to monitor and notify workers of disease and toxic workplace hazards (Knoke et al. 1996). Unions suffered a serious setback when President Ronald Reagan fired the striking air traffic controllers early in his administration, signaling his endorsement of employers' union-busting efforts. Following Margaret Thatcher's lead in Great Britain, Reagan led a conservative crusade against the liberal political and cultural agenda. Republicans tried to curb government controls over the market by expanding military expenditures ("Star Wars"), slashing welfare spending, gutting corporate regulations, cutting taxes on the wealthy, and providing entrepreneurial incentives to stimulate rapid growth. Although the Reagan "revolution" was only partially successful in slowing the growth rate of big government, exploding federal budget deficits would ultimately thwart the Democrats' efforts to re-embark on new social programs such as the vast national health care proposed by Bill and Hillary Clinton. Evidence of Reagan's enduring political legacy was President Clinton's eventual embrace of a smaller federal administration ("the era of Big Government is over"), signified by his signing a 1997 balanced-budget deal with the Republican Congress.

As union power declined, business gained greater sophistication in achieving its political goals by taking advantage of the 1970s Watergate-era reforms in election and lobbying regulations (Vogel 1989). With politicians' re-election chances increasingly dependent on financing extremely costly mass media campaigns, lobbyists manipulated loopholes in campaign-funding laws that allowed large "soft-money" donations by political action committees (Clawson, Neustadl and Scott 1992; Mizruchi 1992). The China-connection funding scandals uncovered after the 1996 presidential election underscored the corrupting impact of soft money in national politics. Because campaign contributions were legally considered to be free speech ("one dollar, one vote"), election results appeared biased in favor of large contributors' public policy interests. If political money bought special access to the corridors of power, lobbying coalitions could push their cases before elected and appointed government officials, thus potentially influencing legislative and regulatory outcomes.

Unfettered capitalism's apparent successes threaten democratic political principles, as Lester Thurow (1996:242) recognized:

> Democracy and capitalism have very different beliefs about the proper distribution of power. One believes in a completely equal distribution of political

power, "one man, one vote," while the other believes that it is the duty of the economically fit to drive the unfit out of business and into economic extinction.

Markets rewarded self-interested actors who relentlessly pursued maximum personal gains without regard to consequences for the common societal good. A constrained U.S. political system was less able or willing to check the increasing inequality of income and wealth, examined in the next section. Whenever organized interest groups clashed against diffuse communitarian values, the former tended more often to prevail politically against broader public interests: farmers harvested crop subsidies that raised consumers' food costs; corporate polluters discharged toxic wastes into the air and water with impunity; gun manufacturers freely marketed handguns and assault rifles despite public opinion favoring stronger controls. A political culture based on rugged economic individualism benefited Wall Street elites at the expense of Main Street:

> For Middle America, the new preoccupation with enterprise and markets to the detriment of public services did have a downside: as public outlays on roads, schools and health came under pressure, the predictable result—worsened commuter gridlock, crowded classrooms and shortchanged hospitals and clinic—confronted ordinary families with either accepting lost services or paying new taxes and fees or higher bills, and ... these losses and pressures became an ingredient of the middle-class squeeze. (Phillips 1993:53)

One public sector enjoying high growth rates was construction of ever more prisons and jails to warehouse a dangerous underclass.

These deep-seated tensions between market capitalism and political democracy were concealed during America's fixation on its long twilight struggle against the Soviet Union. Once that threat had evaporated, these issues surfaced in the shredded safety nets through which large numbers of poor, sick, young, unemployed, and homeless people fell. Growing economic polarization between the haves and have-nots threatened the American Dream of ever-increasing intergenerational prosperity. Its symptoms appeared as sporadic violence by skinheads and militia movements, the chronic drug-induced stupors of inner-city dwellers, and the repudiation of affirmative action policies in California and Texas. The underlying cause was the unhindered triumph of the market principle of "everyone for herself" over the democratic ideals of inclusion and care for the weak and the lost.

Micro-Organizational Trends

The four macro-environmental trends covered in the preceding section had many important impacts on and implications for micro-organizational trends. I discuss them in this section under four topical subheadings: perpetual corporate restructuring; reorganized workplaces; the new employment contract; and rising income inequality in the United States.

Perpetual Corporate Restructuring.   Many corporate managers recalled the 1980s as a decade of downsizing. Employment in the 500 largest U.S. manufacturing companies was 15.9 million workers in 1980, but only 12.4 million by 1989, a drop of 22 percent (Autry and Colodny 1990). A 1985 Conference Board survey of 512 companies found that a majority had closed production facilities or significantly reduced their workforces in the preceding three years (Berenbeim 1986), and a 1993 company survey found that 72 percent had implemented layoffs in the three previous years (Wyatt Company 1993). A 1992 national survey of nearly 3,000 full-time workers revealed that two-fifths of their companies had experienced workforce reductions, with 28 percent cutting back in management employees (Galinsky, Bond and Friedman 1993). Although blue-collar factory workers usually experienced layoffs during business cycle downturns, downsizing began to hit white-collar employees particularly hard. By one estimate up to 0.5 million middle managers and professionals lost their jobs in 300 large companies during the mid–1980s (Willis 1987). Two-thirds of the Fortune 1000 companies both downsized and cut out middle-management layers (Lawler, Mohrman and Ledford 1995). Among companies reporting to the federal Equal Employment Opportunity Commission, covering about 40 percent of the labor force, the number of managers per 100 employees fell from 12.5 in 1983 to 11.2 in 1994, a 10 percent decrease (Markels 1995).

Nor did corporate downsizing stop once economic prosperity revived in the mid–1990s. Although the fortunes of many corporations recovered, others dwindled under relentless competition. Wal-Mart and MCI Communications together created 230,000 jobs, but such familiar names as Kodak, Woolworth, and Xerox continued laying off workers. In 1993 alone, General Motors announced elimination of 69,650 employees; Sears cut 50,000 workers; and IBM, AT&T, and Boeing each axed more than 30,000 jobs. For his role in dismissing 11,200 employees at Scott Paper in 1994 and swiftly slashing half of Sunbeam's 12,000 jobs in 1996 in efforts to revive those companies' sagging performances, corporate fixer Albert J. Dunlap won notoriety as "Rambo in Pinstripes" and "Chainsaw Al."

In many cases, two types of corporate restructurings hammered employees: internal organizational redesign and financial reorganization. I discuss workplace redesign issues in the next subsection. In the 1980s and 1990s financial restructurings that decimated corporate workforces were driven by qualitative changes in company ownership and emerging new ideas about corporate control (Useem 1993). Large shareholders—often giant institutional investors such as pension funds and insurance companies—actively insisted that top managers rebuild their firms to serve stockholder interests through faster growth rates and higher stock prices, even at the expense of company "stakeholders"—its employees, suppliers, customers, and local communities. Contests for control of the largest publicly traded corporations on the stock market took off in the early 1980s. Michael Milken at Drexel Burnham Lambert popularized high-risk "junk bonds" to raise huge amounts of cash for speculative leveraged buyouts (LBOs) by predatory outside raiders or existing top management. A takeover team would proceed to privatize a targeted firm by buying back its publicly held stock at prices irresistible to shareholders. It would then try to operate the company to pay back the high interest on its junk bonds quickly (while just coincidentally turning a nice profit for the new owners). In addition to cutting production costs by slashing production employee and middle-management payrolls, another common restructuring strategy involved selling off business divisions and product lines deemed drags on the company's "core competencies."

Of the Fortune 500 largest manufacturing companies in 1980, one-third were targets of hostile takeover bids and another third ceased to exist as independent businesses by the end of the decade (Cappelli et al. 1997:33). The leveraged buyout wave crested in 1988 when more than 450 mergers and acquisitions that year totaled almost $160 billion and another 120 management-led LBOs spent $60 billion (Useem 1993:24–25). In the largest buyout in U.S. history up to that time, an RJR Nabisco management team led by its chief officer Ross Johnson lost a $25 billion bidding war in 1987 against the venture-capital firm Kohlberg, Kravis and Roberts (KKR). The amusing shenanigans behind that mega-deal also produced an entertaining book (Burroughs and Hellyar 1990) and an eponymous comedy film, *Barbarians at the Gate*, starring James Garner. Not laughing at all were the middle managers and employees who were later squeezed out when KKR sold off various RJR Nabisco units to pay for their gamble.

A major outcome of the 1980s merger, acquisition, and shake-out mania was the rapid decline of the previously popular "conglomerate" corporate structure. This form of organization combined several unrelated business lines, based on a "firm-as-portfolio" concept of growth through diversification (Davis, Diekmann and Tinsley 1994). For example, Harold Geneen constructed International Telephone and Telegraph in the 1950s and 1960s as a multi-industry firm that operated hotels, entertainment, insurance, automotive, defense, electronics, and, yes, even telephone companies. One alleged advantage of the conglomerate strategy lay in its "synergy," the capacity to reduce financial risks while coping with environmental uncertainties. A conglomerate's central administrators could quickly reassign talented top managers to whichever businesses needed them most. Frequent new business acquisitions would sustain rapid conglomerate growth. Unpredictable revenue streams were expected to smooth out across business accounting units, and thus a conglomerate's overall profits would be maximized. By 1980 three out of four Fortune 500 companies operated in two or more unrelated business sectors.

This trend rapidly unraveled in the 1980s, as publicly traded conglomerates appeared ripe for takeover and divestiture of units outside an acquiring company's core industry. By the 1990s the frequency of unrelated diversification among the top U.S. companies had fallen by nearly half (Davis, Diekmann and Tinsley 1994). The rapid bust-up ("deinstitutionalization") of the once prevalent conglomerate form was encouraged by a sea change in business leaders' mental conceptions about how best to organize. Their public remarks began to discredit the firm-as-portfolio model in favor of new strategies involving network structures:

> [P]roducing complete products often entails forming temporary alliances with several specialists and results in a network, or "virtual corporation," composed of formally separate entities rather than a single bounded organization. ... Such "firm-like" arrangements create obvious difficulties for organizational theories that take for granted that the organization is an entity and study analogous processes such as birth, growth, and death, while they create openings for approaches to social structure that take the network as a guiding analogy. (Davis, Diekmann and Tinsley 1994:563 and 567)

The impact of downsizing and financial restructuring reached far beyond the largest corporations. Innumerable medium and small companies supplying parts and services to those giant firms were also forced to shrink their workforces to survive in the lean-and-mean economy (Harrison 1994). Whenever the enthusiasm for unselective downsizing went too far, cutting deeply into corporate muscle as well as fat ("dumbsizing"), employers soon found themselves turning to outside vendors for help. Curiously, middle managers given their pink-slips on Friday sometimes returned on Monday to work for the company as freelance consultants at much higher fees. When big companies shed their permanent in-house support staffs— everyone from lawyers and researchers to grounds keepers and cafeteria cooks—they typically substituted deals with subcontractors and temporary help agencies to provide workers for short-term projects. In 1992, Manpower Inc., with its 560,000 temp employees, replaced the shrinking General Motors as largest private-sector employer in the United States (Swoboda 1993). (In the public sector, the U.S. military remained the nation's largest employing organization.) With fewer permanent employees remaining to perform value-adding work, many companies grew more cautious and selective when hiring new workers. They engaged head-hunting companies to find raidable executive talent, and struck deals with community colleges and commercial enterprises to retrain their older employees in the newest technologies. The interorganizational arrangements for managing human resources are a significant aspect of the networking dynamics explored throughout this book.

Reorganized Workplaces. Internal organizational restructuring complemented the downsizing and financial restructurings described in the preceding subsection. The most dramatic changes involved the flattening of corporate bureaucracies. As first described by Max Weber (1947), the bureaucratic form of control involves detailed job descriptions; fixed rules and regulations applied impersonally; office management through written documents ("the files"); close managerial supervision over a small number of subordinates (span of control); hierarchical flows of information, commands, and decisions; and employee motivation primarily by extrinsic rewards for performance, such as pay and perks. Carried to their logical limits, bureaucratic principles permeated Frederick Taylor's "scientific management" agenda for speeding-up assembly lines, so hilariously caricatured in Charlie Chaplin's 1936 film, *Modern Times.* Tightly integrated sociotechnical systems function best in stable, predictable environments such as manufacturing assembly lines, where workers repeatedly carry out routine actions that don't require them to respond creatively to quickly changing situations. Although bureaucracy's "standard operating procedures" promised to sustain a highly efficient method for coordinating large numbers of workers to achieve collective goals, they could also breed alienation, ritual conformity to orders, and psychological disengagement of employees from their jobs and organizations (Merton 1961). At their pathological worst, bureaucratic workplaces were plagued by employees passively resisting managerial controls or actively sabotaging production schedules. For Weber, the relentless, irreversible spread of bureaucratic capitalism across the twentieth century was just one manifestation of a larger historical trend toward completely rationalizing society that would inexorably imprison all men and women in its "iron cage" (Weber 1952).

Weber's prophecy was wrong. Bureaucratic procedures might be optimal for churning out large volumes of standardized refrigerators and soft drinks for mass consumer markets, but they proved inept at competing in the specialized global product and service markets emerging toward the end of the twentieth century. The trigger for U.S. change was a flood of imported Japanese automobiles and consumer electronics in the 1970s that ate deeply into U.S. producers' domestic market shares. American executives came to believe that the secret of their foreign competitors' successes originated primarily in organizational designs that created a superior "Japanese management system." Ironically, the total quality management (TQM) that Japan embraced to satisfy customer demands was initially formulated by American consultants W. Edwards Deming and Joseph Juran during the

1950s, an era when U.S. employers saw few economic benefits from paying attention to either their employees' or customers' needs and concerns. In a few decades, U.S. companies were frantically scrambling to redesign their plants and offices into flexible organizational structures capable of competing against Japanese firms in the emerging global markets.

When downsizing corporations began firing middle managers in the 1980s, they also eliminated vertical layers of bureaucratic authority between the CEO and frontline production workers in factories and offices. Company headquarters were hollowed out as their tasks and personnel were decentralized to branch locations. In that process, employers devolved decision-making authority downward and re-engineered their business practices to improve employees' psychological commitments to their jobs. All workers were expected to take the initiative in identifying and solving problems without explicit, detailed instructions from above. Rewards went to the people most adept at thinking through the consequences of their actions and capable of combining technical knowledge with superior social skills to get the job done. Firms experimented with job enrichment, quality circles, and pay-for-performance schemes that thrust greater responsibility for self-management onto workers. Rigid job systems were replaced by project assignments where people had to acquire new job "competencies" through cross-training. Progress in their careers increasingly depended on lifelong learning and continual intellectual growth, not time spent in rank. Human resources managers could more selectively recruit, train, and place employees in jobs where their skills were most suitable. Workplaces were physically redesigned to reduce status barriers, putting senior managers at desks in large open areas and abolishing executive washrooms and cafeterias.

Restructuring opened numerous opportunities for network relationships, both inside and outside the organization. Electronic information technologies, allowing data to be transmitted among functional groups, forged lateral communication channels to replace the old vertical bureaucratic paths. Telecommuting to work from home offices mushroomed for millions. "Team work" became a magic mantra by which U.S. companies might achieve the total quality nirvana (Katzenbach and Smith 1993). Self-directed teams must be empowered to control sufficient resources to implement their ideas and their members be held collectively responsible for all results. Corporate outsourcing of many formerly internal functions required specialists who were skilled at negotiating with goods suppliers and service providers. Expensive warehousing operations could be replaced by just-in-time (JIT) delivery systems that require skillful planning and coordination between external vendors and internal production units. Under the new industrial relations regime, unions ideally should become management's partners rather than their adversaries, collaborating in the conversion of old bureaucratic rigidities into flexible new forms (Ferman et al.

1991). Customers, whether inside or outside the organization's boundaries, must be continually consulted throughout the design and production stages, directly communicating to the appropriate teams their requirements for constantly improving quality goods and services. Customer feedback of complaints and compliments should be a vital element in employees' performance evaluations.

Researchers labeled these redesigned workplaces "high involvement practices" (Lawler 1992) or "high performance work organizations" (Osterman 1994a, 1999). According to Edward Lawler III (1996:22), their core logic was embedded in these six principles:

- Organization can be the ultimate competitive advantage.
- Involvement is the most effective source of control.
- All employees must add significant value.
- Lateral processes are the key to organizational effectiveness.
- Organizations should be designed around products and customers.
- Effective leadership is the key to organizational effectiveness.

Just how far such concepts had penetrated into U.S. workplaces was revealed in a 1991 national survey of establishments. About one-third could be characterized as high-performance organizations that combined decentralized decision making, employee job training, performance-based compensation, and firm internal labor markets providing job ladders on which employees can climb steadily upward (Kalleberg et al. 1996:120). Similarly, national surveys of establishments with 50 or more employees found in both 1992 and 1997 that at least half the "core employees" (those most directly involved in producing goods or services) participated in self-managed teams in about 40 percent of the workplaces (Osterman 1999:98–101). Participation by a majority of employees in quality circles, job rotation, or TQM programs increased rapidly, with penetration growing from about one-quarter to more than one-half of the establishments. However, workplaces that combined teamwork with at least two other high-performance practices reached only 25 percent in 1992 and 38 percent in 1997. The survival and diffusion of specific innovative work designs seemed problematic, depending critically on whether the perceived outcomes convinced corporate leaders that the present pain of change would ultimately be repaid by future gains in organizational efficiency, productivity, and profitability:

> The best conclusion is that work reorganization alone does not lead to impressive gains. It pays off only when it is part of a reorganization of the entire production system that includes substantial shifts in other aspects of internal labor markets. When these prerequisites are met, there can be considerable gains. (Cappelli et al. 1997:110–111)

The New Employment Contract.   In the decades after World War I, many large corporations began to develop an implied employment contract[4] that sought to rationalize the uncertain and arbitrary working conditions prevalent in earlier casual, short-term labor markets. The predominant "drive" system relied heavily on foremen playing favorites and bullying workers into compliance with their orders (Jacoby 1985). An expanding U.S. domestic economy required greater predictability and control than could be delivered using the informal hiring and disciplinary arrangements run by company foremen. One outcome of the New Deal's pro-labor legislation was successful pressure by labor unions and government regulatory agencies on firms to adopt standardized employment practices for hours, wages, and working conditions (Kochan, Katz and McKersie 1986). This implicit social contract, predominating well into the 1970s, emphasized strong relationships of mutual obligation between employers and their employees (Osterman 1984; Cappelli 1999). To secure long-term supplies of labor at reasonable cost and to retain employees once they had acquired firm-specific job skills, companies offered: complex pay and benefit packages based more on seniority than on performance merit; elaborate internal labor markets involving company training programs and regular promotion opportunities through graded ranks of occupations; and above all, job security (so-called lifetime employment such as IBM boasted), particularly for core managerial and white-collar employees but increasingly for blue-collar workers as well. These arrangements insulated employees from the whims of competitive labor markets and effectively tied them to their companies through the ups and downs of the business cycle. Even when recessions forced layoffs of blue-collar employees, these relationships assured that most would return when assembly lines began rolling again. In exchange for providing steady employment at comfortable wages, companies could expect reasonable work effort and loyalty from their employees. This rationalized system benefited firms by reducing employee turnover costs (for example, in hiring and training fewer replacement workers) and by enabling greater predictability and control over production schedules and distribution operations. The internalized employment contract was also nurtured by pressures on corporations to conform from external institutions such as unions, governments, courts, and industry competitors. Its popularity was boosted in the 1970s by business leaders' and academic consultants' beliefs that Japan's economic successes arose from a similar model of lifetime employment.

By the 1980s, the traditional contract faced severe challenges from the globalizing economy and technological innovations. Downsizing, mergers, and outsourcing eroded corporate capacities to sustain job security for many employees. Even skilled professionals and experienced managers were fired when their services were no longer needed. In 1974 the Supreme Court ruled that purchasing agents who did not supervise others were "exempt" employees, that is, they could not be considered hourly workers protected under the 1938 Fair Labor Standards Act. Thus, by redesigning jobs to give workers more autonomy in carrying out their tasks, employers gained greater flexibility and reduced their costs by adjusting hours, pay, and working conditions (Cappelli 1999:113–157). Likewise, by leasing short-term workers from temporary help agencies, companies could evade burdensome paperwork requirements in hiring and firing personnel and avoid generous fringe benefits such as medical insurance and retirement pensions. People in nonpermanent employment statuses—including those holding temporary, part-time, subcontracted, and independent consultant jobs—are known as "contingent workers" (Kalleberg and Schmidt 1996). Their ranks grew more rapidly than the labor force expansion as a whole in the 1980s. By one estimate as much as 25–30 percent of the U.S. civilian labor force worked under such externalized employment conditions by the late 1980s (Belous 1989; Applebaum 1992). Part-time employment (less than 35 hours per week) expanded from 16.4 percent in 1970 to 18.0 percent in 1990, with a majority of that growth involuntary because of inability to find full-time work (Tilly 1990; Callaghan and Hartmann 1991).

Small organizations, for example restaurants and construction companies, were especially prone to deploy contingent workers to regulate the ebb and flow of business, but even giant corporations increasingly resorted to such arms-length labor relations. Part-time work and subcontracting issues figured prominently in the 1997 Teamsters Union strike against United Parcel Service of America Inc. (UPS), on top of disputes over control of company pension funds. About 60 percent of the 185,000 unionized jobs at UPS were part-time in sorting and loading operations, and these arrangements had increased sharply: Of 46,000 jobs created at UPS since 1993, 83 percent were part-time. The full-timers, mostly delivery truck drivers, made $19.95 per hour, while the part-timers averaged $11 per hour, although they received some benefits if they stayed long enough at UPS. The Teamsters also rejected the company's initial offer on grounds that subcontracting would reduce promotion chances for some drivers and part-timers. After a two-week strike, the company agreed to increase part-time wages by 35 percent and create 10,000 new full-time jobs over the five-year contract, as well as another 10,000 part-time jobs if UPS could win back its customers. Although the strike showed that the labor movement might sometimes stem the tide toward contingent work, its clout was fairly worthless to the 85 percent of the U.S. private-sector labor force without union representation.

Externalized employment relations also weakened the rationale for companies to collaborate in developing their employees' human capital skills (Osterman 1995a; Cappelli et al. 1997:122–153). Firms offered less on-the-job training because more workers were unlikely to remain on the payroll long enough to return a company's investment through increased productivity.

As responsibility to acquire useful job skills shifted from the employer to the employee, a vicious cycle developed, generating downward spirals in human capital formation. Uncertain about the prospective directions of their careers, workers rationally avoided investing their personal resources in expensive education and training programs for which they might find no future need:

> The net result is less skills investment at exactly the time that more skills investment is needed. The system evolves toward less commitment and less investment just as it should be evolving in the opposite direction. (Thurow 1996:288)

Significant declines in pension and medical coverage in the 1980s also suggested that employers were reducing their long-term commitments to workers through traditional employment-security arrangements (Bloom and Freeman 1992). In 1980, a federal Bureau of Labor Statistics survey of medium and large private-sector firms found that 80 percent of full-time employees were covered by "defined benefit" pension plans, which committed employers to pay future specific amounts to retirees. By 1993 these programs covered only 56 percent of workers. The 1994 BLS small-firm survey revealed that defined benefit plans covered just 15 percent of those employees. "Defined contribution" plans, which calculated payments according to the worker's contributions (for example, profit-sharing, 401(k), and medical savings plans), increased as tax policies changed to allow accumulations on a tax-deferred basis. By the mid–1990s, nearly half the employees of medium and large companies were covered by defined contribution plans, as were a third of small-firm workers. Similar declines occurred in employer-funded health insurance coverage along with rising costs for worker-paid premiums and deductibles. The Census Bureau's employee surveys showed that employer-provided coverage for married men fell from 89 percent in 1979 to 76.6 percent 1992, a 12.5 percent decrease. "Although the decline occurred among all age and education groups, it was most dramatic among the younger, less educated workers" (Olson 1995).

The several trends described above fundamentally combined to rewrite the traditional employment contract. The rigid boundaries between labor markets and firms broke down as both employers and employees looked outside company walls for better deals. Workers struggled to cope with short-term, haphazard career paths requiring them to assume greater accountability for obtaining new job skills (Waterman, Waterman and Collard 1994). Because fewer workers expected to spend their entire working lives at a single organization, they had to prepare to deal with disruptions caused by moving from company to company. Even those employees fortunate to enjoy longer tenure with one firm often found themselves periodically shuttled to new postings. People learned how to survive and even thrive in the new employment climate of reduced career prospects, often by obtaining job skill retraining at their own expense through night school classes and weekend seminars. "Gaming" the corporation became a common practice: Workers accepted projects that would give them useful experiences, skills, and network contacts that enabled them to compete successfully for their next work assignment. In the words of an Intel human resources vice president, "You own your own employability. You are responsible" (O'Reilly 1994:49).

As firms grew lean-and-mean by demolishing their traditional internal labor markets, they typically created two-tier employment structures fraught with tension. A privileged core of employees still enjoyed high job security and good benefits but was immersed in an expanding peripheral workforce having more fragile ties to the corporation. Contingent workers might have cheaper direct labor costs but be much more expensive in lower productivity and morale. They could require more intensive supervision and training, express less commitment and company loyalty, and produce lower-quality work less efficiently. The restructuring process could also increase stress levels and destroy morale if workers felt themselves burdened by heavy work loads and longer hours that conflicted with their family obligations (Cappelli et al. 1997:195–206). The emergence of the external employment contract raised fundamental questions about organizational citizenship in the brave new workplace: Were employees merely human costs to be controlled or were they assets in which employers should invest? What obligations did firms and workers owe one another beyond exchanging hours of labor for a paycheck and a pension?

Rising Income Inequality in the United States. A major result of turmoil in the U.S. political economy was to bring the steady rise in family incomes after World War II to a grinding halt. Figure 1.6 graphs the trend in median constant family incomes. (A "median" divides a distribution of numbers into two equal groups, half with the family incomes in a year above the median value and half with incomes below that value. A transformation into "constant" dollars adjusts the values to remove the effects of inflation; I recalculated family incomes in Figure 1.6 in constant 1998 dollars.) Over the 23 years from 1950 to 1972, median family incomes almost doubled, from $22,448 to $43,347. However, over the next 23 years the trend line remained almost flat. Median family income fluctuated within a narrow band between a low of $39,581 in 1982, a recession year, and a peak of $44,974 in 1989. Only after the recovery from the most recent recession (in 1991) was well under way did family median incomes surpass the 1989 level, reaching $45,262 and $46,737 in 1997 and 1998, respectively. However, if the same rate of increase experienced by the earlier generation had prevailed over the past quarter century, median family incomes would have grown to $85,429 by 1998! By the end of the twentieth century, even the most optimistic believers in the American Dream had been rudely awakened to the new reality of a stagnant standard of living.

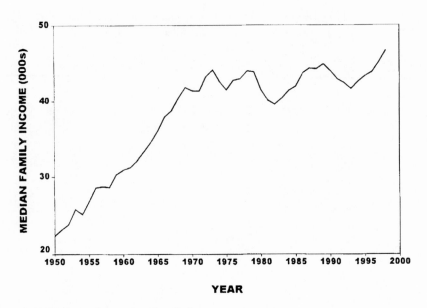

FIGURE 1.6   Stagnating Family Incomes
SOURCE: U.S. Department of Commerce (1991:Table B-4); U.S. Bureau of the Census (1999):Table 750

The family income trend conceals another important aspect of the story. Although the typical family's living standards remained frozen over more than two decades, some Americans enjoyed real improvements while others fell farther behind. This pattern is best illustrated with the different experiences of income "quintiles" (that is, five segments each of which contains exactly 20 percent of all families), ranked from lowest to highest "mean" income. (A mean is calculated by dividing total income by the number of families; it typically yields a somewhat higher value than does the median.) As revealed by Figure 1.7, the increases in mean family incomes from 1967 to 1980 were positive for every quintile, although noticeably lower for the two poorest groups. In other words, all Americans enjoyed real, if modest, increases in their standards of living. However, after 1980 the five quintiles diverged markedly: The 40 percent of families at the bottom of the income ladder actually *lost* real purchasing power, whereas the top 40 percent saw substantial increases. Indeed, the top 5 percent of the income pyramid experienced unprecedented income growth, from $126,000 to $198,000, a 57 percent jump between 1980 and 1994, resulting in their earning one-fifth of total earnings that year. Thus, during the era when median incomes were stagnating, families at the very top reaped enormous gains that pushed them far ahead of those below. This trend toward divergent incomes is evident in

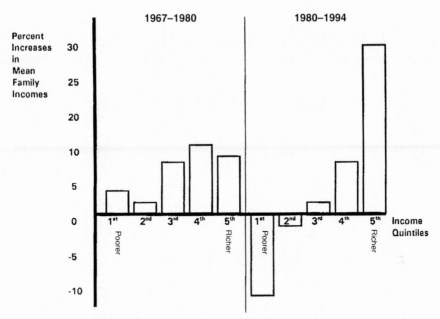

FIGURE 1.7   Diverging Family Incomes across Quintiles
SOURCE: U.S. Bureau of the Census (1999); Exter (1996:49)

Figure 1.8, which tracks the Gini ratio, a measure of family income inequality. A Gini value of 0 indicates perfect equality (every family has the same income), while a value of 1.00 indicates perfect inequality (one family has all the money, everyone else has nothing). The general tendency from 1950 until about 1970 pointed toward slightly increasing equality, but during the next quarter-century the clear trend was toward sharply greater inequality: the rich growing much richer relative to poor and middle-income families.

Social researchers quarreled about the reasons for expanding U.S. income inequality (Danziger and Gottschalk 1993). Many indicted several social and economic trends noted in preceding subsections. The labor force's changing gender composition increased the participation of both two-spouse earners and single-parent households, greatly widening the income disparities between these types of families. Similarly, the number of immigrant workers, who usually earn less than the native born, increased dramatically. College graduates skilled at working with computers competed more effectively for the higher salaries offered by service industries, while high school graduates' wages fell further behind. Changes in federal and state transfer and tax policies, begun under President Reagan in the 1980s and continued under President Clinton into the 1990s, reduced welfare benefits to low-income families, held minimum wages below the pace

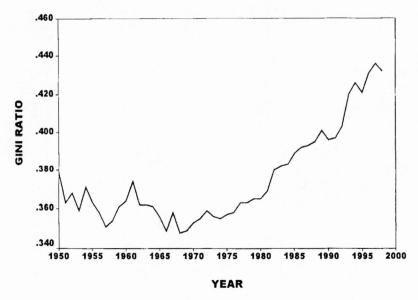

FIGURE 1.8   Rising Income Inequality
SOURCE: U.S. Bureau of the Census (2000:Table F4)

of inflation and allowed the wealthiest families to keep more income. The decline of unionized industries exposed more employees to volatile competitive labor markets. Investor pressures to show quick results forced companies to boost their stock prices by trimming labor costs through restructuring and outsourcing jobs to cheaper labor providers. However, the much-favored villain of foreign competition seemed less important than the productivity drop-off, as noted by two prominent economists:

> The sources of U.S. difficulties are overwhelmingly domestic, and the nation's plight would be much the same even if world markets had not become more integrated. The share of manufacturing in GDP is declining because people are buying relatively fewer goods; manufacturing employment is falling because companies are replacing workers with machines and making more efficient use of those they retain. Wages have stagnated because the rate of productivity growth in the economy as a whole has slowed, and less skilled workers in particular are suffering because a high-technology economy has less and less demand for their services. Our trade with the rest of the world plays at best a small role in each case. (Krugman and Lawrence 1994:49)

Another intriguing source of increased income inequality is the spread of "winner-take-all" markets, where "rewards tend to be concentrated in the hands of a few top performers, with small differences in talent or effort often giving rise to enormous differences in incomes" (Frank and Cook 1995:24; see also Rosen 1981). Real or conjectured limits on the supply of unique talents, coupled with electronic information technologies' capacities to reproduce outstanding performances in massive, cheap copies, can generate vast earnings for a handful of superstars and their agents. We're all familiar with the astronomic salaries commanded by peak movie actors, pop musicians, and athletes. (A 21-year-old basketball player for the Minnesota Timberwolves turned down a six-year, $103 million contract in 1997 because it was "not enough." He later settled for a mere $121 million.) Less publicly visible were contest markets fostering run-away incomes for top scientists, authors, lawyers, business consultants, and corporate chief executive officers. A "dramatic increase in the extent to which American firms compete with one another for the services of top executive talent" (Frank and Cook 1995:70) drove CEO compensation to astronomical levels over two decades. In the 200 largest U.S. firms in 1974, the average CEO earned about 35 times as much the average American manufacturing worker; by 1990 that ratio had grown to 150 to 1 in both manufacturing and services (Crystal 1992:27). The U.S. disproportions greatly exceeded those in Western Europe and Japan (Parker-Pope 1996).

Plan of the Book

In the chapters that follow, I apply diverse theoretical perspectives to analyze trends in the U.S. political economy, seeking to explain their impacts on organizational changes in the twentieth century, especially in the final three decades. Chapter 2 reviews the basic concepts and principles of the five organizational theories that I use extensively throughout the book: organizational ecology, institutionalism, resource dependence, transaction cost economics, and organizational networks. I bring alternative perspectives such as agency theory, social capital theory, organizational learning, and organizational evolution into play on issues where they are most relevant. Chapter 3 provides a broad overview of U.S. organization populations, including for-profit business, governmental, and nonprofit organizations. It analyzes the basic demographic processes of organizational foundings and disbandings, then examines changing structural forms such as the multidivisional corporation and the conglomerate.

The central themes in the following three chapters emphasize both inter- and intra-organizational relations revolving around production patterns and workplace activities. Chapter 4 describes the proliferation of diverse strategic alliances among companies and the critical role of trust in sustaining such partnerships. It explores the origins, development, and consequences of interorganizational collaborations, ranging from large firm-small supplier networks and small-firm networks to regional alliance networks and global organizational systems. Chapter 5 considers the contradictory implications of the changing employment contract from lifetime job security toward greater market-like labor relations. Increasing project-length and temporary employment signaled eroding employee attachments to firms, but high-performance workplaces also sought greater engagement by self-directed work teams. Chapter 6 links new forms of networked organizations to the contrasting strategies of mentoring and networking relations for developing employee careers. It examines social capital formation and its consequences at both the individual and organizational levels of analysis.

The next three chapters concentrate on political processes within and between organizations. Chapter 7 reviews two centuries of changing legal ideas about the governance of corporations. It analyzes the struggles for control between boards of directors and chief executive officers, institutional investor revolts, and new legal theories of stakeholder rights that could transform power and privilege at the top of these organizations. Similarly, Chapter 8 considers how social movements by various identity groups of employees challenged management's workplace prerogatives. The rise and decline of the labor union movement and the steady legalization of the workplace are two major twentieth-century trends with implications for the future transformation of employee rights and protections. Chapter 9 turns to the participation of businesses, trade associations, labor unions, and other interest groups in U.S. public policy making. Controversies over trends in organizational campaign contributions, influence tactics, and lobbying coalitions paint an ambiguous portrait of who, if anyone, really rules the roost.

Finally, Chapter 10 explores the impact of technological changes in national innovation systems, organizational learning processes, and the evolution of new organizational forms. Although complex and chaotic processes inherently limit the capacity of organizational studies to forecast developments with great precision, our collective research endeavors enable us better to understand and explain how the futures of changing organizations emerge immanently from preceding events.

2

Theorizing About Organizations

These terrible sociologists,
who are the astrologers and alchemists
of our twentieth century.
—Miguel de Unamuno, Fanatical Skepticism (1914)

This chapter introduces five basic theories of organizational behavior: organizational ecology theory, institutional theory, resource dependence theory, transaction cost economics, and organizational network analysis. I briefly outline their main concepts and principles, discussing their strengths and limitations for explaining macro level changes. In succeeding chapters, I use these five perspectives as basic analytical tools for examining various facets of organizational performance and transformation. Just as natural science theories help us to make sense of a complex physical and biological world, organization theories are powerful devices for simplifying complicated social realities into more readily comprehensible conceptual images capable of yielding significant insights into basic structures and processes. Careful applications of alternative theoretical perspectives should better enable us to understand the organizational changes transforming the modern world.

These theories are rooted in the field of organization studies, which had emerged by the middle of the twentieth century as a multidisciplinary, multitheoretical paradigm. Their antecedents were the analyses of large public- and private-sector bureaucratic organizations by such pioneering theorists as Max Weber (1947), Robert Michels (1949), Chester Barnard (1938), and Luther Gulick (Gulick and Urwick 1937). Organization studies arose through numerous efforts to comprehend and control the phenomenal growth in scale and scope of organizational activities and their intrusions into the daily lives and well-being of workers, families, and communities. Organization studies continues to draw diverse ideas and inspiration from basic and applied disciplines, including sociology, business management, economics, law, political science, public administration, history, and journalism. Given this field's uneasy mixture of abstract knowledge and pragmatic relevance, organization theories vary in their capacities to guide basic academic research while offering organizational participants practical advice about intervening in the affairs of their corporations and agencies. The ultimate value of any theory lies in its continual ability to generate fresh insights into a steadily changing world, regardless of any immediate applications. Hence, the primary goal of this chapter is to provide enough detail about each theory to be usefully applied to inquiries in subsequent chapters into specific aspects of organizational change.

Theoretical Elements

In general, a useful theory draws an investigator's attention to fundamental features and away from distracting and irrelevant aspects of organizational behavior. For example, most macro theories acknowledge the importance of organization size (whether measured as people, financial resources, or both), but not the color schemes in the physical plant, for explaining such actions as mergers, alliances, and authority reorganization. Theories de-emphasize merely factual descriptions of particular events, such as Corp. X's 2000 fall quarterly earnings. Instead, they stress significant causal relations that are generalizable beyond the specific times and places where they occur, such as how decreasing competition within an industry affects its firms' profit levels.

Ideally, a formal *theory* consists of a set of logically interrelated statements, or theoretical propositions, that explains some significant aspects of observable phenomena. Each *proposition* is a simple sentence that links two or more abstract *concepts*, which are terms defining the key elements of the theory. For example, a theory of organizational mergers should begin by defining its principal concepts, such as organization size, market share, and profit. Its propositions would likely involve statements using these terms to explain the circumstances under which some organizations are expected to combine with others. Thus, propositions might state the expected relation between firms' merger attempts and the merging organizations' sizes, market shares, and profits. Additional theoretical statements might propose how macro-economic conditions and governmental regulatory policies would be expected to affect the merger process.

The ultimate analytical value of theory lies in its capacity to extend our knowledge by generating new insights and understandings. A practical benefit of organization theory for managers and employees would be to apply its insights to improve a company's performance and contributions to the collective well-being of its participants. Without a theory capable of imposing a meaningful order on discrete empirical observations, organization studies would degenerate into an endless compilation of social facts, differing little from descriptive journalism. Because theoretical propositions make assertions about some state of the social world, their truth-value must be assessed with relevant observations. A comprehensive theory also indicates the kinds of data that researchers should collect to test its theoretical claims. A highly successful theory withstands repeated efforts to falsify its propositions, but accumulating disproofs should eventually eliminate an erroneous theory, or at least lead to substantial modifications that remove any contradictions between its propositions and the data (Popper 1959). An exceptionally powerful theory enables researchers to determine whether their findings apply beyond the particular times and places where they originally occurred. If relationships uncovered in one setting fail to replicate in other situations—say, if Japanese management techniques flop when imported into U.S. factories—then analysts must reconsider the theory's *scope conditions*, that is, the limits under which its propositions hold true. Ideally, the continual interplay between analytical theory and empirical evidence progressively improves our ability to identify which social forces in the political economy drive organizational change. The ultimate benefit to society comes from better applied knowledge that helps organizations and their participants avoid making wasteful and harmful mistakes.

The five basic organization theories discussed in the following sections treat a broad range of organizational phenomena spanning multiple levels of analysis. The conceptual scheme in Figure 2.1 indicates this range, using a hierarchy of six widely accepted categories (see, e.g., Scott 1995:57). Three dotted-line icons depict macro levels of analysis:

- The *organizational society* is the totality of all the organizations in a community, a nation, or the international system.
- An *organization population* is a homogeneous set consisting of all organizations of a specific type or form, such as restaurants, newspapers, or hospitals.
- An *organizational field* is a heterogeneous set of functionally interconnected organizations, for example, all the corporations, interest groups, and government agencies that deal with national defense.

Note that the population and field concepts cross-cut one another, because an organizational field typically draws its members from diverse populations. Organizations from different populations participate in a single organizational field whenever they share a common focal interest.

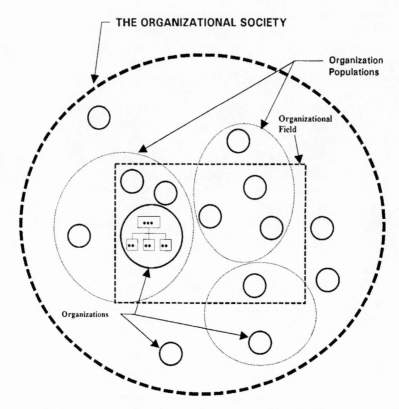

FIGURE 2.1   Levels of Analysis in Organization Theory

Two solid-line icons represent more micro levels of analysis:

- An *organization*, as defined in Chapter 1, is a goal-directed, boundary-maintaining activity system.
- *Organizational subsystems* are the internal structures and processes inside an organization—such as divisions, departments, and work teams—that perform functions contributing to organizational continuity.

Finally, at the lowest level are the real people occupying various roles and positions within each organizational subsystem, depicted in the diagram as tiny filled circles inside one organization's subsystem boxes. These human agents are the owners, directors, top executives, middle managers, and frontline employees whose activities enable each organization to conduct its routine daily and long-range affairs. An even more micro level, not visible in the figure, involves the psychological processes of cognition and emotion occurring within each human actor's mind. Because this book concentrates mainly on macro-organizational phenomena, it puts less emphasis on these processes. However, substantial numbers of organization researchers investigate the social psychologies of participants. Subsequent chapters introduce those theoretical ideas whenever they seem relevant to understanding more macro level behaviors.

Five Basic Organization Theories

Theoretical chaos prevails today in organization studies. No single theoretical approach dominates the discipline in the way that quantum mechanics serves as the core paradigm for physics and the rational actor model reigns in economics. To the contrary, my scrutiny of just six overviews uncovered at least 65 distinctly named theories spanning all levels of analysis (Pfeffer 1982, 1997; Astley and Van de Ven 1983; Clegg 1990; Scott 1998; Hatch 1997).[1] This number is far too vast to attempt an exhaustive review and application to the organizational changes examined in this book. As an alternative, I've selected five macro perspectives that I believe, taken together, best contribute toward a comprehensive explanation of contemporary macro-organizational changes. Although each theory gained considerable attention from organization scholars during the past three decades, none offers "the" definitive explanation covering every important aspect of organizational behavior. As I discuss in the following subsections, these five approaches treat distinct levels of organizational analysis. Although my personal bias favoring network analysis will become evident, I also believe that organization studies will prosper best if each theory's advocates regard other perspectives as providing complementary explanations, rather than as contentious opponents to be defeated and expelled from the debate.

The five basic organization theories I examine at length are organizational ecology theory, institutional theory, resource dependence theory, transaction cost economics, and organizational network analysis. Each theory takes an open-system view of change. That is, each recognizes that organizations are embedded within larger environments of the surrounding political economy and that organizations and their environments mutually influence one another. The precise location of any organization-environment boundary is susceptible to great fluctuations over time, arising from a wide range of social, political, and economic forces at play both inside and outside the organization. Indeed, understanding organizational change is primarily a matter of explaining how interactions of organizations with their political economies expand and contract the boundary over time, altering the numbers, sizes, shapes, and activities of organizations. Although the reciprocal effects between organizations and their environments occur at every level of analysis, the five organization theories differ markedly regarding the levels on which they bestow primary attention. Each theory raises unique substantive questions about organizational structures and behaviors at differing levels of analysis. Hence, when used together judiciously, they can paint a more comprehensive portrait than any single theory taken by itself. In the words of two astute observers, "reliance on basic theories of organization for the study of change may require significant effort in application but should serve to unify the field" (Barnett and Carroll 1995:220). Unfortunately, that utopian prospect remains a distant, rather than immanent, goal.

Table 2.1 summarizes each of the five basic theories according to its primary level of analysis, its key theoretical statement above organizational change, and the main concepts used in its core propositions. This comparison chart makes clear that each theory speaks to a distinctive dimension of organizational structures and processes. In general, they simply do not propose alternative explanations of the same phenomena. Hence, finding empirical evidence to support the claims of one theory is unlikely to lead to refutation of the contentions of other perspectives. Instead, these five theories offer researchers complementary insights into the dynamics of change. Beyond testing the conditions under which a specific theory holds true, organization studies faces a major challenge of forging stronger connections among these distinct approaches. Theorists and researchers should begin to examine how changes occurring at one level of analysis create conditions that compel changes to cascade across other levels. Only by deliberately investigating probable cross-theoretical effects can a theoretical synthesis be initiated that would lead toward a more unitary understanding of organizational change.

Space constraints in this chapter permit only short summaries of each theory's core concepts and principles, with brief illustrations of applications to organizational phenomena and a concluding discussion of their compatibilities. The five basic theories vary in their degree of internal consistency, clarity, and logical rigor. Because these perspectives were constructed over many years through the contributions of numerous analysts, they are plagued by ambiguous assumptions, conceptual contradictions, and logical limitations that restrict their analytical power. Debates continue to rage among scholars over relevant ideas, hypotheses, research methods, data, and interpretations of results. Optimistically, such turmoil indicates an intellectually vital and challenging field. Understanding the fundamental issues at stake in each of these five approaches will add immensely to our subsequent investigation of organizational changes in the twentieth century. Later chapters repeatedly encounter these theoretical concepts, principles, and hypotheses and their empirical research outcomes.

TABLE 2.1   Comparison of Five Open-System Theories of Organizational Change

Theory	*Primary Level*	*Key Change Statement*	*Main Concepts*
Organizational ecology	Population	Organizations that fit best to their environments are more likely to be selected for survival, whereas ill-suited organizations are more likely to perish.	Organization form, Population, Niche, Selection, Foundings, Failures, Growth, Density dependence
Institutionalism	Organization field	Organizations conform to a common form that is legitimated by environmental institutions.	Isomorphism, Legitimacy, Symbols, Taken-for-granted, Norms, Values
Resource dependence	Organization, subunit	Organizations and subunits exchange resources to maximize power, and avoid dependence.	Resources, Exchange, Uncertainty, Power dependence, Autonomy
Transaction cost economics	Transaction decision	Organizations decide whether to make or buy goods and servicesdepending on transaction costs, including administering contracts.	Transactions, Contract, Market, Hierarchy, Hybrid, Opportunism, Efficiency, Bounded rationality
Organizational networks	Multilevel	Organizational structures and actions are both causes and consequences of multiplex relations between and within organizations.	Relations, Centrality, Cohesion, Clique, Structural equivalence, Position, Exchange, Social distance

Organizational Ecology Theory

Organizational ecology theory studies the changing effects of environmental selection processes on organizational populations (Baum 1996). Its concepts and relations can be recast into a rigorously logical theory of change, consisting of a tightly woven formal set of axiomatic assumptions and testable derived hypotheses (Peli et al. 1994). The scope applies primarily to changes occurring at the population level of analysis. That is, the unit that changes is not the single organization but the total number of organizations within some bounded system—geographic, political, market— whose members are all alike with respect to some important characteristic or organizational form. An organizational *form* serves as a blueprint for action, consisting of "rules or procedures for obtaining and acting upon inputs in order to produce an organizational product or response" (Hannan and Freeman 1977:935). Four basic features analysts can use to classify an organization's form are its mission, authority structure, technology, and market strategy (Hannan and Freeman 1984). In practice, most ecology researchers investigate populations identified only by the organization's main product or service, which is roughly equivalent to economists' concepts of the firm's industry or market. Thus, an edited volume included specific chapters on railroads, art museums, radio broadcasters, investment banks, and telephone companies (Hannan and Carroll 1992).

Drawing from principles of institutional theory, Glenn Carroll and Michael Hannan (2000) with Laszlo Polos reconceptualized organizational forms as socially constructed corporate identities. They defined forms as "identities that are externally enforced and that apply to some (form-specific) number of actors" (p. 68). Social identities are codes (sets of rules and signals) specifiying which features an organization may legitimately exhibit, encompassing legal, political, cultural, and technical constraints. Thus, any given organization's form is, to some degree, shaped by the external social actors that develop, enforce, and change the indispensable properties of a social identity code. Violating a code-based identity may generate negative judgments by outsiders that an organization no longer satisfies the requirements to sustain the form. For example, colleges and universities can lose program accreditation by failing to meet quality criteria in facilities, faculties, and curricula set by peer institutions. Both professional norm-enforcing associations and the government exercise powerful influence over permissible organizational forms, for example, by prohibiting the manufacture and sale of alcoholic beverages or consenting to a tax moratorium on Internet commerce. A formidable research implication of the identity-based definition of form is that "several years of close study are required to grasp the important institutional details that provide the key information about forms" (Carroll and Hannan 2000:79). Researchers must immerse themselves in the historical circumstances giving rise to new organizational forms and the events that sustain or change social codes over time.

The primary goals of organizational ecology theory are to explain "how social conditions affect the rates at which new organizations and new organizational forms arise, the rates at which organizations change forms, and the rates at which organizations and forms die out" (Hannan and Freeman 1989:7). Drawing inspiration from biological principles, ecologists depict change as the result of shifting environmental conditions that select new organizational forms for survival and older forms for extinction. The Darwinian metaphor of "survival of the fittest" signifies a tight environment-population coupling. Just as individual biotic organisms cannot alter their anatomies and physiologies, so existing organizations often have great difficulty altering their forms to fit the changed external circumstances. Although the Wright brothers *did* convert their Dayton, Ohio, bicycle shop into an airplane manufactory at the dawn of the twentieth century, such caterpillar-into-butterfly transformations are the relatively rare exception rather than the general rule. Organizational efforts to restructure typically disrupt stable routines, undermine familiar relationships, and require new learning efforts, all of which render an organizational form vulnerable to environmental predators. "Although organizations sometimes manage to change positions on these dimensions, such changes are rare and costly and seem to subject an organization to greater risks of death" (Hannan and Freeman 1984:156). Ecological and evolutionary theories are closely related, differing primarily in the latter's greater interest in the social processes involved in creating and transforming organizations (Aldrich 1999:46–48), whereas the former stresses key demographic processes operating within existing populations (Baum 1996:78–83; Carroll and Hannan 2000). (See Chapter 10 for an extended discussion of evolutionary organizational change.)

Inertia describes an organization's tendency toward inflexibility in responding to environmental challenges by changing its mission, authority structure, technology, or market strategy (Hannan and Freeman 1984; Carroll and Hannan 2000:357–379). When organizational inertia is high, the potential to make adaptive changes is low. Pressures to resist reorganization come from both internal and external sources. The former include sunk investments in buildings, machinery, and personnel; restricted access to subunit information; the organization's internal power structure; and central normative agreements among employees that prevent them from considering alternative responses. Bureaucracies are notoriously inertial structures, fraught with politically vested interest groups willing to fight bitterly against any loss of status and privilege from reorganization. Among the external pressures spurring organizational resistance to change are legal and fiscal barriers to firms entering and leaving markets; constraints on access to environmental information; legitimation by important constituencies; and the "collective rationality problem," where a survival strategy that succeeds for one organization may not be rational if adopted by many (Hannan and Freeman 1977:931–932). For example, a price-cutting war among gasoline companies might succeed only in bankrupting all small corner-station owners rather than driving a rival corporation out of business. In sum, the organizational ecology perspective emphasizes dynamic changes *of* aggregate organizational populations through Darwinian environmental selection mechanisms that replace ill-adapted organizations with new types, rather than through purposefully managed adaptive changes occurring *within* organizations. Selection—who survives, thrives, or dies—is an unintended consequence of fierce competition among firms in capitalist markets where failure is an ever-present possibility.

Organizational ecologists have examined the demographic dynamics of population growth as an interplay between fundamental founding and failure processes (i.e., births and deaths) (Carroll 1984:75). Just as a biological species expands when it enters a fertile niche, an organizational population tends to grow at varying rates after its initial founding point. The *population density*, or total number of organizations existing at a given time in a given population or niche, shapes the growth trajectory through two counterbalanced processes affecting the founding and failure rates: legitimacy and competition. Figure 2.2 depicts an idealized pattern, beginning with the founding of a single organization in the first year. During the first decade, as the small number of foundings is closely matched by many early failures, density remains low and the population grows at a slow rate. Although these new organizations face few competitors for their niche's scarce resources, the form still lacks wide acceptance in the larger society that could increase its chances for survival. Hence, failures remain relatively high until a gradual increase in the sheer density of new-form organizations generates sufficient legitimacy, defined as cognitive perceptions "in the minds of actors that it serves as the natural way to effect some kind of collective action" (Hannan and Carroll 1992:34). Starting around the twelfth year, growth accelerates when foundings greatly outpace failures, leading to a rapid rise in the population's density. However, intensifying competition among the more numerous organizations in this larger population eventually begins to exhaust the niche's resources. The disappearance of easy resources discourages further entrants, pushes specialists into the margins of the niche space, and boosts the failure rate. When the population density reaches a high level, around the sixteenth year in Figure 2.2, the negative competition effect overwhelms the positive legitimacy effect. During the final shake-out period, failures may match or even surpass foundings. The population growth rate drastically slows and even declines somewhat before stabilizing at a level where annual exits roughly balance entries. Such a steady-state population reflects its niche's "carrying capacity" or sustainable resource ceiling, in analogy to deer herds in woods where wolves have disappeared. Chapter 3 further illustrates this growth pattern with data from the U.S. semiconductor industry.

Many research studies of diverse organizational populations generally supported the density-dependence hypothesis. Researchers observed the characteristic growth pattern for labor unions (Hannan and Freeman 1988), newspapers (Carroll and Hannan 1989), trade associations (Aldrich and Staber 1988), and European automobile producers (Hannan et al. 1995). Carroll and Hannan (2000:218–219) summarized a large number of tests, on populations in several major economic sectors, that yielded the expected nonmonotonic growth patterns. However, some insitutionalist critics argued that the population density count is an imprecise measure that fails to capture the full complexity of legitimation and competition processes underlying organizational growth dynamics (Zucker 1989; Baum and Powell 1995; Baum 1996). They claimed that greater realism could be achieved by including more direct measures of legitimation, such as the en-

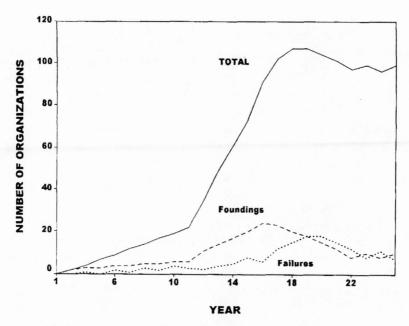

FIGURE 2.2   Organization Population Change

dorsement and sponsorship of new organizational forms by a society's powerful sociopolitical and cultural institutions. Hannan and Carroll (1995) caustically rejected this critique, asserting that their research program routinely examined the impact of institutional environments on vital rates, while offering the additional advantages of theoretical generality and parsimony. In their authoritative exposition on organizational demography, Carroll and Hannan restricted attention to problems of "constitutive legitimation," which are solved once new organizational forms become taken for granted by actors controlling resources (2000:223–225). The debate over concepts and measures of legitimacy seems destined to continue for the foreseeable future.

Ecology researchers also explored the impact of organizational size and age on population change, particularly on mortality rates (Singh and Lumsden 1990). Arthur Stinchcombe (1965) hypothesized a *liability of newness* in which young organizations and new forms are especially vulnerable to failure. Newly formed organizations face formidable obstacles. They must create integrated internal structures, develop trusting relations among relative strangers, coordinate employee roles, and find external customers—all while trying to compete against older and better-established firms with loyal clientele. Environmental selection favors organizational forms that display high reliability and accountability for their actions. The faithful reproduction of structures increases with an organization's age, as does its legitimacy because "old organizations tend to develop dense webs of exchange, to affiliate with centers of power, and to acquire an aura of inevitability" (Hannan and Freeman 1989:81). As new organizational forms become institutionalized over time, their mortalities should decline at an exponential rate.

However, the liability of newness may be confounded with the impact of organizational size on mortality, the *liability of smallness* hypothesis. Most new organizations also tend to be smaller than older organizations, which typically expand the scope and scale of their operations as they mature. Although bigger organizations often develop greater structural inertia (resistance to reorganization), they also possess more resources than smaller organizations to cushion them against environmental shocks. For example, smaller organizations often have more difficulty raising needed capital, suffer more adversely from governmental regulations, and compete less effectively than big corporations in hiring skilled employees (Aldrich and Auster 1986). Researchers investigated the joint effects of age, size, and population density on growth and failure rates of state-chartered credit unions in New York City from 1914 to 1990 (Barron, West and Hannan 1994). They found strong support for the liability of smallness hypothesis: Although larger credit unions grew more slowly, they also failed less often. However, the researchers uncovered no evidence favoring the liability of newness hypothesis: after controlling for age-varying size over the organizational lifespan, aging did not protect older credit unions from failure. To the contrary, a *liability of aging* relationship was evident: Older organizations failed at a significantly faster rate than their youngest competitors, suggesting that bigger organizations may be more vulnerable to environmental shocks. Unfortunately, the analysts lacked data to choose between two explanations of why organizational mortality rose with aging: (1) a liability of obsolescence, in which inertial forces lock organizations into outmoded strategies and structures adopted in their early years, thus rendering these older firms less able to adapt to rapidly changing environments; or (2) a liability of senescence, in which rigid devotion to accumulated rules and routines reduces their efficiency compared to younger, more flexible organizations even in stable environments (Barron, West and Hannan 1994:387). A formalized theory combining these alternative size-and-age liabilities awaits rigorous empirical replications to disentangle the effects of various aging processes (Carroll and Hannan 2000:281–356).

Institutional Theory

Contemporary institutional theory applies to many levels of analysis, ranging from organizational subsystems through populations to the world system. Perhaps its most significant focus is on the *organizational field*, consisting of "those organizations that, in the aggregate, constitute a recognized area of institutional life: key suppliers, resource and product consumers, regulatory agencies, and other organizations that produce similar services or products" (DiMaggio and Powell 1983:148). This concept differs from *industry*, a term referring only to a set of organizations all producing the same product or service. A familiar example of an organizational field is the pop music sector, consisting of bands, talent agencies, recording studios, radio stations, publishers and distributors, concert halls, tour promoters, and fan clubs. Other well-known fields include collegiate athletics, fine arts, commercial banking, medicine, national defense, and international tourism.

Institutional theorists argue that the organizations embedded in a field jointly construct the social realities that then guide their routine actions, thus helping to perpetuate that social system. Because a field's members interact more frequently among themselves than with outside organizations, they tend to develop a shared meaning system, that is, a consensus about the most desirable qualities, values, and behaviors. Institutionalizing a common set of understandings involves "the processes by which social processes, obligations, or actualities come to take on a rule-like status in social thought and action" (Meyer and Rowan 1977:341). Symbolic meanings translate into the social structures and routine practices that permeate organizations' daily life. Universities divide their faculties into a conventional set of disciplinary departments. Corporate cultures find physical expression in the design of workplaces and even such simple rules as which employees may enter parking lots, washrooms, and cafeterias. In a *Dilbert* world, sitting in a cubicle or a coveted window office clearly signals the office pecking order. An institutionalized custom may exhibit ceremonial or mythical aspects that remain unconnected to organizational efficiency or effectiveness (the "red tape" lamented by everyone dealing with such public bureaucracies as the Department of Motor Vehicles). Formal organizational structures and actions may persist as institutionalized customs and habits, without conscious regard for their rationality or instrumental benefits, but simply because alternative possibilities have become meaningless and unthinkable. "In other words, institutionalized acts are done for no other reason than that is how things are done" (Pfeffer 1982:240).

An organizational field's rules and requirements attain a taken-for-granted status among its participants. Institutionalization proceeds by the "elaboration of rules and requirements to which individuals must conform if they are to receive support and legitimacy" (Scott and Meyer 1983:149). As defined by Weber (1947:324–329), *legitimacy* involves normative beliefs governing the proper or acceptable exercise of power in a social situation. Institutional ideas exert subtle influences over organizations and their individual participants, encouraging them to conform without questioning to the field's prevailing norms, cognitions, and regulations regarding the most appropriate structures, beliefs, and behaviors (Scott 1995:35). Normative standards specify the acceptable means that organizations should use to pursue their valued goals, such as following "fair" business practices to produce corporate profits. For example, in 1997 the Federal Trade Commission investigated charges by rival tobacco companies that Philip Morris had violated industry norms by paying retail stores not to install permanent displays of competing cigarettes. Every organization tries to guarantee its continuance by promoting beliefs about legitimacy both among the organization's participants and in the larger society within which it operates. Modern organizations that claim legitimacy on the basis of rational-legal authority (such as private corporate and governmental bureaucracies) ultimately depend on fostering "a belief in the 'legality' of patterns of normative rules and the right of those elevated to authority under such rules to issue commands" (Weber 1947:328). In other words, the exercise of legitimate power within an organization requires that its members implicitly endorse the right of administrators to issue commands and the obligation of subordinates to obey. Strikes over working conditions are open struggles between management and labor to define the legitimate boundaries of workplace authority. In the absence of legitimating beliefs that sustain an enterprise, force and coercion threaten to overthrow the establishment, as Mafia families know only too well.

Applied to an organizational field, the concept of legitimacy means that organizations sanction certain types of formal structures, managerial practices, and expressed values as appropriate and acceptable. Like teenagers, organizations gain peer approval by conforming to prevailing group standards. "Legitimacy is not a commodity to be possessed or exchanged but a condition reflecting cultural alignment, normative support, or consonance with relevant rules or laws" (Scott 1995:45). To achieve acceptance within a field, an organization's ability to demonstrate its technical efficiency or to produce tangible results may be far less important than its embrace of prevailing institutional norms. Many nonmarket organizations that operate with uncertain technologies, such as public schools and hospitals, cannot easily demonstrate that their activities actually produce educated students or healthier communities. Consequently, they adopt the facade of modern bureaucratic design—professionally certified employees, hierarchical command structures, standardized budgetary controls—as visible evidence to the institutionalized environment of their trustworthiness (Meyer and Rowan 1977). By conforming their public demeanors to widely understood and valued formal patterns, legitimated organizations can secure political and monetary resources and thus improve their chances for survival. Note, however, that such organizations' formal structures may be only "loosely coupled" to the actual technical requirements for getting work done. A school's formal bureaucratic features may have little to do with what really goes on inside a classroom between teachers and students. Rather, an organization's public face primarily signals to its important external constituencies that it is reliable, trustworthy, and deserving of their political and financial support.

If a newly created organization radically breaks from the traditional mold that an organizational field and the general public have come to expect, it typically faces a protracted struggle to gain legitimacy. The scramble for scarce resources is complicated by wariness and mistrust of the unknown upstart, which may spell the newcomer's doom before it can attain its full potential. For example, the decades-long effort by health maintenance organizations (HMO) to gain public acceptance for a disease-prevention approach met stiff resistance from a medical profession more comfortable with lucrative fee-for-service doctoring (Wholey, Christianson and Sanchez 1993). This vulnerability of young organizations to environmental resource scarcity is the "liability of newness" principle noted above in the organizational ecology subsection.

Institutional theory stresses how nonlocal political economies create, sustain, and change the institutions that shape individual organizations' structures, beliefs, and actions. Two major sources of external pressures pushing organizations toward conformity to a field's dominant institutions are the national state (through its executive, legislative, and legal systems) and peer organizations (such as business groups, professional associations, and labor unions). As an illustration of the legitimation process, consider how bureaucratic personnel practices—such as centralized employment, job analysis, time-and-motion studies, and promotion and transfer systems—diffused among U.S. industries across the twentieth century (Baron, Dobbins and Jennings 1986). During World War II, the federal government intervened in the military-industrial enterprises, from airplane factories to shipyards, to foster new employment models "by providing incentives to organizations to create or expand personnel departments and bureaucratic controls, and by providing a set of overarching interests that prompted labor-management accommodation" (p. 378). After the war, unions and professional personnel administrators further encouraged the adoption of innovative human resource control practices—such as job codification, systematic promotion, and salary classification—by organizations regardless of their sizes, ages, sectors, and technologies. These legitimizing social forces generated increasing convergence among quite different enterprises around highly similar employee relations systems toward the end of the century.

DiMaggio and Powell (1983) hypothesized that modern institutionalizing processes produce greater *isomorphism*, or homogeneity, among the members of an organizational field. Fast-food restaurants, airlines, hospitals, basketball teams, book publishers, department stores—even armies and navies—each settle on a few basic organizational forms, resulting in a bland sameness from one company to another. Communities from one end of the United States to the other, and increasingly around the globe, display a standardized and dependable economic culture—the McDonaldization and Disneyfication of the world. As organizational fields grow increasingly "structurated" (i.e., well-defined and mature) they wield enormous influence over the organizations within them. In striving to achieve legitimacy and environmental fitness, corporations adopt uniform structures and practices that conform to their field's prevailing norms and standards. Over time, deviant organizations fail to win legitimacy, suffer significant resource losses, and may eventually go out of business. Tobacco companies in the United States were just the most visible victims of changing legal, medical, political, and popular perceptions that threatened their health and survival. When five-year-olds recognized Joe Camel as widely as Mickey Mouse, RJR Nabisco could no longer contend that it marketed cigarettes solely to adults.

Surviving organizations are enmeshed in constraining rules and rationalizing myths that tend toward eliminating all traces of individuality and nonconformity. Three major social mechanisms generate isomorphic changes that reduce organizational variety (DiMaggio and Powell 1983:150):

- *coercive isomorphism*, stemming from political influence and cultural expectations
- *mimetic processes*, deriving from uncertainties that encourage imitation
- *normative pressures*, originating in professional occupations and associations

Government mandates exemplify the coercive power of the state to compel obligations and enforce restrictions on organizations under its jurisdiction. Think of city health inspectors forcing restaurants to clean up their kitchens or shut down. Modern legal systems impose uniform standards of organizational control so that contracting parties can rationally calculate their conditions of exchange and the penalties for failure to comply. Mimetic modeling is an response to environmental uncertainty. By copying the formal structures and innovative practices of apparently successful organizations in a field, imitative organizations seek to cope with ambiguous goals and unclear solutions. Paradigms may diffuse indirectly through employee transfer and turnover, or more explicitly via trade associations and consulting firms that, "like Johnny Appleseeds, spread a few organizational models throughout the land" (DiMaggio and Powell 1983:152). Finally, professional employees such as engineers, accountants, and managers import normative standards into their firms that become replicated across a field:

Two aspects of professionalization are important sources of isomorphism. One is the resting of formal education and of legitimation in a cognitive base produced by university specialists; the second is the growth and elaboration of professional networks that span organizations and across which new models diffuse rapidly. Universities and professional training institutions are important centers for the development of organizational norms among professional managers and their staffs. Professional and trade associations are another vehicle for the definition and promulgation of normative rules about organizational and professional behavior. (DiMaggio and Powell 1983:152)

Whatever its specific homogenizing sources, the institutionalization dynamic conveys an air of inevitability. Theorists tend to stress the stabilizing effect of institutionalized components over their potential for change, although some environmental conditions may stimulate more diversity of forms through decision makers' deliberate designs (Scott 1991:171–172). But the historical tide seems to flow toward homogenizing uniformity within organizational fields. As one dominant form converts organization after organization, the need for external power to coerce compliance is replaced by internalized, taken-for-granted cognition models "in which schemas and scripts lead decision makers to resist new evidence" (DiMaggio and Powell 1991:15). Institutionalizing mechanisms construct the bars for Weber's iron cage that ultimately imprison all modern organizations and their participants.

Resource Dependence Theory

Whereas the ecology perspective emphasizes environmental selection and the institutionalist framework stresses conformity to a dominant social order, resource dependence theory accentuates the importance of power in organizational *adaptation* (Thompson 1967; Pfeffer and Salancik 1978). This approach concentrates primarily on the organizational field level of analysis (see Figure 2.1), but also calls attention to several internal organizational changes. Its basic theoretical premise is that, because no organization can become entirely self-sufficient, each necessarily engages in various resource exchanges with other organizations in its surrounding political economy. Many critical resources—financial capital, labor skills, authority, information—are often scarce and concentrated under the control of a few dominant players. The need to secure steady flows of life-sustaining resources generates a firm's dependence on whichever organizations and institutions control the most critical contingencies for performing its basic tasks and achieving its main goals. An actor possessing an essential resource gains power over those actors who need it, consistent with Max Weber's definition of power as the probability that a person or group can "carry out his own will despite resistance" (Weber 1947:152). For example, local and state governments control large proportions of public school budgets, which are annually besieged by rival claimants ranging from law enforcement to street repair to waste removal. Resource-holders wield their power to obtain compliance by the dependent organizations to their demands about policies and programs.

Organizations try to avoid becoming dependent, while making others more dependent on them. Unlike ecologists, who see structural inertia and external forces as overwhelming managers' feeble attempts to cope with rapid environmental changes, resource dependence theorists explicitly argue that some strategic adaptations are possible through managerial reorganization. Organizations are not totally vulnerable to macro level environmental threats pushing them toward extinction. For example, even small organizations can fight for survival by joining in collective actions with others facing the same external hazards. As agents acting on behalf of their organization, the top leaders can improve the chances of survival by taking political actions intended to avoid or reduce dependence on other organizations for essential resources. Instead of passively reacting to external events, corporate executives actively strive to manipulate relationships with the external political economy to achieve greater freedom of choice and *autonomy*, that is, freedom of independent action. "Administrators manage their environments as well as their organizations and the former may be as important, or even more important, than the latter" (Aldrich and Pfeffer 1976:83). A good illustration was Chrysler chair Lee Iacocca's successful lobbying of the U.S. Congress for a $1.2 billion federal loan guarantee in 1980, which enabled the auto company to survive after surging gasoline prices caused sales to plunge almost 18 percent. Two decades later, Iacocca's successor engineered a $39.5 billion merger with Germany's Daimler-Benz, a deal designed to improve survival chances during an impending shake-out in the global auto industry (Stern and Lipin 1998). Resource dependence principles obviously resonate strongly with the proactive management ideologies popularized in business schools curricula, whose graduating students then later try to implement these ideas as they move up the rungs of the corporate career ladder.

Resource dependence theory is rooted analytically in social exchange concepts that assume "purposive action," that is, rational choices and decision making by actors who seek to gain maximum benefits from socioeconomic transactions (Blau 1964). A fundamental exchange principle is that actor A becomes dependent on actor B to the extent that B controls a resource or behavior highly valued by A, which A can neither do without nor obtain elsewhere. Hence, to acquire that vital resource, A must comply with the exchange conditions B imposes, particularly by paying whatever price B demands. Emerson's power dependence version proposed that, in any exchange relationship, A's dependence is inverse to B's power: the more

A depends on B for an essential resource, the greater is B's power to control A's actions (Emerson 1962). These basic resource imbalance principles apply to social exchanges across many levels of analysis, ranging from small work groups to giant international corporations to national governments.

The classic examples of extreme macro-economic power imbalances are industrial monopolies and oligopolies. One firm secures *monopoly* control of a market when it is the sole seller of a good or service to many buyers and no new seller can enter that market. An *oligopoly* is a small group of firms in a market with barriers that prevent new sellers from entering. Even without an explicit agreement, oligopolists may coordinate their actions to maximize joint profits, thus affecting but not completely controlling the market. A classic example was the Big Three U.S. automobile manufacturers before they faced significant import competition: Consumers paid high prices for lousy cars. Monopoly-like actions may also occur when several firms form a *cartel* whose members explicitly agree to coordinate their production and pricing activities. The most infamous late twentieth-century cartels were the Organization of Petroleum Exporting Countries (OPEC) and the cocaine smugglers of Medellin and Cali, Colombia. OPEC members meet regularly to set production quotas restricting how much oil each nation can pump out of the ground, thereby keeping prices high. The drug lords use violence to blow away rival gangs and thus prevent open competition in powder and crack from driving down prices.

Monopolistic and oligopolistic market structures violate Adam Smith's (1776) "Invisible Hand" conception of pure capitalist competition, in which no firms grow large enough to affect market prices. Monopolists and oligopolists can set prices well above the competitive level by exercising their market power to erect barriers to entry, thereby blocking an influx of new sellers from undercutting prices and profits. Because market domination creates potentially large welfare losses for a society, many governments enforce antitrust laws designed to prevent or break up monopolies, oligopolies, and cartels. For example, as discussed in Chapter 4, Microsoft faced antitrust action by the U.S. Justice Department in the 1990s for using its dominant position in the operating system software market to muscle its competitors and capture the Internet browser market.

At the macro level, resource dependence theory seeks to explain how interorganizational relations emerge from collective struggles to negotiate more advantageous terms for resource exchanges (Cook 1977). Although many political economy factors may affect the degree to which one organization will comply with another's control attempts, three conditions seem especially critical to creating dependencies, both between and within organizations: (1) a resource's importance for sustaining organizational operation and survival, (2) the extent to which an interest group (another organization or a subunit within the organization) exercises discretion over the resource's allocation and use, and (3) the availability of few alternatives (Pfeffer and Salancik 1978:45). Power is situational, shifting with the relative balance of these three factors among actors engaged in resource-exchange relations. Large or increasing power imbalances may trigger a dependent organization's efforts to restore greater equality and autonomy between exchange partners. For example, a less-powerful organization may forge new connections to alternative resource suppliers and customers, pursuing a diversification strategy to gain greater leverage in setting the rates and terms of exchange. However, powerful organizations typically resist efforts to dilute their dominance, resorting to various "bridging strategies" to maintain their advantages (Scott 1998:199–210). Among the more common strategies are:

- *Contracting:* Organizations negotiate long-term agreements to cope with future uncertainties under changing environmental conditions. Firms sign collective bargaining contracts with unions to fix wages and working conditions, avoiding costly production delays from wild-cat strikes and work stoppages. Producers bargain with suppliers and customers to secure reliable inputs of raw materials and outputs for finished goods. Record producers ink deals with rock musicians, who relinquish some of their "artistic control" in return for steady paychecks.
- *Co-optation:* Organizations bring representatives of outside groups into the decision-making process, effectively trading some of their sovereignty for needed resources, information, and political support. As a deliberately co-optive strategy for managing critical dependencies, corporations and nonprofit organizations may allocate seats on their boards of directors to organizations that control essential resources, for example, to financial institutions providing loans or to foundations making grants and donations. The outcomes are interlocking boards that link production firms and finance institutions into complex relational webs (Mintz and Schwartz 1985; Mizruchi 1996). Co-optive linkages constitute conduits for information exchange, political and economic influences going in both directions. The connections may shape such diverse behaviors as investment decisions, market entries and exits, plant locations, corporate acquisitions, and electoral campaign contributions. At an extreme, co-optive strategies may lead to oligopolies and cartels.
- *Strategic alliances:* Temporary collaborative arrangements such as joint ventures and research consortia involve two or more organizations pooling a limited number of resources to pursue a common, limited objective of mutual benefit. For example, firms may cooper-

ate to develop innovative technologies or to enter risky foreign markets. Such collaborative strategies vary in the extent of coordination, trust, and the creation of a formal governance structure to monitor and control the partners' behaviors (see Chapter 4).

- *Mergers and acquisitions:* One organization may try to solve its resource dependence problems by combining with or completely absorbing another, for example, a California "boutique" winery may purchase its own vineyards to assure a dependable flow of grapes. The United States experienced several merger waves during the twentieth century, beginning with the 1895–1905 cycle that eliminated cut-throat competition in many manufacturing industries by creating vertically integrated production facilities under the near-monopoly control of such giant corporations as U.S. Steel, DuPont, General Electric, International Harvester, Standard Oil, Pittsburgh Plate Glass, and the U.S. Rubber Company (Fligstein 1990). The last two merger waves, cresting in the 1980s and 1990s, consolidated the largest firms within many industries (see Chapter 3).
- *Collective action sets:* Because governments play a key role in setting and enforcing the rules under which economic resources may be acquired and exchanged, they are primary targets for political influence activities. Organizations can enhance the likelihood of receiving favorable governmental decisions by pooling some of their resources, forming collective-action coalitions, and coordinating their political efforts (Laumann and Knoke 1987). Trade associations, political action committees, and joint lobbying campaigns by an industry's members are well-known devices by which member organizations yield some individual autonomy to gain greater collective power within the political system (see Chapter 9).

Uncovering the shifting relations among organizations in a political economy is a major objective of the resource dependence approach. Henry Mintzberg (1983), whose iconic image of internal organizational structures appeared in Figure 1.2 in Chapter 1, surrounded this system with an *external coalition* consisting of four general types of players, whom he called "influencers": (1) owners, such as company founders, their family heirs, and major stockholders, including insurance companies and pension funds; (2) employee associations, particularly labor unions and professional societies; (3) associates such as suppliers, customers, partners, and competitors; and (4) publics, including local, state, and national governments as well as organized interest groups and the general populace. These varied external constituents may each bring their power resources to bear in efforts to change an organization's goals. For example, during South Africa's era of racial discrimination, several liberal church activist and leftist political groups launched publicity campaigns intended to embarrass colleges and foundations into divesting their portfolios of stocks in U.S. corporations doing business in that country. Because no single external group likely controls sufficient power resources to impose its interests against the resistance of others, they usually must seek allies with similar interests in the specific issue and try to negotiate compromise deals with influencers holding divergent preferences. Coalition-building processes typically require exchanges of side-payments among potential coalition partners to secure their cooperation or acquiescence. For example, a city's effort to attract a professional baseball team by building a publicly financed stadium may require concessions to businesses, political parties, and interest groups in return for their support. An agreement about a coalition's formal goals often reflects complex deals among the external influencers forming a minimal-winning combination, whose resource contributions are necessary to defeat their opponents. In this perspective, organizations resemble arenas for political combat among conflicting interest groups rather than unitary actors holding fixed and consistent preferences.

Resource dependence principles also apply inside organizations. Power processes may account for both the change and the resistance to change by organizational subunits (see Figure 2.1), particularly for changes in the systems of control and authority that govern participants' work lives:

> [O]rganizational structures are the outcomes of political contests within organizations. Given the various participants interested in controlling the organization, the fact that their preferences and beliefs conflict so that they cannot completely trust one another, and the importance of structure to control, it is clear that the participants will contend over the allocation of discretion and resources and the control of information in organizations as they attempt to gain more influence within the organization. (Pfeffer 1978:38)

In contrast to the external coalition describing how outside actors try to influence an organization's behavior, the *dominant coalition* concept emphasizes the power configuration among its internal decision makers. It "draws attention to the question of who is making the choice" (Child 1972:14). A dominant coalition's members may come from any organizational subunit depicted in Mintzberg's analytical scheme (the top apex, middle line, operating core, technostructure, or support staff; see Figure 1.2 in Chapter 1). Just as resource dependence theory emphasizes exchanges between organizations, a "strategic contingency" analysis of internal power dependence stresses that a subunit's power resides in its ability to cope successfully with major sources of organizational uncertainty. "Thus, intraorganizational dependency can be associated with two contributing variables: (1) the extent to which a subunit copes with uncertainty for other subunits, and (2) the extent to which a subunit's coping activities are substitutable" (Hickson et al. 1971:218). In other words, power flows to those groups possessing political and economic resources that effectively enable them to handle the most critical problems facing the organization. A classic citation is Michel Crozier's (1964) discovery that the maintenance workers in a French tobacco factory were much more powerful than expected given their lowly position in the formal company hierarchy. Because they had destroyed the repair manuals, these workers were the only persons who could patch up breakdowns of essential machinery in the otherwise routine production technology.

In sum, new political interests and coalition realignments within organizations arise in response to changing opportunities and threats occurring in an organization's external political economy. Power flows towards those subunits making the greatest contributions to an organization's survival and prosperity. The changing composition in the dominant coalition reflects the rise and fall of interest groups believed most competent at defending the organization's core technologies and accomplishing its long-range goals in the face of shifting environmental conditions. The selection and removal of the top leaders often reveals these shifting priorities. For example, the control of U.S. hospitals during the twentieth century shifted from the original community owners and trustees to the staff physicians whose medical knowledge could better cope with patients' health uncertainties. Subsequently, most hospital coalitions were dominated by professional administrators who possessed the financial expertise for extracting profits from a vast medical-industrial complex financed through government health care repayment programs (Starr 1982). Chapter 3 returns to this resource dependence theme by examining how changing environmental conditions over the twentieth century transformed corporate power structures, especially the rise and decline of the multidivisional form.

Transaction Cost Economics

Until recently, most economists considered variation in organizational structures to be unimportant for explaining the behaviors of firms operating in perfectly competitive markets (Menard 1996). The neoclassical economic theory of the firm treats organizations as a simple production function where supply-demand schedules efficiently coordinate prices and outputs. The internal structures and processes of the producing firm are opaque and irrelevant. However, in a classic dissenting article, "The Nature of the Firm," first published in 1937, Ronald Coase (1988) asked, first, why do firms emerge at all in a specialized exchange economy? Second, why isn't all economic production performed within one giant, economy-wide organization? In other words, the core question is, when should a firm make rather than buy a good or service? Coase's answer, long ignored by economists, was that "the operation of a market costs something and that, by forming an organization and allowing some authority (an 'entrepreneur') to direct the resources, certain marketing costs are saved" (Coase 1988:40).

Whether an exchange occurs in an open market or inside a firm depends on the real and perceived *transaction costs*. Costs involve discovering and negotiating prices, implementing and monitoring compliance with an exchange agreement, and enforcing the terms of the contract. Other administrative costs include any subsequent adjustments necessary due to omissions and unanticipated irregularities that might occur when economic actors carry out a contract. An organization tends to expand in size until its marginal cost of conducting one additional transaction inside the firm exceeds the cost of making the same exchange in the open market (Coase 1937 [1988:44]). At that point the market-pricing mechanism becomes a more efficient way to coordinate productive resources. In a classic example, Henry Ford, flush with enormous profits from his hugely popular Model T, erected a massive, self-contained factory complex in the 1920s on 2,000 acres of River Rouge marshland near Detroit, Michigan (Lacey 1986:170). Tons of rubber for tires were imported from Fordlandia, the company's Brazilian plantation. Slab-sided Ford lake freighters shipped iron ore and timber from northern Michigan's mines and forests to the Rouge's coking ovens. Ford's blast furnaces then fed their steel plate to giant presses that stamped out doors, hoods, and chassis. After painting, welding, and assembly, the finished autos, tractors, and trucks rolled from the Rouge's grey, smokey buildings onto railcars for transport to Ford dealer showrooms. Coordinating this vast industrial cathedral ultimately proved more costly and less efficient than the decentralized system of subcontracting parts-suppliers created by rival General Motors, which soon surpassed Ford as the nation's top auto manufacturer.

Coase's insights into the make-or-buy question were resurrected in the 1970s by Oliver Williamson (1975, 1979, 1981), who elaborated a transaction cost economics theory about where firms draw economically efficient boundaries between internally organized activities and external market exchanges. As its name implies, the theory's basic unit of analysis is a *transaction*, the transfer of a good or service across a "technologically separable interface"—a fancy term indicating the physical location where one type of economic activity ends and another begins. In an auto assembly plant, spray-painting a car body must precede installing windows and attaching door handles; hence, these activities are socially and spatially segregated into different work units. Other operations might be located in entirely separate organizations; for example, automakers typically buy their car radios from an electronics supply company. One of transaction cost theory's central problems is to explain the conditions under which vertical integration of production occurs: Why are some goods and services produced within an organization and administratively coordinated by a managerial hierarchy, while other production factors are purchased in the market?

Williamson built his approach on two simplified assumptions about human behavior. First, despite their best intentions to act rationally, real economic actors have insufficient cognitive capacities to acquire, process, store, and retrieve all the relevant information. As explicated by Herbert Simon, this *bounded rationality* limitation means that two exchanging parties can never write a perfect "contingent claims contract" that would cover their liabilities in all possible outcomes. Thus, every complex contract is unavoidably incomplete. Second, economic actors are prone to behave *opportunistically*, defined as "self-interest seeking with guile" (Williamson 1975:80). That is, they are tempted to gain advantages by engaging in calculated efforts to mislead, deceive, and confuse their exchange partners (think of used-car salespeople). Hence, because economic transactions display varying degrees of risk, both exchange parties may demand that more explicit safeguards be written into the contract. These security features, such as spelling out the financial penalties for missing deadlines or delivering poor-quality work, are intended to deter or reduce the ever-present temptation to violate contractual agreements among bounded rational and opportunistic actors.

The organizational importance of transaction cost theory lies in its hypotheses about different governance structures (i.e., institutional arrangements) for regulating cooperation and competition among economic units. Transaction costs determine which of three basic governance forms are most efficient for a given set of environmental conditions (Williamson 1994:102):

- *Markets* are classic economic arenas in which wholly autonomous parties engage in resource exchanges.
- *Hierarchies* are formal organizations that place transactions under unified ownership; that is, both buyers and sellers are inside the same enterprise and controlled by an authority empowered to settle disputes.
- *Hybrids* involve long-term contractual relations that preserve each party's autonomy while offering transaction-specific safeguards against opportunistic behavior.

The main force driving changes in governance forms is the rational attempt to economize, that is, to reduce economic waste by minimizing the transaction costs attached to exchanges. Simple, direct exchanges of labor, capital, and intermediate products are most efficiently conducted by market transactions requiring no special governance mechanisms to sustain short-term relations. For example, buying fruits and vegetables at a weekly farmer's market in the town square takes the form of a "spot" market in which goods and money instantaneously change hands between anonymous sellers and buyers. However, for more complex deals that span long periods (for example, ordering a custom-built house from a contractor), the risks from bounded rationality and opportunism increase and thus increase the transaction costs of erecting safeguards against hazards to both buyer and seller. Over time simple markets give way to hybrid governance forms and organizational hierarchies that internalize many kinds of exchanges.

For Williamson (1981), the three most important dimensions along which transactions differ are their frequency, uncertainty, and asset specificity. *Assets*—which can be physical sites, human skills, or dedicated production equipment—increase in *specificity* when the exchanging parties make durable investments that, once put in place, render the asset unavailable for alternative uses without a loss. For example, an employee whose company has invested in on-the-job training to operate and repair a particular machine may find her skill unwanted by any other firm (such locked-in mutual relations are technically called "bilateral dependencies"). A chip supplier that builds a factory to produce unique microprocessors for a computer assembler is vulnerable to its purchaser's production cycles. Hence, whenever both exchange partners' asset specificities increase, the need for adaptive cooperation increases to prevent opportunism by one of the exchange partners. The more specific the assets involved, the stronger an organization's incentives to change its governance form toward stronger integration and coordination. The long-term contractual safeguards built into a hybrid relationship offer more security against opportunistic behavior than provided by open market transactions. In the preceding example, the chip manufacturer and computer assembler are likely to forge a long-term relational contract guaranteeing the purchase of enough microprocessors to cover the supplier's costs of building and running the new plant. Bringing a transaction inside a formal organization's boundary provides even greater protection, because disputes between organizational subunits can be referred to their bureaucratic superiors for resolution. In short, the primary reason why firms come into existence is market failure, arising whenever the neoclassical price mechanism fails to allocate resources efficiently to productive tasks (Clegg 1990:67).

Basic transaction cost ideas explain variation in economic activities and organizational structures involving contracts to produce and distribute goods and services. These applications include "vertical integration, vertical market restrictions, labor organization, corporate governance, finance, regulation (and deregulation), conglomerate organization, technology transfer" (Williamson 1994:86). Other pertinent topics include forming joint ventures and strategic alliances (Hennart 1988); restructuring traditional rule-governed bureaucracies into more discretionary and participatory modes (Aoki 1990); and subcontracting various support-staff functions, hiring temporary employees, and outsourcing job training (Knoke and Janowiec-Kurle 1999). The transaction cost model allegedly even explains why rock musicians squabble over who gets to use their band's name after its members have split up (Cameron and Collins 1997)! A band name is an asset-specific form of reputational capital that guides consumer decisions about future purchases of old albums and new releases. Hence, once a band disbands, some original members may be tempted to earn "rents" by attaching the name to a reconstructed group of inferior quality, as happened with such bands as Pink Floyd, Yes, and the Flying Burrito Brothers.

Transaction cost theory is clearly the most micro-analytic of the five theories I discuss in this chapter. By determining which mechanisms for governing exchanges are the most economically efficient, cost-minimizing calculations drive organizational change. The institutional environment—the surrounding political economy's rules and regulations—may exert major impacts on these calculations. Which governance form an organization ultimately adopts depends on how shifts in such arrangements as property laws, electoral politics, governmental regulations, banking rules, social customs, and other institutional norms enter into a firm's make-or-buy decisions. One consequence of the hypothesized alignment between transactions and governance structures is that changing environmental circumstances eliminate less-efficient forms and lead to a convergence toward a single cost-minimizing organizational form.

Organizational Network Analysis

Organizational network analysis is probably the least-developed of the five theoretical perspectives I examine in this chapter, but I believe that approach holds great potential for knitting together many dimensions of organizational behavior into a comprehensive explanation. Presently, diverse network approaches represent loosely connected sets of concepts, principles, and analysis methods rather than a rigorously deductive system. Their multidisciplinary roots lie in the sociometry of small groups (Moreno 1934), the psychology of sentiments (Heider 1946), cultural anthropology (Nadel 1957), and graph theoretic mathematics (Harary 1959). Contemporary organizational versions propose structural explanations for the behaviors and beliefs of social actors, whether they are corporations, departments, teams, or individual employees. Three basic assumptions underlie the network perspective. First, the social structure of any complex system consists of stable patterns of repeated interactions connecting social actors to one another. Second, these social relations are the primary explanatory units of analysis, rather than the attributes and characteristics of the individual actors. Third, the perceptions, attitudes, and actions of organizational actors are shaped by the larger structural networks within which they are embedded, and in turn their behaviors can change these networks' structures. A major objective of network analysis is to reveal "how concrete social processes and individual manipulations shape and are shaped by structure" (White, Boorman and Breiger 1976:773). In the words of a pioneering network anthropologist, J. Clyde Mitchell, "The characteristics of these linkages as a whole may be used to interpret the social behaviour of the persons involved" (Mitchell 1969:3).

Network theory directs researchers' attention toward a multilevel structural perspective, encompassing the *interorganizational* ties between members of an organizational field, the *intraorganizational* relations among subunits within a single organization, and the *interpersonal* interactions of individual employees (Knoke and Guilarte 1994; Brass 1995). More so than the other organization theories examined above, network analysis has great potential for integrating the macro and micro levels of analysis to produce a unified explanation of structure and actions within and around organizations. An implicit expectation is that the higher-level systems serve as environmental contexts that simultaneously constrain and facilitate the behaviors of lower-level systems. Formal organizations exhibit a dual face: first, as corporate players in national and international political economies, and second, as arenas within which individuals and groups struggle for power and privilege. Even apparently simple market transactions may deviate from the neoclassical model of economic efficiency because of long-standing reciprocal obligations among buyers and sellers (Granovetter 1985). Despite the barriers that higher-level network structures may pose, organizational actors should not be viewed as merely the passive dupes of their network entanglements. Rather, they can be strongly proactive agents who strategically manage their network connections to reduce uncertainties in their rational pursuit of goals (Galaskiewicz 1985). To varying degrees, both organizations and people reactivate or break existing connections, forge new ties to key participants, manipulate information and resource exchanges to gain advantages or avoid costs, and cooperate in collective actions to overcome mutual obstacles. This dynamic aspect of networking paints a patterned but nondeterministic picture of the sources of organizational change.

In addition to its multilevel emphasis, network theory also takes into consideration the *multiplexity* of the relations connecting actors. That is, rather than trying to discover "the" single pattern of ties responsible for all organizational affairs, network analysts acknowledge the simultaneous presence of diverse *relational contents* with differing impacts. Each type of content may display markedly divergent patterns of connections. For example, the structure of a technical advice-giving network among coworkers may bear little resemblance to their patterns of interpersonal trust. The advice network and the trust network might imply contrasting consequences for conflict management and employee morale during a company reorganization (Krackhardt and Hanson 1993). The network perspective argues that a system's overall structure is best conceptualized as combinations of multiplex networks involving several distinct types of relational contents. Although the variety of ties is potentially inexhaustible, a useful general classification involves considering the following five basic relational contents:

- *Resource exchanges*: Transactions in which one actor yields control over a physical good or service to another actor in return for some other kind of commodity (including money). Markets are obvious locations where interorganizational exchanges occur, but numerous resource transactions also occur inside organizations when subunits use a system of "shadow prices" (bookkeeping entries) to track and balance their exchanges.
- *Information transmissions*: Communication exchanges in which technical data, work advice, political opinions, or office rumors flow from one actor to another. A unique feature of an information transmission is that an originating party does not lose control of knowledge by sending it to a recipient; instead, both actors now possess it.
- *Power relations*: Asymmetrical interactions in which one party exerts control over another's behavior either by applying force (coercion) or, more typically, by a superior exercising the taken-for-granted expectation that commands will be obeyed by subordinates ("legitimate power" or authority in Weber's sense). Organizational power to achieve compliance with orders may ultimately rest on exchanging either material resources (taking the form of *domination*) or persuasive information (taking the form of *influence*) (see Knoke 1990a:3–7).
- *Boundary penetrations*: Coordinated actions by two or more actors to reach some mutual objective. In any collaborative relationship, each participant yields some sovereignty to the group in return for eventual gains that could not be produced separately (Coleman 1973). Familiar examples of boundary penetration include interlocking corporate and nonprofit boards of directors, industry committees to set technical standards, strategic alliances for innovation and production, and political campaigns to win concessions from public authorities.
- *Sentimental attachments*: Emotional affiliations among individuals that create solidarity and generate obligations of mutual assistance and support. Kinship, friendship, and respect are well-known sentiments underlying and smoothing out routine interactions in organizations. Trust relations are especially important for sustaining other

kinds of long-term exchanges. Sentimental ties provide latent reservoirs that people can mobilize for extraordinary assistance from others during personal or organizational crises.

Multiple networks can be combined using analysis methods, described in the Appendix and illustrated throughout this book, to identify the overall structure of an organizational system.

By treating the social relationship between a pair of actors (dyad) as the basic unit of analysis, network theory draws attention to a dual perspective on organizational behavior. Theoretical explanations may focus either on the beliefs and behaviors of a specific actor or on the structures and performances of the entire system in which all actors are embedded. First, the *ego-centric* perspective examines a focal person or organization ("ego") and its pattern of direct ties to all significant other actors ("alters"). This approach investigates such structural aspects as the number of ego's ties, their multiplexity and reciprocity, the diversity of alters who can be reached directly or indirectly, and the density of connections among the alters constituting one's ego-centric network. For example, each middle manager in a corporate hierarchy maintains ties to coworkers, subordinates, and superiors, as well as contacts with people in other organizations who could serve as important providers of information, advice, and support in the competition to move up the company ladder (Burt 1992). Second, the *complete network* perspective investigates the totality of multiplex ties among all the actors, for example, all employees within an organization or all the organizations in a field. This approach analyzes various macro-structural features, some parallel to features of the ego-centric approach: the density of existing, compared to potential, ties; the number of indirect links needed to connect every pair of actors; and the extent to which multiplex ties directly connect the same pairs of actors. Although participants may not be fully aware of a complete network, its structures may still affect their members' fates. For example, an industry whose firms are closely connected through dense sets of supportive political, economic, and social ties should be better able to anticipate and adjust to threats from foreign competitors than an industry characterized by a history of suspicion, isolation, and antagonism among its members.

An important structural property of the ego actors embedded in complete networks concerns their *network centrality*. This concept is intimately related to ideas about social power derived from an actor's ability to influence or control others' interactions, for example, by shaping exchanges of information and resources or by brokering deals between unconnected or hostile parties. Three indicators distinguish among various types of centrality according to different connections between an ego and other network members: (1) *degree centrality*, in which central actors have higher total numbers of direct ties to all other actors (i.e., a large ego-centric network size); (2) *closeness centrality*, in which central actors can more quickly interact with all others because they require few intermediaries to relay messages or exchange resources; and (3) *betweenness centrality*, in which central actors can control interactions between many pairs who lack direct connections, because the shortest indirect links between those unconnected pairs must go "through" the more central actors. The power of an actor with high betweenness centrality lies in its ability to find and fill "structural holes" between unconnected actors in a network (Burt 1992). That is, by providing bridges across the structural gaps among disjointed actors, a centrally located broker can transmit, block, or distort valuable resources and information exchanges. The broker's payoff derives from its capacity to extract fees, commissions, and profits for arranging exchanges between parties who are unable to consummate deals directly. The meteoric career of Michael Ovitz, who rose from part-time studio tour guide to top Hollywood agent and transitory president of the Walt Disney Company, embodies the wealth and prestige possible by brokering deals between the "suits" and the "talent" (Slater 1997).

Network researchers often display the results of their analyses as graphic images that powerfully capture the structure of social relations among actors. Figure 2.3 illustrates this procedure, using an artificial 10-actor network in the form of a "kite with a tail," which contains a diversity of structural properties (an insight first noticed by David Krackhardt). Each capital letter represents an actor, and each line refers to a direct social tie between a dyad, for example, to a frequently used two-way communication channel. Although 18 ties occur, another 27 possible direct connections are absent. Both the present and the missing links give this complete network its overall structural image and also account for the different centralities of each participant. Because actor D has the largest number of direct connections (six), it has the highest-degree centrality. In contrast, actor H, with just three ties, has a lower-degree centrality than F, G, A, or B. However, although the seven actors in the "body" of the kite structure are all highly interconnected, they require lengthy indirect routes to reach the two actors in the kite's "tail" (I and J). For example, a message from A can reach J only by traversing a *path* involving a minimum of four links (A-F-H-I-J). Actors F and G both have the highest closeness centralities, because they require smaller average path lengths to reach the other members. Finally, actor H enjoys the greatest betweenness centrality because its strategic location at the juncture of the kite's body and tail allows it to control communications between these two structural locations. If H leaves the network, it would fall apart into two unconnected subsystems.

Analyses of complete networks generally reveal structural properties that are not evident from an ego-centric perspective. In particular, for a system

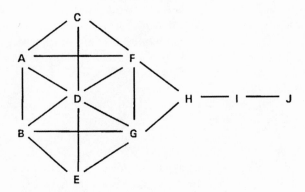

FIGURE 2.3   Ten-Actor Network with a "Kite"
Structure

containing many organizational actors, a smaller number of basic social
positions may be identified by grouping or clustering together subsets of actors who display identical or highly similar patterns of relations. For example, all workers on an automobile assembly line make up a single position
defined by their interchangeable ways of interacting with the plant's foremen, supervisors, and upper managers. Similarly, all firms in a particular
industry jointly occupy the same position, not on the basis of their common
characteristics (such as using the same technologies, hiring similar employees, or pursuing an equivalent market strategy) but because of their similar
patterns of exchanges with other supplying and purchasing organizations.
To assign actors to a jointly occupied structural position, analysts apply
two principles: (1) the degree of similarity between each pair depends on
their total patterns of connections to all other system members; and (2) the
more dissimilar a pair of actors, the greater is their "social distance" and
hence the less likely they are to occupy the same position. In determining
which actors belong to each position, *the absent ties are just as important
as the present ties,* because a pair's similarity must take into account their
entire pattern of relations within a complete network. Whom they interact
with and whom they avoid are equally relevant considerations.

Positional analyses of complete networks usually adopt one of two basic
procedures (Burt 1987). The *cohesion* approach identifies a position only
by the frequency of direct ties among its members. The most cohesive position is a *clique,* whose members are all directly connected by strong ties to
one another (not surprisingly, this term enjoys popular usage by solidarity
groups inside schools, churches, clubs, and workplaces). In Figure 2.3, two
large cliques occur, each consisting of four actors: (BDEG) and (ACDF).
Eleven smaller cliques each involve just three actors: (ABD), (ACD), (ACF),

(ADF), (BDE), (BDG), (BEG), (CDF), (DEG) (DFG) and (FGH). Note that the very popular D, which has the highest-degree centrality, participates in eight of these cliques. Somewhat weaker groupings recognize that not every member of a cohesive subgroup can maintain such maximal connections. *Social circles* consist of members maintaining a high proportion of contacts with one another (Alba and Kadushin 1976). For example, a researcher may define a circle as one that requires half or more of the possible ties to occur. An example of a large circle in Figure 2.3 is the set (ABCDEFG) with 76 percent of the 21 possible communication links. All its members are connected by paths of length two or less.

The second basic approach to identifying members of a network position applies a *structural equivalence* principle. Two organizational actors jointly occupy an equivalent position if they maintain identical or highly similar connections to the other system actors, regardless of whether they are directly connected to one another. In Figure 2.3, the set (CE) are structurally equivalent because they have very similar ties and non-ties to the others, despite the absence of a direct interaction between them. Among real organizations, legal barriers such as antitrust laws may prevent competitive firms from colluding in production and pricing. Nevertheless, two or more companies may occupy an equivalent structural position by virtue of their relations with the rest of the political economy. For example, silicon chip makers who buy their raw materials from the same suppliers, sell their outputs to the same computer manufacturers, and are regulated by the same governmental agencies are effectively indistinguishable. Hence, these interchangeable firms structurally occupy the same production position. By contrast, other chip makers whose buying and selling patterns connect them to unique suppliers and customers would be located in separate network positions.

Given its multilevel outlook, network theory addresses a rich assortment of questions. Analysts explore the sources of network tie formation, the persistence and change in network patterns over time, and the consequences of network structures for organizations and individuals. At the organizational field level of analysis, a variety of social forces generate new interorganizational ties and destroy previous relations. The diffusion of technological innovations is likely to disturb established work-flow patterns. For example, the spread of just-in-time manufacturing techniques—requiring suppliers to deliver parts to a factory gate at the moment of assembly—obviously place higher demands for coordinated schedules across organizational boundaries. New governmental mandates—such as environmental protection rulings or occupational safety and health legislation—are also typical occasions for creating or expanding regulatory agencies that implement and enforce new interorganizational arrangements. Organizations employing professionals such as lawyers, physicians, accountants, or research scientists are inevitably exposed to standards advocated by those employees' professional associations that may conflict with business criteria focused on bottom-line profits. Government efforts to contain escalating health care costs forced for-profit hospitals to restrict their staff physicians' traditional freedom to decide which medical tests and procedures to order for their patients.

Changing customs, norms, and laws may push organizations to transform previously informal interactions into institutionalized networks. For example, during the first half of the twentieth century, network-building processes converted the National Collegiate Athletic Association from a loose mutual-support confederation into a powerful control agent capable of imposing severe financial penalties on member schools caught violating its rules, particularly in recruiting players. "The multiplexity of ties between the NCAA and network institutions increased through the growing number of valued resources and services provided by the association" (Stern 1979:257). These resources included greater financial rewards, legitimacy, and access to participation in the Olympics and football bowl games. A new administrative apparatus arose through complex power struggles between three interest groups in this emerging college sports network: big universities, small colleges, and the NCAA staff. "The historical data suggests [sic] that changes in administration, system coupling, multiplexity of ties, and system resources produced dependence on the NCAA and led increasingly to its dominance over intercollegiate athletics" (Stern 1979:262). These networking dynamics did not cease in the half century after the association won the legal right to enforce its decisions. The big-school versus small-school conflicts over interdependence and autonomy intensified, while the federal government became a major network player through a legislative mandate to equalize the status of women's collegiate athletics.

Network structures exert numerous influences on organizational fields and their members. Thus, the speed at which new technological and social innovations diffuse depends on a network's information-exchange structure, particularly the extent to which the system is centralized or fragmented (Rogers 1995; Valente 1995). Early-adopting organizations are more likely to occupy central positions in the information network and to be influenced through their connections to other initial adopters (opinion-leaders) who directly testify about the advantages of risky opportunities. A second example is how inter-industry competitive relations affect firms' profit margins. Ronald Burt's (1979, 1992) structural autonomy theory argued that if (1) a manufacturing industry is oligopolized, and (2) that industry's firms exchange with many other supplier and consumer markets that are highly competitive, then these two conditions enable companies "to pursue and realize interests without constraint from other actors in the system" (1980:892). In other words, when a network's structural arrangements give firms negotiating advantages, they have better opportunities for producing more profitable returns on their investments. Further, when firms find that their inter-industry networks offer them less autonomy, they will try to improve their positions by acquiring other firms in the most problematic industrial sectors. As a final illustration that network structures can affect system and organizational outcomes, consider how interest groups try to influence public policy legislation. The organizational state model of national policy domains (Laumann and Knoke 1987; Knoke et al. 1996) proposed that successful outcomes require organizations to form "action sets" (coalitions) that pool their political resources for a coordinated campaign involving mass media publicity, membership mobilization, and lobbying of public officials. Organizations occupying the central position in a policy domain's information and resource exchange networks are more likely than peripheral organizations to be recruited into action sets, to acquire high reputations for power, and to influence the outcome of public policy decisions.

The preceding examples could be multiplied many times over, at the interpersonal as well as the intra- and interorganizational levels of analysis. Space limitations prevent further exploration of these aspects here, but the following chapters examine in greater detail the application of network principles to the various aspects of organizational change.

Relations Among Theories

Organizational network theory offers several opportunities for weaving together the varied theoretical strands in organization studies. Because it emphasizes relations between organizational actors at multiple levels of analysis, the network perspective complements the other approaches. For example:

- Organizational populations whose members are more closely interconnected may experience faster growth rates, greater survival prospects, and higher carrying capacities. The original organizational ecology perspective depicted organizations as atomized and competitive rather than interdependent. However, even firms with identical resource needs may cooperate for mutual benefit. They may share information and collaborate in joint ventures, although institutional constraints such as antitrust restrictions may hinder or prohibit the degree of integration. Ironically, although individual organizations' growth opportunities may be hindered by their interorganizational obligations, such commitments may expand population numbers: Assistance to weaker members limits the stronger organizations' development while improving the survival chances of weaker firms.

- Institutional theory recognizes that organizations "are also located in a network or framework of relations which their own activities create but which also acts to shape and constrain their possibilities for action" (Scott 1991:171). The more centrally located an organization is in its field, the greater its exposure to changing legitimacy norms. The high public visibility of central organizations subjects them to stronger pressures to serve as their sectors' opinion-leaders and thus to conform to shifting normative standards. Although intrafield networks enforce homogeneity of beliefs, network ties that link organizations to other sectors serve as conduits for diffusing new standards and, hence, for institutional change.

- Inter- and intraorganizational networks are clearly relevant to resource dependence theory, because other organizations are major resource providers in any political economy. Network connections are channels through which specific environmental pressures become salient to organizational managers. Organizations occupying the central positions in information and resource exchange networks avoid dependence while gaining power and influence over collective actions. Network linkages are susceptible to some degree of manipulation and reshaping by organizational managers who decide which interfirm connections to acquire and which ones to drop. Rational managers proactively pursue strategies of network formation that seek to maximize their companies' autonomy and goal attainment while minimizing their dependence. The more complex, diverse, uncertain, and unstable an organization's external networks, the more differentiated and flexible its internal structures must become to achieve a good fit. Inside an organization, the subunits and persons with ties to important external actors can acquire the financial resources and political support necessary to obtain powerful positions in the firm. An ego's capacity to process diverse information efficiently is enhanced by its access to network alters capable of assisting in sense-making and reducing uncertainty and ambiguity.

- Information-exchange networks help to reduce the collection of transaction cost data required for make-or-buy decisions about making or outsourcing products and hiring or retraining company personnel. Networks are also social mechanisms for building trust between organizational agents, which is vital to sustain recurring exchanges. Trustworthiness reduces the necessity for elaborate contractual and administrative safeguards against environmental uncertainty, limitations of bounded rationality, and temptations of opportunism.

Such instances of convergence between theoretical explanations will be repeated many times over as subsequent chapters explore the fascinating diversity of organizational changes in their many manifestations.

Conclusions

I intend my too-brief review of prominent theories in organization studies to provide a foundation for interpreting the trends and explaining the substantive analyses of organizational change in the following chapters. These five macro level perspectives—organizational ecology, institutional theory, resource dependence, transaction cost economics, and network analysis—have attained satisfactory scope to be applicable to a large array of substantive issues. I will also explicate other theories in chapters focusing on specific topics in organizational behavior. I have not attempted to disguise my personal predilection for organizational network theory, but I also recognize that no single paradigm will likely soon achieve paradigmatic domination. The unique strengths and particular limitations of each approach suggest that they are better used in concert, as intellectual tools to ferret out the multiple meanings of myriad organizational changes. Thus, these complementary theories repeatedly resurface in the pages to come.

3

Resizing
and Reshaping

Corporation, n. *an ingenious*
device for obtaining individual profit
without individual responsibility.
—Ambrose Bierce, The Devil's Dictionary (1906)

In the global telecommunications ocean, a few minnows grow up to be whales. In early October 1997, WorldCom made an unsolicited $30 billion stock-swap bid to take over MCI Communications Corp. Facing huge losses in its local phone services, Washington-based MCI had seemed resigned to marching down the wedding aisle with British Telecommunications. However, pressured by its stockholders, who thought MCI's stock overvalued at $40 per share, BT had reneged and forced MCI to accept just $30 per share. This cheap strategy backfired when WorldCom's aggressive chairman, Bernard J. Ebbers, jumped in with a $41-per-share offer that MCI couldn't refuse (Lipin and Keller 1997). When MCI momentarily balked and rival suitor GTE proposed an even better deal at $45 in cash, Ebbers trumped by offering $51 per share in WorldCom stock. He clinched the then-biggest corporate buyout in history, its total of $37 billion easily beating the $25 billion that KKR had paid in 1988 to take over RJR Nabisco. Pretty shrewd dealing for a company sketched out in 1983 on a napkin in a diner outside Jackson, Mississippi.

A former junior high basketball coach and motel operator, the bearded and cowboy-booted Ebbers, a Canadian transplanted to the Mississippi delta, was a Bernie-come-lately to the tumultuous telecom industry. He had quickly cobbled together WorldCom through a series of billion-dollar takeovers of 50 fiber optic, satellite service, and local phone operators, plus the struggling data networks of Compuserve and America Online. While traditional telephone companies were still sinking billions into copper-wire voice lines, Ebbers acquired 1.2 million miles of fiber optic cable necessary to handle mushrooming data transmission traffic. This aggressive acquisitive strategy won turbocharged investments by Wall Street, enabling his obscure firm to zoom in just five years to the nation's fourth-largest long-distance carrier. The combined MCI WorldCom could now challenge AT&T for the leading share of the long distance communication market. Stodgy AT&T was hemmed in by federal regulatory restrictions against competing in the local phone service market against its "Baby Bell" spin-off companies. Ironically, AT&T had lost its telecom monopoly in the 1980s as a result of an antitrust lawsuit filed by MCI's legendary founder, the late Bill McGowan. With his takeover of MCI, Ebbers would soon reap what McGowan had patiently sown.

The merged MCI WorldCom juggernaut reportedly might control 60 percent of the U.S. traffic on the global computer network, threatening to change the Internet from a peer-oriented community to a market-driven service. "It's important that we at least have some minimal charge," said WorldCom's vice chairman, for allowing small Internet access providers to pass e-mail and exchange Web pages over the "backbone" system of main channels built and operated by MCI WorldCom (Weber and Quick 1997). Charging user tolls on the Internet highway might doom the standard $19.95-a-month unlimited access plans offered by the thousands of local service providers with mere hundreds of customers. The U.S. Justice Department promised to scrutinize the MCI WorldCom deal to see whether it would curb competition. At the same time, in another part of the global telecom ocean, British Telecommunications and GTE were both left standing at the alter with their hopes of becoming world class players in tatters. Despite a cash cushion of $7 billion for selling its 20 percent stake in MCI to WorldCom, BT was especially vulnerable to being shut out of the U.S. market, and back in the United Kingdom it was losing market share to 120 rival local phone companies (Naik 1997). GTE's presence in a full array of communication markets might make it a tempting target for merger with AT&T or alliances with the "Baby Bell" regional companies. Stay tuned to your local station for pending updates from this eternally fascinating soap opera.

The rapid rise of WorldCom Inc. to a central position in the telecommunications industry reflected several major trends that dramatically changed the demographic landscape of the U.S. organizational population. National census figures revealed steadily increasing numbers of organizations but considerable variation in their sizes, whether measured as total employees or financial resources. After massive layoffs and corporate downsizing in the 1980s and 1990s, observers disputed whether smaller or larger firms were mainly responsible for most of the country's job growth. Controversy also swirled around the best ways to conceptualize and measure organizational forms. Recent changes in the government's industrial classification scheme, intended to mirror the increasing importance of high-tech and service trades, promise to make these transformations more difficult to track. During the twentieth century, the multidivisional form of corporate governance displaced all alternative structures among the largest firms. Five massive waves of mergers and divestitures initially expanded, then contracted, the diversity of markets in which the giant companies operated. By the close of the twentieth century, several new forms of networked organizations had emerged to challenge conventional ways of conducting business in the global political economy.

How Many
Business Organizations?

Until the 1970s, no one knew exactly how many business organizations were active in the United States. Unlike some smaller nations, such as Sweden and Norway, the United States conducted no regular census of all organizations. As a result, little reliable data from an earlier era are available about such basic demographic statistics as the numbers and types of organizations, their sizes, and the rates at which this population changed over time. One exhaustive review of earlier research reached a pessimistic conclusion about the accuracy of coverage, usefulness of information collected, and availability of data in forms that could be easily understood: "No consistent method of analysis or reporting is used, and most of the findings are subject to statistical or inferential errors" (King and Wicker 1993:117). Fortunately, that sad situation gradually began to change.

The U.S. Bureau of the Census launched a Standard Statistical Establishment List (SSEL) for all domestic employer and nonemployer businesses (except governments and businesses operated in private households), which also included the separate organizational units of multi-establishment firms.[1] Two technical distinctions are crucial to the portrait of an organizational population. An *establishment* is "an economic unit, generally at a single physical location, where business is conducted or where services or industrial operations are performed" (U.S. Office of Management and Budget 1987:12). A *firm* is a business organization consisting of one or more domestic U.S. establishments under common ownership or control. (In federal economic censuses, the term *company* is a synonym for firm.) Thus an establishment is identical to a firm only for a single-location business such as your neighborhood newsstand. But a multi-establishment firm is an aggregation of all the businesses owned by a parent company. The conglomerate firm General Electric, the fifth-largest U.S. corporation by sales revenue in 1999, runs businesses from powerplant parts manufacturing to the NBC television network. Its diverse establishments produce aircraft engines, kitchen appliances, laundry equipment, electrical distribution systems, and basic materials such as plastics, silicones, laminates, and abrasives. GE operates nearly 150 manufacturing plants across the United States and more than a hundred plants in 25 other countries.

By 1997, the SSEL covered more than 5.3 million single-establishment companies and about 210,000 multi-unit firms representing another 1.6 million establishments, for a total of 6.9 million establishments and 5.5 million firms. The annual total number of U.S. firms and establishments from 1988 to 1997, according to SSEL tabulations, appears in Figure 3.1, along with approximations for total firms from 1981 to 1989 using data provided by the U.S. Department of Labor's Employment and Training Administration (ETA).[2] This period spans two recessions (1981–1982 and 1990–1991) and both subsequent economic recoveries. The ETA trend shows steady growth in the total number of firms, averaging 2.2 percent annual increases during the 1980s, with peaks of 3.5 percent in 1984 and 1987. Both SSEL firm and establishment trend lines increased at lower rates from 1988 to 1997: Annual average gains were 1.37 percent for firms and 1.53 percent for establishments. The only decrease occurred in 1991, when the number of firms fell by 0.5 percent during that recession (but the number of establishments increased slightly). By way of comparison, the U.S. population increased just 16.5 percent from 1981 to 1997, whereas the number of firms grew at double that rate (34.0 percent) over the same period.

The upward trends in Figure 3.1 conceal much turbulent change, created by the numerous business foundings and disbandings (analogous to births and deaths). For example, although the total establishment population grew by only about 91,000 workplaces between 1995 and 1996 (the latest tabulations available), this increase was generated by the creation of 697,457 new establishments that offset the termination of 606,426 organizations. Although the vast majority of businesses disappear by simply ceasing their operations without owing any debts, the number of bankruptcies and business failures ran above 120,000 annually in the 1990s. Another important type of termination among larger organizations is the merger process, examined in greater detail later in this chapter.

Although the SSEL is enormously valuable for measuring aggregate changes in the national business population, its annual tabulations provide cross-sectional snapshots that lack a dynamic perspective. Only detailed analyses that track individual organizations' life histories from their foundings until their failures can reveal the intertwined processes of birth, survival, and mortality. These data are unavailable for all U.S. organizations, but fortunately organizational ecologists have diligently assembled event histories

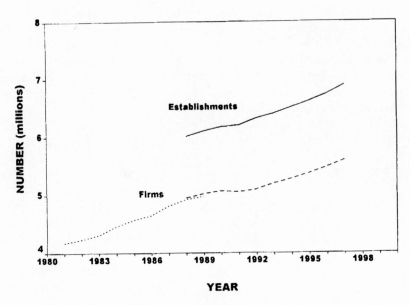

FIGURE 3.1   Firms and Establishments
SOURCE: U.S. Bureau of the Census, "Standard Statistical Establishment List" (SSEL) (2000) and U.S. Small Business Administration (1994)

for many specific populations (Carroll and Hannan 2000). The main limitation of single-industry populations is that their demographic processes may differ in unknown ways from the entire population of U.S. organizations.

Consider, for example, the well-documented emergence of the semiconductor industry after World War II. These firms manufactured the high-tech devices used in computers, such as integrated circuits, random access memories (RAM), and microprocessors. Rapidly changing technologies and markets attracted high-risk entrepreneurs and venture capitalists. The industry's fierce competition and notorious instabilities generated a few huge personal fortunes, including that of Intel's Andrew Grove, as well as numerous company failures. Figure 3.2 displays the first 39 years of growth in this population, compiled from annual listings in the *Electronics Buyer's Guide* by Michael Hannan and John Freeman (1989:225 and 295). Typical for many newly created organizational forms, an initial period of rapid entries into an exploding market (between 1946 and 1969 for semiconductors) saw the numbers of organizations increase exponentially, that is, at an annually compounded rate of change. Note that the peak period for both entries and exits (1969–1973) coincided with the highest population densities (recall that density refers to total number of organizations at a given

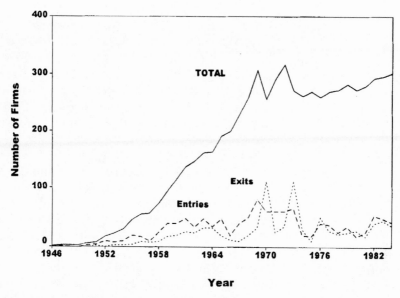

FIGURE 3.2   Growth of Semiconductor Firms
SOURCE: Hannan and Freeman (1989)

time). A volatile shake-out period followed, during which similar levels of entries and exits (through bankruptcy, absorption by other firms, or leaving the industry) eventually stabilized the population at around 300 organizations over the next 15 years. Of the 1,197 companies entering between 1946 and 1984, nearly 900 left the industry.

As discussed in Chapter 2, organizational ecology theory hypothesizes that growth patterns depend on population density. Density captures the opposing effects of legitimacy and competition on growth rates at differing stages in a population's development. The "nonmonotonic density dependence" effect predicts a curvilinear growth pattern: During the early stages when many opportunities abound, a rising population density signals the legitimate acceptance of the new organizational form and thus attracts others to enter the industry at a faster rate. However, after a population reaches its environmental carrying capacity, strong competition for scarcer resources now discourages newcomers. Hence, high population density during this latter stage should decrease the rate of entry. The expected pattern across the population's entire history is an inverse-U relationship between density and entry rates. In the semiconductor case, Hannan and Freeman found a significant relationship of higher population density to increased rate of new-firm entry. However, contrary to theoretical expectations, the hypothesized curvilinearity did not occur for the entire semiconductor population. When Hannan and Freeman separately analyzed subsidiary and independent firms, the curvilinear pattern occurred for the subsidiaries but not for the independent subpopulation. "The entry rates of independent firms do not behave as if they have encountered a carrying capacity" (Hannan and Freeman 1989:243). Interestingly, the subsidiary firms' density also produced a curvilinear effect on the rate at which independent firms entered the semiconductor industry, suggesting highly competitive dynamics between these two subpopulations.

Ecological theory also hypothesizes that the opposing legitimacy and competition processes change the rate of organizational exits. Again the expected pattern is curvilinear with population density, but now following a U-shape as the exit rate first declines then rises with increased population density. The evidence from the entire semiconductor industry strongly supported this theoretical expectation (Hannan and Freeman 1989:296–297). When the subsidiary and independent firm subpopulations were separately analyzed, the expected relationship was significant only for the latter type of organization. Furthermore, a powerful cross-effect occurred in which the subsidiary density increased the exit rate of independent firms, suggesting that the parent organizations were better able to protect their subsidiaries at the expense of the independent companies' survival.

Research on many organizational populations—ranging from labor unions to automobiles to breweries, banks, and newspapers—generally supported the curvilinear density-dependence hypotheses (Hannan and Carroll 1992; Carroll and Hannan 1995). However, one critical review of empirical findings from 1989 to 1995 concluded that, "when population dynamics and population density are modeled together, recent studies find population dynamics effects are generally weaker and less robust" (Baum 1996:85). Data analyses supported the density-dependence hypothesis for organizational foundings by 74 percent of 31 populations and for organizational failures by 55 percent of 22 populations, although the correct predictions were somewhat higher for populations that had passed their peak densities (Baum and Powell 1995). However, Carroll and Hannan (2000:219) noted that most "disconfirming tests that have appeared typically come from analyses of data produced by flawed research designs, notably left-truncated observation schemes that exclude the early history of a population." Such design flaws may seriously distort estimates of a nonmonotonic density effect on rates of foundings and mortality. On balance, the ecological approach to understanding the dynamics of macro level change in organizational populations remains a thriving theoretical perspective in organization studies.

Nonprofit and Government Organizations

Unlike the SSEL, comprehensive censuses of nonprofit organizations are not available for the United States. Nonprofits are a "third sector" of organizations operating neither as government agencies nor to make profits for shareholders (Weisbrod 1988; Gidron, Kramer and Salamon 1992; Salamon and Anheier 1997). The U.S. Internal Revenue Service (IRS) tabulates a wide range of tax-exempt organizations, primarily under Section 501(c) of the federal tax code. The total number of nonprofits tallied by the IRS grew during 1991–1997 from 1.11 million to 1.32 million, a 19.4 percent increase that greatly exceeded the 11 percent growth rate of both business firms and establishments in the same period. The pie charts in Figures 3.3a and 3.3b display the proportions of organizations falling into 10 major IRS classifications in 1991 and 1997, respectively. The largest number was classified under subsection 501(c)(3), religious and charitable organizations, which reached a majority by the latter year.[3] This segment's increase (34.1 percent) was far more spectacular than all other categories combined (6.6 percent). The next two largest nonprofit categories (social welfare organizations and fraternal beneficiary societies) provide many not-for-profit services that benefit their members' private interests but aren't considered charitable in nature (Meckstroth and Arnsberger 1998).

The 501(c)(3) organizations—which range from universities and schools to hospitals, scientific research labs, United Way campaigns, performing arts groups, and environmental support organizations—qualify for this status by serving the public good through programs, services, and grants for charitable purposes. A major tax advantage of this classification is that cash and property contributions made by persons or businesses to these nonprofits are deductible for income tax, estate, and gift tax purposes. To obtain 501(c)(3) status, an organization must operate exclusively for one or more objectives enumerated in the U.S. tax code, must not attempt political influence as a substantial portion of its activities, and cannot participate in any political campaigns. Most 501(c) organizations in the IRS's other 24 tax-exempt categories were not eligible to receive tax-deductible contributions.

No governmental organizations appeared in the SSEL despite the substantial scope of economic activities undertaken in the public administration sector. In 1997 the federal, state, and local governments collectively employed 14.3 percent of the U.S. labor force (three-fifths at the local level) and spent about one-fifth of the gross domestic product (U.S. Bureau of the Census 1999: Tables 534, 649). One difficulty in enumerating the population of public sector organizations is how to determine the governmental equivalents of business firms and establishments. Although the number of "governmental units" in 1997 totaled 87,504, these entities are only broad

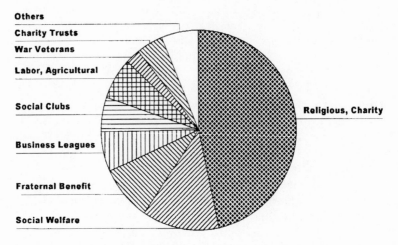

FIGURE 3.3a   Tax-Exempt Organizations, 1991
SOURCE: Internal Revenue Service (1996)

legal jurisdictions that typically embrace hundreds or thousands of specific
organizations performing diverse tasks. Thus, the federal and state governments accounted for just 51 units, while the majority comprised the governments of municipalities (22 percent); towns and townships (19 percent);
school districts (16 percent); and "special districts" such as natural resources, fire protection, and housing and community development (40 percent) (U.S. Bureau of the Census 1999: Table 500).

   The most plausible governmental equivalent to the business firm could be
a specific "agency" that exercises authority over its own budget and personnel matters, for example, a city police department, county library system, or state agriculture department. The concept parallel to a business establishment might be a specific geographic site where work is performed,
such as a police precinct station, branch library, or agricultural extension
office. Complications would arise for such complex entities as hospitals and
universities: Do these organizations comprise unitary work sites, or should
every administrative subunit—from toxicology labs to maternity wards,
from English departments to computer centers—count as a distinct establishment? At the federal level, is the Department of Defense the sole agency,
or should the Army, Air Force, Navy, Marines, and Coast Guard also be
classified as separate agencies? Or should each military branch's ports,
bases, training centers, and weapons depots count as discrete work sites?
Until organizational analysts reach consensus on these definitional criteria,
compiling a comprehensive list of governmental organizations for comparison to the business population will remain elusive. Only a rough idea about

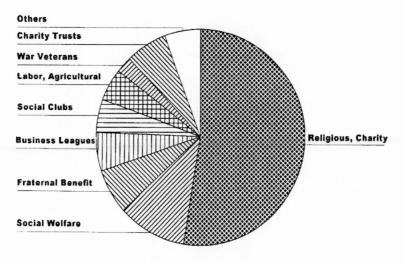

Others
Charity Trusts
War Veterans
Labor, Agricultural
Social Clubs
Business Leagues
Fraternal Benefit
Social Welfare
Religious, Charity

FIGURE 3.3b   Tax-Exempt Organizations, 1997
SOURCE: Internal Revenue Service (1999)

the size of public sector populations can be gleaned from existing directories of specific types, sometimes compiled by professional associations. The most recent numbers available for the 1990s show that the United States had 18,769 law enforcement agencies and 1,500 correctional facilities; 6,097 hospitals, 5,392 mental health facilities, and 19,100 nursing homes; 14,822 school districts with 88,223 public and 8,217 Catholic elementary and secondary schools; 3,706 colleges and universities; and 37,591 libraries (U.S. Bureau of the Census 1999). Several of these categories contain varying mixtures of public, for-profit, and nonprofit organizations.

Organizational Size

Organizational censuses count all firms and establishments as equivalent businesses, but individual organizations vary tremendously in size. Consider the SSEL's percentage distributions for establishments grouped by number of employees in 1997, as displayed in Table 3.1. The first column shows that a majority of the 6.9 million workplaces had just four or fewer workers, while only 2.3 percent employed 100 or more people. Under the U.S. Small Business Administration's definition of a "small business" as one that employs fewer than 500 workers, practically every U.S. establishment would be classified as small (99.8 percent). A more generous definition would recognize that many federal laws regarding pensions, plant closings, and family medical leave have provisions that exempt businesses with fewer

TABLE 3.1   Private-Sector Employment by Establishment Size, 1997

Employment Size (Number of Employees)	Establishment Percent	Employment Percent
0–4 employees	54.5	6.1
5–9 employees	19.6	8.5
10–19 employees	12.4	10.9
20–99 employees	11.1	29.1
100–499 employees	2.1	25.6
500 or more employees	0.2	19.8
Total	99.9*	100.0
(Number of Observations)	(6,894,869)	(105,299,123)

* Totals to less than 100 percent due to rounding.
SOURCE: U.S. Bureau of the Census, "Standard Statistical Establishment List" (SSEL) (2000)

than 50 employees. Other labor regulations come into force only when a workplace hires more than 20 people. Even under this lower size criterion, barely one-eighth of establishments would be classified as "large." One plausible, but very controversial, conclusion is that the United States at the end of the twentieth century remained very much a nation of small businesses.

Quite a different picture emerges, however, when the 105 million private-sector employees in the 1997 U.S. labor force composition are broken down by firm size in the second column of Table 3.1. An apparent paradox arises from the extreme asymmetry in the organization and employee distributions: the median employer is very small but the median employee works in a large organization. Specifically, more than half the establishments (54.5 percent) employ fewer than five people, but almost half the labor force (45.4 percent) draws paychecks from workplaces with 100 or more coworkers. Thus, despite the tiny sizes of most establishments, many employees encounter medium- and large-business environments in their daily work lives. This apparent discrepancy arises because, although the smallest establishments are the most prevalent organizations, the sum of their workforces is also proportionally small. In contrast, although the 160,131 workplaces with 100 or more employees made up just 2.3 percent of all U.S. private-sector establishments, their aggregated workforces approximated their vastly more numerous but so much smaller competitors. The skewed employee-size distributions for Japanese and European Union firms compel similar conclusions that, although small businesses make up the large majority of organizations, the very largest firms employ the largest proportion of their nations' labor forces (Aldrich 1999:10–13). As the trailers for the movie *Godzilla* proclaimed, "Size does matter," but for organization studies, how size matters depends on which yardstick you use.

An examination of the financial resources of firms in different employment-size categories further underscores the impression of great inequality. The IRS estimated that receipts from all business sales totaled $16.7 trillion in 1996. The 0.3 percent of firms with 500 or more employees received more than half this total (53.2 percent), and the 90 percent of firms with fewer than 20 employees accounted for a mere 16.8 percent of total revenue (U.S. Bureau of the Census 1999: Table 877). The highly skewed financial and workforce distributions both support an alternative, and equally controversial, conclusion that a few large U.S. companies economically dominated millions of insignificant small business organizations at the end of the twentieth century.

A relative handful of gigantic firms controlled most of the nation's assets, revenue flows, and organizational workforces. These 800-pound economic gorillas were collectively labeled the Fortune 500 companies (also expanded into Fortune 1000 and Global 500 versions), from annual rankings published by the eponymous magazine.[4] The term symbolized a self-identified peer group that was widely recognized by the business press and in corporate publicity. Many firm names and logos were household words because of consumer familiarity with their products and services. Space limitations prohibit displaying the entire Fortune 500 list for 2000, but Table 3.2 shows the top 25 companies ranked by total revenues, along with their profit rates as a percentage of revenues and numbers of employees worldwide. The staggering scope of operations indicated by these revenue and employment figures is well above the reach of most U.S. firms. Even the smallest Fortune 500 company on the list, an insurance company named ReliaStar Financial with revenues of just $3.0 billion, far surpassed the median SSEL firm in revenues. Given the high visibility, enormous economic impact, frequent involvement in governmental affairs, and easy availability

TABLE 3.2   Top Fortune 500 Companies for 2000, Ranked by Revenues

Rank & Name	Industry	Revenues ($ billions)	Profits (Percent Revenue)	Employees
1 General Motors	Motor vehicles	$189.6	3.2	388,000
2 Wal-Mart Stores	General merchandise	166.8	3.2	910,000
3 Exxon Mobil	Petroleum refining	163.9	4.8	79,000
4 Ford	Motor vehicles	162.6	4.5	364,550
5 General Electric	Electrical	111.6	9.6	340,000
6 IBM	Computers	87.5	8.8	307,401
7 Citigroup	Commercial banking	82.0	12.0	180,000
8 AT&T	Telecommunications	62.4	5.5	107,800
9 Philip Morris	Tobacco	61.8	12.4	137,000
10 Boeing	Airplane manufacturing	58.0	4.0	197,000
11 Bank of America	Commercial banking	51.4	15.3	170,975
12 SBC Communications	Telecommunications	49.4	16.5	204,530
13 Hewlett-Packard	Computers, office equip.	48.3	7.2	84,400
14 Kroger	Food and drug stores	45.4	2.1	213,000
15 State Farm	Insurance	44.6	2.3	76,257
16 Sears Roebuck	General merchandise	41.1	3.5	324,000
17 American Int'l Group	Insurance	40.1	12.4	48,000
18 Enron	Pipelines	40.1	2.2	17,800
19 TIAA-CREF	Insurance	39.4	2.6	5,000
20 Compaq Computer	Computers, office equip.	38.5	1.5	85,100
21 Home Depot	Specialty Retailers	38.4	6.0	157,000
22 Lucent Technologies	Network communications	38.3	12.4	141,600
23 Proctor & Gamble	Soaps, cosmetics	38.1	9.9	110,000
24 Albertson's	Food and drug stores	37.5	1.1	100,000
25 MCI WorldCom	Telecommunications	37.1	10.8	77,000

SOURCE: Fortune (2000) and Hoovers (2000)

of data about these giant businesses, organization researchers frequently confined their investigations to the Fortune 500 and equivalent large companies while excluding medium and smaller businesses. One consequence is a somewhat biased perception of the varieties of sizes, structures, and performances by the organizational population in the U.S. political economy.

Entries and Exits

The ecological approach to organizational change emphasizes (as does the evolutionary perspective discussed in Chapter 10) the importance of organizational *foundings* (births or entry events) and organizational *disbandings* (deaths or exit events) as vital demographic components in organizational population dynamics (Aldrich 1999; Carroll and Hannan 2000). Foundings enable existing organizational forms to reproduce and also promote the emergence of entirely new populations. Organizations end when their participants either stop performing sustaining activities or the entity is absorbed into another organization. The rate of foundings per unit of time minus the rate of disbandings determines the demographic trajectory of organizational population growth or decline. New organizations can enter a population through four basic creation modes (Carroll and Hannan 2000:41–42):

- New founding, typically by startup actions of a single person or a small team of founding partners. This section discusses entrepreneurial founding processes in greater detail.
- Merger of two or more existing organizations that results in a substantially new enterprise. I discuss mergers in greater detail in a later section of this chapter.
- Spin-off from an existing organization; for example, the 1995 split of AT&T into three Fortune 500 companies (AT&T, Lucent Technologies, and Global Information Solutions, later renamed NCR), each specializing in a different aspect of telecommunications and multimedia.
- Migration from another population or industry, such as Westinghouse's transformation from appliance manufacturer into television broadcaster CBS.

Foundings seem to be the predominant entry mode in most organizational populations. Indeed, the discipline of entrepreneurial studies emerged to explore the emergence of new enterprises (Bygrave 1995; Venkatraman 1997; Thornton 1998; Morris 1998). (The French word *entrepreneur* literally means "undertaker," which suggests risk-assuming activities; but the English translation conveys morbid imagery, so everyone uses the foreign word.) Many researchers within this tradition heavily emphasize the motivations, personality traits, and learning experiences of individuals engaged in launching new businesses (e.g., Naffziger 1995). More structural approaches consider how social and institutional conditions shape entrepreneurial efforts and the ultimate successes or failures of organizational startups. Interpersonal networks provide crucial socio-emotional support, diffuse specialized knowledge and information, and connect entrepreneurs to sources of both formal and informal financing (Dubini and Aldrich 1991; Malecki 1997; Aldrich 1999:81–88). Potential new-firm founders also derive competitive advantages through their social embeddedness within ethnic or occupational networks in local communities and regions, such as the industrial districts examined in Chapter 4. Although most entrepreneurs must draw on their personal savings and assets to build their organizations, a few manage to entice substantial resources from more than a thousand U.S. venture capital funds. These funds professionally manage pools of capital invested in equity-linked private ventures (Bygrave 1988; Fiet 1991; Gifford 1997; Gompers 1999). Propelled by the 1990s stock market boom, venture capitalists invested record amounts, rising from $6.2 billion in 1995 to $35.6 billion in 1999 (PricewaterhouseCoopers 2000), and more than 2,500 firms made initial public offerings (IPOs) (Hale and Dorr 2000). Technology-based companies, including hot Internet businesses ("dot.coms"), were the primary beneficiaries of this largesse. However, the number of firms involved in these high-end financial deals constituted just a fractional percentage of all organizational foundings.

The entrepreneurial startup process is sometimes depicted as an orderly sequence of decisions and transitions, applying a biological metaphor of conception-gestation-infancy-adolescent stages (Reynolds and White 1997:6). However, the activities and events surrounding the founding process are much better characterized as disorderly and even chaotic (Aldrich 1999:77–79). Pinpointing the exact time a new entity emerges is problematic. Should the founding date be when a "nascent entrepreneur" has her first serious thoughts about committing time and resources to starting a new business, or when she produces a written business plan, obtains financial support, hires the first employee, or makes the first sale? Not only do these and other startup events occur in varied patterns, but they often stretch across many months or years. Based on a national survey, less than 4 percent of the adult population annually qualified as nascent entrepreneurs, but they collectively launched more than a half million new organizations (Reynolds and White 1997:73). The researchers concluded that "over 90% of new start-ups are either sole proprietorships or controlled by a single family or kin group, which suggests that many of the decisions and resource allocations may not be interpreted, or even identified, with a standard economic or business framework" (p. 208).

Organizations exit from a population through four basic processes (Carroll and Hannan 2000:44):

- Disbanding, either by informally ceasing operations or through formal bankruptcy proceedings that disperse the remaining assets among creditors. Simple disbanding is more likely to occur among small businesses than among large corporations, whose substantial assets are usually taken over by another firm.

- Merging with another organization, which effectively terminates each entity's independent existence and begins a new organization.
- Being acquired, when an acquired organization's resources are submerged within its acquirer's corporate structure. Sometimes the purchased organization retains a vestige of its former identity, especially where a trademark or brand attracts loyal customers. For example, after the Walt Disney Co. bought Miramax Film Corp. from Bob and Harvey Weinstein in 1993, it allowed the brothers to continue producing "art house" films under that label. Disney thus preserved the family-oriented reputation of movies marketed under its own brand.
- Migrating into another population or industry.

Most newly founded organizations face enormous odds against survival and successful growth. Endless disadvantages plague the founders of small, young startups (the entangled liabilities of newness, smallness, and aging are discussed in Chapter 2): entrepreneurial inexperience, insufficient capital resources, feckless employees and disloyal clients, weak supplier and customer networks, ruthless rivalry from established competitors, burdensome governmental paperwork, and lack of public legitimation. Such constraining conditions render new organizations vulnerable to severe environmental selection processes. The high odds of mortality rapidly winnow out many startups. One consequence of these ecological and evolutionary pressures, particularly among for-profit organizations, is that most emergent organizations suffer short, troubled lives and never grow much beyond their initial sizes (measured by employees or revenues). The legendary success stories of a Hewlett Packard or a Wal-Mart, starting in a garage or country store and growing into global Fortune 500 firms, are fairy tales for all but a handful of entrepreneurs. More common are hundreds of thousands of sole proprietorships which, after struggling for months to find and fill a market niche, swiftly exhaust their owners' life savings, and quietly lock their doors, unnoticed and unmourned by passing crowds.

At the population level, high rates of foundings and disbandings facilitate the reproduction and spread of existing organizational forms as well as speed up selection and retention in emerging new populations. Rates of change depend both on influences internal to populations and on external environmental conditions (Baum 1996; Audretsch 1999; Carroll and Hannan 2000; Aldrich 1999:266–273). Primary intra-population factors that increase demographic vital rates include prior foundings and disbandings and increased density dependence. These trends change available resources, sharpen competition, and enhance legitimacy in complex ways. Broad environmental forces that may alter organizational population dynamics include changes in cultural values and norms toward entrepreneurship and corporate welfare; demographic shifts in family formation, immigration, and labor force participation; stocks of specific human capital embodied in entrepreneurs and educated employees; political stability or turbulence; judicial decisions, regulatory rulings, and governmental macro-economic policies (see Chapter 9); national research investment and technological innovation systems (see Chapter 10); and the emergence of new occupational and organizational communities that cooperate and compete with other populations (e.g., Web-based commerce). Some external factors are generic influences affecting the growth patterns of all organizations, whereas others are circumstances unique to particular populations. Hence, comparative research on a variety of organizational populations is crucial for separating general influences from the impact of unique historical circumstances on changing vital rates.

Which Organizations
Create New Jobs?

One topic concerning organizational size that aroused much controversy was job creation. During the late 1980s, a fierce debate erupted over the primary sources of job growth in the United States. David Birch, a business consultant and lecturer at MIT, contended that small businesses hired new workers at much faster rates than mid-sized and large companies, creating eight out of ten new jobs (Birch 1987, 1989). New startup firms were expanding their payrolls at the very time giant corporations from IBM to General Motors to AT&T were busily closing plants and laying off employees in record numbers. (Chapter 5 examines corporate downsizing and restructuring in greater detail.) Birch and his colleagues later claimed that, between 1987 and 1991, firms with fewer than 500 employees created 5.9 million more jobs than they lost, while larger firms experienced a net loss of 2.4 million jobs (Birch, Haggerty and Parsons 1993). Similar analyses led Bruce Phillips at the U.S. Small Business Administration to conclude that firms with fewer than 20 employees, especially those located in states with fast-growing high-tech industries, were generating the most new jobs (1991, 1993). By the 1990s, the image of small business as America's mighty jobs engine had passed into common political rhetoric. Speaking to urban mayors in 1993, President Clinton stated that "small businesses have created virtually all the new jobs in our country in the last ten years. Their inability to create more jobs than larger employers have been shedding is the central cause of stagnant employment in America." In his first State of the Union address, Clinton proposed "the boldest targeted incentives for small business in history," including a permanent investment tax credit (Davis, Haltiwanger and Schuh 1990:170).

Statistics on net job gains from the 1992–1993 SSEL also tend to support the small business job-prowess hypothesis. Although establishments owned by the largest firms, those with more than 500 total employees, generated 5.72 million jobs (either by creating new establishments or expanding the workforces of older ones), they also shed 5.56 million workers for a net gain of just 161,000 new jobs. In contrast, small firm establishments generated 11 times more net new jobs (1,787,000), with 60 percent of this gain concentrated among companies employing four or fewer workers. However, this one-year growth immediately followed the 1991 recession, when many large companies were still laying off workers or reluctant to add new ones:

> Over the course of past business cycles, small firms have always added a more than proportional share of new jobs relative to their employment share. The small business share of net new jobs increases most rapidly during the recovery stage of a cycle, and during the earlier parts of the expansion phase of a cycle. As the economy approaches full employment during the latter stages of an expansion, larger firms tend to produce a larger share of jobs, while the small business share falls somewhat. (U.S. Small Business Administration 1997)

Relying only on the net job-gain calculations touted by Birch and other small-business advocates can lead unwary analysts into a hidden statistical trap. A giant company typically cuts thousands of jobs during a recession, but it usually shrinks in size rather than going entirely out of business (or it might merge with another large company). A small firm more often eliminates all of its jobs by completely ceasing operations. By failing to consider that many small companies simply vanish from the sample, the net-job method usually overestimates the small-business job creation and understates the big-business contribution (Davis, Haltiwanger and Schuh 1990; Nasar 1994:C2).

Evidence to challenge the "myth" that small businesses dominated U.S. job growth came from a painstaking dissection of gross job flows (job creation and destruction) by employer size category. Using 1975–1985 data on the manufacturing sector sampled annually at the establishment level by the Longitudinal Research Database (LRD), Davis and Haltiwanger (1992) uncovered high rates of plant-level job creation and job destruction for both large and small employers, on the order of 10 percent of employment per year (see also Davis, Haltiwanger and Schuh 1994). Although smaller firms and plants created jobs at substantially higher rates than did large firms, they also destroyed jobs at much higher rates. Hence, the survival chances for new and existing jobs were sharply higher for large employers. Plants with fewer than 100 employees reallocated 30 percent of their jobs, but plants with 1,000 or more workers reallocated just 14 percent of their jobs over the 11-year period (Davis and Haltiwanger 1992:841). Additional

LRD analyses revealed that most 1980s growth in manufacturing productivity came not from downsizing factories but primarily from workplaces that also increased employment. "The largest plants are disproportionately represented in the group of plants that increased employment and productivity" (Baily, Bartelsman and Haltiwanger 1994:25; see also Haltiwanger 1999). Researchers must still investigate whether similar creative-destructive dynamics occurred in the 1990s or in nonmanufacturing sectors. Debate about the relative contributions of large and small firms to new and enduring job creation continued to rage, with arguments turning on technical details in quantitative data analysis (see Dennis, Phillips and Starr 1994; Asquith and Weston 1994; Storey 1995; Robson 1996; Carree and Klomp 1996; Kirchhoff and Greene 1998; Davidsson, Lindmark and Olofsson 1998).

A very important implication of the skewed organization-size and revenue distributions and the job-formation findings is that, despite the preponderant numbers of small organizations, collectively they only modestly affect the workplace experiences of the U.S. labor force and the economic life of the nation. Small firms and establishments should not be ignored, but neither can they be considered the major players in our political economy. Medium, large, and gigantic firms encompass the vast majority of the labor force, physical stock, financial assets, profits, and economic growth and contraction processes. Because the largest corporations remained the country's main economic motors, organization researchers continued to pay careful attention to their structures, experiences, and performances.

What Forms of Organizations?

Any answer to the question, "How many different forms of organizations are there?" depends on which features an analyst emphasizes in defining organizational types. In principle, *organizational form* "refers to those characteristics of an organization that identify it as a distinct entity and, at the same time, classify it as a member of a group of similar organizations" (Romanelli 1991:82). Unfortunately, no commonly accepted classification system has been developed, so researchers remain free to choose varied criteria to distinguish similar from different organizations. Both organizational ecology and evolutionary perspectives identify two divergent approaches to classifying organizational forms. Howard Aldrich (1999:35–40) noted that selection processes may operate at two units of analysis: (1) at the micro level within organizations of jobs, routines, and competencies (activities and structures), occurring either singly or in bundles; and (2) at the macro level of bounded entities that contain these activities and structures, such as entire organizations, populations, communities, and groups. Depending on which units of analysis they emphasize, theorists emphasize different distinguishing features of organizational forms.

As a proponent of the first criterion, Bill McKelvey (1982:107) proposed an exceptionally comprehensive taxonomy of organizational forms that embraces "those elements of internal structure, process, and subunit integration which contribute to the unity of the whole of an organization and to the maintenance of its characteristic activities, function or nature." His procedures closely mimicked biologists' methods for identifying unique animal and plant species and constructing family trees showing their evolutionary descent-with-modification (see Mayr and Provine [1988] for overviews of the modern synthesis in biological evolution). The analogy breaks down in the absence of organizational mechanisms rigorously equivalent to the genetic inheritance and mutation processes occurring in biotic populations. To apply McKelvey's taxonomic techniques to classify different organizational forms would require researchers to collect dozens if not hundreds of costly measurements from representative samples of specimen organizations and might result in exceedingly complex and unwieldy formal typologies.

Treating entire organized entities as the unit of selection, organizational ecology theorists Michael Hannan and John Freeman (1977) avoided imposing fixed criteria in pursuing their substantive investigatory interests. They defined an organizational form as:

> a blueprint for organizational action, for transforming inputs into outputs. The blueprint can usually be inferred, albeit in somewhat different ways, by examining any of the following: (1) the formal structure of the organization in the narrow sense—tables of organization, written rules of operation, etc.; (2) the pattern of activity within the organization—what actually gets done by whom; or (3) the normative order—the ways of organizing that are defined as right and proper by both members and relevant sectors of the environment. (Hannan and Freeman 1977:935)

But in Hannan and Freeman's actual research practices, applying even these simple criteria proved impracticable. Instead, "[w]e have relied on the conventional wisdom of participants and observers" but have "usually arrayed the forms along some analytic continuum and focused on variations along the continuum" (1989:63–64). They illustrated this method by their study of 33 precise forms of restaurants (such as pizzerias, doughnut shops, steak houses, hotel restaurants), which were then reclassified into two broad analytic types—"generalists" and "specialists"—according to the range of products and services offered. Carroll and Hannan's (2000:73) redefinition of organizational forms as socially constructed identities hasn't been around long enough to demonstrate its usefulness in guiding empirical research (see Chapter 2).

Given the absence of a theoretical consensus in organization studies about the criteria most useful for classifying organizational variations, the following subsections examine three widely used empirical schemes: legal forms based on firm ownership, industrial forms based on the organization's primary product or service, and structural-relational forms based on arrangements of internal organization configurations and external relationships. Together, these diverse schemas capture much of the changing variation in contemporary organizational types.

Legal Forms

The corporate form was a major social invention that drastically changed the legal status of business organizations. (Chapter 7 explores the legal history of the corporation.) During most of the nineteenth century, businesses took the form of either *sole proprietorships* (single owner) or *partnerships* owned by two or more people. Even today, many small businesses, such as family farms and law firms, are legally organized in these two forms. Their primary characteristic is that *all* of an owner's assets remain at risk if a proprietorship or partnership fails and creditors come knocking at the door. That is, not only the business properties but also the owners' personal homes, automobiles, and bank accounts can be seized and sold to pay company debts, no matter who was responsible for the organizational failure. In the 1980s, thousands of investing partners (called "names") in the giant British insurance pool Lloyd's of London lost their entire life savings because of massive claims from the *Exxon Valdez* oil spill in Alaska, the devastation of Hurricanes Hugo and Andrew, and other natural disasters.

Corporations get around this unlimited liability problem by the legal fiction that a firm is a sovereign person enjoying the same rights, responsibilities, and protections as natural persons (Coleman 1990:531–578). A corporate firm divides its capital assets into shares (equity), which it then sells to individual or institutional shareholders who thereby face only a *limited liability* for the company's debts. If a firm cannot pay its bills and goes out of business, its shareholders are not obligated to pay the creditors from their personal assets. They risk losing only whatever funds they invested in buying the stock. On the upside, shareholders are entitled to receive any company profits that may be distributed as dividends, as well as to reap capital gains by selling their equities when the share value in the stock market rises above their original purchase price. The invention of the corporation enabled giant firms to accumulate huge amounts of capital because equity investors proved much more willing to purchase shares when their personal properties were not legally put at risk.

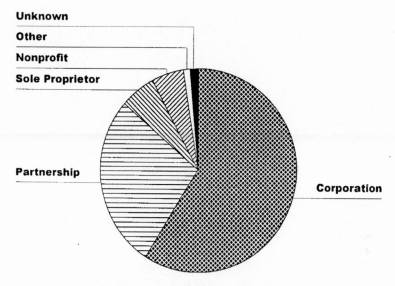

FIGURE 3.4   Legal Types of Firms, 1994
SOURCE: U.S. Bureau of the Census, "Standard Statistical Establishment
List" (SSEL) (2000)

The limited liability corporation rapidly gained ground throughout the
twentieth century, for example, expanding from just half of manufacturing
firms in 1947 to four-fifths a half-century later. The pie chart in Figure 3.4,
showing the 1994 distribution of firm ownership reported in the SSEL, reveals that a majority were corporations (60 percent), followed by sole proprietorships (28 percent). Moreover, the legal form varied strongly with
size: partnerships and proprietorships together accounted for more than
one-third of the firms with fewer than 20 employees, but less than 10 percent of larger firms (83 percent of these larger organizations were corporations). The financial inequality exhibited across types of firms was even
more dramatic. Corporations captured 92 percent of the $14.8 trillion of
estimated firm receipts (sales) in 1994, leaving only table scraps for the
small proprietors and partners to scuffle over.

Industrial Forms

In the 1930s, the federal government began using a complex Standard Industrial Classification (SIC) system to code workers and organizations by
types of industry. The 1987 version of the SIC was a hierarchical system in
which more detailed categories could be aggregated into smaller sets: 1,005

industries were combined into 416 industry groups, then into 83 major groups, and finally into 10 divisions. Table 3.3 displays the firm and employee distributions for nine of the ten divisions (the SSEL does not track organizations in the public administration sector). Just two large divisions, retail trade and services, accounted for the majority of both establishments and employees (columns one and two). The mean number of workers per firms in those two divisions roughly equaled the national average of 15.4 workers (column three). However, larger firms predominated within three divisions—manufacturing (47.4 employees per firm), transportation and communication (20.8), and mining (21.9)—while two divisions contained firms with notably smaller average sizes (construction with 8.3 and agriculture, forestry, and fishing with 6.2 employees per firm).

An industry classification system identifies establishments that operate in the same primary commodity market; that is, they produce similar goods or services for sale. Several theories—notably organizational ecology, resource dependence, and transaction cost economics (see Chapter 2)—emphasize the importance of understanding market environments for explaining organizational behavior. For example, organizations that require similar mix-

TABLE 3.3   Private-Sector Employment by Industry Divisions, 1997

Industry Division (SIC Categories)	Establishment Percent	Employee Percent	Mean Employees per Firm
Agriculture, Foresty, Fishing	1.7	0.7	6.2
Mining	0.4	0.6	21.9
Construction	9.7	5.2	8.3
Manufacturing	5.7	17.7	47.4
Transportation, Communication	4.4	5.9	20.8
Wholesale Trade	7.7	6.5	12.8
Retail Trade	23.2	20.9	13.8
Finance, Insurance, Real Estate	9.9	7.0	10.9
Services	37.2	35.5	14.7
Total	99.9*	100.0	15.4
(Number of Observations)	(6,843,402)	(105,264,799)	—

* Totals to less than 100.0 percent due to rounding
SOURCE: U.S. Bureau of the Census, "Standard Statistical Establishment List" (SSEL) (2000)

tures of resources are more likely to compete against one another to obtain favorable price, quality, and delivery terms from the suppliers of those essential resources. Likewise, institutional theory proposes that companies operating in the same or very similar organizational fields confront common social, economic, and political forces that encourage their adoption of similar structures and practices. Thus, firms in industries engaged in resource exchanges with an equivalent subset of markets should tend to converge toward comparable organizational forms and actions.

A structural equivalence analysis of industry-commodity relations describes the network of market exchanges within which U.S. organizations are embedded. The map in Figure 3.5 was generated by a multidimensional scaling of the Bureau of Economic Analysis's benchmark input-output accounts for 91 commodity markets and major industry groups in 1992 (Lawson 1997). Industries appear close together to the extent that their member establishments purchased similar proportions of input commodities from all industries.[5] For example, although the motor vehicles industry bought nearly one-third of its resources from the automotive parts market, it closely resembled the home appliance industry because both used substantial commodities from the rubber, screw machinery, metal fabrication, service machinery, and wholesale markets. Hence, structural equivalence plots the appliance and motor vehicles industries near one another at the right center of Figure 3.5. In contrast, the apparel and radio-TV industries appear far apart (lower right and upper left, respectively) because their establishments purchased almost entirely different commodity arrays: 63 percent of radio-TV inputs came from the amusements market, but the fabrics and textiles markets together supplied almost the same proportion to apparel producers.

The 91 major industry groups may be further classified into 11 divisions or sectors, approximating the 1987 SIC codes, as indicated by the symbols next to each industry name in Figure 3.5. These sectors help to identify the map's basic orientation (the plus-and-minus scalings on the two axes are arbitrary). The horizontal axis seems to represent a services-versus-manufacturing dimension (from left to right), whereas the vertical axis places the younger, high-tech industries toward the top and the older, extractive industries toward the bottom. With few exceptions, most of the industry groups in a sector occupy distinctly bounded regions in the U.S. market space, suggesting that these industries generally compete against one another for the same input commodities. Thus, all 30 durable manufacturing industry groups cluster at the right side, and most of the 20 nondurable manufacturers fall at the bottom center. The four industry groups in the agricultural sector appear toward the lower left, and most members of the seven other sectors are squeezed into the upper left quadrant of Figure 3.5. Although this 1992 industry map is based on cross-sectional data, similar

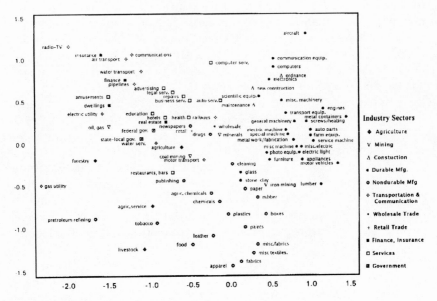

FIGURE 3.5   Industry Similarities, 1992
SOURCE: Lawson (1997)

analyses of input-output tables for 77 product markets from 1963 to 1992 indicate that these network patterns were stable (Burt 1988; 1992:85–89; 1998). Moreover, the network structural locations of producers buying and selling in these markets constrains the profit margin extracted by each industry (Burt 1992; Burt et al. 1999). Unfortunately, researchers' ability to track industry-market network structures into the twenty-first century will be severely hampered by major changes now under way in the federal government's classification system.

Starting with the 1997 Economic Census, the U.S. federal government, in collaboration with its North America Free Trade Association (NAFTA) partners (Canada and Mexico), altered the industry coding scheme to reflect profound transformations in these three political economies. The new North American Industrial Classification System (NAICS) is more consistent in classifying firms and workers according to the actual activities performed by establishments, and it provides greater detail within the rapidly expanding high-tech and service industries. Twenty sectors replaced the ten SIC divisions, including:

- The *Information Sector*, covering the creation, distribution, or provision of access to information: satellite, cellular, and pager communications; online services; software and database publishing; motion pictures; video and sound recording; and radio, television, and cable broadcasting. (Chapter 4 reports an analysis of the strategic alliance network among the largest international firms in this sector.)

- The *Health Care and Social Assistance Sector*, involving industries classified by intensity of care and such new industries as health maintenance organization (HMO) medical centers, outpatient mental health care, and elderly continuing care.
- The *Professional, Scientific, and Technical Services Sector*, for industries relying primarily on human capital, including legal, architectural, engineering, interior design, and advertising services.

Other NAICS categories also identified newly emerging low-tech services that reflect continuing changes in North Americans' busy daily lives: automotive oil change and lubrication shops, casinos and other gambling industries, bed and breakfast inns, convenience stores, credit card issuing, diet and weight reduction centers, environmental consulting, food/health supplement stores, gas stations with convenience food, limited service restaurants, pet supply stores, temporary help supply, and warehouse clubs. Tabulations using both SIC-based and NAICS-based data began appearing in government publications at the end of the twentieth century (U.S. Bureau of the Census 1999). As the SIC was quickly phased out, trend comparisons to previous industry censuses will become increasingly difficult.

Structural-Relational Forms

A third general basis for classifying organizational forms takes into account the recurring relationships among social positions, whether inside or outside an organization's boundaries. Theorists and empirical researchers proposed numerous schemes relying on just a handful of basic criteria. Three classic examples systematically varied in their connections among components. Etzioni's (1961) authority-compliance scheme considered three forms of command-and-obedience relations between organizational managers and lower-level participants: coercive-alienative (e.g., prisons, military), remunerative-calculative (business firms), and normative-moral (churches). Burns and Stalker (1961) generated two ideal types, "mechanical" and "organic," by contrasting polarities in their hierarchical authority, communication patterns, task specialization, and so forth. Mintzberg (1979) proposed five basic organizational forms—simple structure, machine bureaucracy, professional bureaucracy, divisionalized form, and "adhocracy"—depending on the relative sizes and shapes of the five core internal functions (see the generic icon in Figure 1.2). In these and many similar typologies, the underlying principle was how an organization's differentiated subunits are interconnected into a function-ing system. Explaining organizational change then requires examining how hypothesized socioeconomic and political forces, especially those arising from the external environment, compel rearrangements among these basic structural relations.

Because organization studies did not reach consensus about any of the proposed structural-relational typologies, reliable statistics on the national distribution of such organizational forms were simply unavailable. A no-table exception is the multidivisional form of governance used by the largest corporations, examined in the next section. However, several inves-tigators conducted analyses of structural-relational forms in more restricted organizational samples, and their findings appear in Chapter 4 (forms of in-terorganizational relations) and Chapter 6 (forms of workplace structures).

Why Did the
Multidivisional Form Spread?

The multidivisional form (MDF, also known as M-form) was the most renowned structural-relational innovation of the twentieth century, sup-planting all other organizational forms among the largest corporations throughout the world. Business historian Alfred Du Pont Chandler, Jr. de-scribed its primary features using the abstract organizational chart in Fig-ure 3.6:

> In this type of organization, a general office plans, coordinates, and appraises the work of a number of operating divisions and allocates to them the neces-sary personnel, facilities, funds, and other resources. The executives in charge of these divisions, in turn, have under their command most of the functions necessary for handling one major line of products or set of services over a wide geographical area, and each of these executives is responsible for the financial results of his division and for its success in the market place. (Chandler 1962:2)

In contrast to the preceding functional or unitary structure (U-form), in which a firm integrated its internal departments under a single hierarchy with responsibility for different activities, the M-form organization was radically decentralized. It relieved senior executives in the firm's general of-fice of administrative concerns with short-run routine operations. Instead, top management could concentrate on long-run entrepreneurial responsi-bilities for making strategic plans, deciding capital allocations, and guiding the company's destiny. These executives set broad policy guidelines for the entire organization that "determine[d] the present and future allocation of

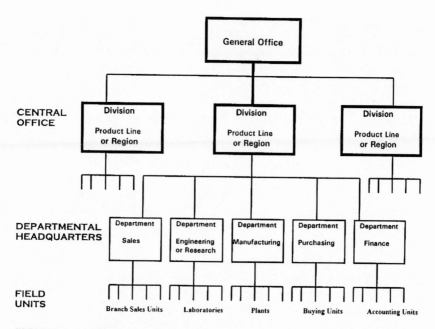

FIGURE 3.6   Alfred Chandler's Multidivisional Structure Chart
SOURCE: Modified from Chandler (1962)

the resources of the enterprise and within the carefully defined interrelationships between the operating units and the general office" (Chandler 1962:311). The division managers were delegated sufficient authority to oversee their units' manufacturing, marketing, and financial operations. They were responsible for making tactical decisions on such matters as product research and development, pricing, and distribution within their own clearly defined markets. Divisional managers and the top team routinely exchanged detailed statistical data about product costs and consumer demand, thus assuring the efficient coordination, forecasting, and evaluation of an MDF company's divisions.

Chandler concluded that four pioneering companies independently invented the multidivisional form during the 1920s: E. I. du Pont, Standard Oil of New Jersey, Sears Roebuck, and General Motors. In 1921, GM adopted a divisional structure devised by its operating vice president, Alfred P. Sloan (1964), to rescue the automobile manufacturer from the sharp recession following World War I. GM's well-known vehicle brands (Buick, Cadillac, Chevrolet, Oldsmobile, and GM Truck; Saturn was added in 1986) each carefully targeted a distinct market niche identified by vehicle price ranges. For example, Chevy prices were slashed to compete for lower-income customers against Ford's long-popular Model T. By 1927 GM's total annual auto sales had permanently overtaken the obstinately centralized Ford Motor Company, which was forced to shut down for six months while it retooled its assembly lines to manufacture the new Model A (Chandler 1964). Only after Old Henry's death following World War II and his grandson's takeover would the Ford Motor Company reorganize itself into an M-form, ironically by hiring a former GM executive to show the way (Lacey 1986). Once the wider business community had discovered the decentralized MDF's advantages, the form diffused rapidly by adoptive imitation. Figure 3.7 demonstrates the march of the MDF across seven decades among the 100 largest U.S. firms (Fligstein 1990:336). Both the U-form and the holding company (a financial device whereby one company bought controlling stock in several firms) virtually vanished in the post-World War II era.

Organizational researchers have proposed five theoretical explanations for the M-form's triumph: diversification strategy compelling structural adjustment; transaction cost efficiencies; resource dependence; institutional legitimacy; and network diffusion. Chandler himself favored an interpretation in which changing organizational strategies required firms to undertake structural reforms to use their skilled human resources more rationally. *Organizational strategies* are "basic long-term goals and objectives of an enterprise and adoption of courses of action necessary for carrying out these goals" (Chandler 1962:13). A strategy involving high-volume production, vertical integration of technically complex functions, geo-

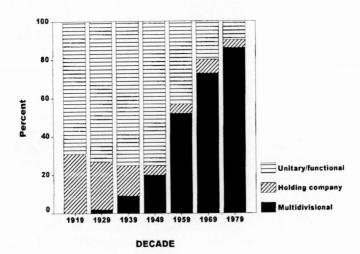

FIGURE 3.7   Spread of the MDF
SOURCE: Fligstein (1990)

graphic dispersion into national and international markets, and entry into diverse new product lines puts severe strains on the top leaders of centralized U-form companies. Thus, any large company pursuing a diversification strategy would be compelled to reorganize into a decentralized M-form to compete in swiftly changing markets (Chandler 1962:13). The MDF innovation was the inevitable choice for large diversified corporations facing identical environmental conditions within the continent-wide American political economy. The multidivisional structure made possible a "continuing effective mobilization of resources to meet both changing short-term market demands and long-term market trends" (Chandler 1962:385).

The transaction cost explanation for MDF diffusion also presumed an organizational search for greater economic efficiency. The expanding size and scale of a U-form organization typically generates "cumulative loss effects, which have internal efficiency consequences" (Williamson 1975:133). Faced with making increasingly diverse and complex decisions, a firm's top administrators encounter growing difficulties in monitoring, coordinating, and controlling their numerous subordinates' voluminous activities. Unable to overcome inherent limitations of imperfect information (bounded rationality), functional managers who joined the top executive team tended to advocate their own divisions' short-term tactical interests, while neglecting broader strategic dilemmas affecting the entire company. Reorganizing a corporation into an M-form allegedly solved these dilemmas by grouping distinct organizational tasks into separate geographic and/or product-line chains of command. Thus the firm's transaction costs decreased and harried top executives found relief from information- and decision overloads. By separating responsibility for strategic and tactical decisions into general and divisional hands, respectively, M-form corporations lessened the chances for error through inattention. Installing effective information and financial accounting systems also enabled the top team to oversee and adjust the division managers' actions before they ran seriously off-track. And the MDF reduced the dangers of opportunism (pursuing "self-interest with guile") by removing divisional managers from participation in the strategic planning process, where they might be tempted to put their units' problems ahead of the company as a whole (Williamson 1983).

The vaunted economic efficiencies gained by converting to M-form governance structures may reflect more wishful mythology than verifiable improvement in organizational performance. The transaction costs saved by separating strategic from operational decision making may be squandered by violating corporate norms and expectations about managerial participation. In a detailed re-analysis of one of Chandler's four paradigmatic MDF cases, Robert Freeland (1996) concluded that General Motors not only had failed to implement a pure M-form during much of its history, but its belated effort at genuine decentralization ultimately proved disastrous for

GM's prosperity toward the end of the century. Between the 1920s and 1950s, the company periodically waffled between (1) a "corrupted" version of Alfred Sloan's 1921 decentralized structure, in which division heads in fact participated informally in strategic decisions; and (2) a more coercive centralized administration, in which the GM general office simply imposed both strategic and operational decisions on its divisions by fiat. In a crucial 1957 reorganization, the general office tried to regain control after an opportunistic Buick division manager's policy initiatives had lost market share and ravaged employee morale. Sloan chaired a special committee to implement a classic M-form that strictly excluded divisional personnel from any role in formulating or approving company-wide policies. Unintentionally, these cost-cutting initiatives succeeded only in undermining the general office's legitimacy in the eyes of its operating division managers. Instead of boosting economic efficiency, imposing this classic M-form provoked divisional resistance and induced perfunctory rather than consummate performances. The conflict propelled a downward spiral of increased centralization and repeated company failures to adjust to the changing automotive environment when foreign auto manufacturers invaded the U.S. market with a vengeance in the 1960s and 1970s. "Ironically, while the new organization succeeded in returning formal authority to the general office, it also smashed the mechanisms for manufacturing consent, laying the groundwork for GM's more extensive and long-lived decline in later decades" (Freeland 1996:509). By overlooking the importance of social norms for motivating exceptional efforts from organizational participants, economic transaction cost theory led to an incomplete understanding of corporate change in unstable environmental conditions (but see Shanley [1996] for a defense of transaction cost efficiencies in the GM case). Freeland inferred from his analysis that if the corporate general officers strictly "adhere to the image of a textbook M-form that relies extensively on fiat and financial control mechanisms, they will substitute bureaucratic compliance of consummate performance and short-term profits for long-term competitive advantage" (1996:518).

A third explanation of the M-form's popularity, resource dependence theory, stressed the importance of political power processes (Pfeffer and Salancik 1978). As discussed in Chapter 2, shifting coalitions of internal and external actors struggle for control over key corporate resources, especially its public stock and its board of directors' seats. Realignments within the dominant coalition typically redirect an organization's goals and its governance structures. From a resource dependence perspective, the triumph of the MDF reflected shifting balances of corporate control among owners (primarily the founding entrepreneurs and their families), financial institutions, and top-level managers. At the beginning of the twentieth century, small family-run and entrepreneur-controlled firms predominated in most sectors of the U.S. political economy. But as the giant diversified companies emerged to service wider national markets, their insatiable demands for huge capital resources from stock issues and bank loans soon dissipated the founding families' power. With ownership so widely dispersed among myriad small shareholders, a top management team could easily use its insider knowledge to gain effective control over company strategy. This "managerial revolution" captured a majority of the largest U.S. corporations because shareholders lacked effective means to oppose the nonowning professional managers and their hand-picked, rubber-stamp boards of directors (Berle and Means 1932). Financial creditors, such as commercial banks, insurance companies, pension funds, and investment houses, also gained control over publicly traded firms by leveraging their monetary clout to put their own officials into corporate board seats (Mintz and Schwartz 1985). By the 1960s, the 200 largest corporations and 50 largest financial companies were connected through more than 600 interlocking directors (Dooley 1969). As major suppliers of capital resources by issuing loans and purchasing bonds, financial institutions were positioned to exercise substantial power over general corporate policies, for example, by insisting on "protective provisions" that restricted dividend payments or future borrowing (Kotz 1978:20). Chapter 9 considers the evidence for and against the existence of a political ruling class rooted in these corporate networks.

Resource dependence theory hypothesizes that both family-dominated and finance-controlled firms were less willing than management-controlled companies to adopt the multidivisional form (Palmer et al. 1987). Family-based coalitions preferred U-forms and undiversified structures that better enabled them to exercise day-to-day control over corporate affairs. Avoiding an MDF reduced the opportunities that nonowning professional managers might pursue undesirable strategies, such as long-term stability and growth in market share, rather than maximizing the owning family's short-term profits. Because family-controlled firms typically situated new plants near the company headquarters community, they also resisted the geographic dispersion that favored an M-form reorganization. Similarly, bank-dominated coalitions preferred to stimulate economic growth within their local service areas. Banks were also reluctant to back the MDF because decentralization tended to undercut corporate needs for the investment expertise provided by financial institutions. An analysis of M-form and U-form structures among 200 U.S. firms, randomly selected from the 1964 Fortune 500 list, supported the hypothesis that both family- and bank-owned corporations were significantly less likely to adopt the M-form, even after controlling for their lower rates of industrial diversity and geographic dispersion (Palmer et al. 1987).

A fourth explanation, based on institutional theory, offered a cultural account of the M-form's spread in the post-World War II era. Neil Fligstein

(1990) agreed with Chandler that the large corporations' decisions to pursue diversification strategies for growth and profits preceded their formal restructuring into multidivisional firms. However, Fligstein argued that market efficiency calculations were less relevant to MDF diffusion than were changing beliefs within the business community about legitimate ways to govern the modern corporation. A socially constructed "finance conception of corporate control" ascended in the 1950s among leaders of the most visible and admired companies in various organizational fields. This ideology depicted the corporation as a portfolio or bundle of financial assets, each earning varying rates of return on the company's investments. Corporate leaders came to believe that divisions and subunits should be purchased, developed, or divested strictly according to their distinct contributions to the firm's immediate bottom-line financial statement:

> Firms in the modern era no longer view themselves as operating in a particular business, but instead view any given business as an investment that must pay off. The rate of return on capital and the potential for that return are viewed as the most important facts by which any product line is evaluated. The basic mode of expansion in the era of financial strategies is no longer sales, but mergers. The decision to merge is made independent of whether or not a product fits with a firm's existing lines. (Fligstein 1991:321)

The people who championed this financial-control strategy for achieving growth and profit were primarily trained in finance and accounting principles, and secondarily in sales and marketing techniques, but not in the manufacturing production expertise of a bygone industrial era. As finance-oriented personnel increasingly ascended to the presidencies of major corporations in the post-World War II period, they obtained sufficient organizational power to implement their preferred diversification strategies. The federal government unintentionally assisted these strategic transformations with judicial decisions and antitrust legislation that changed the legal rules of the business game. The 1950 Celler-Kefauver Act prohibited any vertical and horizontal acquisitions within any single product line that might concentrate a larger share of a given industrial market in fewer corporate hands. Consequently, large companies could grow only by following *product-related strategies* (defined as producing in multiple industries having some functional connection, with less than 70 percent of revenues from a single industry group) and *product-unrelated strategies* (producing in functionally unrelated industries) (Fligstein 1990:261).

Most important, the postwar financial conception of control diffused by imitation among the firms embedded within particular organizational fields. As discussed in Chapter 2, institutional theory argues that such mimetic processes are powerful social mechanisms tending to reduce variation among organizations (DiMaggio and Powell 1983). The initial driving force to embrace new organizational behaviors may differ from the reasons for the continuing institutionalization of organizational practices. Specifically, as Lynne Zucker (1983:13) argued, "the rapid rise and continued diffusion of an organizational form is best interpreted as an instance of institutionalization: early in the process, organizations adopt the new form because it has unequivocal positive effects on productivity, while later adopters view the new form as the most legitimate way to organize formally, regardless of any net productivity benefits." For an organizational field to change, its leaders must both believe in the potential benefits from a new corporate vision and possess sufficient power to enact that belief. "Once some set of organizations in a field has changed its strategies, and once others perceive that the change has resulted in some allegedly superior results, the other actors will follow suit" (Fligstein 1991:316). Regardless of whether such changes actually produce greater performance efficiencies, the followers' socially constructed beliefs about the causes of economic success compel them to embrace the pioneers' ideology and copy their practices.

In the final proposed explanation for MDF diffusion, network theory reinforced the preceding institutionalist account of how the finance-control conception spread. Communication channels distributed information and persuasive arguments about appropriate and inappropriate solutions to common field problems, "establishing a taken-for-granted quality to actions in that field" (Fligstein and Markowitz 1993:192). Firms closely connected to an organizational field's most prominent corporations by a variety of economic, social, and political network ties were quicker to adopt innovative practices than the more marginalized and unconnected firms. Once the number of corporate adopters reached a critical density, the firm-as-portfolio concept became fully institutionalized and thence could serve as the dominant standard of successful strategy for the entire field.

The diversification strategy favored by the financial conception of corporate control also promoted adoption of the M-form as the preferred structure for governing large businesses. Fligstein examined the spread of MDF adoptions among the 100 largest U.S. companies in each decade from 1919 to 1979. Multivariate logistic regression equations for each period gave strong support to his hypothesized relationships (Fligstein 1985, 1987, 1990). Firms that followed a product-related, a product-unrelated, or a merger strategy were more likely to shift from the holding-company or U-form to the M-form governance structure. Companies whose chief executive officers (CEO) came from finance, sales, and marketing backgrounds "introduce the form in order to promote and control their diversification strategy" (Fligstein 1990:364). And the higher the proportion of an industry's firms that had previously adopted the MDF by a decade's beginning, the more likely were other organizations to follow. Contrary to organizational ecology hypotheses about the restraining effects of organizational inertia of rates of change, both older and larger companies were more likely to lead their fields into the M-form promised land.

A more narrowly focused analysis found economic, institutional, and network forces underpinning late MDF adoptions during the 1960s (Palmer, Jennings and Zhou 1993). Of the 105 Fortune 500 industrial companies that hadn't adopted the M-form before 1962, about one-third converted during the following six years. Economic factors such as product-related and product-unrelated diversification and geographic dispersion stimulated M-form adoptions. The researchers found no evidence for the resource dependence, or political power, hypotheses that family ownership or bank control of corporations delayed these late M-form conversions. However, institutional and network effects were significant: CEOs trained in elite business schools and directors embedded in nondirectional corporate interlocks boosted the adoption rate. Management schools socialized their students about preferred business practices, particularly the multidivisional form championed by Chandler. Firms headed by these graduates in the 1960s were more likely to convert to an MDF governance structure. An interlocking director tie is created when one person sits on two firms' boards. A *directional tie* means that the linking director has a principal affiliation with another company, for example, as an owner or top manager. (Most directed ties involve officers of other corporations, often financial institutions such as banking, accountancy, and insurance companies; however, the 1914 Clayton Act prohibits interlocks between firms competing in the same markets.) A *nondirectional link* involves a common board member who has no affiliation to either firm, for example, the head of a civil rights organization or a former U.S. president. The finding that directional ties suppressed M-form adoption while nondirectional ties promoted it is consistent with network theory principles that weaker ties are more effective than strong, cohesive connections for bringing nonredundant information to the attention of corporate leaders. "Thus, nondirectional ties may be more likely than directional connections to provide firms with new and credible information about the MDF" (Palmer, Jennings and Zhou 1993:123). In contrast, top managers of publicly owned corporations may have rejected information favoring the M-form that originated through directional board interlocks, to avoid any appearance of conflict of interest.

An Emerging Multisubsidiary Form?

A few sociologists discerned a shift among large U.S. corporations away from the multidivisional structure toward a multisubsidiary form (MSF) during the late 1980s and early 1990s (see Zey and Camp 1996; Prechel

1997a, 1997b; Zey 1998; Zey and Swenson 1998). The distinguishing feature of the emerging MSF was the restructuring of corporate units as formal subsidiaries rather than as internal divisions. Although divisions are legally embedded inside a corporation, a wholly owned subsidiary is a separate legal entity that may issue its own stock. Hence, by purchasing just 50 percent plus one share to buy a subsidiary, an MSF company acquired complete control without having to own 100 percent of an internal division's assets (Zey 1998:275). The largest U.S. corporations seemed increasingly to adopt a multilayered MSF form, that is, with two or more layers of subsidiaries owning their own subsidiaries. For example, to gain a foothold in the telecommunications sector, General Motors bought 100 percent of Hughes Electronics, a publicly traded satellite and wireless communications firm. Hughes in turn controlled three subsidiaries, including 81 percent of PanAmSat, operator of the world's largest commercial satellite fleet. And PanAmSat itself had two wholly owned subsidiaries (PanAmSat Carrier Services and PanAmSat Communications Carrier Services), which provided international private-line and public-switched telecommunication services.

Between 1983 and 1993, the 100 largest U.S. industrial firms significantly reduced their mean number of divisions from nine to four, while their average number of subsidiaries doubled from 23 to 50 (Prechel 1997a:164). Among the important incentives for a MDF firm to move toward an MSF form were financial and legal protection of corporate assets from tort lawsuits for product defects by erecting a liability firewall (or "corporate veil") between the parent firm and its ventures into high-risk businesses; improved monitoring and managing capacity by embedding product groups in subsidiaries with separate market indicators of performance; reduced dependence on external capital markets and increased financial flexibility for the parent firm, which can sell subsidiaries' stock and use the capital in merger and acquisition strategies; and various corporate tax breaks.

Analyses of the subsidiarization process from 1983 to 1995 were consistent with both resource dependence and political power explanations. Fortune 100 industrial firms with greater long-term debt, more liability-prone product lines, declining shareholder dividends, and higher merger and acquisition involvement were more likely to adopt the MSF form (Prechel, Boies and Woods 1997; Zey 1998). Historic shifts in state and federal governments' business policies in the 1980s were especially important in speeding MSF diffusion. The federal Tax Reform Act of 1986 and Revenue Act of 1987 provided political-legal opportunities for tax-free restructuring of corporate acquisitions, spin-offs, and divisions into legal subsidiaries (Zey and Swenson 1999). Whether these structural changes ultimately translated into enhanced organizational performance, or even better odds of surviving as an independent firm, remained to be demonstrated.

Corporate Merger Waves

Corporate mergers are important demographic processes that change organizational populations by raising termination rates and shrinking total numbers, as well as by transforming an acquiring firm's workforces, financial resources, and internal structures. As the finance conception of corporation control took root in the 1950s, the quickest means for a large company to implement its preferred strategy of greater growth and higher profits through diversification was to acquire an existing business. Organizations could use one of five basic methods to take over a publicly traded company (Ernst & Young 1994:141–158):

- A merger agreement, following a shareholder vote, in which the acquirer buys most or all of the target firm's shares.
- A tender offer, made directly to the target firm's shareholders, that promises to pay a cash "premium" above the current share price in the stock market. If a majority of shareholders are willing to tender (sell) their shares to the bidder, a formal vote is not necessary to gain control. An exchange offer resembles a tender, except the bidder offers securities rather than cash to purchase shares.
- A tender offer for cash for at least a majority of the shares, followed by a merger through shareholder vote.
- Purchase of a controlling portion of a bankrupt or financially distressed company's debt, with the intention to convert that debt into equity as a condition for the debt restructuring.
- A proxy contest in which a noncontrolling group of shareholders backs a slate of directors not supported by the target's top management. The insurgent and management factions each try to solicit enough proxies (power of attorney to vote shares) from the other shareholders to elect their candidates.

The proxy method is implicitly hostile to the target's managers, who are likely to lose their jobs in a post-takeover restructuring, but the first four methods may involve either hostile or friendly takeovers. Although the overwhelming majority of U.S. mergers involved formally voluntary agreements, many allegedly friendly acquisitions might be disguised under implicit threats of "an offer you can't refuse."

Merger waves are recurrent phenomena in U.S. business history (Nelson 1959; Golbe and White 1988; Fligstein 1990; Stearns and Allan 1996). Five major waves spanned the twentieth century. The initial wave, from 1895 to 1905, saw massive horizontal mergers among local and regional competitors that gave birth to such giant national monopolies as General Electric, Du Pont, Standard Oil, American Can, Kodak, and Uniroyal. The second wave, which peaked in the 1920s, integrated vertical markets into manufacturing oligopolies that controlled product prices. Whatever its contribution to the speculative frenzy causing the stock market crash of 1929, this merger wave was effectively dampened by the ensuing Great Depression. The three post-World War II merger waves focused on product-related and product-unrelated diversification strategies. Figure 3.8 charts the rise and fall in annual numbers of announced merger-and-acquisition deals and in the number of divestitures (where a corporation sells one of its subunits to another firm).

The 1960s saw the heyday of the conglomerate kings, who cobbled together such multi-industry megaliths as ITT, Gulf and Western, Ling-Temco-Vought, and Textron (Sobel 1984). Conglomerate mergers flourished because their ambiguous status in both economics and law led to lax federal antitrust enforcement efforts (Aldrich 1979:314–16). The 1960s merger mania crested at more than 6,000 total acquisitions, followed by a fourth wave that peaked in 1986 at barely half that number. The monstrous fifth wave—centered in the information and banking industries—began to swell in 1992 and seemed likely to continue rolling into the next century (Lipin 1998). Annual divestiture trends exhibited similar, although less pronounced, ebbs and flows. However, when merger activity is measured as total financial volume (Figure 3.9, in billions of 1999 dollars), the 1960s and 1980s proved mere foothills to the 1990s Himalayas. The final three years of the twentieth century witnessed successive records for the largest announced corporate mergers in history, between Exxon and Mobil Oil ($77 billion in 1998), MCI WorldCom and Sprint ($108 billion in 1999), and America Online and Time Warner ($166 billion in 2000).

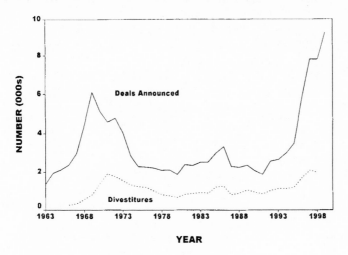

FIGURE 3.8   Mergers and Divestitures
SOURCE: Mergerstat (2000)

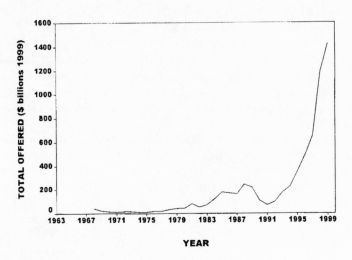

FIGURE 3.9   Total Value Offered for Mergers
SOURCE: Mergerstat (2000)

The 1980s were an especially turbulent period for the U.S. political economy. By the decade's end, 29 percent of the 1980 Fortune 500 companies had been subjected to takeover bids, and roughly one-third of the largest industrial corporations no longer survived as independent organizations (Davis and Stout 1992). Among the 20 largest firms that vanished were seven oil companies, including Gulf, Shell, Getty, and Standard Oil of Ohio (Fligstein and Markowitz 1993). Laissez-faire federal business policies coincided with readily available capital for takeover bids by fringe financiers (Stearns and Allan 1996). To implement its conservative ideological revolution, the Reagan Administration cut corporate taxes, which filled company coffers with quick cash for capital expansion. The Justice Department virtually suspended its antitrust enforcement efforts, and the Supreme Court overturned state laws limiting corporate takeovers. As one contemporary journalist observed, "We have entered the era of the two-tier, front-end loaded, bootstrap, bust-up, junk-bond takeover" (Lipton 1985:A16). The anything-goes follies—Ivan Boesky's illegal insider trades, KKR's leveraged buyouts, and Michael Milken's junk-bond manipulations[6]—were cleverly skewered in Oliver Stone's 1987 muckraking film *Wall Street* (Michael Douglas's infamous "Greed—for want of a better term—is good" speech won him the best-actor Oscar) and in the 1991 Danny DeVito comedy, *Other People's Money*. The number of mergers "sharply increased when the challengers' innovations were imitated by members and the general business community" (Stearns and Allan 1996:714). The wave came to a crashing halt after the October 1987 stock market crash dried up investment money, and federal and state governments finally began cracking down on predatory takeovers. Milken's conviction on racketeering and securities fraud charges sounded the junk bond's death knell (for journalistic and academic analyses of this fascinating era, see Bruck 1988; Lewis 1989; Zey 1993).

Alternative organizational theories sought to explain merger activities and their impacts on both individual firms and the larger political economy. The resource dependence approach asserted that interindustry mergers allow corporation managers to cope with organizational interdependencies by absorbing them into the firm (Pfeffer 1972). One analysis of 854 U.S. large-firm mergers between 1948 and 1969 found that the proportion of mergers across industry lines within the manufacturing sector correlated significantly with the extent of economic exchanges among industries at the start of the period. A replication and extension to 1992 found only small resource dependence effects, which waxed and waned "with periods of antitrust enforcement, the historical incidence within an industry of responding to transaction dependence with mergers, and the degree of concentration in bidder industries" (Finkelstein 1997:805). Some economists promoted a "managerial discipline" interpretation of mergers as rational efforts to improve market efficiencies and increase shareholders' wealth. Hostile takeovers were allegedly triggered when top management failed to sustain a profit-maximizing focus on behalf of the company's shareholders. A "market for corporate control" (Manne 1965) arose whenever outsiders saw a good chance to reap huge financial gains by ousting incompetent or opportunistic managers. For example, takeover artists targeted CEOs who preferred spending "slack" company earnings on fancy office furnishings and corporate jets rather than on expanding production or paying dividends to the stockholders. In transaction cost theory, the historical spread of the MDF drastically weakened top management's ability to resist merger proposals to remove firm-specific assets from their control:

> The diffusion of the M-form structure served to activate competition in the capital market by making takeover a more credible corporate-control technique. Control over corporate assets could thereby be transferred more easily from managements with a greater propensity for slack to those who would use these same assets to realize greater productive value. (Williamson 1987:162)

Economists assumed that stagnating profits and plummeting stock prices signaled an underperforming corporation ripe for the plucking. Raiders could realize windfall capital gains by wresting company control away from the current owners, installing their own management team, selling off profit-bleeding divisions, and pumping the stock price back up by running the restructured firm more efficiently. Even if a takeover bid failed, the very threat of being acquired might pressure a firm's directors to tighten its oversight and discipline poorly performing managers (Mikkelson and Partch 1997). Executives of targeted firms feverishly developed several defense mechanisms to protect their jobs during threatened takeovers, with such colorful labels as:

- Shark repellent: corporate charter amendments erecting higher barriers to takeover
- Anti-greenmail: refusing to pay above-market prices to repurchase shares in exchange for a speculator withdrawing his bid for control
- Poison pills: a dividend issued to current common stockholders entitling them to buy shares at prices more deeply discounted than available to nonowners whenever a takeover was attempted without the board's approval

For a detailed discussion of these and other contrivances, see Jarrell, Brickley and Netter (1988:58–65).

The vast literature in finance economics on mergers and acquisitions generally concluded that the shareholders of a targeted firm were the primary beneficiaries. They typically received stock premiums ranging between 30 and 50 percent above the share price prevailing before a publicly announced takeover attempt (Jensen 1988:22). In contrast, the acquiring firm's shareholders averaged only around 4 percent returns on their investments in hostile takeovers and no gain from friendly mergers. Frederic Scherer (1988) reached a more skeptical conclusion, finding no evidence of improved long-term company profitability following an acquisition. Although busting-up the most inefficient product divisions of overblown conglomerates undoubtedly trimmed some operating expenses, the heavy corporate debts underwriting those acquisitions possibly worsened the 1991 economic recession following the 1980s merger binge.

Institutional and network theorists viewed mergers and acquisitions primarily as the outcomes of socially constructed beliefs about legitimate strategic actions. Rather than purely economically rational cost-benefit calculations, takeover attempts were ultimately shaped by firms' locations within such contexts as organizational fields, power relationships, and interorganizational networks. Even corporate raiders' beliefs that a stock was undervalued and management's resistance to hostile takeovers were shaped by exchanges of persuasive information and imitation of others' actions. Several empirical investigations of the 1980s merger mania revealed how noneconomic factors shaped takeover activity. A longitudinal analysis of the 100 largest companies found no support for the finance economics hypothesis that a firm's higher financial balance (ratio of its net worth to assets) made it more susceptible to takeover (Fligstein and Markovitz 1993). However, consistent with the finance-control concept, the chances of a merger increased if (1) a firm was headed by a finance-oriented CEO, (2) it followed a product-related or product-unrelated strategy, and (3) its board of directors had a higher proportion of members from nonbank financial institutions (insurance companies, pension funds). In the latter case, these "institutional investors were able to convince managers to undertake financial reorganization," (p. 201), supporting the institutional perspective on economic actors embedded in social worlds that shape their perceptions and actions.

Two studies, spanning different portions of the postwar era, uncovered evidence that director networks shaped the merger process. Interlocking directorates are used by corporate elites to optimize their "business scan" of the political economy, to identify potential problems and solutions (Useem 1984). Interlocks allegedly promoted social class cohesion and the diffusion of shared corporate norms about legitimate business practices. They also facilitated corporate defenses against such deviant behaviors as predatory takeover. The first study, covering 1963–1968, found that 37 of the 478 largest industrial firms in 1962 were targets of predatory takeovers, which occurred either when the firm's stock was purchased on the open market or it received a tender offer that it actively opposed (Palmer et al. 1995). Managerial discipline provided the strongest explanation: Companies with undervalued assets attracted predators seeking financial windfalls by eliminating managerial inefficiencies. However, three other socially embedded factors also operated. First, corporations on which other sectors heavily depended for resources were more likely to become the targets of predators seeking to diversify their acquisitions. Second, predators avoided management-controlled corporations and those dominated by inside directors on the firm's board. And third, corporations with many board interlocks to commercial banks avoided being taken over, presumably because outside directors provided information and expertise about mounting an effective defense.

An additional 34 corporations sought friendly combinations with other firms. Although the economic undervaluation of firm assets had no impact on friendly acquisitions, once again network relations proved very important. A target company was more likely to agree to a friendly merger if it had fewer stock-owning inside directors and more board interlocks to industrial firms, commercial banks, and investment banks. "Firms overseen by central directors in the 1960s, especially finance capitalist directors, should have been more successful in the contest to attract the attention of desirable suitors because they were plugged into social networks through which information coursed about attractive and willing partners and desirable suitors" (Palmer et al. 1995:474).

The second study of interlocking directorates also revealed robust network effects on the acquisitions completed by 327 medium and large "focal" firms during the 1980s merger wave (Haunschild 1993). The most important predictor of how many acquisitions a focal firm made during a randomly selected year was its directed board interlocks with other, "tied-to" firms. If a focal firm's top managers sat on the boards of tied-to firms that had completed mergers during the prior three years, they were directly exposed to valuable information about those firms' acquisitive activities. Several such interlocks could provide focal firm managers with reliable data and good examples of merger strategies to be imitated, which were unavailable to companies having few or no network connections to experienced acquirers. The more mergers that the tied-to companies had completed, the greater the number of mergers a focal firm subsequently completed. But this contagion or imitation effect was not linear, peaking instead at around 22 acquisitions during the prior three years. Disaggregation into specific types of merger revealed that the more prior horizontal (competitor), vertical (supplier), or conglomerate (unrelated) acquisitions a tied-to firm made, the more likely it was that the focal firm's acquisitions would involve the same type. Although she uncovered evidence consistent with a social embeddedness perspective on mergers, Haunschild urged more research into how other kinds of network connections are used to transmit information and foster imitation, including links to the business press, professional firms, investment banks, consultants, accounting firms, and professional employees. "We still know little about what dimensions of activities will be imitated under what conditions" (Haunschild 1993:588).

In contrast to the preceding results, Gerald Davis and Suzanne Stout (1992) found no significant network effects (measured by number of director interlocks or board ties to commercial banks) on either merger offers or successful bids received by Fortune 500 firms in the 1980s. Although their findings fully supported no single theoretical approach, financial performance factors produced the strongest impacts: Both greater corporate debt and higher stock values discouraged hostile and other takeover attempts, because lucrative financial gains would not result. However, additional analyses disclosed that network structures influenced the diffusion of corporate resistance to the 1980s takeover wave within the Fortune 500 organizational field (Davis and Greve 1997). The authors compared the adoptions of the poison pill and "golden parachute" defense mechanisms (formal obligations to pay cash to the corporation's top executives in the event of a change in corporate control). They measured a firm's integration into the national corporate elite network by the number of directors it shared with other industrial firms and financial organizations (a median of seven board members, with only 7 percent of firms unconnected). Geographic proximity indicated local network structure, specifically whether a focal firm had the same telephone area code as a prior-adopting firm's headquarters. Although about half the Fortune 500 firms eventually adopted each anti-takeover device, the two network structures differentially affected their diffusion rates:

> Pills spread through shared directors, who acted like Johnny Appleseeds to spread practices from board to board, because they could be readily rationalized by outside directors. The national reach of this network facilitated the rapid spread of this practice. Parachutes spread through regional elite networks, perhaps an informal social comparison process among CEOs. In some cities diffusion was swift, whereas in others the process never took off. Because diffusion was based on local networks rather than national ones, the aggregate effect was a much slower rate of diffusion. (Davis and Greve 1997:32)

These divergent transmission processes implied that differing social forces underlay the acceptance of each innovation. Boards of directors widely regarded poison pills as legitimate defenses to protect the corporation from takeover. Thus, these devices spread contagiously via interorganizational director contacts, especially among directors representing corporations operating in similar industries. But golden parachutes were initially seen as naked self-interest, cynically promoted by top managers to protect their jobs at the expense of their firm's welfare. The absence of strong normative support for parachutes apparently retarded their acceptance among the national corporate elite and thus produced a slower rate of diffusion via regional networks. The results underscored how embedded network relations within an organizational fields could fruitfully combine with the normative perspective of institutional theory to produce a more comprehensive and nuanced explanation of changing organizational practices.

Refocused Organizations

The economic turbulence of the 1980s brought a sea change in the dominant strategy-and-structure model deployed by large corporations. The firm-as-portfolio of diverse business lines gave way to a "back-to-basics" or "lean-and-mean" movement. Giant firms restructured and refocused their activities around a smaller set of "core competencies" by divesting their product-unrelated business lines and acquiring related ones (Bhagat, Shleifer and Vishy 1990; Hoskisson and Hitt 1994). From 1981 to 1987, nearly two-thirds of the acquisitions by the hundred largest U.S. firms and almost three-fifths of their divestitures were related to core businesses (Markides 1995:62). Retrenching firms were more diversified and less profitable than their competitors. Corporations whose managers felt threatened by hostile takeovers also were more likely to refocus. In this trend toward less diversity, large firms shifted from less-centralized toward more-centralized MDFs, in which a company's head office took greater control over divisional operating decisions (Markides 1995:141).

The conglomerate form, so popular in the 1960s, experienced a sharp decline from a 1979 peak in the average number of business groups (Williams, Paez and Sanders 1988). Gulf and Western, known on Wall Street as "Engulf and Devour," sold off its holdings in textiles, glass, paper, tires, and video games, and renamed itself Paramount Communications. Conglomerates with weak financial performance faced significantly higher takeover risks during the 1980s than did the more focused companies in their industries. Davis, Diekmann and Tinsley (1994) investigated the deinstitutionalization of the conglomerate form. They defined a *conglomerate merger* as any purchase where both the acquiring and target firms operated in unrelated industries (using two-digit or four-digit SIC codes). Between 1986 and 1990, fewer than 15 percent of publicly traded Fortune 500 corporations made any conglomerate acquisitions. Just four gigantic corporations (GE, GM, Ford, and International Paper) made more than two such purchases, mainly by expanding into the financial and business service sectors. Thus, most large firms shunned a rapid-growth strategy of taking over unrelated businesses, and almost all also avoided vertical integration by buying their supplier or customer companies. In the 1980s, the Fortune 500 companies increasingly refocused on core competencies: Diversification levels declined by 33 percent at the four-digit and by 44 percent at the two-digit SIC levels.

Why did the firm-as-portfolio model, and the conglomerate form in particular, suffer such swift eclipse? Davis and his colleagues argued that the main driving forces were changing institutional beliefs about most legitimate ways of structuring the largest corporations. The business press and corporate leaders' rhetoric universally condemned the conglomerate form as "the biggest collective error ever made by American business" (Davis, Diekmann and Tinsley 1994:563). Business leaders reassessed what kinds of activities could most effectively be brought inside an organization's boundaries. Specialization, rather than diversity, became the watchword of the day:

> In contrast to the firm-as-portfolio model, which supported bringing virtually any type of business within the organization's boundary, rhetoric around appropriate business practices during the late 1980s and early 1990s has suggested extreme specialization and contracting for any aspects of production outside the firm's "core competence." (Davis, Diekmann and Tinsley 1994:563)

Indeed, the conventional notion of the corporation as a sharply bounded organization appeared to undergo drastic alteration. Extreme specialization and short-term alliances among competing companies, coupled with sub-contracting of many activities to outside firms, gave birth to networked concepts of organizational strategy and structure. An emergent firm-as-network model became a hot topic of speculation in the 1990s by both academic circles and the popular business press.

Conclusions

Throughout the twentieth century, U.S. organizations experienced continual changes of size, shape, and function, resulting in diverse assortments of for-profit companies, nonprofit associations, and governmental agencies. The population of business firms and establishments grew steadily over the final decades of the twentieth century, eventually approaching 7 million. However, these net totals concealed numerous foundings and disbandings as ambitious entrepreneurs launched new businesses and many prior startups failed, either ceasing operations or filing for bankruptcy. Organizational size distributions, whether measured by employees or revenues, revealed that, although the vast majority of organizations were small, financial and human resources were heavily concentrated among proportionally few large corporations. A heated and unresolved debate, with important public policy implications, centered around the question of whether small companies or large firms generated the most new jobs. Although organization studies began deciphering the intricacies of organizational demography, researchers disagreed about suitable criteria for classifying different organizational forms. A new governmental industrial taxonomy rendered comparisons with earlier patterns increasingly problematic. Alternative theoretical explanations abounded about the twentieth-century diffusion of the multidivisional form of governance among large corporations. Some researchers discerned a growing reliance on multisubsidiary forms to maintain flexible corporate control over subordinate business units. The last of five major merger and acquisition waves rolling across the U.S. political economy seemed certain to continue well into the twenty-first century. Business ideology shifted against the conglomerate form and firm-as-portfolio models, as institutional opinion encouraged companies to concentrate on strengthening their core competencies. The next three chapters explore the emergence and consequences of several new networked forms of organizational and workplace structures and practices.

4

Making Connections

I wonder men dare trust themselves with men.
—William Shakespeare Coriolanus (1607)

Marriage between incompatible partners sometimes leads to separation, true for organizations as for couples. As one example, Northwest Airlines and KLM Royal Dutch Airlines tied the knot in 1989, with KLM investing $400 million in the Minneapolis company. The U.S. Justice Department blessed the nuptials with a unique "open skies" antitrust exemption that allowed both airlines to share costs—ground services, sales and marketing, inventory management, computer reservation, and frequent-flyer databases—and profits from routes in the United States and Europe. Over the next decade, the joint venture expanded to serve 400 destinations in 80 countries with more than 60,000 jointly listed monthly flights. When a steep fall-off in air travel during the 1991 Persian Gulf War threatened to bankrupt Northwest, KLM threw in another $50 million and helped the U.S. company to obtain a crucial $250 million loan. By 1994 the U.S. airline's income had returned to the black and the partners had almost doubled their share of the trans-Atlantic market. But the price for rescue was high: In addition to owning more than 20 percent of Northwest stock and controlling three seats on Northwest's board of directors, KLM forced a bylaws change requiring that all major transactions such as mergers, acquisitions, and asset sales obtain a 60 percent "super majority" vote from the board.

When the Dutch company declined a merger offer by three other European airlines and tried to increase its Northwest stockholdings, the Americans suspected that KLM was poised for a stealthy takeover. Northwest proposed an aggressive poison pill plan (see Chapter 3), reducing the super majority to a simple majority vote and limiting any shareholder's stake to 19 percent. KLM counterattacked in the press, publicly threatening a lawsuit to block the governance change. Northwest executives went "'absolutely nuclear,' said one person familiar with the airline. 'In the past, these disagreements have been one person calling to another. But this time it was like having a spat on the front lawn'" (Quintanilla and Carey 1995). By an 11 to 3 vote in late 1995, the board approved the poison pill offering deeply discounted shares to current stockholders, and KLM's three members resigned in protest. The Dutch airline sought to overturn the pill in court. In September 1997, the feuding partners agreed to dissolve their equity ties while strengthening their joint commercial operations. The 10-year deal called for dropping the lawsuits, Northwest spending more than $1 billion buying back all its shares held by KLM, each CEO sitting on the other airline's board, and both companies seeking new ventures with additional partners to penetrate markets in Asia and the Americas. Northwest CEO John Dasburg hailed the divorce settlement: "This alliance has set and will continue to set the industry standard for global alliances."

The stormy Northwest-KLM marriage exemplified unstable partnerships in many industries, from transportation and manufacturing to services and public administration. Strategic alliances and joint ventures among firms emerged and spread widely by the end of the twentieth century as companies sought competitive advantages through interorganizational cooperation and collaboration. Interorganizational relations lie intermediate to two alternative forms of action in a political economy: strictly arm's-length market transactions and bureaucratic hierarchies that tightly internalize all important functions within a single enterprise. This chapter examines the formation, governance, operation, and consequences of interorganizational networks, ranging across levels of analysis from dyads to large- and small-firm networks, from industrial districts to organizational fields. Understanding these diverse phenomena requires applications of network, institutional, transaction cost, and resource dependence theories to explain how these new forms of organizational action fuse economic and political principles of organizational behavior.

Varieties of
Interorganizational Relations

By the 1980s, the cumulating environmental changes described in Chapter 1 began to alter how organizations related to their competitors and customers. Exposed to intensified international competition, companies increasingly tried to survive and thrive by slashing costs and prices, improving production performance, and responding rapidly to technological innovations and fickle consumer preferences. Survival required firms to skip quickly across treacherous and shifting shoals or risk sinking into the economic quagmire. As consumer markets progressively globalized and fragmented, niche opportunities bloomed for specialty products and services. Business-to-business marketing and sales grew increasingly fragmented as industries split into finer-grained segments. Top corporate managers came to believe that huge gains in productivity and profitability could be achieved by destructuring their internal hierarchies. The cumbersome mass production systems run along "Fordist" principles yielded to radically decentralized design, assembly, and distribution systems capable of reconfiguring themselves almost overnight. Entrepreneurs cobbled together the expertise and assets of numerous small enterprises occupying strategic locations within regional economies. Their endeavors spawned supple networks of interdependent companies able to adjust rapidly to shifting environmental conditions.

Incessant pressures to achieve organizational flexibility and specialization drove companies to forge enduring collaborative connections that would allow them to thrive amid quickening creative destruction in the global marketplace. Similar social, economic, and especially political forces incessantly drove state and municipal governments and nonprofit organizations toward legislatively or judicially mandated interagency cooperation and collaboration in community development, social welfare, health and mental health care, even street sweeping and garbage pickup services (Warren 1967; Rogers and Whetten 1982; Milward 1996; Milward and Provan 1998; Galaskiewicz and Bielefeld 1998). Judicial and regulatory barriers, especially enforcement of state and federal antitrust laws, exert substantial constraints on legal forms of inter-firm collaboration. Statutes and court rulings forbid alliances and mergers leading to market power that would allow a firm to charge profitable prices above those prevailing under competition. However, as the U.S. political economy continually changes, so interpretations vary about which kinds of cooperative agreements among rival firms are permissible. Organizations constantly probe the legal boundaries in striking creative interorganizational deals.

Several new interorganizational formations proliferated as organizations searched for new efficiencies and competitive advantages while avoiding both market uncertainties and hierarchical rigidities. Todeva and Knoke (Forthcoming) developed the scheme in Table 4.1 for classifying basic forms of strategic alliances and cooperative agreements appearing in the theoretical and research literatures. (For other recent typologies, see Borys and Jemison 1989; Freeman 1991; Yoshino and Rangan 1995:8; Grandori and Soda 1995; Child and Faulkner 1998:99–108.) The principal theme structuring this classification is that, from bottom to top, collaborating firms experience roughly increasing integration and formalization in the governance of their interorganizational relationships (in contrast to the governance of firms, the theme of Chapter 7). Governance in this context refers to combinations of legal and social control mechanisms for coordinating and safeguarding the alliance partners' resource contributions, administrative responsibilities, and division of rewards from their collaboration. At the bottom of the table are pure market transactions requiring no obligation for recurrent cooperation, coordination, or collaboration among the anonymous exchanging parties. Arm's-length contracts may encourage the participants' expectations about repeated future business transactions, but their exchanges are coordinated primarily through the price mechanism. At the top of Table 4.1 appear hierarchical authority relations in which one firm takes full control, absorbing another's assets and personnel into a unitary enterprise. Coordinated actions among organizational units are legally governed by the ownership rights mechanism. Neither the multidivisional and multisubsidiary corporate forms, nor the acquisition and merger processes examined in Chapter 3, should be considered genuine strategic alliances because the subunits preserve no ultimate independence of action. In between these extremes of market and hierarchy are 11 general alliance forms, or "hybrids," that combine varying degrees of market interaction and bureaucratic integration (Williamson 1975; Powell 1987; Heydebrand 1989). Elaborating and exemplifying these interorganizational forms is the crux of this section.

TABLE 4.1   Varieties of Interorganizational Relations

Hierarchical relations
        Subsidiaries
        Acquisitions
        Mergers

Joint Ventures
Cooperatives
Equity Investments
R&D Consortia
Strategic Cooperative Agreements
Cartels
Franchising
Licensing
Subcontractor Networks
Industry Standards Groups
Action Sets

Market Relations
        Arm's-Length Buy-Sell Contracts

SOURCE: Todeva and Knoke (Forthcoming)

A *strategic alliance* involves at least two partner firms that (1) remain legally independent after the alliance is formed; (2) share benefits and managerial control over the performance of assigned tasks; and (3) make continuing contributions in one or more strategic areas, such as technology or products (Yoshino and Rangan 1995:5). Child and Faulkner (1998:5) clarified the adjective: "They are often 'strategic' in the sense that they have been formed as a direct response to major strategic challenges or opportunities which the partner firms face." Brief definitions and examples of the basic strategic alliance forms in Table 4.1 may be helpful:

- An *action set* is a short-lived organizational coalition whose members coordinate their efforts to influence public policymaking, for example, the passage of legislative acts affecting the coalition members' collective interests (Knoke et al. 1996:21). An action set's cohesion is vulnerable to disintegration by the greater willingness of some participants to strike compromises with opponents. Passage or defeat of a policy decision often rings the death knell of the action set, whose members then join with new partners to fight for their parochial interests on other issues. Chapter 9 examines these political alliances in great depth.
- *Industry standards groups* seek to thwart potentially ruinous competition arising through the introduction of competing technical criteria for consumer and business products. Standards groups range organizationally from ad hoc committees to formal business associations that manage the collective affairs of their member firms. By providing opportunities for technical experts to meet, debate, and choose among alternative proposals, an industry standards group can avoid incompatible solutions such as the 1980s Betamax versus VHS home video cassette recorders (VCR). Having learned a hard economic lesson from that fiasco, in the 1990s the major home entertainment electronics companies negotiated a political solution among proponents of two rival technical standards for digital video disc (DVD) players (De Laat 1999).
- *Subcontractor networks* go beyond simple exchanges set by competitive market prices. A purchaser negotiates long-term prices, production runs, and delivery schedules, thus guaranteeing the supplier a dependable profit margin. The purchaser can demand the right to inspect the suppliers' operations to certify product quality. Well-known examples of such arrangements include the Japanese *keiretsu*, Korean *chaebol*, and the large firm-small supplier networks examined in the next section.
- *Licensing agreements* are sometimes considered market exchanges, but they increasingly stipulate extra-contractual clauses (Grandori

and Soda 1995:202). Under a license, one company typically grants a second firm the right to use the former's patented technologies or production processes for a specified time in return for royalty payments. Both licenser and licensee retain their separate organizational identities and formal autonomy.

- *Franchising* is a tighter form of licensing in which the franchisee takes on the franchiser's brand name identity in a particular geographic market. The popular attraction for the prospective small business owner is the lower failure rate enjoyed by many nationally branded products. Because the corporate home office bears the costs of product development, distribution, marketing, and advertising, the franchisee benefits from a ready-built consumer market. A franchise operator surrenders much freedom of action in the requirement to adhere closely to the parent firm's pricing and standardized service norms. The franchiser preserves centralized management controls to safeguard its interests from abuse by the franchisees, in particular, the corporate image, branded products, and quality reputation. The home office typically leaves routine daily operational decisions to the discretion of its local franchise holders (Reve 1990:148; also Osborn and Baughn 1990), but will discipline a faltering operator for failing to live up to the company's performance standards. We've been overexposed to these organizational forms through advertising bombardments for fast-food restaurants (Wendy's, Dairy Queen), gas stations (Texaco), auto repair shops (Midas, Jiffy Lube), and even plumbing services (Roto-Rooter). The humiliating flop of McDonald's 55-cent Big Mac campaign, where the parent firm forced its franchisees to drop prices in an unsuccessful bid to lure new customers, underscores just how vulnerable a junior partner can be to an 800-pound gorilla's missteps (Gibson 1997).
- *Cartels*, or pools, are unstable alliances formed to constrain competition by cooperatively controlling production and/or prices in specific industries (Fligstein 1990:39). The "trusts" flourishing in late nineteenth-century America—in railways, heating oil, steel, aluminum, sugar, salt—were outlawed by the Sherman Antitrust Act, but cartels periodically arise elsewhere, for example, the oil-producing nations of the Organization for Petroleum Exporting Countries (OPEC). The recurring habit of OPEC members eagerly cheating by unilaterally exceeding their voluntary pumping quotas, which results in ruinously low prices and profits for all members, underscores the flimsy political foundations on which many cartels are erected.
- *Strategic cooperative agreements* encompass contractual networks among buyers and sellers or co-producers that necessitate closer

interorganizational coordination than is possible through the price mechanism (Todeva 1998). These agreements include turnkey, government procurement, and management contracts, as well as international industrial cooperation agreements (Young 1989). A common feature of such arrangements is joint strategic control, with partners collaborating over key decisions and sharing responsibility for performance outcomes. For example, under a management contract, one firm operates a facility on behalf of its owners, a common practice in the commercial real estate industry. Similarly, a turnkey contract specifies that one party construct production equipment or an entire factory according to another's specifications, which may extend to training employees before turning full control of that property over to its owner. Under government procurement contracts (e.g., providing tanks and planes to the U.S. Department of Defense) and international industrial cooperation agreements (e.g., the European Airbus), multinational corporations and governments jointly plan and supervise implementation of production processes.

- *Research and development consortia* are typically created in fast-changing technological fields, such as biomedical and computer industries, where the risks of failed investments are prohibitively expensive for individual firms to bear. By pooling their resources in exchange for claims on any resulting patents, consortium members hope to achieve the benefits of large-scale investment activity (Evan and Olk 1990). Consortia vary in their degree of formalization, with some coordinated through informal social controls and others involving elaborate bureaucratic staffs and contractual incentives. In the late 1980s, 14 firms created SEMATECH to conduct the research, development, and testing that successfully revived the deteriorating U.S. semiconductor industry and recovered market share from its Japanese competitors (Browning, Beyer and Shetler 1995).

- In an *equity investment*, one firm buys a direct financial interest in another through a direct stock purchase, either a majority stake (more than 50 percent of shares) or a minority stake (perhaps as small as 3- to 5-percent). Several firms may jointly purchase the majority of shares in a target firm. An *equity swap* involves mutual stock investments among partners (Yoshino and Rangan 1995). Equity investment alliances do not create new organizational entities but rather provide a partner some financial stake in another company's affairs. Importantly, "the active involvement of the management of the partner-company is retained and the assessment of expertise of the company can be made without complete integration" (Hagedoorn 1993a:132). Equity partnerships abound in science-based industries, such as computer equipment and biotechnology, where large corporations often use minority shareholding to gain access to a startup firm's proprietary technologies. The Northwest-KLM partnership, described at the beginning of this chapter, was a minority equity investment that eventually dissolved because of persistent policy disagreements and mistrust between the partners. In a very complex equity deal, Sony Pictures Entertainment, Bertelsmann, EMI, and Warner Music Group—multinational corporations based respectively in Japan, Germany, England, and the United States—in 1995 bought a combined 50 percent stake in Hong Kong-based Star TV, Asia's most prominent satellite music channel. However, the arrangement kept daily and long-range programming decisions in the hands of Star executives, who were controlled by the venture's primary owner, Australia's Rupert Murdoch (Levin 1995).

- *Cooperatives* are coalitions of small enterprises that independently lack adequate resources to enter a market or to bargain effectively with large suppliers and customers. A cooperative purchasing or marketing program, by combining and coordinating the small producers' resources, enables the collectivity to obtain better market shares and prices for inputs and outputs. Agricultural industries are frequent sites of cooperative movements by farmers and ranchers to regulate supply and demand for food and fiber. The dairy industry's celebrated "Got Milk?" advertising campaign was a highly visible manifestation.

- A *joint venture* occurs when "two or more legally distinct firms (the parents) pool a portion of their resources within a jointly owned legal organization" that serves a limited purpose for its parents (Inkpen 1995:1). Joint ventures may involve 50:50 ownership between two parents or unequal shareholding among multiple partners (Lewis 1990:173–192). Legal ownership and control over the strategic decisions of an equity-based joint venture ultimately resides with the majority investment partners. Nonequity joint ventures are based on shared products or services and control over business operations such as access to new markets. Venture partners may set up a subsidiary legal entity or may take joint control of an existing enterprise. For example, in the early 1990s, IBM, Apple Computer, and Motorola formed Taligent, a jointly managed company to develop and market an integrated PC operating system that would compete against Microsoft Windows. In contrast, in 1994 General Motors and Toyota converted a faltering GM auto assembly plant in Fremont, California, into the New United Motor Manufacturing Inc. (NUMMI), enabling GM to learn about Japanese management techniques while Toyota gained a stronger foothold in the U.S. auto market (Adler 1993).

The analytic typology in Table 4.1 displays fundamental types of interorganizational relations, often involving bilateral agreements between pairs of organizations. However, alliances rarely occur in isolation, and their development is influenced by the larger social contexts in which they arise. One important macro level context is the alliance network, examined in the next section.

Varieties of Alliance Networks

An accelerating rate of strategic alliance formation toward the end of the twentieth century was evident from the explosion of journalistic reports and academic analyses. Dyadic, or pair-wise, collaborations probably make up the large majority of such arrangements. However, a more complex interorganizational configuration is the *alliance network*, consisting of the set of organizations connected through their overlapping partnerships in different strategic alliances. Alliance networks are large-scale, constantly changing social forms that spread across time and space, constituting opportunity structures that simultaneously facilitate and constrain the development of successive collaborative combinations. These loosely coupled concatenations can trigger problems of trust, opportunism, and social control far more complicated than those encountered in simple dyadic affairs. This section examines the empirical evidence about several varieties of strategic alliance networks that formed at the industrial, regional, and organizational field levels of analysis.

Industry Alliance Networks

Industry alliance networks connect organizations whose successive economic inputs and outputs are vital to the production and delivery of specific types of goods or services. These linked chains of activities forge a "web of relatively interdependent activities performed on the basis of the use of a certain constellation of resources" (Hakansson and Johanson 1993:36). Two prominent varieties of industry alliance network are (1) the *large firm-small supplier network*, a form dominant in manufacturing industries during the middle of the twentieth century; and (2) the *small-firm network*, which is both a survival from an early industrial era and a newly re-emergent form in particular political economies of the late twentieth century.

Large Firm-Small Supplier Networks.   The automobile industry was undoubtedly an ideal site to track the oscillating evolution of large industrial firms surrounded by constellations of small suppliers. Susan Helper's detailed reconstruction of the rise of Ford, Chrysler, and General Motors in southern Michigan revealed how a "network of small, innovative auto supplier firms in the Midwest first nurtured, and was nurtured by, the auto assemblers in the period 1890–1925, then was gradually destroyed as the Big Three adopted exit-based supplier relations, and is now (possibly) enjoying a resurgence" (1991:823). Before 1909, numerous small auto assemblers relied on close ties with many financially independent suppliers to create technological innovations that they could install in their machines. These inter-firm relations were often grounded in personal ties among the founding generation of automotive entrepreneurs. However, as rapid market growth consolidated the industry into a few giant corporations controlling their final consumer markets, those unstable outsourcing arrangements gave way to in-house technical functions such as marketing, engineering, and research and development.

These near-monopsonist automakers (sole buyers of other firms' products) instigated fierce competition among their plentiful small components suppliers, playing off against each other dozens of specialists producing a general class of components. As many as six to eight suppliers might bid for an annual single-part contract (e.g., door handles, headlights). Others might be required to license the automaker's key patents rather than manufacture according to their own designs. "[The automakers] also divided up parts into small, easy-to-produce pieces, and hired managers to coordinate the assembly of these parts centrally" (Helper 1993:144). This highly constrained yet uncertain environment, where small suppliers could be ruined if their bids were not accepted, discouraged supplier investments in modern production equipment and just-in-time delivery facilities dedicated to their buyers' needs. A transaction cost explanation of economic efficiency (see Chapter 2) is consistent with both the automakers' internalization of problematic activities and their dispersion of costs among multiple suppliers to improve profit margins (Helper 1993:152). However, that theory fails to anticipate that mutual distrust and suspicion between buyers and sellers led to stagnating technological change, petrified production performance, and the Big Three's increasing nonresponsiveness to customer demands. These outcomes ultimately undermined the very economic gains that buyer-supplier networks were intended to produce.

The adversarial low-bid system, requiring little communication and coordination beyond exchanging basic price and design specifications, prevailed in the U.S. auto industry past mid-century. The small supplier dilemma was that the large automakers tried to reduce their resource dependencies by three strategies, each of which threatened supplier autonomy and survival. First, using a "simple exit" threat, a dominant firm might leave a relationship if a supplier didn't cave in to the buyer's demands. An automaker could choose to award next year's parts contracts to another bidder who offered lower prices and more reliable delivery schedules. Second, using a "voice with cheating" option, a supplier's efforts to build longer-term commitments

based on tradition or personal trust might be thwarted if the automaker reneged by taking the outsourced work back inside the firm, as Ford did when
it bought the Philco radio company in the 1960s (Helper 1991:802). Finally,
by using a "financial integration" strategy, automakers could simply buy a
controlling equity stake in their most technically demanding suppliers. The
large buyer-small supplier practices prevailing from 1910 to 1970 hardly de-
serve the label alliance network, because these lopsided power arrangements
meant that genuine collaborative partnerships among equal contributors
could not develop.

A system of numerous weak suppliers dominated by a handful of corporate giants can remain viable only as long as new competitor firms face prohibitive barriers to entering the industry. Unfortunately, a major consequence of deteriorated communication between buyers and sellers is an
absence of strong incentives for technical innovations and poor control over
the quality inputs and outputs. A captive final-product market meant that
dissatisfied American auto customers had nowhere else to turn. However,
when Japanese auto imports flooded into the U.S. market starting in the
1970s, the Big Three were caught with their parts down. Deserted by droves
of consumers who discovered that Toyota, Honda, and Nissan offered an
unbeatable combination of higher-quality cars at lower prices, Detroit eventually fought back with drastically restructured design and production
strategies, including supplier relations (see Chapter 5). The Big Three
adopted Japanese-style factory management practices and gave their outside
suppliers longer contracts and a greater voice in mutual problem solving.
Ford slashed its suppliers from 5,000 to 2,300 between 1982 and 1987
(Helper 1993:150), while Chrysler pruned its supplier base from 2,500 to
1,140 in the 1990s (Dyer 1996:42). The U.S. automakers reduced protection of their internal component divisions and began routinely offering outsiders three- to five-year contracts. Imitating the famous Japanese *keiretsu*
model of tightly connected producer networks (Gerlach 1992; Lincoln, Gerlach and Takahashi 1992), Chrysler implemented structural reforms that
gave its outside suppliers a greater economic stake in Chrysler's performance (Dyer 1996). According to executives, these changes enhanced interorganizational cooperation and generated "greater trust and more reliable and timely communication of important information" (p. 55). By 1992
Chrysler's profit margin had passed GM and Ford, a remarkable comeback
for a firm on governmental life support during the previous decade.

A genuine large firm-small supplier alliance network is clearly more
costly to administer than an exploitative price coordination system. It requires a collaborative flow of ideas to replace the take-it-or-leave-it dicta-
tion of contract terms. Encouraging vertical disintegration decreases the
dominant firm's bargaining power while risking opportunism by its more
empowered suppliers. However, by offering incentives to participate in in-

novative design and quality-control activities, a giant firm at the heart of an exchange network can benefit from the stronger commitment and creative energies unleashed when junior partners enjoy a more secure voice in their mutually beneficial relationships. The century-long journey by the U.S. auto industry back toward its original pattern resembles the adoption of large-firm, small supplier networks in other contemporary industries exposed to intense technology-based competition, including computer equipment, software, banking, motion pictures (Christopherson and Storper 1986, 1989), and biomedical services (Powell 1996; Powell, Koput and Smith-Doerr 1996).

Small-Firm Networks. In contrast to the alliance networks revolving around a few dominant large manufacturing or service corporations, the small-firm network (SFN) flourished in industries and markets with low economic concentrations. Charles Perrow succinctly described the SFN profile:

> The firms are usually very small—say 10 people. They interact with one another, sharing information, equipment, personnel, and orders even as they compete with one another. They are supplied by a smaller number of business service firms (business surveys, technical training, personnel administration, transport, research and development, etc.) and financial service firms. There are, of course, suppliers of equipment, energy, consumables, and so on, as well as raw material suppliers. Finally, while producers may do their own marketing and distribution, it is more common for there to be a fair number of quite small distributors, which is especially striking because SFNs typically export most of their output. (1992:455)

SFNs arise primarily in highly competitive consumer goods industries such as clothing, toys, food, construction, metalworking, shoemaking, leather goods, ceramics, carpentry, furniture, light machinery, and small electronic goods. Many settings are flighty hothouses of worker-, family- and self-exploitation, featuring low wages, long hours, poor working conditions, and lousy fringe benefits. The next subsection investigates a special SFN case, the industrial district, whose members were embedded in historically unique regions. Here I explore aspects of the SFN situation that transcend geographic particularities.

A critical feature of a SFN is the craft, or flexible-specialization, form of production. Singular or small batches of goods and services are tailor-made to the requirements of particular clients and customers. Further, resource dependence among the network's numerous suppliers, producers, distributors, and customers assures that no single firm can gain an upper hand for very long, because alternative arrangements can be readily found. Given the long-standing and frequently recurring interactions among the participants, deceptions in pricing, quality and delivery are difficult to conceal and dangerous to attempt. Information about bad-faith dealing quickly circulates through the gossip network, and ruined reputations are impossible to recover. Thus, companies seldom succumb to the opportunistic temptations about which transaction cost theorists obsess. Instead, SFN exchanges nurture cooperation and trust relations among the field's embedded firms, building a community of shared fate.

An excellent illustration of how small-firm networks operate was Brian Uzzi's (1996, 1997) ethnographic study of 23 women's better dress apparel firms in New York City. Better dresswear was a midscale market for off-the-rack dresses, skirts, and jackets sewn to orders from department stores and chains. A manufacturer typically designed and marketed its garments to retailers but contracted out their actual production by coordinating the work of textile mills, grading, cutting, and sewing firms. This industry, consisting of thousands of local shops competing in an intense international market, experienced low startup costs and few barriers to new entrants. For his New York study, Uzzi sampled firms headed by chief executive officers with diverse ethnic characteristics: Jewish, Chinese, Anglo, Hispanic, Italian, and Arab. Their companies employed between 2 and 182 workers and had annual sales from $.5 million to $1 billion.

Figure 4.1 depicts a typical ego-centric SFN in this industry. A manufacturer ("jobber") only designs and markets the apparel. Actual production involves coordinating other firms' activities to fabricate the garments. The jobber first creates a "collection" of sample designs using its in-house or freelance designers, then markets the collection to retail stores that place orders for the items. The jobber next fills these orders by managing the sequential movement of semifinished dress goods through a network of grading, cutting, and sewing contractors who produce batches of items in their own shops. The manufacturer also connects with the converter firms that process textile mills' unfinished "griege goods" (cloth without texture, color, or pattern) into the fabric required by the production contractors for the various clothing designs.

In highly competitive small-scale market settings, neoclassical economic theory predicts that social ties have little or no impact on economic behavior. Rather, self-interest restricts efficient transactions solely to the impersonal, arm's-length exchange of price information. Firms are strongly motivated to search continually for lower prices and to switch their orders among new buyers and contractors in an effort to maximize profits and avoid dependence. An alternative *structural embeddedness* perspective argues that "the structure and quality of ties among firms shape economic action by creating unique opportunities and access to those opportunities" (Uzzi 1996:675). A firm located within a network of close ties to other firms will shift from the pursuit of maximum economic gain toward "en-

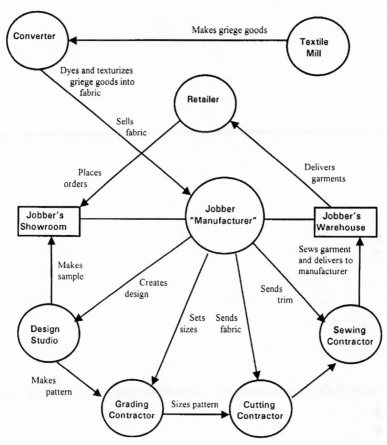

FIGURE 4.1   Typical Interfirm Network in the New York City Better Dress
Industry
SOURCE: Uzzi (1997: 40)

richment of relationships through trust and reciprocity," which cannot be
expressed in prices or contractual provisions (p. 677). For example, company owners may prefer to deal with personal friends, kinsfolk, or members of the same ethnic group, because these social connections permit concessions during credit crunches or delivery delays. An exchange partner's
identity in a system of embedded social ties facilitates transfers of information about company strategies, production techniques, and profit margins,
which allows the partners to solve their coordination and adaptation problems. However, because the precise mechanisms through which such structural benefits arose were not theoretically well understood, Uzzi undertook
his ethnographic inquiry into the apparel industry practices.

Through observation and in-depth interviews, he found that reciprocated embedded ties among the better dress firms originated primarily in third-party referral networks and prior personal relations. Inter-firm connections formed because people know one another from social circles at work, schools, clubs, and kinship. A CEO with personal ties to two unconnected others would act as a go-between, making introductions and vouching for the potential business partners' trustworthiness. Although all companies regularly made one-shot, arm's-length exchanges, their leaders also recognized the importance of those rarer close connections built on trust: "It is hard to see for an outsider that you become friends with these people—business friends. You trust them and their work. You have an interest in what they're doing outside the business" (Uzzi 1997:42). Other informants described how such personal relations subsequently transform into fine-grained information exchanges and joint problem-solving arrangements to coordinate market transactions. As pre-existing social relations develop into multiplex embedded ties, the "calculative orientation of arm's-length ties fades and is replaced with a heuristic decision-making process that economizes on cognitive resources, speeds up decision-making, and inclines actors to interpret favorably the actions and intentions of their network partners in ambiguous situations" (1996:681).

From his fieldwork, Uzzi (1997) constructed several propositions about how social embeddedness governed the operation and outcomes—both positive and negative—of inter-firm networks in ways not predicted by simpler economic rationality models. Networking promoted economies of time by reducing the need to erect contractual safeguards against a partner's opportunism. As one CEO explained, "We have to go to market fast. Bids take too long. He [the contractor] knows he can trust us because he's part of the 'family'" (p. 49). Networks also permitted a closer match to customer preferences than the market price system, avoiding wastage from overproducing unwanted dresses or failing to stock enough fast-selling items. Other likely benefits flowing from embedded network ties included narrower and more efficient searches for new exchange partners; greater reliance on "integrative" agreements (i.e., willingness to go beyond the strict letter of a contract) than on "distributive" deals (i.e., highly detailed contracts); larger, more risk-taking, investments in special-purpose machinery; and less "hostage taking" (demanding that a partner make credible commitments to the business relationship). Paradoxically, over-embedded situations could become harmful if firms remained locked into exclusive exchange obligations that prevent them from acquiring new information and responding to changing market conditions. The optimal configuration mixed arm's-length market ties with embedded social relations to provide the small-firm network and its members with stable expectations that facilitated their mutual economic performances.

The logic of small-firm networks highlights the importance of social factors as mechanisms that shape economic exchanges. Missing from many interpretations are the historical and institutional dimensions that explicitly take into account the cultural contexts in which SFNs are located. Uzzi's study was particularly insightful in exploring ways that interpersonal social relations and ethnic identities could intrude on the utility-maximizing assumptions of micro-economic theory. Studies of historical and contemporary regionally based industrial districts, reviewed in the following subsection, were another major exception to overly economized approaches to market behavior.

Regional Alliance Networks

Although SFNs might arise in any nation, organization researchers devoted special attention to a few regional settings in which unique industrial districts allegedly flourished. Alfred Marshall, the great nineteenth-century English economist, applied the metaphor of "industrial atmosphere" to localized concentrations of skilled workers where "a habit of responsibility, of carefulness and promptitude in handling expensive machinery and materials becomes the common property of all" (Marshall 1986:171). In such milieus, a cultural aptitude for complex industrial work suffuses among the mass of people residing in a relatively confined area, such that "the mysteries of industry become no mysteries; but are as it were in the air, and children learn many of them unconsciously" (p. 25). The family thus plays a crucial role in socializing a set of shared values and work practices that nurture and sustain small enterprises across the generations. This confluence of work and family is evident in contemporary definitions of the *industrial district* as "a socio-territorial entity which is characterized by the active presence of both a community of people and a population of firms in one naturally and historically bounded area" (Becattini 1990:38); and "an exclusive and restrictive locality which has both industrial and residential characteristics" (Goodman 1989: 21).

The two most widely hailed contemporary exemplars of the industrial district are the political economies flourishing in the so-called Third Italy—variously identified as Emilia-Romagna, Umbria, Veneto, and other northeast or north-central regions (Pyke and Segenberger 1992; see the maps in Sforzi 1989)—and portions of southwest Germany—primarily the states of Baden-Württemberg and Hesse (Herrigel 1993, 1996). Other researchers have argued that industrial-district features occur in SFNs of Flanders, Belgium, and Jutland, Denmark (Schmitz and Musyck 1994); Wales and the Basque region of Spain (Cooke and Morgan 1998); Taiwan (Orru 1991); and even Silicon Valley in northern California (Rogers and Larsen 1984; Saxenian 1994). Apart from small firm sizes and close geographic proximity, the modern industrial district's most frequently mentioned features fall into four broad categories:

- *Market structures*: Numerous small, interdependent, specialized firms operate in extremely fragmented consumer goods markets such as apparel and housewares. They seek competitive advantages through the application of high-tech innovations, not by slashing employee wages. Firms respond rapidly to changing fashions with flexible programs, customized goods, and short production runs (Goodman 1989). A fine-grained division of labor integrates them via a subcontracting tie that "allows costs and risks to be spread out between a number of firms, but it also allows production to be based on short-term contracts which can be adjusted to marker requirements ... when the level of demand fluctuates" (Amin 1989:116). Multiplex credit, subcontracting, outsourcing, and joint production relations link together producers, lenders, and customers. "Systems of firms" and "networks of firms" emerge, held together by a "complex and tangled web of economies and diseconomies, of joint and associated costs, of historical and cultural vestiges, which envelope both inter-firm and interpersonal relationships" (Becattini 1989:132).

- *Workplace practices*: Small workshops, located in or near the entrepreneurs' residences, are staffed primarily by members of cohesive families. A strong historical tradition of workmanship promotes the self-confidence and autonomy necessary to adapt to quickly changing conditions, especially by investing in and learning to operate expensive high-tech equipment. The absence of hierarchy and class barriers between entrepreneurs and workers facilitates the free exchange of ideas (Goodman 1989). Entrepreneurs bankroll and subcontract jobs to former workers who set up their own shops. Customers and suppliers participate intimately in product design and marketing.

- *Communal culture*: A common local identity, historically grounded in the community's linguistically and ethnically based culture, facilitates trust relationships among firms and between employers and workers (Schmitz and Musyck 1994). People encounter one another in multiplex relations throughout their lives, socially constructing the personal reputations that form their primary social capital. Cooperative behavior among firms emerges from a "local custom of reciprocal co-operation, directly connected to the more general norm of reciprocity, the real axis of the social culture of the district" (Dei Ottati 1994:531). Pervasive links among producer cooperatives, self-help associations, educational institutions, and other voluntary organizations socialize and diffuse risks in uncertain transactions (Herrigel 1993).

• *Political connections*: Political parties, municipal authorities, and regional governments actively intervene to strengthen the innovative capacities of local industries, providing low-interest loans, grants for new equipment, social welfare supports, and privileged legal classifications, such as Italy's *artigiano* (artisan) laws, which exempt small businesses from taxation, health regulations, and unionization pressures (Lazerson 1993). Legal firms and finance intermediaries knit a region's small enterprises together by brokering information, generating investment capital, and adjudicating disputes (Suchman 1994; Suchman and Cahill 1996).

A fundamental feature of industrial districts is how these distinctive elements combine into a decentralized flexible-production network that yields significant benefits of economic scale, scope, and versatility for its participants. Some analysts view the industrial district not as a mere anachronistic survival from a bygone industrial era but as a potent new sociopolitical formation capable of competing more effectively in a turbulent world economy dominated by large, centralized corporations (Piore and Sabel 1984; Sabel and Zeitlin 1997).

Based on a detailed ethnographic study of the knitwear industry in Modena, Italy, Mark Lazerson argued that a modern, decentralized "putting-out system" of small, family-run firms "represents an attractive alternative to the centralized factory under certain technological, market, institutional, and social conditions" (1995:35). In the early English Industrial Revolution, subcontracting of spinning and weaving to rural cottagers relied on backward technologies and low-wage exploitation of laborers (remember how the eponymous miser of George Eliot's *Silas Marner* accumulated his hoard?). In contrast, to survive in a seasonally volatile fashion market, Modena's decentralized knitwear industry deployed a high-wage, technologically sophisticated network of small firms, sustaining its high-productivity performance through efficient economies of scale and quick turnaround times matching the most modernized clothing factories. Transaction cost theory asserts that transporting and monitoring the quality of intermediate goods across several small-firm boundaries can be prohibitively expensive relative to internalizing the various production stages within a single factory. However, long-term buyer-seller relations, family reputations, and interpersonal trust underpinning Modena's artisan community drastically curtailed the need for elaborate contractual safeguards against theft, embezzlement, shoddy work, and late deliveries. In their capacity to reconcile high wages with low-cost, quality goods, contemporary industrial districts demonstrated the vitality of regionally based SFNs in the modern world economy:

> The Modena knitwear system represents an effective alternative governance form to the vertically integrated firm. From the imbrication of family, community, business, and public structures within a tightly knit space, a sophisticated network links thousands of specialized knitwear suppliers with hundreds of manufacturers to form a sophisticated production system that is at the top of the league in the advanced, industrialized countries. Perhaps because of the high density of ties among small firms, the need for vertically integrated structures is rendered unnecessary. (Lazerson 1993: 221–22)

This obituary for the large corporation seems premature. Other analysts are not so optimistic that the few and scattered European industrial districts, which are almost entirely absent from the United States, offer the best models for future economic development. Industrial district proponents may be guilty of selection on the dependent variable, that is, of investigating only the most visible successes without examining failed or less-triumphant outcomes. Some critics argue that even those highly celebrated cases look suspect on closer scrutiny. For example, Staber (1996) cited 1978–1991 data from local areas of southwest Germany showing their uneven economic performance relative to other regions. The precise contribution of inter-firm linkages was difficult to pin down: "There is no firm evidence that Baden-Württemberg firms are any more embedded locally than firms elsewhere" (Staber 1996:303). Similar questions arose about the potential for transferring the Third Italy model to other regions lacking its distinctive family-firm-association-government configurations (Cooke and Morgan 1994: 114–133; Amin 1993; Schmitz and Musyck 1994).

   If the industrial district sun isn't setting, it may already be eclipsed by larger global economic trends inexorably pulling these delicately balanced SFNs into vast global production and distribution networks. Economic geographers have long theorized that the advantages of territorial *agglomeration* explained the historical tendencies of similar businesses to cluster in particular cities and regions (Scott 1998). Many transaction costs rise with increasing geographic distance, for example, transporting goods and holding frequent face-to-face meetings. To achieve economies of scale by reducing unit costs, firms in the same industry preferred to locate in large, dense, diverse metropolitan conurbations near main suppliers and customers with whom they were interdependent. These spillover effects helped to explain the location decisions of firms in such disparate industries as metalworking (Harrison, Kelley and Gant 1996; Appold 1998), Hollywood filmmaking (Storper and Christopherson 1987), and the semiconductor and computer manufacturers of Silicon Valley and Route 128 around Boston (Scott and Angel 1987; Saxenian 1994).

By the late twentieth century, numerous innovations in communication and information-processing technologies had drastically reduced many industries' dependence on such territorially concentrated agglomerations. More than in any previous era, the large corporation's production activities could be readily decentralized to physically remote, yet socially interlocked, locales while still achieving efficient economies of scale. Flexible arrangements with suppliers, customers, and even competitors transcended previous constraints of time and place. Under such conditions, "local firms and networks are becoming increasingly interlinked with global markets, with corporate hierarchies as well as networks" (Tödtling 1994:83). The interactions between globalizing forces and local political economies increasingly reshaped technological innovation processes and hence the trajectories of both local and regional development. The following subsection examines one such alliance network at the organizational field level of analysis.

Organizational Field Alliance Networks

The small firms involved in industry or regional alliance networks may interact with only a single partner (a dyadic or bilateral alliance), and seldom with more than a dozen partners (multilateral alliance), to achieve a limited economic objective. Most researchers investigate specific alliances as short-term cooperative efforts, without reference to the larger organizational fields within which they are embedded. At any time, a given field contains numerous alliance networks that may compete against rival alliances and traditional single firms. (Gomes-Casseres [1996:35] referred to groups of firms bound together by alliance ties as "constellations.") The overarching structure of the field's alliance networks varies according to the degree of overlap or separation among each particular strategic alliance's partner firms. By simultaneously taking into consideration the entire set of strategic alliances among all organizations in a field, encompassing both their present and absent ties, a macro level phenomenon emerges: the *organizational field network*, or "field-net" for short (Kenis and Knoke 1999). Recall from Chapter 2 that an organizational field is a set of functionally interconnected organizations (DiMaggio and Powell 1983; also Warren 1967). A field-net is defined as the configuration of interorganizational relations among all the organizations that are members of an organizational field. Thus, a field-net consists of a particular pattern of both present and absent links among the entire set of organizational dyads occurring in a specific organizational field. In this treatment of field-nets, an organizational field is not synonymous with a network. That is, to specify a field simply identifies a set of organizational actors that an analyst believes may be relevant to an empirical investigation. No organization maintains direct ties to all the other organizations belonging to a field. Indeed, some organizations may be completely unconnected to all others (i.e., social isolates), while some dyads may be connected only indirectly, through several intermediaries. Thus, a network structure encompasses all absent as well as all present dyadic relations in the field. Combinations of dyadic relations also identify various network substructures, for example, the occurrence of such components as cliques, groups, positions, action sets, structural holes, and so forth (Wasserman and Faust 1994). Characterizing the global structure of interorganizational alliance connections within a field-net is important because this opportunity structure both facilitates and constrains its member organizations' possibilities for successfully pursuing their individual and collective goals. Therefore, describing the pattern of network alliances in a field-net is an indispensable initial step toward explaining organizational changes at both micro and macro levels of analysis.

Explanations of the structure of alliance networks within an organizational field are underdeveloped compared to research on interorganizational relations at lower levels of analysis. To illustrate the potential insights from this approach, I analyze some data from the Global Information Sector (GIS) Project. To set the stage, multiple partnerships among international firms rapidly proliferated in several information industries at the end of the twentieth century. Technological innovations drove many corporate events, beginning with the invention of the personal computer in the 1970s, the court-ordered break-up of AT&T into regional "Baby Bells" in 1984, the rise of the Internet, and the merger of movie studios and broadcast television networks into huge "infotainment" conglomerates in the 1980s. The colorful clash of outsized corporate celebrities who shaped this new electronic era—Ted Turner, Rupert Murdoch, Steve Jobs, Bill Gates, Larry Ellison, Steve Ross, Barry Diller, Sumner Redstone (Auletta 1997)—are pale reminders of the rowdy Robber Barons who begged, seized, or stole vast rail, oil, and steel empires in the previous century. Detailing the history of these tumultuous changes requires numerous books and articles that defy easy summary and would detract from my objective of uncovering the global information field's basic alliance network structure (for exemplary reportage, see Coll 1986; Temin 1987; Ichbiah and Knepper 1991; Scherer 1992; Jackson 1997; Cohan 1997; Yoffie 1997). My purpose in this section is to scan the information sector forest, pausing occasionally to inspect a few strange bushes and birds.

The only direct antecedent to the GIS Project was the MERIT database, assembled and analyzed by Dutch scholars (Hagedoorn and Schakenraad 1992; Hagedoorn 1993b). Using published sources such as newspapers, specialized business journals, and company annual reports, those researchers compiled information on 10,000 cooperative agreements (including 4,000 strategic technology alliances) among 3,500 international firms from 1980 to 1989. The six MERIT industries included computers, microelectronics, telecommunications, industrial automation, software, and telecommunications. They defined strategic alliances as "those inter-firm agreements that can reasonably be assumed to effect the long-term product market positioning of at least one partner" (Hagedoorn and Schakenraad 1992:164). Trends over the decade revealed a sharp rise in numbers of alliances during the mid-1980s, followed by slower rates of increase in network density at the end of the decade (p. 164–5). Separate multidimensional scaling and cluster analyses of the networks of alliance ties among the 45 most active firms in each of the six industries disclosed relatively stable patterns for both halves of the 1980s (p. 185). Many market leaders, as measured by annual sales, played prominent but not dominating roles in strategic partnering. However, little evidence supported an hypothesis that strategic technology alliances were a game led by "second-tier competitors."

The GIS Project examined the changing networks of international strategic alliance from 1989 to 1998 (Genereux and Knoke 1999). As described in Chapter 3, the information sector received official acknowledgment in the North American Industrial Classification System (NAICS). This sector embraces firms that create, distribute, or provide access to different types of information by various means, including satellite, cellular, and pager communications; online services; software and database publishing; motion pictures; video and sound recording; and radio, television, and cable broadcasting. The GIS project retroactively combined the four NAICS information subsectors with selected manufacturing industries (primarily computers, electronic products, and semiconductors). To identify the largest world corporations in these industries, we extracted all relevant names from 10 annual Fortune 500, 1000, and Global 500 lists, then added their closest competitors, as cataloged by Hoovers, an online corporate profile service. After sorting these 400 organizations according to their primary products and services into the four-digit Standard Industrial Classification (SIC) categories directly corresponding to NAICS codes, we ranked them by their most recently available annual revenues. Finally, we selected the top half of each category, resulting in a target population of 145 core firms. About two-thirds were headquartered in the United States, one-sixth in Europe, and the remainder mostly in Asia.

Once we had identified the core GIS companies, we needed an efficient and low-cost procedure for locating all possible interorganizational events that might qualify as joint ventures, strategic alliances, and other types of interorganizational relations between 1989 and 1998. Keyword searches of comprehensive online news archives were the only feasible solution. Although locating events through keyword searches of newspaper and magazine articles and publicity releases may not uncover every joint venture and strategic alliance, it identifies visible events deemed most newsworthy by business reporters, publishers, and corporate public relations departments.[1] To locate articles about interorganizational relations, we searched each company's name in three online archives in union with the key words "alliance or venture." We read headlines and abstracts for tens of thousands of articles, then downloaded the most promising full-length reports. The initial selection criterion only required that an article or press release mention some type of formal relationship between two or more core organizations. This culling yielded approximately 10,000 stories, many referring to the same event or series of events. We entered these raw journalistic and public relations reports into a new searchable database, tagging each distinct event by date of the report, names of all the participating organizations, and a brief description of the primary purpose of the relationship. Our final tally was 2,687 strategic alliances between two or more of the 145 GIS organizations. The rate of alliance formation accelerated across the decade, with the annual number of new events nearly quadrupling, from 107 in 1989 to 400 in 1998.

The majority of alliances involved an agreement between just two core GIS firms, although many also involved smaller and more specialized partners not making the list of 145 core players. Some arrangements were short-term deals, such as NBC and Disney/ABC's partnership with Major League Baseball to broadcast games in 1994–1995, or Microsoft and Compaq jointly offering a holiday promotion of Delta Air Lines companion tickets to software buyers. Other alliances were evidently complex political bargains, for example, a 1995 agreement by Star Television of Hong Kong, a wholly owned subsidiary of Rupert Murdoch's News Corporation, to distribute two NBC cable channels over its satellites to Asian nations. In return, NBC withdrew its complaint to the Federal Communication Commission about violations of U.S. laws prohibiting foreign purchases of U.S. television stations in 1985 by then-Australian Murdoch's Fox Broadcasting subsidiary. Three prominent examples illustrate the complexity of shifting alignments among high rollers playing with huge technological and economic stakes:

- The Tele-TV alliance—formed in 1994 by Bell Atlantic, NYNEX, and Pacific Telesis—sought to develop digital wireless technology to deliver entertainment, data, and home-shopping services to those phone companies' customers. Three years later, the floundering venture laid off half its 200 employees and its chairman resigned. In contrast, the rival Americast partnership between Disney/ABC, GTE, and three other Baby Bells (Ameritech, Bell South, and SBC Communications) apparently thrived by concentrating on fiber optics technology. In 1996 it placed a $1 billion order for Zenith Electronics to build 3 million TV set-top programming boxes. Americast promised to offer programming under its brand name to a potential 200,000 customers in the following year.

- Most of Americast's telephone companies (Ameritech, USWest, GTE, Bell South, and SBC, but not Bell Atlantic) subsequently teamed up with Microsoft, Intel, and Compaq at the end of 1997 to accelerate Internet data transmission over telephone lines. By the next Christmas shopping season, the consortium aimed to market new software and modems that would make Web pages materialize on home computer screens 30 times faster than traditional modems. The telecommunications industry had been working on this technology, known as digital subscriber line, for many years but lacked inter-firm consensus on technical standards. Bill Gates seemed to be playing on both sides in the phone-versus-cable Internet battle. Microsoft had recently invested $1 billion in Comcast, the sixth largest U.S. cable company, to expedite conversion to digital cable modems. And in 1998 Microsoft and Comcast each invested more than $200 million for a 10 percent stake in Time Warners' Road Runner unit, which supplied high-speed Internet access over cable television lines (Fisher 1998).

- In 1991 a coalition of phone, computer, and electronics firms— AT&T, Motorola, Apple, Philips, Sony, and Matsushita—invested in a Silicon Valley startup firm called General Magic. This alliance's main objective was to develop and promote the "personal intelligent communicator," a pocket-sized device for organizing personal notes and appointments and exchanging faxes and computer data by radio waves. In 1994, a rival wireless network venture, Wirelessco, emerged, headed by Sprint and three cable television giants, TCI, Comcast, and Cox. Their chief product was the "personal communications service," or PCS, designed to work like a cellular phone, but operating on different frequencies and providing two-way wireless links for portable computers and information systems. Within two years, that alliance was restructured when TCI and Comcast reduced their stakes to concentrate on their cable businesses. By 1998, the renamed Sprint PCS had signed nearly a million subscribers to its digital wireless service, surpassing rivals PrimeCo (jointly owned by Bell Atlantic, US West Media, and AirTouch Communications) and SBC's Pacific Bell Mobile Services (Jensen 1998).

These events demonstrate that strategic alliances are short-lived affairs for limited purposes, and that partners in one venture become rivals in others. The over-arching structure of these shifting alignments is obscured when analytical attention concentrates on specific individual events rather than the total pattern created by the network connections across the entire set of alliances.

Perhaps the most consequential corporate cleavage within the global information sector during the late 1990s was the steadily widening polarization between Microsoft and Intel, opposed by an array of software and hardware firms that felt threatened by the "Wintel" duo's efforts to gain dominant positions across the personal computer, business network, Internet, and cable transmission markets. During the mid-1990s, several Silicon Valley companies, spearheaded by Sun Microsystems and Netscape Communications, tried to stem Microsoft's increasing Internet penetration. They rallied a hundred firms—including Oracle, Novell, IBM, and Apple— to endorse Sun's Java programming language over Microsoft's Windows as the preferred technical standard in software applications ("applets") for transferring programs across computer systems. In 1996 Netscape, Oracle, IBM, Sony, and three other Japanese firms formed the Navio Corporation to create refined Internet software compatible with consumer electronic devices such as cell phones. A wary John Malone, chair of U.S. cable colossus TCI, rolled the dice at the 1998 Las Vegas Comdex convention by announcing a deal with Sun to deploy both Java and Windows inside his new TV set-top boxes. In a classic case of resource dependency avoidance, Malone apparently was gambling that this "layer cake strategy" could prevent TCI from relying entirely on Microsoft technology despite the substantially higher access costs to consumers (Markoff and Fabrikant 1998). The main thundercloud looming over Gates's skyline was the U.S. Department of Justice's ultimately successful 1998 antitrust suit charging that Microsoft violated the terms of a 1995 consent agreement by bundling its Internet Explorer browser with its omnipresent Windows operating system. A federal judge ruled that bundling effectively leveraged Microsoft's dominance of PC operating systems into a monopoly of Internet browsing software. As of this writing, the judicial penalty of breaking Microsoft into two companies remains unresolved and may involve several years of legal appeals.

A network analysis of the global information sector must move beyond the details of specific partnerships, coalitions, and events to encompass the entire field's changing alliance structures. A detailed examination of the GIS development over the decade would require another book, so I must be content here with an illustrative excerpt. I display the network structure of strategic alliances among the subset of 38 organizations involved in the most new alliances with all GIS firms in 1998. The list of these companies, classified by their major industries in Table 4.2, shows that the majority were active in computers, telecommunications, and software. Two-thirds were U.S.-headquartered, with most of the remainder Japanese and European companies. The triangular matrix in Table 4.3 displays the basic data for mapping this network. Each row-and-column cell entry is the number of alliances formed in 1998 involving a specific pair of organizations. Main diagonal entries show the total number of alliances in which a given organization participated. For example, reading down the first column reveals that Microsoft collaborated in a total of 55 strategic alliances, including 9 ventures with Intel, 15 with Compaq, 7 with IBM, and 10 with Hewlett-Packard, but none with Motorola, Computer Associates Inc. (CAI), Toshiba, France Telecom (FT), and EMC. This network is very dense, with 50 percent of the possible pairs connected in at least one partnership (however, only 22 percent of the dyads had more than a single alliance, and just 10 percent had three or more deals). The most central organizations were Microsoft, Compaq, Cisco, and IBM according to all three basic network centrality measures: degree, closeness, and betweenness (see Chapter 2 and the Appendix). The least central organizations were TCI, FT, and CAI.

TABLE 4.2   Top 38 Global Information Sector Organizations, 1998

COMPUTERS
Compaq Computer
Dell Computer
Fujitsu [Japan]
Hewlett-Packard (HP)
Hitachi [Japan]
International Business Machines (IBM)
Machines Bull (Bull) [France]
NEC [Japan]
Siemens [Germany]
Sun MicroSystems
Unisys

TELEPHONE COMMUNICATIONS
Alcatel [France]
AT&T (ATT)
Bell Atlantic (BA)
Bell Canada Enterprises (BCE)
BellSouth (BS)
Ericsson LM Telephone [Sweden]
France Telecom (FT) [France]
Lucent Technologies
SBC Communications
US West (USW)

CABLE & PAY TV SERVICES
Tele-Communications Inc (TCI)

COMPUTER STORAGE DEVICES
EMC

PREPACKAGED SOFTWARE
Baan [Netherlands]
Computer Associates (CAI)
Microsoft
Netscape Communications
Oracle

SEMICONDUCTORS
Intel
Toshiba [Japan]

COMPUTER COMMUNICATIONS EQUIP
3Com
Cisco Systems

HOUSEHOLD AUDIO-VISUAL
Sony [Japan]
Philips Electronics [Netherlands]

COMPUTER SERVICES
America Online (AOL)

RADIO & TV BROADCASTING EQUIP
Motorola

MOTION PICTURE & VIDEO
Time Warner (TW)
Walt Disney Enterprises

TABLE 4.3 Number of 1998 Strategic Alliances among 38 Global Information Sector Organizations

#	Organization	Values (columns 1 →)
1	MICROSOFT	55
2	INTEL	9 18
3	COMPAQ	15 7 28
4	IBM	7 4 8 28
5	HP	10 0 4 5 30
6	CISCO	4 2 2 1 5 18
7	3COM	2 2 5 5 5 2 16
8	USW	4 2 2 0 1 4 1 14
9	ERICSSON	1 2 2 1 0 1 2 1 9
10	MOTOROLA	0 1 1 1 1 0 1 0 3 10
11	SIEMENS	2 1 1 0 1 1 2 1 2 2 10
12	BAAN	3 1 2 3 1 0 0 0 0 0 0 10
13	DISNEY	2 1 2 1 1 1 0 0 0 0 0 0 4
14	ALCATEL	2 1 1 0 0 2 1 1 1 0 1 0 0 7
15	FUJITSU	4 2 3 4 1 1 2 1 1 0 1 0 0 2 15
16	AOL	2 0 3 3 1 1 0 0 0 0 0 0 1 0 0 | 9
17	NETSCAPE	2 1 2 2 1 1 0 0 0 0 0 0 1 0 1 | 4 8
18	SUN	2 0 1 4 3 1 0 1 1 1 0 1 1 0 0 | 2 2 19
19	ORACLE	3 0 3 3 4 2 1 1 1 1 1 1 0 0 1 | 2 4 2 15
20	CAI	0 0 1 0 0 0 1 0 0 0 1 0 0 0 0 | 1 0 2 1 2
21	AT&T	5 0 3 4 5 3 1 1 0 0 0 0 2 0 0 | 3 2 1 2 0 | 22
22	TCI	2 0 0 0 0 0 0 0 0 0 0 0 0 0 0 | 1 0 0 2 0 0 | 1 6
23	TW	3 0 2 1 1 1 0 0 0 0 0 0 1 0 0 | 1 1 1 1 0 | 1 1 2 8
24	LUCENT	3 1 3 2 3 2 4 2 2 1 1 0 0 2 1 | 0 0 2 0 0 | 2 0 0 18
25	BS	4 2 2 0 0 1 1 2 1 0 1 0 0 1 1 | 0 0 0 0 0 | 1 1 0 0 1 5
26	BA	4 2 3 1 1 2 1 4 1 1 0 1 1 1 1 | 1 1 1 1 0 | 1 1 0 0 3 2 9
27	SBC	2 2 3 0 0 1 1 4 1 0 1 0 1 1 1 | 0 0 0 0 0 | 1 1 0 0 3 2 5 10
28	BCE	6 1 3 0 1 3 2 1 1 1 0 0 1 1 | 0 0 0 0 0 | 1 2 0 0 3 1 2 2 15
29	DELL	3 1 5 5 3 3 4 2 1 1 0 1 1 0 2 | 1 1 1 1 2 | 1 4 0 1 0 0 1 2 0 18
30	SONY	4 2 0 2 1 0 0 0 0 0 0 0 1 0 1 | 1 1 0 1 0 | 1 1 0 1 0 0 0 0 1 0 | 11
31	HITACHI	2 1 2 2 1 1 2 0 1 0 1 0 0 0 2 | 1 0 0 1 0 | 1 0 0 1 0 0 0 0 0 2 1
32	TOSHIBA	0 2 3 3 1 0 4 0 1 1 1 0 0 1 2 | 1 0 0 0 1 | 1 0 0 1 0 0 0 0 0 3 1
33	PHILIPS	1 2 1 0 0 1 0 1 0 0 0 0 0 1 1 | 0 0 0 0 0 | 1 1 0 1 1 0 1 1 0 0 3 1
34	UNISYS	1 1 2 2 2 0 0 0 0 0 0 1 0 0 1 | 0 0 0 1 0 | 1 0 0 1 0 0 0 0 0 3 1
35	NEC	1 0 0 0 0 0 0 0 1 0 1 0 0 2 1 | 1 1 0 | 1 0 0 | 2 0 0 0 0 1 | 1
36	FT	0 0 0 1 0 1 0 0 1 0 0 0 1 0 | 1 0 0 0 0 | 1 0 0 0 0 0 0 0 0 1 0 1
37	BULL	1 0 2 1 0 0 1 0 1 1 0 1 0 0 0 | 1 0 0 0 1 | 1 0 0 0 0 0 0 0 0 0 0 1
38	EMC	0 0 0 0 1 0 0 0 0 1 1 0 0 0 | 1 0 0 0 1 | 1 0 0 0 1 0 0 0 0 0 1

ORG. NUMBERS: 1 2 3 4 5 6 7 8 9 10 11 12 13 14 15   16 17 18 19 20   21 22 23 24 25 26 27 28 29   3(8)

The organizations in Table 4.3 are grouped into five subsets, indicated by the dashed lines, produced by a hierarchical cluster analysis of the alliance data. Each block contains organizations with greater similarity to one another (in terms of their patterns of direct and indirect partnerships) than to the organizations occupying the other blocks. The first block contains the Wintel duo (Microsoft and Intel), along with 5 of the 11 computer companies plus 7 firms from diverse other industries (see Table 4.2). The most active leaders of the anti-Microsoft coalition (Netscape, Oracle, and Sun Microsystems) occupy a smaller second block along with America Online and CAI. Block three is primarily a telecommunications cluster (AT&T, Bell-South, Bell Atlantic, SBC, BCE, and Lucent), but also includes TCI, Time Warner, and Dell. The fourth and fifth blocks seem to be catch-all or residual categories, comprising mainly non-U.S. firms. I generated this classification with UCINET's hierarchical clustering program, analyzing a matrix of proximities based on a transformation of the data in Table 4.3. These proximity measures take into account both distance and reachability between all pairs of organizations without direct alliances.[2] To produce a two-dimensional map of this alliance network structure, UCINET's nonmetric multidimensional scaling program analyzed same proximity matrix, yielding an acceptable two-dimensional fit to the data (stress =.18). Figure 4.2 plots the 38 organizations' locations relative to one another.

Each organization's position reflects its varied connections to all others, either through direct alliances or through indirect links (partners of partners). Contiguity lines encircle the members of the five blocks identified by the hierarchical cluster analysis. In general, companies involved in many collaborations with numerous partners appear near the spatial center (closest to the 0,0 coordinates are Microsoft, Intel, Cisco, HP, and Compaq, all members of the first block), whereas firms with the fewest connections appear on the periphery (e.g., EMC, NEC, FT, Philips). The specific spatial region into which an organization falls depends on its overall pattern of connections. That is, two corporations collaborating with the same partners are close to one another, but a pair choosing different allies are located farther apart. The figure visually confirms that the GIS was still riven by the pro- and anti-Wintel factions in 1998, but it importantly reveals the marginality of the main opponents. Note that Oracle, Netscape, and Sun cluster toward the bottom of Figure 4.2 at a substantial distance from the center of the strategic alliance network. This cluster's location, reflecting those firms' tendencies to choose distinct alliance partners, suggests structural difficulties encountered by its members in forging and sustaining a broader-based group opposed to Gates's predatory tactics. Their nearest potential partners are the telecom companies in the adjacent block.

The GIS strategic alliance map also yields insight into several events occurring in 1998 and subsequently. In an attempt to compete against Microsoft

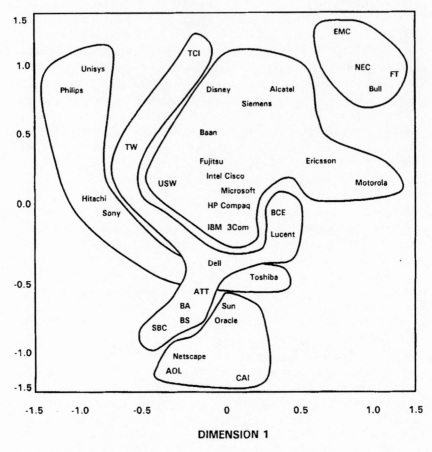

FIGURE 4.2   1998 Global Information Sector Strategic Alliance Network

Network in the rapidly merging e-commerce market, America Online bought Netscape for $4.2 billion in stock. Note AOL's extreme outlier location at the bottom of Figure 4.2. Its nearest neighbor is Netscape, indicating that these firms had formed highly similar alliance ties with other core GIS players. Simultaneously, AOL and Sun Microsystems, both located in the same cluster, announced a joint marketing and development partnership. AOL agreed to purchase about $300 million worth of Sun's computers, and Sun's sales force would sell Netscape's business software (Lohr and Markoff 1998). Thus, AOL's two big deals in late 1998 structurally reinforced its competitive position against Microsoft by merging and linking with two firms connected to similar alliance partners. Commenting on AOL's takeover of his company, Netscape's CEO James Barksdale, observed, "Microsoft represents the ultimate competitor to many parts of this puzzle, though not all. Microsoft cuts a wide swath, so we have to be very clever in trying to dance beneath the elephant's feet. We think this combination makes us a powerful force" (Corcoran 1998:A1). In the federal browser-bundling trial, Microsoft's lawyers immediately argued that the AOL-Netscape merger, by creating an effective new competitor, had effectively undermined the government's charge that Microsoft was a bullying monopolist intimidating the information sector. But the federal judge didn't buy this convoluted logic and refused to dismiss the antitrust suit.

Two ambitious megamergers among core GIS corporations, reflecting deregulatory consequences of the 1996 Telecommunications Act (see Chapter 9), occurred in the telecom cluster. In June 1998, following rebuffed merger discussions with America Online, AT&T paid $32 billion to acquire Tele-Communication Inc.'s cable properties. Note that, although TCI and AT&T belonged to the same alliance block in 1998, they were quite far apart spatially, reflecting their divergent partnerships. Through this purchase, AT&T regained access to potentially one-third of U.S. homes and apartments for the first time since the 1984 federal court decree forced the long-distance carrier to spin off the Baby Bell local phone companies. Using TCI's fiber optic lines, the bulked-up AT&T hoped to create a comprehensive network delivering high-speed Internet computer access, cable TV, and digital phone services to residential customers. The deal intensified the Baby Bells' concerns about accelerating their entry into the long-distance phone market. As Bell Atlantic's CEO put it, "This puts a fire under everyone suggesting those concerns should come down fast now that King Kong and Godzilla just got together" (Schiesel 1998:D3). Fearful of being locked out of the high-speed Internet game, AOL initially demanded that the Federal Communications Commission require AT&T to allow Internet providers open access to its new cable lines. Then, in January 2000, AOL announced it would buy traditional mass media giant Time Warner for $165 billion, the biggest corporate merger in history. Note that this merger involved members of different alliance clusters in Figure 4.2, and that TW was also quite distant from the telecom companies' locations in 1998. In addition to acquiring the content of Time Warner's entertainment empire (HBO, CNN, Warner Brothers films), AOL gained immediate access to 13 million residential cable TV subscribers, effectively trumping AT&T for broadband Internet domination (Hansell 2000). Further consolidation across the boundaries of GIS industries seems likely well into the twenty-first century as both old- and new-media firms try to squeeze competitive advantages from strategic alliances and, ultimately, through mergers and acquisitions.

The preceding detailed case study of recent strategic alliances in the global information sector illustrates how complex network structures are generated by a set of strategic alliances occurring within an organizational

field. Empirical studies of other industrial sectors, such as automobile manufacturing and biotechnology research (Koput, Powell and Smith-Doerr
1997), would reveal similar patterns of distinct partnership blocks competing for advantages. The organizational field network is a potent concept for
developing theoretical explanations of changing interorganizational relations and their consequences for field members. A field-net is an encompassing opportunity structure that influences organizational decisions,
whether linking up with previous allies or seeking new partners. But these
macro level structures are not the only determinants of the formation and
outcomes of alliances. Also important for sustaining collaborative relations
is interorganizational trust, the subject of the following section.

Trust Relations

The initiation and perpetuation of collaborative dyadic social relationships
of any kind, whether marriages between persons or joint ventures among
corporations, hinges on creating and sustaining mutual trust. Actors who
suspect their partners might take advantage of them, if opportunities to
cheat arise, are usually loath to risk the emotional, informational, and resource investments essential to strengthen the pair's relationship. Without
fundamental trust in another's honest intentions to fulfill promises, marriages and strategic alliances alike frequently fail. At the personal level, we
consider a person trustworthy if "the probability that he will perform an
action that is beneficial or at least not detrimental to us is high enough for
us to consider engaging in some form of cooperation with him" (Gambetta
1988:217). Organizational trustworthiness involves similar perceptions
and beliefs about future prospects for an alliance.

At the interorganizational level, trust provides a basis for one firm to
achieve some degree of social control over another's behavior under conditions of high uncertainty. Many companies forge strategic alliances for very
limited purposes with partners that remain serious rivals in their competing
business lines. Autonomous firms seldom willingly yield power and control
to others, yet seek competitive advantages from their partners' technology
and knowledge. The inevitable ambiguities and conflicts arising from efforts to implement a collaborative enterprise pose unique management
problems rarely encountered inside a unitary firm:

> JV subsidiaries and licenses do not involve ongoing shared control by two in-
> dependent firms either. Alliances are different. The new alliances often com-
> bine both competitive and cooperative elements in an environment of shared
> control. Hence the need to master new management skills. (Yoshino and Ran-
> gan 1995:16)

Difficult management situations are further complicated if an interorganizational alliance lacks strong legal and financial safeguards against the partners' temptation to opportunism at the expense of others (i.e., "self-interest seeking with guile" [Williamson 1975:80]). From a transaction cost perspective, trust expectations may provide an efficient mutual deterrent to each partner's opportunism or malfeasance. To the extent that trust substitutes for more formal control mechanisms, such as written contracts, an alliance can reduce or prevent paying several types of transaction costs (Gulati 1995a:88–91). Those costs include the expenses of (1) searching for information about potential partners; (2) contracting a formal agreement that stipulates terms and conditions; (3) monitoring to ensure that every party meets its obligations; and (4) enforcing the contract terms when a partner fails to live up to its agreements (Dyer 1997:536). Writing formal safeguards against all possible moral hazards into a legally enforceable contract is unrealistic and counterproductive if it raises a partner's suspicion that violations should be anticipated. Far less costly protections are available by basing collaborations on a self-enforcing foundation of inter-firm trust.

Trust relations fall conceptually somewhere between the polar logics of hierarchical authority and market prices (Bradach and Eccles 1989:104; also Sako 1992). Two perspectives regarding interorganizational trust differ in their relative emphasis on the predominance of objective and subjective elements in the relationship. A business-risk view stresses that partner trust is based on confidence in the predictability of their behavior, which can be hedged using formal contractual means such as insurance against violations (Luhmann 1979). An alternative psychological conceptualization emphasizes trust as confidence in another's goodwill, of faith in the partner's moral integrity (Ring and Van de Ven 1994). In this approach, trust constitutes a fundamental type of organizational social capital, a strong-tie relationship between a firm and its direct contacts in an organizational field. Organizational attributes and network relations interact over time. As a company builds and reinforces a widespread reputation among its peers for fair dealing and impeccable reliability in keeping its promises, that reputation itself becomes a prized asset that is useful for sustaining the firm's current alliances and forming future ones. Reputed trustworthiness signals to potential partners that an organization is unlikely to behave opportunistically because "such behavior would destroy his or her reputation, thus making the total outcome of the opportunistic behavior undesirable" (Jarillo 1988:37).

The social psychological explanation of trust is rooted in basic social exchange principles, including conformity to such norms as reciprocity, commitment, forbearance, cooperation, and obligations to repay debts (Lewis and Weigert 1985; Stinchcombe 1986; Bradach and Eccles 1989:105). As trust relations became historically institutionalized in modern industrial societies, arm's-length market transactions grew increasingly suffused with various normative connotations (Zucker 1986). These noneconomic principles generated and upheld the moral communities within which trustworthiness conveyed great significance for members' decisions whether to continue or break off relations. Because inter-firm exchanges may be widely separated across time, trust reinforces these economic ties by invoking such principles as balancing exchange levels over the long run and ensuring that the partners' payoffs remain roughly proportional to their contributions to any joint activity. As trust permeates economic transactions, inter-firm relations acquire a dimension of value-rationality (*Wertrationalität*; Weber 1947:14). This motivation embodies the idea of action as an-end-in-itself, in contrast to the means-rationality (*Zweckrationalität*) of cost-benefit calculations exemplified by pure market transactions. In other words, understanding the forms and consequences of strategic alliances among organizations requires taking extra-economic factors into consideration.

What are the macro level sources of trust among organizations? Figure 4.3 proposes that interorganizational alliances emerge over time, with trust occupying a pivotal role between antecedent conditions and consequent alliance formations. Note the feedback loop, which indicates that trust shapes the form of alliance, while events occurring during the alliance implementation process may subsequently transform the interorganizational trust relations. Positive experiences generally reinforce both partners' beliefs about each other's trustworthiness and hence their willingness to continue deepening the relationship. Thus, trust and alliance relations mutually change one another as firms collaborate over time. Alternatively, poor performance, slacking off, and free-riding may lead to deteriorating trust and eventual termination of an alliance, as revealed in the KLM-Northwest story at the beginning of this chapter. The darker dimensions of organizational interactions involve betrayals of trust, which include blocking a partner's competitive advantages, stealing technological secrets, filching customers, and plotting predatory takeovers. The entertainment industry is rife with intrigues and feuds that destroy partnerships. A notorious recent case was the bitter 1996 demise of a joint venture between MCA and Paramount Pictures to operate the USA Network and Sci-Fi Channel on cable TV (McClellan 1996). Following the Seagram Company taking an 80 percent stake in MCA and Viacom buying Paramount, Viacom CEO Sumner Redstone launched Nick at Night's TV Land to rerun vintage television series. Seagram sued Viacom, contending that the joint venture agreement prohibited either partner from starting competing cable services. Redstone countersued, claiming that TV Land was simply a spin-off of existing programming and, besides, Seagram CEO Edgar Bronfman Jr. had reneged on his oral waiver of the noncompete clause in their joint venture. Eventually, after the Delaware Chancery Court ordered the squabbling businesses to figure out how best to dissolve their partnership, Seagram paid Viacom $1.7 billion in cash to buy Viacom's half of their joint venture. Subsequently, Seagram formed a new alliance with Barry Diller's Home Shopping Network, merging big chunks of both partners' TV operations into a new enterprise named USA Networks.

Interorganizational communication networks shape organizational capacities to screen and evaluate initial information about potential alliance partners. These exchanges involve factual data about alters' interests and competencies but also provide indirect evidence about other organizations' trustworthiness through information acquired from knowledgeable peers in an organizational field. The more central an organization's position within a field's communication network, the greater its visibility; hence more informants are available to testify regarding its reliability and integrity. Organizations located in peripheral positions of a field-net have fewer opportunities to become familiar with potential alliance partners and for their own trustworthiness reputations to become vetted by the field. The GIS firms located farthest from the center of the organizational field alliance network in Figure 4.2 (as well as dozens of less-active companies not shown) obtain fewer informational and trust benefits than those organizations occupying more central positions.

A second set of antecedent factors fostering or thwarting trustworthiness are macro-structural conditions. Imbalances in the resources controlled by each organization (such as financial size or market shares) may impede trust creation due to unequal partners' inability to satisfy their reciprocity obligations. Pairs of organizations that share similar or complementary characteristics are more likely to develop strong trust relations. Tacit understandings and taken-for-granted assumptions may be rudely violated when partners have little in common. For example, many cross-border alliances, undertaken between foreign partners to gain entry into local markets, are fraught with pitfalls stemming from incompatible

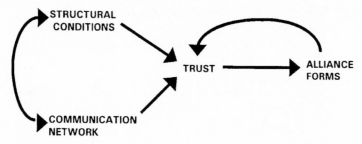

FIGURE 4.3   Trust as an Intervening Factor in the Alliance Formation Process
SOURCE: Knoke (1999)

national cultures (Lewis 1990:253–278; Lorange and Roos 1992:177–204; Bleeke and Ernst 1993:12–13; Gilroy 1993). Even domestic alliances can suffer from clashing corporate cultures. A major instance was the office network software producer Novell Inc.'s disastrous effort to integrate its subsidiary WordPerfect Corp.'s "close-knit and insular" staff with the parent organization's profit-driven style (Clark 1996). After two years of plummeting market share and stock prices, Novell sold WordPerfect to Corel Corp for one-tenth its original $1.4 billion acquisition price.

The feedback loop between trust and alliance depicted in Figure 4.3 implies a temporal dynamic to changing governance forms through accumulating interorganizational experiences (Smith, Carroll and Ashford 1995). Many alliances begin with formal contractual linkages that expose the partners only to small risks. Because the organizations as yet have few bases for trusting one another, equity-based contracts predominate as legal protections against potential opportunism ("hostage-taking" purportedly limits the capacity to act without regard to a partner's interests). Once partners gain confidence in one another through repeated testing, then "informal psychological contracts increasingly compensate or substitute for formal contractual safeguards as reliance on trust among parties increases over time" (Ring and Van de Ven 1994:105). This substitution process was succinctly summarized by Gulati's (1995b) affirmative answer to his question, "Does familiarity breed trust?" Because strong-tie trust relations can counteract firms' fears of a partner's betrayal of confidence, governing alliances through legal documents yields to relations governed by interorganizational trust. Reduced transaction and monitoring costs make informal social control the preferred cost-effective alternative to both market pricing and hierarchical authority. Consistent with these expectations, Gulati's (1995b) analysis of multisector alliances found strong evidence that formal equity-sharing agreements decreased with the existence and frequency of prior ties to a partner (see also Gulati and Gargiulo 1999). Domestic alliances less often involved equity mechanisms than did international agreements, supporting claims that trust relations are more difficult to sustain cross-culturally. In addition to the familiar East-West cultural gulf separating Japanese and Korean from U.S. firms, Western European companies often upheld distinctive norms about the distribution of rewards that required more formal safeguards when allying with U.S. partners.

Andrea Larson's (1992) ethnographic exploration of the formation of dyadic alliances illuminated how social factors, especially trust and reciprocity norms, governed economic transactions. She conducted in-depth interviews in the mid-1980s with informants from seven partnerships created by four small entrepreneurial companies (a telephone distributor, a retail clothing company, a computer firm, and a manufacturer of environmental support systems). Although mutual economic gain was a necessary incentive for an alliance to emerge, sustaining the relationship required a trial period, lasting between 6 and 18 months, during which the partners incrementally built stable and predictable structures to govern their subsequent cooperation. Key dimensions in this critical trial phase were the institutionalization of implicit and explicit rules and procedures and the evolution of clear expectations that became taken for granted by managers in both companies. As a relationship solidified over time, organizational actions grew more integrated and mutually controlled through intertwined operational, strategic, and social mechanisms. In the absence of formal contracts, trust and moral obligations protected each partner from the other's potential opportunism. As the manager of supplier relations for the computer firm described the process by which embedded social ties shaped economic behavior:

It's like working with your own factory. There is full trust. When we call to say, "Don't worry about cost," they know what we mean. They trust us to pay and we trust them to give us a reasonable price. (Larson 1992:95)

Trust and reciprocity norms proved crucial to successful alliance formation, which distinguished these ties from the partners' more typical arm's-length exchanges. As the alliances entered their mature phase, the firms' reputations and identities grew closely enmeshed with their economic transactions. This complex fusion of mutually reinforcing social and economic processes created a distinctive network mode of interorganizational control. Involving neither market-based prices nor hierarchical commands, "social control encompasses self-regulation with a moral dimension in combination with control as jointly determined by and diffused across multiple partners" (Larson 1992:91). However, this governance form was evidently risky, as four of the seven partnerships subsequently either declined or were terminated. Explaining the conditions under which alliances persist or dissolve is a key challenge for organizational network theory and research.

Another challenge for network analysts is to resolve enduring quandaries about the relative capacity of organizations versus individuals qua persona to create interorganizational trust. In general terms, human agency in social action concerns "the capacity of socially embedded actors to appropriate, reproduce, and, potentially, to innovate upon receive cultural categories and conditions of action in accordance with their personal and collective ideals, interests, and commitments" (Emirbayer and Goodwin 1994:1442). Applied to interorganizational contexts, a central question is whether trust relations occur between organizations, or whether trust encapsulates purely interpersonal phenomena. As noted above, some theorists emphasize that trust originates in the social psychology of interpersonal interactions and thus often evokes strong emotional overtones of sharing and caring for the welfare of one's partner (McAllister 1995). As the employees who occupy key boundary-spanning roles try to cope with their organizations' environmental uncertainties, they socially construct bonds of mutual confidence and trust with their counterparts in other organizations that may affect interorganizational behavior. For example, a study of company decisions to switch auditing firms found that the individual attachments of boundary-spanners such as the company's chief executive, financial, and accounting officers attenuated the pressures arising from changing resource needs (Seabright, Levinthal and Fichman 1992). Assuming that only natural persons are capable of expressing beliefs and emotional attachments, then trust resides wholly at the level of individual agents who establish and nurture trust relations on behalf of the organizations they represent. In this perspective only employees, not companies, can carry the substance of interorganizational trust. The potential for intermingling the reputational social capital of people and organizations spawns some knotty dilemmas for intraorganizational control: Exactly *who* legally and morally owns the trust relations in which both companies and employees have invested? This question is not a trivial concern for firms, as reflected by such practices as "noncompete" clauses restricting local television news personalities from working for rival stations after severing their employment ties, and in law suits against lawyers and talent agents who defect to rival firms, taking along their client lists (Tevlin 1997a). In the most extreme instances of trust violation, agents may pilfer major corporate secrets for their new employers, as in Jose Ignacio Lopez's alleged transfer in 1993 of GM purchasing data to Volkswagen.

The intermediary position of trust in the alliance processes proposed in Figure 4.3 should direct research attention toward this portion of the developmental dynamic. Unfortunately, analysts of interorganizational trust relations have concentrated primarily on theoretical and conceptual refinements. Relatively few researchers have tried to measure and test hypotheses about the role of trust in alliance formation and dissolution. (Zaheer and Venkatraman [1995], discussed in the next section, was a notable exception.) Most of the research findings discussed in the next section emphasize how structural conditions, including antecedent alliance networks, shape the subsequent emergence and maturation of new interorganizational collaborations.

Alliance Formation
and Outcomes

What factors explain why companies create alliances, which forms are more likely to occur, and what impacts such collaborations have on the partners' performances? This section examines theoretical explanations and empirical evidence about the formation and outcomes of interorganizational alliances. Conventional economic wisdom holds that firms obviously collaborate to perform production tasks more efficiently and to maximize mutual benefits through exchange. As one insider, NBC Cable president Tom Rogers, put it, "the right alliance can make it possible to implement a good idea" (Fabrikant 1997). In seeking to understand the development and consequences of strategic alliances over time, organization studies should ponder whether a unified theory might eventually be synthesized to explain the full range of alliance forms and their outcomes, or whether distinct theories are necessary to account for different aspects of interorganizational networks (Oliver 1990).

Three prominent explanations of why organizations engage in network relations are institutional, transaction cost, and resource dependence theories (see Chapter 2). Institutional theory draws attention to cultural conditions in organizational environments that define and enforce conformity with prevailing normative standards of conduct. The effort to enhance organizational legitimacy may motivate organizations to adopt particular structures and practices, including interorganizational behaviors, that lack technical or economic-efficiency justification (Scott and Meyer 1994). Thus, firms may pursue alliance formation strategies to increase their sociopolitical legitimacy among constituencies capable of imposing sanctions for nonconformity. For example, nonprofit foundations typically stipulate as a condition for funding that agencies receiving large grants must cooperate with other service providers in their domains (Galaskiewicz and Bielefeld 1998). Similarly, governmental agencies and some professional societies may promote or prohibit interorganizational ties through their rule-setting and enforcement systems. Their surveillance and control mechanisms involve both highly formalized coercive institutions (legislatures, courts, and regulatory commissions) and such informal processes as the diffusion of prescriptive professional ethics and "best-practice" standards. Because the institutional perspective inspired few systematic empirical investigations into the formation and outcomes of interorganizational alliances (Oliver 1990:246), judging the importance of legitimization processes is difficult. However, one analysis of network blockmodels among diverse agencies providing child and youth services in two rural Pennsylvania counties discovered stronger institutionalization in some sectors (health, education, and judicial) than others (mental health and poverty/welfare) (Doreian and Woodard 1999). Ample opportunities clearly abound for investigating how organizations exploit network ties to establish and boost their legitimacy within a field-net.

Transaction cost theory seeks to pinpoint where economically efficient boundaries should be drawn between an organization (hierarchy) and its environment (market), in other words, whether to make or buy a particular function. Oliver Williamson (1975) argued that the most important factor driving organizational efforts to economize is asset specificity, the extent to which investments are specialized to particular recurrent transactions between buyers and sellers. The greater the asset specificity, the more likely are the parties to "make special efforts to design exchanges with good continuity properties" (Williamson 1981:555), thus effectively locking them both into prolonged bilateral exchanges. For example, a corporation requiring only sporadic legal advice is more likely to retain an outside legal firm, whereas a company with persistent legal problems may create its own in-house legal department. Interorganizational ties arise from specialized investments that would lose their value if transferred to another exchange partner. Otherwise, market exchanges will be more cost-efficient. A second core assumption of transaction cost analysis is that at least some actors are "given to opportunism" (Williamson 1981:553), that is, dishonesty and dissembling about preferences and information. The necessity to monitor partner performance and to protect against duplicity raises interorganizational transactions costs, leading to internalization as an alternative to inter-firm collaboration. A theoretical synthesis of transaction cost and social exchange principles identified four conditions favoring the emergence and flourishing of "network governance" (inter-firm coordination) and related social mechanisms to solve coordination and safeguarding problems (Jones, Hesterly and Borgatti 1997:918). These conditions are highly uncertain demand coupled with stable supply, customized (asset-specific) exchanges creating dependencies, complex tasks performed under intense time pressures, and frequent exchanges among network members.

Resource dependence explanations of alliance formation emphasize inherent tensions between organizational resource procurement needs and the desire to preserve freedom of strategic decision making. Intercorporate relations arise from interdependencies and constraints among organizations, that is, situations in which one organization controls the critical resources or capabilities—such as money, information, patents and intellectual property, production and distribution skills, access to foreign markets—needed by another organization. Forging strategic alliances opens conduits to each partner's corporate social capital (see Chapter 6), enabling mutual exchange and combining their information and knowledge resources. These collaborative activities are conducive to developing new intellectual capital and hence to improving both partners' organizational performances (Nahapiet and Ghoshal 1998). Alliances tend to occur more often among interdependent than between independent firms, that is, where complementarity rather than similarity prevails. However, organizational efforts to manage problematic external interdependencies "are inevitably never completely successful and produce new patterns of dependence and interdependence" (Pfeffer 1987:27). Dependence theory argues that network ties arise from managers' efforts to control the most troublesome environmental contingencies through complete or partial absorption (e.g., mergers or joint ventures).

In their desire to acquire critical resources by forming partnerships, organizations risk losing control of their own destinies. Resource dependence generates interorganizational power differentials that constrain firms' opportunities, because organizations tend to comply with demands made by powerful actors in their political-economic environments. "Organizations seek to form that type of interorganizational exchange relationship which involves the least cost to the organization in loss of autonomy and power" (Cook 1977:74). Given a set of potential partners, a company will optimally choose an ally that can best satisfy its resource needs while imposing minimal constraints on its discretionary actions. For example, confronted with several suppliers capable of providing equivalent-quality inputs, a large manufacturing firm is likely to prefer a long-term purchasing deal with the smallest supplier, thereby gaining greater power to set and adjust favorable terms and conditions. Similarly, a small supplier would desire to spread its business across many customers to evade a loss-of-control stemming from its dependence on a single dominant purchaser. These tensions help to explain the oscillating structural forms of the large firm-small supplier networks in the U.S. automobile industry discussed earlier in this chapter.

Few researchers have tested hypotheses about alliance formation drawn explicitly from the transaction cost perspective, and one notable study failed to support its expectations. Zaheer and Venkatraman (1995) tested hypotheses about interorganizational strategies drawn from transaction cost economics and social exchange perspectives, using data from a mail survey of 329 independent insurance agencies. Their two dependent variables were vertical quasi-integration (the percent of total premiums handled by an agency's "focal carrier," the company with which an agency conducted most of its business) and joint action (a multi-item scale measuring planning and forecasting activities with the focal carrier). Although transaction-specific assets predicted quasi-integration, neither uncertainty nor reciprocal investments were statistically significant. Instead, quasi-integration and joint action were both positively related to mutual trust between agency and carrier, a relationship opposite to the transaction cost hypotheses but consistent with social exchange theory.

Resource dependence principles seemed more helpful than transaction cost ideas for understanding alliance formation. Pfeffer and Nowak (1976) found that resource interdependencies (high exchange of sales and purchases) among companies in technologically intensive industries significantly increased joint venturing at the industry level of analysis. Additional support for the resource dependence approach came from research on cooperative networks between new biotechnology firms (NBFs) and established corporations in the 1980s (Barley, Freeman and Hybels 1992; Kogut, Shan and Walker 1992; Powell and Brantley 1992; Smith-Doerr et al. 1999). Complementary resource needs drove strategic alliances, primarily involving exchanges of financial support for technical expertise. The small, innovative R&D laboratories typically lacked funds, public legitimacy, and in-house capability to market their products and maneuver through the federal government's regulatory maze. Hence, they formed alliances with diversified, resource-rich pharmaceutical, chemical, and agricultural companies able to provide sustaining resources. In turn, these established firms welcomed collaborative agreements as a means to acquire tacit knowledge and to learn new technological skills from their NBF partners. As relationships accumulated and stabilized over time, the presence of network positions already occupied by individual organizations blocked latecomers' access to information regarding potential alliance partners. Once the structure of the biotech organizational field-net had solidified, it provided resources for some participants while constraining others' opportunities on the basis of their interorganizational connections. "It is the structure of the network, rather than attributes of the firm, that plays an increasingly important role in the choice to cooperate" (Kogut, Shan and Walker 1992:364).

Two studies of changing network patterns in other organizational fields underscored the impact of past ties on future actions. Leenders (1995) reanalyzed dyadic data from the social service networks of two Pennsylvania counties between 1988 and 1990. Informants named the organizations with which their agencies maintained relations, such as coordinating client treatments or sharing funds and personnel, including ties mandated by the state government. In both counties, estimated dyad-transition models revealed that "reciprocity both increases actors' inclination of creating and maintaining ties and decreases the inclination of withdrawing ties" (Leenders 1995:193). Although he did not use the term *corporate social capital*, the evolution of these interorganizational networks clearly fits such an interpretation (see Chapter 6).

In his study of international corporate alliances, Ranjay Gulati (1995a) found evidence consistent with both resource dependence (which he called "strategic interdependence") and social structural explanations. Using a 1980–1989 panel of 166 corporations operating in three worldwide sectors (U.S., Japanese, and European new materials, industrial automation, and automotive products firms), Gulati conducted event-history analyses on a variety of dyadic alliances ranging from arm's-length licensing agreements to closely intertwined equity joint ventures. Strategically interdependent firms (i.e., those companies operating in complementary market niches) formed alliances more often than did firms possessing similar resources and capabilities. Previously allied firms were more likely to engage in subsequent partnerships, suggesting that "over time, each firm acquires more information and builds greater confidence in the partnering firm" (Gulati 1995a:644). However, beyond a certain point, additional alliances reduced the likelihood of future ties, perhaps prompted by the partners' fears of losing autonomy by becoming overly dependent on one another. (See Gulati and Gargiulo

[1999] for further analyses confirming and extending these results.) Indirect connections within the social network of prior alliances also shaped the alliance formation process: previously unconnected firms were more likely to ally if both were tied to a common third party, but their chances of partnering diminished with greater path distances. Gulati concluded that "the social network of indirect ties is an effective referral mechanism for bringing firms together and that dense co-location in an alliance network enhances mutual confidence as firms become aware of the possible negative reputational consequences of their own or others' opportunistic behavior" (Gulati 1995a: 644). His results reflected a logic of clique-like cohesion rather than status-competition among structurally equivalent organizations.

Corporate managers and social scientists widely believe that interorganizational relations provide performance benefits superior to both markets and hierarchies. Alliances allegedly are "lighter on their feet" than ponderous bureaucratic hierarchies (Powell 1990:303). They enable organizations and their agents to respond rapidly to emerging opportunities and threats, particularly by gaining timely access to swiftly changing technological knowledge and data essential for survival and prosperity. Yet the evidence supporting this claim has remained remarkably slim. Researchers proposed numerous criteria for judging alliance "success," ranging from mere organizational survival to economic performance levels significantly higher than industry norms. For example, in Uzzi's analysis of business failures among 573 New York City better dress apparel firms in 1991, "social capital embeddedness" indicated whether a contractor had a ties to a business group, typically formed with other CEOs who were kin or colleagues from previous jobs. Other network measures combined the proportion of work exchanged between organizations with the degree to which a firm maintained either arm's-length ties or socially embedded connections to partners. Logit analyses showed that firms that "connect to their networks by embedded ties have greater chances of survival than do firms that connect to their networks via arm's-length ties" (Uzzi 1996:694). However, the optimal configuration involved mixtures of both types of personal and interorganizational relations:

> A crucial implication is that embedded networks offer a competitive form of organizing but possess their own pitfalls because an actor's adaptive capacity is determined by a web of ties, some of which lie beyond his or her direct influence. Thus a firm's structural location, although not fully constraining, can significantly blind it to the important effects of the larger network structure, namely its contacts' contacts. (Uzzi 1996:694)

One difficulty in assessing performance outcomes is that most interorganizational ties are created only to achieve limited purposes and are intentionally short lived. Thus, measuring success merely as organizational survival may be an inappropriate yardstick. If an alliance terminates in one partner's acquisition of the other, as apparently happens in the majority of cases (Bleeke and Ernst 1993:18), does that outcome constitute a failure of the alliance? A success for the first organization but a failure for the second? The software geeks who sold their startup company to Bill Gates for millions of (pre-trial) Microsoft shares probably didn't consider themselves business failures.

Organizations enter alliances with many motives and strategic objectives, including speeding entry into new product or geographic markets; accelerating cycle times for developing or commercializing new products; improving product or service quality; gaining technical skills, tacit knowledge, and competencies; sharing costs; spreading risks and uncertainties; and monitoring environmental changes in the political economy. Explaining which successful outcomes occur among these varied goals, and under which conditions, is a Herculean task. Bleeke and Ernst (1993) relied on unpublished reports and interviews with insiders of 150 top companies in the United States, Europe, and Japan to determine that, among 49 cross-border alliances, 51 percent were considered successful by both partners and 33 percent were mutually judged failures. Alliances were "more effective for edging into related business or new geographic markets" (p. 18); acquisitions worked better for core businesses and existing areas. Other conditions leading to success included alliances between equally strong partners, evenly split financial ownership of the joint venture, and autonomy and flexibility for the joint venture to grow beyond the parent firms' initial expectations and objectives.

Empirical evidence regarding the financial outcomes of strategic alliances is scarce, with network studies of investment banking and the stock exchange a notable exception (Eccles and Crane 1988; Baker 1990; Podolny 1993). For example, Chung (1996) analyzed cooperative exchanges among 98 top investment banks involved in new stock issues in the 1980s. He found that the best long-term performers (measured by dollar amounts underwritten) were involved in a strategy of exchange initiation, which also led to subsequently higher popularity and expanded participation in stock deals. However, few researchers have studied whether joint venture partners recover their capital investments, or whether such collaborations yield a higher return than available from alternative resource expenditures. Theorists tend to emphasize only the positive synergies emerging from networks, while ignoring potential dark sides of interorganizational relations, specifically that social embeddedness may exert a drag on market efficiency. For example, Sako (1992:239) speculated that a major disadvantage of obligatory contractual relations is "[r]igidity in changing order levels and trading partners [and] potential lack of market stimulus."

Similarly, the impact of trust on alliance success remains virtually uninvestigated. Trust presumably fosters goal attainment by contributing to the favorable resolution of conflicts, which inevitably crop up during joint operations. Given its subjective basis, high mutual trust is likely to correlate with feelings of satisfaction about the partner's performance and contributions. Researchers should investigate whether collaborators feel their alliance was worthwhile, whether they would be willing to repeat the partnership for other purposes, and whether they would recommend their partners favorably to other firms seeking a collaborator. On the negative side, trust and other obligational norms may attach organizations too strongly to their partners, carrying relations beyond rationally efficient limits by resisting swift dissolution of inefficient or inequitable situations.

Conclusions

Interorganizational relationships came spectacularly into their own toward the end of the twentieth century. Rising uncertainties in technologies and product markets fueled the emergence and proliferation of various equity and nonequity ventures. Mutual trust between partners was crucial to governing and sustaining long-term collaborative agreements between autonomous, rival corporations that might be tempted to opportunistic exploitation or takeover of the joint enterprise. Institutional, transaction cost, and resource dependence theorists tried to explain the formation of strategic alliances by emphasizing the economic and sociopolitical origins of cooperation. Although relatively few empirical analyses sought to test propositions from these perspectives, limited evidence suggests that resource dependence concerns were more important than purely rational cost-benefit calculations in organizational decisions to enter strategic alliances. Beyond the dyadic level of specific agreements, new varieties of alliance networks arose at the industry, regional, and organizational field levels of analysis. Researchers analyzed the propagation of structures of multiple agreements among organizations at every level—large firm-small supplier networks, small-firm networks, regional alliance networks, and global organizational fields—as durable yet continually changing cooperative configurations among competitive firms for the development, production, and distribution of goods and services. Despite high faith among both analysts and practitioners that interorganizational alliances inevitably led to superior performances such as innovation, market share, and profit gains, the available empirical evidence supporting expectations of favorable consequences remained scant. Corporate ties that bind could also blind, preventing timely termination of faltering alliances threatening to drag all partners down. Clearly many opportunities awaited for imaginative research on the outcomes of interorganizational relationships.

5

Changing the Employment Contract

"If only it weren't for the people,
the goddamned people," said Finnerty,
"always getting tangled up in the machinery.
If it weren't for them earth would be
an engineer's paradise."
—Kurt Vonnegut, Player Piano (1952)

The dozen employees working the A-shift on the crankshaft-machining line at the sprawling Saturn factory in Spring Hill, Tennessee, were supposed to perform as a democratic team. Eighteen months after General Motors' innovative small cars began rolling off the assembly line, the crew leaders (CTMs or "charter team members"), machine operators, and trade technicians should have been making decisions by consensus. Instead, A-crew's CTM Scott Prins behaved more like a traditional foreman, telling op tech Nancy Laatz to change how she used the crankshaft-polishing machine. And she didn't take kindly to it:

What had happened was that A-crew had a lot of scrap and less production from the polisher than B-crew. Prins had talked to B-crew's more experienced operator about how he calibrated the machine to avoid scrap, then passed along the information to Laatz who didn't care to hear it. She didn't respect B-crew's operator.

"It was another case of people wanting to reach the same goal," Prins said. "But don't dare tell them how to get there."

He and Laatz did iron the nagging problem out—people-wise and production-wise (A-crew had been losing a half-hour production off the polisher every day they started it up). Prins claimed, "This incident is half the fun of being at Saturn!" (Sherman 1994:268–269)

Despite GM's bold intentions to reform traditional labor-management relations at the Saturn plant, the difficulties encountered in implementing genuine change pointed to a yawning gulf between the promise of theory and the reality of practice. Launched in 1986 with the slogan "a different kind of company, a different kind of car," Saturn was conceived as a co-management partnership between the United Auto Workers union and GM (Adler et al. 1997). In place of the 1,400-page labor contracts governing other GM plants, with precise rules covering every contingency, the 7,300 UAW members at Saturn worked under a 32-page Japanese-style memorandum of agreement. They didn't enjoy the layoff benefits available to other GM workers but were protected against firings except during "unforeseen or catastrophic events or severe economic conditions" (Meredith 1998). After receiving at least 92 hours of intensive job training, Saturn employees could earn performance bonuses up to 20 percent of their base wages, putting their annual incomes well above those of other GM production workers. Production at the Spring Hill plant, built on a "greenfield" site (vacant rural land), was structured around self-managed work teams whose members cross-trained and rotated among all unit tasks. Team members elected their leaders and took responsibility for hiring new members, quality assurance, inventory control, scheduling, and other traditional management tasks. Managerial and union reps at all levels of the organization met periodically to share information and give workers a voice in important company decisions. Half the middle managers were UAW members, breaking down the traditional separation of management and labor. Saturn's task and job design represented "an attempt to synthesize a European sociotechnical approach with the Japanese lean production system" (Adler et al. 1997:63). The firm delegated more decision-making independence to its work teams than was found in most Japan plants.

Despite Saturn's favorable public image, organizational performance in the first decade fell short of GM's initial optimistic expectations. Saturn acquired a cult-like following among customers satisfied with its fixed-price, no-haggle sales and service approach, and its small cars won numerous awards for quality. Yet despite turning a modest operating profit in 1993, Saturn never earned back GM's initial $5 billion investment costs, and the firm's older divisions didn't copy its innovative workplace designs. During the 1990s collapse of the small-car market that accompanied the consumer craze for minivans and sports utility vehicles (SUVs), Saturn workers saw their annual bonuses shrivel from $10,000 to $1,860 by 1998. Conflict erupted among local union factions over Saturn's employment contract. Fearful that GM might invoke the catastrophic events clause, dissident UAW members demanded a referendum to scrap the current memorandum of agreement in favor of the national GM contract. That contract paid laid-off employees 95–100 percent of their base wages until they were offered another job or retired. Saturn workers voted two-to-one to retain the cooperative agreement. However, in July 1997, they authorized the local leaders to call the plant's first-ever strike if negotiations failed to change GM's plans to build future Saturn cars and a new SUV using parts from outside suppliers (Bradsher 1999). And, eight months later, UAW members voted overwhelmingly to toss out the local's entrenched leadership, which had helped to develop and carry out the memorandum of agreement. The new union leaders pledged to rewrite the Saturn memorandum. The future of this unique labor-management partnership seemed clouded as the auto plant entered the twenty-first century.

This chapter starts by comparing the traditional and new employment contracts defining the relationships between firms and workers. As organizations sought greater staffing flexibility by shifting toward more market-based labor relations, employee attachments to their companies eroded. These trends included falling job tenure and increasing numbers of part-time, contingent, and other nontraditional workers with fewer benefits. More flexible work arrangements gave employers greater control over the costs and uncertainties in acquiring labor but weakened their employees' commitments and loyalties. Some firms, particularly in manufacturing industries, transformed their workplaces into high-performance organizations exploiting such innovative human resource practices as self-managed teams and pay-for-work schemes. These potent sociotechnical production systems allegedly generated competitive advantages by unleashing worker participation, commitment, and creativity. Yet despite plausible evidence of productivity improvement, high-performance work practices failed to penetrate very deeply into the U.S. economy, implying significant socioeconomic barriers to implementation. A closer examination of one manufacturing firm's experience with work teams illustrated how subtler forms of employer control permeated modern workplaces. The seeming paradox of flexible staffing arrangements alongside high-performance practices, sometimes occurring within the same plants and offices, embodied contradictory impulses toward hierarchical control and self-directed participation inside contemporary organizations.

The Traditional Employment Contract

National and international turmoil in the final decades of the twentieth century, which drove the extensive restructuring of the U.S. political economy discussed in Chapters 3 and 4, also changed the intra-firm relationships between employers and their employees (Cappelli 1999; Osterman 1999). The massive downsizings, restructurings, mergers, spin-offs, and strategic alliances transformed the traditional employment contract that had prevailed in large bureaucratized corporations since the end of World War II. As depicted in Figure 5.1, this traditional contract sheltered a company's core employees, especially its middle managers and white-collar staff, from exposure to the external labor market during business cycle downturns. Companies provided skills training, generous salaries and fringe benefits, and job security equivalent to guaranteed lifetime employment. In return, employees pledged not only their labor power but unswerving psychological commitment and loyalty to the organization. A pervasive sense of belonging to a "corporate family" cultivated a cooperative spirit that melded organizational participants into a unified collectivity. Strong protective, almost paternalistic, bonds boosted employee morale, which paid off in greater productivity, to the mutual benefit of the firm and its people. *The Organization Man*, William H. Whyte Jr.'s famous portrayal of all-male middle managers in the 1950s, captured the conformist optimism of that prosperous bygone era:

> For the executive of the future, trainees say, the problem of company loyalty shouldn't be a problem at all. Almost every older executive you talk to has some private qualifications about his fealty to the company; in contrast, the average young man cherishes the idea that his relationship with The Organization is to be for keeps. Sometimes he doesn't even concede that the point need ever come to test. (Whyte 1957:145)

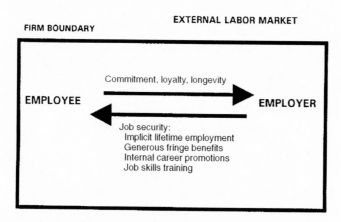

FIGURE 5.1   Traditional Employment Contract

The lifetime employment inducements, provided in the traditional employment contracts of such firms as IBM and Sears, yielded many efficacious results, including low employee turnover, good job performance, firm-specific technical and social skills, organizational commitment and loyalty, and acquiescence with corporate goals. Firms gained docile and predictable workforces unwilling, indeed unable, to relinquish the secure company womb for the uncertainties of the external labor market. Millions of workers struggling without a corporate safety net could only envy the fabled careers of these organization men (and, eventually, organization women).

Corporations structurally embedded their traditional employment contracts in modern bureaucratic personnel systems to manage various employee categories ranging from professionals and middle managers to clerical and blue-collar workers. The employer-employee relationship extended beyond explicitly specified working conditions and pay "to other matters such as grievance procedures, expectations about promotion chances, and stipulations about procedures for making any change in the relationship that might be desired by either party" (Bridges and Villemez 1994:2). Chapter 8 explores the increasing legalization of the workplace and the expanding statutory and case laws regarding due-process protections for employees. This chapter concentrates on workplace transformations from bureaucratic labor-management relations toward more participatory practices.

Two important structural dimensions of bureaucratic employment systems are job formalization and firm internal labor markets. Formalization consists of explicit rules that impersonally govern such behaviors as job classifications, work task activities, authority lines, performance evaluations and rewards, and grievance and disciplinary procedures. Formalization reduces individual employee discretion in performing job tasks by carefully prescribing and proscribing possible actions. For example, clerical workers may be required to prepare letters and invoices in a precise manner to make the most efficient use of their time and energy (Braverman 1974). Although the existence of extensive written documentation—manuals of standard operating procedures—visibly indicates workplace formalization (Kalleberg et al. 1996:75–76), unwritten normative standards that occupants internalize and take for granted are probably more important determinants of how closely formal rules are implemented in actual practice. Radical critics lambaste sophisticated bureaucratic designs that "break up the homogeneity of the firm's workforce, creating many seemingly separate strata, lines of work, and focuses for job identity" (Edwards 1979:133). Polaroid, for example, created roughly 2,100 job titles and pay steps for its 6,397 hourly workers. Formalization makes employee behavior more predictable, thus enabling bureaucracies to achieve high and unvarying levels of performance (p. 146). In addition, a finely stratified division of labor serves as an impersonal control technique for thwarting any collective employee actions that might challenge the power of top management to run the corporation.

The creation of firm internal labor markets (FILMs) was the logical progression of bureaucratic reward-and-control processes (Osterman 1984; Althauser 1989). A FILM is an "administrative unit, such as a manufacturing plant, within which the pricing and allocation of labor is governed by a set of administrative rules and procedures" (Doeringer and Piore 1971:1–2). Common FILM features were hierarchically linked positions comprising job ladders; entry into the ladder only at the bottom rung; and upward promotion within the organization based on demonstrated knowledge, skill, and experience. Some analysts preferred a broader definition that included other formalized features, such as job classifications, wage systems, and rules regarding employment security (Osterman 1994b). Corporations with FILMs concentrated on hiring new workers only into specific lower-level "port of entry" jobs and filling higher-level openings exclusively through internal promotions. Firms provided employees with sufficient formal and informal job training to acquire the firm-specific skills necessary for moving up the corporate ladder (Knoke and Ishio 1994; Osterman 1995a).

The traditional employment contract protected a firm's long-term white- and blue-collar employees against competition from outside job applicants for the better-paid and more responsible positions. For example, an executive trainee might begin as an assistant manager directly supervising a team of sales people in a local office, be promoted to regional sales manager, and eventually achieve a vice presidency at corporate headquarters. Similar hierarchically progressive careers were open to research scientists, marketing and finance personnel, and even clerical workers (e.g., file clerk, pool typist, principal secretary, office supervisor). In unionized plants, a traditional industrial relations system of seniority-based hiring and firing, elaborate job classifications and promotion principles, and compensation rules evolved from collective bargaining struggles of the 1930s and 1940s (Kochan, Katz and McKersie 1994:21–46). Large companies typically built separate FILMs with virtually no opportunities for employees to leap from one type of job ladder to another. For example, a harried loading dock supervisor stood little chance of promotion onto the lowest rung of the finance department, where a certificate of accountancy was the entry ticket.

By the 1980s the rigid relations linking employers and employees began cracking as corporations desperately restructured to survive under increasingly volatile global competition. No longer willing or able to fulfill their expensive lifetime employment promises, many firms abandoned key provisions of the traditional contract for more flexible, market-mediated labor relations. Increasingly, lifelong employment security evaporated as companies shed long-term employees, outsourced projects, subcontracted various organizational functions, purchased labor services from temporary help firms, and even leased entire workforces. After 1972, the most rapidly growing industries in the U.S. economy were business services and engineering and management services (Clinton 1997). Supplying personnel services to other companies in the manufacturing, construction, and service sectors accounted for much of this growth. The next section documents additional evidence about eroding attachments between firms and their employees, which underscored the emergence of a more market-oriented employment contract.

Eroding Firm Attachments

As firms tried to create more flexible workforces, they minimized the presence of expensive full-time, year-round workers. Cumulating evidence of weakening employer-employee attachments over the final decades of the twentieth century included decreasing job tenure, increasing part-time work, growing numbers of contingent and freelance employees, and shifts in employer-provided benefit plans. Time series data revealing these changes came from current population surveys of employees conducted by the U.S. Bureau of the Census for the Department of Labor's Bureau of Labor Statistics (BLS). The trends described in this section spread unevenly across major gender, race, and age demographic categories. Not every change reflected eroding job security relative to employees working in permanent full-time jobs. But taken all together, these patterns suggested that many firms armed their workers with fewer shields against the hazards of the external labor market. Both transaction cost and institutional theories attempt to explain increased flexible staffing as organizationally driven processes rather than as employee desires for more tenuous attachments to their employers.

Job tenure, defined as the length of time an employee has worked continuously for his or her current employer, fell sharply from 1970 to 2000, partly as a result of the many corporate downsizings noted above. However, interpreting length of tenure is problematic because standard measures combine voluntary employee quits with involuntary dismissals through company layoffs and firings. Additionally, quits and dismissals move in opposite directions with cyclical changes in labor market tightness (Cappelli 1999:134). When new jobs are easier to find in a tight labor market, more workers quit, but fewer people are dismissed by their companies because employers cannot easily hire equivalent replacements for terminated employees. As a result, job tenure levels fall in boom times as new labor force entrants find their first jobs and experienced workers move to companies offering them better deals. During recessions the average tenure level rises because companies follow the "last hired, first fired" rule by laying off workers with less seniority. Hence, given these interpretive complications, researchers not surprisingly found contradictory evidence about changes in job stability during recent decades. For example, one study reported substantial decline in overall U.S. job duration from the 1970s to the 1990s (Swinterton and Wial 1995), but others found basically constant levels (Farber 1995; Jaeger and Stevens 1998). Examining only the overall job tenure rate paints a misleading portrait of change, as demonstrated in the next paragraph, which disaggregates the rate by employee ages and genders.

Major job tenure changes were heavily concentrated among certain labor force segments. Figure 5.2 shows changes between 1983 and 1998 in the median number of years spent working continuously for the current employer by 12 age and gender categories. Bars that rise above the "0" line mean that median job tenure increased; bars falling below the line indicate decreased tenure over the period. (Note that this age-category display actually compares the tenure experiences of different generational cohorts; for example, the people 20–24 years old in 1983 had aged into the 35–44 years old category by 1998.) The entire labor force experienced only a modest overall reduction in median tenure in this period, from 5.0 to 4.7 years. Women of all ages enjoyed high job stability: Median tenure fell only slightly in the two youngest female cohorts, slightly increased during the three middle categories, and fell by less than a year and a half among women employees aged 65 or older, when most people begin retiring. In contrast, men endured serious job tenure declines in the three age categories spanning their prime working years between 34 and 65 years old (respectively, falling from 7.3 to 5.5 years, from 12.8 to 9.4 years, and from 15.3 to 11.2 years). Further analyses revealed that older men's job tenure depended markedly on the amount of formal schooling they had achieved. By 1998 median job tenures of employees without high school diplomas had fallen to just 6.4 years among men aged 45–54 years and to 10.1 years for those aged 55–64 years. In contrast, college graduates in those two age brackets enjoyed substantially longer tenures, respectively, of 10.2 and 14.2 years. Declining job stability was especially severe for older workers in several manufacturing industries that had dismantled many internal labor market protections. In particular, job tenure in the motor vehicles and equipment industry was cut in half between 1983 and 1998, from 13.0 to 6.4 years.

Researchers usually bracket part-time workers with the temporary employees considered below, but part-time employment should be seen as a separate phenomenon. Part-time work involves less than 35 hours per week, and full-time work consists of 35 hours or more per week from one or more jobs. Unlike temporary workers hired for preset periods, both part- and full-time employees have implicit or explicit contracts with their employers to work for indefinite duration. Part-timers typically have more

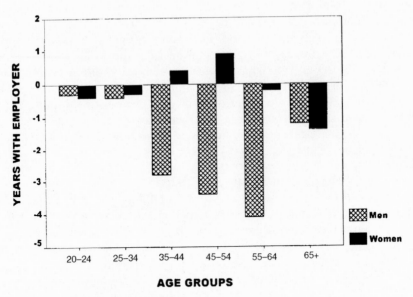

AGE GROUPS

FIGURE 5.2   Changing Job Tenure
SOURCE: U.S. Bureau of Labor Statistics (1999)

job rights and benefits than temps. The percentage of the labor force working part-time doubled from 12 to 25 percent between 1957 and 1997, although much of that increase occurred before the mid-1980s (Belous 1989; Parker 1994; Levenson 1996; U.S. Bureau of the Census 1999). A substantial portion of the change involved rising involuntary part-time work, especially by firms in fast-growing industries requiring flexible staffing arrangements, such as United Parcel Service (Friesen 1997; Fallick 1999). Women were more likely than men to work part-time. By 1997 about two-thirds of the part-time labor force was female, compared to less than half the full-time workers. Both younger (16–21 years) and older (65 years and older) workers tended disproportionately to work part-time (Tilly 1996:18).

In the 1990s, the majority of part-time employees voluntarily reported limiting their hours of work because their life situations prevented full-time work, such as attending school, raising young children, or retiring from a primary career. However, a substantial minority were involuntary part-timers. For example, in 1993 the BLS classified 29 percent of part-timers as involuntary because of slack work, material shortages or repairs, a job starting or ending during the survey week, or inability to find full-time work (Tilly 1996:156, 200). Industry demands for part-time workers fluctuate with the business cycle. The number of involuntary part-timers usually increases during an economic downturn, because many employers temporarily trim workforces without completely laying off their more valuable workers during slack periods. Downsizing companies thereby reduce payroll costs because part-timers require lower or no pension and insurance premiums and are ineligible for more expensive overtime pay.

In contrast to part-time employment, the BLS conceptualized *contingent work* as jobs without "an implicit or explicit contract for ongoing employment" (Polivka 1996) with an expected limit on the job's duration. BLS surveys in 1995 and 1997 used three measures of contingent employment, differing in whether employees expected their jobs to end before or after one year and whether self-employed people and independent contractors were included. The highest estimates of contingent workers in the labor force were 4.9 percent in 1995 and 4.4 percent in 1997 (Hipple 1998). About 43 percent worked part-time in 1997, compared to just 18 percent of noncontingent workers, but only one in ten part-time employees was classified as contingent. A slight majority of contingent workers said that they would prefer permanent jobs. (For detailed analyses of the first BLS contingent work survey in 1995, see Cohany et al. [1998]).

A much broader BLS conceptualization of contingent employment aggregated four types of nontraditional workers without regard to expected job duration: (1) persons self-employed as independent contractors, consultants, and freelance workers but not business operators such as shop owners or restaurateurs; (2) on-call workers, such as construction workers and substitute teachers, who come in only when needed although they may be scheduled for several days or weeks in a row; (3) employees whose wages are paid by a temporary help agency; and (4) workers provided by contract firms, who usually work for only one customer at that customer's worksite, such as landscaping, security, or computer programming. This classification scheme found more than 12.5 million nontraditional employees in 1997, constituting 9.9 percent of the labor force, double the time-restricted contingent worker estimate. Figure 5.3 breaks down their ranks into the four types, revealing that the large majority were independent contractors. Unfortunately, the BLS did not begin tracking contingent and nontraditional employees until the mid-1990s, so data are missing about their changing composition in the U.S. labor force.

Nontraditional workers form a quite heterogeneous bunch. Not all work in low-skill "bad jobs." Many pursue highly paid, professional specialty occupations. Independent contractors tended to be middle-aged white men with college educations holding managerial, sales, or precision production jobs in agricultural, construction, and business services industries. The vast majority (84 percent) preferred their arrangements over traditional jobs, probably because their average earnings were significantly higher than more traditional employees ($619 versus $510 per week for full-time work). Temporary help agency workers tended to be women, young, black

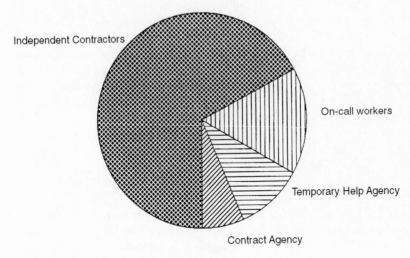

Independent Contractors

On-call workers

Temporary Help Agency

Contract Agency

FIGURE 5.3   Nontraditional Employees
SOURCE: U.S. Bureau of Labor Statistics (1997)

or Hispanic, who held laborer or administrative support jobs such as clerical work. A majority, 60 percent, said they desired better-paying traditional arrangements, obviously hoping to earn more than the temps' median weekly wages of just $329. On-call workers, the second largest nontraditional category, demographically resembled traditional employees, but were somewhat younger. About half worked part-time, the highest of the four types, and half desired more traditional work arrangements. Many were college and university teachers, reflecting the growing presence of non-tenure-track instructors on campuses (Cappelli 1999:167–172). Except for independent contractors, nontraditional workers of all types were less likely than traditional employees to receive health insurance or pension coverage from their employers.

A major shift in company-provided pension plans obligated increasing numbers of employees to shoulder greater responsibility for funding their own retirements. A 1979 BLS survey of medium and large companies (with 100 or more employees) found that 87 percent of workers participated in some form of "defined benefit" plan. Just 10 years later only 42 percent were covered under such plans, and "defined contribution" pension plans claimed 40 percent of all private sector employees (Grossman 1992). Under defined benefit plans, companies bear a heavier obligation to guarantee the retirement incomes of their employees, based on their total years of service. If an employee quits or is laid off after becoming vested (enrolled in the program for some required minimum period), the employer remains liable for paying the guaranteed pension benefits until the former worker dies. Hence, the costs of portable pension plans give firms substantial incentives to prevent worker departures, yet employees lack strong incentives to stay in the firm once they have become vested.

By switching to defined contribution plans, a company reduces the risk of being unable to fund its retirement obligations. These plans require fixed contributions to a retirement fund for each employee, such as stock option and profit-sharing plans, without guaranteeing a fixed pension payout. Additional risk-shifting occurs when employees are encouraged to add directly to their own retirement funds, such as through payments into popular 401(k) plans. The strong emotions surrounding pension fund issues erupted in 1999 when IBM tried to reduce its future liabilities and claim a tax credit by switching from a defined-benefit plan—structured to accumulate half the benefits in employees' final decade of work—into a cash-balance plan designed to accrue benefits steadily throughout an employee's career (*Wall Street Journal* 1999). Public howls of protest from long-serving IBM workers, many of whom stood to lose up to half their pensions' values, forced Big Blue to suspend the conversions. A Senate committee held hearings on cash-balance plans, and the Internal Revenue Service stopped approving new plans until it could determine their legality.

Finally, many companies resisted adopting family-responsive policies to assist employees with strains arising from incompatible work and family responsibilities. The growth of both dual-earner and single-parent households threatened the ability of many employees, particularly working mothers, to provide adequate child care from their personal resources. Childbearing employees (dads and moms alike) need parental leave for birth, adoption, or medical purposes; affordable day care; and alternative work schedules (flexible hours, compressed work weeks, job sharing) to meet the emotional needs of their infants and young children. Parents with older children require after-school, vacation, and summer care services, as well as flex-time and employment leaves to deal with family emergencies. Similar job/family conflicts arise for adult caregivers with elderly parents. Both employers and governments resisted changing corporate and public policies to permit employees to adjust their work hours and work locations around family demands, to return to their jobs after parental leaves, and to receive referrals and subsidies for day care services (Bailyn 1992; Osterman 1995b; Glass and Estes 1997). For example, Republican presidents twice vetoed the Family and Medical Leave Act, at the urging of business lobbyists who opposed mandated expenses and increased governmental regulation of the labor market (see Chapter 8). The version signed into law by President Clinton in 1993 required only unpaid parental leaves with job-protection rights in large establishments, exempting small businesses and persons whose job duties an employer deemed essential.

Voluntary implementation of company work/family programs varied considerably by type of policy, according to surveys of diverse establishments. Only a small minority of employers provided financial assistance for day care (e.g., paid on-site or subsidized off-site). A 1987 BLS survey of establishments with 10 or more employees found that 5 percent offered day care assistance (Hayghe 1988). The 1992 National Establishment Survey (NES) of large workplaces (with 50 or more employees) found just 8 percent offering such services (Osterman 1995a), and the 1991 National Organizations Survey (NOS) of establishments of all sizes found 16 percent with "day care for children, on-site or elsewhere, or help to employees to cover day care costs" (Knoke 1994). In contrast, flexible scheduling was much more prevalent (61 percent in the BLS, 40 percent in the NES, and 63 percent in the NOS), and "maternity or paternity leave with full re-employment rights" was very common (77 percent in the NOS). However, these studies did not determine whether the presence of such policies signaled widespread employee participation in comprehensive programs of family-friendly policies or only token access to benefits for restricted categories of workers (Glass and Estes 1997:300). Certainly, the growing numbers of temporary and other contingent employees remained far less eligible for whatever company benefits their permanent coworkers enjoyed (Christensen 1998:118). The strong inverse correlation between organizational size and work/family programs indicated that many small businesses would not willingly extend generous assistance to their employees in the absence of governmental policies that mandated and underwrote the costs.

Theoretical explanations of increased flexible staffing arrangements stressed changing organizational requirements rather than worker preferences for more temporary, part-time, and contingent employment. Transaction cost analyses depicted company externalization of their employment functions to outside labor providers as a rational decision that maximized efficiency and reduced direct labor costs. Thus, hiring temps and independent contractors avoided administrative paperwork and fringe benefit costs, also enabling firms to discriminate legally in paying lower wages than received by regular full-time employees. Resource dependence arguments pointed to flexible staffing as an important mechanism for companies to manage uncertainties in their varying needs for labor. Institutionalization theories emphasized how growing availability of temp agencies and independent contractors providing high-quality labor services widely legitimated their use, regardless of any actual efficiency or cost reduction. Empirical evidence supporting these alternative theoretical explanations was mixed, reflecting a wide range of samples and complex measures (see the comprehensive review by Kalleberg, Reynolds and Marsden 2000). For example, three surveys using representative samples of diverse U.S. or British establishments uncovered multiple factors related to the greater reliance of different types of flexible staffing (Davis-Blake and Uzzi 1993; Uzzi and Barsness 1998; Kalleberg, Reynolds and Marsden 2000). Although the findings were generally consistent with organizational efforts to reduce costs and cope with labor market uncertainties, numerous other factors affected their adoption of flexible staffing: size and age, bureaucratization, labor-management relations, technology, firm governance, and workforce composition. Increased theoretical understanding of organizational decisions to externalize company employment await more refined indicators and analytical procedures to capture these complex processes.

The New Employment Contract

Some observers tag the growing corporate reliance on the labor market as a "new deal" in employment relationships (Conference Board 1996; Cappelli 1999; Osterman 1999). Figure 5.4 schematically portrays employer-employee relations under this new employment contract. Sharp organizational boundaries no longer insulate workers from the external labor market. Employees face stiff competition from contingent workers brought in for short-duration projects. Some lose their jobs from the outsourcing of various company functions to business service organizations. The formation of a joint venture typically reassigns some employees to the new organization, where they must establish working ties with managers detached by the venture partner. As FILMs are dismantled, long-term employees may be supplanted by more skillful mid-level entrants hired from outside rather than promoted from within. Given the heightened uncertainty about remaining with their firms, workers compulsively engage in informal networking outside the company, trolling continuously for information about possible job openings in other firms. Because corporations no longer assume that their employees will stay for the long haul, they are reluctant to invest substantially in upgrading employees' job skills. Consequently, to stay current with occupational developments, workers pay for their own training from such outside providers as community colleges, vocational-technical schools, and commercial training vendors.

Relationships inside the firm undergo similar transformations toward more market-like transactions. With bureaucratic hierarchies flattened and FILMs dismantled, fewer clearly marked job ladders and career paths are open to ambitious employees. Jobs become restructured around short-term projects, perhaps lasting less than a year. At the project's termination, team members must bid for reassignment to new projects or be kicked out of the company. Instead of orderly and predictable financial rewards for merely adequate job performances, contingent compensation requires exceptional achievements. Employees endure unremitting pressures to make extraordinary efforts, to "hustle" constantly so the ax will fall on someone else. This

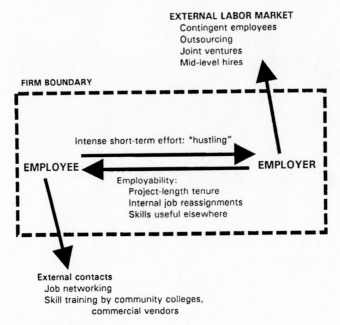

EXTERNAL LABOR MARKET
Contingent employees
Outsourcing
Joint ventures
Mid-level hires

FIRM BOUNDARY

Intense short-term effort: "hustling"

EMPLOYEE   EMPLOYER

Employability:
Project-length tenure
Internal job reassignments
Skills useful elsewhere

External contacts
Job networking
Skill training by community colleges,
commercial vendors

FIGURE 5.4   New Employment Contract

recipe can lead to worker stress, slacking, burnout, demoralization, lowered self-esteem, cynicism, alienation, and other bad stuff (see, e.g., Brockner 1990; Golembiewski, Boudreau and Munzenrider 1996). The weakened bonds between employers and employees rupture the supportive psychological connections sustained under the traditional employment contract. An atmosphere of anxiety, distrust, and back-stabbing spawned by continual downsizings and reorganizations renders employees less company-regarding and committed. Loyalty to oneself and one's career prospects pushes ahead of the company's interest. In place of long-term job security, firms offer only "job employability," learning experiences that might enable them to land subsequent project assignments, either with their current employer or at the next organization they move to. For example, many unskilled employees at Reproco, a business-service firm that subcontracted to perform photocopy work in facilities located on other companies' premises, believed that their interpersonal skills training for dealing with obnoxious customers would prove applicable "to their own small businesses, to different positions in other large corporations, and to higher level positions inside Reproco" (Smith 1996:177). The spirit of the new employment contract was succinctly captured by the response of Andy Grove, CEO of Intel Corporation, when asked what replaced the old idea that "if you worked hard, the company took care of you":

> The only thing you can rely on is your ability to end up where the invisible hand of the economy wants you to be. Our phrase for it is "owning your own employability." We started out originally planning careers like Big Brother. We gave it up; it was too complicated and puts too much of the onus on us. (Lancaster 1994:B1)

Unions traditionally provided some job protection for blue-collar workers from unilateral changes in employment conditions by companies undergoing downsizing and restructuring. They could win legally contracted obligations from firms such as job guarantees, compensation to laid-off union members, and retraining for displaced workers. However, shrinking U.S. union membership rolls, documented in Chapter 8, meant that fewer employees were protected under industrial relation systems stressing job security through collectively bargained labor contracts. Increasingly prevalent were nonunion labor relations models of participatory management that stressed employee involvement in task-related problem solving (Kochan, Katz and McKersie 1994:93–94; Bainbridge 1996). Higher labor mobility between employers undermined "the basic premise of most unions in America: that they can organize a stable set of employees whose careers centered around one employer" (Osterman 1996:170). The new employment contract encouraged white- and blue-collar workers alike to assume that their working careers would extend far beyond the current employer. Their best opportunity lay in acquiring the information and skills to compete as individuals in a constantly changing labor market.

High-Performance Workplace Practices

The trends toward flexible employment arrangements paradoxically accompanied new workplace practices, particularly in manufacturing industries, that placed heavier demands on employee commitments to their firms. These participative designs featured innovative work-flow structures, more cooperative labor-management authority relations, and human resource allocation and compensation systems rewarding group initiatives and individual creative efforts. The Saturn assembly plant exemplified GM's intention to stimulate superior performance by a thoroughgoing redesign of the hierarchical manufacturing workplace. The implementation of numerous technological innovations—particularly in computer-driven automobile, steel, and electronics factories—obligated core workers to acquire both technical and social skills needed to handle complex production machinery and cooperative work relations in the new plants. Beginning in the 1990s, proliferating Internet e-commerce technologies, especially in consumer retailing and business-to-business trade, put high premiums on speedy, quality service in hybrid clicks-and-mortar enterprises. Implementation of such high-performance workplace practices ran against the general tide eroding employee-employer attachments.

Rigid bureaucratic hierarchies, so efficient in churning out mass volumes of standardized products, yielded to sociotechnical systems capable of rapidly adjusting production and delivery schedules in response to shifting customer demands for small batches of high-quality goods and services. Developing these capacities necessitated coordinated worker and manager participation in self-directed groups empowered to solve work problems. Highly participatory initiatives presupposed far more autonomous, creative, and committed employees than firms could reasonably hire using flexible staffing arrangements capable of recruiting only workers with fleeting attachments to the organization. Some companies struggled to integrate a potentially combustible combination of flexible employment arrangements for contingent workers and high-performance practices covering the permanent employees. These incompatible organizational elements uneasily coexisted mainly by "playing different groups of workers off one another, eliciting participation from some by denying participative opportunities to others" (Smith 1997:332). The benefits of self-management enjoyed by high-performance core employees accrued at the expense of dispensable peripheral workers brought in or kicked out as company demands for labor fluctuated.

An implicit social psychological theory of empowerment and human motivation underlay many efforts to redesign workplace social structures (Liden and Arad 1996). Classic bureaucratic factories and offices imposed tightly controlled authority hierarchies on top of fine-grained divisions of labor, dominating deskilled blue-collar and clerical employees by allowing them little discretion in their daily work routines. Management made all important decisions, treating frontline workers as simple biological cogs grafted onto the well-tuned machines forming assembly lines and typing pools. But loss of personal control potentially creates worker alienation, a serious psychological withdrawal from their jobs and organizations displayed in such behavioral symptoms as stress, depression, drug and alcohol abuse, absenteeism, product destruction, and machinery sabotage (Hanisch and Hulin 1991). "Going postal" became the most violent manifestation of alienation from supervisors and coworkers.

In redistributing organizational power from management to lower-level individuals and groups, employers attempted to reduce or eliminate bureaucratic obstacles to raising employee morale and productivity. Jobs would be "enriched" to empower employees with sufficient resources and authority to plan and execute challenging, meaningful whole pieces of intrinsically motivating work (Hackman and Oldham 1976; Rousseau 1977). As employees acquired more control over a broader set of critical work activities, their levels of job satisfaction and commitment would increase and injurious behaviors should diminish. Firms could reap large productivity gains by empowering autonomous, self-directed, cross-functional work teams with responsibility for hiring, firing, training, scheduling, coordinating, evaluating, and rewarding the group members' contributions. "Arrangements that increase the autonomy of teams and their accountability for performance help generate the peer pressure that drives individuals to sacrifice for the team" (Cappelli 1999:218). The emotional bonds forged among team members could help to reclaim some of the corporate loyalties lost when firms shifted toward a more market-based employment contract. Ultimately, heightened employee morale generated through implementation of genuinely participatory work practices might boost both individual and organizational performances to levels unattainable in traditional bureaucratic factories and offices.

At the core of the new workplace designs were innovative management methods, work structures, human resource systems, and labor relations substituting for bureaucratic controls. Among several terms, analysts labeled these work practices: "flexible production" (Piore and Sabel 1984), "new plant revolution" (Lawler 1978), "participatory management" (Drago and Wooden 1991), "high involvement organizations" (Lawler 1992), "transformed work systems" (Applebaum and Batt 1994), and "high performance work organizations" (Osterman 1994a). The most frequently mentioned high-performance work practices included just-in-time inventory systems and quality circles, autonomous or self-managed work teams, flat authority hierarchies, cross-training and job rotation, redesigned physical layouts of plants and offices, information technologies, incentive- or contingent-compensation systems, and a total quality management ideology. A key research question was whether these allegedly high-performance practices constituted a coherent system or could be adopted without regard to their compatibility with one another and with traditional organizational routines. Before examining evidence on the limited penetration of various high-performance work practices into U.S. workplaces, the following subsections describe these innovations in greater detail.

JIT and Quality Circles

Several U.S. workplace innovations of the 1970s and 1980s adapted Japanese management practices that seemed to hold the secret to that nation's successful transformation from shattered war casualty to leading industrial nation. For example, just-in-time (JIT) inventory practices, perfected in Toyota's auto assembly plants, minimized the volume of parts in stock, reduced idle time, and cut waste while improving output quality. By relying on outside suppliers to deliver parts to the factory gate precisely when needed, JIT ideally enabled factories to retool quickly into new special-product lines. A *kanban* or "signal" system for synchronized scheduling used various visual cues—primarily cards but also lights, banners, and flags—to control the efficient flow of materials through the plant doors and around workstations (Monden 1993:6–7). JIT practices required heightened employee vigilance in planning, tracking, and correcting delivery problems and detecting defects throughout the production cycle using such information evaluation techniques as statistical process control (see the subsection on informational technologies below).

Another Japanese innovation, the quality circle (QC), had a brief period of faddish popularity in the United States (R. Cole 1999:93–96). By one estimate, more than 90 percent of Fortune 500 companies had adopted some type of QC program by the peak of the craze in the mid-1980s (Lawler and Mohrman 1985). A quality circle is a group of about a dozen frontline employees and managers from the same work area who come together regularly to discuss problems affecting the group's performance. Facilitated by a supervisory specialist, QC programs typically met voluntarily for about four hours a month, either on company time or after scheduled work. QC members received training in group problem-solving techniques, then collaborated in formulating the circle's recommendations to higher management for solving quality and productivity problems. These interactive suggestion boxes typically produced proposals for saving money by reducing costs while improving the quality of employees' work lives.

As with many business fads appearing so promising when first publicized by professional business gurus, the radiant prospects of quality circles soon tarnished. Many QC programs enabled upper management to diffuse worker resistance by only pretending to show interest in workers' grievances and ideas about running the company. Because QCs "have no decision-making power, managers don't have to give up any control or prerogatives. Also, because they are parallel to the organization's structure, top management can easily eliminate them if they become troublesome" (Lawler and Mohrman 1985:66). With none of their own time or identity invested in QC efforts, company executives could simply approve but not implement the recommendations. Without a serious corporate commitment to genuine employee participation in workplace decisions, many programs deteriorated into superficial, quick-fix gimmicks that were swiftly abandoned once initial enthusiasm faded. The damage to management credibility and worker morale from transparent QC manipulation delayed or prevented some firms from developing more genuine participatory workplace practices.

Work Teams

Work teams, like those implemented at Saturn's Spring Hill plant, transformed traditional hierarchical modes of authority and control. A team approach creates an identifiable, mutually accountable membership group that is assigned a meaningful whole piece of work, enjoys great discretion in determining how best to accomplish its objectives, and receives feedback from the organization about its collective performance. Optimal team size depends on the particular technological requirements for providing a product or service, although few teams seem to exceed 10 members (Katzenbach and Smith 1993:45). Membership typically includes every employee responsible for the transformation of a specific product or service. Manufacturing teams typically handle a complete production segment, such as installing the entire electrical system or all the upholstery in a car. Work teams in service-sector organizations deliver a full range of services to particular customers, for example, designing and carrying out multimedia advertising campaigns for a corporate client or an electoral candidate. A team's customer might be an end-use purchaser outside the organizational boundary or another work-unit inside the company, for example, the auto paint shop that receives the stamping team's door panels for painting. The Swedish automaker Volvo's Uddevalla assembly plant was renowned for its production teams that communicated through car dealers with customers placing orders for specific new vehicles (Berggren 1992). Instead of fragmented work paced by a moving assembly line, with hundreds of worker-bees endlessly tweaking the same nuts and bolts, each 10-person team would assemble an entire car in two stages. Unfortunately, the Uddevalla plant produced vehicles that were too expensive compared to conventional assembly methods (pp. 164–165), so Volvo ultimately terminated its "noble experiment" in craft-like team production.

Many analysts described work teams as "self-managed" because they possessed authority, responsibility, and resources for making and implementing all important decisions about the group's activities. High-performance organizations were characterized by very flat authority structures, which abolished several layers of management including the authoritative foreman's intense supervisory role. Very broad spans of control pushed substantial authority from middle managers down to the lowest production level, blurring the customary distinction between "head work" and "hand work." Support staff personnel were reassigned from separate organizational units to work teams where their technical skills could directly support team missions. Highly autonomous teams enjoyed discretion to hire and fire their own members, schedule work assignments, set production targets, evaluate quality standards, control budgets and databases, discipline and reward member performances, deal directly with customers and suppliers—in short, to perform most small business functions while embedded within a larger organizational context.

Skills Training

Cross-training team members in a variety of job skills was critical to producing flexible staffing, group ownership, and collective pride in the team's output (Stevens and Yarish 1999). Training methods ranged from classroom lecture and group discussion to role-playing and simulation, videotape, self-assessment, and computer-assisted instruction (pp. 145–150). Extensive cross-training enabled individuals to learn how to perform several technical tasks for which the entire team was responsible. As machinery-maintenance and customer-contact skills diffused within the group, the need for close managerial supervision declined. When an employee left the team, disruptions and delays in finding, hiring, and integrating a replacement worker would be minimized if other team members could immediately pick up the vacated tasks. Frequent job rotation also helped to break down the fine-grained division of labor in traditional hierarchies that prevented employees from developing broader organizational perspectives and enlarged capacities for continuous, innovative problem solving. For example, the Phelps Dodge Corporation, a manufacturer of copper and copper-related products, retrained its furnace workers into a team whose members rotated among many relatively narrow jobs such as ladler, tapper, bricklayer, water tender, inspector, control room operator, and so forth. From a firm's perspective, its investments in cross-training pay off with savings from higher worker motivation, more flexible staffing, and increased problem-solving capacity:

> With an enlarged perspective on the work they do, team members are now in a position to recognize connections that were either viewed as inconsequential before or simply unnoticed. This insight then serves to fuel the creative and innovative problem solving that drives the organization toward genuine continuous improvement and creative breakthroughs. Occasionally, these insights lead to innovations that result in cost savings or improvements worth millions of dollars. More often than not, however, the results are of less heroic nature, such as when a few thousand dollars are saved because a team figures out how to modify a furnace so that it can use an ordinary spark plug rather than an expensive specialized one, or when labor and overtime costs are reduced as staffing flexibility and process streamlining are used to increase productivity. Though mundane, such minor daily advances carry a tremendous cumulative weight when aggregated over time and across enough teams (Stevens and Yarish 1999:134)

At least as important as training in task-related technical skills were the interpersonal and decision-making competencies that allowed team members to function as an integrated social group. These skills included "risk taking, helpful criticism, objectivity, active listening, giving the benefit of the doubt, and recognizing the interests and achievements of others" (Katzenbach and Smith 1993:48). Quality circles typically provided valuable instruction in group dynamics but wasted these skills because they lacked authority to transfer learning onto the shop floor and office suite. In contrast, high-performance organizations integrated teams into the firm's daily production processes where their collective decision-making and interpersonal skills contributed directly to smoother work performance. Several unionized manufacturing firms negotiated joint labor-management programs to fund and operate training in vocational skills, safety and health knowledge, communication and personal development, and career counseling for displaced workers (Ferman et al. 1991). Progressive companies recognized a self-interested responsibility to provide recurrent upgrading of employees work skills throughout their careers.

Workplace Layouts

Obsessions with finding the most efficient shop layouts and product flows originated among nineteenth-century industrial engineers. They achieved an apotheosis in Frederick Taylor's "scientific management" method of directly measuring workers' time-and-motion activities to discover how best to maximize labor efficiency (Kanigel 1997). Technical control systems in mass production factories involved the integration of people and equipment into sociotechnical systems: "designing machinery and planning the flow of work to minimize the problem of transforming labor power into labor as well as to maximize the purely physically based possibilities for achieving efficiencies" (Edwards 1979:111–129). The continuous-flow production processes in meat packing disassembly and Fordist auto assembly lines demonstrated that inefficient employee behaviors could be corrected by compelling workers to remain at specific posts where managers could easily monitor and control their repetitive actions. Assembly workers bore heavy psychological and physical burdens in boredom, alienation, and stress injuries. The advent of numerical control machinery (operated by preprogrammed tapes), followed by mini- and microcomputers, merely strengthened management's sociotechnical dominance in the workplace. Japanese plant managers revitalized the technical control approach by insisting that meticulous attention to workplace processes would improve quality, reduce waste, and boost worker morale (Shingo 1987; Monden 1993). The New United Motor Manufacturing Inc. (NUMMI), a Toyota-General Motors joint venture in Fremont, California, demonstrated that an innovative time-and-motion factory regime, implemented by U.S. workers using existing plant and equipment, could transform a troubled loser into a higher achiever (Adler 1993).

In contrast to regimented production layouts under technical control, the employee participation ethos in high-performance organizations favored shop and office floor arrangements that fostered shared responsibility for a whole piece of production:

> Extensive layout changes may be needed in an organization to create work teams. For example, machinery will need to be grouped by product rather than by process. Instead of putting all similar equipment together, an organization must create work cells in which all the equipment that is necessary to produce a particular product is located together. (Lawler 1991:91)

The prevailing high-performance ideology was egalitarian, replacing hierarchical authority and its perks with emphases on individual and group contributions to organizational success through knowledge and expertise. Barriers to effective team communication, such as office walls and cubicles, were torn down. Open-area "bull pens" encouraged direct access and collaboration between teams and upper management. High-performance organizations abolished traditional symbols of the status gap between managers and workers, such as different dress codes, parking lots, washrooms, cafeterias, and recreational areas.

Information Technologies

The proliferation of information technologies (IT) empowered high-performance organizations with new resources for boosting firm and individual productivity. Statistical process control (SPC)—widely deployed in the complex production systems of aerospace, petrochemical, and pharmaceutical industries—used probability methods to monitor the variability of production processes to make sure that outputs stayed within preset upper and lower limits (Williams 1996:286). Control charts and sampling techniques enabled workers to reduce or eliminate defective products and achieve high output yields, minimizing the time needed to satisfy customer orders.

By giving employees greater accessibility to corporate data, organizational IT systems opened up new opportunities for workers to participate in company decisions on a more equal footing with management. Employees could communicate with one another about technical problems and locate expert advisors, possibly among overseas personnel, avoiding a drawn-out approval process by the hierarchical chain of command. Timely access to production and financial databases through company intranets conferred greater flexibility on work teams to detect and quickly correct quality errors, to ramp output up or down to match fickle consumer demand, to plan and adjust work schedules, and to change production and delivery operations to more cost-efficient procedures. Internet, fax, and e-mail links permitted design and production units to interact directly with external suppliers and customers, improving deliveries of products and services better fitted to changing market conditions. Information technologies gave birth to "virtual" factories and retail stores, such as airplane manufacturer AeroTech Service Group and online bookseller Amazon.com. These organizations owned few physical assets and employed few workers but coordinated the made-to-order assembly and/or sale of goods and services produced by networks of other companies (Upton and McAfee 1996; Streitfeld 1998). Chapter 6 explores the rise of virtual companies and other forms of networked organizations sustained by multimedia technologies that abolished previous temporal and spatial barriers.

The creation of computer-assisted design and manufacturing programs (CAD/CAM) vastly accelerated production cycles, compressing the time between project planning and delivery of finished products and services. For example, Boeing used a computerized digital design system, running on the world's largest mainframe installation, to simulate three-dimensional alignments among the 4 million parts in its 777 widebody airliner (Sabbagh 1996). The 777 program cut errors and rework by more than half, bypassing the traditional construction of costly and time-consuming physical mock-ups. It achieved an overall fit of just 0.023 of an inch away from perfect alignment (the width of a playing card), compared to previous aircraft models lining up within one-half inch. Boeing formed 238 design/build teams—comprising engineers, designers, tool makers, finance specialists, manufacturing representatives, suppliers, and customers—to work concurrently on every component and system. However, by themselves computer technologies couldn't guarantee organizational flexibility, as a study of 61 North American paper manufacturing plants revealed (Upton 1995). The length of time needed to make production line changeovers to different paper "grades" (specific weights and pulps) varied enormously, from one minute to four hours. Adjustment speed was uncorrelated with the plants' investments in computer-integrated manufacturing equipment versus reliance on manual changeover teams. Instead, the crucial factors explaining operations flexibility were "determined primarily by a plant's operators and the extent to which managers cultivate, measure, and communicate with them" (Upton 1995:75). The primary lesson was that technical panaceas seldom succeeded without employees who possessed both the technical training and interpersonal skills to adapt new machinery and computer programs to organizational operations. Like every other tool, computers proved only as effective as their human users' abilities to manipulate them creatively.

Total Quality Management

A corporate social movement to implement total quality management (TQM) principles spread rapidly among U.S. high-performance organizations at the end of the twentieth century. Ironically, the quality ideology, pioneered after World War II by U.S. management gurus W. Edwards Deming (1986) and Joseph Juran (1988), was rejected by U.S. mass production firms. American companies reimported the approach only after Japanese corporations demonstrated that TQM principles (*kaizen*, or continuous improvement) enabled them to compete successfully against traditional mass production firms that sacrificed quality output for low-cost goods and services (Ishikawa 1985). Quality improvement efforts gained immense institutional legitimacy and prestige when the business community and the federal government jointly created the Malcolm Baldrige National Quality Award in 1987 to promote the diffusion of innovative best-practices. The award program strongly encouraged nominees to compare their quality programs against other organizations' practices as "benchmarks." The Baldrige guidelines, constantly updated to keep abreast of current developments, were commonly used by top management of larger firms "to assess their company to see where they stood and to target weak areas they uncovered for improvement" (R. Cole 1999:148). Quality diffusion at the international level, promoted by the ISO 9000 standards formulated at Geneva in 1987, accelerated after unification of the European Community markets in the 1990s.

TQM embodied a management philosophy that institutionalized continuous business improvement in product or service quality, defined as meeting or exceeding customer expectations in the market. TQM advocates made several normative assumptions about the best way to combine quality criteria, workplace processes, employees, senior managers, suppliers, and customers to boost organizational quality performance. Given the wide diversity of approaches masquerading under the TQM label (see articles in R. Cole 1995; Cole and Scott 2000), developing a comprehensive and coherent catalog of quality criteria is impracticable. However, Richard Hackman and Ruth Wageman (1995:310–311) summarized four core assumptions common to most TQM programs:

- The costs of poor quality to a firm are much higher than the costs of developing processes to produce high-quality goods and services.
- Employees naturally care about the quality of their work and will take initiatives to improve it, if they have adequate tools and training and if management pays attention to their ideas and removes organizational systems that create employee fear.
- Organizations are systems of highly interdependent parts, whose central problems invariably cross traditional functional lines.
- Hence, "the quality improvement process must begin with management's own commitment to total quality" (p. 311).

The decision to implement a TQM program was a corporate strategy issue, not simply an operational quick-fix or top-down initiative conceived and supervised by senior management (Hill 1991). Many TQM programs were built around four principles for changing organizational structures and processes to improve quality output (Hackman and Wageman 1995:311–312): (1) Management must train and coach employees to assess, analyze, and improve work processes, (2) the frontline workers must analyze and control the root causes of variability in their output quality, (3) "management by fact" calls for systematically collecting and analyzing data at every point in a problem-solving cycle, and (4) all organizational participants must commit to a never-ending quest for quality improvement by learning more about the work they do. To integrate these TQM principles into the organization's structures and routines, firms should engage in several interventions, both inside and outside the organization (pp.312–315). They must learn what customers want and provide products and services meeting their requirements. Partnerships with suppliers should be formed on the basis of quality rather than solely on price. Cross-functional worker teams including participants from all important stakeholder departments should diagnose and solve quality problems. A wide variety of statistical diagnostic tools—control charts, "Pareto analysis" (a method for quantifying sources of quality problems), and cost-of-quality analyses—should be applied "to monitor performance and to identify points of high leverage for performance improvements" (p. 313). Finally, team effectiveness could be enhanced by applying such process-management methods as flow charts, brainstorming, and cause-and-effect diagrams.

Incentive Pay

Traditional organizations rewarded workers primarily through base pay determined by three factors: "the specific job, the need to maintain a certain level of pay equity among employees in the organization, and the need to pay salaries that were competitive with those paid by other employers in the marketplace, industry, or region" (Flannery, Hofrichter and Platten 1996: 83). Pay increases for most workers occurred only through promotions to higher-ranked jobs, cost-of-living adjustments to match inflation, and merit raises. Because employees came to expect annual merit jumps, raises became entitlements rather than rewards pegged to real improvement in individual or organizational achievements. High-performance organizations used several innovative incentive- or contingent-compensation strategies under such labels as gain sharing, win sharing, profit sharing, lump-sum awards, skill-based pay, and team-based pay (Lawler 1991; Schuster and Zingheim 1992; Flannery, Hofrichter and Platten 1996). A common feature of these compensation schemes was to tie variable rewards to individual worker and team performances that added value to the organization. Gain-sharing and profit-sharing plans redistributed some portion of company earnings according to organizational productivity, cost savings, and quality improvements.

By compensating people for the depth and diversity of the new skills they acquired and used, skill-based pay strategies fit well into the high-performance workplace emphasis on flat authority hierarchies, cross-training, and job rotation. Employers could more quickly adjust their workforces to rapid technological changes by rewarding workers for acquiring broader skills and knowledge necessary to deal with these developments. Employees' demonstrable abilities, rather than their job titles, determined their paychecks. For example, hospitals redesigning patient treatment into managed care systems would boost the wages of aides for learning to perform routine technical work, such as drawing blood and administering EKGs, tasks previously handled only by registered nurses (Flannery, Hofrichter and Platten 1996:88). Team-based pay could nurture mutual support and group cooperation, but it might breed ruinous resentment if some members felt they were not adequately compensated for making significantly larger contributions than other members to their team's results. Incentive-based pay differentials that grew too large could have counterproductive impacts on morale. Finding a proper balance between individual and group rewards was critical to designing team-based compensation systems that motivated collective performance rather than goaded employees into self-serving efforts. When carefully designed to align employee and organizational interests, incentive-pay schemes could foster more knowledgeable, accountable, and committed workforces amenable to the continuous learning and skill improvement essential for sustaining flexible, high-performance organizations.

Penetration Problems

By the early 1990s, high-performance and flexible work components still had not penetrated very far into most U.S. workplaces. Two national surveys of diverse workplaces examined the adoption of various practices. The 1992 National Establishment Survey (NES) asked informants whether they had adopted four work practices for workers in the "core" job family. A core job was defined as "the largest group of nonsupervisory workers directly involved in making the product or providing the service at that location" (Osterman 1994a:175). The most common practice was self-directed work teams, present in 55 percent of the establishments, although more than half the core workers participated in work teams in only 41 percent of the workplaces. The extent of penetration of the other work practices was as follows: job rotation 43 percent at any level of penetration, 27 percent with half or more of core workers involved; quality circles 41 and 27 percent, respectively; and total quality management programs 34 and 25 percent. Among manufacturing plants, penetration levels were slightly lower for work teams but a bit higher for the other three practices. Just 9 percent of all establishments simultaneously deployed three of the four work practices for at least half their core workers, and 36 percent adopted none of them (for manufacturing plants, the figures were 12 and 33 percent, respectively). No predominant cluster of practices occurred among the remaining workplaces, indicating that most employers implemented them in random combinations rather than as a coherent package of complementary routines. Osterman concluded that, despite "a veritable explosion of workplace innovations over the past few years ... the majority of workers—by some estimations the vast majority—work without these innovations under traditional arrangements" (Cappelli et al. 1997:99). Whether these practices might diffuse further depended on changing management perceptions of their contributions to overall organizational performance.

I reached a similar conclusion about the limited penetration of high-performance work practices from previously unpublished analyses of the 1997 National Organizations Survey (NOS). Although the NOS included workplaces of all sizes, I selected only the 563 establishments with 50 or more employees for direct comparison with Osterman's NES data. (The NOS establishments were sampled proportional to workplace size, so the descriptive statistics reported next reflect proportions of the U.S. labor force employed in workplaces with the specific practices.) The NOS asked informants whether their establishment involved its core workers in four work practices: cross-training, team work, job rotation, and statistical process control (SPC). Other questions asked whether core workers participated in three types of incentive-pay plans: profit-sharing or bonus programs, group incentives such as gain sharing, and pay for learning new skills. As shown in Figure 5.5, only two high-performance practices—cross-training and team work—were adopted by more than half the workplaces. And only cross-training covered at least half the core workers in the majority of establishments. In 80 percent of the workplaces, a committee of managers and employees met regularly to discuss quality issues, but the NOS did not measure the extent of core worker participation in this TQM activity. A bare majority (51 percent) of workplaces offered at least one of the three incentive-pay schemes to the majority of their core workers. When combinations of the four work practices plus at least one incentive-pay plan are assessed, 61 percent of large U.S. establishments adopted three or more high-performance practices. But only 35 percent of the workplaces involved the majority of their core employees in this many activities.

To explain why some NES establishments adopted any of the four flexible work practices for more than half their core workers and the total number of practices they adopted, Osterman (1994a) estimated multivariate equations using independent variables from various theoretical approaches. He found several factors associated with a greater likelihood of adopting

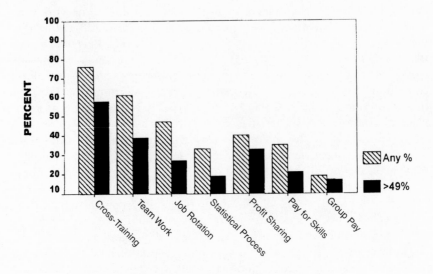

HIGH PERFORMANCE PRACTICE

FIGURE 5.5   High-Performance Practices
SOURCE: National Organizations Survey (1997)

high-performance practices: (1) a work/family "philosophy about how appropriate it is to help increase the well being of employees with respect to their personal or family situations," (2) selling in a market with international competition, (3) using a production process requiring high employee skill levels, (4) following a "high-road" corporate strategy (emphasizing service, quality, and product variety rather than low cost), (5) being a branch or plant of a larger parent organization, and (6) small employee size. Adoption was unrelated to establishment age, unionization, or pressure to produce short-term profits at the expense of long-term investments. Other analyses suggested that flexible work systems were consistent with such human resource practices as innovative pay schemes, extensive training, and efforts to induce greater commitment on the part of the labor force (Osterman 1994a:186). By contrast, neither employment security nor seniority-versus-merit promotion policies were important in predicting whether firms adopted the four flexible work practices.

I performed similar analyses of data from all 1,002 establishments sampled by the 1997 NOS. These results are not directly comparable to Osterman's because I included the full range of establishment sizes, using some different independent variables, and the two dependent measures excluded quality circles but included statistical process control and incentive-pay as two of the five high-performance practices. The two multivariate equations reported in

Table 5.1 use the same 13 predictors or independent variables but two different dependent variables measuring the penetration of high-performance practices. The logistic regression coefficients in the first column show which variables significantly predicted whether an establishment adopted *any* of the five
high-performance practices for half or more of its core workers. The ordered
probit coefficients in the second column indicate which variables significantly
predict how many high-performance practices (between 0 and 5) an establishment was likely to adopt. In both equations, a positive sign for a coefficient indicates that organizations with a particular characteristic were more
likely to adopt high-performance practices, and a negative sign means that an
independent variable was associated with nonadoption.

TABLE 5.1   Multivariate Analyses of Five High-Performance Workplace Practices
Adopted for 50 Percent or More of Establishment Core Employees

Independent Variable	*Logistic Regression: Any Practice*	*Ordered Probit: No. of Practices*
Constant	.18	-.27
Number of Employees (ln)	-.19**	-.06**
Parent Organization	.02	-.04
Foreign Competition	.15	.11*
Family-Friendly Work Scheduling	.31*	.11**
Employability HR Strategy	.36	.22**
Manufacturing Industry	.92**	.41***
Establishment Age (ln)	-.01	-.05
Core Worker Union	-.36*	-.15**
For-Profit Sector	.58*	.24*
Tight Core Labor Market	-.05	.06*
Amount of Market Competition	-.34**	-.13**
Core Worker FILM	.58***	.27***
Formalization	.11	.09**
Log Likelihood	-271.0	-1,096.4
Model Chi-Square	46.2	97.4
N	722	722

Table Notes:
   *   p < .05
  **   p < .01
 ***   p < .001
SOURCE: National Organizations Survey (1997)

Some NOS results in Table 5.1 agreed with Osterman's findings from the NES. Establishments were more likely to adopt any or multiple high-performance practices if they were smaller (natural logarithm of total number of employees), faced competition from foreign organizations; permitted family-friendly work scheduling (child day care services, paid parental leave, and flexible work hours), and pursued an "employability" human resources strategy (offering employees "training and skills that will help them wherever they may work"). Organizational age had no effect, and the positive sign for manufacturing industry was consistent with the NES finding that establishments whose production process required higher worker skills more often adopted innovative work practices. However, being a branch or establishment of a larger parent organization had no effect in the NOS, and the presence of a labor union for core employees significantly decreased high-performance practice adoptions.

Several additional NOS predictors reveal other significant influences: location in the for-profit rather than the nonprofit and public sectors; a tighter external labor market for hiring core employees; less competition in the organization's main market or service area; a more highly developed core-worker firm internal labor market; and a highly developed formalized personnel system, as measured by rules covering seven topics, such as written job descriptions and performance evaluations. The latter two effects indicate that high-performance work practices were neither alternatives to conventional bureaucracy nor incompatible with its survival. Indeed, establishments deploying elaborate bureaucratic personnel systems seemed more prone to implement innovative work practices than were workplaces with absent or weakly developed FILMs and formalization.

Automotive Lean Production

Despite the limited diffusion of high-performance work practices, several industries in the manufacturing sector adopted these techniques because they appeared to offer competitive advantages. The worldwide automobile assembly industry was probably the most thoroughly investigated site of high-performance activity. A seminal investigation of 62 Japanese, European, and U.S. factories, *The Machine That Changed the World* (Womack, Jones and Roos 1990), coined the "lean production" concept to describe the combinations of flexible manufacturing methods and employee relations that enabled Japanese automakers to outperform companies using mass production methods. Traditional auto assembly plants relied on extensive buffers such as high inventories, expansive work spaces, large repair areas, and excess workers to cover absentees. Employees produced batches of subassemblies by "working ahead" to build up stocks that were uncoordinated with activities occurring on the main assembly line. As pioneered by Toyota, lean production involved "eliminating unnecessary steps, aligning all steps in an activity in a continuous flow, recombining labor into cross-functional teams dedicated to that activity, and continually striving for improvement" (Womack and Jones 1994:93). Using a robust just-in-time approach, parts were either delivered by external suppliers or produced on-site just in time to be used on subassembly lines that were tightly integrated with the main assembly line. Subassemblies built just in time were installed in vehicles continuously moving on a conveyor through the shop. Workers were supposed to detect and correct defects immediately so they wouldn't be passed along to the next workstation. For example, any employee who spotted a defective part could pull an "andon cord" to halt the line and summon help.

Lean production advocates referred to it as a flexible work system, which clearly embraced several of the familiar high-performance work practices described in the preceding sections. Its flexibility consisted of the capacity to change product lines rapidly while synchronizing adjustments in human resources to maintain a continuous flow of products under fluctuating demand levels. Lean production obtained these results through "the absence of restrictive rules on work (job classifications), the development of multi-functional workers, job rotation, the ability to widen or narrow the range of jobs done by each worker, the ability to alter workforce size, and the right to assign overtime work" (Rinehart, Huxley and Robertson 1997:26–27). Other high-performance elements in lean production systems included recurrent training for both new hires and experienced workers, off-line employee-involvement or problem-solving groups, suggestion programs, and contingent compensation (MacDuffie and Pil 1997).

The perceived competitive advantages of lean production conferred great legitimacy on this system and promoted its gradual displacement of the traditional mass production model. However, a comparison among 82 auto plants around the world found persistent regional differences in the implementation of high-performance work practices in the early 1990s (MacDuffie and Pil 1997). For example, Korean-owned plants in Korea and Japanese-owned plants in both Japan and North America scored more than twice as high as U.S.-owned plants in North America on a work systems index measuring worker-involvement components. European-owned auto plants in Europe as well as American and Japanese transplants in Europe fell in between. The general trend converged toward high-involvement work and human resource practices, with Australian and European plants the most enthusiastic adopters. However, the Big Three U.S. automakers' implementation of flexible work designs "clearly diverges substantially from the degree of implementation in other regions" (p. 38). Indeed, many GM, Ford, and Chrysler plants either maintained or reverted to more traditional production practices after experimenting with lean production. As noted at the beginning of this chapter, GM's old car divisions failed to adopt Saturn's innovative workplace designs.

High-Performance Impacts

Gains in productivity and quality achieved through lean production could be spectacular. Compared to traditional auto assembly factories using unskilled workers in fragmented labor, lean production plants had 47 percent better quality output, as measured by defects per vehicle assembled, and 43 percent greater productivity, as measured by hours required to assemble a vehicle (Womack, Jones and Roos 1990). The researchers urged that, as the single best way to organize automobile production or any manufacturing activity, "the whole world should adopt [lean production] as quickly as possible" (p. 225). The carefully documented NUMMI case demonstrated that large gains could be achieved with an American workforce (Adler 1993). Absenteeism fell from 20–25 percent to 3–4 percent, and employee grievances dropped from 5,000–7,000 complaints over the three years prior to conversion to just 100 in the next 18 months. NUMMI produced higher-quality products with fewer labor hours than other GM plants, and its workers were nearly as productive as Toyota's prototype plant in Japan (Pfeffer 1994:71–72; Koike 1998).

Firms in other industries that implemented high-performance sociotechnical systems often experienced robust productivity gains (for a detailed review, see Ichniowski et al. 1996). Findings from several research projects in the 1990s illustrate the diversity of organizations studied and performance measured:

- Human resource managers at 30 of 54 existing U.S. steel minimills provided data on employee turnover and manufacturing performance (Arthur 1994). Plants that used a "commitment" HR system were more efficient than plants with a traditional "control" HR system: They needed fewer labor hours to produce a ton of steel, had lower scrap rates (tons of raw steel melted to produce a ton of finished product), and lower rates of employees leaving either voluntarily or involuntarily. A study of 36 of the 60 U.S. steel finishing lines measured performance as monthly "uptime," the percentage of scheduled operating time that a line actually ran (Ichniowski, Shaw and Prennushi 1997). Finishing lines that adopted seven innovative human resources management (HRM) practices—including work teams, incentive compensation, job rotation, and skills training—had significantly greater uptimes than organizations with fewer or none of those practices. Firms achieved "the largest gains in productivity by adopting clusters of complementary practices, and benefit little from making 'marginal' changes in any one HRM practice" (p. 295).
- A 1991 cross-sectional survey of 816 firms representing all major industries provided data to examine the relationship between high-

performance work practices and three firm-level performance indicators (Huselid 1995). Controlling for various organizational and industrial characteristics, the greater the corporate investment in high-performance work practices, the lower the employee turnover rates, the larger the sales per employee, and the higher the corporate financial performance. The estimated magnitudes of these human resources effects were substantial: "A one-standard-deviation increase in such practices is associated with a relative 7.05 percent decrease in turnover, and, on a per employee basis, $27,044 more in sales and $18,641 and $3,814 more in market value and profits, respectively" (p. 667). Analyses of the 218 firms providing data for 1991 and 1993, which corrected for biases due to measurement errors, yielded a slightly smaller estimated market value increase of $15,000 per employee (Huselid and Becker 1996).

- Between 1988 and 1992 only a small percentage of workplaces in the apparel manufacturing industry switched from a traditional bundle assembly system to modular production, which required that teams of 5 to 30 cross-trained operators work together to produce part or all of a garment, and installed a complementary information system linking apparel suppliers with retail customers (Dunlop and Weil 1996). But the business units adopting both processes reduced their lead times (time between ordering fabrics and shipping finished products) by more than three weeks and significantly increased their operating profits by one-third.

- A survey of 973 plants in 21 industries that manufactured diverse metal products (including aircraft engines, elevators, machine tools, precision instruments) estimated the effects of three types of work systems on production hours per unit of output (Kelley 1996). "Participative bureaucracies" combined bureaucratic job formalization and standardized work methods with such high-performance practices as joint labor-management problem-solving committees, autonomous work-group meetings, employer-provided technical classes, and employee stock ownership plans. Their effects varied with type of plant. Branches of multi-establishment firms using this work system derived significant productivity advantages compared to both traditional craft apprenticeship systems and union/seniority-based bureaucracies. However, among single-plant firms, those with internal promotion ladders associated with union work rules and a seniority system fared best.

- A multi-industry study of 108 firms implementing TQM programs between 1981 and 1991 concluded that firms with more advanced TQM attained higher stock returns and long-term financial performance indicators (such as net income to sales and operating income to assets) than did firms with less advanced TQM (Easton and Jarrell 1998).

- A study of 202 customer service and sales employees of a large, unionized regional Bell telephone operating company found that participants in self-managed teams reported higher self-rated service quality and achieved a 9 percent increase in sales per employee compared to traditional mass production (Batt 1999). A further 17 percent boost in sales resulted from self-managed teams using advanced information systems to automate routine tasks and monitor employee performance. However, time spent in TQM meetings produced no quality or sales improvements.

Given such apparent strong links between high-performance work practices and improved organizational efficacy, researchers pondered the reasons for the limited spread of these innovations. "If systems of innovative work practices stimulate productivity, quality, and other dimensions of business performance, why have they not diffused more widely through the economy?" (Ichniowski et al. 1996:325). "Why don't organizations change, even when confronted with fairly convincing evidence concerning the efficacy of alternative management methods and processes?" (Pfeffer 1996:34). Several organization theories implicate diverse socioeconomic obstacles and opportunities for adoption and implementation of innovations. Organizational ecology emphasizes how inertia keeps many older firms locked into traditional behavioral patterns, making nearly impossible their radical conversion into something completely different. Hence, workplace innovations will more likely succeed by launching new organizations on greenfield sites, as General Motors did with its Saturn Corporation. If bloated older firms fail more often in competition against lean-and-mean youngsters, demographic replacement should eventually transform an industry's population into predominantly high-performance organizations.

Institutional theory points to substantial legitimation barriers that can impede the spread of new designs deemed too risky or controversial by important opinion leaders in an industry or sector. Without the active advocacy of prominent actors to vouch for the benefits of untried practices, members of an organization field tend to view an innovation more skeptically and embrace it more slowly. Fields are more susceptible to management fads and fashions when numerous corporate consultants, training programs, accreditation agencies, and governmental regulators spread the gospel to a credulous audience. Organizational imitation lies behind many recurrent crazes over QC, TQM, and similar human resource management practices that confer on their adopters "the value of maintaining an appearance of rationality and remaining at the forefront of managerial thought" (Zbaracki 1998:603). A diffusion process can also work in reverse, when word of mouth from dismayed fans panics prospective enthusiasts into deserting a rapidly sinking tub.

Transaction cost economists stress the prohibitively high costs in many industries of obtaining and verifying information about the productivity gains of innovators, investing in new production technologies, retraining older employees to implement the new work techniques, and suffering inevitable incompetence during a lengthy break-in period until high-performance practices pay back the launch costs. Many cost-benefit calculations favor sticking with known routines in the absence of clearly compelling evidence of economic gains from risky innovations. Firms in industries that face low barriers to new-firm entry, and hence fierce competitive struggles for organizational survival, are most inclined to scrap their inefficient production practices (Williamson 1994:87).

The resource dependence and power perspectives suggest that vested political interests in and around organizations can retard or accelerate adoption of high-performance practices. Shareholders typically prefer quick fixes to the bottom line by downsizing, outsourcing, and spinning off profit-eating units, rather than patient investments in work designs promising illusive profits. In most companies, the human resource professionals lack sufficient status and clout to promote employee participation schemes against opposition from production and finance personnel who generally control the dominant coalition. Unionized workers may feel threatened by loss of union control over job classifications and work assignments entailed in abolishing their firm's traditional bureaucracy (note the Saturn case again). Their resistance may be overcome by selling the new practices as the only alternative to a company's death at the hands of low-cost foreign competitors.

Finally, organizational network explanations highlight how interconnections among producers, suppliers, and customers in an field serve as barriers to simultaneously adopting complementary work practices. For example, a company cannot adopt just-in-time manufacturing without agreement by its suppliers to use the necessary information technologies and radically change their warehousing and delivery practices. Unless all JIT network members simultaneously embrace the ideology that high-performance manufacturing produces mutual benefits, successful implementation will be stalled (Kerwood 1995). Inside an organization, the structure of network relations among workers and managers can support or sabotage any morale boosts and productivity gains from innovative work designs (see Chapter 6).

Although these diverse theoretical arguments about barriers to the diffusion of high-performance work practices appear plausible, none were subjected to rigorous comparative testing with representative empirical samples of diverse organizations. In the absence of such studies, researchers and practitioners alike confronted the unanswered question of why so many organizations continue to scorn credible solutions to their workplace problems. The enthusiasm of many advocates for the new industrial relations should be dampened by the sobering prospect that, for some people caught in their webs, the consequences could be less than wholly benign. The next section considers how normative constraints generated by self-managing work teams can more efficiently, perhaps tyrannically, control employee behavior than does traditional bureaucratic management.

The Trouble with Teams

Critics of lean production expressed skepticism that high-performance practices inevitably foster genuine worker autonomy, participation, and high commitment. Some analysts depicted them as "mean production" devices that disguise the heavy hand of management manipulation under a benign ideology of team spirit. Just-in-time manufacturing firms operating with a lean workforce allowed little margin for errors or buffers against mistakes. Fast-paced and tightly coupled production schedules intensified workplace anxieties, raising employee stress to dysfunctional levels (Smith 1997:321). Workers who fell behind because of supplier delays in delivering crucial parts had to scramble to catch up on lost time. Lean production systems installed information systems that abetted extensive management surveillance of workers on the shop floor (Sewell and Wilkinson 1992). These conditions could trigger employee discontent and conflictual labor-management relations resembling those of traditional Fordist factories, often without union protection from arbitrary, coercive management decisions. For example, one study of a Toyota plant in Kentucky described the work as "monotonous and mind numbing in spite of job rotation, team work, and job enlargement programs" (Besser 1996:25). Research on a joint Canadian venture of Suzuki and General Motors uncovered a demoralized environment "characterized by standardized, short-cycled, heavily loaded jobs" resulting in "a low and declining level of worker commitment and forms of resistance ranging from indifference to collective andon pulls, work stoppages, and strikes" (Rinehart et al. 1997:202). Not exactly a new millennium in industrial relations.

Self-managed teams provided corporations with sophisticated mechanisms for controlling and subtly coercing employees to boost labor productivity while efficiently reducing administrative costs and camouflaging management's retention of ultimate power. The consultative empowerment ideology underlying teamwork shifted responsibility for daily production onto the shoulders of workers, substituting the invisible emotional tyranny of mutual self-monitoring and peer pressure for the constant close supervision exercised in bureaucracies (Sinclair 1992). Team cohesion, loyalty, and spirit became potent motivating forces for curbing individual predispositions toward shirking work duties, "not only by culpable cheating, but also by negligence, oversight, incapacity, and even honest mistakes" (Bainbridge 1996:670). Transaction cost economics explained that self-managed work teams lowered company costs of monitoring labor inputs. Team members had access to information about one another's productive behaviors that was simply too difficult and costly for managers to obtain. "Instead of directly monitoring the inputs of each team member, management can simply monitor the output of the team as a whole" (p. 692).

James R. Barker's masterful ethnographic examination of self-managed work teams in a small industrial firm revealed many nuances of these subtle control mechanisms (1993, 1999). ISE Communications was a management-owned firm that employed 150 people, 90 of whom manufactured voice- and data-transmission circuit boards for the telecommunications industry. In 1988, in an effort to survive in a highly competitive and innovative market, ISE converted its production department to just-in-time manufacturing by three self-managing teams. Three levels of middle management were abolished, and teams reported directly to the vice president for manufacturing. Each team assumed responsibility for fabricating, testing, and packaging its assigned circuit boards. Team members managed their own affairs, making decisions within guidelines set by top management and the company's vision statement; elected one person to serve as information coordinator; and interviewed, hired, and fired new members (Barker 1999:69). By the time Barker began studying ISE two years later, the number of teams had expanded to six and each had developed "a consensus about what values were important to them, what allowed them to do their work, and what gave them pride" (p. 76).

In the initial implementation phase, authority had devolved from the previous hierarchical supervisory system to a loose value consensus that all team members intuitively "knew." However, as ISE hired additional temporary employees to handle the company's expanding workload, new members had to be integrated into existing teams. The basis for a team's authority changed again, into a rational system of objective rules that stated explicit guidelines for doing good work and the penalties for not complying with group norms. "You either obeyed the rules and the team welcomed you as a member, or you broke them and risked punishment" (Barker 1999:79). As teams integrated more temporary workers into the ranks of full-time members, they still expected everyone to follow the rules, as evidenced by attendance charts and careful monitoring of one another's on-the-job behaviors. Although formal rules proliferated and grew increasingly rigid at ISE as team members sought stability and clarity in their work roles, the company did not reinvent its old bureaucracy. Authority remained embedded in the teams and their members' interactions: "The team members themselves still rewarded or punished each other's behavior. They did not give this function to the new facilitators; they kept it for themselves" (p. 86).

Barker claimed that this peer-based control system, which he labeled "concertative control" (Tompkins and Cheney 1985), represented a shift in the locus of legitimate authority from management to workers themselves. Team members collaborated to create the mutually binding rules that structured their daily tasks. Concertative control proved far more effective in achieving compliance than bureaucratic commands issued from above: "It is a powerful and persuasive system that demands our obedience, and we obey because the system reflects our own work values" (Barker 1999:40–41). For example, employees in a bureaucracy might come to work on time because the employee handbook prescribed this behavior and their supervisors had a legal right to demand it. Employees in a concertative organization would show up on time because their teammates now had the authority to demand their willing compliance.

Toward the end of Barker's observation period, an incident illustrated how effectively concertative control could bind its participants. Sharon, a single mother who experienced difficulty getting to ISE at 7 A.M., came late to work again because of a sick child. Her frequent tardiness violated her team's rule against more than four such "occurrences" per month:

> When Sharon showed up, the team reacted in the same way a shift supervisor in ISE's old system might have. The team confronted Sharon immediately and directly. They told her that they were very upset that she was late. They bluntly told her how much they had suffered from having to work short-handed. Stung by the criticism of her peers, Sharon began to cry. The team's tack shifted to healing the wounds they had caused. They told her that they had not meant to hurt her feelings but that they wanted her to understand how her actions had affected them. They asked her to be certain to contact them immediately when she had a problem. The episode closed with the team telling her, "We really count on you to be here, and we really need you here." When I checked a month later, Sharon had not recorded another occurrence. (Barker 1999:86)

A powerful blend of formal rules and peer pressures characterized concertative discipline at ISE. This system was highly effective in eliciting superior team performance, enabling the company to cut costs by 25 percent and gain competitive advantages in its product market. Yet its effects operated insidiously, appearing natural and unobtrusive to the workers. Although concertative control was less overt and oppressive than alternative authority systems, it wasn't exempt from some destructive consequences. Employees heavily invested their identities in the team community, enduring stress and burnout from continuous self-supervision, sacrificing their family time for the team, and damaging the self-esteem of employees who failed to live up to team expectations. Instead of freeing employees from Weber's iron cage of rational bureaucratic rules, concertative control "created a new iron cage whose bars are almost invisible to the workers it incarcerates" (Barker 1999:172). O brave new workplace, that has such people in't!

Conclusions

A new market-based contract between firms and their workers redefined U.S. employment relations at the end of the twentieth century. Life-time job security within a single firm's internal labor market yielded to organizational requirements for more flexible staffing arrangements to control costs and cope with uncertainties in varying demands for labor. Decreasing job tenure, rising part-time employment, increasing contingent workers, and depleted benefit plans characterized the new employment deal, while psychological commitment and loyalty to the organization eroded. Companies offered their nontraditional employees improved work skills and experiences to strengthen their future employability. In a countertrend, some employers tried to create workforces capable of swiftly adjusting production to changing economic conditions by implementing innovative high-performance workplace designs, as exemplified in Saturn's memorandum of agreement. Employee participation programs pushed authority and accountability down to self-managed teams that were empowered to make important staffing and production decisions. By integrating computerized production technologies with creative human resource arrangements, many manufacturing firms devised potent sociotechnical systems that appeared more productive than traditional bureaucratic hierarchies. However, numerous socioeconomic barriers seemed to impede the rapid diffusion of innovative work practices to other sectors. Any tendency to romanticize the high-performance workplace must be balanced against the intense self-monitoring and peer pressures that kept many workers effectively buckled into straight jackets of their own devising.

6

Investing in Social Capital

*Networking, one of my mother's old phrases, musty slang of yesteryear.
Even in her sixties she still did something she called that, though as far
as I could see all it meant was having lunch with some other woman.*
—Margaret Atwood, *The Handmaid's Tale* (1985)

Michael Eisner, the Walt Disney Company's imperious chairman, hired his long-time friend Michael Ovitz to fill the media giant's presidency in August 1995. That job had remained open for months after Frank Wells's death in a helicopter crash. Ovitz had started his Hollywood career humbly, as a tour guide at Universal Studios, followed by a stint in the William Morris Agency's mailroom. It took off when he co-founded the Creative Artists Agency in 1975, which soon became the entertainment industry's premier talent agency, representing a thousand film personalities including Tom Hanks, Barbra Streisand, and Tom Cruise. Ovitz subsequently became Hollywood's most-powerful and most-feared negotiator, personally brokering such megadeals as the Matsushita-MCA merger and Sony's acquisition of Columbia Pictures. In 1995, he had lured CBS news executive Harold Stringer to head Tele-TV, a new video program joint venture of three regional telephone companies. Tele-TV had hoped that the super-agent's connections would procure production deals with the Hollywood studios. But Ovitz's surprise defection to Disney, a firm allied with a rival group of telecommunication companies, left CAA scrambling to hold onto its business and entertainment clients.

Industry observers assumed that Eisner had hired Ovitz to strengthen Disney's ties to top Hollywood talent, to manage its recent $19 billion takeover of Capital Cities/ABC, and eventually to succeed him as chair: "It provides the company with Ovitz's wide network of contacts and skills," said one stock analyst. "Frank Wells was always a sounding board for Eisner. Ovitz will be in a similar role" (Mills 1995:A1). Yet after just 14 acrimonious months, unable to agree with his boss on how best to run the company, Ovitz left the Magic Kingdom "by mutual agreement." Denying rumors of a personal feud, Eisner said, "We have been doing business together while being friends for many years, and I know that both our professional and personal relationships will continue" (Van de Mark 1996). To salve his wounds, Ovitz reportedly took home a $70–90 million severance package. The episode, just one of several rancorous confrontations between Eisner and his former deputies, reinforced Disney's Big Brother image within the movie industry as "Mouschwitz" (Masters 2000).

Although unusually dramatic in its specific events, the Disney episode exemplified the importance of personal networks in connecting employee careers to corporate performances. This chapter examines how network structures and processes occurring inside organizations affect both individuals and their organizations. It describes four new forms of networked organizations—the internal network, the multinational differentiated network, the virtual organization, and the spherically structured network firm—that give employees numerous opportunities to activate their interpersonal connections in the competition for career gains. To navigate the career complexities of these new networked structures, mentoring and networking offer alternative strategies for employees to forge advantageous connections, but each route presents unique prospects and pitfalls. The indispensability of intraorganizational relations requires close inspection of such fundamental network properties as relational contents, strength of ties, and power derived from occupying central positions. These network attributes shape employee perceptions and beliefs and affect a variety of career outcomes ranging from finding jobs to promotions to work performance. Finally, the social capital approach to networks contrasts cohesive and bridging processes at the employee level of analysis and the formation of reputation and status rankings at the organizational level.

Networked Organizations

An exploration of networks within organizations extends the principles of interorganizational relationships examined in Chapter 4 and the creation of high-performance workplaces discussed in Chapter 5. As new connections and partnerships among organizations emerged in the 1980s and 1990s, they changed the patterns of work and communication inside corporate hierarchies, with important consequences for both employee and firm performances. Drawing primarily from a resource dependence perspective, Rosabeth Moss Kanter and Paul Myers (1991) put forward several propositions about the impact of interorganizational relations on power, roles, and relationships inside the partnering organizations. Persons and subunits involved in integrating and coordinating interorganizational relationships would gain power and responsibility within their organizations, displacing employees who were peripheral in interorganizational communication channels. Strategic alliances and joint ventures usually politicize the alliance manager's role, "making it essential for them to be able to juggle a set of constituencies rather than control a set of subordinates or contracted agents" (p. 341). When firm internal relations grow more egalitarian by replacing bureaucratic hierarchies with self-managed teams, employees participate in more consultative activities and autonomous decision making. Interorganizational partnerships reward employees for their participatory skills, including "gathering information, resisting preconceived ideas, testing assumptions, and seeking consensus" (p. 342). Although the theorists did not speculate explicitly about intraorganizational networks, one implication was that firms ought to prize employees who demonstrated superior capacities to construct interpersonal contacts and connections that contributed to achieving organizational goals. Further, successful inter- and intraorganizational networking should yield such career-enhancing benefits as salaries and promotions for its more successful practitioners.

Toward the end of the twentieth century, traditional hierarchical bureaucracies yielded to networked organizational forms in many businesses. These structures consisted of flatter, more decentralized arrangements among subunits and employees, with market mechanisms displacing authoritative commands, short-term projects superseding rigid divisions of labor, and workers assuming greater responsibility for their own employability instead of expecting lifetime job security (see Chapter 5). According to two analysts of the new forms, a networked organization

> creates autonomous units, but it increases the volume, speed, and frequency of both vertical and horizontal communication within the organization to promote collaboration.... The result is an organization with superior performance characteristics for the 1990s. Network management is, in the end, management by empowerment. (Limerick and Cunnington 1993:61)

Networked organizations appear in various configurations, but four analytical forms seem most common: the internal network, the multinational differentiated network, the virtual organization, and the spherically structured network firm. The following paragraphs highlight each form's unique features, as illustrated in Figures 6.1 to 6.4.

An *internal network organization* typically involved informal relations among subunits and employees occurring without regard to the formal authority lines shown in an organizational chart. Figure 6.1 depicts corporate functional units arrayed around a circle rather than the customary pyramid

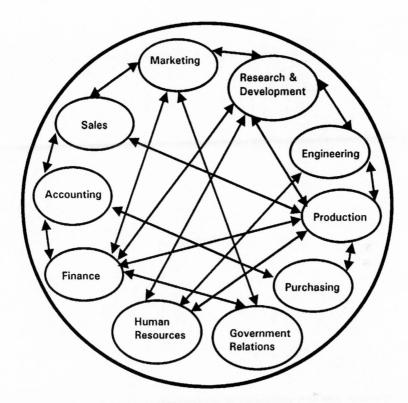

FIGURE 6.1   Internal Network Organization

emphasizing vertical authority relations. The double-headed arrows represent recurrent communication exchanges, resource transfers, or collaborative projects involving inter-unit teams. For example, R&D scientists, engineers, and production workers must work closely together to convert laboratory discoveries into manufacturing processes, whereas identifying potential customers requires consulting with marketing and sales people. Specific unit members, such as department heads or team leaders, serve as the primary agents who conduct negotiations and transactions on behalf of their units' interests. The absence of a central coordinating body in the diagram is deliberate. The CEO and senior executive officers nominally retain authority over their subordinates; in practice, however, exchanging goods, services, and information requires recurrent negotiations in which top managers rarely possess sufficiently detailed knowledge to monitor and control. To adjust rapidly to environmental opportunities and threats, an internal network organization must flexibly reconfigure informal subunit ties without waiting for authorization from top management.

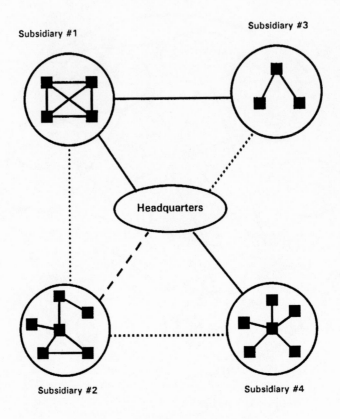

FIGURE 6.2   Multinational Differentiated Network
SOURCE: Adapted from Nohria and Ghoshal (1997:14)

A good illustration of these practices was the Hewlett-Packard Company (HP), whose recent history illustrates how a traditional large bureaucracy transformed itself into an internal network organization through largely unplanned small adjustments to changing external environments. As described by a former HP strategic planning employee, "HP has evolved from an integrated, multidivisional organizational work comprising autonomous divisional operations to a more complex and highly networked structure in which organizations are expected not only to manage more external relationships as part of their everyday operations, but to integrate more fully with other internal operations as well" (Beckman 1996:161). Three major changes radically transformed the company's manufacturing system: consolidation and downsizing of duplicate resources; vertical disintegration and elimination of various noncore production processes; and horizontal integration of such critical processes as strategic investment, product gener-

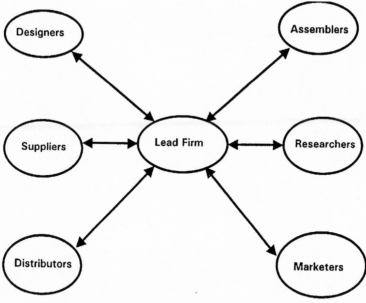

FIGURE 6.3   Virtual Organization

ation, and fulfilling orders. These changes not only required tighter external ties to suppliers and customers but increased levels of internal networking among HP's manufacturing managers and white-collar professional employees. The middle manager's role slowly evolved from exercising direct control over subordinates to influencing other employees' activities, which required cross-boundary management skills unneeded 10 years earlier. To function effectively within this internal network configuration, HP middle managers had to acquire diverse skills:

> Forced to operate in teams, either with internal R&D and marketing partners or with external operators, they must learn to take others' perspectives and to think strategically in integrating others' needs with their own. Interpersonal, negotiation, and business skills are far more critical than technical skills in accomplishing 1994 objectives. (Beckman 1996:173).

The second basic form of networked organization, the *multinational differentiated network* depicted in Figure 6.2, accentuates various organizational subsidiaries in relationship to one another and to the firm's headquarters office (Nohria and Ghoshal 1997:11–16). A prime example was Philips N.V., a multinational corporation (MNC) headquartered in the Netherlands, whose subsidiaries operated in 60 countries ranging from the

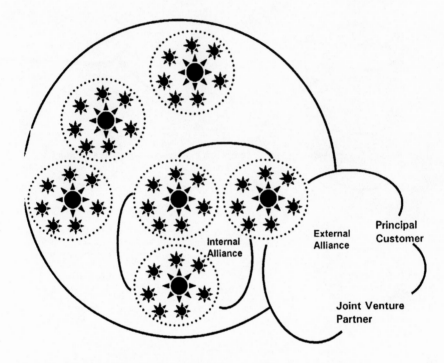

FIGURE 6.4   Spherically Structured Network Firm
SOURCE: Adapted from Miles and Snow (1996:8)

United States and Japan to Nigeria and Peru. Some Philips units were large, fully integrated companies that developed, manufactured, and marketed products ranging from light bulbs to defense systems. Other units were small, single-function establishments employing fewer than 50 people. In general, the structural relations among units within a giant MNC vary along four dimensions: (1) some national subsidiaries are more resource rich and have more complex internal structures than others, (2) headquarter-subsidiary relations differ in the extent of interdependence and local autonomy, (3) subsidiaries vary in how tightly they are integrated through such mechanisms as managers' initial training experiences and career placements, and (4) communication flows, differing in frequency and content within and among the subsidiary and headquarter units, influence a variety of organizational outcomes.

The headquarter-subsidiary configurations adopted by MNCs depend on their environmental contexts, which in turn affect overall corporate performance. Nohria and Ghoshal tested a "requisite complexity hypothesis" that optimal MNC structural complexity would closely match environmental complexity. For 41 MNCs, they measured the degree to which environments required MNCs to be more responsive to global integration or to unique national and local conditions. Similarly, organizational structures varied from ad hoc lack of coherent organizing logic to a highly differentiated network structure. Examples of environmental-structural complexity fit were companies with differentiated networks operating in environments requiring both global and national responsiveness and firms using ad hoc structures in environments where both forces were weak. The 17 MNCs with good structure-environment fits achieved much better organizational performance than the 24 companies with misfitting configurations, as measured by their significantly higher average returns on net assets, asset growth, and revenue growth rates. The findings supported the requisite complexity hypothesis, implying that a differentiated network was not the most favorable MNC structure under all environmental conditions:

> What managers must remember is that it is the *appropriate* level of organizational complexity that leads to effective performance in multi-unit organizations like MNCs.... Unnecessary organizational complexity in a relatively simple business environment can be just as unproductive as unresponsive simplicity in a complex business environment. (Nohria and Ghoshal 1997:189)

A *virtual organization*, the third basic form of networked organization, consists of a lead firm that integrates several other companies to create products or services under the lead firm's brand names. In contrast to the internally networked organization, a virtual corporation extends interunit ties outward. As depicted by the hub-and-spoke image in Figure 6.3, the lead organization subcontracts out various functions to specialized organizations having "core competence," or expertise, not available within the lead firm. Hence, the number of permanent employees on the lead firm's payroll remains relatively small, with most workers performing essential boundary-spanning tasks to coordinate or broker the subcontractors' activities. (The "hollow corporation" is another common name for a virtual organization, underscoring that the lead firm retains few in-house functions.) Although virtual organizations strongly resemble the small-firm networks (SFNs) discussed in Chapter 4, their interunit relationships tend to be more durable and interdependent. Some theorists regarded the virtual corporation as a tightly integrated system with often fuzzy or porous boundaries between its participants. A virtual firm's companies each perform different functions, with electronic linkages growing increasingly cost-efficient through continuous technological advances in corporate intranets. "Organizational learning is not is not a basic objective of the exercise [in contrast to strategic alliances], but rather the creation of a flexible organization of companies, each carrying out one or more functions excellently to deliver a competitive product to the customer" (Child and Faulkner 1998:127). The importance of sophisticated communication networks, information software, and videoconferencing systems for achieving coherence and flexibility among the physically far-flung members of a virtual enterprise cannot be overestimated.

Several very large corporations—including bookseller Amazon.com, clothier Benetton, and shoe seller Nike—exhibited virtual characteristics. For example, British Airways envisioned ultimately leasing rather than owning aircraft and outsourcing everything from maintenance to flight training, eventually supplying little more than its schedule and brand-name recognition (Biddle 1998). More commonly, resource dependence was the mother of virtuality, with insufficient staff as the prime suspect. Netscape, a startup Internet firm that fought a bitter browser war against giant Microsoft before being taken over by America Online, had fewer than 20 employees in 1994. To offset its lack of substantial internal resources, Netscape creatively used the Web to perform virtual marketing, R&D, and finance functions. For example, company engineers posted an error-filled beta version of its Navigator browser on the Internet:

> By downloading the beta, trying it out, and filing their complaints, customers served, sometimes unwittingly, as Netscape's virtual quality assurance team. One month later, one and a half million users had given Netscape's Navigator a trial run. Together they put Navigator through a workout that was far more thorough than anything Netscape's stripped-down staff could have devised. (Yoffie and Cusumano 1999)

The lead firm in a virtually networked organization that coordinates its members' interactions primarily through influence and persuasion, rather than by writing formal contracts or issuing authoritative commands as in a hierarchically structured bureaucracy. Critical to sustaining the virtual organizational form are dedicated employees who, motivated by shared beliefs that cooperation offers greater benefits than competition, can establish and sustain relationships based on trust and confidence. Of course, offering generous stock options, which enable employees to reap potentially huge rewards for their collective hard work, couldn't hurt.

The fourth networked organization form, the *spherically structured network firm*, also resembles a SFN, but with very strong normative constraints to perpetuate its members' collaborative relations. A spherically structured network firm permits quick and efficient connections to multiple partners in the production process, "thus assuring the fullest utilization of its own internal resources and the most agile response to the network as a whole" (Miles and Snow 1996:105). The rotating sphere metaphor alludes to its ability to broker swift connections between units inside the sphere with complementary partners on the outside. As their primary spherical example, Miles and Snow (1996) cited Technical and Computer Graphics (TCG), Australia's largest computer services company, which consisted of 13 independent entrepreneurial firms employing a total staff of about 200 technical specialists. They described TCG as a national innovator in portable data terminals, computer graphics, simulators, bar-coding systems, electronic identification tags, and other information-and-communication applications. In contrast to a virtual corporation with one obvious lead firm, TCG had neither an overall network owner nor formal governance structures, and its member firms did not compete directly head-to-head. Instead, each entrepreneurial member was expected to initiate projects from outside the network and to give preference to the others in choosing subcontractors. Figure 6.4 schematically displays the new-product development process as a three-way partnership among a TCG project-leader firm, an outside joint-venture partner that provides equity capital in return for a stake in the product's future success, and a principal customer whose large advance product order provides additional cash in return for contractual rights in the product.

> [T]he project leader seeks out the participation of other appropriate TCG firms in the product development process. A TCG firm is free to join or not to join the venture, depending on its level of interest and production capacity. After these external and internal alliances have been formed, the project-leader firm serves as the gateway through which information and resources flow for the remainder of the venture. At any given time, many triangular processes such as this are under way at TCG. (Miles and Snow 1996:109)

The emergence of the four basic networked organization forms necessitated alternative employee strategies for building successful careers. These new organizational arrangements abolished the orderly sequence of sheltered lifetime career tracks within a single bureaucratic hierarchy (see Chapter 5). The informal structures and work processes prevalent in networked organizations implicitly offered less-secure employment contracts. Workers moved through successive short-term projects and took greater personal responsibility for acquiring marketable job skills. The "boundaryless career" concept (Arthur and Rousseau 1996) acknowledged that frequent employee movements between firms were no longer limited to Hollywood film crews and large-scale construction projects. To live long and prosper under constantly changing structural conditions, workers became adroit at cultivating ties to their supervisors, coworkers, and subordinates. These interpersonal connections cumulated into complex patterns inside the networked organization, while affiliations arising from career shifts across organizational boundaries generated inter-firm exchanges and mutual dependencies. Mentoring and networking represented alternative employee strategies for getting ahead, both across networked organizations and within conventional bureaucracies. The following sections discuss the advantages and risks, to both firms and employees, of pursuing each career strategy.

Mentoring Protégés

When King Odysseus set off from Ithaca to fight on the Greek side in the Trojan War, he committed his household, and especially his infant son Telemachus, to the care of Mentor, his friend-in-arms, "ordering one and all to obey the old man / and he would keep things steadfast and secure" (Homer 1996:100). Ever since, "mentor" has been synonymous with an older, more experienced person who is dedicated to protecting and guiding a youngster's intellectual maturation. Many college and graduate students experience a close relationship with a teacher who devotes extra time to nurturing the apprentice scholar's academic calling. Inside business corporations, mentoring and "career coaching" activities typically aim at career development only for entry-level managerial and professional employees, not for clerical and blue-collar workers. Theoretical and empirical explanations of mentoring tend to emphasize social psychological processes and individual benefits rather than the organizational implications of embedding mentor-protégé dyads within larger work networks (Kram 1985; Ragins 1995). For example, personality characteristics of the protégé—such as an internal locus of control, high self-monitoring, and emotional stability—increase the likely initiation of a mentoring relationship and predict higher levels of support by the mentor (Turban and Dougherty 1994). The primary advantages that mentors offer to their protégés generally fall under the twin headings of vocational advising and psychological support:

> The mentor may advance the protégé's career by nominating him or her for promotion (sponsorship), by providing opportunities for the protégé to demonstrate competence and special talents (exposure and visibility), by suggesting strategies for achieving work objectives (coaching), by minimizing the likelihood that the protégé will be involved in controversial situations (protection), and by assigning challenging work assignments. In the psychosocial area, the mentor may enhance the protégé's sense of competence and identity by serving as a role model and encouraging the protégé to experiment with new behaviors, and the mentor may provide performance feedback (acceptance and confirmation). Often, mentors serve dual interpersonal roles, acting as an outlet for protégés to discuss confidentially their personal concerns and fears (counseling) and to facilitate informal exchanges of information about work and nonwork experiences. (Noe 1988:66)

Although less often emphasized, a mentor may also benefit from a relationship, for example, by an enlarged reputation reflecting credit for the protégé's future career successes or indirect informational access via the protégé's subsequent network ties. The inherently dyadic nature of a mentor-protégé bond and the prolonged time required to foster these intimate ties (often spanning several years) necessarily limit the frequency of such relationships inside organizations. Most employees do not obtain mentors, and few mentors can guide more than a handful of protégés throughout their careers. Perhaps only one junior executive in four is destined to find a "true mentor" (Keele 1986:58).

Although women were as likely as men to become protégés, junior men were more likely than junior women to have same-gender mentors (O'Neill, Horton and Crosby 1998). This discrepancy stemmed from the still-skewed personnel demographics of many corporations, which made relatively fewer upper-level female executives available as potential mentors for junior women. Some researchers worried that the greater incidence of cross-sex mentoring for junior women provided them with inferior benefits compared to their male peers in same-sex mentoring relationships. Senior white males might be more disposed to function mainly as instrumental career sponsors for their female protégés but were allegedly less prepared to forge the close emotional bonds required to serve as psychosocial confidants. The potential for disruptive sexual involvement and sexual harassment were also an ever-present hazard: A quarter of the professional women in one study admitted to romantic episodes with their male mentors (Collins 1983). Of course, even same-gender mentoring relations weren't fully immunized from the allure of forbidden temptations. More ominously, the false appearance of sexual intimacy could arouse resentments and animosities among coworkers, with detrimental consequences for a junior woman's reputation. However, several research studies indicated that "sponsoring and mentoring benefits women as much as men" in gaining access to work resources, mobility, job satisfaction, and other career outcomes (O'Neill, Horton and Crosby 1998:75; Ragins and Scandura 1994).

Racial and ethnic minorities (African Americans, Hispanics, Asians) faced additional complex challenges and obstacles to establishing successful business mentoring ties. Organizational demographics again imposed familiar structural constraints: The scarcity of upper-level managers with minority-group characteristics inevitably compelled junior minority employees either to seek mentoring ties to senior white males or to forego any possibility of a mentor-protégé experience. Mentorships involving mixed identity-group pairs compounded the inherent difficulties of generating trust, comfort, and emotional intimacy with issues of cultural familiarity, sensitivity, and respect. Based on his study of 22 cross-race (African American and white) "supportive work relationships," David Thomas (1993) concluded that the nature of the relationship depended on both parties' preferred strategies for dealing with their racial differences. Dyads developed true mentor-protégé bonds when both members held symmetrical racial views (either denying and suppressing the racial difference or openly discussing it), whereas asymmetrical views restricted the pair's interactions to purely instrumental career sponsorship without accompanying psychosocial support and friendship. Resource dependence theory, which emphasizes the importance of the structural distribution of organizational power, helped to explain changing patterns of interracial mentoring:

> In particular, I have observed that situations in which Blacks have or are poised to enter positions of power and authority: 1) decrease the White manager's sense of risk in mentoring or sponsoring a member of a different race, 2) increase the White manager's perception of the appropriateness of placing Black people in positions of greater responsibility, 3) increase the White manager's perception of some benefit to him or her derived from engaging in cross-race developmental relationship, and 4) increase the protégé's view that attainment of desired outcomes is possible by engaging in such relationships with Whites. (Thomas 1998:169)

From an organizational perspective, a crucial question is whether mentoring enhances a protégé's work effectiveness. Several researchers analyzing various employee sample surveys concluded that mentors provided protégés with competitive advantages in salary gains, promotions, job assignments, work evaluations, job satisfaction, and subjectively perceived occupational success (e.g., Scandura 1992; Turban and Dougherty 1994). For example, a survey of 244 managers at a large Midwest manufacturing firm found that employees who reported vocational mentoring (e.g., "My mentor has taken a personal interest in my career") earned higher current salaries, while those who received social support (e.g., "I have shared personal problems with my mentor") received more promotions over the course of their careers.

On the negative side, the limited availability and capacity of potential mentors to work with numerous protégés meant that most employees did not enjoy such benefits. Organizations grew wary of appearing unable to offer every employee equal access to career-enhancing opportunities. In the 1980s and 1990s, many companies launched formal assigned-mentor and career-coaching programs. Often designed by human resource consultants, such programs sought to overcome the exclusion of women and minorities from informal ties with senior managers. For example, after the accounting and consulting firm Coopers & Lybrand created a program to match 100 female and minority employees with senior partners, the proportion of fe-

male partners increased by 25 percent (Groves 1998). However, with a subsequent backlash against corporate affirmative action, such efforts suffered
from perceptions that they granted special privileges to certain employees
categorized by race and gender. "Today, many companies see broader benefits to mentoring programs. The programs are often used as a recruitment
tool to show job applicants that the firm is committed to helping employees
succeed.... [and] are often viewed as a way to help retain top performers"
(Olmos 1995). The organizational and career consequences of formally designed mentoring programs, in contrast to dyadic relations that evolve naturally and informally, remain unanswered research questions.

An exclusive focus on the strong interpersonal ties required in mentor-
protégé relationships may ultimately prove less beneficial to both employees and their organizations than a combination of mentoring with social
networking through weak-tie relationships. "Mentor relationships are,
moreover, typically limited to those in higher positions in the organization,
whereas a social network includes ties with superiors, subordinates, subordinates of peers, peers, suppliers, bankers, and anyone else who can provide the person with needed resources" (Keele 1986:64). The next section
considers the importance of networking ties inside work organizations.

Networking Fundamentals

Networking inside organizations, the exchange of work-related communication and social support among employees, is not a new development.
Workers have always engaged in socializing, schmoozing, joking around,
gossiping, politicking, and griping as effective means for learning about
their companies, gathering useful information, and making connections
with other participants occupying good positions who might help advance
their careers. Extrapolating findings from academic network research,
Wayne Baker advised managers to deploy systematic strategies for identifying and building personal and organizationally advantageous connections:
"Networking smart means learning how to network well and applying the
knowledge responsibly... Networking smart means developing relationships that are good for you and your career, good for the people you work
with, good for your organization, and good for your customers" (Baker
1994:xiii-viv). Investigators of real managers' routines found that networking was their predominant behavior, accounting for nearly half of the most
successful managers' activities (Luthans, Hodgetts and Rosenkrantz 1988).
They stressed the conventional distinction between the formal organization, represented in an organizational chart and manual of standard operating procedures, and the "real organization" comprising network connections among employees:

Importantly, however, within every formal organization are one or more informal organizations (shadow organizations, if you wish) with unofficial goals, norms, and relationships. These are groups of employees with common beliefs and goals that transcend the formal organization goals.... Examples include a work-restricting group of production workers or a "good old boy" network of higher level managers who all have relationships quite different than those defined by the formal organization. (Luthans, Hodgetts and Rosenkrantz 1988:121)

Informal networks may hinder effective organizational performance and impede employee career opportunities, for example, by erecting glass ceilings that block the promotion of talented women executives. Harmful outcomes can result when employees construct networks primarily to acquire personal power without regard for collective consequences. Informal networks may also serve adaptive purposes, enabling organizations to perform routine tasks more efficiently, to expedite new project initiatives, and to react swiftly in erupting crises.

Informal networks are never completely independent of the formal division of labor in an organization's authority hierarchy, as demonstrated by research on four types of networks in a large retail chain (Han 1996). A random sample survey of 76 employees at four hierarchical levels in the company's national headquarters (top executives, two managerial classes, and other employees including administrative and support staff) asked them to indicate four types of job-related contacts, both within and between the employees' own corporate divisions: give/receive information, investigate/explain, advise/consult, and negotiate/persuade. A simultaneous analysis of these ties by division and level disclosed that formal hierarchical positions greatly constrained the patterns of employee contacts. Most connections occurred within rather than between divisions, with relationships across divisions taking place mostly at higher levels. Employees' workplace networks grew more dense as their occupational rank increased. Specifically, the higher one's formal status, "the more likely it is that he/she uses negotiate/persuade and advise/consult ties rather than investigate/explain and give/receive ties, the more likely it is that the ties occur across divisional boundaries, and the more likely it is that he/she interacts with alters who are also in higher position" (Han 1996:61). Top executives were less likely to exercise control by issuing direct orders and more prone to try influencing their subordinates by offering suggestions, making requests, or other indirect means. Not surprisingly, lower-rank workers seldom tried to advise or consult and negotiate or persuade those above them, but they were the recipients of advice from their formal superiors. These research findings imply that an organizational chart acts as an underlying scaffolding or template around which employees' informal interactions are draped. The relatively close alignment between formal and informal structures directs theoretical and empirical research attention toward explaining how these twin structures jointly shape workplace interactions.

Three fundamental concepts useful for analyzing intraorganizational networks are relational content, tie strength, and power. The following subsections briefly describe these concepts and their measurements, as a prelude to appraising empirical research on the consequences of networking inside organizations.

Relational Contents

The content of a relationship between two employees is its substantive meaning or the reason for its occurrence. Although the diversity of ties is potentially limitless, a useful classification scheme applicable to both inter- and intraorganizational networks involves five basic contents: resource exchanges, information transmissions, power relations, boundary penetrations, and sentimental attachments (see Chapter 2 and the Appendix for definitions and examples). Network researchers analyzing organizations or workplaces often operationalize various relational contents by presenting employees with separate "name-generator" questions to elicit the identities of coworkers with whom they have specific types of interaction. For example, employees of a newspaper publishing company were asked to "list the names of persons (1) who provided them with inputs to their jobs and to whom they distributed the outputs from their work; (2) with whom they talked frequently about work related topics; and (3) whom they considered close friends. These listing provided the primary basis for three types of networks: work flow, communication, and friendship" (Brass 1985:330–331).

Ronald Burt developed a nine-item relational content series to generate names of coworkers in a computer firm "with whom you discussed matters important to you," "who have contributed most to your professional growth within [the firm]," and "who among the people working for [the firm] has made it most difficult for you to carry out your job responsibilities" (Burt 1992:123). Other important relational contents for studying intraorganizational networks include advice, trust (Krackhardt and Hanson 1993; Ring 1996; Oliver 1997), friendship, support, and cooperation (Ibarra 1995). Different relational contents usually produce markedly different network structures, accentuating the importance of keeping each content separate rather than conflating all connections into a single, comprehensive pattern. The next section demonstrates a procedure for simultaneously analyzing multiplex networks involving different relational contents.

Strength of Ties

Tie strength, another fundamental network property, refers to a quantitative dimension such as the frequency of interaction. The amount of time a dyad's members devote to dealing with one another is a plausible indicator of that relationship's importance. The intensity of emotional intimacy may also measure tie strength. For example, a manager who attends a monthly planning committee with representatives from others departments will probably regard the other committee members as acquaintances rather than as her close friends. But she may consider her workplace team members, with whom she interacts all day long, to be colleagues who owe special loyalty to one another. An early conceptualization of tie strength argued that weak ties provide people with more opportunities to acquire new information and useful resources than do strong ties (Granovetter 1973, 1982). Because intimates generally share the same information and interpretations, a close-knit friendship circle or clique that lacks connections to a larger social system is restricted to recirculating and reinforcing its members' parochial news and views. In contrast, if some clique members also maintain weak-tie links to socially distant groups, they may become conduits for the diffusion of new ideas and practices from one social cluster to another. These bridging actors may also enjoy personal competitive advantages because of their timely access to information about developing situations. To continue the preceding illustration, the planning committee member is more likely to hear from her acquaintances about job openings and project assignment opportunities in other parts of the firm than are managers whose networks are completely encapsulated inside their work teams.

The strong/weak tie distinction highlights critical contrasts between mentoring and networking as employee strategies for getting ahead (Keele 1986). Like kinship, romantic love, and close friendships, a mentor-protégé dyad often involves intense, emotional bonds that reduce the time and energy available for developing extensive weak ties to other employees. Intensity can easily drift into isolation, rendering a protégé dependent on her mentor's willingness to make his personal and business connections available for her advancement. In contrast, a networking strategy that emphasizes crafting an extensive array of weak ties trades off depth for breadth. The advantage of reaching many potential sources of information and instrumental assistance, and of manipulating those primary contacts to broker new connections, compensates for the lack of intimacy in more superficial interactions. Exchanging information for advice and periodically shuffling one's personal network helps to reduce dependence on a few powerful gatekeepers. Relying exclusively on either a strong- or weak-tie strategy is riskier than skillfully blending elements from both approaches, particularly at different career stages. Younger employees often need the support and protection that a mentor can provide, but a wise mentor also pushes her protégés to learn quickly how to network for personal fun and career profit.

Organizations face a tricky dilemma in trying to achieve a stable balance between (1) the decentralization and autonomy necessary for eliciting the fully mobilized creativity of its human resources and (2) the integration and coordination essential to align everyone's efforts toward attaining the organization's performance goals. Firms whose employees have few weak ties connecting them to people outside their immediate workplaces are more likely to suffer from internally disjointed and incohesive structures. If work group factions turn inward, spending too much time talking among themselves, they neglect to cultivate communication connections to key actors who might help them to function better. Fragmented and isolated solidary cliques inefficiently synchronize their input and output tasks with the other groups in an interdependent work-flow sequence. Becoming more effectively networked is increasingly vital to organizational survival and performance. Top managers must fashion sophisticated internal intelligence networks that go around formal chains of command, because subordinates may avoid passing along unpleasant information to their bosses. Underlings frequently fear that, as bearers of bad tidings, they might be scapegoated merely for calling attention to screwed up situations beyond their control. Flexible combinations of weak and strong ties let organizational leaders tap into streams of information about what's really going on inside their company. To cultivate better networking, middle managers and team leaders encourage their subordinates to forge informal connections across unit boundaries, emphasizing the mutual benefits for employees and their firm. Sometimes contrived situations get the sphere spinning, such as luncheons and cocktail parties inviting people from diverse divisions. To revitalize informationally affected sites, firms periodically rotate managers and employees among different units, breaking up entrenched cliques and unfreezing rigid mindsets. Restructuring efforts aimed at replacing bureaucratic hierarchies with a thoroughly networked organization require sustained vigilance to prevent unanticipated consequences:

> The most important change for a company to anticipate is a complete overhaul of its formal structure. Too many companies fail to consider how such a restructuring will affect their informal organizations. Managers assume that if a company eliminates layers of bureaucracy, the informal organization will simply adjust. It will adjust all right, but there's no guarantee that it will benefit the company. Managers would do well to consider what type of redesign will play on the inherent strengths of key players and give them the freedom to

thrive. Policies should allow all employees easy access to colleagues who can help them carry out tasks quickly and efficiently, regardless of their status or area of jurisdiction. (Krackhardt and Hanson 1993)

Power in Organizations

Power is a central concept in intraorganizational network analysis, just as in inter-firm relations (see Chapter 4). From a resource dependence perspective, power is fundamentally a function of network structures and the positions that individual actors occupy within each relevant network (Pfeffer 1987; Cook and Emerson 1984). Both theoretical and empirical analysts expect that actors occupying the central positions of a network gain greater access to information and resources than do actors in more peripheral positions. Consequently, central actors exercise greater influence over organizational actions, decisions, and outcomes. Persons and subunits acquire power by controlling exchanges of essential organizational resources—for example, information in a communication network or money in a financial network—thereby increasing other participants' dependence on them for those resources necessary to perform their tasks. Powerful actors also decrease their own resource dependencies by gaining direct access to valuable resources that are neither controlled nor mediated by others. Network centrality generates power within an organization by freeing employees from constraints on their actions while enabling them to constrain the behaviors of others. Although network structures generate power for employees occupying the more central positions, the reverse causal process also occurs: People seek to establish connections to the most powerful organizational players, expecting to enhance their own power through such contacts. As a result, incumbents of central positions enjoy numerous advantages over peripheral positions. Through their proximity to others in communication exchanges, they can acquire more timely and useful information. They can better control the flow of resources and mobilize support for preferred organizational initiatives. Centrality enables them to mediate and broker deals between interested but unconnected parties. And, through boundary-spanning ties to external organizational actors, they can direct the organization's strategic objectives (e.g., Kanter and Myers 1991). In short, "network centrality increases an actor's knowledge of a system's power distribution, or the accuracy of his or her assessment of the political landscape.... Those who understand how a system really works can get things done or exercise power within that system" (Ibarra 1993a:494).

As discussed in Chapter 2 and the Appendix, three widely invoked measures of an ego-actor's network centrality capture varied aspects of the resource dependence perspective on intraorganizational power (Knoke and

Guilarte 1994; Brass 1995). A simple degree indicator, which counts the total number of direct ties sent to and received from other actors, measures the size of an ego-actor's personal network. It represents the sheer volume of different social contacts directly connected to an employee. Actors with high degrees in a communication network obtain power through their connections to many alternative sources of information, whereas low-degree actors depend on fewer sources that might withhold or distort information. Closeness centrality measures an ego-actor's capacity to reach many other network members either directly or through relatively few intermediaries. More powerful actors have not only a larger proportion of direct ties but also shorter indirect paths that enable rapid message and resource exchanges involving fewer intervening steps. Employees can boost their closeness centrality by forming new connections to alters who themselves have large and nonredundant ego networks, in effect by pursuing the weak-tie expansion strategy described above. Finally, the betweenness centrality measure captures each actor's capacity to mediate, and potentially to control or manipulate, interactions of the other network members. If subsets of an organization depend on a single employee to connect them with the rest of the network, that key person controls the only conduit able to broker connections among various parts of the firm. This structural location enables the go-between to extract a price (most likely in the form of favor-obligations rather than a financial commission) for brokering linkages between unconnected groups. Again, employees can improve their betweenness scores by pursuing a strategy of forging new weak-ties that connect them to previously unconnected clusters of employees. In sum, regardless of specific centrality measures, the most central employees in an organizational unit maintain larger numbers of social and work ties that directly and indirectly connect them to numerous dissimilar coworkers who otherwise cannot easily contact one another. The structural advantages of occupying central positions can translate into both organizational and career benefits through timely access to crucial information and the mobilization of resources to change personal and organizational performance outcomes.

A Small Firm Example

Several abstract concepts discussed above are usefully illustrated using real data from a small entrepreneurial organization collected by David Krackhardt (1990, 1992, 1999). Silicon Systems (a pseudonym) was a West Coast startup computer firm involved in the sales, installation, and servicing of information systems to client organizations, ranging from banks and schools to research labs. The company was wholly owned by three entrepreneur-managers who held equal shares (designated in diagrams by the pseudonyms Steve, Pat and Jim). In 15 profitable years Silicon Systems grew from

224

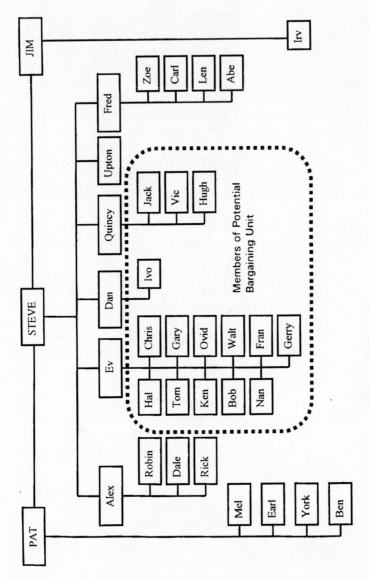

FIGURE 6.5 Organizational Chart of Silicon Systems
SOURCE: Modified from Krackhardt (1999)

these three founders to 36 employees, all of whom worked in a single-story office building, although installers often spent days at the clients' sites. "Thus, employees were familiar with each other to varying degrees, and each had an opinion about every other employee, with the occasional exception of new hires" (Krackhardt 1990:347). The formal organizational chart in Figure 6.5 reveals three hierarchical levels, with most employees reporting to six supervisors under Steve. As part of his larger study on reputation and power, Krackhardt distributed questionnaires to all 36 employees, receiving 33 completed booklets. Two network questions analyzed below are: "Who would you go to for help or advice?" and "Who do you consider to be a personal friend?" These two networks had nearly identical densities (the proportion of actual direct ties to possible ties): 0.11 for friendship and 0.10 for advice. However, ties in the advice network were highly asymmetrical; that is, employees did not reciprocally seek advice from one another. In contrast, the friendship network was much more symmetrical because most dyads tended either to cite or ignore one another. Reciprocation occurred for only 30 percent of the advice ties but for 72 percent of the friendship ties.

Four months after Krackhardt obtained the Silicon Systems network data, several employees started a drive to join a national labor union (Krackhardt 1992). The 15 members of the potential bargaining unit appear inside the dotted box in Figure 6.5. Enough people signed the National Labor Relations Board (NLRB) union authorization cards to hold a certification election. A union official later confirmed that at least 55 percent of the bargaining unit employees had signed up. However, when the NLRB election was held after a two-month campaign, unit members by a 12–3 vote overwhelmingly rejected unionization. Krackhardt explained this change of heart as the effect of employees' network positions on their campaign behaviors. He highlighted the pro- and anti-union stances of eight key employees:

> Chris and Ovid, who were pro-union in sentiment, were quiet and kept to themselves. In contrast, Jack, Hal, and Ivo (also pro-union) were quite vocal about their stand. Dale, Mel and Robin, who were not members of the potential bargaining unit but had close ties with others who were members, vociferously supported the anti-union position.... [T]he key participants who were pro-union were not influential either because they did not take a stand or they were too isolated from the main group in the friendship network. The key anti-union people were influential because they were both in an influential position and were actively proselytizing. (Krackhardt 1999:197)

Chris, an installer with the most friendship ties, was especially troubled about the unionization drive. Although he supported unionization, he did not participate in debates at the organizing meetings. On the day of the vote, Chris asked to be given a "leave" from Silicon Systems rather than make a public commitment on the union issue. He rejoined the firm two days after the NLRB certification vote was taken. Krackhardt attributed Chris's ambivalence to cross-pressures arising from his friendships with employees on both sides, especially with Ovid, who was pro-union but not vocal, and with Robin and Mel, who "were vehemently opposed to the union and told people so" (Krackhardt 1992:234). These two anti-union employees were also close to several other members of the potential bargaining unit, often drinking with them at local bars. In contrast, the three most enthusiastic union supporters—Ivo, Jack, and especially Hal, who was the union's original contact and instigator of the certification drive—had few friends in the unit and their pro-union pleas ultimately proved ineffective.

I reanalyzed Silicon System's advice and friendship networks to produce a graphic display that underscores Krackhardt's (1999) interpretations of the unionization events based on his more elaborate network analyses. UCINET's CONCOR blockmodeling program simultaneously split the employees in these two 36-by-36 actor networks into four blocks based on their structural equivalence across both networks. That is, the employees within a block most closely resemble one another in their patterns of advice seeking and friendships with members of the other three blocks. Next, using the correlations among all employee dyads as measures of similarity, UCINET's multidimensional scaling (MDS) program plotted the relative locations of each employee in a two-dimensional social space.[1] Figure 6.6 shows contiguity lines around the members of each block, and uses different fonts for the employee names to represent their formal roles and unionization positions. All members of the potential bargaining unit appear in bold face italics, while the eight key pro- and anti-union employees are underlined.

Block I at the bottom of the diagram contains the three Silicon Systems owners (Steve, Pat and Jim, in capital letters), along with three of the six supervisors who report directly to Steve (two other supervisors, Alex and Fred, are located nearby in adjacent blocks). Block I is primarily an advice-giving position, occupied by three of the five persons from whom other employees most frequently sought advice (Ev, Steve, and Quincy; Alex and Fred were the other two popular advisors). Blocks II and III at the upper left side include all the potential bargaining unit employees, with two important exceptions. The exceptions are Jack and Hal, both active union supporters, who were isolated from the employees they were attempting to recruit. Although pro-union supporters Chris, Ovid, and Ivo were located in these blocks, so were Robin and Dale, the vocal union opponents. The third strongly anti-union employee, Mel, is much closer to the unit employees than either Jack or Hal. Chris's location on the border between Blocks I and II confirms his central position in Silicon System's friendship network

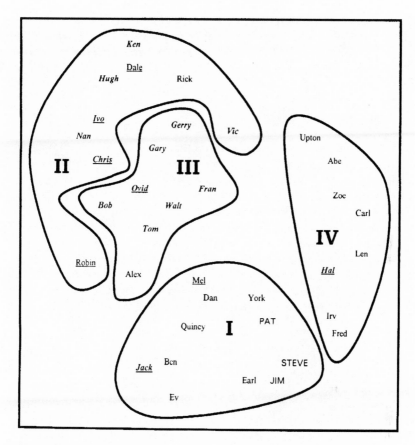

FIGURE 6.6   Social Distance in Advice and Friendship Networks of Silicon Systems

and his high rank in its advice-giving network. (Chris had the largest number of direct friendship ties and the highest betweenness centrality score, indicating his high potential to mediate interactions between pairs of employees [Krackhardt 1992].) However, Figure 6.6 also dramatically reveals the cross-pressures Chris faced, surrounded by Ivo and Ovid from the pro-side and Robin and Dale on the con-side. The spatial configuration demonstrates the capacity of informal networks to reshape the perceptions, attitudes, and actions of individuals caught in their webs of affiliation.

Network Outcomes

Conventional approaches to human resource management investigate the effects of personal attributes and job characteristics without considering how network ties among employees shape their work attitudes and behaviors.

The empirical evidence is relatively sparse but cumulatively implies that ego-centric and intraorganizational networks affect a wide range of phenomena, including "recruitment, selection, socialization, training, performance appraisal, career development, and turnover" as well as "job satisfaction, performance, power, and conflict" (Brass 1995:39). Because space limitations prevent reviewing all these findings in detail, I highlight five studies that must serve as epitomes of the research literature:

- A study of adolescent employees of three MacDonald's restaurants found that voluntary job turnover occurred not at random but through a snowballing effect among workers in structurally equivalent clusters (Krackhardt and Porter 1985, 1986). The effect derived not from the workers' positions in the formal organizational chart but from their connections in the informal communication network. When people saw others leave who had occupied similar network positions as themselves, they interpreted this behavior as a signal about the undesirability of continuing to work for the organization. Hence, job quits were not independent events but tended to occur as clusters of leavers within particular network locations (Krackhardt and Porter 1986). Friendship ties produced an unexpected effect of turnover on the job satisfaction and organizational commitment of the remaining employees. Contrary to a social psychological model that disgruntled leavers would poison others' attitudes toward Mac-Donald's, the friends of leavers actually grew *more* satisfied and committed after their unhappy pals departed compared to employees who were not the leavers' friends (Krackhardt and Porter 1985). One plausible explanation: The disappearance of the "rotten apples" removed significant sources of never-ending complaints about the workplace from the attention of their friends.
- In a study of communication and friendship networks among 140 nonsupervisory employees of a newspaper, Brass (1984, 1985) found that ties beyond the work group and work-flow requirements (vertical and horizontal coordination) affected organizational power reputations. Centrality to the organization's dominant coalition, a clique of four male executives, was strongly related to perceived influence and to actual promotions. Men were more closely tied to this dominant coalition and were rated, by both other employees and supervisors, as more influential than women within the organization. The paths to power for women lay not in networking with other (powerless) women, but in forging ties to the male network. "Women who were part of integrated formal work groups (at least two men and two women) and who were linked (closeness) to the men's network (only male employees considered) were perceived as

more powerful than women who were not" (Brass 1995:61). For the entire sample, centrality within the departmental, men's, and dominant coalition interaction networks was significantly related to promotions into supervisory positions.

- Stephen Barley (1990) examined how work roles and social networks affected the introduction of technological innovations in two hospital radiology departments in the early 1980s. New diagnostic imaging technologies—sonography, computed tomography (CT) scanners, and magnetic resonance imaging (MRI)—produced more highly detailed pictures of patients' internal anatomies than older x-ray methods. These radical innovations disrupted the stable work relations and prestige orders among the radiologists and technicians, whose knowledge and status traditionally had increased with age and tenure. Both hospitals hired young professionals trained under the new modalities, which older employees could not hope to master. The result was a "technologically induced split in the social organization of the two departments" along age and skill fault lines (Barley 1990:91). Structural equivalence analyses of each department's work-related discussion networks diverged dramatically from the formal authority structures (as defined by departmental job descriptions), a typical finding in intraorganizational network analysis. Both blockmodels revealed that the technologists who operated the new modalities were not only similar to one another, their positions in both departments were also more similar to radiologists than to the x-ray techs. "In turn, the x-ray techs were structurally more akin to orderlies and secretaries than to their counterparts in the new modalities" (p. 98). Work roles and social networks combined to mediate the impact of technology on organizational structures, reducing the status and prestige of the previously dominant professionals.

- Another intraorganizational network project sought to explain how gender shaped the conversion of personal networks into corporate advantages. In her study of a New England advertising and public relations firm, Herminia Ibarra (1992) observed differential patterns of homophily (tendency to form same-sex ties) among the 80 male and female employees. Men tended to concentrate their ties primarily on other men across multiple networks (communication, advice-seeking, support, friendship, and influence). Women employees differentiated according to network contents, obtaining social support and friendship from their female coworkers and instrumental access through ties to higher-status men. That is, expressive and instrumental ties coincided for men but were inversely correlated for women. Consequently, men seemed to receive higher returns than women on their social capital investments, in the form of greater network centrality.

• Similar gender-differentiated network propensities occurred among 63 managers of four Fortune 500 corporations (Ibarra 1993b), with men relying more on weak-tie homophilous networks and women forging more strong expressive ties to other women. The relationship between managers' ego-net strategies and their potential for promotion, as judged by supervisors and human resources staff, also differed by gender. High-potential women and low-potential men placed greater relevance on expressive networks, such as trust, whereas high-potential men and low-potential women stressed instrumental ties. Ibarra concluded that women's preferred network strategies disadvantaged them relative to their male peers in the game of getting ahead: "The 'entrepreneurial' network pattern characteristic of successful male managers is less effective for females who many require stronger network ties to achieve the same level of legitimacy and access to resources" (p. 27). A subsequent analysis of minority managers in these firms found that they had more racially mixed, and fewer intimate, network ties (Ibarra 1995). Minority managers with high advancement potential balanced same- and cross-race ties in five networks of varied relational contents, whereas lower-potential managers' networks were dominated by ties to whites. Rather than suggesting an assimilation strategy, Ibarra interpreted her results as consistent with a pluralist approach, where "successful black managers develop instrumental relationships with white sponsors but do not rely on them exclusively for the psychological support they can obtain more readily from other minorities" (p. 697).

All the projects summarized above found evidence of intraorganizational network effects, typically demonstrating that location in more central positions conferred power and other beneficial consequences for employees' careers. These studies just began to expose the underlying complexities connecting actors and relations to outcomes. Several foci for future theorizing and research offer high prospects for scholarly payoffs. Researchers often leave unspecified the precise substantive micro-mechanisms by which intraorganizational networks affect employee perceptions, attitudes, and behaviors. Many social psychological processes might operate simultaneously to translate social structures into personal outcomes, including socialization, role modeling and social comparison, imitation and contagion, information processing, social exchange, and power dynamics, to mention only some obvious possibilities. For example, network centrality may exert its effects primarily by imposing situationally structured opportunities and constraints without regard to particular interpersonal exchanges. Alternatively, more interactive influences may occur, because people socially construct their perceptions during direct contact with other social actors "and network links are the channels through which organizational culture and norms are communicated" (Ibarra and Andrews 1993:280). Employees' cognitive networks, that is, their subjective perceptions of how their coworkers appear connected to one another, may be much more important than those actual interaction patterns in shaping subjective perceptions of power and influence inside a firm (Krackhardt 1990). The lack of longitudinal data on network development contributes to ambiguities about causal directions between network structures and employee outcomes. To some extent most workers, even those remaining blissfully oblivious to the larger informal systems, presumably realize that their direct personal ties influence the quality of their work lives. More savvy and ambitious employees actively manipulate and realign their connections to gain career advantages, which consequently reinforce or change both the ego-centric and the macro-network patterns in their workplaces. Broadway and Hollywood regularly spoof the unintended outcomes of career scheming in such comedies as *How to Succeed in Business Without Really Trying* and *The Secret of My Success*. The magnitude of various network processes undoubtedly differs across organizational contexts, such as industry and firm size, in ways not captured by research restricted to a single site. Implementing a multiple-organization, multiple-wave project to track the evolution of intraorganizational networks would be a costly but welcome improvement over prevalent single-firm, cross-sectional designs that cannot effectively disentangle contextual effects and causal sequences.

Social Capital

The 1990s witnessed a marked resurgence of theoretical interest in social capital, in the form of interpersonal relations, as a resource for instrumental actions both by individuals and organizations to realize their interests. Following suggestions by Loury (1977) and Bordieu (1980, 1986), James S. Coleman (1986, 1988, 1990) defined social capital as social-structural relationships that are assets or resources that facilitate actions by individuals in a specific social system. A person's social capital is not deployable or exchangeable in every situation:

> Like other forms of capital, social capital is productive, making possible the achievement of certain ends that would not be attainable in its absence. Like physical capital and human capital, social capital is not completely fungible, but is fungible with respect to specific activities. A given form of social capital that is valuable in facilitating certain actions may be useless or even harmful for others. Unlike other forms of capital, social capital inheres in the structure

of relations between persons and among persons. It is lodged neither in individuals nor in physical implements of production. (Coleman 1990:302)

Unlike other forms of capital, social capital is jointly owned by both parties in a relationship, with no exclusive property rights for individuals. The formation of network relationships is intimately related to the creation of social capital. However, although networks and social capital are closely related concepts, they are not identical. If relations prove nonbeneficial for attaining an actor's goals and turn instead into constraints that impede performance, then they constitute a social liability (Leenders and Gabbay 1999:3). A common theme in literary works dissecting this phenomenon is the swift degeneration of romantic flings into rancorous marriages.

Physical capital is embodied in material forms such as factories and offices, machines and tools, and transport equipment. Human capital, the focus of much attention by labor economists (Becker 1993; Mincer 1994), consists of the knowledge and skills held by workers, as evidenced by diplomas and certificates of education and training. The intellectual property of organizations embodied in its patents and work routines is another form of human capital. Social capital is less tangible, "created when the relations among persons change in ways that facilitate action" (Coleman 1990:304). Just as physical and human capital both contribute to the economic productivity of persons and organizations, social capital can be mobilized to boost worker and company output. A fundamental proposition is that organizations whose employees have extensive social capital will perform better, just as firms endowed with larger stocks of physical and human capital achieve superior results.

Ambiguity surrounds the concept of social capital as social network ties among individual or corporate actors. Some theorists restrict the term to just the structure of relations themselves, whereas others expand its scope to include potential resources that can be accessed through these networks. People can proactively shape their social relationships to obtain better opportunities and benefits. By forging large volumes of connections to numerous, diverse, and well-endowed contacts, a social actor gains potential access to the assets controlled by those contacts. For example, a CEO who graduated from an elite business school not only could get help from banker alumni with whom she's kept in touch, she could also request referrals from those contacts, tapping into *their* acquaintance networks to put together a complicated funding deal. In effect, the CEO's total social capital is the sum of her direct and indirect network contacts times the financial resources she might leverage via each type of connection. "Social capital is at once the resources contacts hold and the structure of contacts in a network. The first term describes whom you reach. The second term describes how you reach." (Burt 1992:12).

Mark Granovetter's (1985) discussion of how economic transactions are embedded in constraining and facilitating social relations is germane to social capital analysis. *Structural embeddedness* refers to a total configuration of network relations in a social system. *Relational embeddedness* describes the concrete personal ties, such as kinship and friendship, that social actors develop through the history of their interactions with one another. In economists' "undersocialized" model of the market, atomized rational actors impersonally exchange goods at prices without regard to their prior connections. Decisions among available alternatives follow the utility-maximizing principle of choosing that option with the greatest perceived difference between benefits and costs. In contrast, the social embeddedness model of economic behavior asserts the importance of interpersonal networks in creating the trust, identity, and norms that shape economic behavior apart from rational cost-benefit calculations (see the discussion of interorganizational networks in Chapter 4).

Consider the example of a talented employee deciding whether to accept job offers from several rival firms for jobs that pay more and provide greater authority. A purely economic analysis concludes that any rational employee must accept whichever offer maximizes her utility calculations (including staying put if her current employer makes a counteroffer that erases the cost-benefit gap). However, an embeddedness analysis examines the quality of that employee's network ties to her coworkers, including a company-based personal identity, and the negative value of disrupted connections to family and community from moving great physical distances. An employee whose interpersonal relations are infused with highly positive emotional contents might choose to remain at her firm despite greater economic benefits from leaving. Another employee, with weak or antagonist social ties to coworkers, would more quickly snap up the best job offer.

An actor's social capital encompasses many types of beneficial relations, including trust and confidence, obligations and cooperation, information, and even formal authority. The positive consequences of these "moral resources" ultimately depend on shared social norms that sustain and strengthen the cooperative bonds among actors in a social system. The dynamics of social capital formation may parallel other forms of capital growth, with initial investments in riskier relations subsequently paying higher returns to the investors. For example, rural communities and small towns are typically pervaded by extensive webs of mutual social and economic assistance among the residents. Over time, these neighborly exchanges generate high reservoirs of trustworthiness that outstanding obligations to reciprocate will likely be repaid in future times of need. Persons in such interdependent social systems benefit from greater amounts of social capital "credit" on which to draw, as demonstrated by heroic yet futile sandbagging efforts to prevent the Red River from inundating North

Dakota's and Minnesota's riverine towns during spring 1997. Similar endeavors occur in The Netherlands, involving periodic evacuations of thousands of residents from lowland areas.

Mixed competitive and cooperative modalities characterize some forms of network interaction. At times actors mobilize their social capital to gain personal advantages over their adversaries; in other circumstances they jointly coordinate actions for collective benefit. For example, corporate employees engage in self-serving career strategies, seeking out mentors or networking with superiors to advance up the promotion ladder. In contrast, the high-performance workplaces discussed in Chapter 5 stress teamwork and collaborative responsibility for production, encouraging workers to pool their skills and social capital to improve group performance. Similarly, both modalities operate at the level of organizational strategy where plans to achieve global corporate goals are implemented. Firms operating in the same industry generally compete for customer loyalties and form exclusionary supplier relations, yet as described in Chapter 4, they also frequently collaborate in strategic alliances and joint ventures with expectations of mutual gains. An important task for social capital theorists is to explain under which conditions zero- and positive-sum interactions are more likely to occur.

Among several factors shaping the development and destruction of social capital relations in organizations, perhaps the most important is closure. Closure occurs in a three-actor network (A, B, C) when reciprocal ties exist among all three, forming a strong component. Coleman (1988:S108) argued that closure of a social system is conducive not only to the emergence of "effective norms but also for another form of social capital: the trustworthiness of social structures that allows proliferation of obligations and expectations." Network closure encourages the creation of corporate identities and interpersonal trust. The absence of a potential link, for example between actors A and C, weakens the system by reducing the capacity to sanction violators of norms and to develop reputations for trustworthiness. Such an unclosed triad, where C cannot sanction A's ill-treatment of B, enables some members to take advantage of others, for example, by taking a free ride on their accomplishments. In Coleman's approach, the higher network density in a closed system provides more social capital to its members and facilitates beneficial cooperative behaviors. However, he recognized that the effective group norms arising from closure could inhibit autonomy, innovative or deviant behavior, and the realization of personal interests by particular actors. "Evidently, then a constraining social structure is not an asset for the constrained actors. It is negative social capital" (Gabbay 1997:33). In organizations whose employees are highly competitive, individuals' networking strategies may be better explained by the structural hole theory of social capital examined in the next subsection.

Personal Social Capital

Two small but rapidly expanding bodies of theoretical and empirical research applied social capital perspectives on intraorganizational networking to investigate worker and organizational behavior. The first explored how informal social contacts provide advantages over formal channels for finding jobs in the broader labor market. The second considered how intraorganizational networking improves career outcomes such as higher pay and more rapid promotions in firm internal labor markets (for an extensive review, see Flap, Bulder and Völker [1998]).

Success at finding a job depends not only on a candidate's human capital (social background, educational credentials, and work skills) but also on labor market information about job openings and necessary qualifications acquired through social networks. Informal networking often proves a more efficient search mechanism than formal routes such as newspaper advertising, sign-posting, and employment agency referrals. Both employee and employer interests can be better served by relying on extensive weak-ties (e.g., acquaintances and colleagues) that offer more diverse information than is available through impacted strong ties such as close friendships (Granovetter 1973). Mobilizing one's direct and indirect social connections not only lowers an individual's search costs but also reduces firms' transaction costs of locating and screening suitable job applicants. Chances for improved career outcomes are enhanced by the ability to tap into ("borrow") the scarce social resources reachable beyond an actor's immediate social circle. Resources accessed through network relations constitute an individual's social capital, regardless of whether those ties were investments explicitly made by the person in expectation of a future payoff or were overtly mobilized during instrumental actions (Lin 1995). The wider the range and diversity of direct and indirect contacts available to a job-seeker, the greater that person's chances for ultimate success. Social ties seem particularly instrumental pathways to upward occupational mobility. A study of upstate New York job seekers found that accessing and using the social resources of higher-status network contacts improved an applicant's chances of landing a higher-prestige job (Lin, Ensel, and Vaughn 1981). Other analyses uncovering similar effects included a Detroit area survey (Marsden and Hurlbert 1988), two surveys of Dutch managers (De Graaf and Flap 1988; Flap and Boxman 1999), and a retail bank (Fernandez and Weinberg 1997).

Ronald Burt (1992, 1997) formulated a structural hole theory that described social capital as a function of structural arrangements in empirical networks. His approach drew inspiration from several theorizing traditions, including Granovetter's (1973) strength of weak-ties; brokerage processes (Gould and Fernandez 1989); and Georg Simmel's (1955)

analysis of the *tertius gaudens* role ("the third who benefits"), referring to
a triad in which one person profits by encouraging disconnection between
the other two. (Shakespeare's implacable villain, Iago, consummately applied this method to turn Othello fatally against Desdemona.) The structural hole hypothesis equates social capital with opportunities to play the
broker in relations between actors otherwise disconnected in a network.
A structural hole refers to a gap or separation between two actors or
"nonredundant contacts":

> Nonredundant contacts are connected by a structural hole. A structural hole is
> a relationship of nonredundancy between two contacts. The hole is a buffer,
> like an insulator in an electric circuit. (Burt 1992:18)

Figure 6.7 helps to make sense of these circular definitions. Think of the
actors as employees of a small establishment or a department within a
larger organization, with the arrows indicating a communication network
through which they exchange work-related information. Structural holes
separate actor B from both actors A_1 and A_2, indicated by the absence of
direct connections of the former with the latter two. The ego-actor fills
both these structural holes by maintaining direct ties with B and both the
As. Thus, Ego can serve as a broker by passing messages or negotiating
deals between otherwise unconnected pairs. However, no hole exists between A_1 and A_2 because they are directly connected to one another (i.e.,
they are not "nonredundant" contacts). Ego has identical indirect access to
actors 1 and 2 by going through either A_1 or A_2. (The As are structurally
equivalent because they have the same patterns of present and absent ties to
all other system actors.) Given that redundant contacts yield identical information, Ego derives no additional benefits by maintaining direct ties to
both A_1 and A_2. (The four-person clique comprising 1, 2, A_1, and A_2 means
that these actors share identical information.) Note that C is separated
from the four lettered persons and, because actors 5 and 6 are not directly
connected to one another, anyone building a bridge to C would thereby
gain indirect access to two additional sources of unique information. In
other words, this social system is ripe with structural holes just waiting to
be plugged. To maximize efficient information exchange while concentrating time and effort on nonredundant relations, Ego's best strategy would be
to sever connections with one A and create a new tie to C.

Important information and control benefits accrue to managers of organizations with networks that contain many structural holes (Burt 1997:
340–343). The information benefits include access to unique sources of
valuable information, early timing in receiving such information, and referrals by one's direct contacts to more distant third parties. Nonredundant
contacts supply a manager with a broader range of information, alerting her

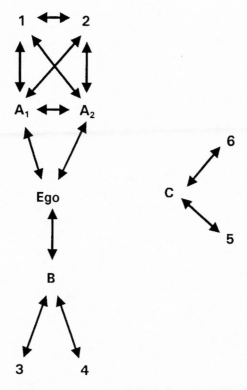

FIGURE 6.7   Structural Holes in an Ego-Centric Network

to emerging prospects and warning of looming threats. The control benefits consist of entrepreneurial opportunities to broker relations inside the organization. As a nexus for communication exchanges, a skilled manager who fills several holes can negotiate rewarding terms for coordinating the actions of otherwise unconnected employees. Bargaining power increases if ego plays two or more contacts against one another, exploiting the alters' lack of direct ties by provoking a competition for their time and attention:

There are several ways control can play out. First, disconnected parties may compete for the same relationship with a third—such as two bidders for the same contract.... Second, disconnected parties can be leveraged against one another—such as leverage gained by a manager playing off the conflicting interests of marketing and finance. Third, two disconnected parties who can add value to one another are introduced by the entrepreneur, who benefits from crafting valuable projects. (Raider and Burt 1996:188)

Structural hole theory is premised on an implicit market-based view of instrumental advantages that individuals can obtain from strategically manipulating their network structures. To become a successful organizational power player, an ambitious managers builds bridges to many heterogeneous contacts because these network patterns generate optimal information and control benefits that reinforce and cumulate over time. Social capital boosts the payoffs to an employee's human capital such as educational credentials and work experience. Individuals who invest their time and energies in constructing extensive work-related personal networks surrounded by structural holes add greater value to their company, and, hence, receive higher rates of career returns on their investments. Managers with networks rich in structural holes receive such rewards as higher salaries and bonuses, quicker promotions, and more preferred project assignments than their hole-poor peers. And the gains from structural holes are greater for managers who operate on a social frontier, defined as "any place where two social worlds meet, where people of one kind meet people of another kind" (Burt 1992:163). Women, minorities, recent entry-level employees, and boundary-spanning employees are all persons on organizational frontiers who can increase their survival chances through entrepreneurial networking in corporate worlds dominated by older, white male managers.

Empirical evidence supporting these theoretical predictions came from a 1989 survey of a large corporation in the electronic components and computing equipment industries (Burt 1992). A sample of 284 upper-level managers (in the three ranks just below vice president) completed sociometric booklets to report their ties to coworkers. Burt combined these data on self-reported tie strength (closeness) to each contact named with data from personnel records about the managers' promotions to their current ranks. He found that structural holes were related both to early promotions (advancement to higher ranks at younger ages than expected for similar managers in the same line of work) and to fast promotions (being at current rank for less time than their peers). Specifically, a lack of structural holes in a manager's network produced small but significant promotion delays, although holes were not identically advantageous to all managers. Hole effects were stronger for managers operating at social frontiers, for managers in remote plants rather than for managers in core plants, for women compared to men, for recently hired managers rather than for managers long with the firm, and for field managers whose sales and service responsibilities involve them with customers outside the firm (Burt 1992:132–134).

Managers' decisions to form network ties within or across their immediate work groups affected their promotion chances. A manager could choose an immediate hierarchical supervisor (e.g., the work group's boss) as the strategic partner at the top of his or her network. Or a manager could build a nonhierarchical (entrepreneurial or opportunity-oriented) network around critical contacts outside the immediate work group, thus spanning corporate structural holes. These alternative choices had contrasting short- and long-term consequences on promotions (Burt 1992:153). A boss-centered network led to an early promotion but was followed by a long period of stagnation in rank. An entrepreneurial network led both to early promotion and to subsequent quick advancement to higher ranks. The consequences of these different types of networks differed markedly by gender. "The worst network for women and entry-rank men is the one best for high-ranking men. Women and entry-rank men with entrepreneurial, opportunity-oriented networks were promoted late to their current rank" (Burt 1992:159). As visible minorities inside a male-dominated firm, women managers benefited initially from a boss-centered strategy but faced subsequent barriers to moving into higher managerial ranks. White males gained from contacts outside their immediate work group who could vouch for their credibility as candidates for top leadership positions.

Further analyses revealed that the value of network social capital depended on competition and legitimacy, both of which correlated with the number of people doing the same work (Burt 1997). Peers "erode the value of social capital to the extent that disorganization among peers intensifies competition between the peers and elicits guidelines from higher authority" (p. 346). Burt measured social capital in terms of network constraint, the extent to which a manager's network was directly or indirectly concentrated on a single contact. In short, the fewer the structural holes, the less social capital. For the computer firm's 170 male senior managers, lower network constraint correlated with earlier promotions. However, the constraint interacted significantly with the number of peers, those holding the same managerial rank in the same business function. That is, each additional person hired to do the same work decreased the impact of social capital on early promotions. This negative effect was strongest among men in the more-senior ranks and those on social frontiers such as nonwhites managing remote plants: "peers most erode the value of social capital to leaders and other boundary-spanning managers who have few or no peers" (p. 357).

Structural hole theory emphasized how individuals could reap personal advantages by forming networks to acquire information and control resources in pursuit of instrumental goals, exploiting gaps in informal network relations, playing unconnected people off against one another, and brokering deals among unconnected parties. This highly manipulative view of social capital contradicted Coleman's notion that solidarity benefits derived from network closure. That is, cohesive informal networks (i.e., an absence of structural holes among system members) increased effective social control in groups with shared norms and sanctions. Following Coleman's approach, Joel Podolny and James Baron (1997) argued that, when competing for career opportunities, network structures conveying coherent and well-defined organizational identities could be as important as positions astride structural holes. Small, cohesive networks could serve as the primary bases of social identity, "conveying a sense of belonging within a collectivity and clear normative expectations associated with one's role" (Podolny and Baron 1997:674). Podolny and Baron collected survey data from a sample of 236 employees of a high-tech engineering and manufacturing corporation on five types of interpersonal networks: task-advice, strategic information, mentoring, friendship or social support, and "buy-in" or fate-control (ties to people whose support was needed for successful pursuit of job-related initiatives). Consistent with structural hole theory, they found that employees with large task-related information and resource exchange networks lacking indirect ties had greater odds of promotion during a one-year interval, but they also found that holes in the buy-in network, which transmitted identities and job expectations, actually decreased upward mobility. Ties to a mentor with fate control did not affect promotion independently of ties to any other person whose buy-in was crucial. Podolny and Baron concluded that

> all structural holes are not of the same color; some are "white holes," propelling the individual upward through the organization and providing socioeconomic benefits, while others are clearly "black holes," holding individuals at a particular rank in the organization and causing negative psychological consequences. (1997:689)

These findings cast doubt on a wholly voluntary, instrumental conception of organizational networks that assumes employees enjoy substantial autonomy to change their social interaction patterns to maximize their benefits from structural holes. Organizational demography and formal authority hierarchies often limit available exchange partners and compel many employees to rely on the same alters for both resource- and identity-based benefits. Even the flexible internal structures of the networked organization forms discussed at the beginning of this chapter may constrain networking processes and their consequences in ways still to be explained theoretically as well as demonstrated empirically.

Organizational Social Capital

The notion that social relations constitute an actor's social capital investments can be generalized to groups and organizations. Just as individual people mobilize their interpersonal contacts' social resources for purposive action, so work teams and corporations activate diverse information and resource networks to achieve their goals. An important but unresolved theoretical question is whether corporate-level social capital resides only in the totality of the personal relations held by a firm's employees. Burt seemed to answer affirmatively: "The social capital of people aggregates into the social capital of organizations" (Burt 1992:9). Organizations certainly derive many benefits through the social connections of their sales people, research scientists, and chief executive officers. For example, powerhouse law firms acclaim the "rainmaker" partner whose personal connections to the business community land the big corporate accounts that the practicing partners service. Chapter 7 explores how the networks formed among persons holding multiple or interlocked seats on corporate boards of directors provide vital conduits for large companies to acquire timely information on changing markets, government affairs, and corporate best-practices. As illustrations of the personal-to-organizational social capital aggregation, consider two recent research studies. An organizational ecology analysis of 1,851 Dutch accounting firms across more than a century found that both human capital (measured by partners' education credentials and tenure) and social capital (measured by partners who had worked in other industries and government, as indicators of ties to potential clients) strongly increased the odds of firm survival (Pennings, Lee and Van Witteloostuijn 1998). A second study, based on data from 15 business units of a multinational electronics company, found that cross-unit social ties among employees was strongly correlated with high levels of inter-unit trust and resource exchange and combination, which led to major product innovations of higher value to the firm (Tsai and Ghoshal 1998).

Corporate social capital also originates in macro level processes that are not just aggregated interpersonal ties. Interorganizational networks of the type examined in Chapter 4 can generate corporate social capital in the form of organizational prestige, reputation, and status. For example, companies making philanthropic contributions to health, welfare, and artistic nonprofit organizations gain prominence and legitimacy in their local community as good corporate citizens (Galaskiewicz 1997; Galaskiewicz and Bielefeld 1998). A network of donation ties provides an invaluable strategic advantage in helping firms to weather uncertainties of the marketplace. Additional research evidence that network connections enhance organizational reputations includes studies of systems of organizations involved in nuclear waste management and photovoltaic cell development (Shrum and Wuthnow 1988), social service delivery (Doreian and Woodard 1999), and U.S. and German labor policymaking domains (Knoke 1998). Organizations in many fields recognize that substantial economic and political benefits can accrue to good reputational capital (ask any tobacco company executive). Several reputation-building professions emerged in the twentieth century to nurture and defend corporate images and identities (Fombrun 1996). Marketers, advertisers, consultants, and public relations specialists created and elaborated tactics ranging from technical demonstrations of product quality, to endorsements by sports and entertainment celebrities, to damage-control spinning in corporate disasters such as the Tylenol poisonings and *Exxon Valdez* oil spill. Developing consumer brand loyalty to encourage repeat product purchases is probably the most pervasive form of organizational reputation-building. A casual walk through any mall testifies to the fashion industry's success at persuading their customers to provide free advertising by wearing designer labels on the outside. Reputation capital at the corporate level was institutionalized in the 1980s with *Fortune* magazine's annual rankings of the most publicly admired firms in dozens of U.S. industries.

Interorganizational network processes help to create and stabilize corporate reputations for high status. Joel Podolny (1993:830) defined status as "the perceived quality of that producer's products in relation to the perceived quality of that producer's competitors' products." When the intrinsic value of goods and services is difficult to measure, status is mediated by an organization's ties to other producers, buyers, and third parties. Reputational defense involves asymmetrical network processes that constrain higher-status organizations' producers from expanding into the lower end of their markets. Higher-status firms have no incentive to extend the linkages desired by lower-status firms, because affiliating with the hoi polloi would jeopardize public perceptions of their superior standing. Groucho Marx's caustic comment, "I wouldn't belong to any organization that wanted me for a member," devastatingly captures the one-way status street. To test his status-based market competition model, Podolny (1993, 1994) analyzed pricing behavior among investment banks that underwrote corporate securities from 1982 to 1987. He measured bank status by "tombstone advertisements" in the major business media that show the syndicates of co-underwriters. These ads arranged bank names hierarchically in a series of prestige brackets that reflect the securities industry pecking order. In multivariate analyses, Podolny found that the percentage spread in debt underwriting (gross spread divided by dollar amount of the bond offering) was negatively related to an underwriter's status rank. As predicted, higher-status banks received a cost advantage from their status that enabled them to underbid their low-cost competitors. The greater the market uncertainty, the more banks formed ties to underwriters with similar organizational status and with those with whom they had past relations. These preferences reinforced and preserved the investment industry's status hierarchy.

Conclusions

The examination of intraorganizational networks in this chapter parallels the investigation of interorganizational relations in Chapter 4. Several networked organizational forms—internal, multinational differentiated, virtual, and spherical—give employees opportunities to build career paths through interpersonal contacts. Mentoring and networking offer employees distinct alternative strategies with unique advantages and drawbacks in the competition to get ahead. Employees can construct and manipulate a variety of informal relationships of various tie strengths to derive personal power by occupying central positions in informal corporate networks, which are only partially constrained by their positions in the company's formal authority hierarchy. Locations within multiple networks—such as advice, trust, and friendship—shape employees' perceptions, attitudes, and instrumental actions. Researchers traced the impact of networks on work outcomes such as employee recruitment and hiring, corporate socialization and job turnover, work performance, and job satisfaction. Women and minority employees often remain disadvantaged relative to white men, who enjoy reinforcing expressive and instrumental networks. From the organizational perspective, employee networks affect company access to the human resources, talents, and productive efforts essential for competing effectively in socially embedded markets. The social capital perspective treats interpersonal connections as valuable assets enabling employees to gain access their contacts' information and resources. Investigators quarreled over whether cohesive, identity-forming ties or extensive connections bridging structural holes proved more beneficial for such instrumental actions as finding jobs and winning promotions. At the corporate level of analysis, social capital is both an aggregation of the interpersonal ties held by a firm's employees and an emergent property of interorganizational relations that create and stabilize reputation and status rankings among corporate peers. An important theoretical and empirical challenge for network researchers is to specify stronger analytical connections across the micro and macro level processes that shape complex webs of relationships and their outcomes inside networked organizations.

7

Governing the Corporation

[Corporations] cannot commit treason,
nor be outlawed nor excommunicated,
for they have no souls.
—Sir Edward Coke (1644)

As General Motors entered the 1990s, the world's largest automaker found itself in serious trouble. Under Chairman Robert Stempel, an engineer with a nice-guy reputation, GM steadily hemorrhaged red ink. By 1992, after losing $16.5 billion in its North American operations, Stempel was forced to announce closure of 21 of GM's 120 factories (McWhirter 1992). With the Ford Motor Company undercutting its labor costs by almost $800 per vehicle, GM's U.S. market share shrank over two decades from one-half to less than one-third. On April 6, 1992, the General Motors board of directors revolted, booting off three GM executives. They also replaced Stempel as head of the board's executive committee with a long-time outside GM director, Robert Smale, a former CEO of consumer products giant Procter & Gamble. Stempel's opponents expected that Smale's strong marketing experience would infuse GM management with a badly needed customer focus. The new board leadership hoped to boost GM's bottom line by getting tough on the company's suppliers, managers, and unions. They further strengthened their hand by installing John Smith Jr., a former head of GM's profitable European operations, as GM president. Smith moved his inner circle of hotshot baby-boomer finance and marketing executives (who called themselves "the cowboys") to a distant technical center, leaving a clueless Stempel to prowl the vacated fourteenth floor of GM's landmark Detroit headquarters. That

244

summer, disgruntled United Auto Workers locals, reacting to Stempel's plant closure announcement, staged wildcat strikes in a vain effort to avert massive layoffs of 74,000 employees over two years. Concerned that the firm wasn't responding with sufficient vigor to union threats, some GM board members launched a "campaign of discreet Stempel-must-go lobbying and far-from-discreet leaks to the press, creating confusion inside and outside GM as to who was running [the company]" (Dickson 1992). Facing imminent ouster, Stempel resigned as company chair in October 1992, bitterly condemning "the chaos of the past several weeks." The board then appointed Smale as board chair and added CEO to Smith's presidential and chief operating officer titles. In a break from corporate tradition, the board stipulated that Smith, who lacked prior GM board experience, would report directly to the worldly Smale, a nonemployee. Over the next five years, the extraordinary Smale-Smith partnership engineered "an excruciating but largely successful turnaround," costing many jobs and depressing share values, which eventually stanched further erosion in GM's share of the U.S. automotive market (Simison and Blumenstein 1997).

The GM board revolt was just the most prominent of several corporate coups d'état in blue-chip companies during that decade, which saw the forced removal of CEOs at Sunbeam, Seagate, IBM, and Kodak, and two successive replacements to founder Steve Jobs at Apple Computer (before its board finally brought Jobs back in 1997 to turn around that troubled company). These dramatic events revealed that governing large corporations was a deadly serious game among company leaders playing political poker for big stakes. Top executives and board members mobilized personal and organizational resources to advance their preferred corporate policies and strategies. Victory in internecine struggles for control and domination often fetched hefty personal rewards, ranging from executive washroom keys and corporate cars to lucrative salaries, bonuses, and stock options. Winners got power and prestige while losers pulled ripcords on their golden parachutes to cushion their fall from grace. However, when high-stakes gamblers neglected to act in the best interests of their organizations, they could also leave bankrupt companies, alienated employees, ruined investors, and devastated communities in their wakes. A crucial normative goal for analysts of organizational change is to identify effective organizational incentives and political control structures that hold top company leaders accountable to numerous stakeholders for the consequences of their decisions and actions.

Power and Authority

Organizational politicking occurs at all levels of analysis, from the loading dock to the board room to the national government. Organizations and their participants regularly engage in political actions inside their boundaries as well as in the larger environment. To explain the eventual outcome of power struggles—who wins and who loses in contests for corporate control—requires an understanding of the rules of the political game and the alternative strategies and tactics that players deploy to get, keep, and use power and authority in the pursuit of collective decisions with big personal payoffs. The concept of political power elicited a vast theoretical and research literature across several disciplines, which cannot be thoroughly encompassed in this brief review. I confine my attention in this and the next two chapters to sociological, managerial, and political science perspectives directly relevant to political activities occurring within and around organizations. A good starting point is to consider the relational nature of power.

Max Weber, the erudite father of German sociology, penned one of the most enduringly serviceable definitions of *power* as a relationship between two or more social actors: "'Power' (*Macht*) is the probability that one actor within a social relationship will be in a position to carry out his own will despite resistance, regardless of the basis on which this probability rests" (Weber 1947:152). Whatever the particular circumstances, Weberian power alludes to the latent coercion, or force, lurking behind every political situation where conflicts of interest arise among the participants. However, Weber further distinguished situations in which assent or consent to commands occurs in the exercise of power, averting the necessity to use force to achieve one's will against resisters. Weber labeled this subjective acceptance *Herrschaft*, variously translated from the German as "domination," "imperative coordination," or most commonly "*legitimate authority*" (Bendix 1960:290–297; Weber 1947:152, 328ff). Weber's famous three pure types of legitimate authority differed across historical contexts, from the traditional bonds between kings and their subjects to the religious charisma connecting cult followers to their guru. In modern organizations, legitimate authority in organizations primarily rested on a rational-legal belief that a valid system of rules defines the rights and obligations of owners, managers, and employees. Expectations that a superior's orders will be obeyed depend on "a belief in the 'legality' of patterns of normative rules and the right of those elevated to authority under such rules to issue commands" (Weber 1947:328). In an ideal rational-legal corporation, all participants always completely agree on both the ends and means for accomplishing some task. Hence, power is not necessary for collective action because unanimous consent voids any need to overcome resistance. More often, some minority of organizational actors holds very intense interests in pursuing certain objectives, while others are either indifferent or only weakly opposed. A faction with intense preferences reveals sufficient power to achieve its goals by overcoming weak and disorganized opponents. However, the stronger the resistance by its adversaries, the more power a group must mobilize to accomplish the same results. For Weber, political power in a specific situation was revealed through social actors' capacities to reach their desired outcomes by using whatever resources, including the legitimate authority provided by their formal positions, would be necessary to overcome both latent and manifest opposition.

Suppose a corporate manager decides to launch a new product that some of her subordinates deem risky and unwise. Because company employees believe in their superior's legitimate authority to make decisions, the manager need not resort to force or coercion to gain her subordinates' compliance with her plans. Her subordinates support the new product marketing campaign, not because they fear losing their jobs or are seduced by their boss's business charisma (although such motives might also be present), but because participants accept her legally sanctioned right as the unit's manager to commit the group members to collective action, regardless of their personal qualms about the project's ultimate outcome. At its core, legitimate power consists of the ability to get things done through appeals to a group's collective beliefs that particular participants, in occupying their distinct structural positions, possess the right to command or the obligation to obey.

Power struggles inside organizations typically revolve around efforts to delegitimate opponents by accusing them of failure to perform their duties in a rational-legal manner. Superiors charge underlings with insubordination for failing to carry out instructions or exceeding the scope of their authority. Subordinates accuse their bosses of overstepping legitimate boundaries between personal and business relations, although fear of retaliation often shields illegitimate activities from detection and punishment (see Chapter 8 for discussions of whistle-blowing and sexual harassment). Conflicts between top executives and their boards of directors, examined below in greater detail, may provoke accusations of violating legal and administrative obligations as organizational agents. Remedies for abuse and misuse of power must be sought within the legal frameworks governing corporate procedures. Thus, the General Motors board followed the bylaws when voting to remove Robert Stempel and his allies from office. In extreme, but unfortunately not rare, instances officials engage in illegal activities for corporate or personal gain. Government sting operations periodically expose public sector organizations as sinkholes of malfeasance and corruption, or just plain refuges of incompetent administrators. For example, Operation Silver Shovel, an eight-year federal investigation into toxic waste dumping in Chicago, netted seven aldermen and three city officials for taking bribes from a mob-connected mole (Novak 2000). Nor are private firms immune from crime in the suites, to judge by an evident global epidemic of corporate felonies ranging from tax fraud, insider trading, and copyright infringement to price fixing, health and safety violations, and sexual harassment (see, e.g., Ruggiero 1996; Mizell 1997; Slapper and Tombs 1999). Lurid as these crimes appear, they underscore the fundamental principle that every organizational action implicitly reveals where the boundary lies between crude power and legitimate authority.

A Political-Organization Model

The predominant approach to organizational power and authority, implicitly drawing from Weber's ideas, is the resource dependence theory proposed by Jeffrey Pfeffer and Gerald Salancik (1978) and elaborated in subsequent publications (Pfeffer 1978, 1981, 1987, 1994). (See Chapter 2 for a summary of the core principles of this perspective.) Contrasting a rational-organization model based on economic efficiency assumptions with a political-organization model based on resource dependence ideas yields some insights into the arrangements of power and authority in organizations:

- An economically *rational organization* is staffed by actors who seek to solve the firm's production problems efficiently and to maximize its economic performance. All participants share the common goal of advancing the organization's collective good. The prevailing ideology is economic efficiency and effectiveness. Power is legitimated authority, distributed unequally across the organization's hierarchically ordered positions. Stable authority serves primarily to facilitate the smooth and rapid coordination of complex tasks. Decision making involves the logical calculation of costs and benefits from each action, using widely available and highly reliable information. Hence, few conflicts should erupt inside the organization, and those that arise are easily resolved by providing clarifying information or by superiors imposing decisions on their subordinates through fiat.

- A *political organization* continually experiences disorderly and unpredictable struggles among coalitions of contentious participants who seek to control decisions for factional benefits. The organization is a nest of interest groups pursuing conflicting goals. The prevailing ideology is win-lose, us-versus-them contests that disregard the organization's collective well-being. Rather than providing accurate information of utility-maximizing decisions, organizational politicians skillfully manipulate data for tactical and strategic gain. Power derives from control over organizational resources, including holding high-level authority positions that enable incumbents to issue commands with some expectation that subordinates will obey. Competing factions seek to advance their preferred organizational actions and goals by acquiring control over sufficient resources to overcome their opponents and to impose their agendas on the entire enterprise.

Because useful resources—financial, technical, legal, and social—are dispersed across diverse positions in the organization, winning coalitions must be forged through bargaining and negotiation. No group's control can be maintained forever, so the game of organizational politics is a ceaseless routine activity. Those who hold a winning poker hand today may find themselves out of chips tomorrow.

These two ideal typical models are extreme exaggerations of the rational economic and political conflict processes that blend together in varying degrees in real enterprises. A combination of power resources and legitimate authority provides the foundation for organizational politics that enable or prevent particular participants from influencing key decisions affecting their collective fates. In every political economy, a complex system of legal statutes and case law exerts potent constraints on the permissible outcomes of struggles among owners, managers, and employees attempting to mold organizational actions to their interests. Explaining the origins of U.S. legal institutions that shaped organizational decision making falls under the rubric of "corporate governance," a multidisciplinary perspective drawing from law, history, economics, and political science (Roe 1994). The next section considers the historical evolution of legal principles that regulate authority relations among the principal actors in modern business corporations.

Legal Theories of Corporate Governance

Over the past two centuries, the power and authority relations of U.S. business organizations were formally encapsulated in statutory and case laws, interpreted by the state and federal courts and enforced by governmental bureaucracies. During the eighteenth and early nineteenth centuries, most economic enterprises were small, family-run proprietorships or partnerships. Legal theory in the United States adhered to an individualist model of economic life "based on visions of production by individual producers and transactions between individuals, all of whom bear responsibility for their own actions" (Bratton 1989:1482). American state governments occasionally granted special charters to larger-scale corporate enterprises, primarily as a legal mechanism to induce private individuals to engage in activities benefiting the public good. Cities and boroughs, churches, charities, and colleges were the most prominent chartered corporations, which prevailing legal theory presumed to require state regulation outside the market-price system. Apart from banks, insurance companies, and transportation firms (canals, toll bridges, and turnpikes), very few general businesses were incorporated as entities receiving special concessions from the state. The law treated a corporation as a "legal fiction" whose special privileges and powers were strictly limited to the explicit rights and obligations stated in its charter of incorporation.

In 1819 the U.S. Supreme Court reviewed a case in which the New Hampshire Legislature rewrote Dartmouth College's colonial charter to dilute the board of trustees' power to dismiss the college president. In his majority opinion, Chief Justice John Marshall described the corporation as "an artificial being, invisible, intangible and existing only in the contemplation of law" (*Trustees of Dartmouth College v. Woodward*, 17 U.S. 518). Under this artificial entity theory, a corporation was created and owed its continued existence to a specific act of the government, rather than through private initiatives undertaken by individual incorporators. This concession view asserted that corporations possessed only such powers as were explicitly granted to them by the state. Thus, state governments retained a legitimate right to regulate the affairs of corporations, notably, by restricting firms to specific activities and to geographic jurisdictions spelled out in their charters (the *ultra vires* doctrine); by prohibiting them from owning other corporations (to prevent them from creating subsidiaries); and by setting limits on their capitalization (to avoid great concentrations of corporate wealth).

The political economy created after the Civil War saw the formation of huge industrial factories and transcontinental railways capable of mass manufacturing and nationwide distribution. This vastly expanded scale and scope of production supplanted small entrepreneurial businesses with joint-stock companies—large managerial hierarchies financed by outside equity investors. The modern business corporation began to take root: ownership by individual shareholders investing in transferable stock, limited financial liability from the claims of creditors, perpetual organizational life, and centralized management separated from the investors (see Handlin and Handlin [1945] and Hovenkamp [1991] for detailed histories). The old legal view of corporations as artificial creations of the state grew increasingly useless for coping with the booming growth and economic distortions instigated by these powerful firms. To accommodate the emergent organizational realities, U.S. law ultimately fashioned a new *natural entity theory* of corporate governance. The corporation was legally reconceptualized as a "corporate personality" arising from natural contractual relations among private individuals. State governments increasingly replaced the special legislative chartering of firms with general incorporation laws that made "corporate charters available simply upon compliance with certain generally applicable filing requirements and submission to standard substantive regulations" (Millon 1990:207). In turn, the states' permissive legal environments stimulated the entrepreneurial propagation of corporate startups.

To pay for their rapid expansion, corporations used two primary financial mechanisms for raising huge volumes of capital resources. First, they issued debt, selling bonds carrying the promise to pay their creditors (debtholders) a fixed amount of interest plus eventual repayment of the entire principal of the loan. Second, they sold shares to equity owners (shareholders) who were entitled to receive dividend payments coming from future corporate profits. Shareholders could also earn capital returns when they sold their shares after the stock price rose above the purchase price. In cases of insolvency or dissolution, the company's board of directors would have to pay all fixed claims of its debtholders, but the stockholders would receive only the residual assets, if any remained. Indeed, failure to fulfill their "directorial duty to creditors" could result in enormous personal liabilities under statutory and common laws. Thus, holding shares was inherently riskier than holding debt. As the residual risk bearers, the shareholders stood to lose or gain when the firm performed poorly or well. Legal analysts argued that only the shareholders were sufficiently motivated to control decisions about how corporate resources should best be deployed, because they had the most direct financial stake in the decision outcomes (Easterbrook and Fischel 1983; Stilson 1995; Cannon and Tangney 1995).

The legal capstone in the institutionalization of the natural entity model of the corporation was the Supreme Court's 1886 decision in *Santa Clara County v. Southern Pacific Railroad.* The Court held that a corporation is legally a person under the 14th Amendment, and thus entitled to the same protections from governmental regulation as enjoyed by individual citizens under the equal protection clause (Horwitz 1987). Corporate entities were now free to act without fear of legal challenges to their pursuit of any lawful business (Dewey 1926). New Jersey liberalized its incorporation laws in 1888, enabling that pioneering state to go from a few hundred to several thousand incorporations within a decade, a proliferation paralleled by Ohio and Pennsylvania despite their more prohibitive incorporation statutes (Roy 1997:171). By lifting restrictions on corporations owning stock in other firms, state laws "gave birth to the holding company, a company that existed solely to own other companies" (Roy 1997:151). Another major consequence of these legal reformulations was to accelerate the consolidation of gigantic national enterprises, such as Standard Oil and U.S. Steel, which, by gobbling up their regional competitors, came to dominate the U.S. economy at the start of the twentieth century (see the discussion of the multidivisional form in Chapter 3).

The courts were slow to develop correspondingly sophisticated theories concerning employee rights and consumer protection. The results were unchecked corporate excesses, including exploitative working conditions, child labor, union suppression, monopoly profits, price-fixing trusts, unsafe food, dangerous transportation, and environmental despoliation. The raucous spirit of that predatory era was vividly captured in the muckraking journalistic exposes of Lincoln Steffens's *The Shame of the Cities* (1904), Ida M. Tarbell's *History of the Standard Oil Company* (1904), and Upton Sinclair's fictional portrait of a filthy Chicago meatpacking plant in *The Jungle* (1906). The slow and fitful implementation of greater legislative, administrative, and judicial restraints on such corporate abuses was the result of century-long social movements for union recognition, workplace health and safety, and consumer and environmental protection (cf. Mayer 1989; Freedman 1994; Aldrich 1997; for discussions of some of these issues see Chapters 8 and 9).

Nexus of Contracts
and Stakeholder Theories

The currently prevailing legal theory of the corporation conceptualized the firm as the private property of its shareholders, existing solely to maximize returns on their investment and not to serve any larger social purposes. Conservative economist Milton Friedman (1970) defended this conception in his famously titled article, "The Social Responsibility of Business Is to Increase Its Profits." Friedman asserted that the corporate executives' only responsibility to their shareholders was "to conduct the business in accordance with their desires, which generally will be to make as much money as possible while conforming to the basic rules of the society, both those embodied in law and those embodied in ethical custom" (p. 56). He concluded that managers had no additional obligations to use corporate resources to promote "social goals," or moral values, such as providing employment, eliminating discrimination, reducing pollution, preventing inflation, and fighting poverty.

Despite placing some constraints on corporate behavior, such as child labor and minimum wage laws, U.S. courts consistently upheld the profit-maximization principle. For example, in 1919 Henry Ford was sued by the Dodge brothers, who in addition to being suppliers to the Ford Motor Company were minority shareholders in that hugely profitable company. The Dodges objected to Ford's effort to limit stock dividends to 5 percent monthly and to plow the remaining profits back into expanding company operations. Ford defended his profit restrictions as his desire "to employ still more men, to spread the benefits of this industrial system to the greatest possible number, to help them build up their lives and their homes." In rejecting the legality of Ford's assertions, the Michigan Supreme Court stated:

> A business corporation is organized and carried on primarily for the profit of the stockholders. The powers of the directors are to be employed for that end.

The discretion of directors is to be exercised in the choice of means to attain that end and does not extend to a change in the end itself, to the reduction of profits or to the nondistribution of profits among stockholders in order to devote them to other purposes. (*Dodge v. Ford Motor Co.,* 170 N.W. Mich. [1919])

Although later judicial rulings permitted corporations to spend some assets for charitable and other nonprofit-related purposes, such philanthropic acts still had to serve the best long-range interests of the firm and hence of its shareholders (Oswald 1998:6). The Delaware Supreme Court concluded that the interests of nonshareholders could be considered only within the narrow context of hostile takeovers, provided that such consideration "bears some reasonable relationship to general shareholder interests" (*Unocal Corp. v. Mesa Petroleum Co.,* 493 A.2d 946 [Del. 1985]). In another takeover case, involving a board's evaluation of outside offers for corporate shares, "circumstances may dictate that an offer be rebuffed, given ... the alternatives available and their effect on the various constituencies, particularly the stockholders" (*Mills Acquisition Co. v. MacMillan, Inc.,* 559 A.2d 1261 [Del. 1989]). Court decisions generally required corporate managers to put their shareholders' desires for profits ahead of the short- and long-term interests of such nonshareholder constituencies as customers, suppliers, employees, and communities where their factories were located.

Consistent with the shareholder-primacy view, several economists and legal scholars proposed that firms could be fruitfully analyzed as a *nexus of contracts* (Alchian and Demsetz 1972; Fama 1980; Fama and Jensen 1983; Macey 1989; Ribstein 1989). Reverting to the nineteenth century's artificial-entity notion of the corporation, these theorists depicted the firm as a market writ small. A bundle of explicit and unwritten private contractual relationships bound together managers, employees, shareholders, consumers, and suppliers. These participants competed to gain optimal arrangements of their risks and opportunities to allocate costs and rewards. As a legal fiction, the corporation became merely an abstract arena or marketplace within which all participants pursue their divergent interests (Millon 1990). Shareholders' effective legal rights were determined by their relative success at striking bargains with the other parties. For example, to entice a hotshot CEO to run a risky "dot.com" startup, venture investors might be forced to concede huge stock options. Or, facing tight supplies of aviation fuel, airline executives should pay premium prices to keep their planes flying, thus cutting into stockholders' quarterly dividends. Top management's main function was to oversee the smooth operation of voluntary bargaining, supervise exchange agreements, and make other adjustments among the participants. As noted above, because shareholders stand last in line for legal claims on a corporation's assets (behind debtholders, whose fixed claims can be contracted out), their investments carried the greatest risk. Hence, the corporate managers owed a special responsibility to protect the shareholders' interests:

> In this capacity, managers act as agents for the shareholder principals. Forced by practical necessity to rely on agents, shareholders face the ever-present risk that managers will fail to act in ways that maximize shareholder financial interests. The costs associated with this risk are called "agency costs." In contrast to creditors and others with fixed claims against corporate revenue, it is the shareholders as residual claimants who ultimately bear these agency costs. If the web of contracts that makes up the firm fails to minimize agency costs, shareholders pay these costs because buyers will pay less for their stock and distributions or liquidation proceeds will be lower than they would have been under more efficient management. (Million 1990:230)

Agency theorists asserted that all other corporate participants (including suppliers, customers, and employees) remained free to bargain to protect their interests. Whatever agreements they reached were private matters among autonomous individuals and should not subjected to government regulation or protection.

Toward the end of the twentieth century, *stakeholder theory*, an alternative to the shareholder-primacy view, gained a precarious foothold in legal scholarship but without definitive judicial rulings regarding its constitutionality (Freeman 1984, 1994; Hill and Jones 1992; Blair 1995). First enunciated by Professor E. Merrick Dodd (1932), the stakeholder model argued that corporations should be socially responsible institutions managed in the public interest, where diverse groups lay conflicting but legitimate claims on the corporation's resources. "Business is permitted and encouraged by the law primarily because it is of service to the community rather than because it is a source of profit to its owners" (Dodd 1932:1149). For example, some later legal commentators advocated that firms were obligated to protect workers and middle managers displaced by corporate reorganizations and bust-up takeovers (Coffee 1988; O'Connor 1991). The schematic in Figure 7.1 depicts various stakeholder groups that might express their interests in the actions taken by a company (Donaldson and Preston 1995). The two-way arrows indicate that all these social actors simultaneously contribute resources to and obtain benefits from the firm. For example, in 1999 Minneapolis-based Honeywell Inc. announced that it would merge with AlliedSignal Corp. and move to New Jersey. City officials extracted a pledge from Honeywell's CEO to continue contributing $7 million in annual donations and employee volunteers to revive a struggling southside Minneapolis neighborhood around the firm's old headquarters complex (St. Anthony 1999).

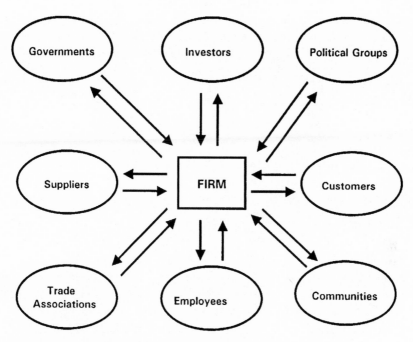

FIGURE 7.1   Stakeholder Model of the Corporation
SOURCE: Donaldson and Preston (1995)

Political receptivity to the social responsibility ideas behind the stake-holder theory was apparent in the "corporate constituency statutes" adopted by 29 U.S. state legislatures during the hostile corporate takeover craze of the 1980s (see the list of states in von Stange 1994:463). These laws permitted (and Connecticut actually required) boards of directors to broaden the traditional business-judgment rule—which constrains directors to act in good faith and in "the best interests of the corporation"—to con-sider how their policy decisions affect current and retired employees, cus-tomers, creditors, suppliers, and local communities (Wallman 1991). Ex-plicit in some statutes and implicit in others was the notion that directors should consider neither the shareholders nor the other constituencies as having the dominant or controlling interest. Some legal scholars argued that these corporate constituency laws, in giving top managers potentially unfettered discretion to redistribute company property from shareholders to the other stakeholders or even into their own pockets, would effectively deny shareholders a voice to complain or protest against management choices (see Mitchell 1997; Orts 1992; von Stange 1994; Leung 1997).

Ironically, despite intentions to protect nonshareholders, legislators passed laws that potentially shift power over societal wealth distribution from open political debates to hidden management self-dealing (Smart 1988). The courts never ruled on whether any constituency statutes, by weakening traditional shareholder claims to a firm's residual assets, violated the U.S. Constitution's provisions against property takings:

> In sum, the constituency statutes, by their broad language, provide for a radical reworking of traditional corporate governance relationships. Under the statutes, management may disregard the best interests of the shareholders in order to further the interests of other stakeholders (or, quite possibly, to further their own interests). The statutes thus permit widespread wealth redistribution from shareholders to protected constituency groups and/or management. Such a redistribution has all the trappings of a traditional regulatory taking. (Oswald 1998:9–10)

Despite the existence of constituency laws for two decades, none of the covered groups sought to enforce their provisions in a specific situation such as a factory closing. The increased corporate merger wave of the 1990s (see Chapter 3) might eventuate in a landmark lawsuit challenging the statutes' constitutionality. Until the controversy over corporate social responsibility is politically and legally resolved, the shareholder primacy conceptualization remains the prevailing legal doctrine underpinning corporate governance.

Board Rules and Realities

Although the United States lacked a uniform body of federal corporation law, many states closely followed Delaware's General Corporation Law. In the century since that tiny state aggressively entered the competition for charters in 1899, it attracted a majority of the largest U.S. incorporations. Delaware's approach to corporate governance was institutionalized nationally through the American Bar Association's Model Business Corporation Act, eventually adopted by 35 states. By statute in all states, a board of directors elected by the shareholders has the legal authority and duty to manage or supervise the corporation's business, although in practice daily decision making is delegated to the corporate officers (Clark 1991:56–57). *Duty to manage* involves selecting competent senior managers, establishing institutional norms and processes, reviewing and shaping strategy, and "a careful and continuous monitoring of the performance of senior management and the enterprise itself" (Varallo and Dreisbach 1996:2).

Two additional classic duties constrain the scope of a board's authority. The duties of loyalty and of care are designed to protect the shareholders' investments from conflicts of interest with management. The *duty of loyalty* requires the directors to make decisions only in the corporation's best interest and not for any personal gain, for example, by selling to or buying from another firm in which they have a stake, or by profiting from insider trading of shares. The *duty of care* obligates directors to inform themselves of all relevant available information before acting, for example when considering whether to accept a takeover bid from another firm. Another core principal of corporate governance, the *business judgment rule*, shields the directors' actions from shareholder lawsuits: When a risky decision turns out badly for the company, the directors' liability is limited if their decision was made with independence (no personal financial interest involved), due care (diligent consideration of the available expert knowledge), and good faith (acting on honest beliefs about the firm's best interests).

This prevailing legal formulation of board formal authority conflicts, however, with much empirical evidence about how publicly held corporations really operated throughout the twentieth century. As two astute observers concluded, directors behaved less like "the corporate potentates the law intends them to be than the management pawns they have too often been" (Lorsch with MacIver 1989:193). The crucial insight of the classic research study, *The Modern Corporation and Private Property* (1932), by Adolph Berle and Gardiner Means, was that professional management's interests had historically become separated from the interests of the shareholders who nominally owned the corporation. Self-interested managers, who controlled but did not own the physical and social means of production, were motivated by drives for greater power, prestige, and job security but not by the short-term profit-maximizing goals of owners. Shareholders, who desired to maintain high liquidity by trading their shares in open stock markets, in effect relinquished responsibility for handling the assets represented by their shares: "The management is more or less permanent, directing the physical property which remains intact while the participation privileges of ownership are split into innumerable parts—'shares of stock'—which glide from hand to hand, irresponsible and impersonal" (Berle and Means 1932:285).

Although the stockholders formally elected the board of directors to supervise managerial performance, diffuse shareholding and diluted responsibility through high stock turnover meant that rarely did a single person or small group own sufficient aggregate shares to control executive decisions in the largest companies.[1] In most large U.S. corporations, the biggest block of stock held by any single shareholder might amount to no more than 1 or 2 percent. Although the Berle-Means managerialism thesis was challenged in detail, especially for smaller corporations and closely held family firms (e.g., Zeitlin 1974; Mizruchi 1982), its general contours remained relevant. In effect, shareholders long ago relinquished formal legal responsibility for constraining management in exchange for receiving regular dividends and share liquidity. Hence, the historical economic transformation between the nineteenth and twentieth centuries—from small, tightly controlled family enterprises to giant, publicly held corporations with numerous passive and diffuse shareholders—put upper management in the dominant position atop the modern corporation's power structure.

Top executives also enjoyed structural control through several formal corporate governance mechanisms that allowed them to perpetuate their power against ineffective challengers. Foremost was their advantage in conducting elections to the board of directors. Any group of insurgent investor activists trying to elect a majority of new directors at an annual shareholders meeting had to secure millions of proxy votes from the scattered shareholders. The proxy solicitation process favored the executive officers, who benefited from far greater access to the corporate proxy machinery (Eisenberg 1976:97–127). Managements could systematically contact shareholders, urging them to sign and mail back the proxy cards that authorized the listed proxies to vote for the current board's recommended slate of candidates. In virtually every election, the current board presented a single slate of candidates for the open seats, a situation resembling the rigged plebiscites held by communist dictators. The proxy rules issued by the Securities and Exchange Commission (SEC) under the 1934 Securities Exchange Act—which required firms to make a full disclosure of the names and financial interests of the directors proposed by management—also permitted a public corporation to pay management's solicitation expenses for legal advice, printing, mailing, and faxing. Many insurgent investors, with only limited access to this proxy machinery, bore much heavier burdens in trying to mount effective challenges to the incumbent candidates. Because corporate officers inevitably dominated the proxy solicitation process, they could effectively guarantee the re-election of their handpicked board members, thereby assuring themselves a free hand in formulating policies, programs, and successor appointments.

Some notable changes occurred in the composition of the largest corporations' boards toward the end of the twentieth century. One analysis of the proxy statements by the 1970 Fortune 500 industrial companies (Smith 1970) found a mean board size of 12.9 members, while my 20 percent sample of Fortune 500 firms in 1998 found a board mean of 11.6 (the median sizes were 12 and 11, respectively).[2] As the two percentage distributions in Figure 7.2 show, this shrinkage in seats occurred primarily because very large boards almost disappeared over the three decades. An even more dramatic shift was the substantial decrease in the numbers of "inside directors," defined in the 1970 study as current firm employees and more broadly in 1998 as current and retired employees plus nonemployees with family ties to current insiders. In 1970, inside directors occupied 57.5 percent of all board seats and almost half the companies (49.7 percent) were "management controlled," meaning that a firm's own managers occupied a majority of director seats. By 1998, inside director seats fell to just 25.3 percent. Inside members controlled a majority of boards in just one-tenth of the firms; the CEO was the sole insider on one-quarter of all boards. (CEOs also served as the board chair in nearly 85 percent of the 1998 companies.)

The formal definitions of inside directors used in both analyses do not mean that outside directors were all independent of management control or influence. As one scholar of corporate law noted more than two decades ago:

> [M]ost directors in most publicly held corporations are closely tied to the chief executive—either economically, through an employment, professional, consulting, or supplier relationship with the corporation, or psychologically, through friendship, prior employment, or the fact that they have been selected and indoctrinated by the chief executive and hold their seats at his pleasure. (Eisenberg 1976:171–172)

This subservient situation appeared to change little over time, despite the much smaller proportions of employees and kin on most boards. The Walt

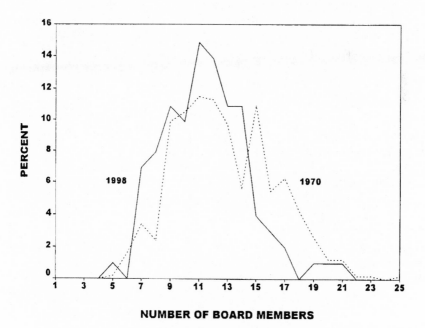

NUMBER OF BOARD MEMBERS

FIGURE 7.2 Board Sizes, 1970 and 1998
SOURCE: Smith (1970); Securities and Exchange Commission (1999)

Disney Company, purveyor of family-oriented entertainment, perennially exhibited an incestuous entanglement. Chaired by company CEO Michael Eisner, Disney's 1999 board included Eisner's personal lawyer, who also chaired the compensation committee; an architect who had designed Eisner's Aspen home and his parents' apartment; the principal of an elementary school once attended by Eisner's (now grown) children; the president of a university to which Eisner donated $1 million; and seven current or former Disney executives (Byrne 2000). Most of the outside directors owned little or no Disney stock. As discussed below, the ratio of inside to outside directors was a significant factor in awarding high financial compensation to CEOs, and Disney seemed no exception.

Another common board practice, whose implications for management influence over board members were less obvious, was paying substantial compensation to the outside directors. In the 1998 Fortune 500 sample, the median annual retainer was $30,000, with an additional $2,500 for chairing a committee and $1,000 per day for attending meetings. Almost all companies (87 percent) also offered their directors a stock grant or stock option, and most allowed a tax advantage by deferring fees until they left office. By requiring directors to hold at least a nominal stake in the firm, one argument went, they would be more disposed to act in the shareholders' best interests. Such modest levels of financial inducement may be mere pocket change for multi-millionaire directors who are executives at other large corporations, but they probably weren't trifling remuneration for the professors, university presidents, former public officials, and nonprofit sector leaders who composed a sizable minority of the corporate directorship. In a 1986 survey, 1,100 directors of Standard and Poor's 400 companies claimed that financial rewards were the least important personal benefit they derived from board membership, behind such psychological and intrinsic rewards as "opportunity to learn" and "seeing new businesses" (Lorsch with MacIver 1989:28).

Most state business statutes specified that directors ordinarily should be elected by shareholders to one-year terms of office (Varello and Dreisbach 1996:15). However, increasing numbers of large firms adopted "classified" or "staggered" boards, which divided the directors into three groups elected in different years to serve three-year terms. This device diffused widely during the 1980s as several corporations fought desperately to evade hostile takeovers by outside investors trying to gain control over their boards through proxy election fights (Useem 1996:160). Fighting a three-year campaign was presumably more difficult and costly than ousting all management candidates in a single election. By 1998, 62 percent of the Fortune 500 sample used a classified board electoral system. Although state laws did not mandate specific committee structures, most boards used nominating and compensation committees. The nominating committee screened and proposed the single slate of candidates for director elections. Not surprisingly, the vast majority of persons running in every election were incumbent board members. Compensation committees reviewed and approved salaries and bonuses for the executive officers and administered the company's stock option plans. Virtually every large corporate board used an audit committee, which recommended certified public accountants for the board's approval, reviewed the company's internal financial and accounting control systems, and monitored the effectiveness of audit efforts. This committee was widely adopted following a 1984 New York Stock Exchange requirement that any U.S. company listed on the NYSE must have an audit committee that "shall consist of at least three directors, all of whom have no relationship to the company that may interfere with the exercise of their independence from management and the company" (New York Stock Exchange 2000). Of course, as noted above, the legal concept of director independence was narrowly construed.

Executive Pay Politics

Executive compensation and dismissals, such as those in the GM case discussed at the beginning of this chapter, were two prominent occasions when political struggles for control of corporate policy surfaced publicly. Paying and firing the CEO were routine and rare actions, respectively, taken by a board of directors to reward or punish the top executive official for real or imagined accomplishments and failures. Numerous research studies sought to explain how these institutional control mechanisms operated, with limited success from applying micro-economic theories of human capital and risk-taking incentives. The political perspective on the relations between corporate officers and the board of directors offered more accurate insights into these aspects of corporate governance.

Another Day, Another Million Bucks

After sex in the workplace, sky-high executive pay kindled the most heated political controversy in the business world. The issue stirred deeply held public opinions about "fairness" and "excess" rewards. Every spring, outraged business and popular media reported the enormous annual compensation packages awarded to CEOs of the nation's largest companies. For example, in 1998 Michael Dell received options on another 6.4 million shares of Dell Computer Corp., despite having just sold off $725 million of his $16 billion stake in the company he founded (Sloan 1999). Editorial writers routinely condemned the "piling of pig on pork," flagrant instances of wealthy business leaders amassing multi-million dollar bonuses after laying off thousands of company employees. Graef Crystal, a former compensation consultant to senior management who repented his misdeeds, embarked on a new career of publicizing "the bloated pay packages of American CEOs, [that] with few exceptions, contain hardly any pay risk" (Crystal 1992:31). On the plausible assumption that spectacularly high executive remuneration should occur only when firms produced better-than-average returns for shareholders, Crystal cited deficient performances throughout the 1980s at such firms as Champion International, ITT, Occidental Petroleum, and W.R. Grace despite their CEOs' lucrative salaries, bonuses, and stock options (Crystal 1992:96–109). Subsequent articles posted on Crystal's Web site slammed Kodak, Computer Associates, Mattel, SBC Communications, Compaq Computer, Colgate-Palmolive, CompUSA and Electronic Data Systems for allegedly awarding top officers disproportionately to those firms' stock price performances.

Not to leave the impression that all CEO paychecks were disconnected from any risk, Crystal cited three "good guys"—Paul Fireman at Reebock, Anthony O'Reilly at H. J. Heinz, and Michael Eisner at the Walt Disney Company—whose contracts allowed large payouts only for major economic performances (but see criticisms below of O'Reilly and Eisner for dominating their boards). The paradigmatic case was Eisner, lured away from Paramount Pictures by Disney in 1984 to rescue that foundering amusement park and movie studio conglomerate. Crystal argued that "Eisner plays the game fairly by assuming a relatively high degree of pay risk" in the especially volatile entertainment industry (Crystal 1992:166). The Disney board, following a compensation consultant's advice, cut a bonus-and-stock-option deal that quickly made Eisner the poster boy for all aspiring CEOs. His initial contract called for (1) freezing his base salary at $750,000 for six years; (2) an option on approximately 2 million Disney common shares at $14 per share with a 10-year exercise period; and (3) an annual bonus of 2 percent of net company earnings, after deducting an amount equal to 9 percent after-tax return on the company's average shareholder equity. For a 10-year contract renegotiated in 1989, Eisner's bonus threshold was raised to 11 percent return on equity. By 1988, Disney's profits had quintupled to $550 million and its stock zoomed from $14 to $66 per share. Eisner's $7 million annual bonus and $104 million on stock-option shares made him the nation's highest-paid company head (Crystal 1991:355). In the 1990s, with Disney stock soaring on mega-box-office receipts from such animated blockbusters as *The Lion King* and *Beauty and the Beast*, his take-home pay went through the roof. Eisner exercised options on 5.4 million shares in 1993, paying just $19.5 million for stock worth $203 million (Bates 1994).

This pittance was eclipsed by Eisner's 1997 contract, developed in part with advice from Crystal, which awarded him options on 8 million Disney shares, estimated to be worth as much as $771 million by 2006. "The package he got is awesome," Crystal said. "But if Sony had tried to lure him away, they would have offered him Tokyo and thrown in Kyoto as a bonus" (Farhi 1997). Disney shareholders also made out splendidly during Eisner's reign, enjoying annual returns of 21.6 percent between 1987 and 1997. However, in 1999 three top Disney executives lost their performance bonuses following a 22 percent plunge in profits due to lackluster consumer products and home video sales (Bates 2000). The big cheese consoled himself with just his $750,000 salary and another $50 million in exercised stock options. Apparently accepting Eisner's plan to turn around earnings growth, Disney shareholders rejected two dissident proposals at the 2000 annual meeting, one to consider cutting executive pay and another to create contested board elections.

Although Michael Eisner defined the Mt. Everest of CEO compensation packages, the Himalayan range is visible in Figure 7.3. As reported annually in the *Wall Street Journal*, the chart shows median values (in millions of 1999 dollars; that is, adjusted for inflation) from the proxy statements of the 350 biggest U.S. businesses.[3] Total executive pay packages more than tripled across the decade, rising from less than $1.0 million in 1989 to $2.85 million in 1999. The major driver was the stock market boom of the late 1990s, which dramatically increased the proportion of CEO income from exercising long-term stock options. In 1989, barely one-third of the CEOs exercised some stock options, accounting for a median value of $300,000, which was just 15 percent of compensation paid to the entire group. By 1999, more than 40 percent of CEOs cashed in their options, raking in an average $2.85 million, which was 41 percent of all compensation paid. (As Figure 7.3 shows, the median value of stock options received by those CEOs exercising them actually exceeded the median total compensation packages for all CEOs in both 1998 and 1999.) To put these figures into a comparative perspective, in 1999 the median annual earnings of full-time U.S. wage and salary workers was $33,000. Thus, the median CEO of the largest firms received income more than 95 times greater. And remember that "median" means half those top executives earned *more* than this amount!

Comparison with executive earnings in other industrial nations provides another slant on the lavish compensation enjoyed by top U.S. managers. Among companies with 1995 revenues above a half billion dollars, total compensation for British CEOs reached 51 percent of U.S. value, while German executives took home 49 percent and the French 45 percent, with Italians trailing far behind at 29 percent (Parker-Pope 1996). As a graphic illustration of these international disparities, when automakers Chrysler and Daimler-Benz merged in 1998, the top five U.S. managers earned an average of $10 million each; the top 10 German executives averaged only $1.1 million apiece (Steinmetz and White 1998). The Chrysler CEO's total

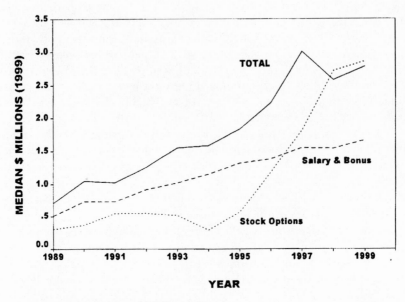

FIGURE 7.3   Median CEO Compensation
SOURCE: *Wall Street Journal* (1989–2000)

package was $16.1 million, more than two-thirds in stock and options, whereas the Daimler-Benz CEO's compensation of $1.9 million included only two-fifths in stock options. Cultural values and historical political pressures, especially stronger labor union representation, restrained European and Japanese executive pay levels to much smaller multiples of ordinary workers' wages than occurred in the United States. In a 1999 survey of mid-size manufacturing firms in 23 countries, a management consultancy company reported that total CEO compensation in the United States was 34 times greater than for employees, whereas in the United Kingdom CEO pay was only 24 times higher than for employees, in France it was only 15 times higher, in Germany 13 times higher, and in Japan 11 times higher (Towers Perrin 2000). Commenting on the narrower pay gaps, the director of a German shareholder protection association stated, "It's the European mentality. The enrichment of an individual on the backs of workers is considered exploitation" (Steinmetz and White 1998:B12). However the cross-national gap may shift toward the American executive pay model as globalization dynamics pressure all corporations to become more competitive in the world market for top managerial talent. Both German and Japanese governments planned to loosen their restrictions on executive stock options (Kroll 1998).

Principals Versus Agents

Agency theory is the predominant explanation among finance economists for executive compensation and its relation to firm performance. It originated as a general perspective on using incentives to gain control over organizational actors' behavior (Jensen and Meckling 1976; Fama and Jensen 1983; Mitnick 1993). Although agency theory shares some intellectual roots with transaction cost economics concerning information and cost-efficiency assumptions (Eisenhardt 1989), it emphasizes risk-sharing among cooperating parties rather than the boundary-setting questions that primarily animate the latter approach. An *agency relationship* is a "contract under which one or more persons (the principal(s)) engage another person (the agent) to perform some service on their behalf which involves delegating some decision making authority to the agent" (Jensen and Meckling 1976:308). An agent is paid for her services and retains some control or autonomy over her specific actions undertaken to achieve the principal's goal. Familiar examples are the Hollywood and sports agents hired by movie stars and athletes to obtain the most lucrative deals from studios and team owners. In business applications, the shareholders (principals) contract via the board of directors with a CEO and top management team (agents) to run the company to maximize profits and hence increase the shareholders' wealth. In most theoretical versions, because principals lack the agent's skills and knowledge (information asymmetry), they cannot accurately assess the quality of an agent's performance. Even the board members, who interact more directly than most shareholders with the manager-agents, do not possess detailed, day-to-day knowledge of company operations and managerial performances. Further, a self-interested agent typically pursues personal goals that do not fully coincide with a principal's aims. Thus, an agent is tempted to divert some of her efforts into activities that may fail to obtain the optimal value desired by her principal. For example, instead of maximizing the firm's current earnings and share value, a CEO may prefer to increase the company's long-term revenue or market share by spending resources on costly pet projects and corporate acquisitions that reduce the stock price. "In the jargon of agency theory, *moral hazard* tempts agents to take advantage of their privileges, producing agency costs for the principal" (Gomez-Mejia and Wiseman 1997:295).

Even worse, an agent may misrepresent or deliberately deceive the principal about her abilities or willingness to perform the job (which goes under the quaint euphemism "adverse selection"). Deceitful and incompetent agents hope to get away with such scams because principals may be unable to verify their agent's honesty and ability at the time of hiring or to assess their subsequent work performance with any accuracy. A persistent theme of agency theory is how best to safeguard the principal's interests against possible agent deceptions. One prevalent practice is to rely on "good old boy networks" to hire and promote male managers with similar social backgrounds, schooling, and entrenched interpersonal ties. This bias arises and persists because of widespread belief that similar social experiences make such candidates more reliable and trustworthy than applicants exhibiting different gender, racial, and social class characteristics. Rosabeth Moss Kanter's classic *Men and Women of the Corporation* (1978) drew attention to the organizational tendency, under conditions of high uncertainty, toward "homosocial reproduction" in selecting socially similar persons for high-prestige, high-reward positions. The result was much greater homogeneity in both board rooms and executive suites than was found in the lower ranks of organizational workforces.

To limit deviant agent efforts, principals could offer efficient incentives and construct monitoring mechanisms that compelled agents to align their interests with those of the principal. Such "agency costs" occurred routinely in supervisor-employee relations inside the firm, for example, for rewarding team productivity and detecting shirking workers. A further complication in agency relations arose whenever a principal and an agent held differing attitudes toward risk taking. In shareholder-CEO situations, the agent was presumed to be risk-averse because her income and wealth were so heavily tied up in that firm. In contrast, individual shareholders were presumably risk-neutral or even risk-prone, because they could more readily minimize potential harms by diversifying their stock portfolios to hold small percentages in many unrelated firms.

Agency theorists were especially concerned with crafting efficient compensation policies that optimally align shareholder and executive interests. Contractual mechanisms that made an executive's compensation contingent on easily observable outcomes—by tying annual bonuses, salary revisions, stock options, and other benefits to the firm's short-term economic performance—sought to reward or punish a CEO for enhancing or contracting shareholder wealth. However, contractually staking an executive's rewards to exceptionally high risks might prove counterproductive. Many factors that shape an organization's financial performance lie beyond direct managerial control. Outcomes such as profits and stock prices are subject to competitive market forces, shifting consumer whims, government regulations, technological changes, and many other forces in the national political economy. Under conditions of high uncertainty, putting ever greater proportions of an executive pay package at risk may simply drive an already risk-averse CEO toward increasingly conservative actions intended to avoid catastrophic damage to her stake. Thus, attempts by shareholders and their board representatives (principals) to make CEOs and other top managers (agents) more accountable by closely linking their compensation to organization performance might actually force them to make less-risky, less-innovative, and more cautious decisions that fail to boost firm performance to levels desired by the principals.

Despite agency theory's elegant simplicity, empirical evidence supporting the hypothesized pay-performance connection was extremely weak. Using data on 2,213 CEOs of 1,295 firms surveyed by *Forbes* magazine between 1974 and 1986, Michael Jensen and Kevin Murphy (1990) analyzed the impact of firm performance (annual change in shareholder wealth, measured as the inflation-adjusted rate of return on common stock) on CEO salaries, bonuses, total compensation, and job dismissal. They found that "changes in both the CEO's pay-related wealth and the value of his stockholdings are positively and statistically significantly related to changes in shareholder wealth" (p. 243). However, the estimated magnitude of the pay-performance sensitivity effect was just $3.25 per $1,000 change in shareholder wealth, explaining barely 3 percent of the variation in CEO pay. The average annual pay increase for CEOs whose shareholders gained $400 million in equity was $37,100, but CEOs whose shareholders *lost* $400 million also saw their pay go up, by $26,300. The difference was slightly more than one week's median income ($9,400) for the sampled CEOs. Jensen and Murphy concluded that the pay-performance relationship was "small for an occupation in which incentive pay is expected to play an important role" (p. 227). Although principal-agency theory is imprecise about how strong a pay-performance effect should be, the Jensen and Murphy findings implied a dismaying absence of substantial management incentives among publicly held corporations. "Highly sensitive pay-performance contracts may not be feasible even under risk neutrality since executives with limited resources cannot credibly commit to pay firms for large negative realizations of corporate performance, and shareholders cannot credibly commit to huge bonuses that amount to 'giving away the firm' for large positive realizations" (p. 244).

Other researchers drew similar conclusions about the limited abilities of principal-agent and economic efficiency theories to explain the decoupling of CEO pay and firm performance (Garen 1994; Haubrich 1994). A careful comparison of the 1930s with the 1980s concluded that pay-performance sensitivities "declined substantially" over a half century (Hadlock and Lumer 1997:179). However, after controlling for firm size, "the only statistically significant difference across time is that smaller firms have higher sensitivities in the modern era" (Hadlock and Lumer 1997:182). Large firms offered better opportunities to limit executive pay risks, because CEOs had more control over layoffs, acquisitions, and divestitures than over stock market performance. A "meta-analysis" of 105 prior studies spanning a variety of data sets and periods concluded that indicators of firm size (return on assets, market share, number of employees and the like) predicted CEO pay much better than did stock price performance:

"The results show that firm size explains more than ten times the amount of variance in executive pay than performance (i.e., 54% vs. 5% respectively) and that firm growth, rather than performance improvement, explains twice the amount of variation in CEO pay adjustments (i.e., 8% vs. 4% respectively)" (Gomez-Mejia and Wiseman 1997:315). Despite the strong impact of firm size on executive compensation, considerable differences in CEO pay remained among corporations of equal size operating in the same industries. Other factors possibly shaping compensation remain unanalyzed, most intriguingly the social and political dynamics of executive compensation discussed in the next two subsections.

Monitoring CEO Behavior

Some agency theorists argued that close monitoring of agents' behavior by principals is an effective alternative to contractual mechanisms. Behavioral criteria encompass the numerous routine tasks and strategic choices made by executives while performing their duties, regardless of successful or failed outcomes. If a principal invests in acquiring information to verify the agent's behavior, the agent is more likely to act in the former's interests (Eisenhardt 1989:60; Fama and Jensen 1983). This proposition should apply to boards evaluating CEOs just as to supervisors monitoring the keystrokes of data entry clerks. Because boards of directors legally represent the shareholders' interests, they may serve as an information-gathering and management behavior-monitoring mechanism (Baysinger and Hoskisson 1990). Implementing behavioral controls over top executives requires that a board obtain information beyond company financial performance data. Instead of rewarding a CEO on the basis of the firm's annual stock price performance, the board might base compensation on its knowledge of her actual behaviors. For example, bonuses could be awarded for investing in R&D projects having long-term payoff prospects rather than giving an immediate but temporary boost to the firm's bottom line. A substantial subjective element may intrude when a principal tries to monitor an agent's behaviors. A well-informed board might perceive consistently poor executive decisions and resist extravagant pet schemes, such as golden parachutes and anti-greenmail policies (see Chapter 3), that seem to benefit management more than the stockholders (Kosnik 1987). Notorious examples of executives bailing out with huge severance packages include $15 million in cash to the head of Florida Power Co. after that floundering firm was sold to another utility company (Sachdev 2000); $24 million to the chair of Long Island Lighting Co., who sank billions into an abandoned nuclear power plant (Halbfinger 1998); and $68.5 million in stock options to the CEO of Chrysler for arranging its acquisition by Daimler-Benz (Smith 2000).

Aligning managerial behavior with shareholders' interest may involve a trade-off between incentives, monitoring, and risk-bearing conditions. In a study of top management contracts used by 435 high-risk firms making initial public offerings in 1984, Beatty and Zajac (1994) measured five monitoring indicators: the ratio of outside board members to total directors, the ratio of outside owner-directors, whether both the board chair and CEO positions were held by the different persons, the presence of nondirector owners with more than 5 percent of total shares, and whether the IPO was venture-capital backed. Riskier firms were significantly less likely to include stock options as incentives in their compensation packages, thus avoiding imposing greater risks on normally risk-averse managers. However, all five monitoring measures consistently showed higher levels with greater firm riskiness and with lower use of stock options. That is, when contracts resulted in top managers holding small or no equity stakes, firms boosted behavior-based compensation policies by "structuring their boards of directors to ensure sufficient monitoring of managerial behavior" (Beatty and Zajac 1994:330).

A key determinant of board power and effectiveness in monitoring top management is whether directors have access to reliable information about the CEO's strategic activities. Baysinger and Hoskisson (1990) argued that inside board directors can better safeguard shareholder interests, because they are more likely than the outside directors to possess accurate knowledge and experience needed to evaluate the quality of a CEO's strategic choices. (As noted above, an inside board member is a current or former firm employee, such as the treasurer, vice-president, or even the CEO herself.) By definition, outside board members have limited experience with the day-to-day decision making occurring inside the firm. Their involvement is often confined to infrequent board meetings, during which they are expected to ratify final policy proposals previously crafted by top management. In contrast, as active participants in the firm, inside board members obtain advantaged insights into the CEO's competence and opportunism. Their much greater access to detailed corporate information enables insiders to argue effectively on behalf of appropriate levels and types of executive compensation. This special governance role of inside directors enables a board to discriminate among various causes of financial misfortune. "That is, through effective internal controls, top management is protected either from the adverse personal consequences of outcomes over which they have no control or from short-term losses that are the result of investments in future cash flows" (Baysinger and Hoskisson 1990:76). To the extent that inside members dominate a board and influence the outsiders to accept their judgments, the board should be less prone to rely on short-term firm-performance indicators and more prone to reward CEOs "on the basis of open and subjective evaluative methods" (p. 77). This benign interpretation of board power games makes the startlingly naïve assumption that insider members would really put shareholder interests ahead of their chief's pay and perks.

A contrary and more plausible perspective assumes that insider board members are inevitably beholden to the CEO both for their presence on the board and for continued employment at the firm. Company officers often develop strong personal ties to the top management team. In any conflict involving shareholder interests, they typically put loyalty to their chief foremost. Consequently, insider board members are highly susceptible to co-optation by the CEO. Being risk-averse, CEOs prefer their boards to make larger up-front cash payments rather than to link executive pay to long-term stock options whose ultimate value is contingent on risky economic events lying beyond the CEO's control. For example, when the speculative bubble in "dot.com" startup companies burst in 2000, many paper millionaires saw their stock options turn worthless overnight—"underwater" in executive-pay jargon.

Insider-dominated boards are less capable of firmly resisting questionable CEO decisions that boost executive benefits yet fail to maximize returns on shareholder investments (Finklestein and Hambrick 1989; Beatty and Zajac 1994). Such dependent boards would also be more prone to award large executive compensation packages that are not anchored to clear evidence of high-quality executive decisions or to firm financial performance indicators. Outsiders bring more detached perspectives, based in their broader experiences with other firms and industries as well as their financial independence from the CEO. They are structurally more predisposed to oppose management's tendency to avoid undertaking projects carrying the high risk returns preferred by shareholders. Thus, outsider-dominated boards would resist rubber-stamping CEO decisions and decoupling compensation from managerial accountability. Given the substantial autonomy acquired by top executives during the early twentieth century separation between corporate ownership and control (the Berle-Means managerialism thesis discussed above), the capacity of most corporate boards to act independently of CEO influence remained suspect. Determining whether boards or managers exert greater influence over executive compensation was ultimately an important answer to the much larger question: Who really governs the modern public corporation?

Some research evidence pointed to complex balances of power between boards and top management in the compensation process (Finklestein and Hambrick 1989; Sridharan 1996). An analysis of 175 manufacturing firms indicated that control over executive pay varied with the concentration of stock ownership and board monitoring. Boards of directors exerted more influence over CEO pay in owner-controlled firms (where the major owner held 5 percent or more of shares) than in management-controlled companies (Tosi and Gomez-Mejia 1989). Less monitoring occurred in these latter firms, and the CEO was more influential in setting her own compensation terms:

> Thus, the interests of owners in management-controlled firms must be represented by persons or groups chosen by, or a part of, management. This condition may lead to the decoupling of CEO compensation from performance because the influence over pay is moved more deeply into the firm, separating control from owners and their representatives. CEOs may take advantage of this freedom and set their pay to protect them against uncertainty. This is possible because of the complicated nature of long-term income and bonuses. (Tosi and Gomez-Mejia 1989:182).

Whether a CEO can successfully manipulate her board into offering a low-risk compensation plan depends on the relative power of each party. Because details about compensation-decision processes occurring behind closed board room doors rarely become publicly visible, investigators draw inferences about the governance process mainly from public data on formal board composition. Among several possible indicators of relatively greater CEO power are the length of the CEO's tenure, the ratio of insider to outsider board members, the number of board members appointed after the CEO assumes office, and whether the CEO and board chair positions are occupied by one person.

In a series of analyses of Forbes 500 and Fortune 500 firms, James Westphal and Edward Zajac explored various political dimensions of CEO pay. For example, boards increasingly adopted formal long-term incentive plans (LTIPs), which purportedly align managerial and shareholder interests by linking executive pay to firm performance (Westphal and Zajac 1994). Between 1972 and 1990, the proportion of 669 large firms formally adopting LTIPs peaked at 76 percent. However, in many firms these policies were merely symbolic statements designed to soothe shareholder worries. Powerful CEOs could fairly easily avoid implementing an LTIP. By the end of the period, only 55 percent of the adopting firms had actually paid any money to their CEOs within the first two years after approving a share grant plan. Ignoring an adopted LTIP was especially likely when the CEO held longer tenure in her job and also occupied the board chair seat (Westphal and Zajac 1994:382).

A further examination of proxy statements disclosed the shifting management rhetoric presented to shareholders to rationalize adoption of an incentive plan (Zajac and Westphal 1995). Later-adopting firms were more likely than earlier approvers to frame their justifications in principal-agency theory terms, and less likely to assert human resources grounds. Where the board was relatively more powerful than the CEO, a proxy statement more often contained agency-theoretic phrases (e.g., emphasizing that the LTIP would increase the CEO's financial stake in boosting company performance). Firms with more powerful CEOs tended to issue proxy statements proclaiming human capital incentives, that is, stressing the need for bigger rewards to "attract and retain" top managerial talent. "While powerful CEOs advertise their value to the firm and rationalize their power over the board by favoring LTIP explanations that reflect romanticized conceptions of corporate leaders, powerful boards favor accounts that emphasize board control over management" (Zajac and Westphal 1995:302). However, the type of rhetorical logic used to justify adopting an LTIP bore no connection to whether the firm actually implemented its LTIP, indicating that public justification of such compensation plans served primarily as a symbolic smokescreen for both boards and top managers.

Corporate compensation politics also operated in selecting board members. Both executives and boards tended to favor *homosocial* selection, that is, choosing persons who are most demographically similar to themselves (Kanter 1978). A social psychological preference for persons with similar gender, race, age, education, and career experiences arises from beliefs that such easily observed personal characteristics are reliable indicators of compatible attitudes, ideologies, goals, and behaviors. Shared identities among group members should facilitate smoother communication, lower conflict, and more comfortable interactions. Top executives prefer new board members who most closely resemble themselves, because they presumably would be more sympathetic and less critical in evaluating and rewarding the CEO. Thus, greater demographic similarity of directors and CEOs should increase the total compensation package but reduce the proportion of executive pay that is contingent on future firm performance.

However, whether a CEO can effectively control the board's nomination process depends on her power relative to the board. In an analysis of 413 large firms from 1986 to 1991, Zajac and Westphal (1995) used the same indicators of CEO and board power from their previous research. They found strong and consistent evidence that the length of CEO tenure, the ratio of inside to outside directors, the fusion of CEO and board chair positions, and lower levels of board stockholding each affected whether new directors were more demographically similar to the CEO or to the current board. CEOs were much more likely than their boards to influence the appointment of new members, indicating managerial entrenchment rather than board control in large enterprises. These findings were consistent with "social psychological studies on the hiring process, which suggest that CEOs (and boards) should favor new director candidates who share common group memberships with them ... [and] with a relatively deliberate, political process whereby CEOs increase board support for their decisions and minimize the risk of dissension by favoring individuals with similar philosophies on strategy and administration, as indicated by demographic characteristics" (p. 77). By recruiting socially similar boards, powerful executives strengthened their coalition of supporters and reinforced their domination of the existing corporate power structure. Furthermore, increasing the CEO-board similarity subsequently changed the executive compensation contract. The greater the change in similarity, the more generous the CEO's total compensation and the smaller the portion of pay conditional on firm economic performance.

These results cast doubt on Baysinger and Hoskisson's (1990) contention that inside board members could better represent the shareholders' interests. Rather, relatively few firms had boards of directors with sufficient independence to resist CEO domination of the board selection processes. Hence, managerial domination over corporate governance grew further entrenched. Even in instances where a board managed to obtain some independence from top management, a CEO confronting a serious loss of power usually could offset the board's autonomy by resorting to ingratiation and persuasion tactics. In a survey of both CEOs and outside directors of 221 large- and medium-size U.S. corporations, Westphal (1998) showed that the impact of board structural change on organizational outcomes triggered CEO countermeasures. He measured board structural independence by a higher ratio of outside to inside board members, separation of CEO and board chair incumbency, increased demographic similarity among board members, and reduced CEO-board friendship ties. CEOs facing board threats to their entrenched power used ingratiation (opinion conformity, flattery, favor-doing) and persuasion (defending current policies, blaming uncontrollable factors) to turn the situation around. These devices effectively canceled any impact that board independence might exert to reduce company diversification strategy, decrease total executive pay, or make CEO compensation more contingent on firm performance. Instead, the more ingratiating and persuasive the CEO, the more favorable these outcomes were to the executive. Ironically, efforts to enhance board independence in the shareholders' interests might prove counterproductive by mobilizing CEO interpersonal manipulations that succeed in reducing the board's overall power.

Getting by with a
Little Help from Friends

Organization researchers began examining the role of corporate social capital as an alternative to economic efficiency explanations of compensation. As discussed in Chapters 4 and 6, *social capital* at the individual level of analysis refers to social-structural relations embedded in interpersonal networks, which people can mobilize to obtain better opportunities and benefits not attainable in the absence of such ties (Knoke 1999:7). Network ties constituting social capital may affect social action independently of an person's human capital assets, such as skills, education, training, and work experience. The social capital of CEOs and directors consists of their personal friendships, common elite institutional affiliations (such as club memberships, same-college attendance, and interlocking directorates on other corporate boards), and shared corporate functional experiences (such as careers in finance or tenancy in top management positions). These connections may facilitate a variety of fundamental social comparison and social influence processes, such as trust, admiration, sympathy, support, reciprocity, status-deference, and conformity. By providing selective access to important information, corporate social capital networks represent a significant reference group for the social construction of status, performance evaluations, and compensation standards. Apparently, alpha males are as potent in corporate suites as in gorilla tribes; perhaps Jane Goodall could start another project?

To ascertain how social capital shaped executive pay, Belliveau, O'Reilly and Wade (1996) analyzed 61 large corporations. They measured social capital as the status (amount and prestige of social resources available through social connections) of both the CEO and the chair of the board's compensation committee. Social similarity within a pair did not influence remuneration, and the absolute amount of social capital status mattered much less than relative status difference between the two persons. High-status CEOs paired with low-status compensation chairs received significantly more pay than low-status CEOs paired with high-status chairs. Consistent with resource dependence theory, the lower-status member of a dyad seemed more likely to accept the pay demands of the partner with more social capital. Given this influence function of social capital, "there is a powerful incentive for CEOs to select lower-status board members" (p. 1586), who can be more easily intimidated into acquiescing in the executive's financial demands.

Cozy ties between CEOs and their board cronies may tolerate laid-back oversight, leading to oversized executive pay packages despite lackluster firm performance. *Business Week*'s ratings of best and worst corporate boards singled out Disney, Occidental Petroleum, Rite Aid, and H. J. Heinz for its 2000 scoldings. In the late 1990s Heinz's flamboyant CEO and chair, Anthony J. F. O'Reilly, became a favorite whipping boy of corporate governance critics. A former professional rugby player, newspaper mogul, and richest man in Ireland, this charismatic marketer (who once toured U.S. military bases with a seven-foot "Private Pickle") had packed the food and drink company's board of directors with company insiders and close friends. Although the board awarded him more than $180 million in total compensation during the 1990s, the company stock lagged significantly behind the wider market at the end of the decade. Before resigning in 1997 after 18 years as CEO, O'Reilly announced a drastic corporate restructuring that closed or downsized one-quarter of Heinz factories around the world, cut a tenth of its workforce, and shed its Weight Watchers slimming classes (Power 1997; Barboza 1999). Asked whether O'Reilly had been forced to resign by relentless criticism from corporate governance activists, one stock analyst concluded, "This guy could not be pushed because he had everyone on the board on his side" (Smart 1997). The new CEO launched yet another campaign to recapture lost market share from private-label companies by aggressively promoting Heinz's bean, pet food, and ketchup brands.

Board interlocks offer another relational network through which CEOs can control corporate power structures by selecting board members who perpetuate a passive, subservient stance on compensation. Outside board members who also serve on other company boards provide information channels through which compensation practices diffuse. Powerful top managers prefer to recruit and retain board candidates with prior experience on passive boards and to avoid candidates from firms whose boards actively monitor and control their CEOs. Similarly, firms with more powerful boards would prefer new directors with activist reputations. These congruent selective-recruitment mechanisms sustain a segmented market for contrasting types of corporate directors. In their analysis of 491 large companies from 1985 to 1992, Zajac and Westphal (1996) showed that low-control boards added passive management-oriented members and subtracted experienced activists. In contrast, high-control boards recruited active, shareholder-oriented directors. Segregation across types of boards was very high, with only 18 percent of observed interlock ties occurring between high-control and low-control boards. "Our findings indicate that while organizational practices spread through the network of interlocking directorates, powerful actors in CEO-board relationships can block or redirect the diffusion of those changes that diminish their control by cutting off interlock ties to other adopters of those practices and steering the diffusion of changes that protect or increase their control over the focal board by adding ties to prior adopters" (p. 526).

Further analyses disclosed that board members who themselves were CEOs of other companies (labeled "CEO-directors") did not invariably support a general norm of reciprocity among CEOs. This norm asserts the obligation to protect a fellow chief executive by opposing greater board control over top management (Westphal and Zajac 1997). "In this system of social interaction among status equals, sufficient trust exists that CEO-directors believe their support for CEOs will be reciprocated at some time in the future" (p. 177). In other words, good ol' boys should really look after each other. Analyses of 422 large firms between 1982 and 1992 revealed that the higher the proportion of CEO-directors, the fewer control-enhancing changes they made in the board structure (e.g., separating the CEO and chair positions, increasing the ratio of outside directors, or increasing the demographic dissimilarity of the board and CEO). However, if CEO-board members had experienced increased board control at their home companies, they were more likely to defect to support greater board control over their fellow CEO in the focal company. Finally, the presence of CEO-directors decreased board support for unrelated diversification and contingent compensation contracts.

The presence of CEO-directors who had suffered reduced diversification and increased pay contingency at their own companies increased the chances of similar changes at the focal company. However, neither undesirable outcome resulted from CEO-directors observing increased board control while serving as outside directors at a third company. In effect, board members who had been forced to pay their dues weren't about to let one of their peers off easily. The overall results provided "strongly consistent evidence that the diffusion of increased board independence and control, as manifested by specific changes in board structure, greater compensation contingency, and reduced diversification, is affected by the CEO-directors' experience at the CEOs' home companies, consistent with the social exchange perspective, but not by CEO-directors' experience as outside directors, contrary to a traditional network diffusion perspective" (Westphal and Zajac 1997:177). That is, rather than spreading through imitation and social learning processes, tighter controls over top executives diffused mainly through personal experiences that led CEO-directors to reduce the structural power of their fellow corporate leaders. These changes occurred mostly at the margins of corporate governance, because board independence didn't diffuse widely among large firms. CEO-directors who experienced losses of structural power accounted for less than 10 percent of corporate boards. Thus, the vast majority of top managers escaped sanctioning by their defecting fellow CEOs.

Farewell to the Chief

The downside of executive compensation is the forced dismissal of a CEO, a relatively rare reason for departure (Weisbach 1988; Jensen and Murphy 1990; Murphy and Zimmerman 1993). The hierarchical authority structure of corporations makes them more susceptible than federated or voluntary organizations to internal social movements that target discontent on company leaders (Zald and Berger 1978; see Chapter 8 for discussion of other organizational social movement). Such unconventional corporate politics tend toward a conspiratorial coup, exemplified by General Motors' ouster to its CEO described at the beginning of this chapter. An *executive coup* involves a small but critically located band of conspirators that swiftly seizes power, usually with the narrow goal of replacing the current leadership by a new executive team mandated to change the firm's direction. This type of turnover differs from routine leadership changes arising through a CEO's planned retirement, where finding a replacement involves a prolonged and public search for a successor. An executive coup must be planned in secrecy and sprung without the CEO's knowledge or public awareness, to thwart counterattack and retaliation. A successful coup requires the plotters to overcome the prevailing business norm of executive loyalty and to gain sufficient support or neutralization of board members and shareholders to force the CEO out. Zald and Berger (1978:837) hypothesized that coup attempts would be more likely to occur in firms that experienced economic poor performance or bad decisions attributable to the CEO; failed to protect their senior executive positions from arbitrary CEO actions; usually promoted CEO successors from within rather than from outside; and provided senior officers with regular contacts with board members, who control the most important power resource, votes.

Finance economists emphasized poor firm performance as the primary explanation of top management dismissals. An analysis (Denis and Denis 1995) of 1,689 firms from 1985 to 1988 found that 55 percent experienced a turnover of the CEO, president, or board chair (some companies experienced multiple departures). However, only 13 percent of these changes were "forced" resignations, as identified by press releases and newspaper reports (although some stated reasons of poor health, retirement, and pursuit of other interests might have disguised nonvoluntary exits). A majority of these forced departures appeared to result not from normal board monitoring but from external events such as shareholder lawsuits, takeover attempts, and large-block shareholder pressures. An event-history analysis disclosed that large and significant operating performance declines preceded the forced CEO removals, and firm improvements followed their departures. In contrast, no significant financial deterioration preceded voluntary executive retirements. "Finally, forced top management changes do not appear to be very timely; managers appear to be forced out only after an extended period of poor performance involving substantial shareholder losses" (Denis and Denis 1995:1055). Another study, analyzing the CEO succession process at 626 firms from 1969 to 1989, came to similar conclusions (Parrino 1997). Forced dismissals also accounted for just 13 percent of all executive changes. Stock price performance was much worse at firms firing their CEOs than at companies with routine retirements. Outsiders were significantly more likely to succeed forced-out CEOs than those who voluntarily retired, suggesting that troubled companies sought fresh executive blood to revive the floundering enterprise.

Choosing a CEO's successor is implicitly a political act, but one which may reflect institutionalized procedures more than overt power struggles between boards and top managers. William Ocasio (1994, 1999) analyzed the political dynamics of CEO succession in 120 large U.S. industrial corporations from 1960 to 1990. He compared two political models predicting opposite effects on rates of executive turnover. First, *institutionalization of power* strengthens as a board commits to specific policies and the CEO's actions become taken-for-granted. "[I]ncumbents may use their power to expend resources, make appointments, and establish networks of influence in ways that consolidate and perpetuate their power" (1994:287). Hence, over time CEOs grow entrenched and insulated from the pressures of poor firm performance. Second, *circulation of power*, reflecting internal political struggles, presumes that environmental turbulence creates opportunities for conflict inside the organization. With time, a CEO's inflexible preferred strategies and programs grow obsolete and unable to produce effective solutions to external problems. As firm performance deteriorates, rivals and enemies emerge to challenge and wrest power from the incumbent top executive. Thus, under conditions of poor company performance, longer CEO tenure should increase the rate of succession.

CEO turnover over the three decades revealed a rising rate of succession during a leader's initial 10 years in office, consistent with the power circulation explanation (Ocasio 1994). However, if a CEO managed to survive into her second decade, the subsequent rate of replacement slowly declined, supporting hypotheses from the institutionalization perspective. The power circulation dynamic was most conspicuous for CEOs hired after 1980, who experienced especially steep rates of removal compared to much lower risks for previous cohorts. The huge 1980s market for large-firm takeovers dramatically raised the vulnerability of corporate executives to contested expulsion. "These results indicate that for recent CEO appointees, the managerialist model of corporate control has been increasingly challenged and the legitimacy of their authority is being eroded. This study predicts that this trend will continue, consistent with recent anecdotal evidence of rising contestation of the power of the CEO and increased turnover in the CEO position" (p.309). One result contrary to long-held beliefs was that a board dominated by inside members, rather than acting as loyal pawns of the chief, were actually more likely to contest and limit the CEO's power, especially under adverse economic conditions.

In further analyses, Ocasio (1999) examined whether institutionalized rules or past succession precedents constrained boards to pick a new CEO from inside or outside the firm. Selection of an outsider offered an opportunity to realign the firm's policies and strategies with the controlling interests of the board. The presence of formal succession rules was indicated by an internal executive labor market for insider CEO succession, based on the job titles of a company's inside directors (e.g., president, chief operating officer, vice chair). Reliance on historical precedents involved prior selections of insider or outsider CEOs, or both. Ocasio's event history analyses revealed that both principles significantly affected board choices: (1) formal rules of insider CEO succession strongly increased insider selection; but (2) in the absence of past precedents, insider succession rates decreased. Applying executive succession rules strengthened a board's commitments to and identification with the company's programs, mission, and identity. By channeling political struggles into constraining normative practices and procedures, board members avoided passively rubber-stamping the departing CEO's heir apparent:

> Reliance on rules of CEO succession and corporate governance also suggests that political maneuverings in organizations are unlikely to be directly expressed or mobilized within the board of directors. This is consistent with a view of managerial power and political dynamics driven by emergent power struggles rather than fixed political coalitions and where overt efforts at social influence, managerial entrenchment, and the institutionalization of executive power are not likely to be effective. (Ocasio 1999:413–414)

Institutional Investors Are Revolting

At the end of the twentieth century, a significant internal challenge arose to managerial dominance over corporation affairs. Large institutional stock owners, such as pension funds and insurance companies, sought to reimpose controls over top management's license to run the show at the expense of shareholder value (Pound 1992). Managers fought back with diverse delaying tactics but were occasionally forced to concede significant changes in formal authority structures or informal power configurations. This section assesses the impacts of the institutional investor revolt on changing corporate governance practices. (For analyses of other social movements arising inside organizations, see Chapter 8.)

A dramatic shift in the ownership of U.S. corporation stocks, from individual shareholders to institutional investors, occurred over three decades. These enterprises include public and private pension funds, investment companies and mutual funds, insurance companies, banks, trust funds, and foundations. As shown in Figure 7.4, total corporate stockholdings swelled from less than $1 trillion in 1973 to more than $15 trillion by 1998, rising rose most rapidly during the stock market boom of the 1990s. Over the entire period, the proportion held by the household sector (which also includes U.S. stocks held by foreign residents and by state and local governments) plummeted from 67 percent to 48 percent.

Among two broad groups of institutional shareholders, insurance companies and pension plans owned a larger portion in 1998 (31 percent) than other institutions such as banks, trust funds, and mutual funds (21 percent).

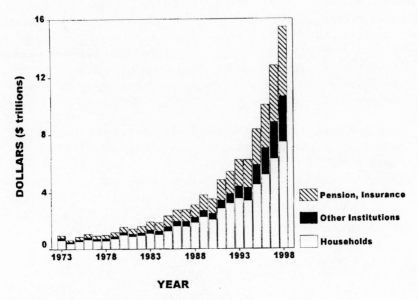

FIGURE 7.4   Institutional Stock Holding
SOURCE: Federal Reserve (1999)

Some researchers estimated that institutions controlled 57 percent of equity in the 1,000 largest U.S. corporations by the mid-1990s (see Brancato [1996] and Useem [1996:25]). The shift in ownership was not unique to the United States, as indicated by comparable growth in total assets held by institutional investors among the two dozen advanced industrial nations: They skyrocketed from $3.2 trillion in 1981 to more than $24.4 trillion in 1995 (Blommestein 1998). This global sea change induced one perceptive analyst to characterize the dawning era as one of "pension fund socialism" (Drucker 1976), while another observer labeled the emergent system as "investor capitalism" (Useem 1996). The waxing dominance of institutional shareholding obviously meant all things to all people.

The colossal stock portfolios at the disposition of professional fund managers gave these institutions potentially enormous influence over financial markets. In particular, the large pension funds faced a classic *exit-voice dilemma* (Hirschman 1970). As the super-sizing of their stock holdings grew, fund managers discovered that they could not simply dump shares whenever they grew disenchanted with a particular firm's underperforming stock. That exit strategy would work only if stock prices remained unaffected by a pension fund's buy-and-sell actions. But because large institutions must trade primarily with one another, any massive sell-off of lousy stocks to buyers also having the same poor opinion of its value would immediately trigger a precipitous plunge in share values, thus further damaging the retirement fund's clients. So the only realistic option for institutional investors to salvage their stakes was to hang onto their poorly performing investments while voicing their dissatisfactions about deteriorating "shareholder value" directly to the firm's management. In Hirschman's (1970:41) words, "Voice is most likely to function in markets with few buyers or where buyers account for an important proportion of total sales, both because it is easier for few buyers than many to combine for effective action and simply because each one may have much at stake and wield considerable power even in isolation." Shareholder activism involved "monitoring and attempting to bring about changes in the organizational control structure of firms (targets) not perceived to be pursuing shareholder-wealth-maximizing goals" (Smith 1996). Other militants discovered that they could use token stockholdings to gain invaluable publicity at annual shareholder meetings for a host of social, environmental, and ethical challenges to corporate policies and practices, ranging from environmental degradation to child labor to investment in apartheid South Africa. During the 1990s, many large-company managers stumbled unwittingly into the investor-activists' cross-hairs.

A handful of very large U.S. state pension funds spearheaded the institutional investor revolt, including the New York State Teachers Retirement System, the Wisconsin Investment Board, and especially the California Public Employees Retirement System (CalPERS), as well as TIAA-CREF, the large college professors' retirement fund (Hawley 1995). The public pension funds reserved seats on the governing boards for elected state officials and their appointees. Given their electoral sensitivities to the voter-employees whose retirements depended entirely on their pension funds' performance, these public officials engaged in anti-management rhetoric and actions to score political points with their constituents (Useem 1996:54–57). Two favorite activist tactics were (1) sponsoring shareholder resolutions on company proxy statements that proposed changes in company governance structures to make a firm more accessible to shareholder influence (e.g., repealing poison pills and staggered director terms; enacting confidential voting and minimum shareholder requirements for directors); and (2) "relational investing," where pension fund managers directly jawboned and cajoled company executives into taking strategic actions to boost share prices.

CalPERS, which by 2000 was managing investments of $172 billion for more than a million California employed and retired beneficiaries, was an especially persistent corporate governance gadfly. It backed investor activist Robert Monks's failed 1991 campaign for election to the Sears Roebuck board of directors; helped to oust the CEOs or change corporate policies at American Express, General Motors, Chrysler, USAir, Westinghouse, IBM, Eastman Kodak, and Time Warner; successfully petitioned the SEC in 1992 to loosen its rules constraining shareholders engaged in proxy fights from communicating openly with one another (see Briggs 1994); pressured companies whose stock it owned to adopt tougher guidelines making directors more attentive to shareholders and less beholden to management; and challenged corporate governance rules in England, France, Germany, and Japan. CalPERS's most publicized effort was an annual "hit-list" of 10 underperforming U.S. corporations, among the 1,500 firms in its portfolio, to receive unwanted public attention and private pressure to shape up:

> The CalPERS Corporate Governance Program annually identifies long-term poor performing companies within the System's domestic equity portfolio. The goal of the program is to implement corporate governance reforms that help to address the root causes of the under-performance, with the goal of enhancing investment returns. Ten companies are identified as among the relative poorest long-term performers in CalPERS domestic stock portfolio and serve as the focus of the System's corporate governance activism. (CalPERS 1999)

Targets in recent years have included Archer Daniels Midland (ADM), Electronic Data Systems (EDS), Apple Computer, Sybase, International Flavors & Fragrances, and Michaels Stores.

Activists launched several national shareholder associations in the 1980s to promote coalition building among institutional investors. The Council of Institutional Investors gathered information, conducted research, and coordinated actions by a network of 111 pension funds with combined assets of $1 trillion. It advocated corporate governance guidelines spelling out shareholder rights and board independence and accountability. The nonprofit Institutional Investor Project at Columbia University, the Investors' Responsibility Research Center (IRRC) in Washington, and the private-sector Institutional Shareholder Services (ISS) served as clearinghouses for information and advice about corporate policies and performances. Following his failed bid for a Sears board seat, Robert Monks formed the Lens activist fund to prospect for companies with a "governance gap that can be closed by shareholder activism" (Monks 1998:136). Oilman T. Boone Pickens, a notorious corporate raider, started the United Shareholder Association (USA) in 1986 to fight anti-takeover measures after he failed to extort a greenmail profit from a hostile takeover bid for Unocal. Before claiming victory and disbanding after seven years, the USA annually targeted 50 worst-offending companies for "shareholder rights campaigns" (it claimed to win 40 percent of proxy votes cast in 1993), and issued annual rankings of firms most responsive to their shareholders, based on economic performance, adherence to shareholder rights, and executive compensation and incentives.

Institutional activists liked to boast that their actions turned around laggard companies and built shareholder value for their beneficiaries. Some evidence from before-and-after studies of targeted firms supported these claims. A study of 96 companies appearing on focus lists of the Council of Institutional Investors from 1991 to 1993 found an average share price increase of 9 percent above the Standard & Poor's 500 index in the following year, while matching portfolios earned significantly lower returns (Opler and Sokobin 1995). These changes, the researchers concluded, "are broadly consistent with the view that coordinated institutional governance activism is effective." A 1995 analysis by pension fund adviser Wilshire Associates found that the stock prices of 42 companies targeted by CalPERS from 1987 to 1994, which had underperformed the S&P 500 index by 66 percent in the five years before the fund took action, subsequently outperformed the index by 41 percent over the next five years (Nesbitt 1994). Another study also spotting this "CalPERS effect" between 1989 and 1993 found that 26 of the fund's 36 targeted companies had either adopted the proposed governance structure resolutions or made sufficient changes to warrant CalPERS's settlement of the dispute (Smith 1996). Stock prices rose significantly for firms with successful targeting events but declined significantly for firms with unsuccessful events. "Overall, the evidence indicates that shareholder activism is largely successful in changing governance structure and, when successful, results in a statistically significant increase in shareholder wealth. However, if the source of the wealth increase is improved operating performance, it is not statistically significant" (Smith 1996).

Many researchers tried to measure the positive and negative consequences of changing corporate governance structures for executive compensation and firm performance, yielding inconsistent findings (for research reports and reviews, see Karpoff, Malatesta and Walking 1996; Akhigbe, Madura and Tucker 1997; Fisch 1997; Klein 1998; Millstein and MacAvoy 1998; Bhagat, Carey and Elson 1999; Guercio and Hawkins 1999; Gillan and Starks forthcoming). For example, both intense scrutiny by professional finance analysts and anti-management resolutions brought to a vote by activists between 1984 and 1994 compelled the Fortune 500 industrial firms to create investor relations departments (Rao and Sivakumar 1999). An analysis of 168 shareholder proposals to restrict executive compensation in 145 companies between 1993 and 1997 suggested that boards responded to shareholder dissatisfaction (Thomas and Martin 1999). Higher levels of voting support for proposals covaried with smaller CEO compensation increases in targeted companies, compared to CEO pay changes at similar-sized firms in the same industry. On the other hand, in a 10-year survey of board composition and firm performance, Bhagat and Black (1999) found scant evidence that greater board independence correlated with higher profitability or faster growth. "In particular, there is no empirical support for current proposals that firms should have 'super-majority-independent boards' with only one or two inside directors. To the contrary, there is some evidence that firms supermajority-independent boards are less profitable than other firms" (p. 921). The ambiguous findings on activist impacts emphasized the necessity for stronger theorizing and more rigorous research designs.

Although institutional activism and shareholder rights movements have also emerged in Japan and several European nations during recent years, documenting any systematic reforms of corporate governance may be premature (Arnold and Breen 1997). However, anecdotal evidence points to incremental changes, spurred by shareholder activists allied with U.S. institutional investors. CalPERS doubled its international equity holdings between 1995 and 1998 and announced alliances with British, French, German, and Japanese shareholder groups to pressure for adoption of such corporate governance principles as smaller boards with independent directors and outside auditors (Flynn 1998; Jackson 1998). In early 1999, the United Kingdom's Hermes Pensions Management joined with the U.S. Lens investment group to force the resignation the Mirror Group's CEO for blocking that British company's takeover by German publishing giant Axel Springer Verlag (Sargent 1999). Telecom Italia and its controlling shareholder, Olivetti, had to scrap a proposed divestiture of its wireless unit after angry minority shareholders protested that the plan trampled on their rights (Rosenberg 1999). And several large Japanese corporations, including Toshiba and Sony, slimmed their bloated insider boards, while the Mitsui Bank refused to back five companies, in which it owned stock, that awarded hefty retirement packages to executives involved in payoff scandals (Tanikawa 1998). American-style investor crusades aimed exclusively at boosting shareholder values seemed implausible in countries like France and Germany, where entrenched stakeholders, such as unions and local governments, still strongly influenced corporate behavior. However, the 1998 formation of a Global Corporate Governance Advisory Board and its Institutional Investors Advisory Group, with representatives of large companies and institutional investors from 16 nations, provided a forum for discussing the eventual creation of international guidelines on corporate governance.

Top corporate managers did not remain passive in the face of aggressive, value-seeking shareholders of the 1980s and 1990s (Davis 1994). They resisted, manipulated, delayed, placated, and where tactically necessary, bent in the storm to keep control of their firms. For example, Chrysler's CEO reached a cease-fire with disgruntled billionaire investor Kirk Kerkorian after a five-year struggle over control of the troubled automaker (Stertz and Phillips 1996). By giving Kerkorian a board seat in return for a pledge not to boost his holdings or try to change Chrysler's management or board, the antagonists avoided a referendum on their opposing positions by the firm's major pension and mutual fund investors. Michael Useem (1993:48–49) noted that several defensive mechanisms originally designed to thwart hostile takeovers in the 1980s market for corporate control, such as poison pills and anti-greenmail policies, also effectively reduced the influence of large institutional investors. Rather than ignoring shareholder interests in the hopes that the activists would go away, executives learned more effectively to manage their investor relationships and cool-off the hotheads:

> Companies now manage their investors in much the same way they manage any constituent group, whether inside or outside the firm. The tactical repertoire includes education, cultivation, and communication. It comprises informal briefings, private tours, daily calls, executed with the professionalism befitting any executive action. Companies reward the large and loyal investor with privileged access; they punish the critical or inaccurate analyst with the cold shoulder. (Useem 1996:168)

Savvy companies gradually learned to construct and influence complex shareholder networks to manage routine interactions that forestalled open struggles for corporate control and reform. Because institutional investors rarely owned more than 1 or 2 percent of a firm's shares, a typical large corporation's investor-affairs staff might deal with dozens or even hundreds of such investor organizations. Many small equity owners were transients due to their frequent portfolio turnovers ("investor drift"; Useem 1996:177). Sustaining collaborative relations required frequent and persistent personalized contacts between executives and investors through a variety of two-way channels to communicate about, advise on, and influence matters of mutual interest. Both the volume and quality of investment information had increased enormously by the end of the twentieth century, especially with the ascent of Internet access to timely corporate data. The relations between U.S. investors and corporations constitute a "nonhierarchical, semi-stable, and personalized" network among co-equals capable of reaching negotiated solutions to governance and performance disputes (Useem 1996:206). The struggles for control and influence over corporate performance, executive compensation, and shareholder value were destined to intensify in the twenty-first century.

Conclusions

The governance of large publicly held corporations has grown increasingly complex and contentious. Conventional legal theory continued to assert shareholder wealth-maximization as the primary purpose for the firm. But the historical separation of top management from shareowners raised a host of conflicting interests in corporate conduct that could not be permanently papered over. Although most chief executives managed to dominate their boards of directors, they grew more vulnerable to challenges from inside as well as outside the company walls. The increased decoupling of CEO pay and firm performance, new legal theories of stakeholder rights, and a militant movement by institutional investors all contributed to an atmosphere demanding greater management accountability for its decisions and missteps. Whether top leaders could continue to resist these pressures depended on how successfully they might deploy their considerable political resources to preserve their corporate power and privileges from the claims of rival interest groups. The next chapter examines some political challenges arising from the lower reaches of the corporate hierarchy.

8

Struggling in
the Workplace

*Man's capacity for justice makes
democracy possible, but man's inclination
to injustice makes democracy necessary.*
—Reinhold Niebuhr, The Children of Light
and the Children of Darkness (1944)

In April 1996, some 2,500 mostly white male employees of the Mitsubishi
Motor Manufacturing plant in Normal, Illinois, poured out of 60 buses
hired by their employer to bring them to the downtown Chicago office of
the U.S. Equal Employment Opportunity Commission. They milled around
in the street, chanting slogans "EEOC, you don't represent me," and "Two
four six eight, we're here to set the story straight" (Grimsley and Brown
1996). Two weeks earlier the federal agency had filed a lawsuit against the
Japanese auto assembler, alleging that many of the 700 women in the
plant's workforce of 4,000 had been subjected to years of groping, sexual
graffiti, and lewd remarks. As detailed in an EEOC memo to the federal
court, the charges involved "incidents in which a male worker forcibly cut
the hair of a female worker; a male worker talked frequently about wanting
to kill women, and said he would force a woman to perform oral sex on
him, and planned to 'blow her away' as he ejaculated; male workers passed
around photos of women engaged in sex with animals; two male workers
taped a woman's hands and feet to a cart and pushed it up and down the
aisles while others laughed" (Grimsley and Swoboda 1997).

The EEOC argued that, by tolerating this sexual harassment, the Mitsubishi management had created a "hostile and abusive work environment" in violation of the 1991 Civil Rights Act. The EEOC class action suit

sought millions of dollars in compensatory and punitive damages and changes in the company's workplace practices. A private suit against Mitsubishi had previously been filed by 29 women employees, many of whom quit their jobs because of the relentless coworker intimidation, managerial retaliation for attempted whistle-blowing, and the refusal by both top company and local United Auto Workers officials to halt male employee behaviors. Their lawyer added claims that company employees sometimes organized sex parties with prostitutes, which were attended by managers who then allowed explicit photos to be passed around at the plant.

Mitsubishi officials launched an aggressive publicity counterattack to deny the allegations. They installed phone banks at the plant for employees to make free calls to their congressional representatives and the press to protest the EEOC charges. They held in-plant rallies, warning employees that the suit threatened the rural Midwest community with loss of many high-wage jobs if sales fell because of the accusations. Management gave workers a paid day off and a meal while attending the EEOC protest in Chicago. Mitsubishi's lawyers petitioned the court for documents on the women involved in the private lawsuit, including their gynecological records and information on credit ratings, divorces, and abortions (Grimsley 1996). Rather than quelling the furor, the company's tactics backfired. Seven Democratic congresswomen denounced the attack on the EEOC. Smelling a public relations serendipity, the National Organization for Women and the Reverend Jesse Jackson's Rainbow Coalition called for a boycott of Mitsubishi products and picketed some car dealerships. The company then hired Lynn Martin, a former U.S. Secretary of Labor and a prominent Illinois Republican, to examine employment discrimination and recommend new workplace policies and practices.

Mitsubishi soon caved in to the mounting pressures, replacing the top two Japanese officials of its U.S. operations and firing or disciplining several male American workers involved in the harassment; reorganizing the Normal plant's human resources procedures following Martin's recommendations, including mandatory sexual harassment training for all employees; and reaching agreement with Jackson and NOW to call off the boycott in return for providing more than $200 million in business opportunities for women and minorities. In late 1997, the company settled the private lawsuit with most of the 29 women for nearly $10 million. And the following spring, as the class action suit went to trial, Mitsubishi negotiated a $34 million settlement with the EEOC, more than triple the previous record amount for a sexual harassment case. By avoiding a trial, the plant and local community were spared further traumatic revelations. "It would have been hardest on the community," said a former appellate court judge who helped to orchestrate the settlement. "They would have heard women [say] how they had been abused by their fellow employees—men who live in the area.... this is a win-win situation" (Grimsley 1998).

The Mitsubishi sexual harassment case propelled into public view several aspects of the usually subterranean struggle for power in corporate and public workplaces. It revealed the relative powerlessness of individual employees in the face of hostility or indifference by their employers. The case illustrated how workers could collectively create a social movement to wrest some measure of justice, and why companies might resist or succumb to demands for more managerial accountability. It pointed to the penetration into factories and offices of pervasive societal controversies over race, gender, and age; to the fragility of the U.S. labor movement; and to changing political mechanisms for concealing or resolving internal organizational conflicts. And, by illuminating the role of a federal regulatory agency in enforcing anti-discrimination statutes, it underscored the expanding legalization of the workplace.

This chapter examines the changing political and legal conflicts that transformed employee relations and strengthened management power in the late twentieth-century U.S. political economy. The early history of the industrial revolution in the United States was replete with bitter struggles among owners, managers, and workers over who would really control the work activities in mills, mines, plants, laboratories, and offices (see Edwards 1979; Jacoby 1985; Burawoy 1985). These battles visibly erupted during the massive labor union organizing drives of the 1930s, often degenerating into bloody strikes over wages and working conditions. Less visible confrontations over managerial prerogatives in the workplace were waged by professional and clerical employees who contested encroachments on their occupational autonomy. Women, racial minorities, and gay and lesbian groups raised legal charges of racial and sexual discrimination by their white male bosses. In reaction to, or anticipation of, interventions by outside political and legal authorities, corporations eventually institutionalized various human resources and personnel procedures designed to restore good employee relations while retaining substantial management control. These normative practices came to assume a taken-for-granted status inside many organizations, operating invisibly as participants routinely went about their daily tasks. However, the underlying divisions of political and economic interests dividing employees and employers, coupled with their unequal positions in organizational power structures, assured that challenge from below would remain an omnipresent specter haunting the workplace.

Social Movements
Inside Organizations

In a seminal article, Mayer Zald and Michael Berger (1978) proposed that the impact of politics and power on organizational change could be fruitfully studied as social movements arising both inside and outside organizational boundaries. They urged the application of a resource mobilization perspective which, first,

> examines the costs of participation in social movement action as well as the distribution of grievances.... Second, it treats mobilization of resources from whatever sources as a central topic. This is especially important in the study of social movements in organizations because such key resources as votes of stock, police intervention, legal support, board member votes and strike funds may come from outside the group of immediate protagonists. Amount and sources of resources and risk-reward ratios are then combined with dimensions of organizational structure and process to explain the forms and rates of social movements in different organizations. (Zald and Berger 1978:829)

They hypothesized that three basic social movement forms—the organizational coup d'état, bureaucratic insurgency, and mass movements—each displayed distinct goals, tactics and strategies, breadths of participation, locations within organizational structures, and collective action outcomes. Chapter 5 examined coups by corporate directors against derelict CEOs. The following subsections explore bureaucratic insurgencies and mass movements inside work organizations.

Insurgents in the Bureaucracy

A *bureaucratic insurgency* differs from a board room coup by aiming, not to replace the top leadership, but to change or reform policies having the nominal support of the organization's legitimate authorities. These policies reflect core norms and values of the corporate culture that transcend particular changes in company leadership. An insurgency mobilizes a limited number of participants, sometimes backed by middle managers or professional and technical staff, possibly carried out in a conspiratorial or other unconventional campaign. Zald and Berger (1978:838–839) cited three subtypes of insurgency: (1) program or product development, such as experimental social service programs not sanctioned by the top leaders of public bureaucracies, or aerospace companies' secretive "skunk works"; (2) policy choice, involving efforts to change the organization's goals, typically by lower-level employees; and (3) whistle-blowing, which Rothschild and Miethe (1994:254) defined as "disclosure of illegal, unethical, or harmful practices in the workplace to parties who might take action." The following discussion illustrates these three varieties of bureaucratic insurgency.

In a *product development movement*, insurgents operate within an organization's overall authority structure, but seek to improve existing programs or to introduce new techniques for accomplishing special objectives without the knowledge and explicit approval of top authorities. Skunk works seldom attract corporate controversy because their small budgets and quick completion cycles don't give their political opponents enough time to notice and mobilize against them. (Cartoonist Al Capp coined the cynical term "Skonk Works" for a noxious alcohol still that was out-of-bounds to ordinary Dogpatch denizens.) Often physically and socially isolated from the main bureaucracy, unconventional insurgents enjoy greater freedom to try out novel ideas with high failure rates. Their insulation from effective administrative control supposedly stimulates skunk workers to creative product development, but may also instigate loafing and goofy behavior not acceptable in more conventional workplaces. One journalist described a band of two dozen 20-something engineers who developed laser weapons for President Ronald Reagan's dubious "Star Wars" anti-missile defense system:

> At the Lawrence Livermore National Laboratory, a Federal site for the design of nuclear weapons and other advanced technologies, about 45 miles east of San Francisco, they are known variously as "O Group" or "Lowell's group" (after Lowell Wood, the founder). They are "eccentric and extraordinarily bright," says a high Livermore official. To a critic within Livermore who opposes the construction of new weapons, they are "bright young hotshots who are socially maladjusted. All their time and energy is spent on science." (Broad 1985)

These juvenile Star Warriors delighted in pranks to relieve the tensions of their deadly serious creative efforts. They once slipped a 20-pound brick into their founder's briefcase, who unknowingly lugged it around the country for months until they clued him in on the joke.

Lax atmospheres such as that in the O Group may help to speed up product innovation but can also produce embarrassing publicity snafus for the parent firm. In 1986 Lockheed's top-secret Advanced Development Company (the original defense industry skunk works, founded in the 1940s) lost track of hundreds of classified documents about the Pentagon's top secret F-19 Stealth fighter. This debacle led to congressional denunciations and the early retirement of four top company officials. Coincidentally, a model plane maker sold a purportedly realistic F-19 plastic assembly kit to hobbyists, based on specs readily available from public sources. The confusing muddle surrounding skunk work programs may be the inevitable price companies pay for the successful innovations produced by the eccentric geniuses attracted to such distinctly nonbureaucratic environments.

In a *policy choice movement*, aggrieved employees collectively try to persuade relevant policymakers that current company or agency practices are detrimental, not only to the workers but to the organization's prosperity and image as well. One rapidly sprouting and quickly successful insurgency was the mobilization of gay and lesbian employees to expand company health insurance and other benefits to their domestic partners. In 1990 just three corporations provided family and bereavement leaves for lesbian and gay employees, and none offered domestic partner health coverage. Despite substantial political opposition to passing federal anti-discrimination legislation, several public universities, the U.S. military, and many corporations voluntarily adopted gay-inclusive policies within a few years. By the end of 1997, more than 200 large companies, representing almost a quarter of firms with at least 5,000 employees, offered domestic partner benefits (Raeburn 2000). By the end of 1999, more than 500 companies, including 81 Fortune 500 firms, had adopted equitable benefits policies. High-tech, medical, and entertainment companies were especially receptive to lobbying by gay and lesbian activist groups. Soon after the Walt Disney Company extended health benefits in 1996 to same-sex partners (but unlike several corporations, not to unmarried heterosexual couples), the Southern Baptist Convention called a boycott of Disney theme parks, films, and toys because of its adult-oriented films and alleged "promotion of homosexuality." The studio issued a sarcastic statement: "We find it curious that a group that claims to espouse family values would vote to boycott the world's largest producer of wholesome family entertainment" (Dickerson 1996). Observers speculated that Baptist parents supporting the boycott would be hard-pressed to resist their children's begging to visit Disney World and watch *The Lion King*.

Evidence from interviews and a survey of 94 Fortune 1000 companies, combined with in-depth case studies, suggested that gay-inclusive policy changes resulted from a political process combining resource mobilization strategies with a focus on organizational institutional values (Raeburn 2000). In linking internal corporate networks to the national gay and lesbian rights movement, activists recruited key corporate executive and human resource supporters to their cause. Successful outcomes depended on how the activists invoked collective identities to promote gay visibility in a framework consistent with, rather than opposed to, existing corporate values and norms (Taylor 1999; Raeburn 2000). Companies whose gay employees were already out of the closet and active, for example by celebrating gay-pride month, were more susceptible to extending domestic partner benefits. Activists who pitched their case solely on an "ideology of ethics" were largely unsuccessful, but groups arguing from an "ideology of profits" generally succeeded. That is, assertions that gay-friendly policies would improve the company's bottom line and enhance its public image more often changed policies than did abstract appeals to fairness and equality. Institutional factors were evident in the diffusion of domestic partner policies within organizational fields: Although the vast majority of early adopting organizations were pressured by their gay employees, late-adopting companies were less likely to require the presence of an activist group. Rather, they seemed to be mimicking the pioneering actions of their field's leaders.

Whistle-blowing involves "the disclosure by organization members (former or current) of illegal, immoral, or illegitimate practices under the control of their employers, to persons or organizations that may be able to take effective action" (Miceli and Near 1992:4). It is a form of political resistance in which a relatively powerless employee attempts to influence a more resourceful and powerful organization to terminate the wrongdoing by some of its participants. Power and resource dependence theories provide the most insightful explanations of the conditions favoring whistle-blowing. A whistle-blower is often a single individual, or at most a small group of dissidents, who undertakes a risky action only after recourse to routine grievance channels fails to convince organizational authorities to rectify an errant situation. Indeed, the bosses themselves may be directly involved in nefarious affairs and prone to retaliate forcibly against the whistle-blower, escalating from ridicule and verbal intimidation to firing or physical violence. Hollywood's best depiction of this phenomenon was a 1984 Meryl Streep melodrama depicting the unsolved murder of Karen Silkwood during her efforts to expose malfeasance at the Oklahoma plutonium plant where she worked. In a more recent case, a major turning point in the fight to penalize tobacco companies for marketing harmful products came after a former research director of the Brown & Williamson Tobacco Corp. claimed on CBS's *60 Minutes* that B&W's CEO had lied under oath to Congress when testifying that he didn't believe nicotine to be addictive. The nefarious tobacco firm then tried to undermine its former employee's credibility by revealing unsavory details of his personal life (Dunlop 1996). This juicy corporate backstabbing, blended with CBS's timidity about risking its own corporate bottom line by airing the show, provided grist for a compelling Hollywood melodrama, *The Insider.*

Because no agency collected systematic data on whistle-blowing cases, tracking changes in their incidence over time was impossible. Researchers knew little about the effectiveness of whistle-blowing as a strategy for creating organizational change or for harming the whistle-blower through retaliation. Most academic researchers studied whistle-blowing primarily as an ethical dilemma or a psychological decision by individual employees (e.g., Barnett, Cochran and Taylor 1993). For example, did personality traits such as self-esteem and moral judgment dispose certain employees to act on their perceptions of questionable activity? What triggered false accusations by disgruntled ex-employees seeking revenge for alleged mistreatment? Missing from many explanations was an emphasis on the types of organizational conditions and institutional contexts that both fostered widespread wrongdoing and provoked or stifled whistle-blowing responses. In several articles, Janet Near and Marcia Miceli speculated about possible situational factors affecting these actions (Near and Miceli 1995; Miceli and Near 1988; Miceli and Near 1992). They hypothesized that an employee would be more likely to blow the whistle on a wrongdoer when an organization clearly signaled its potentially positive responsiveness to complaints, posed a low threat of retaliation, and offered benefits to whistle-blowers such as cash awards. Firms that maintained a supportive climate and culture, such as a well-publicized code of ethics, also probably encouraged whistle-blowing. Similarly, some environmental contexts might favor an employee's decision to act, including a strongly regulated industry and a societal culture that supported whistle-blowers (Miceli and Near 1992:137).

Federal and state laws designed to encourage whistle-blowing seemed to fail in their intended effects (Near, Dworkin and Miceli 1993). Congress created the U.S. Merit Systems Protection Board in 1978 to shield federal workers from reprisals. Although surveys in 1980 and 1983 disclosed that fewer employees reported seeing wrongdoing, the proportion of whistle-blowers who chose to remain anonymous increased, presumably from fear of retaliation. During the 1980s, more than half the U.S. states extended protection to private-sector whistle-blowers against firing or retaliation by their employers. Yet very few employees sought remedies under these statutes and those who did usually met with limited success. Suing under common law apparently offered employees higher monetary damage awards and fewer procedural hassles than those well-intentioned statutory solutions. The authors speculated that one reason why employee lawsuits did not increase after the legislative change was "because organizations that employ them have take actions to encourage internal whistle-blowing, thereby avoiding the problem of external whistle-blowing" (Near, Dworkin and Miceli 1993:408). Further research on several facets of the whistle-blowing phenomenon is necessary for a more complete understanding of this important type of bureaucratic insurgency.

Mass Movements

In contrast to the preceding types of organizational challenges, a key feature of a *mass organizational movement* is the widespread activation of discontented lower-level participants who engage in confrontational collective actions against the top organizational authorities. Organizational mass movements differ from coups and insurgencies by their broader scope and scale. Their goals may range from an expression of minor grievances, to attempts to seize control of the organization, to "redefining the distribution of power, constitution of rules, and norms of society" (Zald and Berger 1978:841). Although a mass movement could be launched by a small conspiratorial protest group, its ultimate success depends on mobilizing the strength of many employees and sympathetic outsiders whose coordinated actions disrupt organizational routines to the point where authorities must either react forcefully to repress the rebellion or capitulate to the movement's demands for change. Zald and Berger (1978) exemplified this phenomenon with student anti-war protests in the 1960s directed against U.S. colleges and with labor union mass strikes in the 1930s to win recognition of the right to represent industrial workers. However, they argued that in the latter case, once a national collective bargaining system achieved public legitimation through congressional legislation and judicial review, labor conflicts largely ceased to exhibit the unconventional political actions of a challenging mass movement. The fully institutionalized industrial relations system involved substantially different mechanisms for recruiting workers; calculating the costs and benefits of striking; and interacting politically with the employers, the public, and the government. The next section examines the successful struggle of business to roll back union power during the latter half of the twentieth century. Another dimension of business-labor conflict surfaces in Chapter 9, which emphasizes changing organizational participation in national political institutions.

Eroding Unionization

I lack the space to recapitulate the convoluted history of trade unions in the United States since their fitful beginnings in the nineteenth century (see Galenson 1960; Bernstein 1971). In brief, the major organizing drives of the Great Depression climaxed in sit-down strikes and employer violence, but ultimately won union recognition to negotiate with employers over wages, benefits, and working conditions in mass production industries from automobiles to steel to mines. Unions received significant support from political allies outside the workplace, particularly from the Democratic Party and President Roosevelt's New Deal administration, which enacted key labor relations legislation to rein in employer power (Tomlins 1985). The preamble of the Wagner Act (National Labor Relations Act of 1935) declared that the policy of the United States was to encourage "the practice and procedure of collective bargaining." Workers were guaranteed the right to form and join labor organizations of their own choosing, free from interference by their employers. Certain individuals were statutorily defined as "employees" entitled to the law's protections. Most notably, agricultural workers and domestic servants were excluded from coverage. The Wagner Act also institutionalized an electoral system to certify union representation through majority vote of the workers in a bargaining unit, defined unfair labor practices by employers, and set up an enforcement mechanism. The National Labor Relations Board (NLRB) supervised union recognition elections and settled labor-management disputes in a court-like manner.

The formal structures of the New Deal transformation remained intact over the following six decades. But the U.S. business community, consistently supported by the Republican Party, set about systematically to weaken labor unions' control over employees and thus to reduce their collective bargaining power. Congress passed the 1947 Taft-Hartley Act over President Harry Truman's veto, permitting the U.S. states to adopt "right-to-work" laws that banned closed union shops. Eventually, 20 mostly Southern and Western states passed such legislation, which kept unions out of small service-sector companies and confined them primarily to the previously organized large mass production industries. Other Taft-Hartley provisions narrowed the definition of "employee" to exclude supervisors from unionization, allowed employers as well as employees to petition the NLRB for union representation elections, and permitted employers to file for decertification elections.

The 1930s labor union organizing victories produced an initial dramatic spurt in unionization of the U.S. labor force. Historians and economists apply the term *union density* to the annual percentage of nonagricultural employees who are union members. Figure 8.1 charts the rise and fall of labor force unionization over the twentieth century.[1] The rapid run-up during the New Deal was consolidated during World War II when the federal government heavily regulated war production industries. Union density plateaued at about 32 percent of the nonagricultural employees during the 1950s. Beginning in the 1960s, a steady erosion of union density began, which accelerated under the Reagan Administration in the 1980s. By 1999 union density had fallen to 13.2 percent, a level not seen since 1936.[2] Removing the much higher unionization levels in the public sector (which held steady around 37 percent through the 1990s), the private-sector union density was even more abysmal, falling to just 9.4 percent in 1999 with no floor in sight. With nonunionized private-sector firms creating the vast majority of new jobs in the booming late-twentieth-century U.S. political economy, the public sector was the sole arena of union expansion. "The unions have a growing alliance with big government because that is where their base is," said a vice president of the U.S. Chamber of Commerce. "Yet the real growth [of employment] is in the private sector" (Burkins 2000:A4).

Analysts proposed various explanations for the post-1950s decline in unionization. Demographic interpretations emphasized changing labor force composition, in which allegedly difficult-to-organize women, racial minorities, and immigrants were the fastest-growing segments. Other accounts attributed deunionization to shifts of employees out of blue-collar jobs in mass production industries, where the union legacy of the New Deal remained strongest (Koeller 1994). The expanding high-tech and business service sectors had generally weak or absent union traditions. These industries employed many professionals and managers, who were legally excluded from collective bargaining coverage. However, such structural transformation explanations found little empirical support in multivariate analyses of surveys or time-series data (Rebitzer 1994; Bender 1997; Bronfenbrenner 1997).

FIGURE 8.1   Unionization of U.S. Labor Force
SOURCE: Freeman (1997:Appendix A, Table 1); U.S. Bureau of the Census
(1998:Table 712)

A power and resource dependence perspective offered a more comprehensive explanation of both rising and declining union density. Richard
Freeman (1997) proposed a general theory in which union density varied
nonlinearly with the relative resources available for union-organizing drives
and for firms opposing unionization. A critical factor was union density itself, the extent to which a product market's workforce had already been organized or covered by collective bargaining contracts. At low densities,
such as existed in the United States before the Great Depression, unions
lacked the strength to fight vigorous campaigns to organize new firms. As
rational actors, targeted companies thus perceived strong incentives to fight
any unionization efforts, including threatening to relocate their plants in
low-wage countries with even weaker union climates. Preventing unionization enabled firms to avoid the disadvantage of paying higher wages and
benefits than their unorganized competitors. On the other hand, if an in-
dustry-wide campaign succeeded and density began to rise rapidly, unions
acquired increased resources to organize, while the remaining nonunion
firms saw fewer competitive advantages from continuing to resist. At some
point, a rational calculation revealed that the costs of caving in fell below
the costs of still fighting. Although Freeman applied his resource dependence theory to explain the union growth spurt of the New Deal, it presumably also explained subsequent shrinking union density. Declining union

density became a self-reinforcing process once firms initially gained enough resources to combat union-organizing drives. When falling density left unions with insufficient resources to sustain new-firm organizing efforts, employers saw substantial gains from avoiding unionization and from deunionizing their workplaces by petitioning the NLRB for decertification elections. A decomposition of union density changes from 1950 to 1980 indicated that deunionization was largely due to decreased organizing efforts by unions and to increased success by management in winning representation elections (Dickens and Leonard 1985). For similar analyses that pointed to plunging union organizing efforts and to rising management opposition, see Freeman and Kleiner (1990), Lawler (1990), Rose and Chaison (1996), and Bender (1997).

One consequence of this shifting balance of power resources from unions to firms was evident in changing NLRB election outcomes. A watershed experience was the 1980 election of Ronald Reagan as president, which signaled a sea change in national political power from labor to business (see Chapter 9 for additional discussion). An ideologically conservative, pro-business Republican, Reagan fired the striking federal air traffic controllers and nominated a majority of anti-union candidates favored by the business community to the five-member NLRB. Under its zealous Chairman Donald Dotson, the NLRB became "far more intently and overtly politicized than any of its predecessors" (Gross 1995:270). Although denying abandonment of official neutrality in labor-management disputes, the Board pursued policy changes that freed employers from many constraints. For example, the NLRB overturned prohibitions on mid-contract plant relocations, on firing employees who tried to organize a union campaign, and on hiring temporary replacement workers during a lockout. Companies swamped the understaffed NRLB under a rising tide of accusations against unions for engaging in flagrantly unfair labor-organizing practices, producing a backlog exceeding 1,600 cases (Noble 1985). Businesses rationally calculated that the longer the overwhelmed courts took to enforce good-faith bargaining, the more likely a union's demoralized supporters would accept a contract no better than the company had offered without a union. Emboldened by the NRLB's shift to pro-business policies, employer resistance made union-organizing campaigns far more difficult and costly in an era when total employment shrank in many basic manufacturing industries:

> [T]he Dotson Board's ruling ended employers' statutory obligation to bargain about many major management decisions, substantially deregulated representation election campaigns, increased management's authority to discipline employees for engaging in activity previously protected by the act, and in many other ways elevated management's authority to manage over statutory obligations. The Dotson Board decisions also weakened unions at a time when the economic situation made them most vulnerable. (Gross 1995:256)

The impact of the Reagan era's pro-business tilt on unionization was evident in a precipitous decline in organizing activity, as revealed by NLRB election results in Figure 8.2.[3] Before 1981, labor union enrollments annually increased by 100,000 or more net new members (employees voting to unionize minus employees voting to decertify). But by 1983, the net gain had collapsed to fewer than half that number. Although the net gains recovered a bit during the Clinton Administration, they never returned to former levels. At this lower rate, the annual net additions replaced only a quarter of the members lost through layoffs, corporate downsizings, firm mergers, and overseas plant relocations. Across the entire period, the proportion of certifying elections won by unions remained fairly stable (just under 50 percent), while management success rates in winning decertification elections also remained unchanged (around 75 percent).

A primary factor behind this downward shift was a sharp decline in the number of NLRB representation elections contested (falling from 37,316 elections from 1975 to 1979 to just 15,190 elections from 1993 to 1997). Confronted by more militant and sophisticated business opponents, union organizers grew more cautious about initiating petitions whenever a successful election result seemed doubtful. (See Chapter 6's case study of a union drive in a small high-tech company, which failed because the outside organizers misunderstood the network dynamics inside the potential bargaining unit.) Coupled with a concentration of efforts on organizing small

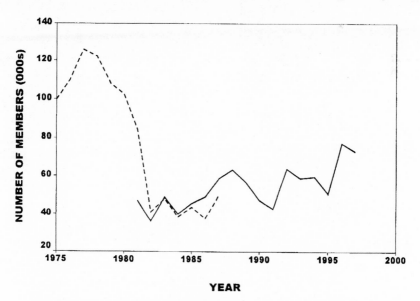

FIGURE 8.2 Net Gain in Union Members
SOURCE: Chaison and Dhavale (1990); National Labor Relations Board (1977–1999)

units (which averaged fewer than 70 employees), such timidity was a sure recipe for continuing the steady erosion of union density. One extrapolation of the 1980s trends led to the startling projection that unionization might decline to just 2 percent of the private-sector labor force in the early twenty-first century (Chaison and Dhavale 1990:371).

Unions lost much ground because companies effectively commanded far greater political and economic resources than organized labor could mobilize. Businesses increasingly waged combative campaigns to block and oust unions from their plants and offices. Both unions and corporations resorted to outside consultants and law firms for assistance in their struggles over employee representation (Bernstein 1980; Lawler 1990). In a sort of arms race, these hired guns fashioned innovative tactics that stimulated defensive countermeasures by their opponents. The legendary union organizer Ray Rogers pioneered aggressive *corporate campaign* tactics, in which a union and its allies carefully orchestrated a series of actions designed to damage a company's business and reputation, thereby pressuring it into making concessions during a labor dispute or organizing drive. In 1980, Rogers helped the Amalgamated Clothing and Textile Workers Union (ACTWU) successfully end a bitter 17-year struggle to unionize 10 J. P. Stevens plants in the South. The ACTWU and sympathetic church groups pressured shareholders of insurance companies owning Stevens bonds, including Manufacturers Hanover Trust and Metropolitan Life; ran ads in local newspapers to attack and embarrass the firm; filed shareholder resolutions at annual meetings; urged union members to pull their money out of banks doing business with Stevens; and attacked the personal reputations of company executives and outside board members. Eventually, three board members resigned to avoid adverse publicity at their home companies, and Stevens agreed to a labor contract. But the firm reportedly insisted on a "Ray Rogers clause," which forbade the ACTWU from ever again conducting a corporate campaign against the company (McFadden 1993).

Other corporate campaigns by unions against American Airlines, the International Paper Company, Hormel, the New York Daily News, Food Lion, Bell Atlantic, and other firms met with varying degrees of success. Business consultants learned how to counterattack effectively, proposing federal legislation to ban some union tactics as unfair labor practices. "That corporate America is so frightened by comprehensive [corporate] campaigns they would move to make them illegal isn't only a measure of how effective we have become, but is a stark reminder that a toothless, weakened labor movement remains a principal goal of the business community," said the United Mine Workers president (Shorrock 1995).

On their side, corporations were never loath to participate in a good street brawl. From the earliest union-organizing days, employers frequently turned to outside labor relations consultants to help them formulate corporate labor-relations strategies. Attorneys were the most prevalent types, providing campaign advice and coordination services from 1975 to 1982 in 73 percent of 201 NLRB certification elections studied by Lawler (1990:99–100). Nonattorney management consultants accounted for most of the remainder. Although favorite tactics emphasized persuasion rather than intimidation, some aggressive consultants verged on the border of legality, such as harassing and firing employees involved in organizing (Tevlin 1997b). "Consultants make extensive use of supervisors, both to conduct union-avoidance activities at the shop floor level and gather information on union activities. There seems to be a somewhat greater likelihood of discrimination against union supporters. These findings most certainly bolster the union view of consultants as 'union busters'" (Lawler 1990:108). A common device was provoking union members to strike, then replacing them with workers who would later vote to end their union affiliation. During the turbulent 1980s, several companies took advantage of a 5–4 Supreme Court ruling that, after filing a Chapter 11 federal bankruptcy petition, a firm could unilaterally eliminate its collective-bargaining agreements while awaiting the bankruptcy court's formal permission to do so. For example, in a desperate effort in 1983 to rescue the floundering Continental Airlines by drastically cutting labor costs, Chairman Frank Lorenzo canceled all contracts with pilots, machinists, and flight attendants after filing under Chapter 11. He laid off three-quarters of the employees and slashed in half the wages and benefits of the remaining employees. These draconian measures ultimately salvaged Continental as a much smaller carrier, after suffering through two bankruptcies. However, Lorenzo's attempt six years later to replicate his terror tactics against striking Eastern Airlines machinists ended with his ouster from that firm by a bankruptcy court judge.

Corporate successes in deunionization also benefited from peculiarly inept union strategies dating back to their New Deal glory years. Campaigns directed from a national headquarters by an oligarchic union leadership could be insensitive to local conditions and employee interests, such as avoiding an alienated community after a bitter organizing drive (Fiorito, Jarley and Delaney 1995; Maranto and Fiorito 1987). Politically liberal unions articulating a clear social-justice ideology proved more successful at winning NLRB elections than were traditional unions stressing only bread-and-butter economic issues (Poland and Beveridge 1992). Kate Bronfenbrenner's (1997) theoretically elegant analysis of 261 NLRB certification election campaigns from 1986 to 1987 supported these insights. In research financially supported by the AFL-CIO, she demonstrated that union strategy explained more variation in election outcomes than other factors such as employer tactics, bargaining unit demographics, and organizer backgrounds. A campaign that deployed a "rank-and-file intensive strategy" increased the likelihood of success because "it generates the worker participation and commitment necessary to withstand aggressive employer anti-union campaigns (which are now commonplace) and to counteract any anti-union aspects of the economic, political, and legal climate" (Bron-fenbrenner 1997:198).

A successful organizing strategy involved six basic components that par-alleled classic social movement recruitment practices: (1) networking that relied on slow, underground, person-to-person contacts at the beginning; (2) emphasizing union democracy and inclusive, interest-representative par-ticipation; (3) building support for the initial contact with employee-voters during the organizing drive; (4) using escalating pressure tactics to build worker commitment and compel the employer to run a fair campaign; (5) stressing issues such as "respect, dignity, fairness, and service quality that go beyond the traditional bread-and-butter issues of wages, fringes, bene-fits, and job security"; (Bronfenbrenner 1997:200) and (6) accentuating the development of an organizing culture that permeated the entire union:

> This result suggests that many unions could improve their organizing success if they adopted a rank-and-file organizing strategy. For most unions, that would involve a dramatic change in their organizing practices. All the rank-and-file organizing tactics investigated in this study were used by less than a third of the campaigns in the sample. If all the organizers had employed elements of rank-and-file intensive campaigns such as representative committees, house-calls, rank-and-file volunteers, building for the first contact, solidarity days, and a focus on new issues, the percentage of elections won by unions, includ-ing those held in large units, would have been significantly higher. (Bronfen-brenner 1997:211)

One signal that the U.S. labor movement had belatedly changed its strat-egy was the 1995 election of John Sweeney to head the 40-year-old AFL-CIO, defeating the candidate of an old-guard leadership on whose watch union density had substantially declined. As president of the service work-ers, Sweeney had doubled his union's membership with an innovative "Jus-tice for Janitors" campaign run along lines suggested by Bronfenbrenner's study. The largely female and immigrant custodians tied up rush hour traf-fic on bridges leading into the nation's capital and picketed the homes of building owners. At the top of Sweeney's list for revitalization was a pledge by the AFL-CIO to spend a third of its annual $60 million operating budget on organizing and to persuade the federation's 79 member unions to com-mit similar proportions of their own budgets. He streamlined the AFL-CIO's top-heavy bureaucracy, creating an Organizing Department staffed by a younger generation of activists with a mandate to rebuild grassroots union power. They launched a "Union Summer," modeled after the 1960s civil rights movement, sending a thousand college student interns into local communities in 1996 to organize new workplaces and to campaign in the fall elections against labor's political party enemies (Hamilton 1996). By

1999, union rolls had increased for the second straight year, with 265,000 new members keeping union density steady at 13.2 percent (Burkins 2000). Only a longer run would reveal whether renewed labor activism, which could make greater inroads by targeting professionals and high-tech workers, might produce more than a momentary blip in the decades-long downward trend in union power.

Legalization of the Workplace

Ironically, even as union power declined in the workplace, statutory and case laws regarding due process protections for employees expanded dramatically. The evolving legal environment increasingly constrained organizational structures and actions as employers attempted both to comply with and to evade anti-discrimination norms. Two broad theoretical approaches offered divergent explanations of how the law and business affected one another (Edelman and Suchman 1997). The materialist perspective depicted organizations as rational, wealth-maximizing social actors. It viewed the law as a system of incentives and penalties intended to coerce companies to adhere to norms imposed by contending forces in the external political economy. From an alternative institutional or cultural perspective, legal systems less *deterred* objectionable corporate behavior than *appealed to* desirable moral and normative commitments. These contrasting approaches were particularly relevant to analysts of the regulatory legal environment, who investigated anti-discrimination, health and safety, antitrust, environmental protection, and similar laws:

> [B]ecause culturalists focus on law as a source of symbol and meaning, rather than as a source of coercive constraint, these researchers tend to emphasize the diffuse and indirect consequences of the legal environment as much as its targeted and direct effects. In this rendition, law serves less as a restraining deterrent for organizational malfeasance than as a supporting framework for all organizational activity. Consequently, organizations often come to embody the underlying logic of the regulatory legal environment even as they try to evade its most burdensome provisions; and, conversely, organizations often come to shape the law through their collective sense-making activities. (Edelman and Suchman 1997:495)

Both material and institutional perspectives portrayed as persistently problematic the inconsistent efforts by private companies and public agencies to comply with equal employment opportunity and affirmative action laws. Legislative acts and regulatory decrees were typically phrased ambiguously, lacking definitions of key terms, allowing alternative interpretations, and providing only weak enforcement and penalty mechanisms. Such equivocations and loopholes gave employers opportunities "to create the appearance of compliance without much change to the racial, ethnic, and gender composition of their work forces" (Edelman 1992:1539). Recurrent high-profile lawsuits by subordinates challenged the actions or behaviors of their superiors, for instance, accusing major corporations of practicing or tolerating sexual harassment (Mitsubishi Motor Manufacturing), racial bias (Texaco), and age discrimination (Wal-Mart and Lockheed Martin). These cases underscored both the persistently arbitrary treatment of employees and the increasingly rights-conscious environments that compelled organizations to pay much greater heed to fairness and due process in their employment relations.

Persistent Occupational Segregation

One root of increasing workplace legalization in the U.S. political economy lay in the enduring inequalities of opportunity and outcome among Americans along gender, racial, ethnic, and age lines (Thurow 1975; Treiman and Hartmann 1981). Inequalities sprang from diverse individual, organizational, and social sources, including insufficient human capital (education, work experience); differential socialization and self-selection into specific occupations; employer biases in hiring, firing, compensating, and promoting employees; and entrenched institutional routines. A key issue remained occupational segregation, the under-representation in more prestigious and better-paying jobs of women, blacks, Hispanics, and other minority groups relative to white males. Figures 8.3, 8.4, and 8.5 show the distributions by gender, race, and ethnicity of workers in 15 broad, nonfarm occupational categories for 1983 and 1996. The horizontal reference lines fall at the labor force rate of the entire group, thus drawing attention to occupational categories where women, blacks, and Hispanics are over- or under-represented. (Over the 13 years, the labor force participation rates rose very little for women [45 and 47 percent] and blacks [9 and 11 percent], but Hispanics jumped from 5 to 9 percent; hence the two reference lines in the third figure.)

The occupational segregation of women was the most dramatic, with huge over-representation in clerical, private household, and other service jobs, and large under-representation in most blue-collar occupations except machine operators. By 1996 the most substantial gain by women was an increase in the executive occupations, which rose from less than one-third to almost 44 percent. Indeed, women held the majority of jobs in several subgroups of that category (medical and health managers, 75 percent; education administrators, 57 percent; financial managers, 54 percent). At the other extreme, very few women worked as mechanics and repairers, in the construction trades, and in extractive occupations (mining). The occupational segregation experienced by blacks and Hispanics, which

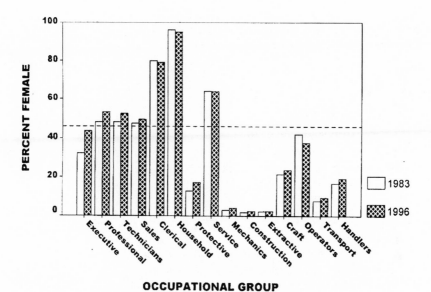

FIGURE 8.3   Female Occupational Groups
SOURCE: U.S. Bureau of the Census (1997:Table 645)

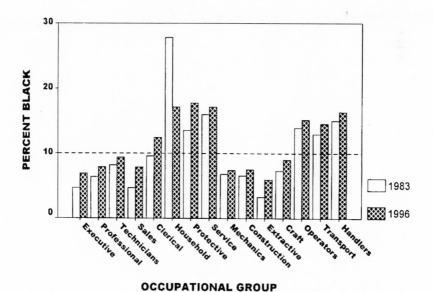

FIGURE 8.4   Black Occupational Groups
SOURCE: U.S. Bureau of the Census (1997:Table 645)

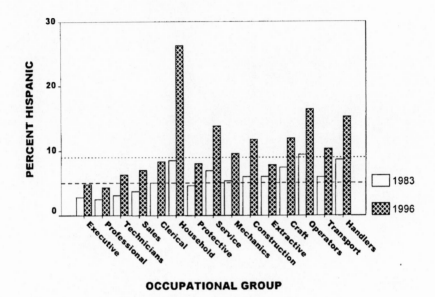

FIGURE 8.5   Hispanic Occupational Groups
SOURCE: U.S. Bureau of the Census (1997:Table 645)

included both men and women, was somewhat less sensational given their smaller presence in the U.S. labor force. In 1996, blacks were most over-represented in private household, protective service, and other services, and most under-represented in extractive and executive jobs. Hispanics experienced a huge over-representation in private household services, machine operation, and equipment handlers, while lagging behind in executive and professional jobs.

One way to summarize the magnitude of occupational segregation is to measure the percentage of a labor force group that would have to shift from over- to under-represented jobs to produce a uniform distribution across the 15 broad occupational categories, exactly equaling that group's labor force participation rate. The women's occupational segregation score fell from 21.4 percent in 1983 to 18.1 percent in 1996, meaning that slightly less than one-fifth of women would have to relocate to a different occupation. For black workers, the score fell from 19.5 to 16.4 percent in the same period. But the Hispanic score increased from 17.3 to 19.3 percent, leaving them the most occupationally segregated of the three groups.[4] These incremental trends did not indicate that gender, race, and ethnic inequalities would likely disappear in the near future. Because even these modest changes also required that men and whites be displaced from occupational categories where they were over-represented, the potential for polarizing resistance and antagonism grew substantially (the backlash by white males accusing employers of "reverse discrimination" in favoring the hiring and promoting of persons from previously dispossessed groups). The progressive legalization of the workplace during the past generation offered one mechanism for regulating and reducing the ferocity of those conflicts.

Preventive Mandates

Workplace legalization originated in a series of executive orders, federal laws, and court decisions created under pressures from the civil rights, women's rights, and other social movements of the 1960s and 1970s. (See Burstein [1985] and Reskin [1998] for insightful analyses of anti-discrimination and affirmative action policies.) In 1961, President John F. Kennedy issued Executive Order 10925, creating a Committee on Equal Employment Opportunity and requiring federal contractors to take "affirmative action" (AA) to assure equal treatment of workers regardless of race, color, or national origin. Four years later, President Lyndon Johnson's Executive Order 11246 mandated that firms with large federal contracts not discriminate against employees or applicants and take affirmative action "to ensure that applicants are employed and employees are treated during their employment without regard to race, color, or national origin" (sex was added to this list in 1967). A major provision of the federal Civil Rights Act of 1964 was Title VII, which banned employment discrimination and created the U.S. Equal Employment Opportunity Commission (EEOC) to enforce the statute. Over time, the EEOC's principal mandate expanded to cover the direct enforcement of four federal laws:

- Title VII of the Civil Rights Act of 1964, as amended in 1972 and 1991, which prohibited private and public employers with 15 or more employees from discriminating "against any individual with respect to his compensation, terms, conditions or privileges of employment, because of such individual's race, color, religion, sex, or national origin." Sexual harassment—unwelcome advances, requests for sexual favors, and other verbal or physical conduct of a sexual nature—was a form of sex discrimination violating Title VII. The Civil Rights Act of 1991 allowed for an award of compensatory damages up to $300,000 per employee if employers engaged in intentional discrimination.
- The Equal Pay Act of 1963 (EPA), which forbade paying different wages to women and men doing substantially similar work in the same establishment.
- The Age Discrimination in Employment Act of 1967 (ADEA), which prohibited discrimination against applicants and employees between

40 and 64 years of age by public and private employers with 20 or more employees.
- The Americans with Disabilities Act of 1990 (ADA), which protected persons in the private sector and state and local government from employment discrimination based on disability.

Several judicial and administrative rulings, most prominently the Supreme Court's 1971 decision in *Griggs v. Duke Power Company*, 401 U.S. 424 (1971) banned employment tests unrelated to job performance and numerical quotas for hiring and promoting women and minorities as compliance strategies.

The extent to which U.S. employers voluntarily complied with EEO/AA rules was difficult to gauge, because organizations without federal contracts and uninvolved in discrimination lawsuits were not required to engage in preventive actions. "The typical components of voluntary affirmative action programs are race- and gender-neutral, while encouraging the race and sex integration of jobs, such as job advertisements that note that the company is an equal opportunity employer" (Reskin 1998:15). Diversity and sexual harassment training became lucrative markets for consultants preying on corporate fears and insecurities about their hiring and promotion practices. Other scant evidence implied that firms and bureaus kept low profiles about their lack of compliance, hoping to avoid arousing the wrath of professional civil rights militants. Employer surveys conducted in five major U.S. metropolitan areas in the early 1990s found slightly less than half the firms reported taking EEO/AA into account when hiring new workers (Holzer and Neumark 1998). In the 1991 General Social Survey (2000), only 44 percent of employed respondents reported that the place where they worked had an affirmation action program or made a special effort to hire and promote minorities. A plausible conclusion was that a majority of U.S. firms probably steered clear of proactive efforts to prevent discrimination in employee hiring, firing, and promotion. Such passivity in personnel practices hindered major change in discriminatory outcomes, as revealed by the trend in employee complaints examined in the next subsection.

EEOC Complaints

Over the 35 years after Title VII went into effect, the volume of private litigation on employment discrimination grew spectacularly. Federal discrimination case filings grew from 350 cases per year in 1970 to a peak of nearly 9,000 in 1983. A multivariate analysis of the 1970–1989 data found that the most important factors behind this trend were increases in the national unemployment rate and broadened statutory definitions of protected workers (Siegelman and Donohue 1990). For example, as corporations retrenched in the downsizing frenzy of the 1980s, laid-off older workers sued their employers under the ADEA. The focus of the lawsuits shifted from alleging biased hiring practices to increasing protections from improper firings for current employees. A similar upward trend occurred in employee discrimination complaints received by the EEOC in the final decades of the twentieth century. As shown in Figure 8.6, new charges of due process violations rose by more than 50 percent between 1989 and the 1994 peak, before leveling off at around 80,000 filings per year.[5] The breakdowns by types of charges, available only for the 1990s, indicate that race and sex discrimination were the two largest categories, but disability filings grew markedly after the EEOC began enforcing the ADA in July 1992. (Because employees often claimed multiple types of discrimination, the total number of charges was less than the sum of specific charges.)

This increasing caseload, coupled with budgetary cutbacks that forced reductions in investigatory staff, meant that the EEOC had built up a huge backlog of unresolved cases by the mid-1990s. The average time to complete cases was expected to double to more than 20 months between 1993 and 1996 (Pryor 1994). Such delays obviously favored businesses by creating difficulties in locating witnesses, obtaining credible witness accounts of alleged discriminatory actions, and securing settlements. If the evidence in a case indicated "no reasonable cause" to believe that discrimination

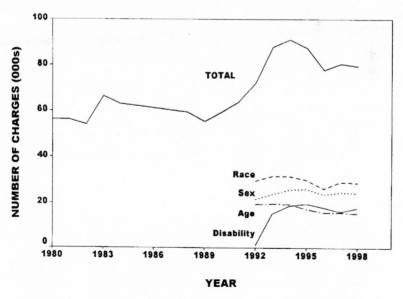

FIGURE 8.6   EEOC Discrimination Charges
SOURCE: U.S. Equal Employment Opportunity Commission (1999)

occurred, the EEOC dismissed the case from its jurisdiction. However, the EEOC gave the employee a right-to-sue letter stating the statutory deadline for filing a private lawsuit. Given their economic powerlessness, very few employees could afford to undertake such civil suits on their own.

If the EEOC found evidence showing reasonable cause, it attempted conciliation. Of more than 614,000 charges resolved by the EEOC between 1992 and 1998, about 57 percent were dismissed for lack of reasonable cause; 30 percent involved administrative closures; 10 percent were settled by the disputants or withdrawn with benefits; and just 3 percent produced a finding of reasonable cause. Fewer than one-third of these latter cases resulted in successful conciliation. If conciliation failed, the EEOC could sue in federal court on behalf of the claimant, although it did so for less than 1 percent of all charges (about 500 suits per year). Remedies available to charging parties included back pay, hiring, promotion, and reinstatement as well as payment of attorney bills, expert witness fees, and court costs. Compensatory and punitive damages might be assessed against an employer where intentional discrimination was found. In 1998, the EEOC obtained $169 million in monetary benefits through settlement and conciliation, and another $90 million through litigation awards. Allegedly, the dissuading effect of these penalties on all employers should far outweigh the financial losses incurred by specific companies and agencies. Yet even multi-million-dollar fines and court settlements probably struck billion-dollar multinational corporations as mosquito stings would a rhinoceros.

Internal Dispute Resolution

An employee filing an EEOC discrimination charge arguably represented the failure by an employer to contain the dispute inside the organization's boundaries. Equal employment opportunity and affirmative action laws and court rulings encouraged corporations to avoid litigation by voluntarily adopting in-house dispute resolution procedures as a means of demonstrating their good-faith efforts to comply with emerging EEO/AA norms. (Chapter 5 examines the changing firm internal labor markets for hiring, training, and promoting employees.) This subsection investigates the spread of innovative organizational policies, programs, and practices to handle employee grievances, including discrimination complaints, sexual harassment charges, and retaliation against whistle-blowers.

With the rising tide of EEOC complaints in the 1990s, employers increasingly adopted internal *alternative dispute resolution* (ADR) procedures, usually involving the intervention or facilitation of a third party to resolve employee complaints. These alternative methods bypassed judges, juries, or other decision-making forums designated by a public authority. ADR began in the 1970s as an internal means to settle disputes of workers covered under collective bargaining agreements. It gained popularity in nonunion organizations after federal laws in 1990 and 1996 required all federal agencies to adopt some form of ADR, and a 1995 EEOC policy encouraged ADR as an alternative to litigation by private-sector employers. Within two decades, the number of state ADR statutes had mushroomed from none to more than 2,000 (Duve 1999). Seeking less costly and time-consuming methods of conflict resolution, many organizations implemented various procedures, ranging from less to more formal:

- *Fact-finding* by a neutral party, either from inside or outside the organization, investigating a complaint and developing findings that could form the basis for a resolution.
- *Negotiation* by direct discussion between the employee and employer with the goal of setting the terms for a resolution.
- *Peer review* by a panel of volunteer employees, possibly including supervisors and managers, working together to resolve complaints.
- *Internal mediation* by a neutral person from inside the company, who helps the disputing parties to negotiate a mutually acceptable agreement.
- *External mediation* by an outside person, without an imposed solution. If mediation fails to produce a settlement, the dispute can still be litigated in the courts.
- *Arbitration* by a neutral person from outside the firm whose decision is usually binding on all parties. That is, an arbitrator's decision cannot subsequently be litigated.

Evidence from two national surveys indicated that ADR made rapid inroads among U.S. businesses. A 1994 EEOC survey of 1,499 private companies with more than 100 employees found that 89 percent used at least one of the six ADR approaches described above to resolve a discrimination complaint. The specific instances ranged from 81 percent for fact-finding and 74 percent for negotiation, to 38 percent for internal mediation, but only 10 and 9 percent for external mediation and arbitration, respectively (Morra 1995). A 1998 survey found much higher incidence of these latter techniques among 606 Fortune 1000 firms (Smoyer 1999). Of employee-related disputes, 79 percent had used mediation and 62 percent had used arbitration at least once during the previous three years, although only about 20 percent reported using either method "frequently" or "very frequently." Both mediation and arbitration were also prevalent methods of resolving commercial, patent or copyright, and contractual disagreements *between* firms, as well as for product liability, personal injury, and environmental disputes with customers and governmental agencies. For example, General Mills, Phillip Morris, the Bank of America, and a dozen other large companies signed a pledge developed by the nonprofit CPR Institute for Dispute Resolution, promising to use mediation first to resolve their Y2K "millennium bug" computer problems such as breach of warranty and misrepresentation (Lepera and Costello 1999). Fortunately, the threat of collapsing civilization from snarled communications and late pizza deliveries proved as overblown as all previous doomsday scenarios.

Evidence showing whether ADR was actually cheaper than conventional litigation remained largely impressionistic, because no central source tracked such data. A large majority of the 1998 survey informants testified that their firms chose mediation or arbitration because it "saves money" and "saves time." A 1996 intensive examination of ADR practices by five private and five federal organizations reflected varied but generally positive experiences (Brostek 1997). Based on limited experience, officials believed that these programs were less costly than formal dispute resolution processes for settling workplace grievances. For example, in the three years after implementing a dispute resolution program in 1993, the international engineering and construction firm Brown & Root reported that its overall costs of handling workplace disputes were less than half the legal fees previously paid to cover employment-related litigation. The number of EEOC cases filed by Brown & Root's workers was cut in half and employment-related lawsuits fell to nearly none. The Hughes Electronics Corporation reported an even steeper reduction in EEOC filings after starting its ADR program in 1993.

Diffusion of
Workplace Legalization

Several organization theorists proposed alternative explanations for the diffusion of workplace legalization throughout the U.S. political economy. Rationalist accounts viewed employee grievance and disciplinary mechanisms as instances of bureaucratization processes within corporations and governmental agencies (Sutton et al. 1994). Large, older, and more hierarchically structured organizations supported law-like norms that achieve economies of scale and reduce uncertainty in the employment relationship. Transaction cost theorists similarly emphasized firm incentives for implementing elaborated governance structures to minimize turnover among highly skilled employees. Nonunionized firms were especially susceptible to creating wholly internalized dispute resolution mechanisms as alternatives to unionization, which would erode management control of the workplace (Williamson 1985:Chapter 10). A resource dependence perspective argued that organizations most heavily dependent on the governmental authorities for resources were more susceptible to normative pressures that are backed by threats of legal sanctions. Hence, public sector agencies and firms holding large federal contracts had significant incentives to comply with legal mandates to reduce the arbitrary treatment of employees and applicants.

Institutional theorists stressed how environmental conditions favored adopting the symbols, rather than the substance, of compliance with due process as a legitimate employer response to the ambiguities and uncertainties that pervade anti-discrimination laws. The socially constructed legal environment became a "central determinant of organizational change, emphasizing legitimacy and survival over efficiency and control as the imperatives that define the form of organizational governance" (Edelman 1990:1402). Organizations most vulnerable to normative environmental pressures should be most prone to institutional isomorphism, that is, to adopt standard due process protections that were widely legitimated by the public legal order. In addition to research on the national state's changing interests in employment nondiscrimination, institutionalists also examined the impact of personnel specialists and labor-law professionals in constructing and interpreting the legal environments confronting employers and employees (Sutton and Dobbin 1996).

Institutional explanations fared better than rationalist approaches in empirical studies of workplace legalization processes. Using a nonrepresentative sample of 52 San Francisco Bay Area firms, Lauren Edelman (1990) examined the diffusion of formal grievance procedures for nonunion employees, defined as any written appeals policy allowing managerial actions to be reviewed at two or more higher levels. Organizations more rapidly implemented nonunion grievance mechanisms if they were located closer to the public sphere, had larger numbers of employees, and had a formal personnel unit. Using a survey of 346 national organizations with 20 or more employees, Edelman (1992) investigated the creation of EEO/AA offices and the adoption of formal rules proscribing employee discrimination. She found similar results, with employers most sensitive to their normative environments (having a union, being a federal contractor) more rapidly creating EEO/AA offices. The strongest determinant of rule formation was the presence of a personnel department. "This strong effect supports my argument that these departments act as 'windows' to the legal environment and are critical to the institutionalization of structural responses to law. However, personnel departments appear to play a greater role in the formation of anti-discrimination rules than in the creation of offices, which suggests that personnel departments help to institutionalize lower-investment symbols of compliance" (Edelman 1992:1565). Given their professional training and ideology, personnel specialists inclined toward formal compliance with due process mandates that avoided challenging and transforming the very organizational power structures on which their livelihoods depended.

Comparable findings occurred in a sample of 279 establishments in spanning 13 industries in three states. Sutton et al. (1994) analyzed the adoption of three due process procedures from 1955 to 1980: employee disciplinary hearings and grievance procedures for nonunion hourly workers and for salaried employees. Rationalist variables such as workplace size, age, and unionization had little impact on rates of initiation. However, all three governance reforms were very responsive to the external environment, rising with the expanded legal and political pressures of the 1970s, but leveling off in the 1980s under the Reagan Administration's attempts to weaken affirmative action. Public agencies and nonprofit associations were more rapid adopters than private firms, as were California employers, whose legislative and judicial climate was more favorable to employee rights. Finally, organizations tied to the national EEO/AA institutional environment through personnel officers and labor attorneys were more likely to create both types of grievance procedures. Personnel management professionals played a critical role in establishing workplace due process procedures because they "actively interpret legal doctrines—typically overstating the legal threat to employers—and disseminate recipes for compliance as a means for enhancing their prestige, autonomy, and authority within organizations" (Sutton et al. 1994:949–950).

The legal changes that brought civil rights protections into the workplace did not guarantee substantive justice through the equitable redress of employee grievances. The creation of fair governance structures might offer more symbolism than substance, as admonished by the institutionalist principle that formal rules often are only loosely coupled with actual organizational practices (Meyer and Rowan 1977). A law-and-society perspective on the social construction of legal environments indicated how organizational agents who handle internal complaints might subtly subordinate employees' legal rights to corporate management interests (Edelman, Erlanger and Lande 1993). Semistructured interviews with 10 EEO/AA "complaint handlers," who were primarily personnel professionals rather than lawyers, revealed that legal considerations played a peripheral part in their orientations toward worker complaints. Rather, given their primary goals of avoiding litigation and restoring good employee relations, these officials typically interpreted the discrimination statutes as requiring fair treatment consistent with good management practices:

> When asked to elaborate [on] what fairness meant, complaint handlers had a variety of responses, but in general they were based more on broad notions of procedural fairness than on the substantive requirements of EEO/AA law. They mentioned consistent treatment, prior notice of rules, protection from retaliation, giving the complainant an opportunity to be heard, and impartial consideration of complaints. Four complaint handlers suggested a more sub-

stantive element of fairness: they said that the resolution should be fair. Only three complaint handlers said that fairness meant consistency with the law. Complaint handlers may construe EEO/AA law as a fair treatment because, as nonlawyers, they need to simplify the complex and amorphous legal doctrines. (Edelman, Erlanger and Lande 1993:514)

Complaint handlers could effectively depoliticize workplace conflicts by categorizing the discrimination complaints of women and minorities as actually managerial or personality problems, rather than as institutionalized sexual and racial discrimination originating deep in the organization's power structures. Claims that might be framed as the absolute right not to be discriminated against by an employer instead were transformed into disputes involving individual interests or personality clashes between particular workers and supervisors. These interpretations could more easily be resolved discreetly though therapy and compromise aimed at restoring good working relations between employees and their supervisors. Internal dispute resolution procedures usually nullified such basic legal safeguards as representation by counsel, limitations on permissible evidence, and burden of proof (Edelman, Erlanger and Lande 1993:519). In sum, organizations implemented formal compliance structures and procedures that, while visibly displaying their symbolic commitments to basic American civil rights ideals, effectively minimized the legal transformation of traditional managerial prerogatives to run the workplace without meaningful interference by either employees or the government.

Employee Ownership

One perennial proposal to reduce, if not eradicate, the inherent conflicts of interest between employers and employees was to transform workers into collective company owners. Worker-owners would simultaneously bear the full financial risks, perform all the productive tasks, and receive any resulting profits as returns to their stockholdings. Resource dependence theory leads to predictions that changing organizational power and control should inevitably and automatically realign the firm's interests with those held by its individual employees. Many extraordinary outcomes should come about if employees run the firm: not only more generous wages and benefits but also better working conditions, better health and safety practices, nonconflictual labor-management relations, and community reinvestment. In principle, professional executives and the board of directors would make only strategic decisions advantageous to the corporation's shareholders, who are concurrently the firm's workforce. Because employees gain many strong incentives to work diligently to reap the full benefits of their labor, both their morale and productivity should rise, making the company more profitable and competitive. Utopian as these outcomes sound, in practice they often ran afoul of numerous pitfalls that impeded their realization.

Although many law firms, accounting agencies, investment banking, and other professional service organizations had long been employee-owned and -operated, a boomlet got underway in 1974 when Senator Russell Long wrote tax-deductible contributions to employee stock ownership plans (ESOPs) into a pension reform bill. The inventor of this conceptual model, San Francisco attorney and investor Louis Kelso, had promoted the idea for decades as "a tool to help restore the economic democracy America once had but lost through technological advance, and to correct the defect in our capitalist system that keeps capitalism from working for the many as well as it does for the few" (Hall 1987). An ESOP created a trust to hold the shares of company stock acquired by the plan through purchases on the open market, from individual shareholders, or from the company's treasury. The trust then allocated shares to individual employee accounts, which they received on retirement or after terminating employment at the firm. One important way for the trust to buy stock was through a leveraged ESOP: A company borrowed money from the plan to buy some of its own stock, securing the loan with corporate assets, then used its earnings to make tax-deductible contributions to the ESOP when repaying the loan (Caver 1996).

After 1974 as many as 11,000 U.S. companies employing about 8 percent of the labor force launched ESOPs. These plans ran the gamut from less than 1 percent to 100 percent stock ownership. Some firms created plans as a means to fight hostile takeover attempts during the 1980s (Scholes and Wolfson 1989), while others made stock-for-concession deals with unions to save their financially endangered hides. In 1994, stockholders of the world's largest airline, United, agreed to sell its pilots and mechanics 55 percent of the company in return for five years of wage cuts to stem a massive flow of red ink. As part of the deal, participating employees picked the new CEO and three of the 12 United Airlines board members. Although UAL, Weirton Steel, and Avis-Rent-A-Car were dramatic examples of large companies taken over by their workers, most of the 2,500 companies with majority-ownership ESOPs were small- or middle-sized businesses, averaging fewer than 600 workers (Worker-Ownership Institute 2000). Typically, retiring or departing owners sold their privately held companies to the employees to avoid paying taxes on their capital gains. After a 1990 tax code revision required employee majority ownership and control for the tax deduction, growth in the total number of plans plateaued at about 10,000 companies. Few of these arrangements involved the extensive employee control and participation in day-to-day decision making in Louis Kelso's original vision. Many more hired professional managers to operate the business, shunting the employee-owners to the sidelines where they passively benefited or suffered from *their* managerial employees' decisions.

Evidence about the actual consequences of worker-ownership was mixed and largely anecdotal. Avis employees doubled their share prices when they sold the company in 1996 to HSF Inc., a real estate sales and hotel licenser. Weirton Steel workers turned around their failing plant within a year of buying it in 1984. However, Rath Packing Company in Waterloo, Iowa, filed for bankruptcy reorganization within three years after its 2,000 workers voted to buy it. And in 1997 the United Airlines pilots union rejected further work concessions demanded by their CEO and threatened to abandon the ESOP when it came up for renewal three years later. One meta-analysis of 43 published studies found that profit-sharing, worker ownership, and worker participation in decision making were all positively associated with higher productivity (Doucouliagos 1995; see also Kumbhakar and Dunbar 1993; Gamble 1998). Another summary of 27 previous investigations of employee ownership and productivity concluded that few strong and significant performance improvements occurred (Blasi, Conte and Kruse 1996). However, many studies were plagued by mixed ownership types and ambiguous productivity measures that rendered them noncomparable (Blum 1997). A meaningful assessment of whether ESOPs really generated the expected performance outcomes depends crucially on whether a plan served merely as a retirement vehicle or allowed genuine worker participation in managerial decisions. Stock ownership alone evoked insufficient sense of control necessary to motivate maximum employee efforts:

> The studies come to a very clear consensus. Employee ownership can, in fact, substantially improve corporate performance, but only when combined with "participative management" programs. By this, the researchers mean programs for employees to have regular and meaningful input into decisions affecting their work. Self-managing teams, employee participation groups, employee advisory committees, and similar structures are often used to accomplish this. Absent this input, employee ownership has no consistent impact on performance. This does not suggest, however, that employee participation itself is adequate. The research on the impact of participation on performance is ambiguous, indicating that it will have an impact only in some cases. (Michael Quarry and Corey Rosen, quoted in Caver 1996:661–662)

In practice, most employee stock ownership plans created a nonprofit organization that permitted workers to reap only financial benefits without enjoying effective management control (Hansmann 1990). That is, no one participated in both control and residual earnings. Firms in which an ESOP owned all the company's equity were seldom controlled by their employees, rather by trustees who operated only as fiduciaries, or agents, on behalf of the workers' financial interests. A company structured solely for beneficial worker-ownership differed little from the classic large investor-owned corporations described by Berle and Means, whose managements were effectively insulated from stockholder control. Once again, corporate executives learned to protect their capacity to act without strong accountability to other stakeholders. "It is naive and ironic to suggest that labor-management relations could improve without changing the structure of power and participation" (Blum 1997:1568). The scattered and tentative experiments with employee ownership of twentieth-century firms provided little evidence that such fundamental changes would soon occur.

Conclusions

Organizations are rarely immune from the conflicts pervading the political economies in which they operate. Increasingly, U.S. workplaces became arenas in which gender, racial, ethnic, sexual orientation, age, and other identity groups challenged the traditional power and privileges enjoyed by white males. Adapting social movement strategies and tactics pioneered in the 1960s, these excluded employees fought for expanded opportunities to compete for better paying and more prestigious jobs. However, collective efforts to institutionalize workplace democracy met with limited success. Business organizations yielded ground only grudgingly, offering largely symbolic concessions while retaining effective control of managerial prerogatives. Simultaneously, crumbling under a ferocious ideological counterattack led by the Republican Party, U.S. labor union rolls fell to levels before the New Deal. Despite an impressive array of federal laws extending anti-discrimination and due process rights to employees, meaningful changes of organizational power were often blunted. Business implementation strategies weakened the impact of workplace legalization, effectively redefining worker-management conflicts as individualized problems requiring therapeutic solutions rather than structural transformation. Even the handful of employee stock ownership plans served more as sources of cheap corporate loans than as genuine experiments in employee participation in strategic decision making. By the end of the twentieth century, titanic struggles for employee power in the workplace had won few grudging concessions, leaving managers firmly grasping the levers of organizational power. The next chapter examines how U.S. corporations successfully manipulated the national political system to thwart numerous challenges to their hegemony.

9

Influencing
Public Policies

*It could be shown by facts and figures that there is no distinctly native
American criminal class except Congress.*
—Mark Twain, *Pudd'nhead Wilson's New Calendar* (1896)

The Telecommunications Act of 1996 culminated a decade-long political
struggle over revamping a 62-year-old hodgepodge of federal legislation
cooked up before the invention of television. Congress sought to create a vast
competitive marketplace capable of dealing with the technological fusion of
digital voice, video, and data services into the new Information Superhighway. The conflict pitted opposing Republican and Democratic ideologies
about the government's role in regulating private enterprise and censoring
TV programming and Internet access. The Republican-controlled Congress
favored a digital free-for-all that removed existing barriers to telecom companies entering new industries, purchasing multiple media in local markets, and
perpetual price regulations. The Clinton Administration wanted to preserve
strong federal regulatory power to safeguard consumer interests in lower
prices and to protect children from exposure to TV violence and cyberporn.
Caught in the middle of this partisan fight, a host of broadcast, cable, and Internet providers repeatedly lobbied congressional committees to water down
draft legislation threatening their monopolistic advantages.

A major snag was how quickly the seven regional "Baby Bell" companies, which provided only local telephone services, should be allowed to
enter the lucrative long-distance market. Long-distance phone providers
such as MCI, Sprint, and especially AT&T (from which the Baby Bells had
been split in a 1984 antitrust settlement) opposed rapid entry of the regional companies. They argued that the Baby Bells should first face stiff
competition in their own local-phone service areas. The regional companies in turn worried that, if cable and cellular companies were allowed to

offer telephone and data services that could "cherry pick" their big corporate accounts, the Baby Bells might be stuck subsidizing high-cost residential voice phones. Other interest groups pursued their narrow advantages: Newspapers lobbied for protection from online publishers, and consumer advocates opposed cable operators launching phone services. Network television broadcasters and civil libertarians objected to the proposed TV show ratings and a "V-chip" enabling parents to block children's access to explicit material. As one wit put it, "All each entity seeks is a fair advantage over its rival" (Lochhead 1994).

After killing the bill in 1994 and delaying its successor the following year, both Congress and the Clinton Administration eventually made enough concessions to telecom industry interests to pass the measure overwhelmingly in early 1996. At the signing ceremony, comedian Lily Tomlin reprised her role of Ernestine the Operator, telling Vice-President Al Gore, "You're not stiff; you're just a techno-nerd" (Mills 1996). Among its many provisions, the Act permitted the Baby Bells to offer long-distance services while also allowing the long-distance carriers to compete in local markets. Phone companies could sell video services to consumers through their own ground lines or by satellite. Broadcasters could own more TV and radio stations serving more people nationwide, although the Act only instructed the Federal Communications Commission to consider whether to allow multiple station ownership within a single local market. The Act gradually freed cable companies from rate regulations and permitted them to offer both phone and cable TV services. And it compelled online service providers to restrict access to indecent material. Within a week of passage, the American Civil Liberties Union and 20 publishers and online firms had filed suit challenging that restriction as "the cyberspace equivalent of book-burning" (Reid 1996). Four months later, a federal judicial panel ruled it an unconstitutional affront to the First Amendment, setting the stage for an eventual Supreme Court decision.

The turbulent transformation of the telecommunications industry, from stodgy monopolistic system into dynamic competitive markets, revealed public policymaking as a serious poker game played by political organizations for big stakes. This chapter examines several important changes in the U.S. national power structure at the end of the twentieth century: growing numbers of interest organizations, increasing mobilization of member resources, expanding repertoires of influence tactics, proliferating political action committees, and colliding coalitions trying to shape the outcomes of national legislative and regulatory decisions. These components of change bear on two core issues in the new political economy: Do business groups, especially large corporations with their vast economic resources, always mobilize sufficient political power to achieve their most important collective interests? Or can opposing political organizations, in particular labor unions and identity groups, occasionally overcome business domination to achieve favorable public policy outcomes? An attempt to answer these questions begins with three basic theoretical approaches to political power structures, summarized in the next section.

Power Structure Theories

Three broad theoretical perspectives on U.S. national power structures, developed by sociologists and political scientists, seek to explain the changing involvement of business interest groups in the U.S. political system: class, elite, and pluralist theories (Knoke 1981; Alford and Friedland 1985). Each approach emphasizes the structural potential for different key political actors to influence public policy decisions made by the elected and appointed officials of the federal government. The ability of business organizations to dominate other social groups depends on whether power resources are monopolized by a ruling social class, by a corporate elite, or are more widely dispersed among competing interest organizations.

In their bluntest Marxist version, *ruling class theories* posited that the state is simply "an executive committee for managing the common affairs of the bourgeoisie" (Marx and Engels 1939). A unified upper class, owning and controlling the means of economic production, dominated the political system, thereby assuring that all major political decisions would favor the interests of that ruling class. This perspective underlay researchers' efforts to discover "who owns America" by revealing that a small proportion of families own huge concentrations of corporate stock and trust assets (Zeitlin 1989). This propertied group constituted a closely interacting social class related through kinship, marriage, schooling, friendship, and other social ties (Domhoff 1983; Dye 1995). The alleged political unity of the upper class arose from its capacity to restrict the policy agenda to only those issues and choices favorable to its interests. The ruling class dominated the national political system by such processes as controlling the mass media (Miliband 1969), propagating ideas and policy proposals through foundations and think tanks (Ricci 1993), and financing presidential and congressional election campaigns (Domhoff 1990).

Elite theories viewed power as concentrated in the top positions of key hierarchical organizations, including large corporations, private foundations, universities, government bureaucracies, and even the military (Mills 1956; Prewitt and Stone 1973). Analysts recognized that elite unity on policy matters and governance of the state was problematic, as divisive external and internal forces continually chipped away this peak coalition. Not only was the working class capable of organizing politically to oppose and thwart the business community's policy preferences, but corporations might split into political factions reflecting their divergent organizational, industrial, and geographic interests. For example, importers and domestic manufacturers held opposing views on tariffs and import quotas, and the health care and insurance sectors took differing positions on cost-containment issues (Mintz 1995).

Power structure research from this perspective illuminated several mechanisms developed to overcome the tendency toward elite fragmentation. Among several significant devices helping to preserve elite unity were interlocking corporate directorships (Mizruchi 1996), policy discussion networks (Moore 1979), and holding multiple leadership positions linking business organizations with major civic institutions (Useem 1979). Analysts of interlocking directorates recurrently found that a small number of New York commercial banks and insurance companies occupied central positions in the large-corporation network, enabling them to exercise "hegemonic control" over the flow of capital to the largest nonfinancial firms (Kotz 1978; Mizruchi 1982; Mintz and Schwartz 1985). As discussed in Chapter 7, company embeddedness in an interlocking director network had demonstrable consequences for several organizational behaviors, such as the adoption of corporate best-practices and takeover prevention strategies. Whether or how cohesive economic ties enabled elites to influence national public policies remained theoretically and empirically vague. Corporate networks might serve as communication channels that reduced business conflict by promoting broader perspectives on common policy interests, thus contributing to elite consensus. However, evidence that corporate interlocks sustained coordinated political action was largely confined to campaign contributions by political action committees, examined later in this chapter.

Finally, *pluralist theories* denied political primacy to any particular class- or identity-based social groupings defined by race, ethnic, gender, age, region, religion, or other attributes (Truman 1951; Dahl 1956). The complex diversity of the U.S. political economy with its fragmented federal, state, and local governments ensured that no enduring political block could effectively and permanently dominate the national political agenda. Constitutional checks and balances provided alternative opportunities for organized interests to influence public policy decisions. A momentary victory by one faction would stimulate counter-action to prevent the monopoly power depicted by the ruling-class model. The key political actors in pluralist theory were career candidates seeking public offices and organized groups mobilizing around very specific issues, such as abortion, gun control, lower taxes, education, and social security. Most citizens belonged simultaneously to several social groups, resulting in cross-cutting rather than cumulative interest cleavages. Individuals most effectively participated in the political system through their affiliation with, or representation by, politically active organizations enjoying legitimate access to political conflicts. The competition between candidates and parties for votes and among politically active interest organizations for the public resources dispensed by office holders tended to produce negotiated redistributive solutions to disputes rather than violently polarized zero-sum contests. Because competitive two-party electoral districts required that politicians receive a majority of ballots to win office, centrist candidates who appealed to broad spectrums of voter interests almost always prevailed over single-issue extremists.

In pluralistic power structures, public institutions, political parties, corporations, and voluntary associations all mobilized and deployed sufficient political resources to gain attention from the officials whose decisions affected their interests. Even politically marginalized groups, such as racial and ethnic minorities, might ultimately mobilize as mass social movements to demand seats at the pluralist bargaining table. Political interest groups continually coalesced, broke apart, and recombined into new electoral blocs to support candidates who plausibly promised to satisfy their constituents' policy demands. In periods between elections, shifting interest group coalitions lobbied legislative parties, executive bureaus, and regulatory agencies for policy decisions. The desire for re-election was a powerful motive for public officials to remain attentive and responsive to their constituents' policy demands.

An important variant of pluralism, *state-centric theories*, highlighted "state managers" (elected and appointed government officials) as a political faction holding distinct policy preferences that were independent from the ruling class or organizational elites (Poulantzas 1978; Krasner 1984). Their structural power primarily rested on the state's legitimate authority and the capacity of public officials to create and use political resources. Because a healthy economy was important to their re-election prospects, state managers necessarily took corporate preferences into account, but in an electoral democracy, public officials also listened seriously to competing demands by other vocal constituencies. In addition, periodically they had to react to major economic and foreign policy crises in ways harmful to some business interests, for example, in delaying favorable trading status to China because of its human rights abuses.

The power structure perspectives summarized in this section offer some useful theoretical concepts and relationships for empirically investigating the changing patterns of business participation in U.S. national politics over the past generation. In particular, consistent with pluralistic assumptions, diverse political organizations that mobilized the resources of their members grew increasingly active in both electoral and lobbying campaigns. Moreover, post-Watergate changes in the institutional rules of the campaign financing and public policymaking games potentially gave large corporations greater influence on the political system, consistent with the elite domination thesis, if not with ruling-class explanations.

Proliferating Political Organizations

Political scientists and sociologists typically distinguish three broad types of organized political organizations: parties, interest groups, and social movement organizations (SMOs). I define a *political organization* as a formally organized, named group that seeks to influence the policy decisions of elected and appointed public officials. (Another term for this type is "collective action organization"; see Knoke 1990b.) Most political organizations are voluntary associations of persons or organizations that pool their members' financial and other resources for use in conventional political actions to affect policymaking. Ironically, under this definition, a political party should not be considered a political organization, because its goal is to elect candidates to public office and only rarely to pressure elected officials for specific policy agendas. The major difference between parties and other political organizations is that party members actually control governmental institutions. Although public bureaucracies might be excluded under the political organization definition, their leaders periodically act to promote the agency's own policy preferences within the government. Similarly, many for-profit corporations behave as political organizations when their legislative affairs officers lobby governments for preferential treatment. In recent decades, the traditional mass membership associations have yielded ground to institutionally based organizations, including corporations, universities, foreign firms and governments, and confederations of U.S. state and local governments like the National League of Cities (Salisbury 1994).

Researchers usually treated interest groups and SMOs as conceptually divergent types of political organizations. Political scientists claimed that interest groups enjoyed regular access to elected officials, and sociologists asserted that SMOs represented outsiders or challengers lacking institutionalized entry into the political system. SMO political tactics were supposedly limited to rallies, demonstrations, or more violent forms of protest (including revolutionary actions intended to overthrow the government) rather than to working within routine political channels including elections and the lobbying commonly associated with interest groups. Some social movements eventually changed into conventional interest groups if they survived their turbulent youths as unruly challengers. For example, the

Symbionese Liberation Army, which kidnapped and converted newspaper heiress Patty Hearst to its violently anarchist cause, was ultimately destroyed by law enforcement agencies, but many civil rights organizations evolved into fully legitimate participants in debates over social and economic issues. Increasingly, SMO analysts emphasized the substantial overlap in tactics and goals between movements and interest groups in democratic polities (McAdam, Tarrow and Tilly 1996). Paul Burstein (1998) convincingly argued that conventional SMO-interest group distinctions were no longer conceptually meaningful nor useful for empirical guidance. "Rather than trying to make the distinction, therefore, we should simply say that a variety of nonparty organizations try to influence political outcomes; the organizations vary in a variety of important ways (tactics, organization, number of members, resources, goals, etc.), but the simple dichotomy between 'interest group' and 'social movement organization' cannot stand up to scrutiny and should be abandoned" (Burstein 1998:45). Instead, various types of nonparty political organizations (which Burstein labeled "interest organizations") all try actively to persuade public officials to make policy decisions favorable to organizational interests.

Political organizations performed two fundamental functions within democratic political systems. First, they aggregated the policy preferences of some category of citizens with common interests, enabling them more effectively to press their demands on policymakers. For example, the American Association of Retired Persons (AARP) formulated its public policy agenda by soliciting the issue preferences of older people through letters, town hall meetings, and surveys. By articulating member demands and pooling the scarce resources of weak individuals, organized interest groups fashioned louder voices less easily ignored by officials who made public policy decisions. However, all interests were not created equal. Because higher socioeconomic status groups more often joined and participated in political organizations, the pressure-group system was biased against mobilizing and representing the viewpoints of less well-organized class, race, gender, and ethnic groups (Verba, Schlozman and Brady 1995; Van Deth 1997). Second, political organizations provided public authorities with channels for communicating policy information and providing benefits to their electoral constituencies. Adroit politicians learned how to compartmentalize the messages and campaign promises they served up to specific electoral segments. A candid pandering revelation occurred in the 2000 South Carolina presidential primary when the main Republican candidates, George W. Bush and John McCain, avoided stating their positions on whether the Confederate flag should stop flying over the statehouse, as demanded by offended African Americans. Only after Bush locked up the nomination did McCain apologize for lying when he called the flag a Southern "symbol of heritage." Elected and appointed officials also tried to manipulate public opinion by selectively targeting which interest organizations received coveted access to present their cases for particular policy decisions.

Public officials and political organizations had mutual interests in delivering policy successes that permitted them both to survive and to re-play the influence game again and again (Browne 1998:226–228). The fragmentation of political power among the numerous policy arenas that make up the U.S. federal system offered several institutional sites—legislatures, executive agencies, regulatory bodies, and courts at the local, state, and national levels—in which aggrieved groups could raise their demands and push their preferred solutions onto the public agenda for debate and resolution. This duality of political organizations at the interface between the state and its citizenry assured that organized interests exerted a crucial, if somewhat constitutionally ambiguous, impact on the outcomes of collective political actions.

Political organizations encompassed a broad range of purposes, including such types as business and trade associations, labor unions, professional societies, neighborhood and community organizations, nationality and racial-ethnic federations, civic service clubs, philanthropies, conservation leagues, fraternities and sororities, and occasionally even churches, recreational, and hobby clubs. National political organizations ranged in membership size from AARP, which claims more than 25 million members, and the U.S. Chamber of Commerce (representing 3 million firms), to small staff organizations with just one or two operatives bankrolled by nonprofit foundations. One interesting type was the so-called citizens' group or public interest group (PIG), which purported to seek neither economic nor sectarian benefits but to promote the broader collective values of the society (Berry 1977). For example, civil rights, civil liberties, environmental protection, feminist, and consumer advocacy associations frequently proclaimed a disinterested policy agenda. However, a closer examination of their supporters and activities suggests that their methods of operation did not differ fundamentally from other political organizations (Schlozman and Tierney 1986:30–35).

The precise number of U.S. political organizations operating at the national level was difficult to gauge. The 1999 edition of the *Gale Encyclopedia of Associations* listed nearly 23,000 nonprofit membership organizations of "national scope," falling into 18 categories ranging from hobby and athletic clubs to scientific, educational, and religious organizations (Maurer and Sheets 1999). The two largest categories were "trade, business, and commercial" (17 percent) and "health and medical" (11 percent), followed by "public affairs" (9 percent), "social welfare," and "cultural" associations (8 percent each). Based on the National Associations Survey I conducted in the mid-1980s, perhaps half of all U.S. national associations qualified as political organizations because they attempted to make their positions on national policy issues known to the federal government (Knoke 1990b:208). The proportions were much higher among labor unions, trade, and professional associations than for organizations with social, leisure, or recreational purposes. Political influence need not be their primary purpose nor compose the majority of their activities, but the indispensable criterion for political organizations is attempting to change or preserve the social, economic, cultural, or legal conditions faced by their members or those on whose behalf they operate.

Trade associations were the major type of political organization seeking "to defend and promote the interests of business firms" (Aldrich and Staber 1988:112). Most trade associations organized businesses operating in fairly narrow industries, although a few purported to represent broader sectors. As illustrations of the range spanned by U.S. trade associations, consider these three cases whose self-descriptions appeared on their Web sites:

- The American Ostrich Association (AOA), located in Fort Worth, Texas, sought to promote the ostrich farming industry, "by providing direction, programs, services, education, and other benefits to support the development of a dynamic and profitable commercial market" for meat, leather, and feathers. Although concentrating on building U.S. consumer awareness, the association purported to represent the interests of ostrich breeders and processors before Congress and government regulatory agencies. However, with fewer than 50 members scattered around the country, the AOA's political clout was certainly dubious.
- The Regional Airline Association (RAA) represented 71 of the 104 U.S. regional airline companies, some of which were independent firms while others were subsidiaries of the major carriers. The RAA's staff and members regularly participated in the industry regulatory process, which included "commenting on proposed requirements, active participation in advisory committees and regulatory negotiations, discussions with federal officials responsible for drafting or setting regulatory policy as well as coordination with other interested industry groups or coalitions to achieve mutual objectives." Chief among these regulatory agencies were the Federal Aviation Administration, Department of Transportation, National Transportation Safety Board, United States Postal Service, Interstate Commerce Commission, Department of Labor, and Immigration and Naturalization Service.
- The American Electronics Association (AEA) represented 3,000 companies in the high-tech sector including the computer, software, semiconductor, telecommunication services, and medical electronics

industries. Its members ranged in size from venerable giants IBM and Microsoft to recent startups Universal Algorithms and Gadzoox Networks. Given this diversity, the issues crowding the AEA's recent political agenda were extensive, spanning federal investment in science and technology, Internet taxation, data encryption and computer export controls, Y2K liability, immigration of skilled workers, patent law reform, and the Clinton Administration's proposed blacklisting of federal contractors "for alleged or actual violations of labor, employment, environment law, tax or antitrust law."

Several "peak associations" or "encompassing organizations" (Grimm and Holcomb 1987) professed to represent the political interests of wide sectors of the business community. The U.S. Chamber of Commerce, the National Association of Manufacturers (NAM), and the Business Roundtable (an association of CEOs of the largest corporations) each maintained a heavy policy advocacy presence in Washington on behalf of their diverse memberships. Similarly, National Small Business United and the National Federation of Independent Business tried to shape federal legislative and regulatory issues affecting the interests of numerous smaller companies.

The trade association was primarily a twentieth-century organizational invention, reacting to the emerging national political economy based on large corporations (see Chapter 7). Their numbers dramatically expanded from barely 100 associations at the end of the nineteenth century. The vital population processes—foundings, deaths, and population growth—followed the familiar dynamics described by organizational ecology theory (Aldrich and Staber 1988; Aldrich et al. 1990, 1994). Recall from Chapter 2 that legitimation and competition selection processes operate in opposing fashion in the proliferation of a new organizational form. After a new type of organization enters a particular socioeconomic niche, that population's survival and expansion depends on attracting sustaining resources from potential members or other organizational sponsors. An S-shape population growth curve typically ensues: slow initial population expansion while the new form lacks wide legitimacy in the society; rapid growth as the form gains wider acceptance and new organizations enter to compete for more abundant resources; a slow-down in population growth as resources become scarcer and competition increases mortality rates and reduces founding rates; finally, population stagnation or decline as the environmental carrying capacity is reached.

Analyses of the expanding U.S. trade association population revealed how this type of political organization created the critical mass essentially for political influence. Figure 9.1 depicts the changing vital rates for this population during the mid-twentieth century (Aldrich and Staber 1988). The rates of association foundings and deaths (terminations due to disbanding, merger, or transformation into another organization) were calculated as the number of each event per year divided by the number of exist-ing organizations. Foundings greatly exceeded deaths until around the 1960s, when the rates began to converge. As a result, the rapid population expansion evident in Figure 9.2 through the middle of the twentieth cen-tury began to slow, eventually stabilizing at around 2,300 national trade as-sociations in the 1980s. By the end of the century, few long-established in-dustries remained unorganized. The only ways that new associations could form were through the emergence of new industries, such as microelectron-ics and biotechnology; the subdivision of an already-organized industry into more homogeneous parts; and the merger or absorption of associa-tions operating in economically declining sectors (Aldrich and Staber 1988:123).

A longitudinal analysis of the factors affecting the foundings and deaths of trade associations found the usual curvilinear density dependence effects hypothesized by organizational ecology theory (Aldrich et al. 1994). That is, with an initial increase in association population density (measured by the total number of organizations), the rate of new foundings increased as the new form acquired greater legitimacy and public acceptance. However, at higher population densities, a competitive resource crowding reduced the rate of new foundings and raised the rate of association disbandings. The magnitude of the density effect for trade associations was much smaller

FIGURE 9.1   Trade Association Vital Rates
SOURCE: Aldrich and Staber (1988)

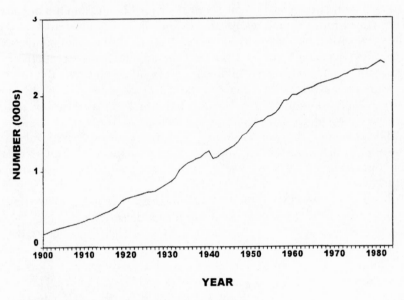

FIGURE 9.2   Trade Association Population
SOURCE: Aldrich and Staber (1988)

than the effect observed in other organizational populations, such as labor unions (see Hannan and Freeman 1989). The researchers concluded that "direct competition between associations is minimized by norms of mutual tolerance or even support, unlike the more resource-driven ecology model, which implies that the negative effects of competition should raise disbandings" (Aldrich et al. 1994:235). Periods of economic growth raised association founding rates but also boosted disbandings, possibly because technological changes drove obsolete firms out of business. Similarly, federal governmental interventions into the economy—during World War I, the 1933–1935 National Industrial Recovery Act (NIRA) of the New Deal, and World War II—differentially altered the vital rates. The federal government sought to coordinate business production and distribution during each of these three national emergencies. Trade association foundings increased in World War I but not in World War II, and the NIRA gave a strong but only temporary boost to both foundings and disbandings. Republican presidential administrations produced an insignificant increase in foundings but a significant decrease in disbandings, implying that "collective action by business has been only modestly affected by which political party is in power" (Aldrich et al. 1994:233). Although that conclusion may be warranted regarding general population dynamics, historical case studies suggest that particular policy events can be as consequential for collective action efforts by trade associations as they are for other types of political organization. For instance, highly publicized incidents such as the 1999 massacre of students at Columbine High School in Littleton, Colorado, stimulated law suits by urban governments against gun makers and increased lobbying against gun restrictions by the National Rifle Association.

The political activities of U.S. political organizations respond to changing national political conditions, including ideological shifts in legislative, regulatory, and judicial climates (Berry 1977:13; Schlozman and Tierney 1986:74–82; Gray and Lowery 1996). For example, during the New Deal, American labor unions established a permanent national policy presence as part of the Democratic Party's electoral coalition. Public interest groups and their liberal sociopolitical agendas flourished during the civil rights, antiwar, feminist, gay and lesbian rights, and other identity-group social movements that erupted during the 1960s. Business advocacy associations flocked to Washington in the 1970s and 1980s in reaction to newly created federal regulatory agencies—such as the Environmental Protection Agency (EPA), Occupational Safety and Health Agency (OSHA), and Consumer Product Safety Commission (CPSC)—which promulgated thousands of pages of federal regulations that provoked their business targets to seek political redress (Vogel 1996). Peak business associations such as the NAM, Business Roundtable, and U.S. Chamber of Commerce took the lead in coordinating a major corporate counterattack against the expanding federal welfare state, ultimately leading to Ronald Reagan's election as president in 1980 with a pledge to "get government off our backs." Congressional procedural reforms in the 1970s, by reducing the power of committee chairmen and fostering government by subcommittees (Oleszek 1978:65), created numerous points of policy access for interest groups to press their claims and grievances.

The magnitude of these changes is evident in Figure 9.3, which plots the number of U.S. trade and professional associations with national headquarters in the Washington, D.C., metropolitan area (Russell 1997; see similar accounts by Schlozman and Tierney 1986; Baumgartner and Leech 1998). The numbers tripled over the quarter century after 1971, reaching nearly 2,400 associations by 1997. The Washington contingent was twice as large as the populations in either of the next largest areas, New York and Chicago. This transformation reflected not only the expanding number of national trade and professional associations but also their increasing concentration in the nation's capital, from 19 percent in 1971 to a peak of 32 percent by 1988, where it stabilized.

In sum, the national political economy faced by interest organizations had grown vastly more crowded by the end of the twentieth century. The expansion from a small population of political organizations into large numbers of claimant groups competing for the attention of public officials

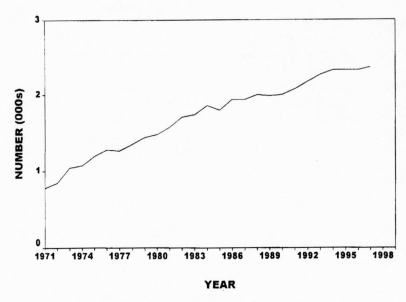

FIGURE 9.3   Associations in Washington, D.C.
SOURCE: Russell et al. (1997)

was more consistent with pluralist theoretical expectations than with either the ruling class or elite theories emphasizing political dominance by a few powerful players. However, the crucial test was not demonstrating growth in sheer weight of numbers, but rather explaining which organized interests tended to prevail in shaping public policies. One clue lay in examining how effectively political organizations mobilized their members' resources in the collective effort to influence governmental decisions.

Mobilizing Member Resources

Forming and sustaining a mass-membership political organization, such as a trade association, was best conceptualized as an exchange between an entrepreneurial organizer and a set of potential members. A leader invested financial capital in some organizational benefits—including favorable public policy decisions—and members paid annual dues to receive these rewards. Many benefits were material goods and services that were either unavailable or more costly to obtain by nonmembers, thus enticing potential participants to join the organization. A typical example was the Regional Airline Association, which offered its members bulletins about aircraft types and operating circumstances; periodic seminars and workshops on human resource management, tax issues, and cabin crew training; monthly legislative updates on congressional activity; and statistical analyses of industry economic trends. Many associations put on annual conferences that provided opportunities for networking, socializing, and nurturing member identification with their organization.

Not all political organizations remained entirely dependent on their mass membership for the resources necessary to live long and prosper. Sometimes an interorganizational grant was crucial at the formative stage in enabling the new association to survive its infancy. For example, the AFL-CIO founded the National Council of Senior Citizens, helped to recruit its initial members from union rolls, and underwrote many NCSC activities. Although committed citizen activists, such as Ralph Nader or John Gardner, occasionally provided the energizing impetus for launching new organizations, many public interest groups relied on patronage from wealthy individuals or foundation sponsors to get up and running (Walker 1983), as well as on favorable mass media treatment to bolster their legitimacy. Trade associations and labor unions could build large war chests through dues and assessments on their members, but PIGs had more limited capacities to tap potential constituents' financial resources. The virtual collapse in the 1990s of an overstaffed Greenpeace underscored the vulnerability of many activist organizations to rapidly dwindling support.

A persisting theoretical conundrum remained explaining why any rational actor would voluntarily contribute to a political organization that offers its members only a public good. A "pure public good" is an indivisible benefit from which no eligible recipient can be excluded. For example, if a farm federation successfully lobbied Congress to enact a federal crop subsidy, any farmer who met the law's conditions could not be prevented from receiving these payments, even if that farmer contributed nothing toward the federation's lobbying to produce this public good. In effect, a nonparticipating recipient of a public good took a "free ride" on the efforts of others. Cost-benefit calculations led to the logical conclusion that a rational (i.e., utility-maximizing) actor should make no resource contributions toward a political organization that offered its members only public goods. A fundamental implication of Mancur Olson's (1965) famous "logic of collective action" explanation was that public goods organizations would fail to mobilize fully their potential supporters. He concluded that such associations remained viable only if they offered "selective incentives," or private goods, to prospective members in exchange for their resource contributions toward organizational lobbying for public goods. These incentives might include magazine subscriptions, group insurance, social gatherings, certification and training programs, and similar benefits from which the organization could effectively exclude noncontributors who failed to pay their dues and assessments. In Olson's formulation, a political organization's policy objectives became reduced to a secondary "by-product" of its members' and supporters' interests in obtaining personal material benefits.

Despite the analytical elegance of his theoretical arguments, Olson's propositions were repeatedly challenged by empirical investigations of the incentive systems implemented by real voluntary organizations. Members frequently responded to diverse inducements apart from personal material gains, including normative and purposive appeals and organizational lobbying for public goods (Moe 1980:201–231; Knoke 1988; 1990b:123–140). For example, right-to-life organizations appealed to their supporters' religious, ideological, and emotional convictions about the illegitimacy of abortion and the necessity to take direct action to shut down clinics and to support election campaigns by prolife politicians. The availability of picnics or printed T-shirts hardly provided a compelling motivation for most participants in such ideological groups.

The internal political economies of many membership organizations were more complex than the rational-actor approach implied. Organizational leaders played important roles in symbolically articulating the threats and opportunities facing their groups and in persuading members to contribute their personal resources toward collective efforts that might run counter to members' utility-maximizing preferences. Even political organizations that pursued largely nonideological agendas, such as professional and trade associations, frequently emphasized public policies as important reasons why firms and people should join and participate. For example, the American Electronics Association's Web site rang all the chimes in urging prospective members to sign up:

> When you join AEA, you immediately increase your insight, credibility and power. You immediately have access to information, networking opportunities, employee benefits, risk management and cost saving programs. Basically? You save money and gain clout. Most importantly you have a voice in Washington with the support of passionate, informed advocates who are helping you shape your business today and tomorrow. Join AEA. (American Electronics Association 2000)

Influencing Public Policies

Popular impressions persisted that U.S. businesses always get the gold mine while the public only gets the shaft. However, pinning down whether and how political organizations influence government officials' policy decisions remained empirically difficult. The proliferation of political action committees (PACs) by corporations, trade associations, labor unions, and public interest groups generated much heated controversy among journalists, academic researchers, and public opinion leaders. The following subsections examine the distribution of PAC contributions to candidates, the variety of tactics marshaled to influence policymakers, the structure of policy communication networks, and the formation of lobbying coalitions among political organizations fighting for their collective political interests. The discussion concludes with a review of the ambiguous research findings regarding the extent of business influence over the outcomes of national public policy battles.

Political Action Committees

Allegations that vast sums of money corrupted public officials and subverted American democracy were summarized in books, aimed at a broad popular audience, with such sinister titles as *Still the Best Congress Money Can Buy* (Stern 1992); *Dirty Little Secrets: The Persistence of Corruption in American Politics* (Sabato and Simpson 1996); and *The Buying of the Congress* (Lewis 1998). By 1998, the average cost of winning a seat in the U.S. House of Representatives had swollen to $674,000, and a Senate victory averaged $4.7 million (Lewis 1998:7). These enormous campaign expenses—for TV advertising, opinion polling, direct mailings, consultants, and PR firms—supposedly rendered successful candidates vulnerable to deep-pocket interest organizations that subsequently extracted political favors from office holders. Career politicians' deep desires to ensure re-election compelled them to cater continually to those political organizations and constituencies offering the campaign cash or votes (and sometimes both) that were the mother's milk of American politics in the late twentieth century.

Some academic researchers concluded that substantial loopholes in the campaign finance laws gave big business exceptional political access and hidden clout in legislative and executive decisions (Clawson, Neustadtl and Weller 1998). However, *overt* contributions-for-votes connections were nearly impossible to detect, meaning that any link between donors and recipients' policy actions operated more subtly. Other researchers saw the business community's capacity to act collectively and to influence political decisions as highly uncertain and conditional on changing circumstances (Mizruchi 1992; Grier, Munger and Roberts 1994). Closer examination of the highly emotional topic of political organizations' involvement in campaign financing revealed evidence to support both interpretations, making definitive resolution of this debate difficult. The very murkiness surrounding the situation permitted the system to muddle along without serious challenge, whereas clear-cut signs of political sleaze might have unleashed a powerful social movement for electoral finance reform.

Although political action committees were invented by U.S. labor unions during World War II, they only flourished after legislative acts and court rulings granted political money the protected status of "free speech." A PAC is an organization "created by interest groups to raise or spend money for the purpose of influencing federal elections" (Gais 1996:5). Ironically, during one of the more blatantly corrupt electoral eras in U.S. history, in 1971 President Nixon signed into law the Revenue Act and the Federal Election Campaign Act (FECA). The Revenue Act set up a voluntary $1 income tax checkoff to encourage public contributions to finance presidential candidates. Congress intended the FECA to restrict the influence of individual fat-cat donors, such as insurance man Clement Stone who had given Nixon's two presidential campaigns more than $5 million. Political committees were required to file regular financial reports that publicly disclosed the names of all contributors donating more than $100 to a candidate (raised to $200 in 1979). A major FECA provision, which was to have unintended consequences for the next generation, encouraged the widespread creation of PACs. Although not overturning federal laws barring direct contributions from labor union and corporate treasury funds to candidates, it formally sanctioned using these moneys to set up and administer affiliated PACs. Their most important functions included soliciting donations from corporate shareholders and from union members and their families (Alexander 1992:37). Thus, PACs could circumvent limits on individual contributions by pooling and coordinating campaign giving from numerous fat cats, workers, or single-issue militants.

A series of congressional amendments to the 1971 FECA and two major Supreme Court decisions put the final provisions of the new campaign financing system into place by the end of the 1970s. An independent six-person, presidentially appointed Federal Election Commission (FEC) collected, monitored, and published detailed contribution and expenditure information (thus creating a cottage industry of political scientists who tortured these massive data sets to give up their secrets). Corporate PACs could use company funds to solicit voluntary contributions from executive and managerial employees and their families. The Supreme Court ruled in *Buckley v. Valeo* 424 U.S. 1 (1976) that unions and corporations could not be limited in the number of PACs their locals and subsidiaries might establish. The Court also permitted PACs to make so-called independent expenditures on behalf of a candidate, as long as these purchases were neither authorized by nor coordinated with the candidate's campaign. Further, the Court also invalidated 1971 FECA restrictions on total campaign spending for House and Senate races. However, it kept limits of $50,000 contributions from the personal wealth of presidential or vice presidential candidates and their immediately families, but only for candidates accepting public funding. The Court, in its majestic impartiality, permitted poor as well as rich candidates to spend as much of their own money as they chose in pursuit of their political dreams. Hence, in the 1996 and 2000 presidential cycles, Malcolm "Steve" Forbes spent tens of millions of his inherited dollars in a dogged bid for the Republican Party nomination.

By the 1980s, PACs began widely deploying new fund-raising and expenditure practices, known as "bundling" and "soft money" donations, to get around the legal limits on individual direct contributions to candidates. Those limits were: (1) from individual donors, $1,000 per federal office candidate per election (primary and general election), $20,000 per year to a national political party, and $5,000 to a campaign committee, with a maximum of $25,000 in total annual contributions; and (2) from federally regulated PACs that gave to at least five candidates, $5,000 each to primary, run-off, and general elections. Bundling involved a party committee or PAC collecting numerous donations from individuals for a specific candidate, often through fund-raising events attended by corporate executives, union leaders, or entertainment celebrities. Then the PAC would ceremoniously hand over the bundled checks to the candidate, very visibly crediting itself as that office-seeker's benefactor. Democratic women candidates backing abortion rights benefited greatly from the bundling practices of a donor network known as EMILY's List, for "early money is like yeast."

The soft money innovation filled party coffers with largely unregulated megabucks (Alexander 1992:66–67). As long as state and local parties did not coordinate efforts with specific campaigns, they could receive and spend unlimited contributions for voter registration, get-out-the-vote drives, and grassroots campaign materials such as bumper stickers and yard signs. Another device for sidestepping campaign spending limits was "issue advocacy," where nominally independent groups placed TV or print ads supporting or opposing a particular policy that, while just happening to mention a specific candidate's name, cleverly avoided such naughty political words as "vote" and "defeat" (Rozell and Wilcox 1999:113). Unregulated soft money excesses compelled one prominent corporate policy association, the Committee for Economic Development (CED), to break from the business community in 1999 by calling for a complete ban. Senator Mitch McConnell, Republican from Kentucky, the leading foe of campaign finance reform efforts, criticized the CED for attempting to impose "anti-business speech controls" (Dewar 1999:A6). Although the House passed a reform bill that would have banned unlimited soft moneys and restricted issue ads, a McConnell-led filibuster killed it in the Senate.

The lax campaign finance regulations threw open the floodgates for a deluge of political money that permanently transformed the national electoral process. The FEC classified PACs as either "nonconnected" if they affiliated with no other organization (many were ideologically based, such as the liberal National Committee for an Effective Congress and the conservative

National Right to Life Committee) or as one of five types connected to a
parent organization: labor unions; corporations; corporations without
stock; cooperatives; and trade, membership, or health-related organizations.
Figure 9.4 depicts the rapid increase of several types of political action committees during the 1970s and early 1980s. Both unconnected and corporate
PACs proliferated, each eventually exceeding more than 1,000, but labor
union PACs stagnated at fewer than 400. Even more rapid increases occurred in the volume of campaign funds raised and spent by these groups.
Total PAC contributions to all federal candidates, mostly to House and Senate candidates, were $35 million in the 1978 election, $140 million in 1986,
and $218 million in 1996 (Federal Election Commission 1999). However
impressive these amounts seem, PAC contributions remained a distinct minority of all campaign funds, accounting for just 26 percent of the $2.7 bil-
lion raked in by Senate and House candidates for the four elections from
1990 to 1996. Of course, these totals did not include individual donations
bundled by PACs nor the soft moneys spread among state and local parties
that indirectly helped their candidates. Thus, PACs could leverage even
modest contributions into future influence with the election victors.

Observers of the PAC game detected two basic strategies of campaign
fund allocation (Sorauf 1992; Clawson, Neustadtl and Weller 1998;
Rudolph 1999). A PAC could follow a *replacement strategy* of attempting

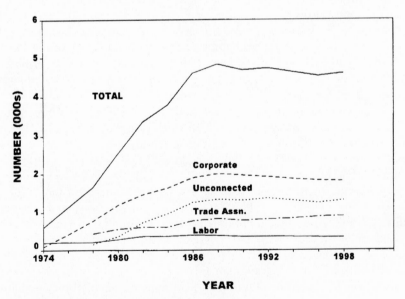

FIGURE 9.4   Political Action Committees
SOURCE: Federal Election Commission (1999, 2000)

to defeat its ideological opponents by backing candidates more disposed to favor the PAC's interests. For example, in 1992 manufacturing firms with plants in Mexico and Canada generally supported free-market Republican candidates running against protectionist Democrats who opposed the North American Free Trade Agreement (NAFTA). However, unseating an incumbent senator or representative often proved very difficult, as congresspersons seeking re-election in recent decades succeeded more than 90 percent of the time. Contributing to the campaigns of unsuccessful challengers simply was an unsound strategy for opening many doors on Capitol Hill. The more pragmatic *access strategy* involved allocating the bulk of PAC contributions to elected officials who occupied governmental positions with the power to block or promote desired legislation. This approach emphasized giving to incumbents of whichever political party currently held the majority in a particular chamber, but abruptly shifting contributions whenever institutional control changed. Indeed, PACs typically funneled political money to specific senators and representatives having expertise and seniority on the committees or subcommittees with jurisdiction over policy matters of vital interest to the PACs and their parent organizations.

Many researchers concluded that labor union PACs tenaciously followed the replacement strategy, but business PACs abandoned that approach in the 1970s for more pragmatic favor-currying with the currently dominant party (see Romer and Snyder 1994; Gaddie 1995; Gaddie and Regens 1997; Rudolph 1999). A key hypothesis was that the contributions from access-oriented PACs would adjust following a change in the political party controlling the federal government. One opportunity to test this proposition came in 1994 when the Republican Party, masterminded by Newt Gingrich's promise to implement a conservative "Contract with America," wrested control of the House of Representatives away from the Democrats for the first time in four decades. With Republicans then setting a new legislative agenda and chairing every House committee and subcommittee, pragmatic PACs should theoretically have increased their subsequent allocations to Republican candidates, while ideological PACs would persist in backing the party most predisposed to support their interests (i.e., Republican for business, Democratic for labor).

Evidence consistent with these inferences appears in Figure 9.5, which contrasts the contributions by corporate, trade-membership-health, and labor union PACs to House candidates for two pairs of elections before and after the 1994 change in House control. When Democrats still controlled the House, corporate PACs gave a small majority of their funds to Republican candidates (56 percent), but after the switch they boosted the GOP's share to 69 percent. This change was consistent with an access-oriented funding strategy. An even more dramatic display of the pragmatic calculation was apparent among PACs in the trade-membership-health category.

Although they gave 58 percent of their campaign funds to Democratic candidates prior to the institutional shakeup, during the next two elections they donated 62 percent of their money to Republicans. Finally, labor union PACs were clearly locked into a replacement-oriented mode. They not only remained inflexible pro-Democratic supporters (93 percent both before and after 1994), but they sharply increased their total contributions for 1996 and 1998 in unsuccessful efforts to reverse the party majority in the House. The increasingly feeble labor union clout was inseparably entwined with their dwindling presence in the U.S. labor force over a half century (see Chapter 8). Thus, while union fortunes inexorably sank or swam with the Democratic Party destiny, the corporate and trade associations crafted a more bipartisan approach to cover their benefit-seeking behinds regardless of electoral vagaries.

PACs could further leverage their political clout by "running in packs," that is, by individual PACs within an industry pooling their resources and collectively coordinating their contributions. Evidence that U.S. businesses achieved such political unity would be more consistent with elite and class theories than with pluralist explanations, which presume that unique considerations drive firms' political actions. An analysis of corporate PAC contributions to House candidates across 124 three-digit SIC industries for 1978–1986 found evidence supporting a profit-maximizing explanation of

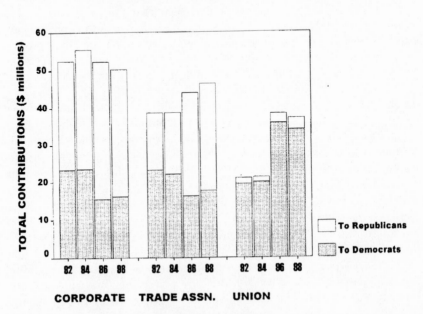

FIGURE 9.5   PAC Money to House Candidates
SOURCE: Federal Election Commission (1999)

collective political action (Grier, Munger and Roberts 1994). Industries collectively made larger campaign contributions when they were: more concentrated (had fewer firms), were more heavily regulated by the government, had more federal antitrust indictments, made larger sales to both the private and government sectors, and faced stiffer competition from imports. These findings implied that total industry investments in political campaigns depended less on the particular circumstances of individual firms than on shared conditions requiring a common governmental response. Mark Mizruchi (1992) investigated how intercorporate networks facilitated coordinated PAC contributions by the 57 largest U.S. manufacturing corporations in 1980. Firms with high levels of interdependence—measured by market constraints (members of an industry limit the ability of other industries to realize profits) and corporate boards indirectly interlocked through directors from the largest banks and insurance companies—were especially likely to donate to the same congressional candidates and to avoid giving to opposing candidates. Although such high levels of business unity were consistent with the ruling class model of corporate political behavior, Mizruchi cautioned that, given the tendency for many large firms to have little to do with one another, "the patterns of political behavior reveal a capitalist class that is far from monolithic" (1992:252). Overall business unity might have been considerably lower if Mizruchi had included smaller organizations than the Fortune 500 firms. Given the unusual circumstances of the 1980 election, which carried the "Reagan revolution" into the White House, longitudinal analyses of broader samples of firms would be essential for determining which social and economic conditions produce changing patterns of business political unity.

Lobbying Tactics

In May 1998, following a series of devastating floods, ice storms, and tornadoes, Congress approved a $2.6 billion emergency natural disaster bill. Tucked deep in the law's provisions was some last-minute relief of a different sort: a $66 million exemption from past-due royalty payments by big oil companies for extracting oil and gas from federal lands. Such behind-the-scenes maneuvers are typical of that industry's legendary political clout on Capitol Hill. "The oil companies lobby in a very coordinated way," said one anonymous staff member for a House energy-related committee. "They rely heavily on the American Petroleum Institute, but they've also got their people. Exxon's lobbyist is very friendly and outgoing and the company is really involved in the royalty issue. On a technical point, Exxon's lobbyist will bring in 11 people to talk to you about it. They are incredibly influential" (Wayne 1998). Edward Rothschild, senior associate of a Washington lobbying firm, marveled at how Mobil and Exxon finessed the most complicated tax rulings. "There were efforts by the Clinton Administration in the last two budget bills to reduce the value of the foreign tax credits. But Exxon and the industry descended and those provisions were quietly eliminated. I don't know who they talked to, but they got the job done" (Wayne 1998).

Over the last four decades of the twentieth century an escalating number of corporations either set up their own government affairs offices in Washington or hired specialists to represent their interests in public policy issues affecting their business. Between 1961 and 1979, the number of firms represented by registered lobbyists in the nation's capital grew from 130 to 650 (Vogel 1996:132). By the late 1980s, almost 4,000 corporations had retained their own "Washington reps" (Heinz et al. 1993:10). The 1998 edition of the *Washington Representatives* directory listed 17,400 government relations advocates, including lawyers, lobbyists, government affairs consultants, registered foreign agents, and executive branch legislative affairs personnel, along with their 11,000 corporate, trade association, and special interest group clients. By mid-1999, the U.S. Senate's Office of Public Records list of registered lobbyists had surpassed 20,500. Similar dramatic growth occurred in the populations of lobbying groups in the U.S. states from 1975 to 1990 as these governments became more involved in such national issues as pollution, antitrust, and tobacco legislation (Gray and Lowery 1996). Although these numbers seem impressive, participants in the Washington policy game account for only a tiny percentage of all U.S. organizations (see Chapter 3).

Thanks to the Lobbying Disclosure Act of 1995, professional firms and organizations that hire lobbyists must now report on which issues they seek to influence and how much they spend to influence legislation, executive-branch enforcement, and regulatory decisions. However, a loophole allows lobbyists to choose which of two inconsistent reporting formulas they apply.[1] Total federal lobbying expenditures increased by 13 percent from 1997 to 1998, from $1.26 billion to $1.42 billion (Center for Responsive Politics 1999). These amounts far exceeded the $207 million in 1997–1998 campaign contributions made by all PACs (Federal Election Commission 2000). For 1998, an average of 38 registered lobbyists collectively spent $2.7 million to lobby each of the 535 senators and representatives. The leading industry was insurance ($77 million), followed by pharmaceuticals/health products ($74 million), telephone utilities ($68 million), and tobacco ($67 million). Labor unions ranked eleventh among broad industry and interest groups in lobbying expenditures ($24 million). The two biggest corporate spenders were tobacco companies ($25 by British American Tobacco, $23 by Philip Morris), which were threatened by federal ratification of a settlement that the state attorneys general had reached with tobacco manufacturers to resolve smoking health claims. In the end, their lobbyists' success in defeating the federal legislation killed the golden geese: Once victory had eliminated the threat to business as usual, tobacco firms cut their lobby expenditures by nearly $40 million for the next year.

Political scientists and sociologists made substantial progress in cataloging the many evolving techniques deployed by political organizations to lobby public policymakers (Schlozman and Tierney 1986:261–385; Knoke 1990b:187–213). A summary of findings from six sample surveys of diverse political organizations and lobbyists (Baumgartner and Leech 1998:152) yielded this typology of tactics, roughly ranked from most to least frequently used:

- Testimony at legislative or agency hearings
- Direct contacts with legislators or other officials
- Informal contacts with legislators or other officials
- Presenting research results
- Coalitions with other groups; planning strategy with government officials
- Mass media: talking to journalists; paid advertising
- Policy formation: drafting legislation, regulations; shaping policy implementation; serving on advisory commissions; agenda setting
- Constituent influence: letter-writing or telegram campaigns; working with influential citizens; alerting legislators to district effects
- Litigation: filing lawsuits or *amici curiae* (friend of the court) briefs
- Elections: campaign contributions; campaign work; candidate endorsements
- Protests or demonstrations
- Other tactics: monitoring; influencing appointments; doing personal favors for officials

Contacting officials and attracting public awareness were relatively low-cost activities, minimally needing only a part-time agent or voluntary worker. Litigation and election work, including the PAC contributions considered above, were much rarer tactics because they typically cost far more than many political organizations could afford. Government officials viewed street protests and court actions as threats and embarrassments, hence political organizations tended to avoid them as tactics of last resort. Stirring up a legislator's constituents was more feasible for large mass-membership organizations, such as labor unions and professional associations, than for trade associations and corporations, whose employees might be regarded as lacking the autonomy enjoyed by the participants of voluntary organizations. Still, public officials could be intimidated by firms that orchestrated massive displays of their employee fears of plant shutdowns and job losses should a particular legislative bill fail to pass. The looming specter of a Chrysler bankrupcty tossing a quarter-million automobile and parts workers out of work in 1979 clearly scared Congress into okaying $1.5 billion in loan guarantees to resuscitate the dying auto company. Such provocative maneuvers obviously were most effective in swaying a legislator's decision when the complaining workers also represented a sizable voting block in that person's district.

Throughout U.S. history, evolving communication technologies have continually created new media—radio, television, mass direct mailings, telephone trees, faxes, and e-mail—which organizations have rapidly adapted in an intensifying political arms race against their competitors. The Internet and World Wide Web are just the most recent inventions pressed into the interest-group battle for the ears and minds of policymakers. Using these techniques to mobilize constituents to pester their elected officials yielded big bangs for the bucks, given that the supreme ambition of every professional politician is re-election. A political organization's clout with officials waxed proportional to the number of voters that it could realistically claim to arouse. However, hiring consultants to drum up colossal volumes of identical postcards, telegrams, and phone calls risked being discredited as phony "astroturf" rather than interpreted as a genuine groundswell of grassroots sentiment (Kollman 1998:157–160).

> A typical tactic is to hire phone solicitors to call unsuspecting citizens, read them a misleading description of a bill and then ask if they wouldn't like to do the equivalent of supporting motherhood or opposing Satan. A spiel might be: "Did you know that Proposal X will raise your rates, throw people out of jobs and increase the federal deficit? Are you opposed to those things?" The unsuspecting people who answer the phone say "Sure." Suddenly, letters, telegrams and faxes appear on Capitol Hill in their names expressing fervent opinions about a bill they may never have heard of before the call and still may know virtually nothing about. (Buffalo News 1999:F6)

A similarly sleazy tactical innovation was the notorious push-poll. It tried to alter public opinion in a tight race by directly passing negative information to voters in the guise of a conventional phone survey purporting to tally public opinions. An allegedly independent "pollster" (actually a campaign worker for candidate X) first ascertained that a respondent favors candidate Y. Then he might ask, "Would you still support candidate Y if you knew she had voted to raise your taxes/admitted using drugs/been accused of adultery?" The survey results were never tallied, because the sole purpose was to poison the perceptions of potential supporters of the push-poller's opponent.

The ultimate aim of all lobbying tactics, the legitimate as well as the unethical ones, transcended simply gaining and maintaining a political organization's access to policymaking officials. Access alone was insufficient to influence policymakers to support the organization's political interests. Successful lobbyists deployed the multitude of advocacy tricks enumerated above to accomplish three primary functions that, taken together, constituted a generic lobbying strategy: "getting attention, communicating with contacts about mutual information needs, and reinforcing for lobbying targets the value of their continuing to give the lobbies attention" (Browne 1998:81):

- *Winning attention* and keeping the publicity spotlight concentrated on a political organization's issues encompassed multifaceted public relations activities targeted to the electorate, mass media reporters, and other interest organizations as well as to various public officials. These activities included placing op-ed pieces in newspapers, appearing on radio and TV talk shows, holding press conferences, testifying at policy hearings, commissioning opinion polls, issuing research reports, and offering to draft technical language for inexpert legislative or regulatory staffs.
- The *contact* game suggested the shopworn caricature of lobbyists as back-slapping, glad-handing loudmouths who connivingly dispensed booze, broads, and bucks to corrupt politicians in sleazy hotels in exchange for their committee and floor votes. Although this image retains a bit of truth—reinforced by the Koreagate and Abscam congressional bribery scandals of the 1980s—most contacts involved more mundane forms of persistent schmoozing between interest group agents, elected officials, and top government appointees. Foundational relationships consisted of the interpersonal currying of durable political friendships, developing interpersonal trust, sharing of credible knowledge, and keeping one another apprised of potential problems arising from policy decisions. Political money, customarily intimated as a "gift" that forges networks of obligation between givers and recipients (Clawson, Neustadtl and Weller 1998:29–62), might get a lobbyist's foot in the door. But only an incessant exchange of reliable political information would keep it open. A single failure to provide accurate data, particularly concerning how an issue affected voters in a legislator's district, could banish a duplicitous agent and her organization forever from the politician's portal.
- Performing the *reinforcement* function meant that "lobbyists keep coming back, showing their issues are still alive, reinforcing both their access and previously discussed policy matters" (Browne 1998:75). Given exceptionally short political attention spans at all levels and the cacophony of voices clamoring for lawmakers' attention to their agendas, a capacity to keep an organization playing in

the lobbying game over the long haul was highly prized. Successful lobbyists, like old horseshoe champions, just never stop pitching.

To adapt their strategies to changing conditions, political organizations generally preferred to sign up lobbyists with excellent public relations skills who could deal effectively with the highest-level governmental contacts. Some agents were in-house counsel, but many advocates were "hired guns" from Washington, D.C., legal and consulting firms. Both transaction cost and principal-agent theories proposed that a political organization made cost-benefit calculations when deciding whether to invest resources in developing its own governmental affairs staff, make contracts with outside specialists, join other organizations in a lobbying coalition (including the members of its industry's trade association), or follow a mixture of strategies to achieve its policy influence objectives (Mitnick 1992; Kaufman, Englander and Marcus 1993). The more often an organization encountered recurrent political problems and the greater the technical or legal expertise needed to deal with uncertainties, the more likely it was either to create its own permanent lobbying unit or to retain the long-term services of an outside firm. If an organization only occasionally needed to negotiate with public policymakers about simple issues, a short-term contract with an outside lobbyist would be more realistic.

Agency theory emphasized that problems could arise whenever an agent (a lobbyist) acted on behalf of a principal (a corporation). Hiring an outside advocate increased an organization's costs of monitoring and safeguarding the hired gun's representation of the firm's policy interests in dealings with governmental players. The ever-present temptation of opportunism exposed any principal to potential agent deceptions about the vigor of its lobbying effort and the quality of deals struck with policymakers. Due to bounded rationality and information asymmetry, agents might fail to act on behalf of a principal's best interests for four reasons: They didn't understand what the principal wanted, they disagreed with the principal's goals, they lacked sufficient skills to act effectively, or they deliberately shirked by devoting insufficient effort to achieving the best results (Getz 1993:247). A principal's attempts to resolve these problems by exercising control over the agent could prove so costly that a more efficient alternative would be to create a permanent in-house lobbying staff that could be more easily supervised and controlled.

Another problem was the greater risk aversion of agents relative to principals, because the price of failure was often much higher for the former (e.g., they'd soon find themselves without any clients). As discussed in Chapter 7 in the context of CEO compensation, one common way to control an agent and to induce an exceptional performance is to offer big incentives. Only the largest corporations and associations could regularly afford the high fees charged by the elite lobbying firms lining K Street in

Washington (a.k.a. Gucci Gulch). For leading the successful 1998 fight to kill the federal anti-smoking agreement with the state attorneys general, cigarette makers paid $7 million to the Washington lobbying firm Verner Liipfert, which not coincidentally boasted among its partners two former Senate majority leaders (Republican Bob Dole and Democrat George Mitchell). The result was well worth the lobbyists' fee, because the tobacco companies saved billions.

Further principal-agent complexities arose for trade associations claiming to speak for the policy interests of an entire industry. Because the firms making up an industry often faced unique situations, some members might feel that the industry group could not adequately represent their interests on particular policy issues. In instances where a trade association was internally divided, dissenting organizations might decide to undertake their own corporate lobbying efforts. For example, after automakers Daimler and Chrysler merged, the American Automobile Manufacturers Association was dissolved by its remaining U.S. members, Ford and General Motors. Nine companies formed a new lobbying group in 1999, the Alliance of Automobile Manufacturers (AAM): Ford, GM, DaimlerChrysler, Germany's Volkswagen and BMW, Sweden's Volvo, and Japan's Toyota, Nissan, and Mazda. AAM lobbied U.S. lawmakers about safety and environmental issues but avoided labor and trade matters on which their members disagreed, such as Japanese tariffs and import regulations that make selling U.S. vehicles in Japan difficult. Instead, Ford and GM had to pursue individual lobbying strategies on trade policies. The six overseas AAM companies also maintained their memberships in the rival Association of International Automobile Manufacturers (AAIM) because, as its president said, "we have services the new organization [AAM] won't be able to provide" (K. Cole 1999).

Policy Communication Networks

Twentieth-century political organizations needed timely and accurate information about policy issues and events that could affect their interests. Although much policy information was available through public mass media, some truly invaluable insights could be acquired only through interactions with other significant players. The global structure of information exchanges, constituting a communication network connecting consequential political organizations, served simultaneously as constraint and opportunity for gaining access to crucial intelligence. Peripheral, out-of-the-loop organizations—with few direct ties to key policy players—had much difficulty gaining hearings for their interests. Central organizations—with numerous links to diverse participants—enjoyed greater capacity to coordinate their actions with other powerful actors, boosting the chances of achieving their policy goals. Occupying an advantageous position within an information exchange network was a significant power resource. A central position gave political organizations better means to identify potential allies and adversaries, to reveal positions and preferences on issues, to formulate strategies and tactics for collective actions to influence policy decisions, and to inform policymakers about preferred legislative or regulatory outcomes.

Network analysts revealed that global patterns of information exchange among political organizations were structured around their common interests in national policy domains. A policy domain comprised the set of organizations and institutions engaged in conflicts over specific proposals to solve substantive policy problems, such as national defense, education, agriculture, or welfare. Research on the U.S. national energy and health policy domains in the 1970s (Laumann and Knoke 1987) and a comparison of the U.S., German, and Japanese labor policy domains in the 1980s (Knoke et al. 1996) uncovered very dense communication networks connecting these core political organizations. The labor policy domain proved an especially relevant arena in which to investigate whether business dominates public policymaking. Unlike more tranquil policy domains, corporate interests in controlling labor conditions encountered vigorous opposition from labor unions. In each of the three U.S. domains, researchers asked informants from more than a hundred political organizations (trade associations, labor unions, professional societies, public interest groups, federal executive agencies, and congressional committees) with which organizations they exchanged important policy information. The density of communication ties (the ratio of reported to all possible exchanges) was .38 for the U.S. labor domain and .30 in both the energy and health domains.

Diagrams representing the communication network structures in the three domains showed that organizations expressing similar issue interests and policy preferences tended to occupy the same regions. In a two-dimensional plot of the labor policy organizations' path distances (i.e., the number of direct or indirect steps required to connect a pair of organizations), most unions, business associations, and federal agencies were located in three distinct sectors (Knoke et al. 1996:112). Similarly, sharp cleavages occurred within the energy domain between consumers and several types of energy producers, and in the health domain between consumers, clients, researchers, and health providers (Laumann and Knoke 1987:242 and 246). This partitioning into specialized policy segments reflected a tendency for political organizations to communicate primarily with their friends and potential allies and to avoid passing information on to organizations with which they share few common interests.

Every domain's communication structure also revealed that governmental actors and interest groups with broad policy agendas filled the central locations. Thus, the center of the energy domain was occupied by the White

House, Department of Energy, and key House and Senate energy and re-sources committees. This core group was closely surrounded by such major labor unions and trade associations as the AFL-CIO, United Automobile Workers, American Petroleum Institute, Edison Electric Institute, American Gas Association, American Mining Congress, and National Automobile Dealers Association (Laumann and Knoke 1987:243–245). Despite the di-vergent and sometimes antagonistic policy interests of these organizations, their close proximity to the center of the domain's communication network indicated that these major political actors maintained high levels of infor-mation exchange with potential opponents. Open communication carried risks as well as benefits:

> Given the information problems in the early stages of issue formation, contact-ing groups that will eventually oppose your point of view gives them signifi-cant information that they might not have otherwise had. At a minimum, it can alert them that a policy change is afoot. It also conveys one's position, and it could convey extensive information about the political environment. As a strategic blunder, direct contact can provide the impetus for latent opposition to mobilize, expanding the scope of conflict. As a tactical matter, it is clearly in a group's interest to let its opponents address the information problems on their own. (Hula 1999:54)

To lower the risks of aiding one's opponents, political organizations con-fined the transmission of sensitive tactical and strategic information to other actors who shared their preferred policy outcomes. Communications with potential foes were more likely to serve as warnings and deterrents, signaling the intensity of an organization's interests and its intentions to fight for its objectives on particular policy events.

Figure 9.6 maps the positions of political organizations occupying the center of the U.S. labor domain communication network in 1988, when the Reagan Administration controlled the federal executive branch. The 0.71 density of information exchanges among this core group of 20 most reput-edly influential labor policy organizations (identified from a checklist filled out by all 117 organizations) was more than twice the density among the re-maining 97 organizations. Hence, drawing arrows to represent the flow of information would have produced an incomprehensible image. Instead, the figure plots locations by using path distances between all pairs of organiza-tions as the distance measure. That is, the farther apart a pair's locations, the less likely they were to send and receive direct communications. Two major blocks reflect the sharp ideological cleavage that structured this do-main for many decades. At the upper right is a tight cluster of congressional Democrats, unions, and two interest groups (the ACLU and AARP), which generally advocated liberal, pro-labor policies. At the left is a somewhat more diffuse cluster of congressional Republicans, the Reagan White House and Department of Labor, and three peak business associations (NAM, Business Roundtable, U.S. Chamber of Commerce), which usually supported conservative, pro-business policies.

Note that two powerful labor organizations—the Teamsters Union and the AFL-CIO—are not embedded within the liberal-labor block but reside in very close proximity to the business cluster. This placement doesn't mean that these two unions cozied up to the business community. Indeed, the next subsection reveals that labor and business were antagonists across nu-

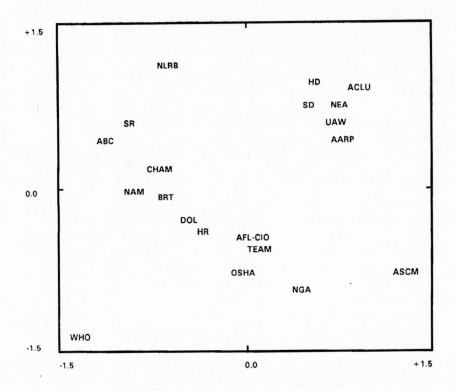

AARP: American Association of Retired Persons
ABC: Association of Builders and Contractors
ACLU: American Civil Liberties Union
AFL-CIO: American Fedn of Labor
ASCM: Am. Fedn of State, County, Municipal Workers
BRT: Business Roundtable
CHAM: Chamber of Commerce of the United States
DOL: Department of Labor
HD: House Labor Committee Democrats
HR: House Labor Committee Republicans

NAM: National Assn. of Manufacturers
NEA: National Education Association
NGA: National Governors Association
NLRB: Nat. Labor Relations Board
OSHA: Occup. Safety & Health Admin.
SD: Senate Labor Committee Democrats
SR: Senate Labor Committee Republicans
TEAM: Teamsters Union
UAW: United Automobile Workers Union
WHO: White House Office

FIGURE 9.6   Labor Policy Communication Network

merous policy fights. Rather, the close proximity between these key business and labor organizations indicates substantial direct communication exchanges that enabled players on both sides of the ideological fence to become better apprised about the labor domain's policy developments. Without recurrent contacts between foes as well as friends, political conflict might deteriorate into rancorous and unrelenting hostility. A communication network connecting key political participants provided an opportunity structure for a more conciliatory resolution of policy disputes.

Lobbying Coalitions

Exchanging policy-relevant information with other political organizations was an important prerequisite for engaging in political action but was insufficient to explain organizational attempts to influence policymakers' decisions. Engaging in policy discussions was a relatively low-cost activity, because participants can quickly move into or drop out of contact with one another. The complexity and density of interorganizational communication networks made their boundaries amorphous and rendered large, diffuse discussion groups unwieldy as effective policy-influencing instruments. More promising insights followed from examining the formation of advocacy coalitions whose member organizations cooperatively pursued collective policy goals.

The expanding population of Washington political organizations and the complexities of gaining access to federal institutions increasingly necessitated coalitional behavior to achieve policy objectives. Organizations could leverage their political influence by pooling resources, especially their technical and political expertise, to create an effective division of labor for contacting governmental targets. Public officials might be more easily impressed, even convinced, by arguments advanced through a broadly united front than by clashing claims proffered by individual organizations. Hence, the main incentive for joining a collective action was the reduction of resource costs while increasing the chances of achieving a successful political outcome.

A serious drawback to collaborative lobbying was the same free-riding problem encountered in creating voluntary membership organizations. Many rewards from political action were collective benefits from legislation and regulation, for example, reducing the corporate tax rate or blocking an increase in the minimum wage. By definition, no firms could be excluded from receiving such public-goods benefits, even if they contributed few or no resources toward procuring these policies. Following Olson's (1965) cost-benefit logic, no rational, utility-maximizing organization should join a lobbying coalition for two reasons: Its actions would have almost no impact on obtaining the collective good and it would maximize its gains by contributing nothing yet enjoying whatever benefits the other participants might succeed in producing. To overcome the negative calculations, coalitions had to offer potential participants selective incentives to join. That is, only the contributing organizations received some benefits apart from the public policy outcome available to everyone. For example, membership in a coalition might bring access to contacts and insider information and an enhanced reputation as a powerful player in the policy game. The temptation to take a free ride was much lower within a small group, such as an industry with only a few dominant firms, particularly if some organizations stood to reap large gains from the attainment of a public-good policy. For example, domestic automobile manufacturers could substantially increase their profits if the federal trade representative successfully pressured Japan to open its home market to U.S. imports. In such small-numbers situations, contributing organizational resources to a collective lobbying effort to provide a public-good policy made sense.

Political organizations whose interests were implicated in a policy decision had to choose among joining a lobbying coalition, engaging in solitary lobbying, or remaining inactive. Olson's free-rider hypothesis predicted coalition participation would be more likely among corporations in highly concentrated industries than in highly competitive sectors with numerous small firms. Some organizations could take a "cheap ride" (Hula 1999:25), lending their names to a coalition's membership list, perhaps even making nominal appearances at meetings, in exchange for symbolic rewards of publicly demonstrating their commitment to a popular political cause (Browne 1998:146). A study of 130 transportation, education, and civil rights organizations in the early 1990s investigated the impact of selective incentives on joining coalitions or working alone (Hula 1999). Organizations chose lobbying strategies that enabled them to claim credit and enhance their long-term reputations in Washington as "having a unique and recognized identity as a significant and legitimate voice in the policy process" (p. 95). If lobbyists judged that their group could claim credit and reputational benefits by pursuing independent actions, they were less disposed to participate in coalitions. A study of 172 organizations lobbying on five policy proposals in 1993 found that fewer than one-third worked alone (Hojnacki 1997). An organization with very narrow issue interests was more likely to spend its time and energy working by itself. When opponents were strong and well-organized, the benefits of working in a coalition became more apparent. Organizations trying to recruit key partners to a coalition had to convince the holdouts that their presence and participation would boost the probability of a successful outcome beyond what they could accomplish through solo efforts.

Network analysts investigated the effects of interorganizational ties on political action. A study of 57 large manufacturing companies examined joint appearances to testify at congressional hearings from 1980 to 1987 (Mizruchi 1992). The frequency of inter-firm agreement was almost four times higher than opposition (207 versus 56 cases), with many statements using virtually identical language, clearly indicating prior coordination. The strongest predictors of policy agreement between pairs of firms were location in the same primary industry, common stockholders, directly inter-locked boards of directors, and indirect board interlocks through financial institutions (Mizruchi 1992:169). The effect of direct ties on joint testi-mony was even stronger than their impact on common PAC contributions. Decisions about campaign donations could easily arise without explicit communication, but joint appearances before a congressional committee entailed interaction:

> The testimony of representatives from two or more firms often consists of joint statements or is nearly verbatim. In other cases there is virtually no overlap, which raises the possibility that an explicit division of labor was engineered. Firms with direct interlock ties are in a better position to communicate than are firms with indirect ties. (Mizruchi 1992:174)

Comparative research on the U.S., German, and Japanese labor policy domains investigated the effects of network position on organizational rep-utations and political action (Knoke et al. 1996). The more central an orga-nization in both the communication network (measured by policy informa-tion exchanges) and the support network (measured by resource exchanges), the higher was its reputation as an especially influential player in labor pol-icy. Similarly, greater centrality in both networks led to more involvement across numerous legislative events in six types of political influence activi-ties, including coalitions with other organizations. In the U.S. and German cases, the communication centrality effect was much stronger than the sup-port centrality effect on both organizational reputations and political activ-ities; the pattern in Japan was just the reverse (Knoke et al. 1996:120). De-tailed analyses of specific legislative decisions showed that most national labor policy fights were conducted by relatively small *action sets*, defined as coalitions of organizations that hold the same preferred event outcome (passage or failure of a bill), communicate directly or indirectly with one another about policy affairs, and consciously coordinate their policy influ-ence activities (pp. 21–22). Labor unions and business associations were the primary coalition leaders in all three nations, frequently taking oppos-ing positions on legislative bills and almost never collaborating in the same action set even on rare occasions when they preferred the same policy out-come. Only minorities of the 117 core U.S. labor policy domain organiza-tions expressed interest in the outcomes of each of the 25 congressional bills examined. On average fewer than 37 organizations advocated either the passage or failure of a bill (p. 140). Slightly more than half participated in action sets, which averaged fewer than 10 members (however, two legislative events produced no action sets, and nine others just one action set favoring the bill's passage).

Very few prominent coalitions were institutionalized as permanent fixtures on the policy scene. For example, the Washington Business Group on Health, created by the Business Roundtable in 1974, lobbied for decades on the health care interests of 200 large corporations (Mintz 1995). Most often, action sets were constructed as short-term coalitions to fight collectively over a specific policy event, then to disband after political authorities rendered their decision. Subsequently, new action sets coalesced, composed of different participants lured by the particular policy interests at stake in a new policy proposal. These changing alliances were not random assemblages of political organizations. Policy domains were routinized political arenas comprising a limited range of potential participants, problems, and procedures for putting proposals onto the national agenda. Consequently, many coalitions were assembled and led by an enduring core group of organizations, primarily the peak or encompassing organizations possessing broad mandates to defend and advance the policy interests of sizable domain segments (Hojnacki 1997).

I illustrate the underlying stability of political cleavages despite substantial turnover in action set members from event to event by examining three major proposals on Congress's labor policy agenda for 1987–1988: (1) to create a High Risk Occupational Assessment Board of epidemiologists and medical experts to monitor and notify workers of their exposure to disease and chemical hazards in the workplace, (2) to raise the minimum wage in steps from $3.35 to $4.65 by 1990, and (3) to enable workers in large firms to take unpaid parental or disability leaves with continued employer-paid health insurance benefits. Organized labor and its Democratic allies in Congress supported the three bills, whereas the Reagan Administration, Republican Party, and business organizations opposed these provisions as unwarranted intrusions into management control of the workplace.

Figure 9.7 displays the overlapping action sets formed around these three events. The business sector (led by the Chamber of Commerce, National Association of Manufacturers, and Business Roundtable) and the Reagan Administration (led by the Department of Labor) each formed separate action sets opposing the bills. The labor unions (led by the AFL-CIO and nine other labor unions such as the United Auto Workers [UAW] and the National Education Association [NEA]) organized three distinct pro-passage coalitions. A separate action set emerged to support the family leave bill, consisting mainly of women's interest groups (led by the National Organization for Women, NOW). Note that the leading organizations in every instance fell into the intersection of the three overlapping circles representing their block's action sets. Moreover, each policy proposal saw some participants who joined the fight for just one or two events. For example, NOW also joined the AFL-CIO's minimum wage coalition, but stayed away from the occupational risk-board fight.

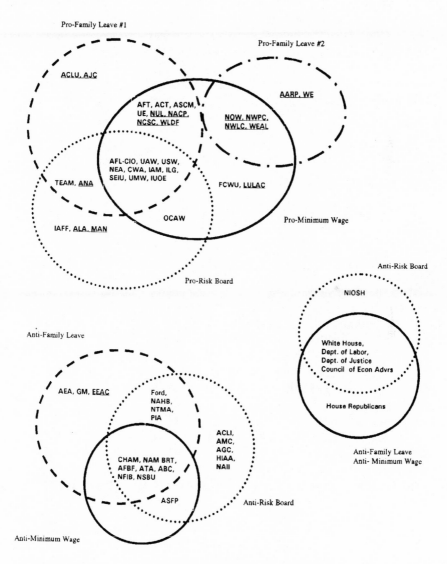

FIGURE 9.7   Lobbying Coalitions for Three Labor Policy Events

One clue about the transient nature of action sets comes from examining the apparent policy interests of their members. The underlined acronyms in Figure 9.7 refer to organizations that were neither labor unions, trade associations, nor federal agencies. The three business coalitions were highly homogeneous. Thus, the arguments for opposing each bill could concentrate on their negative impacts for particular industries. In contrast, the three labor-led action sets also attracted numerous ethnic, racial, gender, and occupational identity organizations, including the American Jewish Congress (AJC), National Urban League (NUL), National Association for the Advancement of Colored People (NACP), League of United Latin American Citizens (LULAC), American Association of Retired Persons (AARP), American Nurses Association (ANA), and American Lung Association (ALA). Diversity could be a source of political power when approaching legislators with strong political ties to these constituencies, but it also created difficulties in keeping a coalition's attention focused on common goals and not fighting and fragmenting over the partners' insular interests.

Who Wins?

Did PAC contributions and lobbying coalitions have any demonstrable impact on the outcomes of U.S. policy decisions? Did business always win fights over the political issues closest to its interests? Critics who railed against the campaign financing system assumed that political money, and the access it supposedly bought to legislators and regulators, had an inherently corrupting influence on government policymakers. How else, they argued, to explain the absence of effective tobacco- and gun-control laws, weak safety standards for food and drugs, high prices for sugar and cable TV, low corporate tax rates, and millions of families without health insurance? (See Lewis [1998] for an exhaustive litany of federal policies and programs apparently tailored to benefit particular interest groups.) Yet, academic researchers rarely found a smoking pistol: campaign contributions that clearly bought congressional members' votes on legislation of interest to PACs (e.g., Grenzke 1989; Hall and Wayman 1990; Goidel, Gross and Shields 1999:52–54). Showing a simple correlation between PAC contributions and the votes cast for or against a particular high-visibility event was relatively easy. For example, House members who received large business PAC funds tended to favor the passage of NAFTA in 1993 (Steagall and Jennings 1996). However, properly specified multivariate analyses that controlled for a variety of other influences on congressional decisions, particularly constituents' opinions unfiltered by political organizations, usually yielded scant support for a blatant money-vote connection:

Employing sophisticated statistical techniques and large numbers of cases, scholars have generally failed to turn up consistent evidence that representatives' campaign contributions directly affect their roll call decisions. Only when scholars aggregate together all of a representative's PAC contributions, or all of his or her corporate PAC contributions, and relate these to broad indexes of support for labor or business is money found to have statistically significant effects. At such high levels of aggregation, however, money becomes a proxy for other important interest group activities, principally Washington and grass roots lobbying. (Wright 1996:136–149)

Some analysts remained skeptical about the conventional wisdom asserting that interest groups exerted an inevitable stranglehold on politicians through the campaign finance system. In this alternative view, political organizations achieved their greatest influence by providing meaningful information about electorally relevant resources that most closely match specific officeholders' career motivations and electoral requirements (Hansen 1991; Krehbiel 1991; Burstein and Eaton 2000). Rational officials needed to know whether satisfying political organizations' demands would boost or harm their re-election chances with the voters. Did the money, campaign workers, and media coverage resources that groups offered, in return for access and consideration of their policy interests, help or hurt a candidate's popularity with voting constituents? The obligations incurred by PAC dollars did not carry identical political value everywhere: Tobacco company donations remained assets in farmland Kentucky and North Carolina but were an electoral kiss of death in health-conscious Oregon and Washington. The simple money-equals-policies equation couldn't adequately capture the complex interactions among organizational resources, constituent opinions, and politicians' instincts for self-preservation. Although these informational dynamics resembled the fluid functionality of the pluralist model, they also suggested possible new directions for future theorizing about the public policy impacts of political organizations in democratic societies.

PAC money seemed to exert little independent influence over roll call votes after taking into account a senator's or representative's political party, personal ideology, perceived constituency preferences, and similar factors. However, decisions made on the House and Senate floors might not be valid sites to observe overwhelming effects. If trade association and corporate PACs genuinely pursued access strategies, then perhaps campaign contributions were simply one lure among many in the lobbyists' tackle boxes. Political access involved obtaining preferential treatment from policymakers for meetings and phone calls to pitch the mutual benefits from supporting an organization's preferred policy solutions. A pragmatic political organization targeted most of its campaign funds to its governmental "friends" who were known to be predisposed to support the interest organization's agenda (Austen-Smith 1995). Then, these donations served as invaluable access tickets, enabling a group's lobbyists to visit legislative or regulatory offices for chats and to receive invitations to testify at committee hearings.

By assisting elected and appointed officials behind the scenes to shape technically arcane details of legislative and regulatory proposals, lobbyists reaped the fruits planted by campaign funds. This view of political money as mainly a door-opening device was consistent with John Wright's (1990) analyses of two controversial bills considered by the House Ways and Means and the Agriculture Committees in 1985. He concluded that the representatives' committee votes were best explained, not by PAC money, but by the total number of contacts they had with groups on each side of the issue. "Consistent with the popular notion that money 'buys' access but not votes, campaign contributions influenced voting decisions indirectly through lobbying" (1990:433–434). Similarly, interest groups achieved greater subjective success in influencing federal agency rule-making through formal procedures (e.g., commenting on proposed rules, participating at public hearings). However, participating in coalitions did not significantly affect perceived influence through such informal methods as contacting agency officials or mobilizing members (Furlong 1997).

Class and elite theorists asserted that large corporations and their owners enjoyed an enormously privileged position in American society that enabled them to dominate governmental decisions for their own profits and political advantages. Special access to policymakers through campaign contributions and lobbying efforts was the most visible, but not the sole, instrument of power. Other mechanisms included ideological domination, through corporate control of mass media, and policy formation through planning institutes, foundations, and think tanks that developed and propagated favorable proposals (Domhoff 1978, 1990). Democratic governments were also structurally dependent on business for a prosperous economy. "The primary foundation of business power is the ability to make day-to-day business decisions unless and until the government intervenes" (Clawson, Neustadtl and Weller 1998:96). Elected politicians were so eager to sustain a robust "business confidence" climate—essential heavy corporate investments to generate the high growth, profits, and wages on which their re-election hopes depended—that they obsessively pandered to business demands (Block 1977; Mitchell 1997:61–78).

All these processes conferred a unique political legitimacy on the business community in general and large corporations in particular. One implication for this perspective was that business would seldom, if ever, lose to its opponents in major policy fights where its vital interests were at stake. Class and elite researchers generally found what they expected to see. For example, despite the alleged political weakness of business during the Great Depression, commercial farmers and plantation owners successfully blocked federal subsidies to farm laborers; business leaders forced abandonment of the New Deal's attempted close regulation of the economy through the National Recovery Administration; and the Social Security Act of 1935 adopted business-oriented provisions designed by the Rockefeller network of foundations and think tanks (Domhoff 1996). In 1978, labor unions tried to amend the National Labor Relations Act to expedite the settlement of unfair labor practices claims and to strengthen sanctions against employers who violate existing labor laws. A broad coalition of corporate and trade association lobbyists mobilized top business leaders and grassroots members to crush this modest reform, marking "the last major attempt to stem the declining influence of organized labor in the United States through federal legislation" (Akard 1992:607).

For pluralist theorists, business didn't benefit from a particularly privileged position relative to other interest organizations, despite typically superior financial resources and more compelling incentives for engaging in policy influence actions. Policy outcomes hinged more on how astutely the opposing sides mobilized their supporters and deployed available political resources to persuade policymakers. Corporate interests did not automatically prevail, particularly when their opponents presented a more compelling case about the substantive merits and the political gains to politicians for supporting their preferred outcome. Changing political climates, reflected in election returns, could shift enough fence-straddling legislators to spell victory or defeat for business organizations.

Consider the disparate outcomes of the three bills analyzed in Figure 9.7. Although the Democrat-controlled House passed the high-risk notification proposal in 1987, it was never "marked up" by the Republican-controlled Senate labor committee. Although supported by a few companies such as IBM and General Electric, the bill was opposed by many corporate lobbyists who argued convincingly that "it would create an unnecessary new bureaucracy and expose employers to lawsuits that could drive them to bankruptcy" (Aiges 1987). Republicans also successfully stalled the minimum wage raise throughout the eight-year Reagan Administration. Although George Bush made a 1988 campaign promise to allow an increase, as president in 1989 he vetoed an increase from $3.35 to $4.55. Shortly thereafter he cut a deal with the Democrat-controlled Congress to hike the minimum wage to $4.25 over the next two years. The new law also expanded tax credits to low-income families and included a special "training wage" for teenage workers, both provisions favored by business interests. President Bush also twice vetoed the family leave bill, echoing business complaints that it would impose financial hardships on firms, despite the exemption of more than 90 percent of companies from its provisions. After Democrats regained the presidency in the 1992 elections, the Family and Medical Leave Act was the first bill Clinton signed into law. Business and labor interests both won and lost on these three issues.

An incremental pattern of policy adjustments, in which neither side achieved continual domination over its opponents, was more consistent with pluralist theory than class or elite theories. A pattern of alternating successes and failures emerged from examining a long series of public policy fights over a common issue. In his painstaking case study of federal clean air legislation from 1967 to 1981, David Vogel (1996:322–395) charted the intense efforts by various corporations, unions, and environmental groups to influence pollution regulations for automobiles, factories, and power plants. Business organizations were not always successful in achieving their goals. Rather, relative political effectiveness varied with four sets of factors: "the pattern of opposition and support from other interest groups, how well [business] lobbying is organized, the perceived merits of their position, and the geographic distribution of their production" (p. 381). Interest groups that assembled a broader coalition against weak or disorganized opponents were more likely to win. For example, coal producers achieved their objective of weakening emission standards in the 1967 Clean Air Act because they received substantial support from other industries and faced no effective opposition. But in the 1970 fight to amend the Clean Air Act, a broad coalition of environmental organizations successfully tightened auto emission standards because "the auto manufacturers made no attempt to mobilize or involve their independent dealers," the peak business associations made "rather ineffectual lobbying efforts," and divided industry interests prevented inter-industry coordination (pp. 346–347). Business learned these harsh lessons before the intense fight over the 1977 amendments, where the auto makers prevailed in loosening emission standards. The explanation for this remarkably quick turnaround was a cohesive coalition that car companies forged with other organizations, including the independent auto dealers, auto service companies, and other small businessmen. In particular, the United Auto Workers union defected from the environmentalists to support the manufacturers over the question of job losses from higher pollution standards.

Despite years of research and debate, the jury is still out on whether class, elite, or pluralist theories, or some new theoretical approach yet to be clearly articulated, offered better accounts of the corporate community's influence on public policy formation. The testimonies provided by case studies and systematic data analyses remained open to alternative interpretations. The most plausible judgment of the indictment that business dominated U.S. public policymaking was a third verdict, available only in Scottish courts: "not proved."

Conclusions

Public policy arenas grew increasingly crowded at the end of the twentieth century as the numbers of political organizations, lobbyists, and consultants flocking to Washington swelled to epidemic dimensions. Institutional changes in electing officials, legislating, and regulating public affairs made the game of access and influence more complicated and costly to play. Organizations deployed diverse influence tactics to pressure policymakers, ranging from formal and informal contacts to mobilizing grassroots constituencies. Although buckets of PAC money seemed to grease political organizations' entries into policymakers' offices and committees, demonstrating unambiguous links between dollars and votes proved nearly impossible. Lobbying activities grew so incessant that business groups and their opponents were forced to run flat-out just to stay even with one another. Information networking and coalition formation became indispensable processes for political organizations to remain conversant about issue developments and to attract policymakers' attention to their preferences. Short-term action sets struggling for incremental advantages on specific policy proposals split apart and reassembled into new configurations for subsequent policy fights. The centrifugal pulls of narrow industrial, occupational, and geographic interests split fragile alliances and diluted interest organizations' ability to achieve their political goals. Sustaining even temporary political unity within the business community was a formidable endeavor, let alone achieving a comprehensive domination over the national political economy. In the pluralist constellations of late twentieth-century U.S. politics, corporations and trade associations were just the brightest stars, not the entire universe.

10

Learning
to Evolve

He that will not apply new remedies must expect new evils; for time is the greatest innovator.
—**Francis Bacon, *Of Innovations* (1625)**

The Monsanto Company, a giant St. Louis-based agribusiness corporation, wanted to buy the nation's largest cotton seed breeder company, which had just won U.S. patent approval for a promising genetic engineering process. The Delta & Pine Land Company's 1998 patent involved creating molecular switches that would force food and fiber plants to produce toxic proteins that sterilized their seeds (Specter 2000). Thus, farmers couldn't save their harvested seeds to plant next year's crop, a common practice among impoverished cultivators in developing nations. Instead, they would be forced to buy new seeds annually from Monsanto and other corporate seed producers. Bioengineering foes dubbed these self-sterilizing plants Terminators, after the Arnold Schwarzenegger robotic killer. They demonized "Monsatan" as the poster child for greedy corporations reaping huge profits by pushing dangerous biotechnologies that threatened to break down the natural order. The anti-biotech movement harvested a media bonanza by hyping unverified claims that gene-altered corn pollen blowing onto milkweed leaves was destroying the larvae of the much-beloved Monarch butterfly (Weiss 1999). With public protests forcing many European governments to restrict recombinant DNA products from their markets, the commercial future for biotechnology looked increasingly bleak.

Thrown on the defensive, multinational corporations championed the benefits of genetically modified crops for improving health and raising living standards in developing nations. For example, European scientists cre-

ated "Golden Rice" by splicing three genes that enable ordinary rice ker-
nels to carry beta carotene, which is then broken down into Vitamin A during human digestion. These plants could help to prevent the vitamin deficiencies in millions of poor children around the world that lead to blindness
and death from related infections (Gugliotta 2000). With almost mission-
ary zeal, Monsanto CEO Robert B. Shapiro proclaimed that his company's
practices differed only in degree from traditional cross-breeding to improve
plant and animal quality:

> This is an important moment in human history. The application of contempo-
> rary biological knowledge to issues like food and nutrition and human health
> has to occur. It has to occur for the same reasons that things have occurred for
> the past ten millennia. People want to live better, and they will use the tools
> they have to do it. Biology is the best tool we have. (Specter 2000:60)

Agribusinesses fought a losing public relations battle against renegade
agronomists, socially conscious churches, environmental organizations like
Greenpeace, and Third World democracy movements. American public
opinion on the issue began drifting toward the Europeans' skepticism and
outright opposition to "Frankenfoods." In early 2000, Monsanto withdrew
its bid for Delta & Pine, merged with a pharmaceutical firm to create Phar-
macia Corporation, and planned to divest its agricultural units. Several
other drug makers—including American Home Products, Britain's As-
traZeneca, and Switzerland's Novartis—also decided to shuck their
agribusinesses (Morrow 2000). However, the humanitarian and commercial attractions of biotechnology remained too alluring, especially for poor
nations with swelling multitudes to feed, to assume that the controversy
would quickly fade away.

The fierce biotechnology debate reflected the potent stew of astonishing
technologies, voracious commercial appetites, popular privacy anxieties,
and intrusive governmental regulations swirling around organizations and
institutions at the start of the twenty-first century. This concluding chapter
examines some near-term developments and their implications for future
organizational structure and action. Chaos and complexity theories explain
why real events thwart researchers' best efforts to predict future trends precisely, yet offer the possibility of understanding and explaining large-scale
system behavior. Evolutionary theories based on variation, selection, and
retention processes offer alternative possibilities for anticipating innovative
directions without promising precise predictions.

With the Cold War's end, national innovation systems shifted away from
heavy governmental investment in military technologies and toward greater
reliance on private-sector funding of research and development. Complex
networks of industry, university, and multilevel government relations began

emerging. Learning theories at both the organizational and population levels of analysis pointed to explicit tradeoffs between exploring and commercially exploiting inventions and discoveries. Innovator organizations, which include both small entrepreneurial enterprises and large corporations with huge R&D budgets, will be the major sources for key technological breakthroughs leading organizations down new evolutionary pathways. Therefore, uncovering the details of innovation journeys undertaken in such innovator organizations is crucial to understanding potential future developments. In the final section, I review the central themes of this book and contemplate where organization studies may plausibly travel next.

Chaos and Complexity
Thwart Predictability

Self-proclaimed futurologists (e.g., Minkin 1995; Naisbitt 1994) regularly release copious lists of predictions and forecasts, generated by largely inexplicable and nonreplicable procedures, that show scant improvement over ancient augurs inspecting bird entrails. Their prognostications could easily be derailed by an unforeseen catastrophic event, on the order of magnitude of a global thermonuclear war, that throws a star-mangled spanner into the works. Less drastic disruptions start with technological breakthroughs that rapidly shift the political economy onto new trajectories. The preceding century witnessed numerous transforming inventions that were largely unanticipated and inconceivable at its beginning: powered airflight, radio and television, atomic energy, computers and the Internet. In hindsight (always a smug vantage point), we can see that fiction writers speculating about the future erred by extrapolating short-term situations into long-term trends (O'Neill 1981:18–38). As examples, Rudyard Kipling (1913) assumed that lighter-than-air Zeppelins would prevail over the fragile airplanes of his day, and H. G. Wells (1933) imagined the first moon trip would occur more than a century later by firing a spaceship through an enormous gun barrel. Arthur C. Clarke, one of the century's more perceptive science fiction writers (his collaboration with director Stanley Kubrick on *2001: A Space Odyssey* remains a classic of the genre), proposed geosynchronous orbiting communication satellites several decades before they were launched. He also predicted language translating machines by 1970, manned planetary landings by 1980, wireless transmission of energy by 2000, weather control by 2015, interstellar probes and robots of human complexity by 2025, gravity control by 2050, near-light speeds by 2075, and self-replicating factories by 2090 (Clarke 1958). Clarke has already missed the mark on several forecasts, but only the shape of things to come will tell about the others. (For amusing lists of other predictions that both did and did not materialize during the past century, see Makridakis 1990:90–102.) My point in drawing attention to failed prophecies is not to embarrass their instigators but to underscore the difficulties of attempting to peer accurately into the far future. The main obstacle may lie, not so much in the prophets' inabilities to take into account sufficient numbers of variable factors as in the intrinsic indeterminacies lurking within all highly complex systems, great and small.

Efforts to predict precise changes in complex systems are thwarted by nonlinear relationships among key variables that render system outcomes extremely sensitive to small variations in initial conditions. In a linear relation, inputs and outputs are related proportionally; for example, doubling the number of employees exactly doubles a firm's output (i.e., following a straight line formula $Y = 2X$ where Y is output and X is input). But nonlinear relations yield disproportional changes. For example, suppose that an exponential effect occurs where doubling the number of employees yields a four-fold increase in the firm's output (i.e., $Y = X^2$). Chaos theory explains how tiny perturbations can rapidly reverberate through a complex system, producing significantly different outcomes than would have occurred in their absence (Gleick 1987; Anderla, Dunning and Forge 1997). Unpredictable trajectories arise from minute fluctuations and small measurement errors occurring at the beginning of a process. Developed to forecast weather, analyze fluid turbulence dynamics, and control subatomic oscillations in electronic devices, research based on chaos theory revealed inherent limits to modeling complex interactions. The farther an equation's calculations carried into the future, the more likely its predictions fell far from the actual results. The implicit futility of attempting to predict long-term cause-and-effect sequences lies behind Edward Lorenz's famous question, "Does the flap of a butterfly's wings in Brazil set off a tornado in Texas?" Maybe, but more often it draws a bird's attention, and bye-bye butterfly.

Chaos in scientific usage does not indicate the random behavior, disorder, and confusion of ordinary vocabulary. Writing about biological evolution, Stuart Kaufmann (1995:17) argued that "the failure to predict does not mean failure to understand or to explain. Indeed, if we were confident we knew the equations governing a chaotic system, we would be confident we understood its behavior, including our incapacity to predict in detail its long-term behavior." Paradoxically, even a forecasting model consisting of relatively simple, mathematically deterministic, nonlinear equations may exhibit chaotic behavior. Chaotic systems can display cyclical irregularities, that is, yield recognizable *patterns* in the trajectory traced by changes while remaining ultimately indeterminate about precise longitudinal *paths* followed over an extended time (Dooley and Van de Ven 1999). Although nonlinear dynamic equation outputs are not predictably related to their inputs, not every pattern is equally feasible. Both chaotic and nonchaotic dynamic systems may contain "attractors," fixed points around which movements oscillate periodically through time, for example, as planets orbit a star in recurring cycles. Disturbing such systems does not change their basic behavioral patterns, as the perturbed trajectories return to their equilibrium oscillation around the attractor. In chaotic systems governed by nonlinear equations, "strange attractors" produce stable, cyclical patterns that never exactly repeat themselves. Graphic plots of the trajectories generated by a chaotic system with a strange attractor often visually reveal gradually changing movements over time but confined within fairly circumscribed boundaries or limits. However, abrupt changes may cause system motions to jump irregularly from one strange attractor to another, yielding another stable and nonperiodic pattern of continuous change.

As a purely hypothetical example of chaos in a social system, aggregate stock price indexes (such as the Dow Jones Industrials or S&P 500) might bounce unpredictably between relatively narrow bounds, never exactly repeating the same daily pattern of ups and downs. Suppose an intrusive external event, such as a declaration of war or a central bank interest hike, triggers a huge market collapse because panicking investors try to sell more shares than buyers want to purchase at a high price (e.g., the spring 2000 puncturing of Internet company share prices). When the market eventually stabilizes, the index values would again fluctuate chaotically around a new attractor having much lower bounds. Empirical efforts to apply chaos theory to explain economic activity generally yielded negative results (Creedy and Martin 1994; Dechert 1996). Most researchers uncovered no evidence of chaotic behavior in the random movements of stock market indexes for several countries (Ramsey 1996; Mayer-Foulkes and Feliz 1996; Brooks 1998; Pandey, Kohers and Kohers 1998), although a few analysts detected chaotic patterns in stock markets (Lux 1998; Jasic 1998), bankruptcies (Lindsay and Campbell 1996), and free-floating monetary exchange rates (Ellis 1994). One pessimistic inference from chaos arising in simple nonlinear systems is that "model building and estimation for forecasting purposes may be insurmountably difficult. Even with the correct model, reasonably accurate predictions will only be possible for very short time horizons" (Ellis 1994:195).

Other social sciences treated chaos concepts more as sexy metaphorical icons than as rigorous ideas susceptible to empirical examination (Smith 1995; Shelly and Wagner 1998). Consequently, organization researchers largely avoided modeling and interpreting dynamic organizational data as nonlinear temporal processes of complex systems involving sensitivity to initial conditions, feedback loops, emergent properties, chaotic equilibria, and unpredictable outcomes. A notable recent exception was the Minnesota Innovation Research Program (MIRP), which investigated innovation as nonlinear chaos processes that advance organizational learning through discovery. "By uncoupling actions and outcomes, a chaotic process facilitates the construction of repertoires of action experiences, outcome beliefs, and contextual practices. These repertoires increase an organization's capacity for creative learning" (Van de Ven et al. 1999:17). Chaotic patterns were evident in the early time-series of monthly events at the 3M Corporation of St. Paul, Minnesota, during its development of a surgically implanted cochlear device, an electronic device to give profoundly deaf persons a sensation of hearing (Cheng and Van de Ven 1996; Dooley and Van de Ven 1997). In its initial five years before the emergence of a dominant design (1981–1985), program participants sought to invent a cochlear implant device that would both win Food and Drug Administration approval and capture market share. These shared program goals and other institutional constraints limited individual program participants' freedom of action: the FDA's regulatory review process, common sources of basic knowledge from university labs, and shared mental models and interpretive schemas arising from common professional training and organizational socialization. These institutional factors acted interdependently; for example, the push for FDA approval and first-mover market advantage drove 3M employees into frenzied activities to complete the implant development for clinical trials. The test results were interpreted and fed back into subsequent program actions. Such complex nonlinear local and global feedback loops produced potentially chaotic event patterns at the beginning of the development cycle, followed by a more orderly periodic pattern as the failing cochlear implant device encountered market-entry problems. Finally, 3M terminated the cochlear implant program in 1989.

A close cousin of chaos, complexity theory, attempted to explain and model the general behaviors of nonlinear systems—ranging from rain forests to automated software agents to multinational corporations—as complex adaptive systems (CAS). Any interacting network of self-organizing actors, following rules and exchanging information among themselves and with the environment, may collectively behave as though it were a single entity. By simplifying complexity and identifying emergent properties in CAS, complexity theory tried to model the behavioral patterns of the whole group, even though the actions of any single member remain unpredictable (Waldrop 1992; Casti 1994; Axelrod and Cohen 2000). Like chaos, initial adaptations of the complexity theory in the social sciences were more metaphorical than rigorous (Byrne 1998; Nijkamp and Reggiani 1998). In organization studies, complexity analysts could investigate the transformation of centralized hierarchical systems into improvised, self-organized actions by local agents (Stacey 1995; Anderson 1999a), for example, in banks (Kurtyka 1999) and nursing homes (Anderson and McDaniel 1999). Given strong overlap of explanatory concepts between complexity and organizational evolution theory, I examine their shared variation and selection mechanisms in the next section.

The general dearth of serious theoretical and empirical attention to chaotic and complexity theories by the social sciences in general, and by organization analysts in particular, simultaneously represented investigatory deficiencies and opportunities for future theory construction. Prime candidates for the application of deterministic chaos ideas included forecasting the growth patterns of organizational populations, explaining organizational adaptation to changing environments, and accounting for the emergence of stable "networks of networks" (Marion 1999). However, just as chaos theory posits that the outcomes of complex systems are ultimately indeterminate, so must remain any predictions that chaos principles will eventually improve our understanding of organizational change.

Evolutionary Alternatives

Like chaos and complexity theories, evolutionary perspectives also assumed indeterminacy in organizational change. Drawing inspiration from biological theories of speciation, evolutionary explanations in economics and organization studies emphasized how random and systematic factors generated variation in institutional and organizational forms, structures, and practices, then selected and retained particular successful outcomes for survival and persistence within a population (Campbell 1969; Nelson and Winter 1982; Nelson 1994; Aldrich 1979, 1999:21–33). The three generic sequences in the evolutionary model consisted of:

- Initial *variations* in organizational form, which may arise from the conscious strategic choices of entrepreneurs and managers, by imitation and learning from successful companies, or through haphazard and unplanned innovative activities. The model is "indifferent to the ultimate source of variation, as planned and unplanned variations both provide raw material from which selection can be made" (Aldrich 1979:28). Like genetic mutations among one-celled creatures swimming in the primordial soup, chance variations in organizational structures and processes might give their adopters a competitive advantage in the struggle to survive. Some variations seemed to carry an historical "imprint" of the era during which that form emerged (Stinchcombe 1965). Thus, modern construction firms continued to display the informal, nonbureaucratic structures typical of the family-run companies founded in the nineteenth century.
- *Selection*, which, once variation emerged within a population, ultimately depended on how well the new form fit its environment. Se-

lection occurred primarily through the competition for scarce resources. A new form's survival depended on finding resources in an
environmental niche where it could outcompete alternative forms,
analogous to biotic mutations that allowed air-breathing lungfish to
leave the water for land (Aldrich and Pfeffer 1976). A *niche*, another
basic concept borrowed from biology, is a localized environment
consisting of all combinations of resources and other constraints
(such as government support, public opinion, and judicial rulings)
that are sufficient to sustain an organizational form. For example,
federal deregulation of the U.S. airline industry in the 1970s literally
opened new air space for startup commuter lines to feed passengers
into regional hubs operated by the major carriers. The commuter
companies thrived by servicing small towns that the big airlines ignored as yielding too-thin profit margins. Similar opportunistic population expansions occurred in the German beer brewing (where
new technologies enabled micro-breweries to thrive) and Toronto
day-care populations (which benefited from changing work/family
patterns of women) (see, respectively, Swaminathan and Wiede-
mayer 1991; Baum and Oliver 1992). Niche characteristics affected
the type of organizational forms most likely to survive, particularly
when environmental conditions become unstable and unpredictable.
In brief:

Specialist organizations maximize their exploitation of the environment over a
relatively narrow range of environmental conditions and have little slack or
excess capacity. Generalist organizations can survive over a wide range of environmental conditions but are not not optimally suited to any single conditions.
The trade-off is between security or risk reduction and efficiency or the exploitation of the particualr environment in greater depth. (Pfeffer 1982:182)

- The *retention* stage, which ensured that a selected form would be
  perpetuated rather than die out in a population. The well-known biological reproductive process of genetic inheritance across generations had no identical mechanism in socially created organizations.
  Nelson and Winter (1974) coined the term "routines" to denote particular practices or capabilities that determined what firms did and
  how productively in specific situations. Some optimal combinations
  of corporate learning, employee socialization, and formalized institutions bolstered the participants' commitment to preferred technologies and social organizational practices. These processes enabled
  the selected structures and behaviors to persist within an organizational population. Ironically, these same retention mechanisms could
  also generate an ossifying inertia that prevented organizations from

adapting to changing environmental conditions. Note that analysts did not equate the evolution of new forms with progressive improvement in organizational efficiency, especially where market pressures were weak or absent, as in public-sector bureaucracies. Rather, they depicted an endless cycle of macro level changes that blossomed over time into the wide diversity of organizations characterizing modern societies.

Evolutionary theories predict neither the exact pace at which nor the specific mechanisms through which the generic variation-selection-retention processes operate. Rather, these complex dynamics function blindly without following a prescribed path or blueprint for reaching a known or predetermined destination. (In contrast, teleological theories of development and change assume that actors and social systems purposefully set and pursue specific end states or goals; Van de Ven and Poole 1995.) Evolutionary explanations of organizational change depict an intersection between internal organizational processes and outside forces, in which "external events interact with an organization's own actions to drive the pace, pattern, and direction of change" (Aldrich 1999:198). However, a specific direction of change resulting from their interaction is not preordained by the starting internal configurations and environmental conditions. Indeed, the path followed might be just one among several alternative routes that could have been taken. Hence, explanatory propositions from organizational evolution perspectives are typically expressed in an algorithmic, or conditional, rather than a deterministic mode. That is, evolutionary theories only assert that, if particular environmental circumstances arise in the context of certain organizational arrangements, then some varieties of organizational outcomes are more likely than others to occur. The concept of *equifinality* recognizes that more than one route can lead to a given outcome.

Paradoxically, despite the indeterminacy of evolutionary change, its dynamics may exhibit considerable *path dependence*. This concept refers to a sequence of unique historical events that fixes a system on a course that can be neither retraced nor effortlessly altered by subsequent events. Evolving organizations do not always attain optimal fit, especially in turbulent environments, but may lock into inefficient forms of behavior. As selection and retention operate cumulatively over time to push developments in particular directions, alternative paths shut down. Organizational change trajectories converge on a narrowing range of options for subsequent transformations, and retracing a path back to pick up an alternative branch grows increasingly unlikely (Arthur 1989). Such renowned cases of technological lock-in as the internal combustion automobile engine (which triumphed over steam-powered vehicles), the QWERTY typewriter keyboard, VHS home video recorders, digital video discs, and Microsoft's DOS personal computer operating system illustrate how, through chance, an inferior technology may gain an insurmountable lead over allegedly superior alternatives (David 1985; Cusumano, Mylonadis and Rosenbloom 1992; Grindley 1995; Liebowitz and Margolis 1999). Once a critical mass of adopters had jumped on the bandwagon (i.e., adopted a specific technical standard), and many firms began producing new applications for that technology, the increasing economic returns to scale enjoyed by the favored innovation assured that its rivals never overcame their initial competitive disadvantages. Of course, skillful strategic maneuvering by corporations with heavy stakes in the outcome, as well as protective or laissez-faire governmental policies toward monopolies, could steeply tilt a playing field toward the eventually triumphant technology. Micosoft's long reign as the dominant operating system for personal computers, coupled with its efforts to monopolize the Internet browser market, was crafted with business practices eventually deemed predatory by a federal judge. The government proposed, and the judge agreed, that breaking up Microsoft would derail path dependence in the software industry by spawning competitive technologies.

Interactions between internal circumstances and environmental conditions may not produce the most efficient new organizational forms in an economic sense, but instead "reflect the historical path laid down by a meandering drift of accumulated and selectively retained variations" (Aldrich 1999:33). Unique, chance events may also play important roles in generating variation in the raw materials upon which shifting environmental conditions operate to select the fit from the unfit organizational forms. A smooth, gradual evolutionary trend through continuous incremental developments is vulnerable to disruption by unforeseen catastrophic events (think asteroids and dinosaur extinction, or wars and government collapse). In a well-known case of path dependence and catastrophe, U.S. auto manufacturers had by the mid-twentieth century locked into traditional bureaucratic factories using machine-paced assembly processes to build large, gas-guzzling cars (see Chapter 5). When two 1970s oil price shocks jolted the auto market, the Big Three firms could not quickly change their production and sales strategies (Alm and Weiner 1984). Unable to transform their operations to meet consumer demands for small, fuel-efficient, high-quality vehicles, their domination of the domestic U.S. market was toppled by Japanese imports. By definition, abrupt and violent metamorphoses that rapidly and radically transform populations and individual organizations are far rarer than gradual and continuous evolutionary changes. However, the potential for major discontinuities to spawn large-scale revolutionary transformations across entire organizational populations severely limits efforts to apply evolutionary principles to forecast the precise direction of future changes.

The ultimate indeterminacy of evolutionary paths should not deter analysts from undertaking theoretical and empirical efforts to identify plausible internal and environmental conditions that may already be shaping the future course of organizations in the twenty-first century. Because evolutionary perspectives cannot specify which mechanisms would be most likely to generate change, analysts may freely deploy the entire panoply of organization theories to flesh out the particulars. Thus, organizational ecology dynamics, institutional arrangements, power and resource dependence, transactional economics, and network analysis each emphasize different sources of organizational variation on which evolutionary selection and retention processes operate. These diverse perspectives, as well as organizational and population learning theories, help to explain several dimensions in the evolution of innovation. At the societal and international levels, the most important institutions shaping the creation and diffusion of new science and technology were the national innovation systems, examined in the next section.

National Innovation Systems

National innovation system refers to the diverse institutions and policies governing a nation's capacity to create, develop, and adopt new technologies (Freeman 1987; Lundvall 1992; Nelson 1993; Edquist 1997). Such systems include formal organizations arranged as "a hierarchical, multidimensional network of public and private institutions interacting non-linearly in a given historical context" (Leoncini 1998:75). These organizations are integrated with higher education, regulatory, and international trade programs and policies designed to improve innovative capacity and foster economic growth (Peters, Groenewegen and Fiebelkorn 1998). Researchers in innovation studies use aggregate research and development (R&D) expenditures as key indicators of a nation's capacity to solve complex problems. The U.S. National Science Foundation, chief tracker of R&D statistical trends, classifies expenditures under three broad categories according to their intended objectives:

- *Basic research* aims to gain comprehensive knowledge or understanding of a subject under study without specific applications in mind. Classic examples include projects inquiring into the fundamental properties of subatomic particles, the origins of the universe, and human impacts on global climate change. Basic research in industry also advances scientific knowledge without specific commercial objectives, although such ulterior interests may be latent. Automobile company investigations of solar alternatives to the internal combustion engine illustrate this approach.
- *Applied research* seeks to gain knowledge to meet specific needs, for example, to improve battlefield communications between troops and commanders. Applied investigations by for-profit firms are ori-

ented toward specific commercial objectives, such as marketing new drug treatments and genetically modified crops, exemplified by the Monsanto case discussed at the beginning of this chapter.

• *Development* involves the systematic use of scientific knowledge gained from basic research "directed toward the production of useful materials, devices, systems, or methods,"(National Science Foundation 1998:4-9) including the construction of prototypes. A project to demonstrate the feasibility of a universal verbal-language translation machine is a long-anticipated development.

Basic research involves exploration of unknown terrain, whereas both applied and developmental research emphasize intensive exploitation of existing fundamental knowledge. These distinctions are central issues in the organizational and population learning perspectives examined in the following two sections.

Governmental policies, industrial strategies, and international competition dramatically transformed the U.S. national innovation system over the latter half of the twentieth century. After World War II, political concerns about communism and cancer steered federal R&D spending toward defense-related applied technologies and basic research in biomedical sciences. These efforts "provided a powerful impetus to the development and commercialization of new civilian technologies in commercial aerospace, semiconductors, computers and computer software" (Mowery 1998:640). A unique convergence of government R&D funding patterns and permissive antitrust policies with domestic financial institutions fostered the generous private capitalization of new high-tech firms. As these pioneering enterprises and industries matured, they eventually shifted the U.S. national innovation system toward decreased resource dependence on the public purse. The major structural changes included:

(1) increased reliance by US firms on sources of R&D outside their organizational boundaries, through such mechanisms as consortia, collaboration with US universities and federal laboratories, and strategic alliance with other US and foreign firms; (2) expanded performance of R&D offshore by US firms and increased performance by non-US firms of industrial R&D within the United States; (3) increased reliance by US universities on US and foreign industry for research funding and expanded efforts by US universities to license and otherwise realize commercial returns from the results of academic research. (Mowery 1998:646)

Figure 10.1 displays the constant-dollar trends in U.S. R&D expenditures from 1960 to 1999 as reported by the National Science Foundation (1999). The most notable feature is the yawning divergence between federal government and private industry R&D spending as the Cold War began winding down in the late 1980s. After federal share peaked and fell in 1987, profit-making companies were entirely responsible for the strong upward surge in R&D spending, especially in the final decade of the century. Projections for the year 2000 estimated that industry would account for 70 percent of the record $267 billion total, the federal share would hold steady at 25 percent (down from 50 percent as recently as 1980), and universities and nonprofit foundations together would spend less than 4 percent (Guidera 2000). As a percentage of total U.S. gross domestic product, R&D spending declined from 2.7 percent in 1991 to 2.4 percent in 1994 before rebounding to 2.6 percent in 1997.

A further breakdown of 1997 expenditures by sectors revealed the evolving functions of research and development activity in the United States. The relative decline in federal funding came largely from its substantial withdrawal of support for defense- and energy-related R&D conducted by private industry. The Department of Defense eventually accounted for less than half of the federal total, down from two-thirds at the height of the Reagan Administration's defense buildup in 1986. Among federal nondefense sectors, health R&D was the largest and most rapidly expanding function, with AIDS-related research the fastest-growing category. Within the private sector, firms in service-sector industries accounted for almost

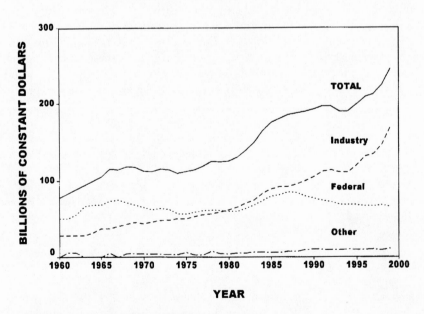

FIGURE 10.1   R&D Expenditures
SOURCE: National Science Foundation (1999)

one-quarter of all R&D investments, largely due to the spectacular growth in spending in computer programming, communication services, and biotechnology, particularly by pharmaceutical firms. Among manufacturing industries, chemicals, transportation equipment, and electrical equipment companies exhibited the largest R&D increases. Across all funding sources, development projects account for a larger proportion (62 percent) than both applied research and basic research combined (22 and 16 percent, respectively).

Comparisons with other advanced capitalist nations reveals similar R&D trends. In 1995, the United States accounted for approximately 44 percent of the world's R&D total, far outdistancing second-place Japan. However, if only nondefense expenditures were considered, the other Group of Seven nations (Japan, Germany, France, United Kingdom, Italy, and Canada) altogether spent about 18 percent more than the United States (National Science Foundation 1999). In all these nations, public funding of R&D declined, primarily from government cutbacks in defense spending, while industry's share grew substantially (Mowery 1998:645). Consequently, national innovation systems grew to resemble one another in their increasing reliance on for-profit firms, as well as the increasing prevalence of funding sources outside their national boundaries. International cooperation in basic research mega-projects such as atomic physics, space exploration (the international space station), and mapping the humane genome reflected governmental financing constraints on major instrumentation and facility investments.

The globalization of private-sector R&D also accelerated through research consortia, strategic technology alliances, joint ventures, licensing, and other interorganizational collaborations (see Chapter 4). Foreign sources made up growing shares of domestic R&D investments in many countries, and numerous multinational firms established research labs outside their home bases. In 1994, U.S. firms' R&D investments abroad were roughly equivalent to the amount spent inside the U.S. by affiliates of foreign companies. By 1996, more than 670 R&D facilities owned by foreign companies were located in the United States, more than one-third by Japanese corporations (Dalton and Serapio 1998). Firms tended to adopt a global R&D approach primarily to tap knowledge from competitors and universities (a home-base augmenting strategy where information flowed from foreign laboratories to the central home lab) or to support their overseas production facilities and adapt their standards to local consumer demands (a home-base exploiting strategy). One study of 238 foreign labs found about 45 followed a home-base augmenting and 55 percent a home-base exploiting strategy (Kuemmerle 1997). An analysis of product-embodied R&D diffusion among 10 advanced nations, primarily involving information and communications technologies, found that the proportions of technology obtained through imports increased over three decades for all countries except Japan, with the United States the most important source (Papaconstantinou, Sakuri and Wyckoff 1998). A strong implication was that national innovation systems were evolving into an increasingly integrated global system.

Given the expanded leading role of industry in R&D funding, some analysts detected the emergence of a "triple helix," an innovation network interconnecting industry, university, and governmental organizations (Etzkowitz and Leydesdorff 1997, 2000). In particular, higher education institutions in the United States and European Union experienced transitions away from ivory-tower teaching and basic research missions toward more active participation in local and regional economic growth and development. Alternative technology transfer mechanisms such as publications and patents generated distinct transaction costs in turning scientific and technical knowledge into marketable commercial products and services. Basic university research matured in the twentieth century, with government grants allocated through peer review of proposed projects' scientific merits. Strong professional norms legitimated the open publication of research results and faculty won academic prestige, but not much money, for discovering basic scientific knowledge. In contrast, developmental research programs funded by industry contracts typically erected proprietary protections, using patents to restrict other researchers' access to data and knowledge. Applied projects attracted participants by offering large personal financial rewards through royalties and stock options, rather than peer acclaim.

With the relative decline in governmental R&D funding, intense competition for research money forged new connections between firms and universities. As their professors and research units increasingly entwined with private firms through spin-offs, startups, joint ventures, and consultancies, higher education institutions confronted conflicts over their core norms and missions. These tensions were exemplified in the emergence of small, knowledge-based biotechnology companies around prestigious universities in New England and the San Francisco Bay Area (Liebeskind et al. 1996; McMillan, Narin and Deeds 2000; Giesecke 2000; see also Chapter 4 on strategic alliances in this industry). Genetic research scientist-entrepreneurs working on recombinant DNA in academic settings foresaw enormous personal financial gains by capitalizing their startup companies through initial public offerings. Large pharmaceutical firms and agribusinesses such as Monsanto invested in the biotechs' projects, hoping to commercialize their drug and crop inventions. These competing and collaborating networks compelled many universities to revise their intellectual property policies to cope with the clashing organizational cultural values between academic openness and corporate secrecy. International disputes over corporate attempts to patent the human genome, genetically modified plants and animals, and even traditional folk remedies (Pollack 1999; Gosselin and Jacobs 2000) revealed the deep quagmires into which universities, industries, and governments could stumble.

Another core strand in the triple helix network was the emergence of more complex R&D relations between industries and governments. From an evolutionary perspective, these efforts bred wider variations for the political economy to select. Governments ranging from international to local levels encouraged and underwrote private-sector innovation efforts. Europe's Airbus Industrie—a supra-national consortium heavily subsidized by the French, British, German, and Spanish governments—ultimately surpassed its sole rival Boeing to become the world's leading manufacturer of jumbo jets (Thornton 1995; McGuire 1997). The U.S. federal government's Small Business Innovation Research (SBIR) program annually awarded $1.2 billion in grants to small high-tech businesses. These companies were not required to repay the funds but could keep any commercial intellectual properties rights resulting from their awards. State and local governments also competed to attract research investments into their jurisdictions, which they considered indispensable to their long-term economic prosperity. Nonprofit organizations played key mediating roles in integrating money and ideas. For example, the steering committee of the Minnesota Seed Capital Network, launched in 1999 to connect fledgling high-tech companies with equity investors, included representatives from the University of Minnesota, large corporations, venture capital firms, private investors, banks, law firms, accounting firms, and small high-technology companies (Olson 2000). The evolution of national innovation systems toward complex triple helices implicated the organizational and population learning dynamics examined in the following two sections.

Organizational Learning

Organizational learning perspectives offer promising approaches to understanding key components of evolutionary change. Evolutionary processes tend to select those organizations in a population that exhibit high "absorptive capacity" (Cohen and Levinthal 1990), the ability to acquire, assimilate, and apply new information and knowledge. A firm's environmental fitness depends heavily on its *organizational learning* system, defined as "a system of actions, actors, symbols and processes that enables an organization to transform information into valued knowledge which in turn increases its long-run adaptive capacity" (Schwandt 1997:343). Learning is intimately intertwined with innovation and suffused with technology adoption and adaptation issues. Organizational learning processes involve behaviors embedded in *routines*, recorded in collective organizational memory and transmitted from old to new individual members by formal and informal socialization mechanisms (Cyert and March 1963; Nelson and Winter 1982). According to a definition proposed by Barbara Levitt and James G. March, practically anything an organization does qualifies as a routine:

> The generic term "routines" includes the forms, rules, procedures, conventions, strategies, and technologies around which organizations are constructed and through which organizations are constructed and through which they operate. It also includes the structure of beliefs, frameworks, paradigms, codes, cultures, and knowledge that buttress, elaborate, and contradict the formal routines. Routines are independent of the individual actors who execute them and are capable of surviving considerable turnover in individual actors. (Levitt and March 1988:320)

As metaphorical genes, routines store and pass on organizational codes, enabling organizations to reproduce their structures, processes, and outputs despite often high rates of individual participant turnover. Organizations store and transmit their routines in a variety of repositories or collective memory devices, such as documents, employee training courses, standard professional practices, organizational cultural ceremonies, and corporate narratives. Learning and sense-making activities (Weick 1995) involve social psychological dynamics that create collective interpretations and understandings of organizational events through shared stories, interpretive paradigms, and socially constructed identity frames.

Organizational learning is not identical to individual learning, the various human capital formation processes, such as education and training, by which individuals acquire knowledge useful for performing their work tasks. The intrapersonal cognitive processes involved in individual consciousness, biological memory (storage and retrieval), and application to novel situations (creativity) at best have only crude parallels to learning mechanisms at the organizational level. However, organizations and persons can and do learn from one another. All organizations socialize their new participants to existing collective beliefs about legitimate ways to behave, and organizations in turn absorb and incorporate some of the knowledge introduced by the new members. Hence, basic demographic processes, such as rates of employee turnover and interorganizational collaboration, shape organizational learning.

Both organizations and individuals learn directly from their own experiences as well as vicariously by observing the consequences of others' behaviors. Experiential learning cycles— scanning the environment, deciding and acting, acquiring performance feedback, reflecting and modifying behavior—may require costly trial-and-error efforts to improve performance. This slow process can be short-circuited by patterning one's own activities after observations of others' behaviors and their consequences. Some firms merely copy their competitors' products, using "reverse-engineering" to dissect gadgets and rebuild them with slight variations to avoid copyright or patent infringement. A notorious example was the cloning of IBM personal computers by startup firms, which eventually drove Big Blue out of that market segment. Most effective vicarious learning transcends unreflective imitation or avoidance, instead entailing collective filtration through symbolic representations and social interpretations of multiple potential meanings embedded in the observed behaviors (Peteraf and Shanley 1997). Actors tend to fall back on their customary framing and labeling habits to decipher the cause-and-effect connections between actions and their consequences, thus biasing the lessons derived from vicarious learning toward preconceived directions.

Whether learning cycles occur directly or vicariously, the more strongly that prior learning is cumulatively reinforced and encapsulated in organizational routines, the more difficulty firms experience in acquiring new routines through future learning. Organizational ecology theorists conceptualized this resistance to change as a structural inertia that prevented firms from changing quickly enough to survive abrupt alterations in environmental conditions such as technological inventions, shifting market demand, or political realignments. Instead of learning how to adjust their core forms and functions, many companies succumbed to overwhelming external selection forces, disappearing either through disbanding or absorption by competitors (see Chapter 3).

In contrast, the power and resource dependence perspectives emphasized the potential for some firms to survive and prosper by adapting to altered conditions. Although large organizations controlling substantial economic and political resources could exert some influence over their environments, organizational learning presumably also improved their capabilities of breaking the chains of conventional routines. Organizations might hire new employees versed in the latest technologies while retraining their older ones, restructure corporate practices under the tutelage of management consultants experienced at turning around troubled firms, and actively pursue strategic alliances with other companies with the aim of learning new production and administrative techniques. A central theoretical issue for evolutionary theory was to determine under what conditions selection or adaptation processes would more likely effect organizational change and the relative contributions of learning to either outcomes.

Learning theorists proposed several fundamental forms or styles of learning with contrary implications for successful organizational change (see reviews in Huber 1991; Dodgson 1993; Yeung et al. 1999). Chris Argyris and Donald Schön (1978, 1996) introduced a distinction between single- and double-loop organizational learning. In single-loop learning, an organization processed internal and external information about how well or poorly it performed under current circumstances, taking the firm's goals and values for granted. A firm adjusted its routine actions to achieve or maintain some targeted performance level, such as quality products or market share. Using data on machinery downtime, scrappage, and flow-through rates, production engineers could detect errors and modify factory operations to improve output levels. After rolling out a new operating procedure, firms often experienced dramatic productivity gains revealed by learning curve patterns, that is, the number of hours of labor needed to produce a unit of output, which usually fall at decelerating rates as total output rises. For example, businesses as diverse as jet aircraft manufacturers and pizza franchises typically exhibited downward-sloping learning curves indicative of fewer quality complaints and late deliveries, respectively, as they gained experience (Argote 1999:8–9). Organizational learning rates, varying tremendously across firms, were a major source of competitive advantage through reducing costs and raising quality. An important explanatory goal was identifying the internal and environmental causes of this variation. However, the short-term, incremental performance improvements revealed by organizational learning curves occurred within a stable framework of unchallenged assumptions about company goals, values, and routines. They did little to prepare an organization for long-term changes vital to survival and prosperity.

By contrast, double-loop learning reassesses core assumptions about organizational missions and their underlying values and beliefs. It not only facilitates periodic evaluations of how a firm is performing in relation to its goals, but also stimulates exceptional challenges to the very validity of those goals. By confronting inconsistencies between organizational purposes and the objectives motivating first-loop learning, "double-loop learning allows the organization to be more flexible in the face of future changes by suggesting alternative causal theories and by augmenting the repertoire of actions that an organization possesses" (Thomas, Gioia and Ketchen 1997:309). An organization's culture might either fail or regenerate by disclosing contradictions, such as irreconcilable pressures to turn short-term profits and the need for longer-term investments. To shake General Electric out of its bureaucratic business-as-usual rut during the downsizing 1980s, CEO Jack Welch launched a "Workout" program that forced everyone to question how the firm was conducting its diverse businesses (Kanter, Stein and Jick 1992:430–431). Holding hundreds of town meetings throughout the company over two years, three day-long Workout sessions required small groups of GE managers and employees from diverse ranks and functions to criticize conventional practices and to make collective recommendations for changes, with protection from retribution and immediate managerial feedback on their proposed actions (Stewart 1991). This massive organizational learning effort formed a vital part of Welch's larger restructuring strategy that transformed GE into a lean conglomerate striving to be first or second in each of its diverse industries.

Intimately related to the tensions inherent in single- and double-loop learning is the competition within organizations to control scarce resources for exploiting existing opportunities or for exploring new possibilities (March 1991). This allocation choice is usually depicted as a zero-sum tradeoff, between either implementing and refining existing routines to increase the firm's immediate financial returns or investing in innovative efforts leading to the creation of alternative technologies and administrative practices that might increase its future returns. In evolutionary conceptualizations of change, greater exploration generates variation in organizational populations, and increased exploitation boosts a firm's chances of selection. "Effective selection among forms, routines, or practices is essential to survival, but so also is the generation of new alternative practices, particularly in a changing environment" (p. 73). Finding an appropriate balance between these two processes is tricky because over-emphasizing one learning style relative to the other may lead to maladaptive outcomes. On the one hand, organizations that successfully pursue excessive exploitation run a risk of falling into competency traps, that is, becoming increasingly efficient at using specialized technologies that eventually become obsolete (Levitt and March 1988:322). On the other hand, concentrating exclusively on exploratory learning risks fails to derive the full benefits from each invention. For decades, Japanese and Korean electronics companies enjoyed many exploitative successes by rapidly commercializing products developed from the basic research discoveries of U.S. firms, such as transistors, semiconductors, and digital recording. Belatedly, the U.S. electronics industry learned to extract greater mercantile value from its exploratory capabilities.

One difficulty in striking a viable balance between exploitation and exploration lies in asymmetries of each strategy's potential payoffs over time. The consequences of exploitation yield relatively more certain, quick, and reliable organizational rewards than the less-predictable returns from experimenting with new ideas, markets, and relationships (March 1991:74). March's simulation studies of mutual individual-organizational learning demonstrated that these tradeoffs were affected by contextual features such as cost-benefit arrangements and ecological interactions. In a simulated closed organization, high rates of learning resulted in individuals quickly becoming more homogeneous with respect to common knowledge (socialization to the organization's "code of beliefs"). Slower learning rates sustained higher variability within the organization by allowing "for greater exploration of possible alternatives and greater balance in the development of specialized competences" (p. 80). In an open organization, levels of knowledge about the organizational code deteriorated with higher environmental turbulence but stabilized at moderate levels when individual turnover brought in new participants whose beliefs differed from the code. March interpreted these results as prescribing optimal change rates for achieving a balance between exploitation and exploration:

> Mutual learning leads to convergence between organizational and individual beliefs. The convergence is generally useful both for individuals and the organization. However, a major threat to the effectiveness of such learning is the possibility that individuals will adjust to an organizational code before the code can learn from them. Relatively slow socialization of new organizational members and moderate turnover sustain variability in individual beliefs, thereby improving organizational and average individual knowledge in the long run. (March 1999:85)

Future researchers will have to discover whether these simulation outcomes also occurred inside real organizations engaged in creating and commercializing innovative products. The exploration-exploitation dilemma conveyed different implications for population-level learning processes, as discussed in the next section.

Population-Level Learning

In contrast to learning occurring primarily inside individual organizations, learning processes operating at the population level also shape organizational evolution. Anne Miner and Pamela Haunschild (1995:118) defined *population-level learning* as "systematic change in the nature and mix of organizational action routines in a population of organizations, arising from experience." An entire collection of organizations acquires some new routine as a consequences of interorganizational contacts and shared exposure to key events. Such changes might arise through selective imitation, when organizations within a population copy and retain one another's useful routines, similar to the contagious diffusion in a viral epidemic. Alternatively, learning also occurs when the entire population itself acquires a new collective routine. For example, in the communications technology explosion at the end of the twentieth century, many firms found themselves unable to connect their new devices to other companies' products to create a reliable, user-friendly information-processing network. Consequently, telecommunication and computer corporations formed several consortia and committees with sufficient expertise and authority to iron out company differences and develop common standards for this population's members. The Enterprise Computer Telephony Forum brought together more than a hundred companies—including such key international players as AT&T, British Telecom, Fujitsu, Nokia, Novell, Siemens, and Sun Microsystems—

to promote interoperability agreements among the members' diverse approaches (Edwards 1996). Over time, the information-organization population's cumulating experiences in creating and successfully enacting many standards forums enabled this population to acquire a collective routine for dealing with shared problems arising from the rapid pace of innovation at the firm level.

Population-level learning may occur through a variety of mechanisms corresponding to the selection process of evolutionary theory (Miner and Haunschild 1995:137–149). Fundamental processes for transmitting population routines include:

- *Mimetic organizational interaction,* in which other population members copy or imitate a new routine invented or somehow acquired by one organization. Contact transmission involves direct communication with such sources as interlocking directors, professional and social networks, and public statements delivered by company personnel. Researchers lack clear evidence about whether populations mainly copy routines believed to produce useful outcomes or only those known to be successful.

- *Broadcast transmission,* in which a single source such as a peak association or governmental agency diffuses new practices or structures to a target population. For example, federal equal opportunity and affirmative action guidelines prompted the widespread adoption of particular personnel routines designed to protect firms from employee lawsuits charging sex, race, and age discrimination (see Chapter 8).

- *Population leaning of routines* that cannot be executed by a single organization, hence requiring cooperative interaction among organizations. Examples include the "creation of industry associations, of standards boards, of lobbying groups, research consortia, or tacit pricing collusion" (Miner and Haunschild 1995:146). These supra-organizational bodies typically lack coercive power over their members, so must operate via consensus and persuasion to diffuse new routines to the population.

Not all population-level learning experiences prove beneficial over the long run. The "Red Queen" effect (Van Valen 1973; Barnett and Hansen 1996), named after Lewis Carroll's *Through the Looking Glass* character who ran very fast yet never advanced, refers to reciprocal learning among competing populations. In a cyclical co-evolutionary arms race, all populations incrementally change in a never-ending contest merely to sustain their level of environmental fitness. A population experiencing longer and more intense direct competition is itself more likely to become a stronger competitor. The timing of population learning may also contribute to its chances for survival and prosperity (Miner and Haunschild 1995:130–133). Some populations acquire new routines too early or too late to contribute to performance improvements for their member organizations. For example, when firms from different nations compete, one national organizational population may too quickly lock into a technologically inferior routine, while its competitor populations avoid that trap by waiting to see which dominant standard emerges. The Japanese electronic industry's losing bet on Betamax video cassette recorders remains a paradigm of inappropriate population learning.

The population-level learning approach to change eclectically draws many concepts and principles from institutionalist, ecological, network, and evolutionary theories (Miner and Mezias 1996; Miner and Anderson 1999). In particular, it is compatible with the familiar variation-selection-retention cycle posited by general evolutionary models. However, population learning theorists emphasize different dimensions than the other approaches; for example, they stress organizational rationality more than the institutionalists and are less concerned with changing organizational form than the ecologists. Moreover, by calling attention to the co-evolution of routines and organizations, population-level learning directs researchers toward differences with organizational learning processes. Distinct dynamics can produce divergent outcomes at the organizational and population levels. In particular, "populations of organizations may be less likely to drift towards excessive exploitation of past learning, and more likely to drift towards excessive exploration of new learning, than individual organizations" (Miner and Haunschild 1995:160). Because populations typically lack a cohesive hierarchical authority structure, their member organizations collectively face few effective constraints and incentives to inhibiting radically new ideas and adopting highly risky routines. The main obstacles are selection processes in competitive markets that ultimately prune out the more inept and unlucky population members.

Initial empirical efforts to test population-level learning hypotheses concentrated more on simulation and case studies (e.g., Ginsberg, Larsen and Lomi 1999; Anderson 1999b) than analyses of large comparative data sets (e.g., Baum and Ingram 1998). A good exemplar of the latter method was a study of mimetic transfers of routines among 2,506 U.S. radio stations in 160 local markets between 1984 and 1992 (Greve 1999; also Greve 1996). Stations owned by a branch system (i.e., a nonlocal broadcasting network) were more likely than single-market stations to serve as conduits for imitative learning of new programming formats over long geographic distances. Affiliation with a branch system increased a station's audience share, as measured by Arbitron reports, probably reflecting the greater resources

provided by such systems or their acquisition of successful independent sta
tions. However, audience share fell with a system's longer experience in op
erating its current stations outside the local market following the Reagan
Administration's 1980 streamlining of governmental regulations. "This negative effect shows that transfers of routines occur but that this long-distance
learning is harmful to the branch's performance" (Greve 1999:74). Only
replicated research will demonstrate whether similarly inappropriate transfers of routines across local contexts also occur within other organizational
populations whose corporations operate extensive branch systems.

Innovator Organizations

The dual paired concepts of exploitation/exploration and single-/double-
loop learning imply a continuum between *reproducer organizations*, which
import and adapt existing technologies and practices developed elsewhere,
and *innovator organizations*, which create significant departures from
known routines (Aldrich 1999:80). Because their small sizes and constrained market positions imposed unrelenting struggles for survival, the
large majority of U.S. organizations lacked adequate resources to engage in
extensive double-loop and exploratory learning activities. Consequently,
they concentrated on more efficient exploitation of existing technologies
and managerial practices, trying to wring smidgens of competitive advantage by more cleverly applying known processes. Two types of organizations made up the innovator minority capable of sustaining exploratory
learning: small startup companies whose entrepreneurs willingly undertook
huge risks on unproven technologies, and large corporations, such as 3M
and Hewlett-Packard, which possessed sufficient slack resources to sustain
systematic research and development efforts. Although relatively few of
these endeavors paid off in major discoveries and inventions that dramatically transformed the organizational landscape, such innovator organizations probably created the preponderance of radical advances deemed the
most powerful drivers of evolutionary change.

Innovations are primary sources of the variation on which the basic evolutionary processes of selection and retention operate in changing organizations. In its broadest definition, an innovation is any departure from existing technologies or managerial practices (Kimberly 1981). Innovations
range from minor tweaking of standard operating procedures to key discoveries and inventions whose applications transform entire civilizations,
such as steam-powered machines, which launched the Industrial Revolution; the moving assembly line, which made products cheaply available to
mass consumer markets; and Post-it notes, which reminded us to pick up
the dry cleaning. Recent major innovations include high-performance

ctices (see Chapter 5), the Internet, and wireless communica-
which dramatically overhauled manufacturing, consumption,
activities.

technical and administrative innovations involve only modest, in-
al adjustments that comfortably fit into ongoing organizational
res and processes. However, technological breakthroughs or discon-
ues, "innovations that dramatically advance an industry's price versus
ormance frontier," often trigger periods of organizational turmoil that
minate only when a new dominant design emerges (Anderson and Tush-
nan 1990:604). Historical comparisons of technological cycles in the cement, glass, and minicomputer industries revealed that both the duration of
turmoil and the type of firm instigating a standard design were conditional
on how the discontinuity affected existing competencies. An innovation
might build on or destroy organizations' technological advantages: New
entrants into an industry inaugurated competence-destroying breakthroughs; established firms initiated competence-enhancing breakthroughs.
Established organizations were threatened by competence-destroying innovations requiring them to abandon their known skill bases and routines,
while the new entrants were unencumbered by commitments to old know-
how. The researchers concluded that similar technological cycles shaped the
course of organizational evolution:

> As technology evolves, organizations are faced again and again with a set of
> recurring challenges: pioneering or being threatened by substitute technology;
> adopting some version of a breakthrough innovation in the face of extraordi-
> nary rates of variation; recognizing, shaping, or adopting an emerging stan-
> dard; surviving in an environment in which technology advances incrementally
> and competitive advantage depends on continuous improvement instead of
> novelty. (Anderson and Tushman 1990:628)

The prevalence of such traumatic innovations should not be exaggerated.
Only 16 technological discontinuities occurred during the 203 industry-
years studied by Anderson and Tushman. Most innovations were minor,
competence-enhancing developments that could be easily integrated into
existing organizational operations. But the relatively rare breakthrough innovations were primarily responsible for disruptive quantum leaps in the
evolutionary trajectory of an industry. Innovative discontinuities spawned
the "perennial gales of creative destruction" in entrepreneurial capitalism,
identified more than half a century ago by the Austrian economist Joseph
Schumpeter. Macro-economic transformations never arose from micro level
streams of incremental changes, but only through equilibrium-displacing
innovations that forever altered the very system giving them birth: "Add

successively as many mail coaches as you please, and you will never get a railway thereby" (Schumpeter 1942:64).

Given the critical importance of innovator organizations, uncovering the essential details of their innovative processes is vital for understanding how they contribute to evolutionary dynamics and, hence, for understanding organizational change. Analysts frequently depicted an innovation (from the Latin *novus*, meaning new) as following an orderly life cycle of clearly defined stages through which all innovator organizations pass in precise sequence, with success or failure as the ultimate outcome. For example, Hage (1980:209–210) posited four steps of evaluation, initiation, implementation and routinization, and Rogers (1995) described a linear sequence of invention, development, production, testing, diffusion, and adoption. However, case studies of organizational innovations often revealed more complex and messier progressions. Based on comparisons among the 14 MIRP longitudinal studies, Van de Ven et al. (1999) developed an empirically grounded, generic model of the *innovation journey*, which they defined as a "nonlinear cycle of divergent and convergent activities that may repeat over time and at different organizational levels if resources are obtained to renew the cycle" (p. 16). Divergence involved exploratory behaviors expanding in various directions; convergent behaviors integrated and narrowed exploitation in a specific direction. Both phases were "enabled by resource investments and are constrained by external rules and internal discovery of an organizational arrangement and the infusion of resources from external sources" (p. 186). As summarized in Table 10.1, the innovation journey consisted of three broad periods (initiation, development, and implementation/termination), each involving several activities among various participants. Despite its sequential appearance, the innovation journey entailed nonlinear learning processes, through discovery under divergent, chaotic conditions and through testing under more stable, convergent conditions (p. 203). Detailed case studies of three innovations indicated that the analytical model captured core processes that were fundamentally equivalent across differing organizational structures and settings.

Although successful intentional innovations provide substantial variations for evolutionary selection, the chosen variations either must be retained or die out in an organizational population. Various intra- and interorganizational networks shape the process of diffusion of new technologies and administrative practices from a few innovator organizations to vaster numbers of reproducer organizations that exploitatively replicate and adapt these outputs to their own contexts. Barriers inhibiting the spread of innovations and transfer of complex knowledge include the strength of inter-unit ties (Hansen 1999), cutthroat market competition, bureaucratically centralized control structures, incompatible organizational

TABLE 10.1 Common Elements in the Innovation Process

THE INITIATION PHASE

1. Gestation in extended period lasting several years
2. Shocks from internal and external sources trigger concenrated efforts
3. Plans developed and submitted to controllers for resources to launch development

THE DEVELOPMENTAL PHASE

4. Proliferation of numerous ideas and activities on divergent, parallel, convergent paths
5. Setbacks and mistakes cause resource and development time lines to diverge
6. Shifting succes-failure criteria trigger power struggles between project managers and resource controllers
7. Innovation personnel participate in highly fluid, emotionally charged ways
8. Investors and top management frequently involved as checks-and-balances
9. Relationships with other organizations lock innovation units into specific action courses with unintended consequences
10. Involvement with competitors, trade associations, government agencies to create supportive infrastructure

THE IMPLEMENTATION/TERMINATION PHASE

11. Adoption of innovation by linking, integrating new and old or fitting innovation to local situation
12. Termination by implementing innovations or when resources run out

SOURCE: Based on Van de Ven et al. (1999:23–25)

cultures, and legal restrictions on intellectual property (patents and copyrights). An innovation's ultimate success may depend less on any intrinsic technical merits than on the likelihood that subsequent innovations will build on its foundations. The more intense the competition within the technological niche an innovation occupies, the lower its chances for survival (Podolny and Stuart 1995; Stuart 1998). Among the chief cooperative mechanisms for interorganizational learning and sharing are strategic alliances, consortia, personnel movements between firms (Aldrich 1999:31), industry conventions and conferences (Argote 1999:180), information clearinghouses, trade and professional associations ("communities of practice"), and informal communication ties among top management teams.

A Vision, Instead
of a Conclusion

Prospects for changing organizations in the twenty-first century emanate from the diverse twentieth-century trends of business, work, and politics examined in the preceding chapters of this book. Right up to the spring 2000 meltdown of NASDAQ dot.com stocks, business gurus and popular media raved about the imminent birth of a "New Economy." It was supposedly midwived by miraculous computing and communication technologies; clicks-and-mortar Internet e-commerce; and hyper-connected global trade routes that were radically transforming how people managed businesses, performed jobs, elected leaders, enjoyed family life, and pursued leisure activities. Many utopian speculations erroneously posited massive ruptures with past practices and institutions. But the fundamental economic laws of supply and demand were never suspended, nor have product markets and business cycles vanished, nor will legal protections of private property be repealed; governments cannot ignore their constituents' vital interests; and businesses will not soon abandon their primary goal of turning a profit. Whatever new political economy eventually emerges will most likely involve an evolutionary slouch toward a subsequent system that bears a strong resemblance to its predecessor. Therefore, like the two-faced Roman god Janus, we must continually gaze upon the past for clues about future directions of changing organizations.

Twentieth-century Americans witnessed numerous remarkable shifts in the sizes and shapes of organizational forms. Small-family proprietorships gave way to gigantic multidivisional corporations operating in nationwide markets, industrial districts preserved protective niches for small artisans, multi-industry conglomerates rose and fell, downsizing firms retrenched toward core competencies, strategic alliances and joint ventures proliferated, and networked organizations constructed permeable boundaries that blurred the distinctions between organizations and environments. Successively cresting waves of mergers and acquisitions consolidated large enterprises in most industries, surrounded by diffuse small-firm networks thriving on business-to-business services. The steady global advance of multinational firms eroded the distinctions between U.S., European, and Japanese companies, binding the world ever more tightly in webs of commerce and a creeping consumer culture.

The employment contract between firms and their employees shifted from traditional, almost paternalistic, lifetime job security toward more market-driven labor relations. Career patterns increasingly involved contingent arrangements, creating divisions between privileged permanent employees and temporary workers. Flexible workplace designs emphasized short-term projects, self-managed team work, and peer social control. These arrangements required high levels of worker commitment and loyalty, incompatible with the apathy and anxiety fostered by the new employment contract. Innovative high-performance workplaces promised to boost productivity using potent sociotechnical systems, but socioeconomic barriers limited their diffusion in most organizations. In an increasingly uncertain corporate arena, mentoring and networking assumed greater importance for both employee career advancement and company performance. Social capital, embedded in networks of interpersonal ties, differentially benefited or disadvantaged male, female, white, and minority employees. Organizations faced dilemmas of designing fair and effective human resources policies and procedures to motivate every employee to exert peak effort.

The legal foundations of organizational continuity seemed to reach a mature form, yet some elements appeared ill-adapted to the changing political economy. Legal doctrines enshrined the primacy of shareholder wealth-maximization as the paramount corporate objective. The separation of ownership from managerial control in publicly held corporations transferred real power to top management. Although boards of directors legally represented their companies' interests, chief executive officers effectively retained informational advantages in corporate governance. But widening disconnections between firm performance and CEO pay, new legal concepts of stakeholder rights, and institutional investor revolts tested corporate leaders' political survival skills. Social movements challenging managerial prerogatives erupted periodically within the lower ranks, as various identity groups asserted their claims to more equitable treatment. Over the century, labor unions gained public legitimacy, organized a substantial portion of the U.S. labor force, then steadily declined in membership and political clout. A feisty business community fought back, blunting the employee-empowerment thrust of anti-discrimination and due process laws. Progressive legalization of the workplace evolved into management tools to control the workplace by shunting worker complaints into individualized resolutions.

The U.S. national political system became frozen in an increasingly dysfunctional framework, where legal campaign bribes cast growing public doubt on the acceptability of electoral, lobbying, and legislative processes and their outcomes. Both major parties amassed swollen soft-money war chests from corporate, labor, and other interest-group political action committees. Some observers alleged that a ruling class of wealthy families and corporations dominated public policymaking to their direct benefit; others saw more equitable and pliant struggles for transitory access and influence. In specific policy domains, information networking and short-term coalitions among political organizations mobilized and applied diverse political tactics to cajole incremental policy decisions from politicians worried about their re-election chances. Although scant convincing evidence overtly connected campaign contributions to subsequent policy decisions, public qualms about legal political bribery might ultimately jeopardize the democratic system's legitimacy.

As the world entered the twenty-first century, the pace of organizational change seemed poised to accelerate. With global markets expanding and national political boundaries crumbling, inflexible organizations grew increasingly vulnerable to discontinuities arising from complex, turbulent environments. Heightened interdependencies increased the importance of social networks, knowledge, and trust relationships to coordinate the actions of people and organizations. Knowledge-creating and learning organizations and populations gained comparative advantages over their competitors in the struggle to survive and flourish. Prospective innovations in information processing and communication heralded an imminent explosion of devices and applications that would compel organizations to restructure how they managed their workplaces and their methods of operating. One fascinating vision of transformed information infrastructures, based on a hardware and software system called Oxygen under development at MIT's Laboratory for Computing Science and Artificial Intelligence Lab, was sketched by its long-term director (Dertouzos 1999). At Oxygen's core was an integrated collection of eight technologies: a multipurpose handheld device combining the functions of cell phone, computer, visual display, camera, and infrared detector; office wall and car trunk computers to regulate sensors, controllers, phones, fax machines, cameras, and microphones; a novel net to connect collaborators and devices wherever they may be physically located; built-in speech understanding for human-machine communication; knowledge access to search, extract, and triangulate information from the Web; automation of routine and repetitive tasks onto electronic "bulldozers"; collaboration technology to track tasks as they progress; and customization technology to tailor information to individual needs and habits. By unchaining workers and customers from desktop machines, Oxygen technologies could become "the foundations on which any new activities that help us do more by doing less will be built. For the next few decades at least, they are the steering wheel, the gas pedal and the brakes we seek—as well as the forces leading to a full-fledge Information Marketplace" (Dertouzos 1999:53). Whether this particular technological vision materializes, or some alternative system takes root, is less relevant to understanding future organizational trends. Far more puzzling is how such

intentional innovation designs nonetheless propel the trajectories of organizational change in unpredictable new directions.

A central challenge for all students of organizational change is how best
to concentrate our full array of theories and empirical methods on explaining how and why various macro level transformations occur. The theoretical principles and research results discussed throughout this book highlight
some broad conclusions, albeit inferences that must remain more tentative
than definitive. Given the vast array of socioeconomic and political forces
impinging on organizations, the sources of their actions and outcomes are
extremely complex, often chaotic, and largely unpredictable. Nevertheless,
intellectual efforts to understand organizational change despite the inherent
impossibility of making accurate forecasts remains a valuable collective research objective. Macro level organizational changes are neither wholly
random nor entirely incomprehensible, particularly in retrospect and in
broad outline.

Rather than falling for the specious illusion that organization studies
could uncover precisely quantified natural laws forming an organizational
physics and chemistry, the optimal model to adopt is the metaphor of undi-
rected biological evolution. In biology, future transformations of an organic
species depend heavily on interactions between randomly changing natural
environmental conditions and the chance genetic mutations that generate
sufficient variations for natural processes to select optimally fit new creatures. Similarly, transformations of organizational populations are most ap-
propriately conceptualized as interactions involving the unpredictably
changing political economy with autonomous technological and administrative innovations that yield new organizational forms and behaviors better fit to the altered environment. Explaining the appearance of new biological species also requires detailed knowledge of chemical and physical
processes at the cellular and molecular levels of analysis. Analogously, constructing a comprehensive account of macro-organizational change requires that analysts apply multilevel, multidisciplinary methods to uncover
the underlying dynamic processes.

Organization theories are our collective intellectual tools for understanding and explaining organizational change. In emphasizing organizational
ecology, institutionalism, resource dependence, transaction cost economics,
and especially network analysis, I have acclaimed these theories' many contributions to our knowledge of organizational change. By directing analytical attention to a small number of core concepts and relationships, each
perspective empowers its adherents to isolate, from a welter of unique historical events, a handful of key principles pertaining to organizational
structures and actions. But a dangerous disadvantage lurks in the temptation to stress one theoretical approach to the exclusion of all others. Like
small children with shiny new hammers, scholars engrossed in an exciting

theory come to believe that everything needs the same academic pounding. The results are as likely to be shattered data as cumulative knowledge. Throughout this book, I have assumed that no single theory could comprehensively account for everything of interest and importance to investigators of tangled organizational events. My reading and interpretation of the insights gathered by hundreds of thinkers, toiling diligently in dozens of theoretical vineyards, has convinced me that significant advances in understanding organizational change demand familiarity with and appreciation of many alternative viewpoints. Organization studies undoubtedly still lacks the collective wisdom to integrate its numerous theoretical approaches into an encompassing framework. But unless organization students keep that ultimate objective in mind, we will neglect significant opportunities to achieve dramatic gains in theoretical vigor to guide our empirical labors.

I close by observing that the adjective "corporate," which figured so prominently throughout this book, applies equally to business organizations and to communal groups. After all, its Latin origins merely refer to a body. Unfortunately, contemporary corporations too often behave as though they have neither hearts nor souls. My fervent hope is that, for everyone struggling to achieve some measure of dignity and freedom as moral agents in a world increasingly dominated by corporate actors, changing organizations will ultimately infuse that adjective with its other meaning.

Appendix:
Basic Network Concepts

In this appendix I briefly review some basic ideas in network analysis of social relationships, including core concepts and principles, data collection procedures, and methods of analysis. I provide brief substantive illustrations of these ideas, using research examples from both the individual and organizational levels of analysis. This nontechnical introduction should provide readers with sufficient vocabulary to understand the network structures and processes discussed in this volume. For extensive technical and substantive reviews of network analysis, consult Knoke and Kuklinski (1982), Burt and Minor (1983), Mizruchi (1994), Brass (1995), Wasserman and Galaskiewicz (1994), and Wasserman and Faust (1994). This appendix is a revision of portions appearing in Knoke (1999).

Identifying Actors
and System Boundaries

Networks are social constructions arising from the continual exchanges and joint activities among participants in a social system, defined as a "plurality of actors interacting on the basis of a shared symbol system" (Parsons 1951:19). The recurrent pattern of relations connecting the actors constitutes that system's social structure. The actors belonging to a network may be designated at varying levels of analysis: individuals (children in a kindergarten class); small groups (work teams on an automobile assembly line); formal organizations (corporations in a business association); coalitions (lobbying alliances); even nations (members of the World Trade Organization). More complex network structures may bring together actors from multiple levels of analysis, for example, connecting individual patients, nurses, and physicians with the emergency room, maternity ward, laboratory, and housekeeping units of a community hospital.

Identifying the boundaries of a social system, and hence its size, requires the researcher to specify which potential members must be considered relevant or irrelevant to the social system's functioning. An investigator using a *nominalist* strategy typically achieves conceptual closure by including all actors that possess one or more key characteristics (Laumann, Marsden and Prensky 1983). Nominal designations often restrict network membership to incumbents occupying formal positions, for example, to directors of the Fortune 500 companies or middle managers at Apple Computer. Involvement in particular activities may also define the boundary, as in Laumann and Knoke's (1987:97–98) stipulation that the U.S. energy or health policy domains' core organizations participate in five or more legislative, judicial, mass media, or lobbying events. The contrasting *realist* approach to boundary specification assumes that system participants themselves can best identify who belongs and who is excluded. Uncovering the subjective meanings that network participants consciously experience requires the researcher to designate "a substantively defined criterion of mutual relevance or common orientation among a set of consequential actors" (Knoke and Laumann 1982:256). Typically, potential network members carry out a reputational evaluation that ranks the other actors according to their importance to the system's performance. Actors enjoying high reputations, indicating that their peers believe they must be taken into account, are included, but actors with low or no reputations are dropped because of their marginal impact on the system.

The nominal and real approaches may be combined to ensure that no crucial system participants are omitted. For example, to study the power elite in a medium-sized German city, researchers conducted an initial canvass that located leaders by their top positions in six institutional sectors (Pappi 1984). This list was then reduced by asking a panel of knowledgeable "sector experts" to designate which leaders were most important in community affairs. Finally, the researchers asked these 78 leaders to supplement the target list with names of influential persons they felt had been omitted. Only two new persons received three or more nominations, indicating that the project had reached closure on the community power structure's boundary.

Total and
Ego-Centric Networks

If a social system encompasses a small number of actors, researchers may be able to obtain information about the relations linking all system participants, making up a *total network*. "Small" in this context means anywhere from a dozen to several hundred actors. Mariolis (1975) compiled data on board of director interlocks among the 797 top U.S. enterprises in 1969. Knoke et al. (1996) gathered network data on various types of interactions among the 117, 126, and 122 peak organizations in the U.S., German, and Japanese labor policy domains, respectively. A basic requirement for reconstructing a total network among N actors is that each actor be able to report on the presence or absence of a tie to all other system members, typically by checking a previously compiled list (see example questionnaires for the U.S. energy and health domains reprinted in Laumann and Knoke 1987:401–500).

Some social systems are either too large or too weakly connected for researchers to attempt to collect completed network ties among all members. In such instances, the only feasible alternative is to draw a representative sample from the target population and to elicit the direct network ties of each sampled actor (an *ego-centric network*). For example, a high-tech firm studied by Burt (1992) employed 3,303 managers below the vice-presidential level. Because these managers had few direct or indirect connections to most other managers, the appropriate research design was to sample 547 managers and ask about their personal social and work-related sociometric ties (Burt 1992:119). In contrast to the total-network method of listing all system actors, the ego-net procedure identifies a unique set of *network alters*, typically through a self-administered name-generator protocol (see the example reprinted in Burt 1992:123). The respondent first writes down the names of the most important people with whom a specific type of interaction occurred during a particular time. Then, the informant ego describes each alter's key attributes, such as age and gender, the nature of her ties to each alter (e.g., closeness and frequency of contacts), as well as her beliefs about which alters have direct ties among themselves. Importantly, because the alters named by ego are not subsequently interviewed, ego's self-reported information remains unconfirmed. The ego-net approach is the only plausible network methodology for general population surveys (Marsden 1987) and large samples of diverse organizations (Kalleberg, Knoke and Marsden 1995).

Operationalizing a network depends on actors reporting about all their *dyadic* (pairwise) links to all other system actors. Subsequently, both ego-centric and total networks can be reconstructed by aggregating the information from all these dyadic connections. Because the number of dyads expands geometrically with network size, analysts face practical constraints on the size of any network they can expect to obtain. A system of N actors contains $(N^2 - N)$ dyads (not counting self-ties); for example, a 100-actor network has 9,900 dyads, while a 1,000-actor system contains nearly a million pairings. Respondent fatigue places realistic limits on their ability and willingness to report about their potential connections within a total network. Although informants will usually read and check off a list containing a few dozen or even a hundred names, they might balk when confronted with a task of several hours' duration. Similarly, when solicited for their ego-networks with the name-generator method, respondents might readily supply a dozen alters but be unable to comply with instructions to identify a hundred casual acquaintances. If analysts seek to collect data about several relational contents (see the following subsection), these repetitions will further reduce the size of the network that the researchers can reasonably expect to operationalize.

Network
Relational Contents

After determining where to draw network boundaries and how many actors to include, the next task is to decide what type of substantive relationship to measure. A network's *relational content*, sometimes called its *type of tie*, refers to a relatively homogeneous linkage among the actors. For example, "neighboring" ties might be operationalized as homeowners lending tools to one another; "advising" could be construed as task assistance between office workers. Most broadly, relational contents seem to fall into two general categories, transactions and joint actions. A *transaction* is an exchange in which one actor yields rights of control over some physical commodity or intangible value to another actor, often in expectation of eventual reciprocation. A giver's loss of control may be temporary (e.g., loaning weekend use of one's cabin to a friend) or permanent (e.g., physicians donating services to a low-income clinic). *Joint actions* require actors to participate together in an event located in specific time and space, but do not require relinquishing control over resources to others. A minimal connection is mere co-presence, for example, software firms attending the annual Las Vegas COMDEX trade fair. More intense joint activity involves coordinated efforts to achieve a common goal, for example, lobbying the Congress in support of or opposition to legislative proposals (Knoke et al. 1996).

An analyst's choice of which type of network content to investigate should be guided by the project's theoretical objectives: What substantive relationship does the researcher expect to find useful for understanding important actor and system behaviors? In practice, *multiplex ties* link social actors into complex webs, necessitating an a priori decision about which network contents to operationalize and which ones to ignore. Consequently, no such creature as "the network" exists among a set of actors. Instead, different networks may be operationalized for differing analytical objectives, and more than one type of relational content may be gathered by a single project. Stating universally valid criteria about which contents will prove valuable for all purposes is a futile exercise. Instead, researchers' selections ultimately depend on their detailed knowledge of the particular phenomena they seek to explain.

Magnitude of Ties

At the same time that network informants report about their dyadic ties to other system actors, they indicate the magnitude or value of each tie. At a minimum, only a dichotomous coding — presence (1) or absence (0) of ties — might be recorded; for example, ego checks each name on a list to reveal from whom advice was sought during some period specified by the researcher. The absence of checks for some possible alters yields important data, because network structure depends as much on gaps ("holes") as on direct actor-to-actor connections. More detailed codings of tie magnitude assign scalar values to each existing dyad to reflect the ties' relative strength or weakness. For persons, tie strength usually refers to intensity of commitment to the partner, exemplified by emotional attachments and/or frequency of interactions. For example, a friendship study requested egos to differentiate among their alters as to which people were their "casual," "close," and "best friends" (Leenders 1996). Note that tie-strengths are not necessarily reciprocated for any dyadic choices, especially if respondents' subjective impressions are elicited. Even seemingly "hard" behavioral indicators, such as the frequency of meetings and communications, are notoriously susceptible to recall biases that may connote how salient such events were for each participant. Hence, preserving all potential asymmetries in reported tie-strength (including the special case of present-absent ties) is important for detecting variation in network forms. For organizations, magnitudes of relations may involve highly reliable data, for example, the dollar amount of outstanding loans from commercial banks to manufacturing firms, or the number of a corporation's officers who sit on other companies' boards of directors. Clearly, such transactions and joint activities will rarely be symmetrical, reflecting fundamental role differentiation and power imbalance in interorganizational networks.

Mark Granovetter's classic article, "The Strength of Weak Ties" (1973), discussed the crucial contribution of differential tie magnitudes for social capital processes. Based on sociometric evidence about how men found their jobs, Granovetter's central insight was that a person's most instrumentally valuable connections often are not his strong relationships (such as friendship and kinship circles). Because all participants in these heavily connected local structures already know one another, information quickly circulates and each actor soon knows what everyone else knows. Alternatively, a job-seeker would be more successful by mobilizing his weak ties to reach more socially distant and diversified sets of actors, for example, by forging compound connections enabling him indirectly to traverse social bridges (e.g., contacting the "acquaintances of friends"). These connections enable a person to gain access to potential new sources of information and assistance, more likely leading to a new job. Hence, weak ties actually provide the strongest pathways to one's building social capital. Given the impacted character of strong-tie networks, some researchers condemn mentoring relations as potential career traps for young workers and advocate that employee opportunities be nurtured by active weak-tie networking with diverse associates (Keele 1986).

Another consideration for network data collection is which time frame should be covered: too short and important but infrequent relations may be overlooked; too long and dormant ties might mistakenly be treated as current. Unfortunately, the temporal dimension is not well-integrated into researchers' practices. Most network projects yield static snapshots of a long-established network, without revealing their origins, evolution, and ultimate fates. For example, we have little knowledge about whether informal ties between employees of different companies subsequently generate formal alliances between organizations, or what conditions tend to produce the opposite pattern. Despite evident theoretical payoffs from understanding network dynamics, data collection has not kept pace with recent developments in analysis methods that provide many useful techniques for investigating network changes over time (Wasserman and Iacobucci 1988; Snijders 1996; Frank 1991; Zeggelink 1994; Leenders 1995).

Network Forms

Basic network forms describe elementary properties connecting system actors regardless of their specific relational contents. Most of these concepts pertain to total networks, but some are also applicable to ego-centric nets. Network researchers estimate these descriptive measures using computer programs, such as UCINET and GRADAP, that manipulate chooser-by-chosen matrices containing the dyadic information collected from respondents. As a visual aid to understanding, refer to the hypothetical *graph* and its associated binary *adjacency matrix* in Figure A.1. Think of the {ABCD} subset as a production department whose members are all located in one building, while the {WXYZ} subset is a geographically dispersed sales force. Actors A and W are these units' respective heads. The relational content shown here might be a regular communication relationship regarding work tasks as collected from an organizational survey. In a matrix, each row represents a potential sender and each column a receiver of dichotomous social ties. A "1" entry indicates that the row actor reported sending communication to the receiving column actor, while "0" means that no connection occurred. Graphs depict actors as labeled points and their relations as directed arrows, with the arrowheads pointing from sending actors to receiving targets. Corresponding to the matrix entries, the graph in Figure A.1 shows that every communication tie was reciprocated; hence all 10 arrows are two-headed.

The simplest descriptive measures of system connectedness just count the numbers of ties observed in the network. The network's *volume* is the total number and its *density* is the proportion of observed ties to the number of possible connections

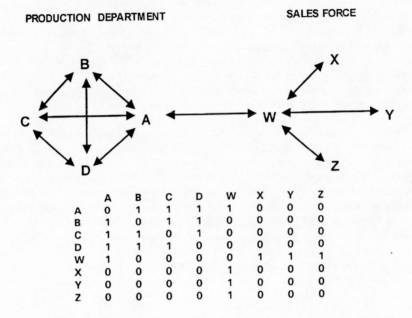

PRODUCTION DEPARTMENT

SALES FORCE

	A	B	C	D	W	X	Y	Z
A	0	1	1	1	1	0	0	0
B	1	0	1	1	0	0	0	0
C	1	1	0	1	0	0	0	0
D	1	1	1	0	0	0	0	0
W	1	0	0	0	0	1	1	1
X	0	0	0	0	1	0	0	0
Y	0	0	0	0	1	0	0	0
Z	0	0	0	0	1	0	0	0

FIGURE A.1.   Graph and Matrix Representations of a Hypothetical Eight-Actor Network

not counting self-ties ($N^2 - N$ for an N-actor system). The example has a volume of 20 ties and a density of $(20/56) = .357$. However, the two work units are internally more connected than the total network: densities of the production department and the sales force are 1.00 and .50, respectively. Volume and density may also be calculated for each actor's ego-centric networks. For example, actor C is directly connected to four alters, all of whom have direct ties to one another; hence, C's ego-net volume = 4 and its density = 1.00. But, W's ego-centered net comprises four alters who have no ties among themselves, yielding ego-net volume = 4 and density = 0.

An actor's degree of *connectedness* to the system can be computed by summing the number of non-zero entries in the matrix's rows (*out-degrees*) and columns (*in-degrees*), or alternatively by counting the number of arrows each point sends or receives. Thus, department heads A and W are the best-connected actors, both having out-degrees and in-degrees = 4; next come B, C, and D with in-degrees = out-degrees = 3, trailed by the dispersed salespeople X, Y, and Z with only one 1 degree of connection via their boss. In general, in-degrees represent an actor's popularity among other system members; out-degrees reflect an actor's tendency toward expansiveness in choosing others. An actor who neither sends nor receives ties with anyone (0 in- and out-degrees) is a social *isolate*, and would appear in a graph as a disconnected point without arrows.

Networks enable actors to become indirectly as well as directly connected to other system participants. A matrix can be successively multiplied by itself to reveal the minimal *path length* required to connect each pair of actors. Visually, a path can be traced by following the directed arrows connecting a given pair of actors, with its length calculated as the number of steps (the sum of intervening direct ties) to connect that dyad. For example, for Z to pass a message to C would require traversing a minimal path of length = 3: (Z-W) + (W-A) + (A-C). The four production members all have 1-paths to each other (direct ties), but the salespeople must use 2-paths to reach one another. The total network is fully connected after three steps: Everyone is *reachable* through paths of length 3 or less. However, if the A-W direct tie were severed, the network would disaggregate into two mutually unreachable groups. The A-W tie forms a *bridge* that ties system actors together. Similarly, actors A and W are *cut points*, because removing either one would disrupt the network's connectivity. In effect, these two leaders can serve as *brokers* who mediate relations between the two units, for example, by coordinating customer orders with schedules of production activities.

These visual observations imply that A and W enjoy unique and powerful roles in the system, an insight confirmed by measures of actor *centrality* (see Freeman 1977, 1979). Basically, a central actor participates in a large volume of social relations, with refined centrality concepts differentiating among the type or "quality" of the connections involved. An actor's power within a network derives from its capacity to reach others or to become a focus of attention of other system members. As discussed above, the simplest centrality measure is an actor's *in-degrees*, measuring the sheer volume of ego-centric contacts received from alters, regardless of their individual situations. *Closeness centrality* captures the extent to which ego maintains connections to many alters who themselves have many non-overlapping ties, thus enabling ego to reach numerous others by paths of relatively short length. In the example, A and W each have the highest closeness scores (70), and B, C, and D enjoy somewhat higher closeness (50 each) than the less-connected X, Y, and Z (43.8 each). *Betweenness centrality* reflects an actor's ability to serve as a go-between who mediates many connections between subgroups, thereby potentially leveraging greater impact on system activities. To the extent that ego serves as a key conduit for brokering inter-alter connections, its power may be disproportionate to its nominal system location. Because the salespeople are less connected than are the production employees, W has a higher betweenness score than does A (15 to 12); the other six actors' betweenness centrality scores are all 0. In addition to ego-level centralities, various global centralization indices permit comparisons of total networks having different numbers of actors.

A final set of network forms involves grouping actors into clusters or *positions* within total networks, leading to simplified depictions of internal structures in terms of the social roles played by subsets of network actors. Two generic approaches involve cohesion (strength of ties) and equivalence (structural, automorphic, regular) criteria. A *clique* is a network subset in which all dyads are maximally connected (all reciprocal direct ties occur, yielding a density of 1.00). By this rigorous definition, only the {ABCD} cluster is a genuine clique. More relaxed stipulations, such as *n-cliques* and *k-plexes*, tolerate lower levels of subgroup densities. For example, {WABCD} and {AWXYZ} are both 2-cliques, because all members in a subset are reachable by two or fewer steps.

Other useful network positions are identified through equivalence principles. Two actors are *structurally equivalent* to the extent that they display identical or very similar patterns of ties to all third alters in the system, regardless of their ties to one another (Sailer 1978). For example, firms in an industry that buy from the same sources and sell to the same customers are fundamentally interchangeable from the market's perspective. In the example, the four equivalent *blocks* are {A}, {W}, {BCD}, and {XYZ}. Rather than displaying the full eight-actor matrix or graph, the reduced structurally equivalent version involves just four positions. Its *blockmodel image*, where "1" indicates all possible ties within or between positions are present and "0" means no intra/inter-positional connections, is:

	A	BCD	W	XYZ
A	1	1	1	0
BCD	1	1	0	0
W	1	0	1	1
XYZ	0	0	1	0

As noted above, although the members of block {BCD} are fully connected among themselves, the {XYZ} position is internally disconnected. A further aggregation, requiring less than complete equivalence, would merge the two department leaders' positions with their respective subordinates' blocks. Positional analyses may reveal a network's underlying competitive structure by identifying blocks whose members may be rivals for the attentions of other positions and those positions that may lack sufficient internal connectivity to undertake collective actions.

Finally, *automorphic equivalence* provides another approach to identifying network positions using isomorphic principles from graph theory (Borgatti and Everett 1992). Network actors i and j are automorphically equivalent if, after removing the "names" of the actors from the nodes, nodes i and j are impossible to distinguish. In the example, the sets of automorphically equivalent actors are {AW}, {BCD}, and {XYZ}. In contrast to structural equivalence, which puts A and W into separate positions because they supervise different individuals, they are automorphically equivalent because they are connected to corresponding others—their work-unit subordinates.

Notes

Chapter 1

1. Calculated from data in World Bank (1999:230–231). The other high-income nations, with per-capita GNP of $7,970 or more, were Argentina, Australia, Austria, Belgium, Canada, Denmark, Finland, Greece, Ireland, Israel, The Netherlands, New Zealand, Norway, Portugal, South Korea, Singapore, Slovenia, Spain, Sweden, and Switzerland.

2. The 8-by-8 matrix of trade flows in U.S. dollars was submitted to the UCINET network software for multidimensional scaling. Data were treated as an asymmetrical similarity matrix, using Gower's classic metric ordination procedure. A two-dimensional solution yielded a fit with a moderately high stress of 0.24. See the Appendix for further details about network analysis principles and methods.

3. Golden (1994:11) provided these average growth rates (percent per year): *Country 1950–73 973–84 1984–90* United States 2.5 1.0 1.0 Germany 6.0 3.0 1.9 Japan 7.7 3.2 3.4

4. Few employers have formal written contracts with their employees, but rely instead on implicit or "psychological contracts" that are open to ambiguity and misunderstandings about standards set and promises kept (Rousseau 1995).

Chapter 2

1. These theories are Administration; Affect-based; Agency; Bounded Rationality; Bureaucracy; Circuits of Power; Coalitional; Cognitive; Comparative Structure; Conflict; Contingency; Cooperative Systems; Cultural; Cybernetic; Decision-Making; Decision-Process; Economic/Market Failure; Economic History; Efficiency-Effectiveness; Enactment; Ethnomethodology; Evolutionary; Expectancy; Feminist; Garbage Can; Goal-Setting; Human Relations; Individual Economic; Institutional; Institutionalist; Language in Organizations; Market; Marxist/Class; Negotiated Order; Network; Operant Conditioning; Organizational Ecology; Organizational Learning; Organizing; Pluralism; Political; Political Economy; Population Ecology; Post-Modernist; Power; Resource Advantage; Resource Dependence; Retrospective Rationality; Role; Scientific Management; Social Constructionist; Social Context; Social Information Process; Social Learning; Socialization; Socio-Technical; Strategic Contingency; Strategic Management; Strategic Process; Strategy-Structure; Structural Contingency; Structural-Functional; Symbolic-Interpretive; Systemic; and Transaction Cost Economics.

Chapter 3

1. *Businesses* are defined as legal or administrative entities that have been assigned an Employer Identification Number (EIN) by the Internal Revenue Service. Units include divisions, subsidiaries, companies, and other affiliated organizations. The SSEL's information on single establishments is updated continuously with employment and payroll data based on payroll tax records and receipts data based on IRS income tax records. Information about multi-unit companies' establishments is updated annually based on a company organization survey and an annual survey of manufacturers.

2. The ETA firm counts reported by the U.S. Small Business Administration (1994:38) are "based upon state employment security agencies' quarterly reports, 1994." Because total firms in the SSEL series were 89 to 90 percent of the ETA's figures for the six years when both series overlapped (1988–1993), I multiplied the ETA series by .895 to approximate the SSEL counts.

3. The figures do not include all section 501(c)(3) groups "because certain organizations such as churches, integrated auxiliaries, subordinate units and conventions or associations of churches, need not apply for recognition of exemption unless they desire a ruling" (Internal Revenue Service 1996, 1999). The "other" category also includes organizations classified as 501(d)–(f), 521 (farmers' cooperatives), taxable farmers' cooperatives, and nonexempt charitable trusts.

4. To qualify for the Fortune 500 list, companies must publish their financial data and report their figures to a government agency. Subsidiaries of foreign companies incorporated in the United States are excluded. Revenues include discontinued operations if they are published. Profits are calculated after taxes, extraordinary credits or charges, and cumulative effects of accounting changes. The revenues and profits in Table 3.2 refer to the fiscal year ended December 31, 1999. Employee numbers were obtained from Hoovers' online service (<http://www.hoovers.com>).

5. The summary input and output tables, in producer prices aggregated from 498 detailed industries, were estimated from several economic censuses. Because 85 to 100 percent of each commodity is produced within a single industry (the "make" or production relation), only the "use" table (input or consumption) contains sufficient variation to reveal the differentiated industry structure. Each industry's purchases of commodities from the 91 market sectors were first standardized to sum to 100 percent. Then Pearson correlation coefficients (r) were calculated for all pairs of industries, where higher correlations indicated greater equivalence in the proportions of all commodities purchased by a pair. This 91-by-91 matrix of correlations was then entered into UCINET's multidimensional scaling program with instructions to generate a two-dimensional solution. The stress value for the two-dimensional fit (.24) is somewhat higher than desirable and could be improved by fitting a third dimension (stress = .16). But the small gain in accuracy comes at the price of greater visual complexity without substantially changing the industries' relative structural positions.

6. A leveraged buyout (LBO) occurs when a small investment group buys out a company's public shareholders by borrowing against the assets of the acquired firm. They then pay off this debt with cash from the firm or by selling some company assets. "Junk bonds" pay higher interest yields than investment-grade corporate bonds because their interest and principal payments are unsecured. Junk bonds are

safer than shares because the bondholders must be paid off before the stockholders if a firm goes out of business. For discussions of the role of junk bonds in 1980s takeovers, see Taggart (1988) and Yago (1991).

Chapter 4

1. Our primary source was the Information Access Company's keyword-searchable online InfoTrac Searchbank *General Business File ASAP*. Original sources in that archive were more than 400 business general and specialty magazines, major newspapers, and wire services. To supplement the InfoTrac findings, we searched two other online services: University Microfilms International's *Newspaper Abstracts* of article summaries from 25 U.S. national and regional newspapers from 1989 to 1998, and the general business and financial sources archive of Reed-Elsevier's *Lexis-Nexis Academic Universe* Company News file.

2. The *distance* between two organizations is the length of the shortest path connecting them, whose "strength" is the magnitude of its weakest link (measured as the number of alliances between pairs). *Reachability* for a pair of organizations is the value of an optimum path, whose value is the strongest path. Dividing path strength by path length yields a measure of path distance between pairs that takes into account the number of alliances among intermediaries.

Chapter 6

1. This two-dimensional specification produced a barely acceptable fit, with a stress coefficient of 0.26. A three-dimensional MDS specification improved the stress somewhat (to .19) but did not change the substantive interpretation of the plot.

Chapter 7

1. Berle and Means used a 20 percent stock concentration to distinguish between minority and management control (1932:93). In contrast, the Securities and Exchange Commission considered just 5 percent sufficient for "block control"; see Zeitlin's (1974) informative discussion about methodological difficulties in empirically identifying who controls a corporation.

2. I randomly sampled 21 percent of the 500 firms listed by *Fortune* in 1999, then coded information about their board characteristics as reported in their most recent proxy statements filed with the Securities and Exchange Commission. Three of the 104 proxy reports were unavailable from 1998 or 1999 and were excluded from my calculations. Because the 1970 Fortune 500 list did not include nonmanufacturing firms, I also compared the 1998 mean board sizes of the 46 manufacturing firms and the 55 nonmanufacturing companies and reached the same conclusions.

3. Total compensation consisted of salaries, bonuses, gains from exercising stock options, long-term incentive payouts, and the value of restricted stock at the time of grant. The figure also separately shows the sum of salary and bonuses (for all CEOs) and the median cashed stock options (only for the subset of CEOs who exercised their options).

Chapter 8

1. The estimates of union density as a percentage of nonagricultural employees for 1900–1995 come from Freeman (1997:Appendix A, Table 1). His series is primarily based on various Bureau of Labor Statistics published series spliced to estimates of the Bureau of National Affairs using the Current Population Survey. I estimated densities for 1996–1998 by adjusting the CPS rates reported in the *Statistical Abstract of the United States 1998* (U.S. Bureau of the Census 1998:Table 712). Because these densities included agricultural employees, to be consistent with Freeman's series, I reduced them to 0.95 of the reported CPS percentages. This proportion precisely equilibrated the preceding three years where the Freeman and CPS series overlapped.

2. The regression slopes for five 10-year intervals yield these estimated linear percentage changes in union density over a half-century: 1950s, +0.5 percent (not significantly different from zero); 1960s, –4.07 percent; 1970s, –4.09 percent; 1980s, –7.55 percent; 1990s, –2.89 percent.

3. Data for 1975–1987 from Chaison and Dhavale (1990:Table 1); for 1982–1997 from annual issues of the *NLRB Election Report*. Inconsistent counts for the overlapping years stem from differing procedures for calculating gains in new units and losses in represented units.

4. Reskin (1998:22) reported somewhat higher figures for redistributing five gender-race groups into the occupational distribution of men in 1990: 29 percent for black and Hispanic men, 54 percent for white women, 58 percent for Hispanic women, and 60 percent for black women. However, she did not report the number of occupational categories used to compute these values. Reskin (p. 53) also found that gender and racial occupational segregation scores decreased from 1970 to 1990, falling from 67 to 53 percent for all women and from 37 to 27 percent for blacks.

5. Under a 1978 executive order, the EEOC dealt separately with federal employee complaints, which doubled from 17,000 to 34,000 cases between 1991 and 1997. It also contracted with 90 state and local Fair Employment Practices Agencies that annually processed another 48,000 cases using federal guidelines.

Chapter 9

1. The Lobbying Disclosure Act formula does not require reporting of any state, local, or grassroots lobbying expenditures, and the Internal Revenue Code method, which requires these amounts, applies a narrower definition of the covered public officials. Subsidiaries operating in different industries than their parent organizations are not included in the parents' totals. Given prevalent filing errors and the absence of any verification and correction mechanisms, information reported to the House and Senate is not completely accurate and directly comparable across lobbying organizations.

References

Adler, Paul S. 1993. "The 'Learning Bureaucracy': New United Motor Manufacturing, Inc." *Research in Organizational Behavior* 15: 111–194.

Adler, Paul S., Thomas A. Kochan, John Paul MacDuffie, Frits K. Pil and Saul Rubinstein. 1997. "United States: Variations on a Theme." In *After Lean Production: Evolving Employment Practices in the World Auto Industry.* Ed. Thomas A. Kochan, Russell D. Lansbury, and John Paul MacDuffie. Ithaca: ILR Press, pp. 61–83.

Aiges, Scott. 1987. Wire service report from Washington by State News Service. June 1.

Aiken, Michael, and Jerald Hage. 1968. "Organizational Interdependence and Intraorganizational Structure." *American Sociological Review* 33: 912–930.

Akard, Patrick J. 1992. "Corporate Mobilization and Political Power: The Transformation of U.S. Economic Policy in the 1970s." *American Sociological Review* 57: 597–615.

Akhigbe, Aigbe, Jeff Madura, and Alan L. Tucker. 1997. "Long-term Valuation Effects of Shareholder Activism." *Applied Financial Economics* 7: 567–573.

Alba, Richard D., and Charles Kadushin. 1976. "The Intersection of Social Circles: A New Measure of Social Proximity in Networks." *Sociological Methods and Research* 5: 77–102.

Alchian, Armen A., and Harold Demsetz. 1972. "Production, Information Costs, and Economic Organization." *American Economic Review* 62: 777–795.

Aldrich, Howard E. 1979. *Organizations and Environments.* Englewood Cliffs, NJ: Prentice-Hall.

Aldrich, Howard E. 1999. *Organizations Evolving.* Thousand Oaks, CA: Sage Publications.

Aldrich, Howard E., and Ellen Auster. 1986. "Even Dwarfs Started Small: Liabilities of Age and Size and Their Strategic Implications." In *The Evolution and Adaptation of Organizations.* Ed. L. L. Cummings and Barry Staw. Greenwich, CT: JAI Press, pp. 33–66.

Aldrich, Howard E., and Jeffrey Pfeffer. 1976. "Environments of Organizations." *Annual Review of Sociology* 2: 79–105.

Aldrich, Howard E., and Udo Staber. 1988. "Organizing Business Interests: Patterns of Trade Association Foundings, Transformations, and Death." In *Ecological Models of Organizations.* Ed. Glenn Carroll. New York: Ballinger, pp. 111–126.

Aldrich, Howard E., Udo Staber, Catherine Zimmer, and John J. Beggs. 1990. "Minimalism and Organizational Mortality: Patterns of Disbanding Among U.S. Trade Associations, 1900–1983." In *Organizational Evolution: New Directions.* Ed. Jitendra V. Singh. Newbury Park, CA: Sage Publications, pp. 21–52.

Aldrich, Howard E., Udo Staber, Catherine Zimmer, and John J. Beggs. 1994. "Minimalism, Mutualism, and Maturity: The Evolution of the American Trade Association Population in the Twentieth Century." In *Evolutionary Dynamics of Organizations*. Ed. Joel A.C. Baum and Jitendra V. Singh. Newbury Park, CA: Sage Publications, pp. 223–238.

Aldrich, Mark. 1997. *Safety First: Technology, Labor, and Business in the Building of American Work Safety, 1870–1939*. Baltimore, MD: Johns Hopkins University Press.

Alexander, Herbert E. 1992. *Financing Politics: Money, Elections, and Political Reform*. Washington, DC: Congressional Quarterly Press.

Alford, Robert P., and Roger Friedland. 1985. *Powers of Theory: Capitalism, the State, and Democracy*. Cambridge, UK: Cambridge University Press.

Alm, Alvin L., and Robert J. Weiner (eds.). 1984. *Oil Shock: Policy Response and Implementation*. Cambridge, MA: Ballinger.

Althauser, Robert P. 1989. "Internal Labor Markets." *Annual Review of Sociology* 15: 143–161.

American Electronics Association. 1999. "About AEA." http: //www.aeanet.org/aeanet/public/about/index.html> (May 16, 2000).

Amin, Ash. 1989. "A Model of the Small Firm in Italy." In *Small Firms and Industrial Districts in Italy*. Ed. Edward Goodman and Julia Bamford. London: Routledge & Kegan Paul, pp. 111–122.

Amin, Ash. 1993. "The Globalization of the Economy: An Erosion of Regional Networks?" In *The Embedded Firm: On the Socio-economics of Industrial Networks*. Ed. Gernot Grabher. London: Routledge, pp. 278–295.

Amin, Ash, and Nigel Thrift (eds.). 1994. *Globalization, Institutions, and Regional Development in Europe*. New York: Oxford University Press.

Anderla, Georges, Anthony Dunning, and Simon Forge. 1997. *Chaotics: An Agenda for Business and Society in the 21st Century*. Westport, CT: Praeger.

Anderson, Kay E., Philip M. Doyle, and Albert E. Schewnk. 1990. "Measuring Union-Nonunion Earnings Differences." *Monthly Labor Review* 113: 26–38.

Anderson, Philip. 1999a. "Complexity Theory and Organization Science." *Organization Science* 10: 216–232.

Anderson, Philip. 1999b. "Collective Interpretation and Collective Action in Population-Level Learning: Technological Choice in the American Cement Industry." *Advances in Strategic Management* 16: 277–307.

Anderson, Philip, and Michael Tushman. 1990. "Technological Discontinuities and Dominant Designs: A Cyclical Model of Technological Change." *Administrative Science Quarterly* 35: 604–633.

Anderson, Ruth A., and Reuben R. McDaniel Jr. 1999. "RN Participation in Organizational Decision Making and Improvements in Resident Outcomes." *Health Care Management Review* 24: 7–16.

Aoki, Masahiko. 1990. "The Participatory Generation of Information Rents and the Theory of the Firm." In *The Firm as a Nexus of Treaties*. Ed. Masahiko Aoki, Bo Gustafson, and Oliver Williamson. London: Sage Publications, pp. 26–52.

Applebaum, Eileen. 1992. "Structural Change and the Growth of Part-Time and Temporary Work." In *New Policies for the Part-Time and Contingent Workforce*. Armonk, NY: M. E. Sharpe, pp. 1–14.

Applebaum, Eileen, and Rosemary Batt. 1994. *The New American Workplace: Transforming Work Systems in the United States.* Ithaca: ILR Press.

Appold, Stephen J. 1998. "Agglomeration, Interorganizational Networks, and Competitive Performance in the U.S. Metalworking Sector." *Economic Geography* 71: 27–54.

Argote, Linda. 1999. *Organizational Learning: Creating, Retaining, and Transferring Knowledge.* Boston: Kluwer Academic Publishers.

Argyris, Chris, and Donald Schön. 1978. *Organizational Learning: A Theory of Action Perspective.* Reading, MA: Addison-Wesley.

Argyris, Chris, and Donald A. Schon. 1996. *Organizational Learning II: Theory, Method, and Practice.* Reading, MA: Addison-Wesley.

Arnold, Corinna, and Kerry Breen. 1997. "Investor Activism Goes Worldwide." *Corporate Board* 18(103): 7.

Arthur, W. Brian. 1989. "Competing Technologies, Increasing Returns and Lock-in by Historical Events." *Economic Journal* 99: 116–131.

Arthur, Jeffrey B. 1994. "Effects of Human Resource Systems on Manufacturing Performance and Turnover." *Academy of Management Journal* 37: 670–687.

Arthur, Michael B., and Denise M. Rousseau (eds.). 1996. *Boundaryless Career: A New Employment Principle for a New Organizational Era.* New York: Oxford University Press.

Asquith, Daniel, and J. Fred Weston.1994. "Small Business, Growth Patterns and Jobs." *Business Economics* 29(3): 31–34.

Astley, Graham, and Andrew Van de Ven. 1983. "Central Perspectives and Debates in Organizational Theory." *Administrative Science Quarterly* 28: 245–273.

Audretsch, David B. 1999. "Entrepreneurship and Economic Restructuring: An Evolutionary View." In *Entrepreneurship, Small and Medium-Sized Enterprises and the Macroeconomy.* Ed. Zoltan J. Acs, Bo Carlsson, and Charlie Karlsson. Cambridge, UK: Cambridge University Press, pp. 79–96.

Auletta, Ken. 1997. *The Highway Men: Warriors of the Information Superhighway.* New York: Random House.

Austen-Smith, David. 1995. "Campaign Contributions and Access." *American Political Science Review* 89: 566–581.

Autry, R., and M. M. Colodny. 1990. "The Fortune 500: Hanging Tough in a Rough Year." *Fortune* 121(April): 338–345.

Axelrod, Robert, and Michael D. Cohen. 2000. *Harnessing Complexity : Organizational Implications of a Scientific Frontier.* New York: Free Press.

Axelsson, Björn, and Geoffrey Easton (eds.). 1992. *Industrial Networks: A New View of Reality.* London: Routledge.

Baily, Martin N., Eric J. Bartelsman, and John Haltiwanger. 1994. "Downsizing and Productivity Growth: Myth of Reality?" Washington, DC: Bureau of the Census Center for Economic Studies. Working Paper 94-4.

Bailyn, Lotte. 1992. "Changing the Conditions of Work: Responding to Increasing Work Force Diversity and New Family Patterns." In *Transforming Organizations.* Ed. Thomas A. Kochan and Michael Useem. New York: Oxford University Press, pp. 188–201.

Bainbridge, Stephen M. 1996. "Participatory Management Within a Theory of the Firm." *Iowa Journal of Corporation Law* 21: 657–730.

Baker, Wayne E. 1990. "Market Networks and Corporate Behavior." *American Journal of Sociology* 96: 589–625.

Baker, Wayne E. 1994. *Networking Smart: How to Build Relationships for Personal and Organizational Success.* New York: McGraw-Hill.

Barboza, David. 1999. "Heinz to Shed Units and Jobs In an Overhaul." *New York Times,* February 18: C1.

Barker, James R. 1993. "Tightening the Iron Cage: Concertive Control in Self-Managing Teams." *Administrative Science Quarterly* 38: 408–437.

Barker, James R. 1999. *The Discipline of Teamwork: Participation and Concertive Control.* Thousand Oaks, CA: Sage Publications.

Barley, Stephen R. 1990. "The Alignment of Technology and Structure Through Roles and Networks." *Administrative Science Quarterly* 35: 61–103.

Barley, Stephen R., John Freeman, and R. C. Hybels. 1992. "Strategic Alliances in Commercial Biotechnology." In *Networks and Organizations: Structure, Form and Action.* Ed. Nitin Nohria and Robert G. Eccles. Boston: Harvard Business School Press, pp. 311–347.

Barnard, Chester L. 1938. *The Functions of the Executive.* Cambridge, MA: Harvard University Press.

Barnett, Tim, Daniel S. Cochran, and G. Stephen Taylor. 1993. "The Internal Disclosure Policies of Private-sector Employers: An Initial Look at Their Relationship to Employee Whistleblowing." *Journal of Business Ethics* 12: 127–136.

Barnett, William P., and Glenn R. Carroll. 1995. "Modeling Internal Organizational Change." *Annual Review of Sociology* 21: 217–236.

Barnett, William P., and Morten T. Hansen. 1996. "The Red Queen in Organizational Evolution." *Strategic Management Journal* 17: 139–157.

Baron, James N. 1984. "Organizational Perspectives on Stratification." *Annual Review of Sociology* 10: 37–69.

Baron, James N., Frank R. Dobbin, and P. Devereux Jennings. 1986. "War and Peace: The Evolution of Modern Personnel Administration in U.S. Industry." *American Journal of Sociology* 92: 350–383.

Barron, David N., Elizabeth West, and Michael T. Hannan. 1994. "A Time to Grow and a Time to Die: Growth and Mortality of Credit Unions in New York City, 1914–1990." *American Journal of Sociology* 100: 381–421.

Bates, James. 1994. "Eisner Earns $203 Million But No Bonus." *Los Angeles Times,* January 4: D1.

Bates, James. 2000. "No Bonuses for Eisner, 3 Other Disney Execs." *Los Angeles Times,* January 20: C1.

Batt, Rosemary. 1999. "Work Organization, Technology, and Performance in Customer Service and Sales." *Industrial and Labor Relations Review* 52: 539–563.

Battelle Memorial Institute. 2000. "Forecast Predicts Significant Increase in R&D Spending for Year 2000." Press release. <http://batelle.org/News/00/default.stm> (January 5, 2000).

Baum, Joel A. C. 1996. "Organizational Ecology." In *The Handbook of Organization Studies.* Ed. Stewart R. Clegg, Cynthia Hardy, and Walter R. Nord. London: Sage Publications, pp. 76–114.

Baum, Joel A. C., and Christine Oliver. 1992. "Institutional Embeddedness and the Dynamics of Organizational Populations." *American Sociological Review* 57: 540–559.

Baum, Joel A. C., and Paul Ingram. 1998. "Survival-Enhancing Learning in the Manhattan Hotel Industry, 1989–1980." *Management Science* 44: 996–1016.

Baum, Joel A. C., and Walter W. Powell. 1995. "Cultivating an Institutional Ecology of Organizations." *American Sociological Review* 60: 529–538.

Baumgartner, Frank R., and Beth L. Leech. 1998. *Basic Interests: The Importance of Groups in Politics and in Political Science.* Princeton: Princeton University Press.

Baumol, William J., Sue Anne Batey Blackman, and Edward N. Wolff. 1989. *Productivity and American Leadership: The Long View.* Cambridge, MA: MIT Press.

Baysinger, Barry, and Robert E. Hoskisson. 1990. "The Composition of Boards of Directors and Strategic Control: Effects on Corporate Strategy." *Academy of Management Review* 15: 72–87.

Beatty, Randolph P., and Edward J. Zajac. 1994. "Managerial Incentives, Monitoring and Risk Bearing: A Study of Compensation, Ownership, and Board Structure in Intitial Public Offerings." *Administrative Science Quarterly* 39: 313–335.

Becattini, Giacomo. 1989. "Sectors and/or Districts: Some Remarks on the Conceptual Foundations of Industrial Districts." In *Small Firms and Industrial Districts in Italy.* Ed. Edward Goodman and Julia Bamford. London: Routledge & Kegan Paul, pp. 123–135.

Becattini, Giacomo. 1990. "The Marshallian Industrial District as a Socioeconomic Notion." In *Industrial Districts and Inter-Firm Co-operation in Italy.* Ed. Frank Pyke, G. Becattini, and W. Sengenberger. Geneva: International Labor Office.

Becker, Gary S. 1993. *Human Capital: A Theoretical and Empirical Analysis with Special Reference to Education.* 3d ed. Chicago: University of Chicago Press.

Beckman, Sara L. 1996. "Evolution of Management Roles in a Networked Organization: An Insider's View of the Hewlett-Packard Company." In *Broken Ladders: Managerial Careers in the New Economy.* Ed. Paul Osterman. New York: Oxford University Press, pp. 155–184.

Belliveau, Maura A., Charles A. O'Reilly, and James B. Wade. 1996. "Social Capital at the Top: Effects of Social Similarity and Status on CEO Compensation." *Academy of Management Journal* 39: 1568–1593.

Belous, Richard S. 1989. *The Contingent Economy: The Growth of the Temporary, Part-time, and Subcontracted Workforce.* Washington, DC: National Planning Association.

Bender, Keith A. 1997. "The Changing Determinants of U.S. Unionism: An Analysis Using Worker-Level Data." *Journal of Labor Research* 18: 403–423.

Bendix, Reinhard. 1960. *Max Weber: An Intellectual Portrait.* New York: Doubleday Anchor.

Berenbeim, R. E. 1986. *Company Programs to Ease the Impact of Shutdowns.* New York: Conference Board.

Berggren, Christian. 1992. *Alternatives to Lean Production: Work Organization in the Swedish Auto Industry.* Ithaca: ILR Press.

Berle, Adolf, Jr., and Gardiner C. Means. 1932. *The Modern Corporation and Private Property.* New York: Macmillan.

Bernstein, Irving. 1971. *The Turbulent Years.* New York: Houghton Mifflin.

Bernstein, Jules. 1980. "Union-Busting: From Benign Neglect to Malignant Growth." *University of California, Davis Law Review* 3: 17–36.

Berry, Jeffrey M. 1977. *Lobbying for the People: The Political Behavior of Public Interest Groups.* Princeton: Princeton University Press.

Besser, Terry L. 1996. *Team Toyota: Transplanting the Toyota Culture to the Camry plant in Kentucky.* Albany: State University of New York Press.

Bhagat, Sanjai, and Bernard Black. 1999. "The Uncertain Relationship Between Board Composition and Firm Performance." *The Business Lawyer* 54: 921–963.

Bhagat, Sanjai, Andrei Shleifer, and Robert W. Vishny. 1990. "Hostile Takeovers in the 1980s: The Return to Corporate Specialization." In *Brookings Papers on Economic Activity: Microeconomics 1990.* Ed. M. N. Baily and C. Winston. Washington, DC: Brookings Institution, pp. 1–84.

Bhagat, Sanjai, Dennis C. Carey, and Charles M. Elson. 1999. "Director Ownership, Corporate Performance, and Management Turnover." *The Business Lawyer* 54: 885–919.

Biddle, Frederic M. 1998. "British Airways Moves Closer to Being 'Virtual Airline.'" *Wall Street Journal,* June 25: B4.

Birch, David L. 1987. *Job Creation in America: How Our Smallest Companies Put the Most People to Work.* New York: Free Press.

Birch, David L. 1989. "Change, Innovation, and Job Generation." *Journal of Labor Research* 10: 33–38.

Birch, David L., A. Haggerty, and Wayne Parsons. 1993. *Who's Creating Jobs?* Cambridge, MA: Cognetics Inc.

Blair, Margaret M. 1995. *Ownership and Control: Rethinking Corporate Governance for the Twenty-First Century.* Washington, DC: Brookings Institution.

Blasi, Joseph, Michael Conte, and Douglas Kruse. 1996. "Employee Stock Ownership and Corporate Performance among Public Companies." *Industrial and Labor Relations Review* 50: 60–79.

Blau, Peter M. 1964. *Exchange and Power in Social Life.* New York: Wiley.

Bleeke, Joel, and David Ernst. 1993. *Collaborate to Compete: Using Strategic Alliances and Acquisitions in the Global Marketplace.* New York: Wiley.

Block, Fred. 1977. "The Ruling Class Does Not Rule: Notes on the Marxist Theory of the State." *Socialist Revolution* 7: 6–28.

Blommestein, Hans J. 1998. "Impact of Institutional Investors on Financial Markets." In *OECD Proceedings Institutional Investors in the New Financial Landscape.* Paris: Organisation for Economic Co-operation and Development, pp. 29–106.

Bloom, David E., and Richard B. Freeman. 1992. "The Fall of Private Pension Coverage in the United States." *American Economic Review* 82: 539–545.

Blum, Hunter C. 1997. "ESOP's Fables: Leveraged ESOPs and Their Effect on Managerial Slack, Employee Risk and Motivation in the Public Corporation." *University of Richmond Law Review* 31: 1539–1570.

Bollier, David. 1998. *Work and Future Society: Where Are the Economy and Technology Taking Us?* Washington, DC: Aspen Institute.

Bolton, Michele Kremen. 1993. "Organizational Innovation and Substandard Performance: When Is Necessity the Mother of Innovation?" *Organization Science* 4: 57–75.

Bonacich, Philip. 1987. "Power and Centrality: A Family of Measures." *American Journal of Sociology* 92: 1170–1182.

Bordieu, Pierre. 1980. "Le Capital Social: Notes Provisoires." *Actes de la Recherche en Sciences Sociales* 3: 2–3.

Bordieu, Pierre. 1986. "The Forms of Capital." In *Handbook of Theory and Research for the Sociology of Education.* Ed. John G. Richardson. Westport, CT: Greenwood Press, pp. 241–258.

Borgatti, Stephen P., and Martin G. Everett. 1992. "Notions of Position in Social Network Analysis." *Sociological Methodology* 22: 1–35.

Borys, Bryan, and David B. Jemison. 1989. "Hybrid Arrangements as Strategic Alliances: Theoretical Issues in Organizational Combinations." *Academy of Management Review* 14: 234–249.

Boyett, Joseph H., Stephen Schwartz, Laurence Osterwise, and Roy Bauer. 1993. *The Quality Journey: How Winning the Baldrige Sparked the Remaking of IBM.* New York: Dutton.

Bradach, Jeffrey L., and Robert G. Eccles. 1989. "Price, Authority, and Trust: From Ideal Types to Plural Forms." *Annual Review of Sociology* 15: 97–118.

Bradsher, Keith. 1999. "Labor's Peace with G.M. Unraveling at Saturn." *New York Times,* July 22: A1.

Brancato, Carolyn Kay. 1996. *Institutional Investors and Corporate Governance.* New York: Conference Board.

Brass, Daniel J. 1984. "Being in the Right Place: A Structural Analysis of Individual Influence in an Organization." *Administrative Science Quarterly* 29: 519–539.

Brass, Daniel J. 1985. "Men's and Women's Networks: A Study of Interaction Patterns and Influence in an Organization." *Academy of Management Journal* 28: 327–343.

Brass, Daniel J. 1995. "A Social Network Perspective on Human Resources Management." *Research in Personnel and Human Resources Management* 13: 39–79.

Brass, Daniel J., and Marlene E. Burkhardt. 1992. "Centrality and Power in Organizations." In *Networks and Organizations: Structure, Form and Action.* Ed. Nitin Nohria and Robert G. Eccles. Boston: Harvard Business School Press, pp. 191–215.

Bratton, William W. 1989. "The New Economic Theory of the Firm: Critical Perspectives From History." *Stanford Law Review* 41: 1471–1527.

Braverman, Harry. 1974. *Labor and Monopoly Capital: The Degradation of Work in the Twentieth Century.* New York: Monthly Review Press.

Bridges, William P., and Wayne J. Villemez. 1994. *The Employment Relationship: Causes and Consequences of Modern Personnel Administration.* New York: Plenum.

Briggs, Thomas W. 1994. "Shareholder Activism and Insurgency Under the New Proxy Rules." *Business Lawyer* 50: 99–149.

Broad William J. 1985. "The Secret Behind Star Wars." *New York Times,* August 11: 6: 32.

Brockner, Joel. 1990. "Scope of Justice in the Workplace: How Survivors React to Co-Worker Layoffs." *Journal of Social Issues* 46: 95–106.

Bronfenbrenner, Kate. 1997. "The Role of Union Strategies in NLRB Certification Elections." *Industrial and Labor Relations Review* 50: 195–212.

Brooks, Chris. 1998. "Chaos in Foreign Exchange Markets: A Skeptical View." *Computational Economics* 11: 265–281.

Brostek, Michael. 1997. *Alternative Dispute Resolution: Employers' Experiences with ADR in the Workplace.* Washington, DC: Government Accounting Office. Report GAO/GGD-97-157.

Browne, William P. 1998. *Groups, Interests, and U.S. Public Policy*. Washington, DC: Georgetown University Press.

Browning, Larry D., Janice M. Beyer, and Judy C. Shetler. 1995. "Building Cooperation in a Competitive Industry: SEMATECH and the Semiconductor Industry." *Academy of Management Journal* 38: 113–151.

Bruck, Connie. 1988. *The Predators' Ball: The Junk Bond Raiders and the Men Who Staked Them*. New York: Simon & Schuster.

Buffalo News. 1999. "They Don't Want Your Input, They Just Want Your Name: Astroturf Lobbying Creates Phony 'Grass Roots'." *Buffalo News*, December 31: F6.

Burawoy, Michael. 1985. *The Politics of Production: Factory Regimes Under Capitalism and Socialism*. London: Verso.

Burkins, Glenn. 2000. "Labor Union Membership Increases Second Year in Row to 16.48 Million." *Wall Street Journal*, January 20: A2.

Burns, Tom, and George M. Stalker. 1961. *The Management of Innovation*. London: Tavistock.

Burroughs, Bryan, and John Hellyar. 1990. *Barbarians at the Gate*. New York: Harper & Row.

Burstein, Paul. 1985. *Discrimination, Jobs, and Politics: The Struggle for Equal Employmnet Opportunity in the United States Since the New Deal*. Chicago: University of Chicago Press.

Burstein, Paul. 1998. "Interest Organizations, Political Paarties and the Study of Democratic Policies." In *Social Movements and American Political Institutions*. Ed. Anne Costain and Andrew McFarland. Boulder: Rowman & Littlefield, pp. 39–56.

Burstein, Paul, and April Linton Eaton. 2000. "The Impact of Political Parties, Interest Groups, and Social Movement Organizations on Public Policy: Some Recent Evidence and Theoretical Concerns." Paper presented to American Sociological Association Meeting, Washington, DC.

Burt, Ronald S. 1979. "Disaggregating the Effect on Profits in Manufacturing Industries of Having Imperfectly Competitive Consumers and Suppliers." *Social Science Research* 8: 120–143.

Burt, Ronald S. 1980. "Autonomy in a Social Topology." *American Journal of Sociology* 85: 892–925.

Burt, Ronald S. 1987. "Social Contagion and Innovation: Cohesion Versus Structural Equivalent." *American Journal of Sociology* 92: 1287–1335.

Burt, Ronald S. 1988. "The Stability of American Markets." *American Journal of Sociology* 94: 356–395.

Burt, Ronald S. 1992. *Structural Holes: The Social Structure of Competition*. Cambridge, MA: Harvard University Press.

Burt, Ronald S. 1997. "The Contingent Value of Social Capital." *Administrative Science Quarterly* 42: 339–365.

Burt, Ronald S. 1998. "Partitioning the American Economy for Organizational Research." Manuscript, University of Chicago Graduate School of Business and Department of Sociology.

Burt, Ronald S., and Michael J. Minor (eds.). 1983. *Applied Network Analysis*. Beverly Hills, CA: Sage Publications.

Burt, Ronald S., Miguel Guilarte, Holly J. Raider, and Yuki Yasuda. 1999. "Competition, Contingency, and the External Structure of Markets." Manuscript, University of Chicago Graduate School of Business and Department of Sociology.

Bygrave, William D. 1988. "The Structure of Investment Networks of Venture Capital Firms." *Journal of Business Venturing* 3: 137–157.

Bygrave, William D. 1995. "Mom-and-Pops, High-Potential Startups, and Intrapreneurship: Are They Part of the Same Entrepreneurship Paradigm?" *Advances in Entrepreneurship, Firm Emergence, and Growth* 2: 1–19.

Byrne, David S. 1998. *Complexity Theory and the Social Sciences: An Introduction.* London: Routledge.

Byrne, John A. 2000. "The Best & the Worst Boards." *Business Week*, January 24: 142.

Callaghan, Polly, and Heidi Hartmann. 1991. *Contingent Work: A Chart Book on Part-Time and Temporary Employment.* Washington, DC: Economic Policy Institute.

CalPERS. 1999. "Corporate Governance Program." <http://www.calpers-governance.org> (April 29, 1999).

Cameron, Samuel, and Alan Collins. 1997. "Transaction Costs and Partnerships: The Case of Rock Bands." *Journal of Economic Behavior and Organization* 32: 171–183.

Campbell, Donald T. 1969. "Variation, Selection, and Retention in Sociocultural Systems." *General Systems* 16: 69–85.

Cannon, Kimble C., and Patrick J. Tangney. 1995. "Protection of Minority Shareholder Rights under Delaware Law: Reinforcing Shareholders as Residual Claimants and Maximizing Long-Term Share Value by Restricting Directorial Discretion." *Columbia Business Law Review* 1995: 725–784.

Cappelli, Peter. 1999. *The New Deal at Work: Managing the Market-Driven Workforce.* Boston: Harvard Business School Press.

Cappelli, Peter, Laurie Bassi, Harry Katz, David Knoke, Paul Osterman, and Michael Useem. 1997. *Change at Work.* New York: Oxford University Press.

Carlton, Jim. 1996. "Apple Posts Big Loss, Plans More Layoffs." *Wall Street Journal,* April 18: B9.

Carree, Martin, and Luuk Klomp. 1996. "Small Business and Job Creation: A Comment." *Small Business Economics* 8: 317–322.

Carroll, Glenn. 1984. "Organizational Ecology." *Annual Review of Sociology* 10: 71–93.

Carroll, Glenn, and Michael T. Hannan. 1989. "Density Dependence in the Evolution of Populations of Newspaper Organizations." *American Sociological Review* 54: 524–541.

Carroll, Glenn R., and Michael T. Hannan (eds.). 1995. *Organizations in Industry: Strategy, Structure, and Selection.* New York: Oxford University Press.

Carroll, Glenn R., and Michael T. Hannan. 2000. *The Demography of Corporations and Industries.* Princeton, NJ: Princeton University Press.

Castells, Manuel. 1996. *The Rise of the Network Society.* Cambridge, MA: Blackwell.

Casti, John L. 1994. *Complexification: Explaining a Paradoxical World Through the Science of Surprise.* New York: HarperCollins.

Caver, Paul. 1996. "Employee-Owned Airlines: The Cure for an Ailing Industry?" *Journal of Air Law and Commerce* 61: 639–681.

Center for Responsive Politics. 1999. *Influence Inc.: The Bottom Line on Washington Lobbying*. Washington, DC: Center for Responsive Politics.

Chaison, Gary N., and Dileep G. Dhavale. 1990. "A Note on the Severity of the Decline in Union Organizing Activity." *Industrial and Labor Relations Review* 43: 366–373.

Chandler, Alfred D., Jr. 1962. *Strategy and Structure: Chapters in the History of Industrial Enterprise*. Cambridge, MA: MIT Press.

Chandler, Alfred D., Jr. 1964. *Giant Enterprise: Ford, General Motors, and the Automobile Industry*. New York: Harcourt, Brace & World.

Cheng, Yu-Ting, and Andrew H. Van de Ven. 1996. "Learning the Innovation Journey: Order Out of Chaos?" *Organization Science* 7: 593–614.

Child, John. 1972. "Organization Structure, Environment, and Performance: The Role of Strategic Choice." *Sociology* 6: 1–22.

Child, John, and David Faulkner. 1998. *Strategies of Cooperation: Managing Alliances, Networks and Joint Ventures*. New York: Oxford University Press.

Christensen, Kathleen. 1998. "Countervailing Human Resource Trends in Family-Sensitive Firms." In *Contingent Work: American Employment Relations in Transition*. Ed. Kathleen Barker and Kathleen Christensen. Ithaca: ILR Press, pp. 103–125.

Christopherson, Susan, and Michael Storper. 1986. "The City as Studio: The World as a Back Lot: The Impact of Visual Disintegration on the Location of the Motion Picture Industry." *Environment and Planning D: Society and Space* 4: 305–320.

Christopherson, Susan, and Michael Storper. 1989. "The Effects of Flexible Specialization on Industrial Politics and the Labor Market: The Motion Picture Industry." *Industrial and Labor Relations Review* 42: 331–347.

Chung, Seungwha (Andy). 1996. "Performance Effects of Cooperative Strategies Among Investment Banking Firms: A Loglinear Analysis of Organizational Exchange Networks." *Social Networks* 18: 121–148.

Clark, Don. 1996. "Software Firm Fights to Remake Business After Ill-Fated Merger." *Wall Street Journal*, January 12: A1.

Clark, Don. 1997. "Intel's Tumble Underscores the Debate Over Coming Changes in PC Hardware." *Wall Street Journal*, August 25: B8.

Clark, Robert C. 1991. "Agency Costs Versus Fiduciary Duties." In *Principles and Agents: The Structure of Business*. Ed. John W. Pratt and Richard J. Zeckhauser. Boston: Harvard Business School Press, pp. 55–79.

Clarke, Arthur C. 1958. *Profiles of the Future: An Inquiry into the Limits of the Possible*. New York: Harper & Row.

Clawson, Dan, Alan Neustadtl, and Denise Scott. 1992. *Money Talks: Corporate PACs and Political Influence*. New York: Basic Books.

Clawson, Dan, Alan Neustadtl, and Mark Weller. 1998. *Dollars and Votes: How Business Campaign Contributions Subvert Democracy*. Philadelphia: Temple University Press.

Clegg, Stewart R. 1990. *Modern Organizations: Organization Studies in the Postmodern World*. London: Sage Publications.

Clinton, Angela. 1997. "Flexible Labor: Restructuring the American Work Force." *Monthly Labor Review* August: 3–27.

Coase, R. H. 1988. *The Firm, the Market, and the Law.* Chicago: University of Chicago Press, 1988.

Coffee, John C. Jr. 1988. "Shareholders Versus Managers: The Strain in the Corporate Web." In *Knights, Raiders, and Targets: The Impact of the Hostile Takeover.* Ed. John C. Coffee Jr., Louis Lowenstein, and Susan Rose-Ackerman. New York: Oxford University Press, pp. 78–134.

Cohan, Peter S. 1997. *The Technology Leaders: How America's Most Profitable High-tech Companies Innovate Their Way to Success.* San Francisco: Jossey-Bass.

Cohany, Sharon R., Steven F. Hipple, Thomas J. Nardone, Anne E. Polivka, and Jay C. Stewart. 1998. "Counting the Workers: Results of a First Survey." In *Contingent Work: American Employment Relations in Transition.* Ed. Kathleen Barker and Kathleen Christensen. Ithaca: ILR Press, pp. 41–68.

Cohen, Wesley M., and Daniel A. Levinthal. 1990. "Absorptive Capacity: A New Perspective on Learning and Innovation." *Administrative Science Quarterly* 35: 128–152.

Cole, Kenneth. 1999. "Lobby Firm Is Global: U.S. and Foreign Carmakers Team Up to Tackle Industry Issues." *Detroit News*, January 8: B1.

Cole, Robert E. (ed.). 1995. *The Death and Life of the American Quality Movement.* New York: Oxford University Press.

Cole, Robert E. 1999. *Managing Quality Fads: How American Business Learned to Play the Quality Game.* New York: Oxford University Press.

Cole, Robert E., and W. Richard Scott (eds.). 2000. *The Quality Movement and Organization Theory.* Thousand Oaks, CA: Sage Publications.

Coleman, James S. 1973. "Loss of Power." *American Sociological Review* 38: 1–17.

Coleman, James S. 1986. "Norms as Social Capital." In *Economic Imperialism: The Economic Approach Applied Outside the Field of Economics.* Ed. Gerard Radnitzky and Peter Bernholz. New York: Paragon House, pp. 133–155.

Coleman, James S. 1988. "Social Capital in the Creation of Human Capital." *American Journal of Sociology* 94: S95–S121.

Coleman, James S. 1990. *Foundations of Social Theory.* Cambridge, MA: Harvard University Press.

Coll, Steve. 1986. *The Deal of the Century: The Breakup of AT&T.* New York: Atheneum.

Collins, N. 1983. *Professional Women and Their Mentors.* Englewood Cliffs, NJ: Prentice-Hall.

Conference Board. 1996. *The New Deal in Employment Relationships: A Council Report.* No. 1162–96-CR. New York: Conference Board.

Cook, Karen S. 1977. "Exchange and Power in Networks of Interorganizational Relations." *Sociological Quarterly* 18: 62–82.

Cook, Karen S., and Richard M. Emerson. 1984. "Exchange Networks and the Analysis of Complex Organizations." *Research in the Sociology of Organizations* 3: 1–30.

Cooke, Philip, and Kevin Morgan. 1994. "Growth Regions Under Duress: Renewal Strategies in Baden Württemberg and Emilia-Romagna." In *Globalization, Insti-*

tutions, and Regional Development in Europe. Ed. Ash Amin and Nigel Thrift. New York: Oxford University Press, pp. 91–117.

Cooke, Philip and Kevin Morgan. 1998. The Associational Economy: Firms, Regions, and Innovation. Oxford: Oxford University Press.

Corcoran, Elizabeth. 1998. "AOL Closes Deal to Buy Netscape for $4.2 Billion." Washington Post, November 25: A1.

Creedy, John, and Vance L. Martin (eds.). 1994. Chaos and Non-linear Models in Economics: Theory and Applications. Aldershot, UK: Elgar.

Crozier, Michel. 1964. The Bureaucratic Phenomenon. Chicago: University of Chicago Press.

Crystal, Graef. 1991. "CEO Compensation: The Case of Michael Eisner." In Executive Compensation: A Strategic Guide for the 1990s. Ed. Fred K. Foulkes. Boston: Harvard Business School Press, pp. 353–365.

Crystal, Graef. 1992. In Search of Excess: The Overcompensation of American Executives. New York: Norton.

Cusumano, Michael A., and Richard W. Selby. 1995. Microsoft Secrets. New York: Free Press.

Cusumano, Michael A., Yiorgos Mylonadis, and Richard S. Rosenbloom. 1992. "Strategic Maneuvering and Mass-Market Dynamics: The Triumph of VHS over Beta." Business History Review 66: 51–94.

Cyert, Richard, and James G. March. 1963. A Behavioral Theory of the Firm. Englewood Cliffs, NJ: Prentice-Hall.

Daft, Richard L. 1995. Organization Theory and Design. 5th ed. Minneapolis-St.Paul: West Publishing.

Dahl, Robert. 1956. A Preface to Democratic Theory. Chicago: University of Chicago Press.

Dalton, D. H., and M. G. Serapio Jr. 1998. Globalizing Industrial Research and Development. Washington, DC: U.S. Department of Commerce Technology Administration.

Danziger, Sheldon, and Peter Gottschalk. 1993. Uneven Tides: Rising Inequality in America. New York: Russell Sage Foundation.

David, Paul A. 1985. "Clio and the Economics of QWERTY." American Economic Review, Papers and Proceedings 75: 332–337.

Davidsson, Per, Leif Lindmark, and Christer Olofsson. 1998. "The Extent of Overestimation of Small Firm Job Creation: An Empirical Examination of the Regression Bias." Small Business Economics 11: 87–100.

Davis, Gerald F. 1994. "The Corporate Elite and the Politics of Corporate Control." Current Perspectives in Social Theory, Supplement 1: 215–238.

Davis, Gerald F., and Henrich R. Greve. 1997. "Corporate Elite Networks and Governance Changes in the 1980s." American Journal of Sociology 103: 1–37.

Davis, Gerald F., Kristina A. Diekmann, and Catherine H. Tinsley. 1994. "The Decline and Fall of the Conglomerate Firm in the 1980s: The Deinstitutionalization of an Organizational Form." American Sociological Review 59: 547–570.

Davis, Gerald F., and Suzanne K. Stout. 1992. "Organization Theory and the Market for Corporate Control: A Dynamic Analysis of the Characteristics of Large Takeover Targets, 1980–1990." Administrative Science Quarterly 37: 605–633.

Davis, Steven J., and John Haltiwanger. 1992. "Gross Job Creation, Gross Job Destruction, and Employment Reallocation." *Quarterly Journal of Economics* 107: 819–863.

Davis, Steven J., John Haltiwanger, and Scott Schuh. 1990. "Published Versus Sample Statistics from the ASM: Implications for the LRD." *Proceedings of the American Statistical Association, Business and Economics Statistics Section*: 52–61.

Davis, Steven J., John Haltiwanger, and Scott Schuh. 1994. "Small Business and Job Creation: Dissecting the Myth and Reassessing the Facts." In *Labor Markets, Employment Policy and Job Creation*. Ed. Lewis C. Solmon and Alec R. Levenson. Boulder: Westview Press, pp. 169–199.

Davis-Blake, Alison, and Brian Uzzi. 1993. "Determinants of Employment Externalization: A Study of Temporary Workers and Independent Contractors." *Administrative Science Quarterly* 38: 195–223.

De Graaf, Nan Dirk, and Hendrik Derk Flap. 1988. "With a Little Help From My Friends." *Social Forces* 67: 452–472.

De Laat, P. B. 1999. "Systemic Innovation and the Virtues of Going Virtual: The Case of the Digital Video Disc." *Technology Analysis & Strategic Management* 11: 159–180.

Dechert, W. Davis (ed.). 1996. *Chaos Theory in Economics: Methods, Models and Evidence*. Cheltenham, UK: Elgar.

Dei Ottati, Gabi. 1994. "Trust, Interlinking Transactions and Credit in the Industrial District." *Cambridge Journal of Economics* 18: 529–546.

Deming, W. Edwards. 1986. *Out of the Crisis*. New York: Cambridge University Press.

Denis, David J., and Diane K. Denis. 1995. "Performance Changes Following Top Management Dismissals." *Journal of Finance* 1: 1029–1057.

Dennis, William J., Jr., Bruce D. Phillips, and Edward Starr. 1994. "Small Business Job Creation: The Findings and Their Critics." *Business Economics* 29(3): 23–30.

Dertouzos, Michael L. 1999. "The Future of Computing." *Scientific American* (August): 52–55.

Dewar, Helen. 1999. "Civic, Business Leaders Back 'Soft Money' Ban." *Washington Post*, October 5: A6.

Dewey, John. 1926. "The Historic Background of Corporate Legal Personality." *Yale Law Journal* 35: 655–678.

Dickens, William T., and Jonathan S. Leonard. 1985. "Accounting for the Decline in Union Membership, 1950–1980." *Industrial and Labor Relations Review* 38: 323–334.

Dickerson, Marla. 1996. "Baptists Urge Disney Boycott Over Values." *Los Angeles Times*, June 13: D1.

Dickson, Martin. 1992. "GM's Revolution Devours Its Creator." *Financial Times*, October 27: 25.

DiMaggio, Paul, and Walter Powell. 1983. "The Iron Cage Revisited: Institutional Isomorphism and Collective Rationality in Organizational Fields." *American Sociological Review* 48: 147–160.

DiMaggio, Paul, and Walter Powell. 1991. "Introduction." In *The New Institutionalism*. Ed. Walter Powell and Paul DiMaggio. Chicago: University of Chicago Press, pp. 1–38.

Dodd, E. Merrick Jr. 1932. "For Whom Are Corporate Managers Trustees?" *Harvard Law Review* 45: 1145–1148.

Dodgson, Mark. 1993. "Organizational Learning: A Review of Some Literatures." *Organization Studies* 14: 375–393.

Doeringer, Peter B. (ed.). 1991. *Turbulence in the American Workplace*. New York: Oxford University Press.

Doeringer, Peter, and Michael Piore. 1971. *Internal Labor Markets and Manpower Analysis*. Lexington, MA: D. C. Heath.

Domhoff, G. William. 1978. *The Powers That Be: Processes of Ruling-Class Domination of America*. New York: Vintage Books.

Domhoff, G. William. 1983. *Who Rules America Now?* Englewood Cliffs, NJ: Prentice Hall.

Domhoff, G. William. 1990. *The Power Elite and the State: How Policy Is Made in America*. Hawthorne, NY: Aldine de Gruyter.

Domhoff, G. William. 1996. *State Autonomy or Class Dominance? Case Studies on Policy Making in America*. New York: Aldine de Gruyter.

Donaldson, T., and L. E. Preston. 1995. "The Stakeholder Theory of the Corporation: Concepts, Evidence, and Implications." *Academy of Management Review* 20: 65–91.

Donaldson, Thomas, and Lee E. Preston. 1995. "The Stakeholder Theory of the Corporation: Concepts, Evidence, and Implications." *Academy of Management Review* 20: 65–91.

Dooley, Kevin J., and Andrew H. Van de Ven. 1997. "The Nonlinear Dynamics of Innovation." *Society for Chaos Theory in Psychology and the Life Sciences* 4: 3–4.

Dooley, Kevin J., and Andrew H. Van de Ven. 1999. "Explaining Complex Organizational Dynamics." *Organization Science* 3: 358–372.

Dooley, Peter C. 1969. "The Interlocking Directorate." *American Economic Review* 48: 147–160.

Doreian, Patrick, and Katherine L. Woodard. 1999. "Local and Global Institutional Processes." *Research in the Sociology of Organizations* 16: 59–83.

Doucouliagos, Chris. 1995. "Worker Participation and Productivity in Labor-Managed and Participatory Capitalist Firms: A Meta-analysis." *Industrial and Labor Relations Review* 49: 58–77.

Drago, Robert, and Mark Wooden. 1991. "The Determinants of Participatory Management." *British Journal of Industrial Relations* 29: 177–204.

Drucker, Peter F. 1976. *The Unseen Revolution: How Pension Fund Socialism Came to America*. New York: Harper & Row.

Dubini, P., and Howard E. Aldrich. 1991. "Personal and Extended Networks Are Central to the Entrepreneurial Process." *Journal of Business Venturing* 6: 305–313.

Dunlop, John T., and David Weil. 1996. "Diffusion and Performance of Modular Production in the U.S. Apparel Industry." *Industrial Relations* 35: 334–355.

Dunlop, R. G. 1996. "The Tobacco Wars: Wigand's Credibility." *Louisville Courier-Journal*, March 28: 1A.

Duve, Christian. 1999. "Dispute Resolution in Globalization Context." *New York Law Journal*, April 12: 9.

Dye, Thomas R. 1995. *Who's Running America?: The Clinton Years*. Englewood Cliffs, NJ: Prentice Hall.

Dyer, Jeffrey H. 1996. "How Chrysler Created an American Keiretsu." *Harvard Business Review* 74 (July-August): 42–56.

Dyer, Jeffrey H. 1997. "Effective Interfirm Collaboration: How Firms Minimize Transaction Costs and Maximize Transaction Value." *Strategic Mangement Journal* 18: 535–556.

Easterbrook, Frank, and Daniel Fischel. 1983. "Voting in Corporate Law." *Journal of Law and Economics* 26: 418–426.

Easton, George S., and Sherry L. Jarrell. 1998. "The Effects of Total Quality Management on Corporate Performance: An Empirical Investigation." *Journal of Business* 71: 253–307.

Eccles, Robert G., and Dwight B. Crane. 1988. *Doing Deals: Investment Banks at Work*. Boston: Harvard Business School Press.

Economic Report of the President Transmitted to the Congress February 1995. Washington, DC: Government Printing Office.

Economic Report of the President Transmitted to the Congress February 1999. Washington, DC: Government Printing Office.

Edelman, Lauren B. 1990. "Legal Enviornments and Organizational Governance: The Expansion of Due Process in the American Workplace." *American Journal of Sociology* 95: 1401–1440.

Edelman, Lauren B. 1992. "Legal Ambiguity and Symbolic Stuctures: Organizational Mediation of Law." *American Journal of Sociology* 97: 1531–1573.

Edelman, Lauren B., Howard S. Erlanger, and J. Lande. 1993. "Employers' Handling of Discrimination Complaints: The Transformation of Rights in the Workplace." *Law and Society Review* 27: 497–534.

Edelman, Lauren B., and Mark C. Suchman. 1997. "The Legal Environments of Organizations." *Annual Review of Sociology* 23: 479–515.

Edquist, C. (ed.). 1997. *Systems of Innovation, Technologies, Institutions and Organizations*. London: Pinter.

Edwards, Morris. 1996. "Standards for CTI: Hard Choices Ahead." *Communications News* 33(9): 72.

Edwards, Richard. 1979. *Contested Terrain: The Transformation of the Workplace in the Twentieth Century*. New York: Basic Books.

Eisenberg, Melvin A. 1976. *The Structure of the Corporation: A Legal Analysis*. Boston: Little, Brown.

Eisenhardt, Kathleen M. 1989. "Agency Theory: An Assessment and Review." *Academy of Management Review* 14: 57–74.

Ellis, Jenny. 1994. "Non-linearities and Chaos in Exchange Rates." In *Chaos and Non-linear Models in Economics: Theory and Applications*. Ed. John Creedy and Vance L. Martin. Aldershot, UK: Elgar, pp. 187–195.

Emerson, Richard M. 1962. "Power-Dependence Relations." *American Sociological Review* 27: 31–41.

Emirbayer, Mustafa, and Jeff Goodwin. 1994. "Network Analysis, Culture, and the Problem of Agency." *American Journal of Sociology* 99: 1441–1454.

Ernst and Young. 1994. *Mergers and Acquisitions*. 2d ed. New York: Wiley.

Etzioni, Amitai. 1961. *A Comparative Analysis of Complex Organizations*. New York: Free Press.

Etzkowitz, Henry, and Loet Leydesdorff (eds.). 1997. *Universities in the Global Economy: The Triple Helix of University-Industry-Government Relations*. London: Cassell Academic.

Etzkowitz, Henry, and Loet Leydesdorff. 2000. "The Dynamics of Innovation: From National Systems and 'Mode 2' to a Triple Helix of University-Industry-Government Relations." *Research Policy* 29: 109–123.

Evan, William M., and P. Olk. 1990. "R&D Consortia: A New U.S. Organizational Form." *Sloan Management Review* 31(3): 37–46.

Exter, Thomas G. 1996. *The Official Guide to American Incomes*. 2d ed. Ithaca: New Strategist Publications.

Fabrikant, Geraldine. 1997. "Cooperation Counts." *New York Times*, December 15: D12.

Fallick, Bruce C. 1999. "Part-time Work and Industry Growth." *Monthly Labor Review* 122(3): 22–29.

Fama, Eugene. 1980. "Agency Problems and Theory of the Firm." *Journal of Political Economy* 88: 288–306.

Fama, Eugene F., and Michael C. Jensen. 1983. "Separation of Ownership and Control." *Journal of Law and Economics* 26: 301–325.

Farber, Henry S. 1995. "Are Lifetime Jobs Disappearing? Job Duration in the United States: 1973–1993." *Industrial Relations Section, Working Paper 341.* Princeton, NJ: Princeton University.

Farhi, Paul. 1997. "Disney Chief May Reap $771 Million from Stock Options." *Washington Post*, February 22: D1.

Federal Election Commission. 1999. "Campaign Finance Reports and Data." <http://www.fec.gov/finance_reports.html> (August 25, 1999).

Federal Election Commission. 2000. "Campaign Finance Reports and Data." <http://www.fec.gov/finance_reports.html> (May 16, 2000).

Federal Reserve. 1999. "Flow of Funds Accounts of the U.S.: Annual Flows and Outstandings. 1973–1981; 1982–1990; 1991–1998." <http://www.federalreserve.gov/releases/z1/current/data.htm> (April 24, 1999).

Ferman, Louis A., Michele Hoyman, Joel Crutcher-Gershenfeld, and Ernst J. Savoie (eds.). 1991. *Joint Training Programs: A Union-Management Approach to Preparing Workers for the Future*. Ithaca: ILR Press.

Fernandez, Roberto M., and Nancy Weinberg. 1997. "Sifting and Sorting: Personal Contacts and Hiring in a Retail Bank." *American Sociological Review* 62: 883–902.

Fiet, J. O. 1991. "Network Reliance by Venture Capital Firms and Business Angels: An Empirical and Theoretical Test." In *Frontiers of Entrepreneurial Research*. Wellesley, MA: Boston College, pp. 445–503.

Finkelstein, Sydney. 1997. "Interindustry Merger Patterns and Resource Dependence: A Replication and Extension of Pfeffer (1972)." *Strategic Management Journal* 18: 787–810.

Finkelstein, Sydney, and Donald Hambrick. 1989. "Chief Executive Compensation: A Study of the Intersection of Markets and Political Processes." *Strategic Management Journal* 10: 121–134.

Fiorito, Jack, Paul Jarley, and John Thomas Delaney. 1995. "National Union Effectiveness in Organizing: Measures and Influences." *Industrial and Labor Relations Review* 48.613–635.

Fisch, Jill E. 1997. "Corporate Governance: Taking Boards Seriously." *Cardozo Law Review* 19: 265–290.

Fisher, Lawrence M. 1998. "Microsoft and Compaq to Buy 10% Stakes in Road Runner." *New York Times*, June 16: D4.

Flannery, Thomas P., David A. Hofrichter, and Paul E. Platten. 1996. *People, Performance, and Pay: Dynamic Compensation for Changing Organizations*. New York: Free Press.

Flap, Henk D., and Ed Boxman. 1999. "Getting a Job as a Manager." In *Corporate Social Capital and Liability*. Ed. Roger Th. A. J. Leenders and Shaul M. Gabbay. Boston: Kluwer Academic Publishers, pp. 196–216.

Flap, Henk D., Bert Bulder, and Beate Völker. 1998. "Intra-organizational Networks and Performance: A Review." *Computational and Mathematical Organization Theory* 4(2): 109–147.

Fligstein, Neil. 1985. "The Spread of the Multidivisional Form, 1919–79." *American Sociological Review* 50: 377–391.

Fligstein, Neil. 1987. "The Intraorganizational Power Struggle: The Rise of Finance Presidents in Large Corporations, 1919–79." *American Sociological Review* 52: 44–58.

Fligstein, Neil. 1990. *The Transformation of Corporate Control*. Cambridge, MA: Harvard University Press.

Fligstein, Neil. 1991. "The Structural Transformation of American Industry: An Institutional Account of the Causes of Diversification in the Largest Firms." In *The New Institutionalism*. Ed. Walter Powell and Paul DiMaggio. Chicago: University of Chicago Press, pp. 311–36.

Fligstein, Neil, and Linda Markowitz. 1993. "The Finance Conception of the Corporation and the Causes of the Financial Reorganization of Large Corporations, 1979–89." In *Sociology and Social Policy*. Ed. William Julius Wilson. Greenwich, CT: JAI Press, pp. 185–206.

Flynn, Julia. 1998. "Bosses under Fire." *Business Week*, November 30: 22.

Fombrun, Charles J. 1996. *Reputation: Realizing Value from the Corporate Image*. Boston: Harvard Business School Press.

Fortune. 2000. "Fortune 500–2000." <http://www.fortune.com/fortune/fortune500> (March 15, 2000).

Frank, Ove. 1991. "Statistical Analysis of Change in Networks." *Statistica Neerlandica* 3: 283–293.

Frank, Robert H., and Philip J. Cook. 1995. *The Winner-Take-All Society*. New York: Free Press.

Freedman, Russell. 1994. *Kids at Work: Lewis Hine and the Crusade Against Child Labor*. New York: Clarion Books.

Freeland, Robert F. 1996. "The Myth of the M-Form? Governance, Consent, and Organizational Change." *American Journal of Sociology* 102: 483–526.

Freeman, Christopher. 1987. *Technology Policy and Economic Performance: Lessons from Japan*. London: Pinter.

Freeman, Christopher. 1991. "Networks of Innovators: A Synthesis of Research Issues." *Research Policy* 20: 499–514.

Freeman, Edward R. 1984. *Strategic Management: A Stakeholder Approach.* Marshfield, MA: Pitman.

Freeman, Edward R. 1994. "A Stakeholder Theory of the Modern Corporation," In *Ethical Theory and Business.* Ed. Tom L. Beauchamp and Norman E. Bowie. Englewood Cliffs, NJ: Prentice-Hall, pp. 66–76.

Freeman, Linton C. 1977. "A Set of Measures of Centrality Based on Betweenness." *Sociometry* 40: 35–41.

Freeman, Linton. 1979. "Centrality in Social Networks: I. Conceptual Clarification." *Social Networks* 1: 215–239.

Freeman, Richard B. 1997. *Spurts in Union Growth: Defining Moments and Social Processes.* Cambridge, MA: National Bureau of Economic Research. Working Paper No. 6012.

Freeman, Richard B., and Morris M. Kleiner. 1990. "Employer Behavior in the Face of Union Organizing Drives." *Industrial and Labor Relations Review* 43: 351–365.

Friedman, Milton. 1970. "The Social Responsibility of Business Is to Increase Its Profits." *New York Times Magazine,* September 13: 33.

Friesen, Jane. 1997. "The Dynamic Demand for Part-time and Full-time Labour." *Economica* 64: 495–507.

Furlong, Scott R. 1997. "Interest Group Influence on Rule Making." *Administration & Society* 29: 325–347.

Gabbay, Shaul. 1997. *Social Capital in the Creation of Financial Capital: The Case of Network Marketing.* Champaign, IL: Stipes Publishing.

Gaddie, Ronald Keith. 1995. "Investing in the Future: Economic Political Action Committee Contributions to Open-Seat House Candidates." *American Politics Quarterly* 23: 339–354.

Gaddie, Ronald Keith, and James L. Regens. 1997. "Economic Interest Group Allocations in Open-Seat Senate Elections." *American Politics Quarterly* 25: 347–362.

Gais, Thomas. 1996. *Improper Influence: Campaign Finance Law, Political Interest Groups, and the Problem of Equality.* Ann Arbor: University of Michigan Press.

Galaskiewicz, Joseph. 1985. "Interorganizational Relations." *Annual Review of Sociology* 11: 281–304.

Galaskiewicz, Joseph. 1997. "An Urban Grants Economy Revisited: Corporate Charitable Contributions in the Twin Cities, 1979–91, 1987–89." *Administrative Science Quarterly* 42: 445–471.

Galaskiewicz, Joseph, and Wolfgang Bielefeld. 1998. *Nonprofit Organizations in an Age of Uncertainty.* New York: Aldine de Gruyter.

Galenson, Walter.1960. *The CIO Challenge to the AFL.* Cambridge, MA: Harvard University Press.

Galinsky, Ellen, James T. Bond, and Dana E. Friedman. 1993. *The Changing Workforce.* New York: Families and Work Institute.

Gambetta, Diego. 1988. *Trust: Making and Breaking Corporate Relations.* New York: Blackwell.

Gamble, John E. 1998. "ESOPs: Financial Performance and Federal Tax Incentives." *Journal of Labor Research* 19: 529–541.

Garen, John E. 1994. "Executive Compensation and Principal-Agent Theory." *Journal of Political Economy* 102: 1175–1199.

General Social Survey. 2000. "Data and Information Retrieval System." <http://www.icpsr.umich.edu/GSS99/index.html> (March 30, 2000).

Genereux, Anne, and David Knoke. 1999. "Identifying Strategic Alliances in the Global Information Sector, 1989–1998." Paper presented to EGOS Colloquium, Warwick, UK.

Gerlach, Michael L. 1992. *Alliance Capitalism: The Social Organization of Japanese Business.* Berkeley: University of California Press.

Getz, Kathleen A. 1993. "Selecting Corporate Political Tactics." In *Corporate Political Agency: The Construction of Competition in Public Affairs.* Ed. Barry M. Mitnick. Newbury Park, CA: Sage Publications, pp. 242–267.

Gibbs, W. Wayt. 1997. "Taking Computers to Task." *Scientific American* 277(July): 82–89.

Gibson, Richard. 1997. "Worried McDonald's Plans Dramatic Shift and Big Price Cuts." *Wall Street Journal,* February 26: A1.

Gidron, Benjamin, Ralph M. Kramer, and Lester M. Salamon (eds.). 1992. *Government and the Third Sector: Emerging Relationships in Welfare States.* San Francisco: Jossey-Bass.

Giesecke, Susanne. 2000. "The Contrasting Roles of Government in the Development of Biotechnology Industry in the US and Germany." *Research Policy* 29: 205–223.

Gifford, Sharon. 1997. "Limited Attention and the Role of the Venture Capitalist." *Journal of Business Venturing* 12: 459–482.

Gillan, Stuart L., and Laura T. Starks. (forthcoming). "Corporate Governance Proposals and Shareholder Activism: The Role of Institutional Investors." *Journal of Financial Economics.*

Gilroy, Bernard Michael. 1993. *Networking in Multinational Enterprises: The Importance of Strategic Alliances.* Columbia: University of South Carolina Press.

Ginsberg, Ari, Eric R. Larsen, and Alessandro Lomi. 1999. "The Organizational Ecology of Strategic Interaction." *Advances in Strategic Management* 16: 81–112.

Glass, Jennifer L., and Sarah Beth Estes. 1997. "The Family Responsive Workplace." *Annual Review of Sociology* 23: 289–313.

Gleick, James. 1987. *Chaos: Making a New Science.* New York: Viking.

Goidel, Robert K., Donald A. Gross, and Todd G. Shields. 1999. *Money Matters: Consequences of Campaign Finance Reform in U.S. House Elections.* Lanham, MA: Rowman & Littlefield.

Golbe, Devra L., and Lawrence J. White. 1988. "Mergers and Acquisitions in the U.S. Economy: An Aggregate and Historical Overview." In *Mergers and Acquisitions.* Ed. Alan J. Auerbach. Chicago: University of Chicago Press, pp. 25–47.

Golden, James R. 1994. *Economics and National Strategy in the Information Age: Global Networks, Technology Policy, and Cooperative Competition.* Westport, CT: Praeger.

Golembiewski, Robert T., Robert A. Boudreau, and Robert F. Munzenrider. 1996. *Global Burnout: A Worldwide Pandemic Explored by the Phase Model.* Greenwich, CT: JAI Press.

Gomes-Casseres, Benjamin. 1996. *The Alliance Revolution: The New Shape of Business Rivalry.* Cambridge, MA: Harvard University Press.

Gomez-Mejia, Luis, and Robert M. Wiseman. 1997. "Reframing Executive Compensation: An Assessment and Outlook." *Journal of Management* 23: 291–374.

Gompers, Paul A. 1999. "Resource Allocation, Incentives and Control: The Importance of Venture Capital in Financing Entrepreneurial Firms." In *Entrepreneurship, Small and Medium-Sized Enterprises and the Macroeconomy.* Ed. Zoltan J. Acs, Bo Carlsson, and Charlie Karlsson. Cambridge, UK: Cambridge University Press, pp. 206–235.

Goodman, Edward. 1989. "Introduction: The Political Economy of the Small Firm in Italy." In *Small Firms and Industrial Districts in Italy.* Ed. Edward Goodman and Julia Bamford. London: Routledge & Kegan Paul, pp. 1–30.

Gosselin, Peter G., and Paul Jacobs. 2000. "Clinton, Blair to Back Access to Genetic Code." *Los Angeles Times,* March 14: C1.

Gould, Roger V., and Roberto M. Fernandez. 1989. "Structures of Mediation: A Formal Approach to Brokerage in Transaction Networks." In *Sociological Methodology 1989.* San Francisco: Jossey-Bass, pp. 89–126.

Grandori, Anna, and Giuseppe Soda. 1995. "Inter-firm Networks: Antecedents, Mechanisms and Forms." *Organization Science* 16: 183–214.

Granovetter, Mark. 1973. "The Strength of Weak Ties." *American Journal of Sociology* 78: 1360–1380.

Granovetter, Mark. 1982. "The Strength of Weak Ties Revisited: A Network Theory Revisited." In *Social Structure and Network Analysis.* Ed. Peter V. Marsden and Nan Lin. Beverly Hills, CA: Sage Publications, pp. 105–130.

Granovetter, Mark. 1985. "Economic Action and Social Structure: The Problem of Embeddedness." *American Journal of Sociology* 91: 481–510.

Gray, Virginia, and David Lowery. 1996. *The Population Ecology of Interest Representation: Lobbying Communities in the American States.* Ann Arbor: University of Michigan Press.

Grenzke, Janet M. 1989. "Shopping in the Congressional Supermarket: The Currency Is Complex." *American Political Science Review* 33: 1–24.

Greve, Henrich R. 1996. "Patterns of Competition: The Diffusion of a Market Position in Radio Broadcasting." *Administrative Science Quarterly* 41: 29–60.

Greve, Henrich R. 1999. "Branch Systems and Nonlocal Learning in Populations." *Advances in Strategic Management* 16: 57–80.

Grier, Kevin, Michael C. Munger, and Brian E. Roberts. 1994. "The Determinants of Industry Political Activity, 1978–1986." *American Political Science Review* 88: 911–926.

Grimm, Curtis M., and John M. Holcomb. 1987. "Choices Among Encompassing Organizations: Business and the Budget Deficit." In *Business Strategy and Public Policy: Perspectives from Industry and Academia.* Ed. Alfred A. Marcus, Allen M. Kaufman, and D. R. Bream. Westport, CT: Quorum Books, pp. 105–118.

Grimsley, Kirstin Downey. 1996. "Auto Plant Sexual Harassment Case Divides Community." *Washington Post,* April 17: A1.

Grimsley, Kirstin Downey. 1998. "Community Still Split in Aftermath of Mitsubishi Settlement." *Washington Post,* June 15: A9.

Grimsley, Kirstin Downey, and Frank Swoboda. 1997. "Mitsubishi Managers Blamed for Environment at Plant; EEOC Says Supervisors Created, Tolerated 'Sexually Hostile and Abusive' Situation." *Washington Post,* September 16; C1.

Grimsley, Kirstin Downey, and Warren Brown. 1996. "Mitsubishi Workers March on EEOC." *Washington Post*, April 23: A1.

Grindley, Peter. 1995. *Standards Strategy and Policy: Cases and Stories*. New York: Oxford University Press.

Gross, James A. 1995. *Broken Promises: The Subversion of U.S. Labor Relations Policy, 1947–1994*. Philadelphia: Temple University Press.

Grossman, Glenn M. 1992. "U.S. Workers Receive a Wide Range of Employee Benefits." *Monthly Labor Review* (September): 36–39.

Groves, Martha. 1998. "Mentor Program Adds Diversity to Corporate Climb." *Los Angeles Times*, March 4: Business, Part D: 1.

Guercio, Diane Del, and Jennifer Hawkins.1999. "The Motivation and Impact of Pension Fund Activism." *Journal of Financial Economics* 52: 293–340.

Guidera, Mark. 2000. "R&D Spending Boom Forecast for U.S. Firms." *Baltimore Sun*, January 1: C9.

Gugliotta, Guy. 2000. "Gene-Altered Rice May Help Fight Vitamin A Deficiency Globally." *Washington Post*, January 14: A6.

Gulati, Ranjay. 1995a. "Does Familiarity Breed Trust? The Implications of Repeated Ties for Contractual Choices in Alliances." *Academy of Management Journal* 38: 85–112.

Gulati, Ranjay. 1995b. "Social Structure and Alliance Formation Patterns: A Longitudinal Analysis." *Administrative Science Quarterly* 40: 619–652.

Gulati, Ranjay, and Martin Gargiulo. 1999. "Where Do Networks Come From?" *American Journal of Sociology* 104: 1439–1493.

Gulick, Luther. and L. Urwick (eds.). 1937. *Papers on the Science of Administration*. New York: Institute of Public Administration.

Hackman, J. Richard, and G. R. Oldham. 1976. "Motivation Through the Design of Work: Test of a Theory." *Organizational Behavior and Human Performance* 16: 250–279.

Hackman, J. Richard, and Ruth Wageman. 1995. "Total Quality Management: Empirical, Conceptual, and Practical Issues." *Administrative Science Quarterly* 40: 309–342.

Hadlock, Charles J., and Gerald B. Lumer. 1997. "Compensation, Turnover, and Top Management Incentives: Historical Evidence." *Journal of Business* 70(2): 153–187.

Hage, Jerald. 1980. *Theories of Organizations: Forms, Processes, and Transformation*. New York: Wiley.

Hagedoorn, John. 1993a. "Strategic Technology Alliances and Modes of Cooperation in High-Technology Industries." In *The Embedded Firm: On the Socioeconomics of Industrial Networks*. Ed. Gernot Grabher. New York: Routledge, pp. 116–137.

Hagedoorn, John. 1993b. "Strategic Technology Partnering During the 1980s: Trends, Networks, and Corporate Patterns in Non-core Technologies." *Research Policy* 24: 207–231.

Hagedoorn, John, and Jos Schakenraad. 1992. "Leading Companies and Networks of Strategic Alliances in Information Technologies." *Research Policy* 21: 163–190.

Hakansson, Hakan, and Jan Johanson 1993. "The Network as Governance Structure: Interfirm Cooperation Beyond Markets and Hierarchies." In *The Embedded Firm: On the Socioeconomics of Industrial Networks*. Ed. Gernot Grabher. London: Routledge, pp. 35–51.

Halbfinger, David M. 1998. "In Deal, LIPA and Utility End Clash Over Pay to Ex-Officers." *New York Times*, December 22: B1.

Hale and Dorr LLP. 2000. "The National and Regional IPO Market." <http://www.haledorr.com/archive_pub.html> (March 31, 2000).

Hall, Richard L., and Frank W. Wayman. 1990. "Buying Time: Moneyed Interests and the Mobilization of Bias in Congressional Committees." *American Political Science Review* 84: 797–820.

Hall, William. 1987. "Employee Ownership 4: ESOPs Win Their Spurs." *Financial Times*, April 13: 32.

Haltiwanger, John. 1999. "Job Creation and Destruction by Emnployer Size and Age: Cyclical Dynamics." In *Entrepreneurship, Small and Medium-Sized Enterprises and the Macroeconomy*. Ed. Zoltan J. Acs, Bo Carlsson, and Charlie Karlsson. Cambridge, UK: Cambridge University Press, pp. 239–285.

Hamilton, Gary G. (ed.). 1996. *Asian Business Networks*. Berlin: Walter de Gruyter.

Han, Shin-Kap. 1996. "Structuring Relations in On-the-Job Networks." *Social Networks* 18: 47–67.

Handlin, Oscar, and Mary F. Handlin. 1945. "Origins of the American Business Corporation." *Journal of Economic History* 5: 1–23.

Hanisch, Kathy A., and Charles L. Hulin. 1991. "General Attitudes and Organizational Withdrawal: An Evaluation of a Causal Model." *Journal of Vocational Behavior* 39: 110–128.

Hannan, Michael T., and Glenn Carroll. 1992. *Dynamics of Organizational Populations: Density, Legitimation, and Competition*. New York: Oxford University Press.

Hannan, Michael T., and Glenn Carroll. 1995. "Theory Building and Cheap Talk About Legitimation: Reply to Baum and Powell." *American Sociological Review* 60: 539–544.

Hannan, Michael T., Glenn Carroll, Elizabeth A. Dundon, and John C. Torres. 1995. "Organizational Evolution in a Multinational Context; Entries of Automobile Manuffacturers in Belgium, Britain, France, Germany, and Italy." *American Sociological Review* 60: 509–528.

Hannan, Michael T., and John Freeman. 1977. "The Population Ecology of Organizations." *American Journal of Sociology* 82: 929–964.

Hannan, Michael T., and John Freeman. 1984. "Structural Inertia and Organizational Change." *American Sociological Review* 49: 149–164.

Hannan, Michael T., and John Freeman. 1988. "The Ecology of Organizational Mortlity: American Labor Unions, 1836–1985." *American Journal of Sociology* 94: 25–52.

Hannan, Michael T., and John Freeman. 1989. *Organizational Ecology*. Cambridge, MA: Harvard University Press.

Hansell, Saul. 2000. "Media Megadeal." *New York Times*, January 11: A1.

Hansen, John Mark. 1991. *Gaining Access: Congress and the Farm Lobby, 1919–1981*. Chicago: University of Chicago Press.

Hansen, Morten T. 1999. "The Search-Transfer Problem: The Role of Weak Ties in Sharing Knowledge across Organization Subunits." *Administrative Science Quarterly* 44: 82–111.

Hansmann, Henry. 1990. "When Does Worker Ownership Work? ESOPs, Law Firms, Codetermination, and Economic Democracy." *Yale Law Journal* 99: 1749–1816.

Harary, Frank. 1959. "Graph Theoretic Methods in the Management Sciences." *Management Science* 5: 387–403.

Harrison, Bennett. 1994. *Lean and Mean: The Changing Landscape of Corporate Power in the Age of Flexibility.* New York: Basic Books.

Harrison, Bennett, Maryellen R. Kelley, and Jon Gant. 1996. "Innovative Firm Behavior and Local Milieu: Exploring the Intersection of Agglomeration, Firm Effects, and Technological Change." *Economic Geography* 72: 233–258.

Hatch, Mary Jo. 1997. *Organization Theory: Modern, Symbolic, and Postmodern Perspectives.* Oxford: Oxford University Press.

Haubrich, Jospeh G. 1994. "Risk Aversion, Performance Pay, and the Principal-Agent Problem." *Journal of Political Economy* 102: 258–276.

Haunschild, Pamela R. 1993. "Interorganizational Imitation: The Impact of Interlocks on Corporate Acquisition Activity." *Administrative Science Quarterly* 38: 564–592.

Hawley, James P. 1995. "Political Voice, Fiduciary Activism, and the Institutional Ownership of U.S. Corporations: The Role of Public and Noncorporate Pension Funds." *Sociological Perspectives* 38: 415–435.

Hayghe, Howard. 1988. "Employers and Child Care: What Roles Do They Play?" *Monthly Labor Review* 111: 38–44.

Hays, Laurie. 1995. "The Outsider's New In Crowd: Five IBM Lifers." *Wall Street Journal,* January 12: B1.

Heider, Fritz. 1946. "Attitudes and Cognitive Organization." *Journal of Psychology* 21: 107–112.

Heinz, John P., Edward O. Laumann, Robert L. Nelson, and Robert H. Salisbury. 1993. *The Hollow Core: Private Interests in National Policymaking.* Cambridge, MA: Harvard University Press.

Helper, Susan. 1991. "Strategy and Irreversibility in Supplier Relations: The Case of the U.S. Automobile Industry." *Business History Review* 65: 781–824.

Helper, Susan. 1993. "An Exit-Voice Analysis of Supplier Relations: The Case of the US Automobile Industry." In *The Embedded Firm.* Ed. Gernot Grabher. London: Routledge, pp. 141–160.

Hennart, Jean-Francois. 1988. "A Transaction Costs Theory of Equity Joint Ventures." *Strategic Management Journal* 9: 361–374.

Herrigel, Gary. 1993. "Power and the Redefinition of Industrial Districts; The Case of Baden-Württemberg." In *The Embedded Firm.* Ed. Gernot Grabher. London: Routledge, pp. 227–251.

Herrigel, Gary. 1996. *Industrial Constructions: The Sources of German Industrial Power.* New York: Cambridge University Press.

Heydebrand, Wolf V. 1989. "New Organizational Forms." *Work and Occupations* 16: 323–357.

Hickson, D.J., C. R. Hinings, C. A. Lee, R. E. Schneck, and J. M. Pennings. 1971. "A Strategic Contingencies' Theory of Intraorganizational Power." *Administrative Science Quarterly* 16: 216–229.

Hill, Charles W., and Thomas M. Jones. 1992. "Stakeholder-Agency Theory." *Journal of Management Studies* 29: 131–154.

Hill, Stephen. 1991. "Why Quality Circles Failed but Total Quality Management Might Succeed." *British Journal of Industrial Relations* 29: 541–568.

Hipple, Steven. 1998. "Contingent Work: Results from the Second Survey." *Monthly Labor Review* (November): 22–35.

Hirschman, Albert O. 1970. *Exit, Voice, and Loyalty: Responses to Decline in Firms, Organizations, and States.* Cambridge, MA: Harvard University Press.

Hojnacki, Marie. 1997. "Interest Groups' Decisions to Join Alliances or Work Alone." *American Journal of Political Science* 41: 61–87.

Holzer, Harry J., and David Neumark. 1998. "Are Affirmative Action Hires Less Qualified? Evidence from Employer-Employee Data on New Hires." *Journal of Labor Economics* 17: 534–569.

Homer. 1996. *The Odyssey.* Translated by Robert Fagles. New York: Viking.

Hoovers. 2000. "Hoover's Companies—A to Z." <http://www.hoovers.com/company/all/list/0,2504,116,00.html> (March 15, 2000).

Horwitz, Morton J. 1987. "*Santa Clara* Revisited: The Development of Corporate Theory." In *Corporations and Society: Power and Responsibility.* Ed. Warren J. Samuels and Arthur S. Miller. Westport, CT: Greenwood Press, pp. 13–63.

Hoskisson, Robert E., and Michael A. Hitt. 1994. *Downscoping: How to Tame the Diversified Firm.* New York: Oxford University Press.

Hovenkamp, Herbert. 1991. *Enterprise and American Law, 1836–1937.* Cambridge, MA: Harvard University Press.

Huber, George P. 1991. "Organizational Learning: The Contributing Processes and Literatures." *Organization Science* 2: 88–115.

Hula, Kevin W. 1999. *Lobbying Together: Interest Group Coalitions in Legislative Politics.* Washington, DC: Georgetown University Press.

Huselid, Mark A. 1995. "The Impact of Human Resource Management Practices on Turnover, Productivity, and Corporate Financial Performance." *Academy of Management Journal* 38: 635–672.

Huselid, Mark A., and Brian E. Becker. 1996. "Methodological Issues in Cross-Sectional and Panel Estimates of the Human Resource-Firm Performance Link." *Industrial Relations* 35: 400–422.

Ibarra, Herminia. 1992. "Homophily and Differential Returns: Sex Differences in Network Structure and Access in an Advertising Firm." *Administrative Science Quarterly* 37: 422–447.

Ibarra, Herminia. 1993a. "Network Centrality, Power and Innovation Involvement: Determinants of Technical and Administrative Roles." *Academy of Management Journal* 36: 471–501.

Ibarra, Herminia. 1993b. "Untangling the Web of Interconnections: An Exploration of Competing Explanations for Gender Differences in Managerial Networks." Mimeographed document, Harvard University Graduate School of Business Administration, Cambridge, MA.

Ibarra, Herminia. 1995. "Race, Opportunity, and Diversity of Social Circles in Managerial Networks." *Academy of Management Journal* 38: 673–701.

Ibarra, Herminia, and Steven B. Andrews. 1993. "Power, Social Influence and Sense Making: Effects of Network Centrality and Proximity on Employee Perceptions." *Administrative Science Quarterly* 38: 277–303.

Ichbiah, Daniel, and Susan L. Knepper. 1991. *The Making of Microsoft: How Bill Gates and His Team Created the World's Most Successful Software Company.* Rocklin, CA: Prima Publishing.

Ichniowski, Casey, Kathryn Shaw, and Giovanna Prennushi. 1997. "The Effects of Human Resource Management Practices on Productivity: A Study of Steel Finishing Lines." *American Economic Review* 87: 291–313.

Ichniowski, Casey, Thomas A. Kochan, David Levine, Craig Olson, and George Strauss. 1996. "What Works at Work: Overview and Assessment." *Industrial Relations* 35: 299–333.

Ingram, Paul, and Tal Simons. 1995. "Institutional and Resource Dependence Determinants of Responsiveness to Work-Family Issues." *Academy of Management Journal* 5: 1466–1482.

Inkpen, Andrew. 1995. *The Management of International Joint Ventures: An Organizational Learning Perspective.* London: Routledge.

Internal Revenue Service. 1996. "1995, Exempt Organizations and Other Entities Listed on Exempt Organizations and Business Master File. 1995 IRS Annual Data Book Report. Format 123 ver. 1a, Excel ver. 4." <http: //www.irs.gov/tax_stats/soi/ex_iad.html> (March 30, 2000).

Internal Revenue Service. 1999. "1994–1997, Exempt Organizations and Other Entities Listed on Exempt Organization Business Master File. 1997 IRS Annual Data Book. Format Lotus 123 ver. 1a, Excel ver. 4." <http: //www.irs.gov/tax_stats/soi/ex_iad.html> (March 30, 2000).

Ishikawa, Kaoru. 1985. *What Is Total Quality Control? The Japanese Way.* Englewood Cliffs, NJ: Prentice-Hall.

Jackson, Tim. 1997. *Inside Intel: Andy Grove and the Rise of the World's Most Powerful Chip Company.* New York: Dutton.

Jackson, Tony. 1998. "Shareholder Value: Obstacles May Be More Deep-Seated Than Expected." *Financial Times,* May 14: 10.

Jacoby, Sanford. 1985. *Employing Bureaucracy: Managers, Unions, and the Transformation of Work in American Industry, 1900–1945.* New York: Columbia University Press.

Jaeger, David A., and Ann Huff Stevens. 1998. "Is Job Stability in the United States Falling? Reconciling Trends in the Current Population Survey and Panel Study of Income Dynamics." Paper presented at the Russell Sage Foundation Conference on Job Stability and Security.

Jarillo, José Carlos. 1988. "On Strategic Networks." *Strategic Management Journal* 9: 31–41.

Jarrell, Gregg A., James A. Brickley, and Jeffrey N. Netter. 1988. "The Market for Corporation Control: The Empirical Evidence Since 1980." *Journal of Financial Economics* 19: 127–168.

Jasic, Teo. 1998. "Testing for Nonlinearity and Deterministic Chaos in Monthly Japanese Stock Market Data." *Zagreb International Review of Economics and Business* 1: 61–82.

Jensen, Michael C. 1988. "Takeovers: Their Causes and Consequences." *Journal of Economic Perspectives* 2: 21–48.

Jensen, Michael C. 1998. *Foundations of Organizational Strategy.* Cambridge, MA: Harvard University Press.

Jensen, Michael C., and Kevin J. Murphy. 1990. "Performance Pay and Top-Management Incentives." *Journal of Political Economy* 98: 225–264.

Jensen, Michael C., and William H. Meckling. 1976. "Theory of the Firm: Managerial Behavior, Agency Cost and Ownership Structure." *Journal of Financial Economics* 3: 305–360.

Johnson, Ian. 1997. "Latest Merger Boom Is Happening in China, and Bears Watching." *Wall Street Journal,* July 30: A1.

Jones, Candace, William S. Hesterly, and Stephen P. Borgatti. 1997. "A General Theory of Network Governance: Exchange Conditions and Social Mechanisms." *Academy of Management Review* 22: 911–945.

Juran, Joseph. 1988. *Juran on Planning for Quality.* New York: Free Press.

Kalleberg, Arne L., David Knoke, and Peter V. Marsden. 1995. "Interorganizational Networks and the Changing Employment Contract." *Connections* 18: 32–49.

Kalleberg, Arne L., David Knoke, Peter V. Marsden, and Joe L. Spaeth. 1996. *Organizations in America: Analyzing Their Structures and Human Resource Practices.* Newbury Park, CA: Sage Publications.

Kalleberg, Arne L., Jeremy Reynolds, and Peter V. Marsden. 2000. "Externalizing Employment: Flexible Staffing Arrangements in U.S. Organizations." Mimeographed document, University of North Carolina.

Kalleberg, Arne L., and Kathryn Schmidt. 1996. "Contingent Employment in Organizations: Part-Time, Temporary, and Subcontracting Relations." In *Organizations in America: Analyzing Their Structures and Human Resource Practices.* Arne L. Kalleberg, David Knoke, Peter V. Marsden, and Joe L. Spaeth. Newbury Park, CA: Sage Publications, pp. 253–275.

Kanigel, Robert. 1997. *The One Best Way: Frederick Winslow Taylor and the Enigma of Efficiency.* New York: Viking.

Kanter, Rosabeth Moss. 1977. *Men and Women of the Corporation.* New York: Basic Books.

Kanter, Rosabeth Moss, and Paul S. Myers. 1991. "Interorganizational Bonds and Intraorganizational Behavior: How Alliances and Partnerships Change the Organizations Forming Them." In *Socioeconomics: Toward a New Synthesis.* Ed. Amitai Etzioni and Paul R. Lawrence. Armonk, NY: M.E. Sharpe, pp. 329–44.

Kanter, Rosabeth Moss, Barry Stein, and Todd Jick (eds.). 1992. *The Challenge of Organizational Change: How Companies Experience It and Leaders Guide It.* New York: Free Press.

Karpoff, Jonathan M., Paul H Malatesta, and Ralph A. Walking. 1996. "Corporate Governance and Shareholder Initiatives: Empirical Evidence." *Journal of Financial Economics* 42: 365–395.

Katzenbach, Jon R., and Douglas K. Smith. 1993. *The Wisdom of Teams: Creating the High-Performance Organization.* Boston: Harvard Business School Press.

Kaufman, Allen M., Ernest J. Englander, and Alfred A. Marcus. 1993. "Selecting an Organizational Structure for Implementing Issues Management: A Transaction Costs and Agency Theory Perspective." In *Corporate Political Agency: The Construction of Competition in Public Affairs.* Ed. Barry M. Mitnick. Newbury Park, CA: Sage Publications, pp. 148–168.

Kaufmann, Stuart. 1995. *At Home in the Universe: The Search for Laws of Self-Organization and Complexity.* New York: Oxford University Press.

Keele, Reba. 1986. "Mentoring or Networking? Strong and Weak Ties in Career Development." In *Not as Far as You Think: The Realities of Working Women.* Ed. Lynda L. Moore. Lexington, MA: Lexington Books, pp. 53–68.

Kelley, Maryellen R. 1996. "Participative Bureaucracy and Productivity in the Machined Porducts Sector." *Industrial Relations* 35: 374–399.

Kenis, Patrick, and David Knoke. 1999. "A Network Theory of Organizations: How Field-Nets Shape Tie-Formation Rates." Paper presented to American Sociolgical Association Meeting, Chicago.

Kennedy, Paul. 1987. *The Rise and Fall of the Great Powers: Economic Change and Military Conflicts from 1500 to 2000.* New York: Random House.

Kerwood, Hazel A. 1995. "Where Do Just-In-Time Manufacturing Networks Fit? A Typology of Networks and a Framework for Analysis." *Human Relations* 48: 927–950.

Kimberly, John. 1981. "Managerial Innovation." In *Handbook of Organizational Design, Vol. I.* Ed. Paul C. Nystrom and William H. Starbuck. New York: Oxford University Press.

King, Jeanne C., and Allan W. Wicker. 1993. "Demography for Organizational Populations: Methodological Review and Applications." *Advances in Entrepreneurship, Firm Emergence, and Growth* 1: 83–143.

Kipling, Rudyard. 1913. *The Writings in Prose and Verse of Rudyard Kipling.* New York: Charles Scribner's Sons.

Kirchhoff, Bruce A., and Patricia G. Greene. 1998. "Understanding the Theoretical and Empirical Content of Critiques of U.S. Job Creation Research." *Small Business Economics* 10: 153–169.

Klein, April. 1998. "Firm Performance and Board Committee Structure." *Journal of Law and Economics* 41: 275–301.

Knoke, David. 1981. "Power Structures." In *Handbook of Political Behavior Vol. 3.* Ed. Samuel L. Long. New York: Plenum, pp. 275–332.

Knoke, David. 1988. "Incentives in Collective Action Organizations." *American Sociological Review* 53 (June): 311–329.

Knoke, David. 1990a. *Political Networks: The Structural Perspective.* New York: Cambridge University Press.

Knoke, David. 1990b. *Organizing for Collective Action: The Political Economies of Associations.* New York: Aldine de Gruyter.

Knoke, David. 1994. "Cui Bono? Employee Benefits Packages." *American Behavioral Scientist* 37: 963–978.

Knoke, David. 1998. "The Organizational State: Origins and Prospects." *Research in Political Sociology* 8: 147–163.

Knoke, David. 1999. "Organizational Networks and Corporate Social Capital." In *Corporate Social Capital and Liability.* Ed. Roger Th. A. J. Leenders and Shaul M. Gabbay. Boston: Kluwer Academic Publishers, pp. 17–42.

Knoke, David, and Edward O. Laumann. 1982. "The Social Organization of National Policy Domains: An Exploration of Some Structural Hypotheses." In *Social Structure and Network Analysis.* Ed. Peter V. Marsden and Nan Lin. Beverly Hills, CA: Sage Publications, pp. 255–270.

Knoke, David, and James H. Kuklinski. 1982. *Network Analysis.* Beverly Hills, CA: Sage

Knoke, David, and Lisa Janowiec-Kurle. 1999. "Make or Buy? The Externalization of Company Job Training." *Research in the Sociology of Organizations* 16: 85–106.

Knoke, David, and Miguel Guilarte. 1994. "Networks in Organizational Structures and Strategies." *Current Perspectives in Social Theory, Supplement* 1: 77–115.

Knoke, David, and Yoshito Ishio. 1994. "Occupational Training in Organizations: Job Ladders and Unions." *American Behavioral Scientist* 37: 992–1016.

Knoke, David, Franz Urban Pappi, Jeffrey Broadbent, and Yutaka Tsujinaka. 1996. *Comparing Policy Networks: Labor Politics in the U.S., Germany, and Japan.* New York: Cambridge University Press.

Kochan, Thomas A., Harry C. Katz, and Robert B. McKersie. 1986. *The Transformation of American Industrial Relations.* New York: Basic Books.

Kochan, Thomas A., Harry C. Katz, and Robert B. McKersie. 1994. *The Transformation of American Industrial Relations.* [First ILR Press ed.]. Ithaca: ILR Press.

Koeller, C. Timothy. 1994. "Union Activity and the Decline in American Trade Union Membership." *Journal of Labor Research* 15: 19–32.

Kogut, Bruce, Weijian Shan, and Gordon Walker. 1992. "The Make-or-Cooperate Decision in the Context of an Industry Network." In *Networks and Organizations: Structure, Form and Action.* Ed. Nitin Nohria and Robert G. Eccles. Boston: Harvard Business School Press, pp. 348–365.

Koike, Kazuo. 1998. "NUMMI and Its Prototype Plant in Japan: A Comparative Study of Human Resource Development at the Workshop Level." *Journal of the Japanese and International Economies* 12: 49–74.

Kollman, Ken. 1998. *Outside Lobbying: Public Opinion and Interest Group Strategies.* Princeton, NJ: Princeton University Press.

Koput, Kenneth W., Walter W. Powell, and Laurel Smith-Doerr. 1997. "Strategies of Learning and Industry Structure: The Evolution of Networks in Biotechnology." *Advances in Strategic Management Research* 14: 229–254.

Kosnik, Rita D. 1987. "Greenmail: A Study of Board Performance in Corporate Governance." *Administrative Science Quarterly* (32): 163–185.

Kotz, David. 1978. *Bank Control of Large Corporations in the United States.* Berkeley: University of California Press.

Krackhardt, David. 1990. "Assessing the Political Landscape: Structure, Cognition and Power in Organizations." *Administrative Science Quarterly* 35: 342–369.

Krackhardt, David. 1992. "The Strength of Strong Ties: The Importance of Philos in Organizations." In *Networks and Organizations: Structure, Form and Action.* Ed. Nitin Nohria and Robert G. Eccles. Boston: Harvard Business School Press, pp. 216–239.

Krackhardt, David. 1999. "The Ties That Torture: Simmelian Tie Analysis in Organizations." *Research in the Sociology of Organizations* 16: 183–210.

Krackhardt, David, and Jeffrey R. Hanson. 1993. "Informal Networks: The Company Behind the Chart." *Harvard Business Review* (July-August): 104–111.

Krackhardt, David, and Lyman W. Porter. 1985. "When Friends Leave: A Structural Analysis of the Relationship Between Turnover and Stayers' Attitudes." *Administrative Science Quarterly* 30: 242–261.

Krackhardt, David, and Lyman W. Porter. 1986. "The Snowball Effect: Turnover Embedded in Communication Networks." *Journal of Applied Psychology* 71: 50–55.

Kram, K. E. 1985. *Mentoring at Work.* Glenview, IL: Scott, Foresman.

Krasner, Stephen. 1984. "Approaches to the State: Alternative Conceptions and Historical Dynamics." *Comparative Politics* 16: 223–246.

Krehbiel, Kieth. 1991. *Information and Legislative Organization.* Ann Arbor: University of Michigan Press.

Kroll, Luisa. 1998. "Catching Up." *Forbes,* May 18.

Krugman, Paul R. 1990. *The Age of Diminished Expectations: U.S. Economic Policy in the 1990s.* Cambridge, MA: MIT Press.

Krugman, Paul R. 1994. *Peddling Prosperity: Economic Sense and Nonsense in the Age of Diminished Expectations.* New York: Norton.

Krugman, Paul R., and Robert Z. Lawrence. 1994. "Trade, Jobs and Wages." *Scientific American* (April): 44–49.

Kuemmerle, W. 1997. "Building Effective R&D Capabilities Abroad." *Harvard Business Review* (March-April): 61–70.

Kumbhakar, Subal C., and Amy E. Dunbar. 1993. "The Elusive ESOP-Productivity Link: Evidence from U.S. Firm-Level Data." *Journal of Public Economics* 52: 273–83.

Kurtyka, Jerry. 1999. "The Science of Complexity: A New Way to View Industry Change." *Journal of Retail Banking Services* 21: 51–58.

Lacey, Robert. 1986. *Ford: The Men and the Machine.* Boston: Little, Brown.

Lamphere, Louise, Patricia Zavella, Felipe Gonzales, with Peter B. Evans. 1993. *Sunbelt Working Mothers: Reconciling Family and Factory.* Ithaca: Cornell University Press.

Lancaster, Hal. 1994. "You, and Only You, Must Stay in Charge of Your Employability." *Wall Street Journal,* November 15: B1.

Larson, Andrea. 1992. "Network Dyads in Entrepreneurial Settings: A Study of the Governance of Exchange Relationships." *Administrative Science Quarterly* 37: 76–104.

Laumann, Edward O., and David Knoke. 1987. *The Organizational State: A Perspective on the Social Organization of National Energy and Health Policy Domains.* Madison: University of Wisconsin Press.

Laumann, Edward O., Peter V. Marsden, and David Prensky. 1983. "The Boundary Specification Problem in Network Analysis." In *Applied Network Analysis.* Ed. Ronald S. Burt and Michael J. Minor. Beverly Hills, CA: Sage Publications, pp. 18–34.

Lawler, Edward E., III. 1978. "The New Plant Revolution." *Organizational Dynamics* 6(3): 2–12.

Lawler, Edward E., III. 1990. "The New Plant Revolution Revisited." *Organizational Dynamics* 19(2): 5–14.

Lawler, Edward E., III. 1991. "The New Plant Approach: A Second Generation Approach." *Organizational Dynamics* 20(1): 5–15.

Lawler, Edward E., III. 1992. *The Ultimate Advantage: Creating the High-Involvement Organization.* San Francisco: Jossey-Bass.

Lawler, Edward E., III. 1996. *From the Ground Up: Six Pinciples for Building the New Logic Corporation.* San Francisco: Jossey-Bass.

Lawler, Edward E., III, and Susan A. Mohrman. 1985. "Quality Circles After the Fad." *Harvard Business Review* 63(1): 64–71.

Lawler, Edward E. III, Susan A. Mohrman, and Gerald E. Ledford. 1995. *Creating High Performance Organizations: Practices and Results of Employee Involvement and Total Quality Management in Fortune 1000 Companies.* San Francisco: Jossey-Bass.

Lawson, Ann M. 1997. "Benchmark Input-Output Accounts for the U.S. Economy, 1992 Make, Use, and Supplementary Tables." *Survey of Current Business* (November). <http://www.bea.doc.gov/bea/pubs.htm> (December 18, 1997)

Lazerson, Mark H. 1993. "Factory or Putting-out? Knitting Networks in Modena." In *The Embedded Firm.* Ed. Gernot Grabher. London: Routledge, pp. 203–226.

Lazerson, Mark H. 1995. "A New Phoenix? Modern Putting-Out in the Modena Knitwear Industry." *Administrative Science Quarterly* 40: 34–59.

Leenders, Roger Th. A. J. 1995. *Structure and Influence: Statistical Models for the Dynamics of Actor Attributes, Network Structure and Their Interdependence.* Amsterdam: Thesis Publishers.

Leenders, Roger Th. A. J. 1996. "Evolution of Friendship and Best Friendship Choices." *Journal of Mathematical Sociology* 21: 133–148.

Leenders, Roger Th. A. J., and Shaul M. Gabbay (eds.). 1999. *Corporate Social Capital and Liability.* Boston: Kluwer Academic Publishers.

Leoncini, Riccardo. 1998. "The Nature of Long-Run Technological Change: Innovation, Evolution and Technological Systems." *Research Policy* 27: 75–93.

Lepera, Christine, and Jeannie Costello. 1999. "The Use of Mediation in the New Millennium." *New York Law Journal,* May 6: 3.

Leung, Wai Shun Wilson. 1997. "The Inadequacy of Shareholder Primacy: A Proposed Corporate Regime that Recognizes Non-Shareholder Interests." *Columbia Journal of Law and Social Problems* 30: 587–634.

Levenson, Alec R. 1996. "Recent Trends in Part-time Employment." *Contemporary Economic Policy* 14: 78–89.

Levin, Mike. 1995. "Majors Take 50% Stake in Star's TV Music Channel." *Billboard,* January 14: 6.

Levitt, Barbara, and James G. March. 1988. "Organizational Learning." *Annual Review of Sociology* 14: 319–340.

Lewis, Charles. 1998. *The Buying of the Congress: How Special Interests Have Stolen Your Right to Life, Liberty, and the Pursuit of Happiness.* New York: Avon Books.

Lewis, H. Gregg. 1986. *Union Relative Wage Effects: A Survey.* Chicago: University of Chicago Press.

Lewis, Jordan D. 1990. *Partnerships for Profit: Structuring and Managing Strategic Alliances.* New York: Free Press.

Lewis, Jordan D., and A. Weigert. 1985. "Trust as a Social Reality." *Social Forces* 63: 967–985.

Lewis, Michael. 1989. *Liar's Poker: Rising Through the Wreckage on Wall Street.* New York: Norton.

Liden, Robert C., and Sharon Arad. 1996. "A Power Perspective of Empowerment and Work Groups: Implications for Human Resources Management Research." *Research in Personnel and Human Resources Management* 14: 205–251.

Liebeskind, J., Amalya Oliver, Lynne Zucker, and M. Brewer. 1996. "Social Networks, Learning, and Flexibility: Sourcing Scientific Knowledge in New Biotechnology Firms." *Organization Science* 7(4): 428–442.

Liebowitz, Stan J., and Stephen E. Margolis. 1999. *Winners, Losers and Microsoft: Competition and Antitrust in High Technology.* Oakland, CA: Independent Institute.

Limerick, David, and Bert Cunnington. 1993. *Managing the New Organization: A Blueprint for Networks and Strategic Alliances.* San Francisco: Jossey-Bass.

Lin, Nan. 1995. "Les Resources Sociales: Une Theorie du Capital Social." *Revue Francaise de Sociologie* 36: 685–704.

Lin, Nan, Walter M. Ensel, and John C. Vaughn. 1981. "Social Resources and Strength of Ties: Structural Factors in Occupational Status Attainment." *American Sociological Review* 46: 393–405.

Lincoln, James R., Michael L. Gerlach, and Peggy Takahashi. 1992. "Keiretsu Networks in the Japanese Economy: A Dyad Analysis of Intercorporate Ties." *American Sociological Review* 57: 561–585.

Lindsay, David H., and Annhenrie Campbell. 1996. "A Chaos Approach to Bankruptcy Prediction." *Journal of Applied Business Research* 12(4): 1–9.

Lipin, Steven. 1998. "Murphy's Law Doesn't Apply: The Conditions Are Perfect for Continued Growth in Mergers." *Wall Street Journal,* January 2: R6.

Lipin, Steven, and John J. Keller. 1997. "WorldCom's MCI Bid Alters Playing Field for Telecom Industry." *Wall Street Journal,* October 2: A1.

Lipton, Mark. 1985. "Takeover Abuses Mortgage the Future." *Wall Street Journal,* April 5: A16.

Lochhead, Carolyn. 1994. "Landmark Legislation on Telecommunications." *San Francisco Chronicle,* February 21: A1.

Lohr, Steve, and John Markoff. 1998. "Conquering the Internet." *New York Times,* November 24: A1.

Lorange, Peter, and Johan Roos. 1992. *Strategic Alliances: Formation, Implementation, and Evolution.* Cambridge, MA: Blackwell Business.

Lorsch, Jay W., with Elizabeth MacIver. 1989. *Pawns or Potentates: The Reality of America's Corporate Boards.* Boston: Harvard Business School Press.

Loury, G. 1977. "A Dynamic Theory of Racial Income Differences." In *Women, Minorities, and Employment Discrimination.* Ed. P. A. Wallace and A. LeMund. Lexington, MA: Lexington Books, chapter 8.

Luhmann, Niklas. 1979. *Trust and Power.* Chichester, UK: Wiley.

Lundvall, Bengt-Ake (ed.). 1992. *National Systems of Innovation: Towards a Theory of Innovation and Interactive Learning.* London: Pinter.

Luthans, Fred, Richard M. Hodgetts, and Stuart A. Rosenkrantz. 1988. "Networking Activities." In *Real Managers.* Cambridge, MA: Ballinger, pp. 119–133.

Lux, Thomas. 1998. "The Socio-economic Dynamics of Speculative Markets: Interacting Agents, Chaos, and the Fat Tails of Return Distributions." *Journal of Economic Behavior and Organization* 33: 143–165.

Macey, Jonathan. 1989. "Externalities, Firm-Specific Capital Investments, and the Legal Treatment of Fundamental Corporate Changes." *Duke Law Journal* 1989: 173–201.

MacDuffie, John Paul, and Frits K. Pil. 1997. "Changes in Auto Industry Employment Practices: An International Overview." In *After Lean Production: Evolving Employment Practices in the World Auto Industry.* Ed. Thomas A. Kochan, Russell D. Lansbury, and John Paul MacDuffie. Ithaca: ILR Press, Pp. 9–42.

Makridakis, Spyros G. 1990. *Forecasting, Planning, and Strategy for the 21st Century.* New York: Free Press.

Malecki, Edward J. 1997. "Entrepreneurs, Networks, and Economic Development: A Review of Recent Research." *Advances in Entrepreneurship, Firm Emergence, and Growth* 3: 57–118.

Manne, Henry G. 1965. "Mergers and the Market for Corporate Control." *Journal of Political Economy* 73: 110–120.

Maranto, Cheryl L., and Jack Fiorito. 1987. "The Effect of Union Characteristics on the Outcome of NLRB Certification Elections." *Industrial and Labor Relations Review* 40: 225–240.

March, James G. 1991. "Exploration and Exploitation in Organizational Learning." *Organization Science* 2: 71–87.

March, James G. 1999. *The Pursuit of Organizational Intelligence.* Malden, MA: Blackwell.

Mariolis, Peter. 1975. "Interlocking Directorates and Control of Corporations." *Social Science Quarterly* 56: 425–439.

Marion, Russ. 1999. *The Edge of Organization: Chaos and Complexity Theories of Formal Social Systems.* Thousand Oaks, CA: Sage Publications.

Markels, Alex. 1995. "Restructuring Alters Middle-Manager Role But Leaves It Robust." *Wall Street Journal,* September 25: A1.

Markides, Constantinos C. 1995. *Diversification, Refocusing, and Economic Performance.* Cambridge, MA: MIT Press.

Markoff, John, and Geraldine Fabrikant. 1998. "TCI Seeks Variety in Software and Suppliers for TV Boxes." *New York Times,* January 12: D1.

Marsden, Peter V. 1987. "The Core Discussion Networks of Americans." *American Sociological Review* 52: 122–131.

Marsden, Peter V., and Jeanne S. Hurlbert. 1988. "Social Resources and Mobility Outcomes: A Replication and Extension." *Social Forces* 88: 686–717.

Marshall, Alfred. 1986. *Principles of Economics.* 8th ed. London: Macmillan.

Marx, Karl, and Friedrich Engels. 1939. *The Communist Manifesto.* Authorized English translation, edited and annotated by Frederick Engels. New York: New York Labor News Co.

Masters, Kim. 2000. *The Keys to the Kingdom: How Michael Eisner Lost His Grip.* New York: Morrow.

Maurer, Christine, and Tara E. Sheets (eds.). 1999. *Encyclopedia of Associations.* 34th ed. Detroit: Gale Group.

Mayer, Robert N. 1989. *The Consumer Movement: Guardians of the Marketplace.* Boston: Twayne.

Mayer-Foulkes, David, and Raul Anibal Feliz. 1996. "Nonlinear Dynamics in the Stock Exchange." *Revista de Analisis Economico* 11: 3–21.

Mayr Ernst, and William B. Provine (eds.). 1988. *The Evolutionary Synthesis: Perspectives on the Unification of Biology.* Cambridge, MA: Harvard University Press.

McAdam, Doug, Sidney Tarrow, and Charles Tilly. 1996. "To Map Contentious Politics." *Mobilization* 1: 17–34.

McAllister, Daniel J. 1995. "Affect- and Cognition-Based Trust as Foundations for Interpersonal Cooperation in Organizations." *Academy of Management Journal* 38: 24–59.

McClellan, Steve. 1996. "MCA, Viacom Battle over TV Land." *Broadcasting and Cable,* May 6: 32.

McFadden, Robert D. 1993. "2 Get Ready to Lock Horns at The Daily News." *New York Times,* January 12: B3.

McGuire, Steven. 1997. *Airbus Industrie: Conflict and Cooperation in US-EC Trade Relations.* New York: St. Martin's Press.

McKelvey, Bill. 1982. *Organizational Systematics: Taxonomy, Evolution, Classification.* Berkeley: University of California Press.

McMillan, G. Steven, Francis Narin, and David L. Deeds. 2000. "An Analysis of the Critical Role of Public Science in Innovation: The Case of Biotechnology." *Research Policy* 29: 1–8.

McWhirter, William. 1992. "Who's in the Driver's Seat?" *Time*, October 26: 55.

Meckstroth, Alicia, and Paul Arnsberger. 1998. "A 20-Year Review of the Nonprofit Sector, 1975–1995." *SOI Bulletin* (Fall): 149–171.

Menard, Claude. 1996. "Why Organizations Matter: A Journey Away from the Fairy Tale." *Atlantic Economic Journal* 24(4): 281–300.

Meredith, Robyn. 1998. "Many at the Saturn Auto Factory Are Finding Less to Smile About." *New York Times*, March 6: A1.

Mergerstat. 2000. "More Than 30 Years of M&A Activity." <http://www.mergerstat. com/free_reports/free_reports_m_and_a_activity.html> (March 15, 2000).

Merton, Robert K. 1961. "Bureaucratic Structure and Personality." In *Complex Organizations: A Sociological Reader*. Ed. Amatai Etzioni. New York: Holt, Rinehart, pp. 47–59.

Meyer, John W., and Brian Rowan. 1977. "Institutionalized Organizations: Formal Structure as Myth and Ceremony." *American Journal of Sociology* 83: 340–363.

Miceli, Marcia P., and Janet P. Near. 1988. "Individual and Situational Correlates of Whistle-Blowing." *Personnel Psychology* 41: 267–282.

Miceli, Marcia P., and Janet P. Near. 1992. *Blowing the Whistle: The Organizational and Legal Implications for Companies and Employees*. New York: Lexington Books.

Michels, Robert. 1949. *Political Parties: A Sociological Study of the Oligarchical Tendencies of Modern Democracy*. Translated by Eden and Cedar Paul. Glencoe, IL: Free Press.

Mikkelson, Wayne H., and M. Megan Partch. 1997. "The Decline of Takeovers and Disciplinary Managerial Turnover." *Journal of Financial Economics* 44: 205–228.

Miles, Raymond E., and Charles C. Snow. 1996. "Twenty-First-Century Careers." In.*The Boundaryless Career: A New Employment Principle for a New Organizational Era*. Ed. Michael B. Arthur and Denise M. Rousseau. New York: Oxford University Press, pp. 97–115.

Miliband, Ralph. 1969. *The State in Capitalist Society*. New York: Basic Books.

Millon, David. 1990. "Frontiers of Legal Thought I: Theories of the Corporation." *Duke Law Journal* 1190: 201–259.

Mills, C. Wright. 1956. *The Power Elite*. New York: Oxford University Press.

Mills, Mike. 1995. "Disney Hires Michael Ovitz, Hollywood's Star Dealmaker: Super-Agent Named to No. 2 Position." *Washington Post*, August 15: A1.

Mills, Mike. 1996. "Ushering in a New Age in Communications: Clinton Signs 'Revolutionary' Bill into Law at a Ceremony Packed with Symbolism." *Washington Post*, February 9: C1.

Millstein, Ira M., and Paul W. MacAvoy. 1998. "The Active Board of Directors and Performance of the Large Publicly Traded Corporation." *Columbia Law Review* 98: 1283–1321.

Milward, H. Brinton. 1996. "Symposium on the Hollow State: Capacity, Control and Performance in Interorganizational Settings." *Journal of Public Administration and Theory* 62: 193–195.

Milward, H. Brinton, and Keith G. Provan. 1998. "Principles for Controlling Agents: The Political Economy of Network Structure." *Journal of Public Administration Research and Theory* 8(2): 203–221.

Mincer, Jacob. 1994. "Human Capital: A Review." In *Labor Economics and Industrial Relations: Markets and Institutions*. Ed. Clark Kerr and Paul D. Staudohar. Cambridge, MA: Harvard University Press, pp. 109–141.

Miner, Anne S., and Philip Anderson. 1999. "Industry and Population-Level Learning: Organizational, Interorganizational, and Collective Learning Processes." *Advances in Strategic Management* 16: 1–30.

Miner, Anne S., and Pamela R. Haunschild. 1995. "Population Level Learning." *Research in Organizational Behavior* 17: 115–166.

Miner, Anne S., and Stephen J. Mezias. 1996. "Ugly Duckling No More: Pasts and Futures of Organizational Learning Research." *Organization Science* 7(1): 88–99.

Minkin, Barry Howard. 1995. *Future in Sight: 100 Trends, Implications & Predictions That Will Most Impact Businesses and the World Economy into the 21st Century*. New York: Macmillan.

Mintz, Beth. 1995. "Business Participation in Health Care Policy Reform: Factors Contributing to Collective Action within the Business Community." *Social Problems* 42: 408–428.

Mintz, Beth, and Michael Schwartz. 1985. *The Power Structure of American Business*. Chicago: University of Chicago Press.

Mintzberg, Henry. 1979. *The Structure of Organizations*. Englewood Cliffs, NJ: Prentice-Hall.

Mintzberg, Henry. 1983. *Power in and Around Organizations*. Englewood Cliffs, NJ: Prentice-Hall.

Mitchell, J. Clyde. 1969. "The Concept and Use of Social Networks." In *Social Networks in Urban Situations*. Ed. J. Clyde Mitchell. Manchester, UK: Manchester University Press, pp. 1–50.

Mitchell, Neil J. 1997. *The Conspicuous Corporation: Business, Public Policy and Representative Democracy*. Ann Arbor: University of Michigan Press.

Mitnick, Barry M. 1992. "The Theory of Agency and Organizational Analysis." In *Ethics and Agency Theory: An Introduction*. Ed. Norman E. Bowie and R. Edward Freeman. New York: Oxford University Press, pp. 75–96.

Mitnick, Barry M. (ed.). 1993. *Corporate Political Agency: The Construction of Competition in Public Affairs*. Newbury Park, CA: Sage Publications.

Mizell, Louis R., Jr. 1997. *Masters of Deception: The Worldwide White-Collar Crime Crisis and Ways to Protect Yourself*. New York: Wiley.

Mizruchi, Mark S. 1982. *The American Corporate Network 1904–1974*. Beverly Hills, CA: Sage Publications.

Mizruchi, Mark S. 1992. *The Structure of Corporate Political Action: Interfirm Relations and Their Consequences*. Cambridge, MA: Harvard University Press.

Mizruchi, Mark S. 1994. "Social Network Analysis: Recent Achievements and Current Controversies." *Acta Sociologica* 37: 329–343.

Mizruchi, Mark S. 1996. "What Do Interlocks Do? An Analysis, Critique, and Assessment of Research on Interlocking Directorates." *Annual Review of Sociology* 22: 271–298.

Moe, Terry. 1980. *The Organization of Interests: Incentives and the Internal Dynamics of Political Interest Groups*. Chicago: University of Chicago Press.

Monden, Yasuhiro. 1993. *Toyota Production System: An integrated Approach to Just-in-Time*. 2d ed. Norcross, GA: Industrial Engineering and Management Press.

Monks, Robert A.G. 1998. *The Emperor's Nightingale: Restoring the Integrity of the Corporation in the Age of Shareholder Activism*. Reading, MA: Addison-Wesley.

Moore, Gwen. 1979. "The Structure of a National Elite." *American Sociological Review* 44: 673–691.

Moreno, Jacob L. 1934. *Who Shall Survive?* Washington, DC: Nervous and Mental Disease Publishing Co.

Morra, Linda G. 1995. "Employment Discrimination: Most Private-Sector Employees Use Alternative Dispute Resolution." Washington, DC: Government Accounting Office.

Morris, Betty. 1997. "Big Blue." *Fortune*, April 14: 68–81.

Morris, Michael H. 1998. *Entrepreneurial Intensity: Sustainable Advantages for Individuals, Organizations, and Societies*. Westport, CT: Quorum Books.

Morrow, David J. 2000. "Rise, and Fall, of 'Life Sciences': Drugmakers Scramble to Unload Agricultural Units." *New York Times*, January 20: C1.

Mowery, David C. 1998. "The Changing Structure of the US National Innovation System: Implications for International Conflict and Cooperation in R&D Policy." *Research Policy* 27: 639–654.

Murphy, Kevin J., and Jerold L. Zimmerman. 1993. "Financial Performance Surrounding CEO Turnover." *Journal of Accounting and Economics* 16: 273–316.

Nadel, S. F. 1957. *The Theory of Social Structure*. Glencoe, IL: Free Press.

Naffziger, Douglas. 1995. "Entrepreneurship: A Person Based Theory Approach." *Advances in Entrepreneurship, Firm Emergence, and Growth* 2: 21–50.

Nahapiet, J., and Sumantra Ghoshal. 1998. "Social Capital, Intellectual Capital, and the Organizational Advantage." *Academy of Management Review* 23: 242–266.

Naik, Gautam. 1997. "BT's Plan to Be Global Telecom Player May Have Collapsed with Its MCI Bid." *Wall Street Journal*, November 11: B8.

Naisbitt, John. 1994. *Global Paradox: The Bigger the World Economy, the More Powerful Its Smallest Players*. New York: William Morrow.

Nasar, Sylvia. 1994. "Myth: Small Business as Job Engine." *New York Times*, March 25: C1.

National Labor Relations Board. 1977–1999. *NLRB Election Report*. Washington, DC: Government Printing Office.

National Organizations Survey. 1997. *Machine Readable Data File*. University of Minnesota [producer] 1997. Inter-university Consortium for Political and Social Research (ICPSR) [distributor] 2000.

National Science Foundation. 1998. *Science and Engineering Indicators 1998*. Washington, DC: Government Printing Office.

Near, Janet P., Terry Morehead Dworkin, and Marcia P. Miceli. 1993. "Explaining the Whistle-Blowing Process: Suggestions from Power Theory and Justice Theory." *Organization Science* 4: 393–411.

Near, Janet P., and Marcia P. Miceli. 1995. "Effective Whistle-Blowing." *Academy of Management Review* 20: 679–708.

Nelson, Ralph L. 1959. *Merger Movements in American Industry, 1895–1956.* Princeton, NJ: Princeton University Press.

Nelson, Richard R. (ed.). 1993. *National System of Innovation.* New York: Oxford University Press.

Nelson, Richard R. 1994. "Evolutionary Theorizing about Economic Change." In *The Handbook of Economic Sociology.* Ed. Neil Smelser and Richard Swedberg. Princeton, NJ: Princeton University Press, pp. 108–136.

Nelson, Richard R., and Sydney Winter. 1974. "Neoclassical Versus Evolutionary Theories of Economic Growth: Critique and Perspective." *Economic Journal* 84: 886–905.

Nelson, Richard R., and Sydney Winter. 1982. *An Evolutionary Theory of Economic Change.* Cambridge, MA: Harvard University Press.

Nesbitt, Stephen L. 1994. "Long-term Rewards from Shareholder Activism: A Study of the 'CalPERS Effect'." *Journal of Applied Corporate Finance* 6(4): 75–80.

New York Stock Exchange. 2000. "Listed Company Manual." <http://www.nyse.com/listed/listed.html> (June 13, 2000).

Nijkamp, Peter, and Aura Reggiani. 1998. *The Economics of Complex Spatial Systems.* Amsterdam: Elsevier Science, North-Holland.

Noble, Kenneth B. 1985. "In 50 Years, Unions Move from Fans to Foes of Labor Board." *New York Times,* July 9: A14.

Noe, Raymond A. 1988. "Women and Mentoring: A Review and Research Agenda." *Academy of Management Review* 13: 65–78.

Nohria, Nitin, and S. Ghoshal. 1997. *The Differentiated Network: A New Model for Organizing Multinational Corporations.* San Francisco: Jossey-Bass.

Novak, Tim. 2000. "Federal Mole Gets 39 Months: Silver Shovel Corruption Probe Ends." *Chicago Sun-Times,* March 18: 3.

Ocasio, William. 1994. "Political Dynamics and the Circulation of Power: CEO Succession in U.S. Industrial Corporations, 1960–1990." *Administrative Science Quarterly* 39: 285–312.

Ocasio, William. 1999. "Institutionalized Action and Corporate Governance: The Reliance on Rules of CEO Succession." *Administrative Science Quarterly* 44: 384–416.

O'Connor, Marleen A. 1991. "Restructuring the Corporation's Nexus of Contacts: Recognizing a Fiduciary Duty to Protect Displaced Workers." *North Carolina Law Review* 69: 1189.

Oleszek, Walter J. 1978. *Congressional Procedures and the Policy Process.* Washington: Congressional Quarterly Press.

Oliver, Amalya L. 1997. "On the Nexus of Organizations and Professions: Networking Through Trust." *Sociological Inquiry* 67: 227–245.

Oliver, Christine. 1990. "Determinants of Interorganizational Relationships: Integration and Future Directions." *Academy of Management Review* 15: 241–265.

Olmos, David R. 1995. "They've Been There, Done That—And Now They're Passing It on to Others." *Los Angeles Times,* March 13: Business, Part 2: 22.

Olson, Craig A. 1995. "Health Benefits Coverage Among Male Workers." *Monthly Labor Review* 118(3): 55–61.

Olson, Mancur. 1965. *The Logic of Collective Action: Public Goods and the Theory of Groups.* Cambridge, MA: Harvard University Press.

Olson, Randall. 2000. "High-Tech, Low-Profile: 'New Economy' Companies and Their Financial Backers Can Thrive in Minnesota, But a Stronger Network Is Needed to Stitch Them Together." *Minneapolis Star Tribune,* May 1: Business 3.

O'Neill, Gerard K. 1981. *2081: A Hopeful View of the Human Future.* London: Jonathan Cape.

O'Neill, Regina, Sylvia Horton, and Faye J. Crosby. 1998. "Gender Issues in Developmental Relationships." In *Mentoring Dilemmas: Developmental Relationships Within Multicultural Organizations.* Ed. Audrey Murrell, Faye J. Crosby, and Robin J. Ely. Mahwah, NJ: Lawrence Earlbaum Associates, pp. 63–80.

Opler, Tim C., and Jonathan Sokobin. 1995. "Does Coordinated Institutional Activism Work? An Analysis of the Activities of the Council of Institutional Investors." Mimeographed document, Ohio State University, Columbus. <http://www.timopler.com/ciiweb> (June 18, 1999).

O'Reilly, Brian. 1994. "The New Deal: What Companies and Employees Owe One Another." *Fortune,* June 13: 44–52.

Orru, Marco. 1991. "The Institutional Logic of Small-Firm Economies in Italy and Taiwan." *Studies in Comparative International Development* 26: 3–28.

Orts, Eric W. 1992. "Beyond Shareholders: Interpreting Corporate Constituency Statutes." *George Washington Law Review* 61(November): 16–134.

Osborn, Richard N., and C. Christopher Baughn. 1990. "Forms of Interorganizational Governance for Multinational Alliances." *Academy of Management Journal* 33: 503–519.

Osterman, Paul (ed.). 1984. *Internal Labor Markets.* Cambridge, MA: MIT Press.

Osterman, Paul. 1994a. "How Common Is Workplace Transformation and How Can We Explain Who Does It?" *Industrial and Labor Relations Review* 47: 173–188.

Osterman, Paul. 1994b. "Internal Labor Markets: Theory and Change." In *Labor Economics and Industrial Relations: Markets and Institutions.* Ed. Clark Kerr and Paul D. Staudohar. Cambridge, MA: Harvard University Press, pp. 303–339.

Osterman, Paul. 1995a. "Skill, Training, and Work Organization in American Establishments." *Industrial Relations* 34: 125–146.

Osterman, Paul. 1995b. "Work/Family Programs and the Employment Relationship." *Administrative Science Quarterly* 40: 681–700.

Osterman, Paul (ed.). 1996. *Broken Ladders: Managerial Careers in the New Economy.* New York: Oxford University Press.

Osterman, Paul. 1999. *Securing Prosperity: The American Labor Market: How It Has Changed and What to Do About It.* Princeton, NJ: Princeton University Press.

Oswald, Lynda J. 1998. "Shareholders v. Stakeholders: Evaluating Corporate Constituency Statutes Under the Takings Clause." *Iowa Journal of Corporation Law* 24: 1–18.

Palmer, Donald, Brad Barber, Xueguang Zhou, and Yasemin Soysal. 1995. "The Friendly and Predatory Acquisition of Large U.S. Corporations in the 1960s." *American Sociological Review* 60: 469–500.

Palmer, Donald, P. Devereaux Jennings, and Xueguang Zhou. 1993. "Late Adoption of the Multidivisional Form by Large U.S. Corporations: Institutional, Political and Economic Accounts." *Administrative Science Quarterly* 38: 100–131.

Palmer, Donald, Roger Friedland, P. Devereaux Jennings, and Melanie E. Powers. 1987. "The Economics and Politics of Structure: The Multidivisional Form and the Large U.S. Corporation." *Administrative Science Quarterly* 32: 25–48.

Pandey, Vivek, Theodor Kohers, and Gerald Kohers. 1998. "Deterministic Nonlinearity in the Stock Returns of Major European Equity Markets and the United States." *Financial Review* 33: 45–63.

Papaconstantinou, G., N. Sakuri, and A. Wyckoff. 1998. "Domestic and International Product-Market R&D Diffusion." *Research Policy* 27: 301–314.

Pappi, Franz Urban. 1984. "Boundary Specifications and Structural Models of Elite Systems: Social Circles Revisited." *Social Networks* 6: 79–95.

Parker, Robert E. 1994. *Flesh Peddlers and Warm Bodies: The Temporary Help Industry and Its Workers.* New Brunswick, NJ: Rutgers University Press.

Parker-Pope, Tara. 1996. "So Far Away." *Wall Street Journal,* April 11: R12.

Parrino, Robert. 1997. "CEO Turnover and Outside Succession: A Cross-Sectional Analysis." *Journal of Financial Economics* 46: 165–197.

Parsons, Talcott. 1951. *The Social System.* Glencoe, IL: Free Press.

Peli, Gabor, Jeroen Bruggeman, Michael Masuch, and Breanndan O. Nuallain. 1994. "A Logical Approach to Formalizing Organizational Ecology." *American Sociological Review* 59: 571–593.

Pennings, Johannes M., Kyungmook Lee, and Arjen van Witteloostuijn. 1998. "Human Capital, Social Capital, and Firm Dissolution." *Academy of Management Journal* 41: 425–440.

Perrow, Charles. 1992. "Small-Firm Networks." In *Networks and Organizations: Structure, Form and Action.* Ed. Nitin Nohria and Robert G. Eccles. Boston: Harvard Business School Press, pp. 445–479.

Peteraf, Margaret, and Mark Shanley. 1997. "Social Learning and the 'Fundamental Paradox' of Transaction Cost Economics." *Advances in Strategic Management Research* 14: 193–222.

Peters, Lois, Peter Groenewegen, and Nico Fiebelkorn. 1998. "A Comparison of Networks Between Industry and Public Sector Research in Materials Technology and Biotechnology." *Research Policy* 27: 255–271.

Pfeffer, Jeffrey. 1972. "Merger as a Response to Organizational Interdependence." *Administrative Science Quarterly* 17: 382–394.

Pfeffer, Jeffrey. 1978. "The Micropolitics of Organizations." In *Environments and Organizations.* Ed. Marshall Meyer and Associates. San Francisco: Jossey-Bass, pp. 29–50.

Pfeffer, Jeffrey. 1981. *Power in Organizations.* Cambridge, MA: Ballinger.

Pfeffer, Jeffrey. 1982. *Organizations and Organizational Theory.* Cambridge, MA: Ballinger.

Pfeffer, Jeffrey. 1987. "A Resource Dependence Perspective on Intercorporate Relations." In *Intercorporate Relations: The Structural Analysis of Business.* Ed. Mark Mizruchi and Michael Schwartz. New York: Cambridge University Press, pp. 25–55.

Pfeffer, Jeffrey. 1994. *Competitive Advantage Through People: Unleashing the Power of the Workplace.* Boston: Harvard Business School Press.

Pfeffer, Jeffrey. 1996. "When It Comes to 'Best Practices'—Why Do Smart Organizations Occasionally Do Dumb Things?" *Organizational Dynamics* 19(Summer): 33–44.

Pfeffer, Jeffrey. 1997. *New Directions for Organization Theory: Problems and Prospects.* Oxford: Oxford University Press.

Pfeffer, Jeffrey, and Gerald R. Salancik. 1978. *The External Control of Organization: A Resource Dependence Perspective.* New York: Harper & Row.

Pfeffer, Jeffrey, and Philip Nowak. 1976. "Joint Ventures and Interorganizational Interdependence." *Aministrative Science Quarterly* 21: 398–418.

Phillips, Bruce D. 1991. "The Increasing Role of Small Firms in the High-Technology Sector: Evidence from the 1980s." *Business Economics* 26: 40–47.

Phillips, Bruce D. 1993. "The Growth of Small Firm Jobs by State, 1984–88." *Business Economics* 28(2): 48–53.

Phillips, Kevin. 1993. *Boiling Point: Democrats, Republicans, and the Decline of Middle-Class Prosperity.* New York: Random House.

Piore, Michael, and Charles F. Sabel. 1984. *The Second Industrial Divide: Possibilities for Prosperity.* New York: Basic Books.

Podolny, Joel M. 1993. "A Status-Based Model of Market Competition." *American Journal of Sociology* 98: 829–872.

Podolny, Joel M. 1994. "Market Uncertainty and the Social Character of Economic Exchange." *Administrative Science Quarterly* 39: 458–483.

Podolny, Joel M., and James N. Baron. 1997. "Relationships and Resources: Social Networks and Mobility in the Workplace." *American Sociological Review* 62: 673–693.

Podolny, Joel M., and Toby E. Stuart. 1995. "A Role-Based Ecology of Technological Change." *American Journal of Sociology* 100: 1224–1260.

Poland, Diane, and Andrew A. Beveridge. 1992. "Does Union Matter? An Analysis of 81,418 NLRB Union Representation Elections, 1972–87." Paper presented to annual meetings of the American Sociological Association.

Polivka, Anne E. 1996. "A Profile of Contingent Workers." *Monthly Labor Review* (October): 10–21.

Pollack, Andrew. 1999. "Patenting Life: Biological Products Raise Genetic Ownership Issues." *New York Times,* November 26: A1.

Popper, Karl. 1959. *The Logic of Scientific Discovery.* New York: Basic Books.

Poulantzas, Nicos. 1978. *State, Power, Socialism.* London: NLB.

Pound, John. 1992. "Raiders, Targets, and Politics: The History and Future of American Corporate Control." *Journal of Applied Corporate Finance* 5(3): 6–18.

Powell, Walter W. 1987. "Hybrid Organizational Arrangements: New Form or Transitional Development?" *California Management Review* 30(1): 67–87.

Powell, Walter W. 1990. "Neither Market Nor Hierarchy: Network Forms of Organizations." *Research in Organizational Behavior* 12: 295–366.

Powell, Walter W. 1996. "Inter-organizational Collaboration in the Biotechnology Industry." *Journal of Institutional and Theoretical Economics* 152: 197–216.

Powell, Walter W., Kenneth W. Koput, and Laurel Smith-Doerr. 1996. "Interorganizational Collaboration and the Locus of Innovation: Networks of Learning in Biotechnology." *Administrative Science Quarterly* 41: 116–145.

Powell, Walter W., and Peter Brantley. 1992. "Competitive Cooperation in Biotechnology: Learning Through Networks?" In *Networks and Organizations: Structure, Form and Action.* Ed. Nitin Nohria and Robert G. Eccles. Boston: Harvard Business School Press, pp. 366–394.

Power, Carol. 1997. "Heinz Board Might Lack Some Essential Ingredients." *The Irish Times*, September 19: 52.

Prechel, Harland. 1997a. "Corporate Form and the State: Business Policy and Change from the Multidivisional to the Multilayered Subsidiary Form." *Sociological Inquiry* 67: 151–174.

Prechel, Harland. 1997b. "Corporate Transformation to the Multilayered Subsidiary Form: Changing Economic Conditions and State Business Policy." *Sociological Forum* 12: 405–439.

Prechel, Harland, John Boies, and Tim Woods. 1997. "Debt, Mergers and Acquisitions, and Transformation to the Multilayered Subsidiary Form." Paper presented to the American Sociological Association Meetings, Toronto.

Prewitt, Kenneth, and Alan Stone. 1973. *The Ruling Elites: Elite Theory, Power, and American Democracy*. New York: Harper & Row.

PricewaterhouseCoopers. 2000. "Moneytree U.S. Report, Full Year & Q4 1999 Results." <http: //www.pwcmoneytree.com/> (March 31, 2000).

Pryor, David H. 1994. "EEOC's Expanding Workload; Increasing in Age Discrimination and Other Charges Call for New Approach." Washington, DC: General Accounting Office. Report HEHS–94–32.

Pyke Frank, and W. Sengenberger (eds.). 1992. *Industrial Districts and Local Economic Regeneration*. Geneva: International Labor Office.

Quintanilla, Carl, and Susan Carey. 1995. "Successful Northwest, KLM Partnership Hits the Skids." *Wall Street Journal*, November 2: B6.

Raeburn, Nicole C. 2000. "The Rise of Lesbian, Gay, and Bisexual Rights in the Workplace." Ph.D. dissertation, Ohio State University.

Ragins, Belle Rose. 1995. "Diversity, Power, and Mentorship in Organizations: A Cultural, Structural and Behavioral Perspective." In *Diversity in Organizations*. Ed. M. Chemers, M. Costanzo, and S. Oskamp. Newbury Park, CA: Sage Publications, pp. 91–132.

Ragins, Belle Rose, and T.A. Scandura. 1994. "Gender Differences in Expected Outcomes of Mentoring Relationships." *Academy of Management Journal* 37: 957–971.

Raider, Holly J., and Ronald S. Burt. 1996. "Boundaryless Careers and Social Capital." In *The Boundaryless Career: A New Employment Principle for a New Organizational Era*. Ed. Michael B. Arthur and Denise M. Rousseau. New York: Oxford University Press, pp. 187–200.

Ramsey, James B. 1996. "If Nonlinear Models Cannot Forecast, What Use Are They?" *Studies in Nonlinear Dynamics and Econometrics* 1(2): 65–86.

Rao, Hayagreeva, and Kumar Sivakumar. 1999. "Institutional Sources of Boundary-Spanning Structures: The Establishment of Investor Relations Departments in the Fortune 500 Industrials." *Organization Science* 10: 27–42.

Rebitzer, James B. 1994. "Structural, Microeconomic and Institutional Explanations for Union Decline in the United States." *Economic Review* 45: 41–52.

Reid, Calvin. 1996. "Outcry Over Telecom Anti-smut Act; ACLU Files Free Speech Suit." *Publishers Weekly*, February 12: 16.

Reskin, Barbara F. 1998. *The Realities of Affirmative Action in Employment*. Washington, DC: American Sociological Association.

Reve, Torger. 1990. "The Firm as a Nexus of Internal and External Contracts." In *The Firm as a Nexus of Treaties*. Ed. Masahiko Aoki, Bo Gustafson, and Oliver Williamson. London: Sage Publications, pp. 133–161.

Reynolds, Paul D., and Sammis B. White. 1997. *The Entrepreneurial Process; Economic Growth, Men, Women, and Minorities*. Westport, CT: Quorum Books.

Ribstein, Larry E. 1989. "Takeover Defenses and the Corporate Contract." *Georgetown Law Journal* 78: 71–151.

Ricci, David M. 1993. *The Transformation of American Politics: The New Washington and the Rise of Think Tanks*. New Haven, CT: Yale University Press.

Rice, Ronald E., and Carol Aydin. 1991. "Attitudes Toward New Organizational Technology: Network Proximity as a Mechanism for Social Information Processing." *Administrative Science Quarterly* 36: 219–244.

Rinehart, James, Christopher Huxley, and David Robertson. 1997. *Just Another Car Factory? Lean Production and Its Discontents*. Ithaca: ILR Press.

Ring, Peter Smith. 1996. "Fragile and Resilient Trust and Their Roles in Economic Exchange." *Business and Society* 35: 148–175.

Ring, Peter Smith, and Andrew H. Van de Ven. 1994. "Developmental Processes of Cooperative Interorganizational Relationships." *Academy of Management Journal* 19: 90–118.

Ritzer, George. 1989. "The Permanently New Economy: The Case for Reviving Economic Sociology." *Work and Occupations* 16: 243–272.

Robson, Geoffrey B. 1996. "Unraveling the Facts about Job Generation." *Small Business Economics* 8: 409–17.

Roe, Mark. 1994. *Strong Managers, Weak Owners*. Princeton, NJ: Princeton University Press.

Rogers, David L., and David A. Whetten. 1982. *Interorganizational Coordination: Theory, Research and Implementation*. Ames: Iowa State University Press.

Rogers, Everett M. 1995. *Diffusion of Innovation*. 5th ed. New York: Free Press.

Rogers, Everett M., and Katherine Larsen. 1984. *Silicon Valley Fever*. New York: Basic Books.

Romanelli, Elaine. 1991. "The Evolution of New Organizational Forms." *Annual Review of Sociology* 17: 79–103.

Romer, Thomas, and James M. Snyder, Jr. 1994. "An Empirical Investigation of the Dynamics of PAC Contributions." *American Journal of Political Science* 38: 745–769.

Rose, Joseph B., and Gary N. Chaison. 1996. "Linking Union Density and Union Effectiveness: The North American Experience." *Industrial Relations* 35: 78–105.

Rosen, Sherwin. 1981. "The Economics of Superstars." *American Economic Review* 71: 845–858.

Rosenberg, Hilary. 1999. "Hark! The Shareholders Are Restless in Europe." *New York Times*, December 12(3): 4.

Rothschild, Joyce, and Terance D. Miethe. 1994. "Whistleblowing as Resistance in Modern Work Organizations: The Politics of Revealing Organizational Deception and Abuse." In *Resistance and Power in Organizations*. Ed. John M. Jermier, David Knights, and Walter R. Nord. London: Routledge, pp. 252–273.

Rousseau, Denise M. 1977. "Technological Differences in Job Characteristics, Employee Satisfaction, and Motivation: A Synthesis of Job Design Research and Sociotechnical Systems Theory." *Organizational Behavior and Human Performance* 19: 18–42.

Rousseau, Denise M. 1995. *Psychological Contracts in Organizations: Understanding Written and Unwritten Agreements*. Thousand Oaks, CA: Sage Publications.

Roy, William. 1997. *Socializing Capital: The Rise of the Large Industrial Corporation in America*. Princeton, NJ: Princeton University Press.

Rozell, Mark J., and Clyde Wilcox. 1999. *Interest Groups in American Campaigns: The New Face of Electioneering*. Washington, DC: Congressional Quarterly Press.

Rudolph, Thomas J. 1999. "Corporate and Labor PAC Contributions in House Elections: Measuring the Effects of Majority Party Status." *Journal of Politics* 61: 195–206.

Rueschemeyer, Dietrich, Evelyne Huber Stephens, and John D. Stephens. 1992. *Capitalist Development and Democracy*. Chicago: University of Chicago Press.

Ruggiero, Vincenzo. 1996. *Organized and Corporate Crime in Europe: Offers That Can't Be Refused*. Brookfield, VT: Dartmouth Publishing.

Russell, John J. 1997. *National Trade and Professional Associations of the United States*. 32d ed. New York: Columbia Books.

Sabato, Larry J., and Glenn R. Simpson. 1996. *Dirty Little Secrets: The Persistence of Corruption in American Politics*. New York: Times Books.

Sabbagh, Karl. 1996. *21st Century Jet: The Making and Marketing of the Boeing 777*. New York Scribner.

Sabel, Charles F., and J. Zeitlin (eds.). 1997. *World of Possibilities: Flexible and Mass Production in Western Industrialization*. Cambridge, UK: Cambridge University Press.

Sachdev, Ameet. 2000. "Florida Progress CEO Gets $15-Million." *St. Petersburg Times*, March 7: 1A.

Sailer, Lee D. 1978. "Structural Equivalence: Meaning and Definition, Computation and Application." *Social Networks* 1: 73–90.

Sako, Mari. 1992. *Prices, Quality and Trust: Inter-firm Relations in Britain and Japan*. Cambridge, UK: Cambridge University Press.

Salamon, Lester M., and Helmut K. Anheier. 1997. *Defining the Nonprofit Sector: A Cross-national Analysis*. New York: Manchester University Press.

Salisbury, Robert H. 1994. "Interest Structures and Policy Domains: A Focus for Research." In *Representing Interests and Interest Group Representation*. Ed. William Crotty, Mildred A. Schwartz, and John C. Green. Washington, DC: University Press of America.

Sargent, Joseph. 1999. "Incurring Shareholder Wrath." *Global Finance* 13(3): 8.

Saxenian, AnnaLee. 1994. *Regional Advantage: Culture and Competition in Silicon Valley and Route 128*. Cambridge, MA: Harvard University Press.

Scandura, Terri A. 1992. "Mentorship and Career Mobility: An Empirical Investigation." *Journal of Organizational Behavior* 13: 169–174.

Scherer, Frederic M. 1988. "Corporate Takeovers: The Efficiency Arguments." *Journal of Economic Perspectives* 2: 69–82.

Scherer, Frederic M. 1992. *International High-technology Competition.* Cambridge MA: Harvard University Press.

Schiesel, Seth. 1998. "Venture Promises Far Faster Speeds for Internet Data." *New York Times,* January 20:A1.

Schlozman, Kay Lehman, and John T. Tierney. 1986. *Organized Interests and American Democracy.* New York: Harper & Row.

Schmitz, Hubert, and Bernard Musyck. 1994. "Industrial Districts in Europe: Policy Lessons for Developing Countries?" *World Development* 22: 889–910.

Scholes, Myron S., and Mark A. Wolfson. 1989. "Employee Stock Ownership Plans and Corporate Restructuring: Myths and Realities." Cambridge, MA: National Bureau of Economic Research Working Paper 3094.

Schumpeter, Joseph. 1942. *Capitalism, Socialism, and Democracy.* New York: Harper & Row.

Schuster, Jay R., and Patrick K. Zingheim. 1992. *The New Pay: Linking Employee and Organizational Performance.* New York: Lexington Books.

Schwandt, David R. 1997. "Integrating Strategy and Organizational Learning: A Theory of Action Perspective." *Advances in Strategic Management Research* 14: 337–359.

Scott, A. J., and D.P. Angel. 1987. "The U.S. Semiconductor Industry: A Locational Analysis." *Environment and Planning* A 19: 875–912.

Scott, Richard, and John Meyer. 1983. "The Organization of Societal Sectors." In *Organizational Environments: Ritual and Rationality.* Ed. John W. Meyer and W. richard Scott. Beverly Hills, CA: Sage Publications, pp. 129–154.

Scott, Richard, and John Meyer. 1991. "The Organization of Societal Sectors: Propositions and Early Evidence." In *The New Institutionalism in Organizational Analysis.* Ed. Walter W. Powell and Paul J. DiMaggio. Chicago: University of Chicago Press, pp. 108–140.

Scott, Richard, and John Meyer. 1994. *Institutional Environments and Organizations: Structural Complexity and Individualism.* Thousand Oaks, CA: Sage Publications.

Scott, W. Richard. 1991. "Unpacking Institutional Arguments." In *The New The New Institutionalism.* Ed. Walter Powell and Paul DiMaggio. Chicago: University of Chicago Press, pp. 164–182.

Scott, W. Richard. 1995. *Institutions and Organizations: Attempting a Theoretical Synthesis.* Thousand Oaks, CA: Sage Publications.

Scott, W. Richard. 1998. *Organizations: Rational, Natural, and Open Systems.* 4th ed. Englewood Cliffs, NJ: Prentice-Hall.

Scott Morton, Michael S. (ed.). 1991. *The Corporation of the 1990s: Information Technology and Organizational Transformation.* New York: Oxford University Press.

Seabright, Mark A., Daniel A. Levinthal, and Mark Fichman. 1992. "Role of Individual Attachments in the Dissolution of Interorganizational Relationships." *Academy of Management Journal* 35: 122–160.

Securities and Exchange Commission. 1999. "SEC Company Filings." <http://freeedgar.com> (March 30, 1999).

Sewell, Graham, and Barry Wilkinson. 1992. "'Someone to Watch Over Me': Surveillance, Discipline and the Just-in-Time Labour Process." *Sociology* 26: 271–289.

Sforzi, Fabio. 1989. "The Geography of Industrial Districts in Italy." In *Small Firms and Industrial Districts in Italy.* Ed. Edward Goodman and Julia Bamford. London: Routledge & Kegan Paul, pp. 153–173.

Shanley, Mark. 1996. "Straw Men and M-Form Myths: Comment on Freeland." *American Journal of Sociology* 102: 527–536.

Shelly, Robert K., and David G. Wagner. 1998. "Chaos in Social Theory: Explaining Complex Events with Simple Ideas." *Sociological Focus* 31: 357–372.

Sherman, Joe. 1994. *In the Rings of Saturn.* New York: Oxford University Press.

Sherman, Stralford. 1992. "Are Strategic Alliances Working?" *Fortune* (September): 77–78.

Shingo, Shigeo. 1987. *Non-Stock Production.* Cambridge, MA: Productivity Press.

Shorrock, Tim. 1995. "Business Groups to Fight Campaigns by Unions." *Journal of Commerce*, September 22: 2B.

Shrum, Wesley, and Robert Wuthnow. 1988. "Reputational Status of Organizations in Technical Systems." *American Journal of Sociology* 93: 882–912.

Siegelman, Peter, and John J. Donohue III. 1990. "Studying the Iceberg from Its Tip: A Comparison of Published and Unpublished Employment Discrimination Cases." *Law and Society Review* 24: 1133–1170.

Simison, Robert L., and Rebecca Blumenstein. 1997. "Smale May Stay on GM Board Beyond Age 70." *Wall Street Journal*, December 22: B1.

Simmel, Georg. 1955. *Conflict and the Web of Group Affiliations.* Translated by Kurt H. Wolff and Reinhard Bendix. New York: Free Press.

Sinclair, Armanda. 1992. "The Tyranny of a Team Ideology." *Organization Studies* 13: 611–626.

Sinclair, Upton. 1096. *The Jungle.* New York: The Jungle Publishing Co.

Singh, Jitendra V., and Charles J. Lumsden. 1990. "Theory and Research in Organizational Ecology." *Annual Review of Sociology* 16: 161–195.

Slapper, Gary, and Steve Tombs. 1999. *Corporate Crime.* Harlow, UK: Longman.

Slater, Robert. 1997. *Ovitz: The Inside Story of Hollywood's Most Controversial Power Broker.* New York: McGraw-Hill.

Sloan, Alfred P. 1964. *My Years with General Motors.* Garden City, NJ: Doubleday.

Sloan, Allan. 1999. "CEOs Display Their Spring Green: It's the Season of Financial Disclosure." *International Herald Tribune*, March 10: 19.

Smart, Christopher J.. 1988. "Takeover Damages and Non-Shareholders: Who Should Be Our Brothers' Keeper?" *Columbia Business Law Review* 1988: 301–339.

Smart, Tim. 1997. "O'Reilly Retires After 10 Years As Chief Executive of Heinz." *Washington Post*, December 3: B13.

Smith, Ephraim P. 1970. "Interlocking Directorates Among the 'Fortune 500'." *Antitrust Law and Economics Review* 3(4): 47–52.

Smith, Joel J. 2000. "Dealmaker Gets Big Payoff: DCX Co-chairman Is Rewarded with Huge Stock Options." *Detroit News*, January 27: A1.

Smith, Ken G., Stephen J. Carroll, and Susan J. Ashford. 1995. "Intra- and Interorganizational Cooperation: Toward a Research Agenda." *Academy of Management Journal* 38: 7–23.

Smith, Michael P. 1996. "Shareholder Activism by Institutional Investors: Evidence from CalPERS." *Journal of Finance* 51: 227.

Smith, R. David. 1995. "The Inapplicability Principle: What Chaos Means for Social Science." *Behavioral Science* 40: 22–40.

Smith, Vicki. 1996. "Employee Involvement, Involved Employees: Participative Work Arrangements in a White-Collar Service Occupation." *Social Problems* 43: 166–179.

Smith, Vicki. 1997. "New Forms of Work Organization." *Annual Review of Sociology* 23: 315–339.

Smith-Doerr, Laurel, Jason Owen-Smith, Kenneth W. Koput, and Walter W. Powell. 1999. "Networks and Knowledge Production: Collaboration and Patenting in Biotechnology." In *Corporate Social Capital*. Ed. R. T. A. J. Leenders and S. Gabbay. Boston: Kluwer Academic Publishers, pp. 390–408.

Smoyer, Divonne. 1999. "Business World's Preference for ADR is Growing." *Legal Times*, February 22: S38.

Snijders, Tom A. B. 1996. "Stochastic Actor-Oriented Dynamic Analysis." *Journal of Mathematical Sociology* 21: 149–172.

Sobel, Robert. 1984. *The Rise and Fall of the Conglomerate Kings*. New York: Stein & Day.

Solomon, Robert. 1994. *The Transformation of the World Economy, 1980–93*. New York: St. Martin's Press.

Sorauf, Frank J. 1992. *Inside Campaign Finance: Myths and Realities*. New Haven, CT: Yale University Press.

Specter, Michael. 2000. "The Pharmageddon Riddle." *New Yorker*, April 10: 58–71.

Sridharan, Uma V. 1996. "CEO Influence and Executive Compensation." *Financial Review* 31: 51–66.

St. Anthony, Neal. 1999. "Twin Cities Can Weather Buyouts, as Past Shows." *Minneapolis Star Tribune*, June 13: 1A.

Staber, Udo. 1996. "Accounting for Variations in the Performance of Industrial Districts: The Case of Baden-Württemberg." *International Journal of Urban and Regional Research* (June): 299–316.

Stacey, Ralph D. 1995. "The Science of Complexity: An Alternative Perspective for Strategic Change Processes." *Strategic Management Journal* 16: 477–495.

Starr, Paul. 1982. *The Social Transformation of American Medicine: The Rise of a Sovereign Profession and the Making of a Vast Industry*. New York: Basic Books.

Steagall, Jeffrey W., and Ken Jennings. 1996. "Unions, PAC Contributions, and the NAFTA Vote." *Journal of Labor Research* 17: 515–521.

Stearns, Linda Brewster, and Kenneth D. Allan. 1996. "Economic Behavior in Institutional Environments: The Corporate Merger Wave of the 1980s." *American Sociological Association* 61: 699–718.

Steffens, Lincoln. 1904. *The Shame of the Cities*. New York: McClure, Phillips.

Steinmetz, Greg, and Gregory L. White. 1998. "Chrysler Pay Draws Fire Overseas." *Wall Street Journal*, May 26: B1.

Stern, Gabriella, and Steven Lipin. 1998. "Proposed Chrysler, Daimler-Benz Merger Could Spark Reshuffling of Auto Industry." *Wall Street Journal*, May 7: A10.

Stern, Philip M. 1992. *Still the Best Congress Money Can Buy*. Washington, DC: Regnery Gateway.

Stern, Robert N. 1979. "The Development of an Interorganizational Control Network: The Case of Intercollegiate Athletics." *Administrative Science Quarterly* 24: 267–284.

Stertz, Bradley A., and Dave Phillips. 1996. "Chrysler, Kerkorian Call 5-year Truce." *Detroit News*, February 9: A1.

Stevens, Michael J., and Michael E. Yarish. 1999. "Training for Team Effectiveness." In *Supporting Work Team Effectiveness: Best Management Practices for Fostering High Performance*. Ed. Eric Sundstrom. San Francisco: Jossey Bass, pp. 126–156.

Stewart, Thomas A. 1991. "GE Keeps Those Ideas Coming." *Fortune* (August 12): 40–47.

Stilson, Anne E. Conaway. 1995. "Reexaminign the Fiduciary Paradigm at Corporate Insolvency and Dissolution: Defining Directors' Duties to Creditors." *Delaware Journal of Corporate Law* 20: 1.

Stinchcombe, Arthur L. 1965. "Social Structure and Organizations." In *Handbook of Organizations*. Ed. James G. March. Chicago: Rand McNally, pp. 142–193.

Stinchcombe, Arthur L. 1986. "Norms of Exchange." In *Stratification and Organization*. New York: Cambridge University Press, pp. 231–67.

Storey, David J. 1995. "Symposium on Harrison's 'Lean and Mean': A Job Generation Perspective." *Small Business Economics* 7: 337–340.

Storper, Michael, and Susan Christopherson. 1987. "Flexible Specialization and Regional Industrial Agglomeration: The Case of the U.S. Motion Picture Industry." *Annals of the Association of American Geographers* 77: 104–107.

Strassmann, Paul A. 1997. *The Squandered Computer.* New Canaan, CT: The Info Economics Press.

Streitfeld, David. 1998. "Paper Money on the Net: Amazon.com Rewrites Bookselling Script." *International Herald Telephone*, July 11–12: 11.

Stross, Randell E. 1993. *Steve Jobs and the NeXT Big Thing.* New York: Atheneum.

Stross, Randell E. 1996. *The Microsoft Way: The Real Story of How the Company Outsmarts Its Competition.* New York: Addison-Wesley.

Stuart, Toby E. 1998. "Network Positions and Propensities to Collaborate: An Investigation of Strategic Alliance Formation in a High-technology Industry." *Administrative Science Quarterly* 43: 668–698.

Suchman, Mark C. 1994. "On the Advice of Counsel: Legal and Financial Firms as Information Intermediaries in the Structuration of Silicon Valley." Ph.D. dissertation, Department of Sociology, Stanford University, Stanford, CA.

Suchman, Mark C., and Mia L. Cahill. 1996. "The Hired-Gun as Facilitator: Lawyers and the Suppression of Business Disputes in Silicon Valley." *Law and Social Inquiry* 21: 679–712.

Sutton, John R., and Frank Dobbin. 1996. "The Two Faces of Governance: Responses to Legal Uncertainty in U.S. Firms, 1955–1985." *American Sociological Review* 61: 794–811.

Sutton, John R., Frank Dobbin, John W. Meyer, and W. Richard Scott. 1994. "The Legalization of the Workplace." *American Journal of Sociology* 99: 944–971.

Swaminathan, Anand, and Gabriele Wiedenmayer. 1991. "Does the Pattern of Density Dependence in Organizational Mortality Rates Vary Across Levels of Analysis? Evidence from the German Brewing Industry." *Social Science Research* 20: 45–73.

Swinterton, Kenneth A., and Howard Wial. 1995. "Is Job Stability Declining in the U.S. Economy?" *Industrial and Labor Relations Review* 48: 293–304.

Swoboda, Frank. 1993. "Growing Ranks of Part-Time Workers Are Finding Fewer Benefits." *Washington Post,* September 12.

Taggart, Robert A. 1988. "The Growth of the 'Junk' Bond Market and Its Role in Financing Takeovers." In *Knights, Raiders, and Targets: The Impact of the Hostile Takeover.* Ed. John C. Coffee Jr., Louis Lowenstein, and Susan Rose-Ackerman. New York: Oxford University Press, pp. 5–24.

Takahashi, Dean. 1997. "How the Competition Got Ahead of Intel in Making Cheap Chips." *Wall Street Journal,* February 12: A1.

Tanikawa, Miki. 1998. "Shareholder Rights? In Japan?" *Business* (November 9): 70E12.

Tarbell, Ida M. 1904. *The History of the Standard Oil Company.* New York: Mc-Clure, Phillips.

Taylor, Verta. 1999. "The Rise of Gay, Lesbian, and Bisexual Rights in the Workplace." Mimeographed document, Department of Sociology, Ohio State University, Columbus.

Temin, Peter. 1987. *The Fall of the Bell System: A Study in Prices and Politics.* New York: Cambridge University Press.

Tevlin, Jon. 1997a. "Non-compete Clauses Are a Growing Trend." *Minneapolis Star Tribune,* May 23: D1.

Tevlin, Jon. 1997b. "Kinder, Gentler Union Busting." *Minneapolis Star Tribune,* November 3: D1.

Thomas, David. 1993. "Racial Dynamics in Cross-race Developmental Relationships." *Administrative Science Quarterly* 38: 169–194.

Thomas, David. 1998. "Beyond the Simple Demography-Power Hypothesis: How Blacks in Power Influence White-Mentor-Black-Protégé Developmental Relationships." In *Mentoring Dilemmas: Developmental Relationships Within Multicultural Organizations.* Ed. Audrey Murrell, Faye J. Crosby, and Robin J. Ely. Mahwah, NJ: Lawrence Earlbaum Associates, pp. 157–170.

Thomas, James, Dennis A. Gioia, and David J. Ketchen, Jr. 1997. "Strategic Sense-Making: Learning Through Scanning, Interpetation, Action, and Performance." *Advances in Strategic Management* 14: 299–329.

Thomas, Randall S., and Kenneth J. Martin. 1999. "The Effect of Shareholder Proposals on Executive Compensation." *University of Cincinnati Law Review* 67: 1021–1081.

Thompson, James D. 1967. *Organizations in Action: Social Science Bases of Administrative Theory.* New York: McGraw-Hill.

Thornton, David Weldon.1995. *Airbus Industrie: The Politics of an International Industrial Collaboration.* New York: St. Martin's Press,

Thornton, Patricia. 1998. "The Sociology of Entrepreneurship." *Annual Review of Sociology* 25: 19–46.

Thurow, Lester C. 1975. *Generating Inequality: Mechanisms of Distribution in the U.S. Economy.* New York: Basic Books.

Thurow, Lester C. 1996. *The Future of Capitalism: How Today's Economic Forces Shape Tomorrow's World*. New York: William Morrow.

Tilly, Chris. 1990. *Short Hours, Short Shrift: Causes and Consequences of Part-time Work*. Washington, DC: Economic Policy Institute.

Tilly, Chris. 1996. *Half a Job: Bad and Good Part-time Jobs in a Changing Labor Market*. Philadelphia: Temple University Press.

Todeva, Emanuela. 1998. "Network Structures in International Business: A Review of the Research Agenda." Paper presented to 25th annual conference of the Academy of International Business. London.

Todeva, Emanuela, and David Knoke. (forthcoming) "Strategic Alliances and Corporate Social Capital." *Kölner Zeotschrift für Sociologie unde Socialpsychologie*.

Tödtling, Franz. 1994. "The Uneven Landscape of Innovation Poles: Local Embeddedness and Global Networks." In *Globalization, Institutions, and Regional Development in Europe*. Ed. Ash Amin and Nigel Thrift. New York: Oxford University Press, pp. 68–90.

Tomlins, Christopher L. 1985. *The State and the Unions: Labor Relations, Law, and the Organized Labor Movement in America, 1880–1960*. Cambridge, UK: Cambridge University Press.

Tompkins, Phillip K., and George Cheney. 1985 "Communication and Unobtrusive Control in Contemporary Organizations." In *Organizational Communication: Traditional Themes and New Directions*. Ed. Robert D. McPhee and Phillip K. Tompkins. Newbury Park, CA: Sage, pp. 179-210.

Tosi, Henry L., Jr., and Luis Gomez-Mejia. 1989. "The Decoupling of CEO Pay and Performance: An Agency Theory Perspective." *Administrative Science Quarterly* 34: 169–189.

Towers Perrin. 2000. "1999 Worldwide Total Remuneration Survey." <http://www.towers.com/towers/hot.html> (April 24, 2000).

Treiman, Donald J., and Heidi I. Hartmann (eds.), 1981. *Women, Work, and Wages: Equal Pay for Jobs of Equal Value*. Washington, DC: National Academy Press.

Truman, David B. 1951. *The Governmental Process*. New York: Knopf.

Tsai, Wenpin, and Sumantra Ghoshal. 1998. "Social Capital and Value Creation: The Role of Intrafirm Networks." *Academy of Management Journal* 41: 464–476.

Turban, Daniel B., and Thomas W. Dougherty. 1994. "Role of Protégé Personality in Receipt of Mentoring and Career Success." *Academy of Management Journal* 37: 688–702.

Turnbull, Peter, Nick Oliver, and Barry Wilkinson. 1992. "Buyer-Supplier Relations in the U.K. Automotive Industry: Strategic Implications of the Japanese Manufacturing Model." *Strategic Management Journal* 13: 159–168.

United Nations. 1997. *International Trade Statistics Yearbook. Vol. 2: Trade by Commodity*. New York: United Nations.

United Nations. 1997. *International Trade Statistics Yearbook. 46 V. 2: Trade by Commodity*. New York: United Nations.

Upton, David M. 1995. "What Really Makes Factories Flexible?" *Harvard Business Review* 73(July-August): 74–84.

Upton, David M., and Andrew McAfee. 1996. "The Real Virtual Factory." *Harvard Business Review* 74(July-August): 123–133.

U.S. Bureau of Labor Statistics. 1997. "Contingent and Alternative Employment Arrangements, February 1997." <http://stats.bls.gov/newsrels.htm> (September 29, 1999).

U.S. Bureau of Labor Statistics. 1999. "Employee Tenure in 1998, September 23, 1999." <http://stats.bls.gov/newsrels.htm> (September 28, 1999).

U.S. Bureau of the Census. 1997. *Statistical Abstract of the United States 1997.* 117th ed. Washington, DC: Government Printing Office.

U.S. Bureau of the Census. 1998. *Statistical Abstract of the United States 1998.* 118th ed. Washington, DC: Government Printing Office.

U.S. Bureau of the Census. 1999. *Statistical Abstract of the United States 1999.* 119th ed. Washington, DC: Government Printing Office.

U.S. Bureau of the Census. 2000. "Historical Income Tables—Families." <http://www.census.gov/hhes/income/histinc/f04.html> (March 15, 2000).

U.S. Bureau of the Census. 2000. "Standard Statistical Establishment List (SSEL)." <http://www.census.gov/econ/www/mu0600.html> (March 15, 2000).

U.S. Department of Commerce. 1991. *Money Income of Households, Families, and Persons in the United States: 1990.* Current Population Reports: Consumer Income Series P-60, No. 174.

U.S. Equal Employment Opportunity Commission. 1999. "Enforcement Statistics and Litigation." <http://www.eeoc.gov/stats/enforcement.html> (May 24, 1999).

U.S. Office of Management and Budget, Statistical Policy Division. 1987. *Standard Industrial Classification Manual 1987.* Washington, DC: Government Printing Office.

U.S. Small Business Administration. 1994. *The State of Small Business: A Report to the President.* Washington, DC: Government Printing Office.

U.S. Small Business Administration. 1997. *Facts About Small Business.* Washington, DC: SBA Office of Advocacy.

Useem, Michael. 1979. "The Social Organization of the American Business Elite and Participation of Corporate Directors in the Governance of American Institutions." *American Sociological Review* 44: 553–571.

Useem, Michael. 1984. *The Inner Circle: Large Corporations and the Rise of Business Political Activity in the U.S. and U.K.* New York: Oxford University Press.

Useem, Michael. 1993. *Executive Defense: Shareholder Power and Corporate Reorganization.* Cambridge, MA: Harvard University Press.

Useem, Michael. 1996. *Investor Capitalism: How Money Managers Are Changing the Face of Corporate America.* New York: Basic Books.

Uzzi, Brian. 1996. "The Sources and Consequences of Embeddedness for the Economic Performance of Organizations: The Network Effect." *American Sociological Review* 61: 674–698.

Uzzi, Brian. 1997. "Social Structure and Competition in Interfirm Networks: The Paradox of Embeddedness." *Administrative Science Quarterly* 42: 35–67.

Uzzi, Brian, and Zoe I. Barsness. 1998. "Contingent Employment in British Establishments: Organizational Determinants of the Use of Fixed-term Hires and Part-time Workers." *Social Forces* 76: 967–1005.

Valente, Thomas W. 1995. *Network Models of the Diffusion of Innovations.* Cresskill, NJ: Hampton Press.

Van de Mark, Donald. 1996. "Ovitz at Disney." *Cable News Network,* December 12.

Van de Ven, Andrew H., and Marshall Scott Poole. 1995. "Explaining Development and Change in Organizations." *Academy of Management Review* 20: 510–540.

Van de Ven, Andrew H., Raghu Garud, Douglas E. Polley, and Sankaran Venkataraman. 1999. *The Innovation Journey.* New York: Oxford University Press.

Van Deth, Jan W. 1997. *Private Groups and Public Life: Social Participation, Voluntary Associations and Political Involvement in Representative Democracies.* London: Routledge.

Van Valen, Lee. 1973. "A New Evolutionary Law." *Evolutionary Theory* 1: 1–30.

Varallo, Gregory V., and Daniel A. Dreisbach. 1996. *Fundamentals of Corporate Governance: A Guide for Directors and Corporate Counsel.* Chicago: Section of Business Law, American Bar Association.

Venkatraman, Sankaran. 1997. "The Distinctive Domain of Entrepreneurship Research." *Advances in Entrepreneurship, Firm Emergence, and Growth* 3: 119–138.

Verba, Sidney, Kay Lehman Schlozman, and Henry E. Brady. 1995. *Voice and Equality: Civic Voluntarism in American Politics.* Cambridge, MA: Harvard University Press.

Vogel, David. 1978. "Why Businessmen Distrust Their State: The Political Consciousness of American Corporate Executives." *British Journal of Political Science* 8: 45–78.

Vogel, David. 1989. *Fluctuating Fortunes: The Political Power of Business in America.* New York: Basic Books.

Vogel, David. 1996. *Kindred Strangers: The Uneasy Relationship Between Politics and Business in America.* Princeton, NJ: Princeton University Press.

von Stange, Gary. 1994. "Corporate Social Responsibility through Constituency Statutes: Legend or Lie?" *Hofstra Labor Law Journal* 11: 461–497.

Waldrop, M. Mitchell. 1992. *Complexity: The Emerging Science at the Edge of Order and Chaos.* New York: Simon & Schuster.

Walker, Jack L. 1983. "The Origins and Maintenance of Interest Groups in America." *American Political Science Review* 77: 390–406.

Wall Street Journal. 1989-2000. "Executive Pay." Annual reports published every April: Section R.

Wall Street Journal. 1999. "Controversy Besetting New Pension Plan Rises with IBM's Retreat." September 20: A1.

Wallman, Steven M. H. 1991. "The Proper Interpretation of Corporate Constituency Statutes and Formulation of Director Duties." *Stetson Law Review* 21: 163.

Warren, Roland. 1967. "The Interorganizational Field as a Focus for Investigation." *Administrative Science Quarterly* 12: 396–419.

Wasserman, Stanley, and Dawn Iacobucci. 1988. "Sequential Social Network Data." *Psychometrika* 53: 261–282.

Wasserman, Stanley, and Joseph Galaskiewicz (eds.). 1994. *Advances in Social Network Analysis.* Thousand Oaks, CA: Sage Publications.

Wasserman, Stanley, and Katherine Faust. 1994. *Social Network Analysis: Methods and Applications.* New York: Cambridge University Press.

Waterman, Robert H., Jr., Judith A. Waterman, and Betsey A. Collard. 1994. "Toward a Career Resilient Workforce." *Harvard Business Rveiew* (July-August): 87–95.

Wayne, Leslie. 1998. "Companies Used to Getting Their Way." *New York Times,* December 4: C1.

Weber, Max. 1947. *The Theory of Social and Economic Organization.* New York: Free Press.

Weber, Max. 1952. *The Protestant Ethic and the Spirit of Capitalism.* New York: Scribner.

Weber, Thomas E., and Rbecca Quick. 1997. "Would WorldCom-MCI DealLift Tolls on Net?" *Wall Street Journal,* October 2: B1.

Weick, Karl E. 1995. *Sensemaking in Organizations.* Thousand Oaks, CA: Sage Publications.

Weisbach, Michael S. 1988. "Outside Directors and CEO Turnover." *Journal of Financial Economics* 20: 431–460.

Weisbrod, Burton A. 1988. *The Nonprofit Economy.* Cambridge, MA: Harvard University Press.

Weiss, Rick. 1999. "Biotech vs. 'Bambi' of Insects? Gene-Altered Corn May Kill Monarchs." *Washington Post,* May 20: A3.

Wells, H.G. 1933. *The Shape of Things to Come.* London: White Lion Publishers.

Westphal, James D. 1998. "Board Games: How CEOs Adapt to Increases in Structural Board Independence from Management." *Administrative Science Quarterly* 43: 511–537.

Westphal, James D., and Edward J. Zajac. 1994. "Substance and Symbolism in CEO's Long-term Incentive Plans." *Administrative Science Quarterly* 39: 367–390.

Westphal, James D., and Edward J. Zajac. 1997. "Defections from the Inner Circle: Social Exchange, Reciprocity, and the Diffusion of Board Independence in U.S. Corporations." *Administrative Science Quarterly* 42: 161–183.

White, Harrison C., Scott A. Boorman, and Ronald L. Breiger. 1976. "Social Structure from Multiple Networks, I: Blockmodels of Roles and Positions." *American Journal of Sociology* 81: 730–780.

Wholey, Douglas R., Jon B. Christianson, and Susan M. Sanchez. 1993. "The Effects of Physician and Corporate Interests on the Formation of Health Maintenance Organizations." *American Journal of Sociology* 99: 164–200.

Wholey, Douglas R., and J. W. Huonker. 1993. "Effects of Generalism and Niche Overlap on Network Linkages among Youth Service Agencies." *Academy of Management Journal* 36: 349–372.

Whyte, William H. Jr. 1957. *The Organization Man.* New York: Doubleday Anchor Books.

Williams, Blair R. 1996. *Manufacturing for Survival: The How-to Guide for Practitioners and Managers.* Reading, MA: Addison-Wesley.

Williams, Jeffrey R., Betty Lynn Paez, and Leonard Sanders. 1988. "Conglomerates Revisited." *Strategic Management Journal* 9: 403–414.

Williamson, Oliver E. 1975. *Markets and Hierarchies: Analysis and Antitrust Implications.* New York: Free Press.

Williamson, Oliver E. 1979. "Transaction Cost Economics: The Governance of Contractual Relations." *Journal of Law and Economics* 22: 3–61.

Williamson, Oliver E. 1981. "The Economics of Organization: The Transaction Cost Approach." *American Journal of Sociology* 87: 548–577.

Williamson, Oliver E. 1983. "Organization Form, Residual Claimants, and Corporate Control." *Journal of Law and Economics* 26(2): 351–366.

Williamson, Oliver. 1985. *The Economic Institutions of Capitalism: Firms, Markets, Relational Contracting.* New York: Free Press.

Williamson, Oliver. 1987. "Comment: Shareholders and Managers—A Risk-Neutral Perspective." In *Knights, Raiders, and Targets: The Impact of the Hostile Takeover.* Ed. John C. Coffee Jr., Louis Lowenstein, and Susan Rose-Ackerman. New York: Oxford University Press, pp. 159–167.

Williamson, Oliver. 1994. "Transaction Cost Economics and Organization Theory." In *The Handbook of Economic Sociology.* Ed. Neil J. Smelser and Richard Swedberg. Princeton, NJ: Princeton University Press, pp. 77–107.

Willis, R. 1987. "What's Happened to America's Middle Managers." *Management Review* 76: 24–33.

Wolff, Edward N. 1985. "The Magnitude and Causes of the Recent Productivity Slowdown in the United States: A Survey of Recent Studies." In *Productivity, Growth, and U.S. Competitiveness.* Ed. William J. Baumol and Kenneth McLennan. New York: Oxford University Press, pp. 29–57.

Womack, James P., and Daniel T. Jones. 1994. "From Lean Production to the Lean Enterprise." *Harvard Business Review* (March-April): 93–103.

Womack, James P., Daniel T. Jones, and Daniel Roos. 1990. *The Machine That Changed the World.* New York: Rawson Associates.

Worker-Ownership Institute. 2000. "The Role and History of Employee Ownership Companies."<http://www.workerownership.org/history.html[greaterthan greaterthan] (June 7, 2000).

World Bank. 1999. *World Development Report 1999/2000: Entering the 21st Century—Development.* New York: Oxford University Press.

Wright, John R. 1990. "Contributions, Lobbying, and Committee Voting in the U.S. House of Representatives." *American Political Science Review* 84: 417–438.

Wright, John R. 1996. *Interest Groups and Congress: Lobbying, Contributions, and Influence.* Boston: Allyn & Bacon.

Wyatt Company. 1993. *Measuring Change in the Attitudes of the American Workforce.* New York: Wyatt WorkUSA, Wyatt Company.

Yago, Glenn. 1991. *Junk Bonds: How High Yield Securities Restructured Corporate America.* New York: Oxford University Press.

Yeung, Arthur K., David O. Ulrich, Stephen W. Nason, and Mary Ann Von Glinow. 1999. *Organizational Learning Capability.* New York: Oxford.

Yoffie, David B. (ed.). 1997. *Competing in the Age of Digital Convergence.* Boston: Harvard Business School Press.

Yoffie, David B., and Michael A. Cusumano. 1999. "Building a Company on Internet Time: Lessons From Netscape." *California Management Review* 41(3): 8–28.

Yoshino, Michael Y., and U. Srinivasa Rangan. 1995. *Strategic Alliances: An Entrepreneurial Approach to Globalization.* Cambridge, MA: Harvard University Press.

Young, S. 1989. *International Market Entry and Development: Strategies and Management.* Hertfordshire, UK: Harvester Wheatsheaf.

Zachary, G. Pascal. 1994. "Microsoft Will Remain Dominant Despite Pact in Antitrust Dispute." *Wall Street Journal,* July 18: A1.

Zaheer, Akbar, and N. Venkatraman. 1995. "Relational Governance as an Interorganizational Strategy: An Empirical Test of the Role of Trust in Economic Exchange." *Strategic Management Journal* 16: 373–392.

Zajac, Edward J., and James D. Westphal. 1995. "Accounting for the Explanations of CEO Compensation: Substance and Symbolism." *Administrative Science Quarterly* 40: 283–308.

Zajac, Edward J., and James D. Westphal. 1996. "Director Reputation, CEO-Board Power, and the Dynamics of Board Interlocks." *Administrative Science Quarterly* 41: 507–529.

Zald, Mayer N., and Michael A. Berger. 1978. "Social Movements in Organizations: Coup d'Etat, Insurgency, and Mass Movements." *American Journal of Sociology* 83: 823–861.

Zbaracki, Mark J. 1998. "The Rhetoric and Reality of Total Quality Management." *Administrative Science Quarterly* 43: 602–636.

Zeggelink, Evelien P.H. 1994. "Dynamics of Structure: An Individual Oriented Approach." *Social Networks* 16: 295–333.

Zeitlin, Maurice. 1974. "Corporate Ownership and Control: The Large Corpration and Capitalist Class." *American Journal of Sociology* 79: 1073–1119.

Zeitlin, Maurice. 1989. "Who Owns America? The Same Old Gang." In *The Large Corporation and Contemporary Classes.* Ed. Maurice Zeitlin. New Brunswick, NJ: Rutgers University Press, pp. 142–161.

Zey, Mary. 1993. *Banking on Fraud: Drexel, Junk Bonds, and Buyouts.* Hawthorne, NY: Aldien de Gruyter.

Zey, Mary. 1998. "The Transformation of Corporate Control to Owners and Form to the Multisubsidiary: 1981–1993." *Research in Organizational Change and Development* 11: 271–312.

Zey, Mary, and Brande Camp. 1996. "The Transformation from Multidimensional Form to Corporate Groups of Subsidies in the 1980s: Capital Crisis Theory." *Sociological Quarterly* 37: 327–351.

Zey, Mary, and Tami Swenson. 1998. "Corporate Tax Laws, Corporate Restructuring, and Subsidiarization of Corporate Form, 1981–1995." *Sociological Quarterly* 39: 555–581.

Zey, Mary, and Tami Swenson. 1999. "The Transformation of the Dominant Corporate Form from Multidivisional to Multisubsidiary: The Role of the 1986 Tax Reform Act." *Sociological Quarterly* 40: 241–267.

Ziegler, Bart. 1997. "Gerstner's IBM Revival: Impressive, Incomplete." *Wall Street Journal,* March 25: B1.

Zucker, Lynne G. 1983. "Organizations as Institutions." *Research in the Sociology of Organizations* 2: 1–47.

Zucker, Lynne G. 1986. "Production of Trust: Institutional Sources of Economic Structure, 1840–1920." *Research in Organizational Behavior* 8: 53–111.

Zucker, Lynne G. 1989. "Combining Institutional Theory and Population Ecology: No Legitimacy, No History." *American Sociolgical Review* 54: 542–545.

Index